Third Edition

Writing That Works

How to Write Effectively on the Job

Third Edition

Writing That Works
How to Write Effectively on the Job

Walter E. Oliu
U.S. Nuclear Regulatory Commission

Charles T. Brusaw
NCR Corporation (retired)

Gerald J. Alred
University of Wisconsin—Milwaukee

St. Martin's Press
New York

Executive Editor: Susan Anker
Copy Editor: Barbara Hoffert
Production Supervisor: Christine Pearson
Cover design: Ben Santora

Library of Congress Catalog Card Number: 87–060516
Copyright © 1988 by St. Martin's Press, Inc.
All rights reserved.
Manufactured in the United States of America.
21098
fedcba

For information, write to:
St. Martin's Press, Inc.
175 Fifth Avenue
New York, NY 10010

ISBN: 0–312–00275–0
Instructor's Edition ISBN: 0–312–01286–1

Preface

Writing That Works, Third Edition, is designed for students with varied academic backgrounds and occupational interests whose jobs will, or already do, require writing skills. Each chapter provides abundant and realistic examples drawn from a wide range of occupations, as well as carefully structured exercises and writing assignments. The text is unusually comprehensive, and probably few instructors will wish to assign every chapter. We have therefore built into the book sufficient flexibility to allow instructors to choose the sections they consider most important for a particular class. (In addition, our Instructor's Manual contains a suggested syllabus for a 16-week course.) At the same time, we feel that this text is inclusive enough to serve as a reference tool for a student long after the course is over, since no course can possibly cover all the writing concerns students will encounter once they are on the job.

For the Third Edition we have retained the three-part organization of the text—an organization designed to facilitate both the teaching and learning of various types of writing. Part One is an introduction to the writing process. The five chapters in this part guide students through all the steps of the process—planning, organizing, writing (including a separate chapter on how to highlight key ideas), and revising—with special emphasis on the questions a writer must ask when approaching any writing task: What is my purpose in writing? For whom is the writing intended? How much information must I include? By page 37 students are familiar with the most common organizational patterns; by page 57 they have been introduced to the principles of effective paragraph writing, including transition between sentences and paragraphs and successful openings and closings. And by page 76 the students have studied the ways of achieving emphasis in writing—with the active and passive voices, subordination, word order, and introductory words and phrases. For the Third Edition, the information on revision in Chapter 5 has been reorganized to group related tasks more closely and the Revision Checklist has been expanded.

Part Two—Chapters 6 through 15—looks at the writing process at work, considering in particular the various kinds of on-the-job writing and the strategies appropriate to each. Part Two opens with a chapter that presents the range of rhetorical strategies that should be part of every writer's basic equipment: instructions, process explanation, description, comparison, division and classification, definitions, cause and effect, persuasion, and summarizing. Each rhetorical method is illustrated by one or more job-related examples and the chapter includes a new section on summarizing information. Chapter 7 discusses the principles of business correspondence, focusing on the importance of goodwill and the "you" viewpoint; this chapter also includes typical letter and memo formats. For the Third Edition, the section on memo writing in Chapter 7 has been expanded. Chapter 8 then goes on to describe the various types of business correspondence, including order letters, inquiry letters, transmittal letters, acknowledgment letters, complaint letters, adjustment letters, refusal letters, collection letters, and sales letters.

Chapters 9 through 11 discuss reports, with separate chapters on the informal report, the formal report, and research techniques (which include not only library research but interviews, questionnaires, and first-hand observations). For the Third Edition, we have expanded the research chapter to cover a wealth of new reference sources, including a new listing of on-line data bases in the section on computerized information retrieval. In addition, the documentation section has been updated in line with the second edition of the *MLA Handbook for Writers of Research Papers*. Chapter 12 looks at proposal writing, with coverage of both internal proposals and external, or sales, proposals (both solicited and unsolicited). Comprehensive examples of both internal and external proposals are provided.

Chapter 13 takes up the preparation of tables, charts, and other visual aids. Chapter 14 discusses not only the preparation and delivery of oral presentations but also a vitally important skill that is too often ignored: effective listening. The last chapter is a practical, step-by-step guide to finding a job, with special emphasis on the preparation of effective resumes and of application and follow-up letters. Sample resumes are provided both for students with little or no job experience and for those with a great deal of experience.

Finally, Part Three of *Writing That Works* is a highly accessible Writer's Guide, with instructional material on spelling and vocabulary building, as well as a handbook of grammar, punctuation, and mechanics. The handbook is based on materials drawn from our *Handbook of Technical Writing* and *Business Writer's Handbook* (both published by St. Martin's Press). In an effort to make the handbook section as useful and accessible as possible, we have cross-referenced it with the chapter on revising. For the Third Edition, we have added a completely new section to the Writer's Guide: an illustrated introduction to word processing. This section features a set of guidelines to help students use word processing as a writer's tool to maximum effect. Last, at the very end of the book is a correction chart, with page references to appropriate passages in the text discussion and the handbook.

For their assistance with the Third Edition, we wish to recognize the contributions of William Van Pelt of the University of Wisconsin–

Milwaukee, who wrote the section on word processing, and Judy McInish, Law Librarian, District of Columbia Public Defender Service, for her valuable work in updating and expanding the information on library research in Chapter 10.

In addition, we would like to express our appreciation to the following instructors for their helpful comments and recommendations for the Third Edition: Vernon Ball, Chattanooga State Technical Community College; Santi Buscemi, Middlesex County College; Robert Gentry, Texas State Technical Institute; Louis Kasdan, Fairfield University; and Louise Vest, New Mexico State University–Las Cruces.

Finally, we want to thank Susan Anker of St. Martin's Press for her thoughtful editorial guidance.

Contents

Part One   THE WRITING PROCESS   1

1 Getting Started   3
Using a Systematic Approach to Writing *4*
Determining Your Purpose *5*
Determining Your Reader's Needs *5*
Generating, Gathering, and Recording Ideas and Facts *9*
Establishing Your Scope *12*
Organizing Your Ideas *13*
Successful Writing *14*
Chapter Summary *17*
Exercises *17*

2 Organizing Your Information   20
Outlining *21*
Methods of Organization *25*
Chapter Summary *37*
Exercises *37*

3 Writing the Draft   43
Paragraph Unity *45*
Paragraph Length *48*
Paragraph Coherence *48*
Writing an Opening *52*
Writing a Closing *54*
Chapter Summary *57*
Exercises *57*

4 Achieving Emphasis   62
Active and Passive Voice *62*
Subordination *66*
Introductory Words and Phrases *70*
Parallel Structure *71*
Lists *73*
Other Ways to Achieve Emphasis *74*
Chapter Summary *76*
Exercises *77*

5 Revising   **80**
    Revising Tactics *81*
    Revising for Accuracy and Completeness *83*
    Revising for Basics *83*
    Revising for Style *97*
    Revising for Mechanics *106*
    Physical Appearance *111*
    Revision Checklist *112*
    Chapter Summary *113*
    Exercises *113*

Part Two   THE PROCESS AT WORK   **121**

6 Writing for Specific Purposes   **123**
    Instructions *123*
    Explaining a Process *129*
    Description *132*
    Comparison *137*
    Division and Classification *140*
    Definition *143*
    Cause and Effect *148*
    Persuading Your Reader *151*
    Summarizing Information *154*
    Chapter Summary *155*
    Exercises *156*

7 Principles of Business Correspondence   **162**
    Writing Letters *163*
    The Memorandum *181*
    Chapter Summary *190*
    Exercises *191*

8 Types of Business Letters   **194**
    The Order Letter *194*
    The Inquiry Letter *195*
    Response to an Inquiry Letter *198*
    The Transmittal Letter *200*
    The Acknowledgment Letter *203*

The Complaint Letter *203*
The Adjustment Letter *208*
The Refusal Letter *210*
The Collection Letter Series *213*
The Sales Letter *218*
Chapter Summary *224*
Exercises *225*

9 Informal Reports   **229**
Writing the Report *230*
The Parts of the Report *230*
Types of Reports *231*
Chapter Summary *249*
Exercises *250*

10 Researching Your Subject   **254**
In the Library *255*
Taking Notes *271*
Plagiarism *278*
Interviewing *279*
Using a Questionnaire *281*
Other Sources of Information *287*
Documentation *288*
Chapter Summary *297*
Exercises *298*

11 Formal Reports   **301**
Order of Elements in a Formal Report *301*
Transmittal Letter or Memorandum *302*
Front Matter *303*
Body *311*
Back Matter *325*
Graphic and Tabular Matter *328*
Chapter Summary *329*
Exercises *329*

**12 Proposals and Other Kinds of On-the-Job
       Communication**   **331**
Proposals *331*
Minutes of Meetings *358*
Job Descriptions *362*
Creating Business Forms *365*

Chapter Summary   *370*
Exercises   *370*

13   Creating Tables and Illustrations   **374**
Tables   *375*
Graphs   *377*
Computer Graphics   *387*
Drawings   *389*
Photographs   *392*
Flowcharts   *393*
Organizational Charts   *396*
Maps   *397*
Chapter Summary   *398*
Exercises   *399*

14   Making an Oral Presentation   **402**
Preparing an Oral Presentation   *403*
Delivering an Oral Presentation   *409*
Effective Listening   *414*
Chapter Summary   *415*
Exercises   *416*

15   Finding a Job   **417**
Locating the Job You Want   *417*
Preparing an Effective Resume   *420*
Writing an Effective Letter of Application   *436*
Conducting Yourself Well During the Interview   *439*
Sending Follow-up Letters   *444*
Chapter Summary   *448*
Exercises   *448*

Part Three   THE WRITER'S GUIDE   **451**

Section A   Spelling and Vocabulary   **453**

1   Spelling   **453**
1.1   The Silent *e* Rule of Thumb   *456*
1.2   Hard and Soft Sounds   *457*
1.3   Adding to Basic Words   *458*
1.4   Doubling Final Consonants   *461*
1.5   Prefixes and Suffixes   *462*

1.6   Words with *ie* or *ei*   *463*
1.7   Contractions   *463*
1.8   Abbreviated Spellings   *464*
1.9   Word Groups of Frequently Misspelled Words   *464*

2   Vocabulary   **466**
Choosing the Right Word   *467*
The Word-Part Approach   *470*
2.1   Roots   *471*
2.2   Prefixes   *476*
2.3   Suffixes   *485*

**Section B   Handbook of Grammar, Punctuation,
and Mechanics**   **488**

3   Parts of Speech   **488**
3.1   Nouns   *488*
3.2   Pronouns   *492*
3.3   Adjectives   *500*
3.4   Verbs   *503*
3.5   Adverbs   *515*
3.6   Conjunctions   *519*
3.7   Prepositions   *520*
3.8   Interjections   *522*

4   Phrases, Clauses, Sentences, and Paragraphs   **522**
4.1   Phrases   *522*
4.2   Clauses   *524*
4.3   Sentences   *527*
4.4   Paragraphs   *542*

5   Punctuation   **546**
5.1   Commas   *546*
5.2   Semicolons   *553*
5.3   Colons   *555*
5.4   Periods   *556*
5.5   Question Marks   *559*
5.6   Exclamation Marks   *560*
5.7   Parentheses   *560*
5.8   Hyphens   *561*
5.9   Quotation Marks   *563*

5.10 Dashes *565*
5.11 Apostrophes *566*
5.12 Slashes *568*
5.13 Brackets *569*

6 Mechanics **569**
6.1 Numbers *570*
6.2 Acronyms and Initialisms *573*
6.3 Abbreviations *575*
6.4 Ampersands *578*
6.5 Capital Letters *578*
6.6 Dates *583*
6.7 Italics *584*
6.8 Symbols *586*
6.9 Proofreaders' Marks *588*

Section C   Word Processing **590**
Hardware *591*
Software and Computer Systems *593*
Word Processing and the Writing Process *594*
Tips on Using the Word Processor to Improve
Writing Skills *594*

Index **596**

part one

THE WRITING PROCESS

Part One discusses the principles of effective writing that apply to all on-the-job writing tasks. Whatever your purpose or audience, you must plan the amount and type of information to include, where to obtain it, and how best to organize it before you begin writing the first draft. After completing the draft, you must review it to see how well it communicates to its intended audience: key ideas must be emphasized; information checked for factual accuracy; language scrutinized for grammatical correctness, consistency, and preciseness; the text reviewed for coherence and conciseness; and finally, the draft given a detailed proofing for crucial mechanical concerns such as punctuation and spelling.

1

Getting Started

Christine Thomas was aware of both a potential problem and an opportunity at HVS Data Processing Services. An administrative assistant, she knew that the computer service offered by HVS could easily attract new customers if only the president and founder of the small company, Harriet Sullivan, would expand HVS's equipment and staff. HVS had, in fact, turned away customers because its computer equipment was loaded to capacity handling its 49 current business customers. Even more troubling, HVS had promised to cover emergency or overload back-ups for these customers. Christine knew it was only a matter of time before HVS would be forced to refuse computer time to a valued customer. Something had to be done.

Christine had for the last month kept careful records of the number of customers she turned away. She had also researched the costs of new equipment and additional staff. She was convinced that even though HVS was just over two years old, the time to expand had come.

So, with all the information at hand and confident of the value of her suggestion, Christine wrote the following memo to Harriet Sullivan:

```
DATE:      December 3, 19—

TO:        Harriet Sullivan

FROM:      Christine Thomas    CT

SUBJECT:   Expansion of HVS Capabilities
```

> The number of customers being turned away is steadily growing. Further, we may need to refuse computer time for emergency or overload backups for our present customers.
> By purchasing a VT–8000 computer and expanding our staff by two, we could triple the number of customers and ensure emergency and overload backup for new and current clients.
> Please consider my suggestion that we expand HVS.

Two days later, Christine Thomas's memo was returned to her with the note "Too soon to make such a move" written across the bottom.

Christine Thomas was not only disappointed but also puzzled. She knew that her suggestion was timely and reasonable because she had checked all the facts before writing the memo. Yet she had failed to convince Harriet Sullivan.

USING A SYSTEMATIC APPROACH TO WRITING

In writing her memo, Christine Thomas committed the most common of all mistakes made by people who write on their jobs: she lost sight of the purpose of her memo and overlooked the needs of her reader. Christine had been so convinced of the rightness of her suggestion that she forgot that her reader was not familiar with the information her research had produced and could not see the situation from her perspective. Had she kept her purpose and her reader clearly in mind, Christine would then have been able to generate ideas, establish her scope, and organize her ideas in a way that might have ultimately achieved her objective.

The last three steps are important: even with her reader and her purpose clearly in mind, Christine would still not have been ready to write her memo to Harriet. She would simply have established a framework in which to develop her memo. Some writers, once they have identified their purpose and their reader, don't know what to do next and stare at a blank piece of paper waiting for inspiration.

A systematic approach helps writers over this hurdle. Before beginning to write, careful writers not only identify their purpose and reader but think seriously about the content of their writing and the form this information should take. This process involves first listing all the ideas and facts that they might wish to include, then refining the list by examining each item in it from the perspectives of reader and purpose, and finally organizing the resulting list in a way that satisfies their purpose and their reader's needs. You should complete each of the following steps before beginning to compose any important document:

1. Determine your purpose.
2. Determine your reader's needs.
3. Generate, gather, and record ideas and facts.
4. Establish the scope of coverage for your topic.
5. Organize your ideas.

DETERMINING YOUR PURPOSE

Everything you write is written for a purpose. You want your reader to know, to believe, or to be able to do something when he or she has finished reading what you have written. Determining your purpose is the first step in preparing to write, for unless you know what you hope to accomplish by your writing, you cannot know what information should be presented.

Purpose, then, gives direction to your writing: the more precisely you can state your purpose at the outset, the more successful your writing is likely to be. Christine Thomas, if asked, might have said that her purpose was "to expand HVS's computer facilities"—but expansion was the *result* she wanted, not the precise *purpose* of her memo. Further thought on her part would have led her to recognize the more specific goals of the memo itself.

To make sure that your purpose is precise, try to put it in writing. In most cases, you can use the following formula to guide you:

My purpose is to _____ so that my reader _____ .

Using this formula, Christine Thomas might have come up with the following statement of purpose:

My purpose is to *explain the advantages of expanding our equipment and staff* so that my reader *will be persuaded to buy the VT-8000 and hire two new employees.*

With this statement of purpose, Christine would have recognized that her purpose was more complicated than it had at first appeared and that she would have to present persuasive evidence if her writing was to be effective.

DETERMINING YOUR READER'S NEEDS

Remember that your job as a writer is to express your ideas so clearly that your reader cannot misinterpret them and that an important element of the purpose formula is the phrase "so that my reader. . . ." Simply identifying the response you would like is very different from actually achieving it. Although a purpose statement addresses a problem from the writer's point of view, the reader's needs must also be taken into account. Yet all too often writers forget that they have readers and write essentially to themselves, focusing solely on *their* purposes.

After you have stated your purpose, ask yourself "Who is my reader?" Often you will know who your reader is. For example, if you are writing a memo to your boss attempting to convince him or her to fund a project, you know who your reader is. In another situation, however, you might be writing a letter to someone you do not know in another company. In this case, you would try to imagine your reader, taking into consideration what you know about that company, your reader's position in the company or department, and your reader's responsibilities regarding the topic you are writing about. You could not know what his or her needs were until you knew at least this much about him or her.

Your Reader's Background

Obviously, when you know enough about your reader that you can actually picture him or her responding to what you have written, you have an advantage. But even when you know your reader very well, a little reflection is necessary. In Christine Thomas's case, without careful thought she might have answered the question from only one point of view:

> My reader is Harriet Sullivan, and she's been my boss for two years. We've worked together since she founded the company, so she'll no doubt understand that I have her best interest in mind.

Had Christine thought more carefully about Harriet *as the reader of the memo* rather than as her friend and boss she might have answered the question differently:

> My reader is Harriet Sullivan, president of HVS Data Processing Service. Harriet founded HVS two years ago with modest savings and a substantial loan. Cautious, industrious, and a stickler for detail, Harriet has built HVS into a sound business and is now beginning to see some return on her investment. She is not an expert in the technical aspects of data processing and has had little time to keep up with innovations in the field. Instead, Harriet is an able manager, but one who is sometimes slow to recognize the value of the advice her more technically oriented subordinates can offer.

This portrait of Harriet would have enabled Christine to raise two essential questions, the answers to which would have helped her frame her memo:

1. What information does my reader need to understand what I'm writing about?
2. What is my reader's basic attitude likely to be toward what I'm writing about?

These questions—which might be rephrased "What does my reader probably know?" and "What does my reader probably think?"—are always worth investigating. Suppose your purpose is to explain your plan for bypassing a malfunctioning piece of equipment that is causing a production bottleneck. If your reader were an associate, these questions would be easier to answer than if your reader were the president of your company, someone you know only by name and title. In the first case, your reader is a colleague who understands the equipment, the terminology you will use, and the production system. In the second case, your reader is a decision maker primarily interested in the "big picture"—the broader implications of the bottleneck and the feasibility of your plan to correct it. This reader would probably not know the technical details of the day-to-day operation of your production system and would likely have neither the time nor the inclination to learn them simply to understand your explanation. You would have to write to the company president in terms that would be comprehensible to a typical executive. The company president, having read your explanation, would want to know whether to investigate your plan further or to replace the malfunctioning equipment.

Your Reader's Point of View

Keep in mind that your reader, whether a coworker, a customer, or a company president, is interested in the problem you are addressing more from his or her own point of view than from yours. Imagine yourself in your reader's position. For instance, if you were working for a bicycle manufacturer and your purpose were to write a set of assembly instructions so that people who buy your new model 1050J could get from opening the carton to riding the bicycle with a minimum of frustration, you would have to break down the assembly process into a sensible series of easy-to-follow steps. You would avoid technical language and anticipate questions that your readers would be likely to have. You would make it unnecessary for them to consult other sources to follow your directions. You would not explain the engineering theory that is responsible for the bicycle's unique design; your reader would be more interested in riding the bicycle than in reading such details, however fascinating they might be to you. If you ventured into theory at all, it would be for a specific reason such as to explain why a particular step in the assembly process had to be completed before the next. You would also include assembly diagrams, a list of parts, and a list of the tools necessary for assembly.

You would approach the situation differently if you were preparing assembly instructions for a bicycle dealer. You could feel free to use standard technical terms without defining them, and you would probably reduce the number of steps necessary for assembly by combining related steps because your reader, the dealer, would be familiar with bicycle assembly and be able to follow a more sophisticated set of instructions. Your reader would not need a list of tools required for assembly; the dealer's shop would no doubt have all the necessary tools and the dealer would know which ones to use. You might well, in a separate section, include some theoretical detail, too. The dealer could possibly use this information to explain to customers the advantages of your bicycle over a competitor's.

Writing for Multiple Readers

When you write for a group of readers who are similar in background and knowledge—all operators, for example, or all programmers—you should picture in your mind a typical representative of that group and then write directly to that person. Occasionally, however, you may write a document that will be used by many different types of people. For example, you might write a technical report that would be used by technicians, salespeople, and executives. In such a situation, you might deal with each audience separately in clearly identified sections of your document: you might write an executive summary for the executive, include an appendix for the technician, and address the body of the report to the salespeople. (See Chapter 11 for an explanation of the different parts of formal reports.) When you cannot segment your writing this way, determine who your primary reader is and then make certain that you meet all of that reader's needs. Then meet the needs of your other readers only if you can do so without placing a burden on your primary reader.

For example, if your primary reader is an executive and your secondary reader is a technical specialist, you should not include a large amount of technical detail that would obscure the main point for the executive, even though the technician might find such detail interesting. But you could include a small section containing detailed technical information for the specialist without interfering seriously with your message to the executive, especially if you label such a section "Technical Analysis," or something else appropriate.

GENERATING, GATHERING, AND RECORDING IDEAS AND FACTS

When you have determined your purpose and analyzed your reader's needs, you must decide what information will satisfy the demands of both. There are several techniques you can use.

Brainstorming

A good way to start is to interview yourself so that you can tap into your own knowledge and experience. You may find that you already have enough information to get started. This technique, commonly known as brainstorming, may also suggest additional ways of obtaining information.

To begin, create a list containing as many ideas as you can think of about the general subject of the document you plan to write and jot them down in random order *as they occur to you.* (This type of research may be done by a group as well as alone.) Jot down what you know and, if possible, where you learned of it, using a chalkboard, a pad of paper, or notecards. (Notecards are especially useful if you are working alone because they can be easily shuffled and rearranged.) For every idea noted, ask yourself the following questions, as expressed in a short poem by Rudyard Kipling:

> I keep six honest serving-men
>   (They taught me all I knew);
> Their names are What and Why and When
>   And How and Where and Who.

Newspaper reporters have long used these questions as a guide to make sure that they have answered the questions their readers are likely to have about a particular story: *What* happened? *Why* did it happen? *When* did it happen? *How* did it happen? *Where* did it happen? *Who* was involved? Rarely will you be able to apply all these questions to any single on-the-job writing situation, but the range of information that they cover can be useful in helping you to start getting your ideas down on paper.

Once you have assembled a list of ideas, examine each item and decide whether it contributes to your purpose or satisfies your reader's needs. Then mark the item with a "P" for purpose or an "R" for reader. Some items will satisfy both your purpose and your reader; other items will appear to satisfy only one, and still others will appear to have nothing to do with either. Often you will mark an item first with one letter and then see that the other applies as well. The order in which you write

Items for memo to Harriet Sullivan

R.P Harriet needs to see financial benefits of expansion

P.R Our old computer showing signs of rheumatoid arthritis

P.R Employee morale down because of overwork

R.P We could triple number of customers (give estimate)

~~How the VT-8000 was developed~~

R List cost of data entry person and operator

R.P Income would more than pay for expansion (give estimate)

~~R VT-8000 can be color coordinated~~

RP We can't attract new customers with old equipment

R.P Easy to implement VT-8000 ~~(see brochure)~~

~~RP VT-8000 service people use radio-dispatched trucks~~

R.P Peripheral VT-3033 equipment could be added later

R.P Buying an entire new system would disturb routine

~~P VT-8000 would make my job easier~~

R VT-8000 is noisy

P.R VT-8000 is compact and easy to operate

P Soundproofing would be inexpensive and we need it anyway

R List costs of new equipment and operation

R.P (~~give number of~~ ^many direct requests turned away

    We run 3 shifts on our VT-3400 but don't keep up

P.R Briefly describe VT-8000 capacity

R.P Buying now will give us an edge on our competitors

R.P We could advertise in: Computer Times for new staff

down the letters will indicate whether you consider the item to be more important for your reader or for your purpose.

When you have finished marking your list, eliminate any item that is not marked. Be sure to reconsider an unmarked item from the perspectives of both your purpose and your reader, making certain that it fits neither before eliminating it. Ideally, you will have a comprehensive list of items beside which you have placed both a "P" and an "R," although many items will no doubt belong more to one than the other, and you may find that some will belong exclusively to one or the other. The more common ground your purpose and your reader's needs share, the more effective your writing is likely to be.

As you read over the items on your list, you will find that those items relating clearly to both your purpose and your reader's needs are easiest to deal with. Trickier are items that your reader might need but that would get in the way of your purpose. Harriet Sullivan, for example, would want to know that the VT-8000 Computer's printer is noisier than the printer that VHS is presently using; Christine Thomas, on the other hand, would be reluctant to mention this fact, since it would appear to be counterproductive to her own purpose. To reconcile Harriet's interests and her own, Christine would have to note the noise problem but also point out that soundproofing can be installed easily and inexpensively.

Turning a writer's list of ideas into a reader's list of information should be neither difficult nor mysterious; thoroughness is the key. Christine Thomas, for example, might have generated the well-balanced list on page 10, using one or more of the methods described here. Such a list will give you a tentative idea of the content of the project. It will probably be sketchy or missing information, thus helping to show where additional research is needed. It will also help integrate the various details of the additional research.

Other Sources of Information

Brainstorming may not produce all the information you need. To get enough information to meet your reader's needs adequately, formal, systematic research into your subject may be necessary. In such cases, you should have some idea of how thoroughly you will cover your subject. In other words, to consult the appropriate sources you will have to know how much detail is required. If you know what you are looking for and you know where to find it, research presents few problems.

The *library* provides books, articles, reference works, and other written material for your research. A personal *interview* with an expert can provide you with up-to-date information not readily available in printed material. A *questionnaire* permits you to obtain the views of a group of people without taking the time and expense necessary for numerous personal interviews. These different sources of information are discussed in detail in Chapter 10, "Researching Your Subject."

ESTABLISHING YOUR SCOPE

Having refined your list of ideas and facts, you must review it once again to establish your scope. Your scope is the degree of detail you decide is necessary to cover each item in your list; and, as before, you must consider this aspect of preparation in terms of your purpose and your reader's needs. This step is really a refinement of the last: as you contemplate each item, ask yourself, "Am I including enough information to support my purpose? Am I including enough information to satisfy my reader's needs? Have I included unnecessary information that only gets in the way of meeting my purpose and my reader's needs?" Often you will find that you are omitting important facts or figures and will have to research your subject further to come up with them. At other times, you will find that your list is cluttered with unnecessary detail.

Increase in number of customers: 45 in 1st yr — 50 in 2nd yr
Six customers turned away equal to our largest account
21 direct requests refused
VT-8000 easy to maintain and is expandable
Give Harriet Sullivan copy of brochure on VT-8000
Increased income: $37,000 (1st yr) — $64,000 (2nd yr.)
Cost of operator ($19,000/yr) and data entry person ($12,000)
VT-8000 would triple our capacity
Surplus income expected: $27,880 (underline)
Current systems can't handle state-of-art VRX software
Can't attract new customers with our VT-3400
VT 8000 is fast, reasonably priced, and high capacity
VT 8000 costs $16,330 (break out items)
We can't offer improved service to <u>current</u> customers with VT-3410
VT-8000 is compact and will not disturb routine.

Had Christine Thomas drawn up the list on page 5 and then reviewed it to establish her scope, she would have discovered that many of the items on her list needed detailed information to satisfy her reader's concerns. Entries such as "Harriet needs to see financial benefits of expansion" would tell her that she had to provide some figures. However, other items requiring more detail might be more difficult to identify: "Income would more than pay for expansion" sounds reasonable enough, but Harriet would want to know how much more and in what period of time. On page 12 is an example of the preceding list after the scope has been established.

Be on guard, though, when establishing your scope. Writers who have much knowledge of a subject tend to "unload" information on readers who have no time or need to wade through a boring catalog of topics or a mass of details to get to the point. In establishing your scope, always be guided by your reader's needs and your purpose.

ORGANIZING YOUR IDEAS

Once you have established your scope, you should have a list of the ideas and facts to be included in your writing. Examine this list and look for relations among the items in it. Group the related ideas and arrange them under headings—short phrases that identify the kind of items in each group. Once you have established these groups, consider the order in which you would like to present them. In other words, determine which arrangement of groups would most effectively serve your purpose and your reader's needs. As you assemble and arrange the groups of ideas, feel free to rework the items in your groups—adding, deleting, and moving ideas around until you feel that you have the best possible organization. Following is a satisfactory organization of the preceding list.

```
Problems with Present System

        Turning away customers (21 last month)—6 equal to our
            biggest accounts
        Current computer can't handle state-of-the-art VRX
            software
        We can't offer improved services to our best customers
        We can't attract new customers with an old, limited sys-
            tem
```

<u>VT–8000 as a Solution</u>

> VT–8000 is a fast, reasonably priced, high-capacity computer
> VT–8000 would triple our capacity
> Cost of new equipment (list) and operating personnel (list)
> Increased income produced by expansion (list for projected two years)

<u>Advantages of Expansion</u>

> Surplus income would be $27,880
> VT–8000 requires little maintenance
> VT–8000 requires less-skilled staff than VT–3400
> VT–8000 is compact and fits our space
> VT–8000 can expand with peripherals
> Expansion will not disturb routine (VT–8000 is compatible)
> Include brochure for Harriet

To organize larger and more complex subjects a more formal outline is often helpful. Chapter 2 discusses outlining techniques in detail.

From these groups of items, presented in the order shown, Christine could have written a rough draft and polished it into a final memo that not only might have achieved its purpose but also would have demonstrated Christine's skill and effectiveness to her boss.

SUCCESSFUL WRITING

Soon after she received the disappointing response to her memo, Christine found the courage to step into Harriet's office. Christine explained, "I've really investigated the situation, and I'm sure my suggestion would be to our best interests. Perhaps if I gave you more information, you'd reconsider my suggestion." Harriet thought for a moment and then said, "All right. Give me the figures and major benefits tomorrow. If they are convincing, I'll talk to Fred Sadowski, our accountant, as soon as I get the chance." Christine Thomas left Harriet Sullivan's office both relieved and determined that this time she would convince Harriet.

After writing a statement of purpose; determining the needs of her reader; generating, gathering, and recording ideas and facts; and establishing her scope, Christine organized the items that she wanted to cover.

She then wrote the following memo. Notice that as she drafted and revised the memo, Christine found it advantageous to alter her original headings.

DATE: December 5, 19—

TO: Harriet Sullivan

FROM: Christine Thomas   *cT*

SUBJECT: Advantages of Expanding HVS Computing Facili-
            ties

As we discussed earlier, because our computing facilities currently operate at maximum capacity, we are turning new customers away in growing numbers and will soon have to deny present customers computer time for emergencies or overload backups. By purchasing a new VT–8000 minicomputer and expanding our staff, we could respond to new service requests, provide better service to valued customers, and attract new customers who would not have previously considered using our service.

Last month we turned away 21 new service requests. At least 6 of these requests were equal to the largest accounts we currently serve. Furthermore, since our aging mainframe computer cannot handle the latest software available from VRX Systems, we can neither offer improved, faster services to our most profitable accounts (such as First International Savings and Loan) nor attract the new customers who are eager to take advantage of the most recent advances in computer technology.

The VT–8000 is a very fast, reasonably priced minicomputer with massive peripheral memory capacity in the form of removable disk packs. This machine would triple our current processing capacity and enable us to use the full range of new VRX software now available. The following details show how purchasing the VT–8000 system would triple our number of customers and pay for itself within two years.

Cost of New Equipment	
VT–8000 minicomputer	$ 12,500
Two 3033 disks and disk drives	1,800
One VT80 computer terminal	980
New VRX software	1,050
Total cost of equipment	$ 16,330

<u>Increases in Annual Operating Budget</u>

Salaries:	Computer operator	$ 19,000
	Data entry technician	12,000
Total increase in annual		
operating budget		$ 31,000

<u>Total Costs</u>

First year	$ 47,330
Second year	26,200
Two-year total cost	$ 73,530

<u>Increased Income Generated by Expansion</u>

First-year estimate (45 new	
customers)	$ 37,010
Second-year estimate (50 new	
customers) plus the 45 of	
the first year	$ 64,400
Total	$101,410

Since the purchase of the VT-8000 system is a one-time investment a profit of $27,880 will be generated by the end of the second year. The estimates are based on the $751 average annual value of accounts over the past two years.

Other advantages of the VT-8000 minicomputer are as follows:

- It requires little maintenance and therefore suffers minimal downtime.
- It is easy to operate and thus requires less highly trained staff.
- It is extremely compact and will easily fit into space already available in our computer room.
- Additional peripheral equipment, such as disk drives and remote terminals, can be added at minimal cost if we decide to expand the facility again at a later date.

Because this system is reliable, easy to install, and easy to operate, we could have it running in three weeks with little disturbance of our normal office routine. More importantly, buying the VT-8000 will provide a cost-effective solution to the current problem of overburdened computing resources and will clear the way for meeting the demands of a growing base of customers. Although the VT-8000 printer is somewhat noisier than the VT-3400 printer, soundproofing the computer room is something that we had planned to do anyway.

On the basis of these details, I recommend that we expand
HVS services by purchasing the VT–8000 system. An enclosed
brochure describes the system in more detail. I will be happy
to provide additional information about the system at your
request.

Christine's story had a happy ending: Harriet was impressed with
Christine's memo and within a month ordered the VT-8000. Furthermore,
Christine was promoted to office manager, taking over many of Harriet's
duties in the expanded organization.

CHAPTER SUMMARY

Successful writing on the job is the result of careful preparation.
Successful writers prepare by precisely defining the purpose of their
writing, determining the identity and needs of their reader or readers
as specifically as possible, generating a list of ideas and facts, and establishing their scope. Then they organize their writing by logically grouping
their ideas and facts. Once organized, the ideas and facts can be converted
to a rough draft, then polished into final form. These two steps—writing
and revising—are the subjects of Chapters 3 and 5.

EXERCISES

1. Using the pattern suggested in this chapter, create a statement of
   purpose for a memo you could write. Select a problem at your place
   of employment (past or present) or on your campus—for instance,
   inadequate parking, poor cafeteria services, or lack of tuition reimbursement for job-related courses. Aim your memo at a reader who
   could make a decision regarding your suggestion. Be sure to give
   the reader's name and position in your statement of the objective.

2. Using the method for generating ideas described in this chapter,
   create a list of items for the subject selected for Exercise 1. Try to
   list at least 15 to 20 items—don't worry if some seem inappropriate,
   just keep listing.

3. Eliminate the items in your list from Exercise 2 that clearly do not
   meet the reader's needs or contribute to your objective. Then establish
   your scope and rewrite the resulting list.

4. Group the items in your revised list from Exercise 3 in three or more categories. Next, arrange the items in each category in sequence.

5. Using the outline created in Exercise 4, write the memo suggesting a solution to the problem.

6. For three of the following topics, or topics of your own choosing, list one possible purpose for a document and then list the kinds of information that would be needed to meet that objective. (Be sure to give *kinds* of information and not *sources* of information.) Since the following topics are broad, you will need to select some particular aspect of the broader topic. Be sure to identify your reader.

Topics

personal computers	music
highway construction	sports
real estate	electronics
office procedures	computer programming
welding	television
photography	occupations

EXAMPLE: Subject: Auto repair

Reader: The average driver

Objective: To instruct the average driver to remove and reinstall a carburetor for a 1985 Chevrolet so that it can be cleaned.

Kinds of Information: Required tools and new parts or new materials; location of the carburetor; detailed instructions on how to remove and reinstall the carburetor.

7. Find an article on a subject of interest to you in two different types of publications—for example, a newspaper and a newsmagazine, a magazine like *Popular Science* and a technical journal, and so on. After you have read the two articles, respond to the following:

   a. Compare the approaches taken in each article toward the intended audience. Look specifically for the presence or absence of technical terms, the kind and number of illustrations used, and the audience's apparent knowledge of the subject.

b. Create statements of purpose for each article, as if you had been the writer.

c. How well do you think the writers met the needs of their readers? (Respond only after you have completed *a* and *b*.)

8. Using the techniques described in this chapter, write a memo describing how you perform your job (or a job you've had) for an employee who may be replacing you while you are on vacation. Write two versions of this assignment:

a. For an employee hired through a temporary job service from outside the organization.

b. For an employee who works in your department but not in the same job.

9. Discuss similarities and differences between writing for the reader in 8*a* and writing for the reader in 8*b*.

10. Discuss the similarities and differences between writing on the job and writing for a general composition class.

11. Prepare a memo for your manager asking for tuition reimbursement to attend this or another course you are taking. Assume that the memo will be sent elsewhere for further approval. Use the course and text descriptions as well as the syllabus as you prepare your memo. Remember that the effectiveness of the memo will depend on how well you are able to help your reader see the value of this course. You may wish to attach supporting material (within reason); this material may not be counted as adding length to your memo. The length of the memo should be two or three double-spaced pages.

2

Organizing Your Information

When a motion picture is made, the scenes are usually shot out of the sequence in which they will appear in the finished film. Different shooting locations, actors' schedules, weather conditions, and many other circumstances make shooting out of sequence necessary. If it were not for a skilled film editor, the completed film would be a jumble of randomly shot scenes. The film editor, following the script, carefully splices the film together so that the story moves smoothly and logically from one event to the next, as the screen writer planned. Without a plan, no such order would be possible: the film editor would have no guide for organizing the thousands of feet of film.

Organizing a film and organizing a written document are obviously different tasks, but they have one element in common—both must be planned ahead of time. For a film, planning means creating a script. For a written document, it means organizing the information into a sequence appropriate to the subject, the purpose, and the reader.

Organizing your information before you write has two important advantages. First, it forces you to reexamine the information that you plan to include in your writing to be sure that you have sufficient facts and details to satisfy your reader's needs and achieve the purpose of your writing. Second, it forces you to order the information logically, so that your reader understands it as clearly as you do.

OUTLINING

For relatively short items, like memos and letters, you may need to jot down only a few notes to make sure that you haven't left out any important information and that you have arranged the information in a logical order. Longer documents generally require more elaborate planning; when such planning is necessary, the formal outline provides the best means.

An outline consists of phrases arranged according to the logical development of your subject. To create an outline, you begin by dividing your topic into its major sections. If these sections need to be subdivided, you divide them into their major parts. Then you identify all items by a number or a letter, according to the following system.

```
  I. Major section
     A. First-level subsection
        1. Second-level subsection
           a. Third-level subsection
              1) Fourth-level subsection
```

Outlining permits you to recognize at a glance the relative importance of divisions within your subject. Your subject will seldom require this many divisions, but the system allows for a highly detailed outline if one is necessary.

When you are ready to write, you should know your topic well enough that you can identify its major sections. Write them down. Then consider them carefully to make sure that they divide the topic logically. Assume, for example, that you are writing an article about computers for a company magazine. You might start with the following major sections.

```
  I. Development of computers
 II. Types of present applications
III. Future and potential benefits
 IV. Potential benefits to mankind
```

After a moment's reflection, you might decide that you can combine "present" and "future." A few more moments of thought might convince you that you can also combine "applications" and "benefits." So you might substitute the following two major sections for the original four.

```
  I. Development of computers
 II. Present and future applications and benefits
```

You quickly decide, however, that you have put too much into your second major section, so you make another effort.

```
  I. Development of computers
 II. Present applications
III. Future benefits
```

Now you are satisfied that you have arrived at the appropriate major sections for your topic.

Once you have established your major sections, look for minor divisions within each section. For example, you might first arrive at the following minor divisions within your first major section.

```
  I. Development of computers
     A. Early efforts not practical
     B. New industry created
 II. Present applications
     A. Business
     B. Social
III. Future benefits
     A. Economic
     B. Social
```

This outline is a start, but it is weak. The minor divisions are too vague to be useful. After considering these weaknesses, you might produce the following revision.

```
  I. Development of computers
     A. History of computing aids
     B. Development of the computer to a practical size
     C. New industry created around the more compact com-
        puter
 II. Present applications
     A. Business applications of the computer
     B. Social, scientific, and technical applications of
        the computer
III. Future benefits
     A. Potential impact of the computer on business and
        industry
     B. Potential social impact of the computer
```

Now you are ready to insert any notes that you may have compiled under the appropriate major and minor divisions.

I. Development of computers
    A. History of computing aids
        1. Abacus as man's first computing tool
        2. First electronic computer patented in 1944
    B. Development of the computer to a practical size
        1. Early computers very large, impractical for commercial use
        2. First electronic computer weighed 30 tons, took 1,500 square feet of floor space
        3. Introduction of transistor in 1958 made computer commercially practical
    C. New industry created around the more compact computer
        1. Transition from research phase to commercial application phase
        2. Corporate competition
II. Present applications
    A. Business applications of the computer
        1. Route long-distance telephone calls and set type
        2. Monitor airline reservations
        3. Replace typewriters as word processing devices
        4. Keep records and aid project management
        5. Communicate mail electronically
    B. Social, scientific, and technical applications of the computer
        1. Prepare weather forecasts
        2. Direct city traffic
        3. Maintain data banks on crime and criminals
        4. Monitor the condition of patients in hospitals
        5. Compare chemical characteristics of drugs
        6. Navigate ships and planes
        7. Monitor the performance of automobile engines
III. Future benefits
    A. Potential impact of the computer on business and industry
        1. More efficient day-to-day operations
        2. Greater productivity
        3. More leisure time for employees, enhancing the recreation industry
    B. Potential social impact of the computer
        1. Make education and government more effective
        2. Help find cures for diseases, translate languages, land jetliners without human aid

When you have finished, you have a complete outline. It is only a *rough* outline, however, because you still must check for a number of things. For example, you will need to make sure that corresponding divisions are equally important (that major divisions are equal to one another and minor divisions are equal to one another).

NOT
    II. Present applications
        A. Economic applications of the computer
        B. Social, scientific, and technical applications of the computer
        C. Future benefits

BUT
    II. Present applications
        A. Economic applications of the computer
        B. Social, scientific, and technical applications of the computer
    III. Future benefits

Make sure that all division heads at any one level are in parallel form. If you begin one with a noun phrase, for example, make sure that all heads at that level begin with noun phrases.

NOT
PARALLEL
    A. Potential economic impact of the computer
    B. The computer's potential social impact

PARALLEL
    A. Potential economic impact of the computer
    B. Potential social impact of the computer

Make sure that all topics are divided logically. A head must be divided into at least two parts if it is to be divided at all.

NOT
SUBDIVIDED
    A. Retailer benefits
        1. Permits direct transfer of purchase price to retailer's account

SUBDIVIDED
    A. Retailer benefits
        1. Permits direct transfer of purchase price to retailer's account
        2. Provides daily printout of vital records

Scan your outline for completeness, determining whether you need additional information. If you find that your research is not really complete, now is the time to return to your sources and dig out the missing data.

Finally, the outline is only a means to an end, not an end in itself. Don't view it as being cast in concrete. If you suddenly see a better way to organize your material while you are writing the draft, depart from your outline and follow the better approach. The main purpose of the outline is to bring order and shape to your writing *before* you begin to write the draft. But don't hesitate to improve upon the outline *as* you write the draft.

METHODS OF ORGANIZATION

The method of organization comes naturally for some types of writing. Instructions for operating a piece of machinery are arranged step by step. A trip report usually follows a chronological sequence. When a subject does not lend itself to one particular sequence, you can choose the best sequence, or combination of sequences, by considering your purpose in writing and your reader's needs. Suppose, for example, that you report on a trip to several offset-printing companies to gather information on the most efficient way to arrange equipment in the printing shop where you work. You would probably organize the report of the trip chronologically, but your description of the various shop layouts, emphasizing the physical locations of the equipment, would be organized spatially. If you went on to make recommendations about the most workable arrangement for your shop, you would present the most efficient arrangement first, the second most efficient arrangement next, and so on. Thus the recommendations portion of the report would be organized according to decreasing order of importance.

The most common ways to organize, or sequence, information in on-the-job writing are the following:

- step by step
- chronological
- spatial
- decreasing order of importance
- increasing order of importance
- general to specific
- specific to general

Step by Step

In the step-by-step sequence, you divide your subject into steps and then present the steps in the order in which they occur. This arrangement is most effective way to describe the operation of a mechanism, such as an internal combustion engine, or to explain a process, such as the administration of cardiopulmonary resuscitation. Step by step is also the logical method for writing instructions. For example, the instructions for using a pay telephone follow a step-by-step sequence.

For local calls:

1. Deposit coin.
2. Listen for dial tone.
3. Dial number.

The greatest advantage of presenting your information in a step-by-step sequence is that it is easy for your reader to understand and follow because the sequence of steps in your writing corresponds to the natural sequence of the process. If you were to write instructions for the proper way to process film, for example, you would present the information in a step-by-step sequence:

OUTLINE

I. Developing
  A. In total darkness, load film on spindle
  B. Enclose in developing tank
  C. Do not let film touch tank or other film
  D. Add developing solution
  E. Turn lights on
  F. Start timer: set for seven minutes
  G. Agitate for five seconds; then agitate for five seconds every half minute

II. Stopping
  A. Drain developer from tank
  B. Add stop bath
  C. Rinse 30 seconds in stop bath, agitating continually

III. Fixing
  A. Drain stop bath from tank
  B. Add fixing solution
  C. Fix for two to four minutes
  D. Agitate for five seconds, then agitate for five seconds every half minute

IV. Washing
  A. Remove tank top
  B. Remove film from tank and wash for 30 minutes under running water

V. Drying
  A. Hang film, placing drip pan beneath
  B. Sponge gently to remove excess water
  C. Allow film to dry completely, at room temperature

PROCESSING FILM

<u>Developing</u>. In total darkness, load the film on the spindle and enclose it in the developing tank. Be careful not to allow the film to touch the tank walls or other film. Add the developing solution, turn the lights on, and set the timer for seven minutes. Agitate for five seconds initially and then every half minute.

<u>Stopping</u>. When the timer sounds, drain the developing solution from the tank and add the stop bath. Agitate continually for 30 seconds.

<u>Fixing</u>. Drain the stop bath and add the fixing solution. Allow the film to remain in the fixing solution for two to four minutes. Agitate for five seconds initially and then every half minute.

<u>Washing</u>. Remove the tank top and wash the film for at least 30 minutes under running water.

<u>Drying</u>. Suspend the film from a hanger to dry. It is generally advisable to place a drip pan below the rack. Sponge the film gently to remove excess water. Allow the film to dry completely.

When you present your information in steps, you must carefully consider the needs of your reader. Do not assume that your readers are as familiar with your subject as you are; if they were, they wouldn't need your instructions. Even for a simple process, be sure that you list *all* steps and that you explain in adequate detail how each step is performed. Sometimes you must also indicate the purpose or function of each step.

In some instructions or process descriptions, the steps can be presented in one sequence only. The steps for using a pay telephone, for example, must be carried out in the sequence in which they are listed. In many other instructions or process descriptions, the steps can be presented in the sequence that the writer thinks is most effective.

Chronological

In a chronological sequence, you arrange events in the order in which they occur in time, beginning with the first event, going on to the next event, and so on until you have reached the last event. Trip reports, work schedules, minutes of meetings, and certain accident reports are among the types of writing in which information may be organized chronologically.

In the following report, a firefighter describes the events of a fire at a lumber mill. After providing important background information, the writer presents the events according to the sequence in which they occurred.

OUTLINE

```
  I. Setting
     A. Pile of combustible by-products stored near two
        buildings
     B. Fire building used as electric shop and storage area
        for lumber
     C. Fire building contained flammable liquids
     D. Fire building contained sprinkler system

 II. Cause of fire
     A. Spontaneous ignition of combustible by-products,
        which spread to second building
     B. Fire aided by 40-mph wind

III. Events of fire
     A. 6 a.m.: Fire first noticed
     B. 7 a.m. (approx.): Plant superintendent arrived and
        wet smoldering area
     C. 1:20 p.m.: Fire resumed in same area
     D. 1:25 p.m. (approx.): Fire department called
     E. Fire spread to second building: pumping equipment
        activated 15 to 30 minutes later
```

WOODWORKING PLANT FIRE[1]

Exposed Building Destroyed	July 24, 19—
Notification Delayed	Burney, California

Wood bark, sawdust, and wood chips were stored in three piles about 100 feet south of one building at this lumber mill and 150 feet west of a second building. The second building, called the "panel plant," consisted of one story and a partial attic and was used in part as an electric shop and in part for the storage of finished lumber. About six pallet loads of Class I flammable liquids in 55-gallon drums

---

[1] "Bimonthly Fire Record." *Fire Journal* 72 (March 1977), p. 24.

were stored in the western section. The building contained a sprinkler system.

Fire, caused by spontaneous ignition of the piled bark, spread to sawdust and chip piles, then to the chip-loading facilities, and finally to the panel plant. A 40-mph wind was blowing in the direction of the panel plant.

A watchman first noticed the fire in the bark pile about 6:00 a.m. He notified the plant superintendent, who arrived more than an hour later, hosed down the smoldering bark pile, and set up several irrigation sprinklers to wet the area.

At about 1:20 p.m., smoke was seen at the further end of the bark pile. The hose was not long enough to reach this area and the local fire department was called, nearly eight hours after the fire was originally discovered.

The fire burned up into the hollow joisted roof of the panel plant. The sprinklers were on a dry system and, from accounts of witnesses, it is estimated that the fire pump was not started until after the fire had been burning in the panel plant for 15 to 30 minutes.

The plant was a $350,000 loss. . . .

This report follows a chronological sequence because the time in which the events occurred and the intervals between events are crucial to an understanding of how the fire developed. Consequently, the chronological sequence is the best method for organizing this report.

Spatial

In a spatial sequence, you describe an object or a process according to the physical arrangement of its features. Depending upon the subject, you may describe the features from top to bottom, from side to side, from east to west (or west to east), from inside to outside, and so on. Descriptions of this kind rely mainly on dimension (height, width, length), direction (up, down, north, south), shape (rectangular, square, semicircular), and proportion (one-half, two-thirds). Features are described in relation to one another:

> One end is raised six to eight inches higher than the other end to permit the rain to run off.

Features are also described in relation to their surroundings:

> The lot is located on the east bank of the Kingman River.

The spatial method of organization is commonly used in descriptions of buildings and laboratory equipment, in proposals for landscape work, in construction-site progress reports and, in combination with a step-by-step sequence, in many types of instructions.

The following description of a small house relies on a bottom-to-top, clockwise (south to west to north to east) sequence, beginning with the front door:

OUTLINE

```
  I. Ground floor
     A. Front hall and stairwell
     B. Dining room
     C. Kitchen
     D. Bathroom
     E. Living room
 II. Second floor
     A. Hallway
     B. Southwest bedroom
     C. Northwest bedroom
     D. Bathroom
     E. Bathroom
     F. Master bedroom
```

INTERIOR OF A TWO–STORY, FIVE–ROOM HOUSE

The front door faces south and opens into a hallway seven feet deep and ten feet wide. At the end of the hallway is the stairwell, which begins on the right–hand (east) side of the hallway, rises five steps to a landing, and reverses direction at the left–hand (west) side of the hallway. To the left (west) of the hallway is the dining room, which measures 15 feet along its southern exposure and ten feet along its western exposure. Directly to the north of the dining room is the kitchen, which measures ten feet along its western exposure and 15 feet along its northern exposure. To the east of the kitchen, along the northern side of the house, is a bathroom that measures ten feet (west to east) by five feet. Parallel to this bathroom is a passageway having the same dimensions as the bathroom and leading from the kitchen to the living room. The living room, which measures 15 feet (west to east) by 20 feet (north to south), occupies the entire eastern end of the floor.

On the second floor, at the top of the stairs is an L–shaped hallway, five feet wide. The base of the ''L,'' over the front door, is 15 feet long. The vertical arm of the ''L'' is 13 feet long. To the west of the hall is the southwest

bedroom, which measures ten feet along its southern exposure
and eight feet along its western exposure. Directly to the
north, over the kitchen, is the northwest bedroom, which
measures 12 feet along its western exposure and ten feet
along its northern exposure. To the east, at the end of the
hall, is a bathroom, which is five feet wide along the northern side of the house and seven feet long. To the east of
this bathroom and also along the northern side of the house
is the master bathroom, which is ten feet square and is entered from the master bedroom, which is directly over the
living room. Like the living room, the master bedroom measures 15 feet along the northern and southern exposures of
the house and 20 feet along the eastern exposure.

Decreasing Order of Importance

When you organize your information in decreasing order of importance, you begin with the most important fact or point, then go on to
the next most important, and so on, ending with the least important.
Newspaper readers are familiar with this sequence of information. The
most significant information always appears first in a news story, with
related but secondary information completing the story.

Decreasing order of importance is an especially appropriate method
of organization for a report addressed to a busy decision-maker, who
may be able to reach a decision after considering only the most important
points—and who may not even have time to read the entire report. This
sequence of information is useful, too, for a report written for a variety
of readers, some of whom may be interested in only the major points
and others in all the points. The following outline presents an example
of such an approach.

OUTLINE

    I. Most qualified candidate: Mildred Bryant, acting chief
        A. Positive factors
            1. Twelve years' experience in claims processing
            2. Thoroughly familiar with section's operations
            3. Strong production record
            4. Continually ranked ''outstanding'' on job ap-
               praisals
        B. Negative factors
            1. Supervisory experience limited to present ten-
               ure as acting chief
            2. Lacks college degree required by job description

II. Second most qualified candidate: Michael Bastick, claims coordinator
   A. Positive factors
      1. Able administrator
      2. Seven years' experience in section's operations
      3. Currently enrolled in management-training course
   B. Negative factors
      1. Lacks supervisory experience
      2. Most recent work indirectly related to claims processing
III. Third most qualified candidate: Jane Fine, administrative assistant
   A. Positive factors
      1. Skilled administrator
      2. Three years' experience in claims processing
   B. Negative factors
      1. Lacks broad knowledge of claims procedures
      2. Lacks supervisory experience

MEMORANDUM

TO: Mary Vincenti, Chief, Personnel Department
FROM: Frank W. Russo, Chief, Claims Department   *FwR*
DATE: November 13, 19—
SUBJECT: Selection of Chief of the Claims Processing Section

The most qualified candidate for Chief of the Claims Processing Section is Mildred Bryant, who is at present acting chief of the Claims Processing Section. In her 12 years in the Claims Department, Ms. Bryant has gained wide experience in all facets of the department's operations. She has maintained a consistently high production record and has demonstrated the skills and knowledge that are required for the supervisory duties she is now handling in an acting capacity. Another consideration is that she has continually been rated ''outstanding'' in all categories of her job-performance appraisals. However, her supervisory experience is limited to her present three-month tenure as acting chief of the section, and she lacks the college degree required by the job description.

Michael Bastik, claims coordinator, my second choice, also has strong potential for the position. An able administrator, he has been with the company for seven years. Further, he is presently enrolled in a management—training course at the university. He is ranked second, however, because he lacks supervisory experience and because his most recent work has been with the department's maintenance and supply components. He would be the best person to take over many of Mildred Bryant's responsibilities if she should be made full—time chief of the Claims Processing Section.

Jane Fine, my third—ranking candidate, has shown herself a skilled administrator in her three years with the Claims Consideration Section. Despite her obvious potential, my main objection to her is that, compared with the other top candidates, she lacks the breadth of experience in claims processing that would be required of someone responsible for managing the Claims Processing Section. Jane Fine also lacks on—the—job supervisory experience.

Increasing Order of Importance

When you want the most important of several ideas to be freshest in your reader's mind at the end of your writing, you organize your information by increasing order of importance. This sequence is useful in argumentative writing when saving your strongest points until the end suits your purpose and your perception of your audience. The sequence begins with the least important point or fact, then moves to the next least important, and builds finally to the most important point at the end. You lead your reader to the conclusion you want him or her to reach by building your case inductively.

Writing organized by increasing order of importance has the disadvantage of beginning weakly, with the least important information. This can cause your reader to become impatient before reaching your main point. But for writing in which the ideas lead, point by point, to an important conclusion, increasing order of importance is an effective method of organization. Reports on production or personnel goals are often arranged by this method, as are oral presentations. Below is an example of this approach.

OUTLINE

  I. Staffing problem
    A. Too few qualified electronics technicians
    B. New recruiting program necessary
  II. Recruitment of veterans
    A. Relied heavily on veterans in past
    B. Fewer veterans now available

       C. Want ads aimed at veterans less successful than in
          past
  III. Apprentice program
       A. Providing insufficient numbers
       B. Fewer high school graduates entering program
   IV. Technical colleges
       A. Provide pool of trained technicians
       B. Recommend recruiting from this group

MEMORANDUM

To: William D. Vane, Vice President, Operations
From: Harry Matthews, Personnel Department   *HM*
Date: December 3, 19—
Subject: Recruiting Qualified Electronics Technicians

To keep our company staffed with qualified electronics technicians, we will have to redirect our recruiting program.

In the past dozen years, we have relied heavily on the recruitment of skilled veterans. An end to the military draft, as well as attractive reenlistment bonuses for skilled technicians now in uniform, have all but eliminated veterans as a source of trained employees. Our attempts to reach this group through ads in service and daily newspapers have not been successful recently. I think that the want ads should continue, although each passing month brings fewer and fewer veterans as job applicants.

Our in-house apprentice program has not provided the needed personnel either. High school enrollments in the area are continually dropping. Each year, fewer high school graduates, our one source of trainees for the apprentice program, enter the shop. Even vigorous Career Day recruiting has yielded disappointing results. The number of students interested in the apprentice program has declined proportionately as school enrollment has dropped.

The local and regional technical schools produce the greatest number of qualified electronics technicians. These graduates tend to be highly motivated, in part because many have obtained their education at their own expense. The training and experience they have received in the technical programs, moreover, are first-rate. Competition for these graduates is keen, but I recommend that we increase our recruiting efforts and hire a larger share of this group than we have been doing.

I would like to meet with you soon to discuss the details
of a more dynamic recruiting program in the technical
schools. I am certain that with the right recruitment campaign we can find the skilled personnel essential to our
expanding role in electronics products and services.

General to Specific

In a general-to-specific sequence, you begin your writing with a general statement and then provide facts or examples to develop and support
that statement. For example, if you begin a report with the general
statement "Companies that diversify are more successful than those that
do not," the remainder of the report would offer examples and statistics
that prove to your reader that companies that diversify are, in fact,
more successful than companies that do not.

A memorandum or report organized in a general-to-specific sequence
discusses only one point—the point made in the opening general statement. All other information in the memo or report supports the general
statement, as in the following example.

OUTLINE

The company needs to locate additional suppliers of circuits
because of several related events.

    I. The current supplier is reducing output.
   II. Domestic demand for our calculators continues to in-
      crease.
  III. We are expanding into the foreign market.

LOCATING ADDITIONAL CIRCUIT SUPPLIERS

**GENERAL
STATEMENT**
On the basis of information presented at the Supply Committee meeting on April 14, we recommend that the company
locate additional suppliers of integrated circuits. Several related events make such an action necessary.

Our current supplier, ABC Electronics, is reducing its
output. Specifically, we can expect a reduction of between
800 and 1,000 units per month for the remainder of this fiscal
year. The number of units should stabilize at 15,000 units
per month thereafter.

Domestic demand for our calculators continues to grow.

**SUPPORTING
INFORMATION**
Demand during the current fiscal year is up 25,000 units
over the last fiscal year. Sales Department projections for
the next five years show that demand should peak next year

at 50,000 units and then remain at that figure for at least
the following four years.

Finally, our overseas expansion into England and West
Germany will require additional shipments of 5,000 units
per quarter to each country for the remainder of this fiscal
year. Sales Department projections put calculator sales for
each country at double this rate, or 20,000 units in a fiscal
year, for the next five years.

Examples and data that support the general statements are frequently accompanied by charts and graphs. Guidelines for creating and
presenting illustrations are given in Chapter 13.

Specific to General

When you organize information in a specific-to-general sequence,
you begin with specific information and build to a general conclusion.
The examples, facts, and statistics that you present in your writing support the general conclusion that comes at the end. For example, if your
subject were highway safety, you might begin with details of a specific
highway accident, go on to generalize about how that accident was similar
to many others, and then present recommendations for reducing the
probability of such accidents. If your purpose is to persuade a skeptical
reader by providing specific details, this method is useful because it
suspends the general point until your case has been made. This method
of organization is somewhat like increasing order of importance in that
you carefully build your case and do not actually make your point until
the end. Here is an example:

OUTLINE

   I. Study of 4,500 accidents involving nearly 7,200 front-
      seat passengers showed only 20 percent wore seat belts.
  II. Studies show front-seat passengers without belts are
      four times as likely to be killed as those wearing
      belts.
 III. Estimated 40 percent of front-seat passenger car
      deaths could be prevented if seat belts were worn.
  IV. Survival chances in an accident are greater with seat
      belts.

THE FACTS ABOUT SEAT BELTS

STATISTIC   Recently a government agency studied the use of seat
belts in 4,500 accidents involving nearly 7,200 front-seat

passengers of the vehicles involved. Nearly all these accidents occurred on routes that had a speed limit of at least
40 mph. Only 20 percent of all the front-seat passengers
were wearing seat belts, and the study showed that those
not using seat belts were more than four times as likely to
be killed as those using them.

**GENERAL
CONCLUSION**   A conservative estimate is that 40 percent of the front-
seat passenger car deaths could be prevented if everyone
used the seat belts that the law requires the manufacturer
to put into each automobile. If you are in an accident, your
chances of survival are far greater if you are using your
seat belt.

CHAPTER SUMMARY

This chapter has presented the most commonly used methods of
organizing information in job-related writing: step by step, chronological,
spatial, decreasing order of importance, increasing order of importance,
general to specific, and specific to general. Some subjects lend themselves
naturally to a particular method. Other subjects can be organized in
more than one way; you must choose the best method on the basis of
your reader's needs and the purpose of your writing.

A simple outline will help you to organize the information into a
logical sequence before you begin to write. Preparing an outline gives
you a chance to reexamine your information and order it in such a way
that your reader will understand it as clearly as you do.

EXERCISES

1. Below is a sample of a poorly developed outline. Prepare a new outline
   in which the weaknesses are corrected.

COMPANY SPORTS

I. Intercompany sports
   A. Advantages to the company
      1. Publicity
      2. Intercompany relations
   B. Disadvantages
      1. Misplaced emphasis
      2. Athletic participation restricted
II. Intracompany sports
   A. Wide participation
   B. Physical fitness

C. Detracts from work

D. Risks injuries

2. The following list contains both major and minor heads. Select the heads that you feel should be major heads and arrange them in the appropriate sequence. Then select the minor heads that should go under each major head and arrange them in the appropriate sequence. Put each next to the appropriate Roman numeral or capital letter. Use the following definitions:

CONDUCTION: the transmission of cold or heat *through solid material.*

AIR INFILTRATION: the transmission of cold or heat *through cracks and other open spaces.*

Report on a Plan to Remodel a 50-Year-Old House to Make It More Energy Efficient

I. ——————————— Insulation

   A. ——————————— Introduction

   B. ——————————— Heat Loss Through Conduction

   C. ——————————— Scope of the Report

II. ——————————— Storm Doors and Windows

   A. ——————————— The Solutions

   B. ——————————— Procedure Used to Prepare the Report

III. ——————————— Heat Loss Through Air Infiltration

   A. ——————————— The Problems

   B. ——————————— Weatherstripping

   C. ——————————— Purpose of the Report

   D. ——————————— Caulking

3. Key all the following notes to the topic outline you created. Use the following definitions:

WINDOW SASH: the frame holding the panes of a window

WINDOW CASING: the framework in a wall within which the window sash is set

- Specific costs are not discussed.
- Caulking is a flexible adhesive that is used to insulate against air infiltration.
- Fiberglass (six inches thick) should be installed between the unfinished basement and the floor.

- Recommend a remodeling plan to make the house more energy efficient.
- Window sashes and casings fit loosely.
- The best weatherstripping is the spring-bronze or felt-hair type.
- The cost of insulating is recovered in fuel savings in five years.
- The proposed plan does not specify methods or materials.
- The house will be warmer in winter and cooler in summer.
- Lack of insulation means that much of the heat passes through the walls and ceilings by conduction.
- Caulking should be done after weatherstripping.
- The history of the house was studied.
- Storm windows and doors also reduce conduction through the glass by half.
- The windows and doors were checked for air leaks.
- Weatherstripping is insulating material that is installed around windows and doors in an outside wall to help insulate against air infiltration.
- Each cavity between the studs in the walls should be filled with foam.
- Fuel bills will be lower.
- Doors and windows, made of thin materials, waste vast amounts of heat.
- Eight inches of insulation should be installed in the attic.
- To ensure watertight weatherstripping, windows should be sealed and new window latches should be installed.
- Caulking provides an airtight seal between the doors and windows and the building materials.

The report deals with the causes of heat loss and the solutions being recommended to solve the problem.

- The house was built at a time when little insulation was used.
- A storm window or door is an extra window or door in an outside wall to help insulate against air infiltration.
- Insulation is material that resists the conduction of heat and cold. It is installed in attics and walls of the homes.
- Doors do not close tightly.
- Such openings allow cold air to enter and hot air to escape.
- Insulation provides comfort and a pleasant sense of well-being.
- Storm windows and doors should be installed to help reduce air infiltration.
- Conduction through doors and windows is even worse.
- The structure of the building and its foundation were studied.

4. Create an outline for one of the following topics, organizing it in a *step-by-step* sequence. Using the outline, write a paper of assigned length on the topic.

    a. Changing a washer in a wash basin faucet
    b. Starting and banking a fire in a wood-burning stove
    c. Tuning a six-string acoustic guitar
    d. Opening a checking account
    e. Sharpening a chain-saw blade
    f. Splicing together two pieces of movie film
    g. Bathing a bedridden adult
    h. Repairing a broken window
    i. Borrowing money on a life insurance policy
    j. Maturing of a monarch butterfly egg to an adult

5. Create an outline for one of the following topics, organizing it by a *chronological* sequence. Using the outline, write a paper of assigned length on the topic.

    a. A report on an accident
    b. Instructions for breeding, raising, and selling puppies or other pets
    c. A description of the life cycle of a typical fruit, from blossom to ripe fruit, in one growing season

6. Create an outline for one of the following topics, organizing it in a *spatial* sequence. Using the outline, write a paper of assigned length on the topic. Without relying on illustrations, describe the topic clearly enough so that a classmate, if asked, could create an accurate drawing or diagram based on your description.

    a. The layout of your apartment or of a floor in your home
    b. The layout of the reference room or other area of the school library
    c. The dimensions and pertinent features of the grounds of a public building
    d. The layout of a vegetable or flower garden
    e. The layout of the shop, office, or laboratory where you work
    f. Instructions for disinfecting a hospital room, exterminating insects in a kitchen or other area, or painting or wallpapering a room

7. Create an outline for one of the following topics, organizing it by a *decreasing-order-of-importance* sequence. Using the outline, write a paper of assigned length on the topic.

    a. Your job qualifications
    b. The advantages to you of living in a particular city or area of the country
    c. The importance of preventive maintenance of a machine or piece of equipment with which you are familiar

   d. The importance of preventive care in one health-related area (diet, exercise, dental care, and so on)

8. Create an outline for one of the following topics, organizing it by an *increasing-order-of-importance* sequence. Using the outline, write a paper of assigned length on the topic.

   a. The college courses that you believe will be most important to your career (discuss no more than five)
   b. Why smoking should or should not be permitted in the classroom or on the job
   c. The advantages of learning to pilot a small airplane
   d. The reasons why you need a pay raise
   e. The advantages of a home solar-heating system
   f. A proposal to change a procedure where you work

9. For this exercise, use a *general-to-specific* sequence. Choose one of the following statements, then support it with pertinent facts, examples, anecdotes, and so on. Outline the information and write a paper of assigned length based on the outline.

   a. Volunteer jobs provide valuable experience in the working world.
   b. For families on limited means, budgeting is essential.
   c. The mark of a capable administrator is willingness to delegate authority.

10. For this exercise, use a *specific-to-general* sequence. For one of the following sets of data, study the trends or patterns that are presented, draw your own conclusions, and state the conclusions in a plausible general statement. Outline the information that supports your main point, and write a paper of assigned length based on your outline. Alternatively, as a basis for this exercise you may select other information from lists and tables in current yearbooks, almanacs, or newspapers.

   a. Deaths from Motor Vehicle Accidents in the United States

1978	51,500
1977	48,849
1976	44,520
1975	45,853
1974	46,402
1973	55,511
1972	56,278

b. Vocational Training in the United States, 1979

Type of Training	Men (18–24)	Women (18–24)
Office	300,000	1,100,000
Nursing, health	63,000	432,000
Trades	1,100,000	384,000
Engineering	277,000	19,000
Agriculture and home economics	83,000	46,000
Other	153,000	93,000

3

Writing the Draft

If you have gathered and recorded enough information to meet your purpose, reader's needs, and scope, as described in Chapter 1, and if you have prepared an outline, as described in Chapter 2, you are well prepared to write a rough draft. Yet writing the draft for most people remains a chore—if not an obstacle.

One technique experienced writers use to get started is to think of writing a rough draft as simply transcribing and expanding the notes from the outline into paragraphs without worrying about grammar, style, or such mechanical aspects of writing as spelling. Refinement will come with revision, the details of which are discussed in Chapter 5.

Another technique is to write the rough draft quickly, concentrating entirely upon converting your outline to sentences and paragraphs. Write directly to your reader—as though you were explaining your subject to someone across the desk from you.

Whatever technique you use, don't worry about a good opening— that can wait until you've constructed your paragraphs. Just start. Concentrate on *ideas,* without attempting to polish or revise. Writing and revising are different activities. Keep writing quickly to achieve unity, coherence, and proportion.

As you write your rough draft, remember that the first rule of good writing is to *help your readers.* Your function as a writer is to communicate certain information to them. So do not try to impress them with a fancy writing style. Write in a plain and direct style that is comfortable and natural for both you and for them.

Also keep your readers' level of knowledge of the subject in mind.

Doing so will not only help you write directly to them but it will also tell you which terms you must define. (Review Chapter 6, Writing for Specific Purposes, for guidelines on when to define.)

Above all, don't wait for inspiration to write the rough draft—treat writing the draft as you would any on-the-job task. The following are tactics that experienced writers use to start, keep moving, and get the job done; you will discover which ones are the most helpful to you.

Tips for Writing the Rough Draft

- Set up your writing area with the equipment and materials (paper, dictionary, source books, etc.) you will need to keep going once you get started. Then hang out the "Do Not Disturb" sign.
- Use whatever writing tools, separately or in combination, are most comfortable for you: pencil, felt-tip pen, typewriter, word processor, etc.
- Remind yourself that you are beginning a version of your writing project that *no one* else will read.
- Remember the writing projects you've *finished* in the past—you *have* completed something before and you *will* this time.
- Start with the section that seems most easy to you. Your reader will neither know nor care that you first wrote a section in the middle.
- Give yourself a time limit (ten or 15 minutes, for example) in which you will write continually regardless of how good or bad your writing seems to you. The point is to *keep moving*.
- Don't let anything stop you when you are rolling along easily—if you stop and come back, you may not regain the momentum.
- Stop writing before you're completely exhausted; when you begin again, you may be able to regain the momentum.
- Give yourself a small reward—a short walk, a soft drink, a short chat with a friend, an easy task—after you have finished a section.
- Reread what you've written when you return to your writing. Often, seeing what you've written will trigger the frame of mind that was productive.
- Use a tape recorder to prepare a rough draft. (Try this strategy with a small document first; some writers find that they become very wordy on tape recorders, and others are intimidated by the machine.)

The most effective way to start and to keep going, however, is to use a good outline as a springboard and a map for your writing. The outline also serves to group related facts and details. Once these facts are grouped, you are ready to construct unified and coherent paragraphs— the major building blocks of any piece of writing.

Suppose you were responsible for writing the report of a committee examining possible locations for a new distribution center. One part of your outline might concern the way in which the committee narrowed 30 possible locations to three.

OUTLINE

I. Method Committee Used to Narrow Locations
   A. Committee considered 30 locations
   B. Committee eliminated 20 locations because of problems with labor supply, tax structure, and so forth
   C. Committee selected three cities to visit
   D. Committee visited Chicago, Minneapolis, and Philadelphia
   E. Committee's observations follow in the report

From this group of items, you could write the following paragraph:

> The committee narrowed 30 possible locations for the new distribution center to three. Twenty possibilities were eliminated almost immediately for reasons ranging from unfavorable tax structures to inadequate labor supplies. Of the remaining ten locations, the committee selected for intensive study the three cities that seemed to offer the best transportation and support facilities: Chicago, Minneapolis, and Philadelphia. The committee then visited these three cities, and its observations on each follow in this report.

Because the sentences in the paragraph evolved from the items listed in the group, every sentence is directly related to one central idea—narrowing the selection of possible locations for the distribution center to three cities. Notice that the paragraph does not contain the committee's final recommendation or the specific advantages of each of the three cities. Those details will follow later in the report. To include such details in this paragraph would make the paragraph stray from its one central idea. In fact, the function of any paragraph is to develop a single thought or idea within a larger piece of writing.

PARAGRAPH UNITY

When every sentence in a paragraph contributes to developing one central idea, the paragraph has *unity*. If a paragraph contains sentences that do not develop the central idea, it lacks unity. The following is a later paragraph from the report in which possible locations for the new distribution center are evaluated. Does this paragraph have unity?

Probably the greatest advantage of Chicago as the location for our new distribution center is its excellent transportation facilities. The city is served by three major railroads. In fact, Chicago was at one time the hub of cross-country rail transportation. Chicago is also a major center of the trucking industry, and most of the nation's large freight carriers have terminals there. We are concerned, however, about the delivery problems that we've had with several truck carriers. We've had far fewer problems with air freight. Both domestic and international air cargo services are available at O'Hare International Airport. Finally, except in the winter months when the Great Lakes are frozen, Chicago is a seaport, accessible through the St. Lawrence Seaway.

Every sentence in this paragraph should have been about *the advantages of Chicago's transportation facilities*. Three sentences, however, do not develop that central idea: the sentence about Chicago as the former hub of rail transportation, and the two sentences about delivery problems. These sentences are italicized below:

Probably the greatest advantage of Chicago as the location for our new distribution center is its excellent transportation facilities. The city is served by three major railroads. *In fact, Chicago was at one time the hub of cross-country rail transportation.* Chicago is also a major center of the trucking industry, and most of the nation's large freight carriers have terminals there. *We are concerned, however, about the delivery problems that we've had with several truck carriers. We've had far fewer problems with air freight.* Both domestic and international air cargo services are available at O'Hare International Airport. Finally, except in the winter months when the Great Lakes are frozen, Chicago is a seaport, accessible through the St. Lawrence Seaway.

Now read the paragraph without the italicized sentences. Each of the remaining sentences is directly related to the central idea, and the paragraph has unity.

Probably the greatest advantage of Chicago as the location for our new distribution center is its excellent transportation facilities. The city is served by three major railroads. Chicago is also a major center of the trucking industry, and most of the nation's large freight carriers have terminals there. Both domestic and international air cargo services are available at O'Hare International Airport. Finally, except in the winter months when the Great Lakes are frozen, Chicago is a seaport, accessible through the St. Lawrence Seaway.

One way to make sure that your paragraph has unity is to provide a *topic sentence,* which is a sentence within a paragraph that clearly states the central idea of that paragraph. If every sentence in the paragraph directly relates to the topic sentence, the paragraph will have unity.

Notice that all the sentences in the following paragraph directly relate to the topic sentence:

> *Probably the greatest advantage of Chicago as the location for our new distribution center is its excellent transportation facilities.* The city is served by three major railroads. Chicago is also a major center of the trucking industry, and most of the nation's large freight carriers have terminals there. Both domestic and international air cargo service is available at O'Hare International Airport. Finally, except in the winter months when the Great Lakes are frozen, Chicago is a seaport, accessible through the St. Lawrence Seaway.

Beginning a paragraph with the topic sentence helps both the writer and the reader. The writer has no difficulty constructing a unified paragraph because every sentence can be measured against the topic sentence and the central idea it expresses. And the reader knows immediately what the paragraph is about because the opening sentence states the central idea. Busy readers, especially, appreciate being told at once what a paragraph will deal with. For this reason, topic sentences are usually the first sentences of paragraphs in on-the-job writing.

Occasionally, however, a topic sentence may be placed somewhere other than at the beginning of a paragraph. A topic sentence may be the last sentence of a paragraph, for example. Placing the topic sentence at the end of a paragraph emphasizes the central idea because all the sentences build up to that idea. Notice how the sentences in the following paragraph lead up to the topic sentence:

> A study by the Department of Agriculture revealed that insect damage in our region increased from 15% to 23% between 1975 and 1977. During this past year, many farmers reported a 30% increase in insect damage over damage that had occurred the previous year. Furthermore, another recent study found that certain destructive insects are migrating north into our area. *Clearly, we should prepare for increased insect damage in the coming year.*

Although a topic sentence placed at the end of a paragraph provides a forceful conclusion, it also makes reading the paragraph more difficult. Especially in on-the-job situations, where time is at a premium, the reader may become irritated at having to plow through details to reach the main point of a paragraph. Therefore, it is best to place topic sentences at the ends of paragraphs only occasionally.

PARAGRAPH LENGTH

Paragraph length should be tailored to the reader's convenience. Specifically, a paragraph should help the reader by providing a physical break on the page as well as by signaling a new idea. Long paragraphs can intimidate your reader by failing to provide manageable subdivisions of thought. Overly short paragraphs have a disadvantage too: they may make it difficult for the reader to see the logical relationships between ideas in your writing. A series of short paragraphs can also sacrifice unity by breaking a single idea into several pieces.

Although there are no fixed rules for the length of paragraphs, paragraphs in on-the-job writing average about 100 words each, with two or three paragraphs to a double-spaced, typewritten page. Paragraphs in letters tend to be shorter; two- or even one-sentence paragraphs are not unusual in letters. The best advice is that a paragraph should be just long enough to deal adequately with the central idea stated in its topic sentence. A new paragraph should begin whenever the subject changes significantly.

PARAGRAPH COHERENCE

An effective paragraph has not only unity but *coherence;* that is, it takes the reader logically and smoothly from one sentence to the next. When a paragraph is coherent, the reader clearly recognizes that one sentence or idea leads logically to the next, which in turn leads to the sentence or idea that is next, and so on. Consider the following paragraph. Does each sentence or idea lead logically and clearly to the one that follows?

> Most adjustable office chairs have nylon hub tubes that hold metal spindle rods. To ensure trouble-free operation, lubricate these spindle rods occasionally. Loosen the set screw in the adjustable bell. Lift the chair from the base so that the entire spindle rod is accessible. Apply the lubricant to the spindle rod and the nylon washer, using the lubricant sparingly to prevent dripping. Replace the chair and tighten the set screw.

Because each sentence in the paragraph says something about how to lubricate an adjustable office chair, the paragraph has unity. Yet the paragraph does not move as smoothly from one sentence to the next as it could. Nor does the paragraph make as clear as possible how each idea relates to the others. Transitional devices, as discussed below, will achieve both these goals.

Transitions Between Sentences

Transitional devices are words and phrases that help the reader to move smoothly from one sentence to the next and to see the logical relationships between the sentences. Notice how the simple technique of putting the steps in sequence (see the italicized words and phrases) provides effective transitions between ideas in the sample paragraph:

> Most adjustable office chairs have nylon hub tubes that hold metal spindle rods. To ensure trouble-free operation, lubricate these spindle rods occasionally. *First,* loosen the set screw in the adjustable bell. *Then* lift the chair from the base so that the entire spindle rod is accessible. *Next,* apply the lubricant to the spindle rod and the nylon washer, using the lubricant sparingly to prevent dripping. *When you have finished,* replace the chair and tighten the set screw.

Now, because the transitional devices provide coherence, the reader can follow the writer's step-by-step instructions easily. The word *first* indicates that the statement following is the first step in lubricating the rods. The words *then* and *next* point out the logical, step-by-step relationship of the instructions that follow. The phrase *when you have finished* tells the reader that the lubricating process is finished and that a new instruction will follow.

The following list includes other words and phrases that commonly function as transitional devices:

- To express result: *therefore, as a result, consequently, thus, hence*
- To express example: *for example, for instance, specifically, as an illustration*
- To express comparison: *similarly, likewise*
- To express contrast: *but, yet, still, however, nevertheless, on the other hand*
- To express addition: *moreover, furthermore, also, too, besides, in addition*
- To express time: *now, later, meanwhile, since then, after that, before that time*
- To express sequence: *first, second, third, then, next, finally*

Some of the words and phrases given above are nearly synonymous but imply somewhat different logical connections. Be sure that the transitional device you choose conveys the precise meaning you intend.

Another transitional device is the use of pronouns, such as *he, she, they,* and *it.* Because pronouns refer to a person or thing mentioned in a previous sentence, they bind sentences and ideas together. Notice the use of pronouns as transitional devices in the following paragraph:

It **refers to punch press**

They **refers to first-shift employees**

He **refers to Bill Taylor**

> We have recently discovered a problem with the #41 *punch press*. *It* consistently fails to retract fully when *it* is shut off at the end of the second shift. *First-shift employees* are concerned that this condition poses a safety hazard. *They* believe that the press could go through a cycle after the power has been turned on. *Bill Taylor,* a second-shift supervisor, reports that the maintenance department does not consider the problem to be a safety hazard. *He* has pointed out to me, however, that when the power is turned on, the safety shield is not in place. *He* believes that this fact warrants a thorough analysis of the problem.

Although pronouns can be excellent transitional devices, they confuse the reader if the person or thing to which the pronoun refers is not perfectly clear.

CONFUSING   Midcity College is located in the central business district of the city. *It* is very large.

It is confusing because the reader must guess whether *it* refers to the college, the business district, or the city. In such a case, repeating a word is better.

BETTER   Midcity College is located in the central business district of the city. The *college* is very large.

The problem of pronoun reference is discussed in Chapter 5.

Another transitional device that links sentences and ideas is the repetition of key words and phrases. Notice how repetition of the key words and phrases in the paragraph below moves the paragraph forward:

> Over the past several months, I have heard complaints about the Merit Award *Program*. Specifically, many employees feel that this *program* should be linked to annual *salary increases*. They believe that *salary increases* would provide a much better incentive than the current $150 to $300 *cash awards* for exceptional service. In addition, these *employees believe* that their supervisors consider the *cash awards* a satisfactory alternative to salary increases. Although I don't think this practice is widespread, the fact that the *employees believe* that it is justifies a reevaluation of the Merit Award Program.

Transitions Between Paragraphs

Transitional devices used to link sentences can also be effective for transition between paragraphs. The repetition of a key phrase, for example, connects the first paragraph below with the one that follows.

Consumers spend more money for plumbing repairs than for any other home repair service. The most common repair that plumbers make is the clearing of drains. Since the kitchen *sink drain* is used more often than any other drain in the home, that is the drain that is most often clogged.

Clearing the *sink drain* yourself is easier than you might expect. You probably have all the tools you need. . . .

Another transitional device for linking paragraphs is to begin a paragraph with a sentence that summarizes the preceding paragraph. In the following excerpt from a report, notice how the first sentence in the second paragraph summarizes the ideas presented in the first paragraph:

Each year, forest fires in our region cause untold destruction. For example, wood ashes washed into streams after a fire often kill large numbers of fish. In addition, the destruction of the vegetation along stream banks causes water temperatures to rise, making the stream unfit for several varieties of cold-water fish. Forest fires, moreover, hurt the tourist and recreation business, for vacationers are not likely to visit flame-blackened areas.

The opening sentence summarizes the examples from the preceding paragraph

These losses, and many other indirect losses caused by forest fires, damage not only the quality of life but also the economy of our region. They also represent a huge drain on the resources and manpower of the Department of Natural Resources. For example, our financial investment last year in fighting forest fires. . . .

If used sparingly, another effective transitional device between paragraphs is to ask a question at the end of one paragraph and answer it at the beginning of the next. This device works well in the following example:

Transition using a question and answer

Automation has become an ugly word in the American vocabulary because it has sometimes meant the displacement of employees from their jobs. But the all-important fact that is so often overlooked is that automation invariably creates many more jobs than it eliminates. The vast number of people employed through automation in the American automobile industry, compared with the number of people who had been employed in the harness-and-carriage-making business, is a classic example. Almost always, the jobs that have been eliminated by automation have been menial, unskilled jobs, and the people who have been displaced have been forced to increase their skills. The result has been better and higher-paying jobs for many workers. *In view of these facts, is automation really bad?*

There is no question that automation has made our country wealthy and technologically advanced. Furthermore, it has freed many people from boring and repetitive work. . . .

When you use this transitional device, make sure that the second paragraph does, in fact, answer the question posed in the first. And, again, do not use this device too often. Your reader may find it monotonous and gimmicky.

WRITING AN OPENING

As discussed earlier in this chapter, you do not need to begin your draft by writing the opening; however, understanding the purposes of an opening and the strategies for writing one can help you start the draft.

What should the opening statement of your writing do? It should (1) identify your subject and (2) catch the interest of your reader.

Most readers of on-the-job writing are preoccupied with other business when they begin to read a memo, letter, or report. Therefore, you must catch their interest and focus their attention on the subject you are writing about. Even if your readers are required to read what you've written, catching their interest at the outset will help ensure that they pay close attention to what follows. And if you are attempting to persuade your readers, you *must* catch their interest if your writing is to succeed.

To catch your reader's interest, you first must know your reader's needs (as discussed in Chapter 1). An awareness of those needs will help you to determine which details your reader will find important and thus interesting. Consider the following opening from a memo written by a personnel manager to her supervisor. This opening not only states the subject of the report but also promises that the writer will offer solutions to a specific problem. And solutions to problems are always of interest to a reader.

MEMORANDUM

To: Paul Route, Corporate Relations Director
From: Sondra L. Rivera, Personnel Manager
Date: November 1, 19—
Subject: Decreasing Applications from Local College Grad-
          uates

This year only 12 local college graduates have applied for jobs at Benson Tubular Steel. Last year over 30 graduates applied, and the year before 50 applied. After talking with several college counselors, I am confident that we can solve the problem of decreasing applications from local colleges.

> First, we could resume our advertisements in local stu-
> dent newspapers. . . .

For most types of writing done in offices, shops, and laboratories, openings that simply get to the point are more effective than those that provide detailed background information. Furthermore, the subject of a memo or report is often, by itself, enough to catch the reader's interest. The following openings are typical; however, do not feel that you must slavishly follow these patterns. Rather, always first consider the purpose of your writing and the needs of your reader and then tailor your opening accordingly.

Correspondence

> Mr. George T. Whittier
> 1720 Old Line Road
> Thomasbury, WV 26401
>
> Dear Mr. Whittier:
>
> You will be happy to know that we have corrected the error
> in your bank balance. The new balance shows . . .

Progress Report Letter

> William Chang, M.D.
> Phelps Building
> 9003 Shaw Avenue
> Parksville, MD 29099
>
> Dear Dr. Chang:
>
> To date, 18 of the 26 specimens you submitted for analysis
> have been examined. Our preliminary analysis indi-
> cates . . .

Longer Progress Report

> PROGRESS REPORT ON REWIRING THE SPORTS ARENA
>
> The rewiring program at the Sports Arena is continuing
> ahead of schedule. Although the cost of certain equipment
> is higher than our original bid had indicated, we expect to
> complete the project without exceeding our budget, because
> the speed with which the project is being completed will
> save labor costs.
>
> Work Completed
>
> As of August 15th, we have . . .

Memorandum

```
                          MEMORANDUM

    To:        Jane T. Meyers, Chief Budget Manager
    From:      Charles Benson, Assistant to the Personnel Direc-
               tor
    Date:      June 12, 19—                          C B
    Subject:   Budget Estimates for Fiscal Year 19—

        The personnel budget estimates for fiscal year 19— are
    as follows:  . . .
```

Notice that all these openings get directly to the point; they do not introduce irrelevant subjects or include unnecessary details. They give the readers exactly what they need to focus their attention on what is to follow. (For examples of openings for special types of writing, such as application letters, complaint letters, and formal reports, refer to specific entries in the index.)

WRITING A CLOSING

A closing not only ties your writing together and ends it emphatically but also may make a significant point. A closing may recommend a course of action, offer a value judgment, speculate on the implications of your ideas, make a prediction, or summarize your main points. Even if your closing only states, "If I can be of further help, please call me" or "I would appreciate your comments," you are showing consideration for your reader and thereby gaining your reader's goodwill.

The way you close depends on the purpose of your writing and the needs of your reader. For example, the committee report on possible locations for a new distribution center could end with a recommendation. A report studying a company's annual sales could end with a judgment about why sales are up or down. A report for a retail department store about consumer buying trends could end by speculating on the implications of these trends, perhaps even suggesting new product lines that the store might carry in the future. A lengthy report could end with a summary of the main points covered to pull the ideas together for the reader.

The following closings, shown paired with the openings previously illustrated to provide a context, are typical.

Correspondence

Mr. George T. Whittier
1720 Old Line Road
Thomasbury, WV 26401

Dear Mr. Whittier:

You will be happy to know that we have corrected the error
in your bank balance. The new balance shows . . .

Polite, helpful Please accept our thanks for your continued business, and
closing let us know if we can be of further help.

Sincerely,

Michael Fosse

Michael Fosse
Branch Manager

Progress Report Letter

William Chang, M.D.
Phelps Building
9003 Shaw Avenue
Parksville, MD 29099

Dear Dr. Chang:

To date, 18 of the 26 specimens you submitted for analysis
have been examined. Our preliminary analysis indicates . . .

Closing that These results indicate that you may need to alter your test-
recommends a ing procedure to eliminate the impurities we found in speci-
response mens A–G and K.

Sincerely,

Marion Lamb

Marion Lamb
Research Assistant

Longer Progress Report

PROGRESS REPORT ON REWIRING THE SPORTS ARENA

The rewiring program at the Sports Arena is continuing
ahead of schedule. Although the cost of certain equipment
is higher than our original bid had indicated, we expect to
complete the project without exceeding our budget, because
the speed with which the project is being completed will
save labor costs.

Work Completed

As of August 15th, we have . . .

Closing that makes a prediction   Although my original estimate on equipment ($20,000) has been exceeded by $2,300, my original labor estimate ($60,000) has been reduced by $3,500; therefore, I will easily stay within the limits of my original bid. In addition, I see no difficulty in having the arena finished in time for the December 23 Christmas program.

Memorandum

MEMORANDUM

To: Jane T. Meyers, Chief Budget Manager
From: Charles Benson, Assistant to the Personnel Director
Date: June 12, 19——
Subject: Budget Estimates for Fiscal Year 19——

CB

The personnel budget estimates for fiscal year 19—— are as follows . . .

Closing that offers a judgment   Although our estimate calls for a substantially higher budget than in the three previous years, we believe that it is justified by our planned expansion.

MEMORANDUM

To: Paul Route, Corporate Relations Director
From: Sondra L. Rivera, Personnel Manager
Date: November 1, 19——
Subject: Decreasing Applications from Local College Graduates

SLR

This year only 12 local college graduates have applied for jobs at Benson Tubular Steel. Last year over 30 graduates applied, and the year before 50 applied. After talking with several college counselors, I am confident that we can solve the problem of decreasing applications from local colleges.

First, we could resume our advertisements in local student newspapers . . .

Closing that summarizes main points   As this report has indicated, we could attract more recent graduates by (1) increasing our advertising in local student newspapers, (2) resuming our co-op program, (3) sending a representative to career day programs at local colleges and

```
high schools, (4) inviting local college instructors to
teach in-house courses here in the plant, and (5) encouraging
our employees to attend evening classes at various colleges.
```

As these examples show, a good closing is concise and ends your writing emphatically, making it sound finished. Any of the methods for closing can be effective, depending on the purpose of your writing and the needs of your reader. Be careful, however, not to close with a cliché or a platitude, such as "While profits have increased with the introduction of this new product, *the proof is in the pudding.*" Also be careful not to introduce a new topic in your closing. A closing should always relate to and reinforce the ideas presented in the opening and body of your writing.

CHAPTER SUMMARY

Gathering the details you need (discussed in Chapter 1) and grouping them in an outline (discussed in Chapter 2) will enable you to write a good rough draft. When writing the rough draft, remember that your task is to produce only a "draft," not a polished piece of writing. Polish will come with revision (discussed in Chapter 5).

The basic building blocks of the rough draft are paragraphs. To be effective, paragraphs must have unity, appropriate length, and coherence. *Unity* is achieved when every sentence in a paragraph relates to the single central idea stated in the topic sentence. *Appropriate length* is based on the reader's convenience and the topic. The paragraph should not be so long that it overwhelms the reader with details nor so short that it fails to focus adequately on one idea. *Coherence* is achieved when the ideas are arranged in a logical order and transitional devices link sentences and paragraphs, enabling the reader to move smoothly from sentence to sentence and from paragraph to paragraph.

Good openings identify the subject of the writing and catch the reader's interest. Good closings not only show consideration for the reader but may also recommend a course of action, make a prediction, offer a judgment, speculate on the implications of the ideas presented in the writing, or summarize the main points.

EXERCISES

1. Underline the topic sentences in the following paragraphs.

    a.   Whether you use a hand mower, a power reel mower, or a rotary power motor to cut your lawn, the blades should be sharp enough to trim the grass cleanly without bruising or tearing the leaves. Both the cutting edge of the bedknife or reel-type mower and the reel blades should be sharp, and the reel should be set firmly against the bedknife. Make any necessary adjustments of the bedknife or of the roller (which determines the height of cut) on a flat surface, such as a concrete walk or floor. Rotary mower blades in particular require frequent sharpening. On most rotary mowers, height of cut is fixed by adjusting the wheels in holes or slots on the mower frame.

b.   One property of material considered for manufacturing processes is hardness. Hardness is the internal resistance of the material to the forcing apart or closing together of its molecules. Another property is ductility, the characteristic of material that permits it to be drawn into a wire. The smaller the diameter of the wire into which the material can be drawn, the greater the ductility. Material may also possess malleability, the property that makes it capable of being rolled or hammered into thin sheets of various shapes. Engineers, in selecting materials to employ in manufacturing, must consider the materials' properties before deciding which ones are most desirable for use in production.

c.   People who raise houseplants must periodically replace the soil that serves as the growing medium for most indoor plants. When the soil of plants housed in small pots needs to be replaced, the plant is usually "potted up"—that is, transplanted to a pot of the next largest size. The plant, with its root ball intact, is removed from the small pot, and fresh dirt is piled into the larger container, with space allowed for the root ball. The plant is then carefully inserted into the new soil. For plants already in the largest-sized pots, the indoor gardener may take the plant, along with its root ball, out of the pot, discard the remaining earth, put in a similar amount of fresh dirt, and then return the plant to its original container.

2. Read the following paragraph and then complete the exercises pertaining to it.

Frequently, department managers and supervisors recruit applicants without working through the corporate personnel office. Personnel departments around the country have experienced this problem. Recently, the manager of our tool design department met with a graduate of MIT to discuss an opening for a tool designer. The graduate was sent to the personnel department, where she was told that no such position existed. When the tool design manager asked the personnel director about the matter, the manager learned that the company president had ordered a hiring freeze for two months. I'm sure that our general employment situation will get better. As a result of the manager's failure to work through proper channels, the applicant was not only disappointed but bitter.

    a. Underline the topic sentence of the paragraph.

    b. Cross out any sentences that do not contribute to paragraph unity.

3. Underline the transitional words and phrases in the following paragraphs.

    a.   Homeowners should know where the gutters on their houses are located and should be sure to keep them in good repair, because gutters are vulnerable to various weather conditions. On many houses, gutters are tucked up under or into the eaves, so that they appear as little more than another line or two of trim. As a result, many homeowners are not even aware that their houses have gutters. Unless the gutters are well maintained, however, the thousands of gallons of water that may fall onto the roof of the average house each year can easily damage or weaken the gutters. During the winter months, the weight of snow and ice may pull gutters away from the house or loosen the down-spout straps. Clogged and frozen down spouts may also develop seam cracks. When spring comes, these seam cracks sometimes create leaks that may allow heavy rains to flood the yard or the house instead of draining properly into the sewer system. In addition, melting snow that flows freely off the roof may go down the house wall, wetting it sufficiently to cause interior wall damage.

    b.   The causes of global climate change remain in dispute. Existing theories of climate, atmospheric models, and statistical data are inadequate to provide planners with information on future weather patterns. In the long run, research may lead to reliable forecasts of climate. For the present, however, planners have no choice but to heed expert judgments about the world's future climate and its effect on agriculture and other sectors of the economy.

4. Each of the following pairs of sentences lacks a transition from the first sentence to the second. From the list of transitional devices on page 49, select the most appropriate one for each sentence pair. Then rewrite the sentences as necessary.

    a. Ms. Silvenski arrived at the post office just before closing time. She was not able to mail her package because it had not been wrapped according to post office specifications.

    b. An improperly cut garment will not hang attractively on the wearer.

When you sew, you should be sure to lay out and cut your pattern accurately and carefully.

c. The Doctors Clinic was able to attain its fund-raising goal on time this year.

Mercer Street Hospital was forced to extend its fund-raising deadline for three months.

d. When instructing the new tellers, the branch manager explained how to deal with impatient customers.

The personal-banking assistant told the new employees that they should consult her if they had difficulty handling those customers.

e. There are several reasons why a car may skid on ice.

The driver may be going faster than road conditions warrant.

5. The sentences in the following paragraphs have been purposely placed in the wrong order. Rearrange the sentences in each paragraph so that the paragraphs move smoothly and logically from one sentence to the next. Indicate the correct order of the sentences by placing the sentence numbers in the order in which the sentences should appear.

a.   (1) If such improvements could be achieved, the consequences would be very significant for many different applications. (2) However, the most challenging technical problem is to achieve substantial increases in the quantities of electrical energy that can be stored per unit weight of the battery. (3) The overall process yields about 70 percent of the electricity originally put into the battery. (4) A storage battery is a relatively efficient way of storing energy.

b.   (1) Each atrium is connected to the ventricle below by a valve that allows blood to flow in only one direction. (2) The two upper chambers are called atria, and the two lower chambers are called ventricles. (3) The ventricles are also connected by one-way valves to the main outgoing blood vessels. (4) The organ is divided into four chambers. (5) The heart is a fist-sized, heavily muscled organ located approximately in the center of the chest.

6. Bring something to class that you have written either in this (or another) class or at your job. Under the direction of your instructor, take the following steps.

a. Circle all the words or phrases that provide transition between each sentence.

b. If you find two sentences that do not have adequate transition, place as "X" in the space between them.

    c. For these sentences that seem not to have adequate transition, insert a word, phrase, or clause that will improve the transition.

7. Write a paragraph in which you develop one of the following topic sentences. Be sure that the paragraph is both unified and coherent; follow the guidelines offered in this chapter.

    a. I chose [name your major] because I am interested in [name one quality such as "working with numbers" or "helping people"].
    b. On-the-job writing courses show why the principles of good writing are important.
    c. Working at a part-time (or full-time) job has helped me appreciate my education in three specific ways.
    d. Business ethics today is simply good business.

8. Write an opening paragraph for two of the following topics. The audience for each topic is specified in parentheses.

    a. My favorite instructor (to someone nominating him or her for a teaching award).
    b. Ways to improve employee motivation (to the president or head of the organization that employs you).
    c. Ways to improve student advising at your school (to the "Dean of Students" or an equivalent position).
    d. What to look for in a first apartment (to a friend who's looking).
    e. The advantages of budgeting (to a spendthrift friend).

4

Achieving Emphasis

Effective writing is *emphatic* writing—it highlights the facts and ideas that the writer considers most important and downplays those that the writer considers less important. By focusing the reader's attention on the key elements in a sentence, emphatic writing enables the reader to determine how one fact or idea in a sentence is related to another. Emphatic writing, then, is a technique by which writers can make their material more accessible to their readers.

Writers employ a number of methods to achieve emphasis in their sentences. This chapter discusses the use of active and passive voice, subordination, introductory words and phrases, parallel structure, lists, and a number of other devices.

ACTIVE AND PASSIVE VOICE

If you were going to relate the information contained in the following two sentences to someone in conversation, which version would you use?

EXAMPLE 1   The complicated equipment is operated skillfully by the x-ray technician.

EXAMPLE 2   The x-ray technician operates the complicated equipment skillfully.

You would probably choose Example 2 because it conveys its message more directly than Example 1. By making the x-ray technician the *actor* (or *doer*) in the sentence, Example 2 readily communicates the fact that it is the technician's initiative that turns the equipment into a working tool. Example 1, in contrast, downplays the role of the operator; the focus of the sentence is on the x-ray equipment as the *receiver* of the action. The technician, though still the performer of the action, appears in a *by* phrase at the end of the sentence, rather than as the subject of the sentence.

What accounts for the difference in "feel" between the two sentences is that Example 2 is in the active voice, while Example 1 is in the passive. A sentence is in the *active voice* if the subject of the sentence acts; it is in the *passive voice* if the subject is acted upon.

In general, the active voice is the more emphatic of the two. The reader can move quickly and easily from *actor* (the subject) to *action performed* (the verb) to *receiver of the action* (direct object); in passive-voice sentences, the reader often has to reach the end of the sentence to find out who (or what) performed the action that the subject received.

ACTIVE VOICE
Sheila Cohen *prepared* the layout design for the new pump. (The subject, *Sheila Cohen,* acts on *the layout design*—the direct object.)

PASSIVE VOICE
The layout design for the new pump *was prepared* by Sheila Cohen. (The subject—*the layout design*—receives the action.)

Passive-voice sentences tend to be longer than active-voice sentences for two reasons. First, a verb in the active voice often consists of only one word (in this example, *prepared*), whereas a verb in the passive voice always consists of at least two words (*was prepared*). Second, passive-voice sentences tend to be longer because they frequently require a *by someone* or *by something* phrase to complete their meanings. The active-voice version of the Sheila Cohen sentence contains 10 words; the passive-voice version contains 12.

Note the word order and verb forms in these examples:

PASSIVE
Up to 460 pages of text *can be stored* on a single disk.

ACTIVE
A single disk *can store* up to 460 pages of text.

PASSIVE
Instructions on how to use the automatic teller *are described* in the brochure.

ACTIVE
The brochure *describes* how to use the automatic teller.

PASSIVE
The circuit-breaker switches *are lubricated* by maintenance personnel every three months.

ACTIVE
Maintenance personnel *lubricate* the circuit-breaker switches every three months.

The chief advantage of the active voice is that, by clearly stating who is doing what, it gives the reader information quickly and emphatically. A straightforward style is especially important in writing instructions. Compare the following two versions of a paragraph giving nurses directions for treating a serious burn. The first version is written entirely in the passive voice; the second uses the active.

PASSIVE VOICE   The following action must be taken when a serious burn is treated. Any loose clothing on or near the burn is removed. The injury is covered with a clean dressing, and the area around the burn is washed. Then the dressing is secured with tape. Burned fingers or toes are separated with gauze or cloth so that they are prevented from sticking together. Medication is not applied unless it is prescribed by a doctor.

ACTIVE VOICE   Take the following action when treating a serious burn. Remove any loose clothing on or near the burn. Cover the injury with a clean dressing and wash the area around the burn. Then secure the dressing with tape. Separate burned fingers or toes with gauze or cloth to prevent them from sticking together. Do not apply medication unless a doctor prescribes it.

If you were the nurse who had to follow these instructions, which version would you find easier to read and understand?

Occasionally, of course, the passive voice can be useful. There are times, for example, when the doer of the action is less important than the receiver of the action, and the writer can emphasize the receiver of the action by making it the subject of the sentence.

EXAMPLE   The new medical secretary was recommended by several doctors.

The important person in this sentence is the medical secretary, not the doctors who made the recommendation. To give the secretary—the receiver of the action—the needed emphasis, the sentence should be written in the passive voice.

The passive voice is also useful when the performer of the action either is not known or is not important.

EXAMPLE   The valves were soaked in kerosene for 24 hours. (*Who* soaked them is not important.)
The wheel was invented thousands of years ago. (*Who* invented it is not known.)

Consider that principle at work in a longer passage.

EXAMPLE   Area strip mining *is used* in regions of flat to gently rolling terrain, like that found in the Midwest and West. Depending on applicable reclamation laws, the topsoil from the area to be mined may *be removed, stored,* and later *reapplied* as surface material during reclamation of the mined land. Following removal of the topsoil, a trench *is cut* through the overburden to expose the upper surface of the coal to be mined. The length of the cut generally corresponds to the length of the property or of the deposit. The overburden from the first cut *is placed* on the unmined land adjacent to the cut. After the first cut *has been completed,* the coal *is removed* and a second cut *is made* parallel to the first.

If you were to specify a doer in this passage, you might write *the operator,* referring to the person operating the equipment that performs these tasks. Using *the operator* in each sentence, however, would soon get monotonous and, finally, pointless. The writer might even want to leave open the possibility of several doers: operators, mining companies, or an industrial society in general. The proper focus of this passage, however, is on what happens and in what sequence, not on who does it. The passive voice is also commonly used when the writer wants to avoid identifying the performer of an action.

EXAMPLE   The guilty employee was placed on disciplinary probation. (The writer does not want to say *who* placed the guilty employee on probation.)

As you write—and as you revise—select the voice, active or passive, that is appropriate to your purpose. In most cases you can express your ideas more simply and more emphatically in the active voice, especially if you are writing instructions or making a report in which you intend to emphasize *who did what* (for example, which employee performed which subtask of a large project). And if you are describing a complicated piece of equipment, the active voice will probably provide better clarification of how one part interacts with another part. If, on the other hand, you are explaining a process in which the *doer* is not known or is not important, the passive voice is likely to be more effective. In whatever kind of writing you do, be careful to maintain consistency of voice. Avoid making an awkward switch from active to passive (or vice versa), either within a sentence or between sentences.

REVISE   After the test for admission to the training program had been taken by ten applicants, each one wrote a brief essay on his or her career plans.

TO   After the ten applicants had taken the test for admission
to the training program, each one wrote a brief essay on
his or her career plans.

SUBORDINATION

Read the following passage.

The computer is a calculating device. It was once known as a mechanical brain. It has revolutionized industry.

Reading the passage—a group of three short, staccato-like sentences—is something like listening to a series of drum beats of identical tone. The writing, like the music, is monotonous, because every sentence has the same subject-verb structure. Further, the writing is unemphatic because every idea is given equal weight. The passage can be revised to eliminate the monotonous sentence structure and to place stress on the most important idea: the computer has revolutionized industry.

The computer, *a calculating device once known as a mechanical brain,* has revolutionized industry.

The key to transforming a series of repetitive, unemphatic sentences is *subordination,* a technique in which a fact or an idea is subordinated to—that is, made less important than—another fact or idea in the same sentence. You can subordinate an element in a sentence in three basic ways:

- make it a dependent clause
- make it a phrase
- make it a single modifier

With all three methods, the less-important element can be combined with the more-important element to form one unified sentence.

Ways of Subordinating

Clauses. A *subordinate clause* (also called a *dependent clause*) has a subject and a predicate but by itself is not a sentence. Rather, it must be joined to a sentence (called an *independent clause*) by a connecting word. That is, when two sentences are joined by subordination, one sentence becomes the independent clause, and the other sentence, introduced by a connecting word, becomes the dependent clause. The words most commonly used to introduce subordinate clauses are *who, that, which, whom, whose* (relative pronouns) and *after, although, because, before, if, unless, until, when, where, while* (subordinating conjunctions). A few word groups are also used to introduce subordinate clauses—*as soon as, even though, in order that, so that.*

In the following examples, two sentences are turned into one sentence that contains a subordinate clause.

REVISE   Virginia Kelly has become a printing press operator at the Granger Printing Company. She graduated from the Midcity Graphic Arts School last month.

TO   Virginia Kelly, *who graduated from the Midcity Graphic Arts School last month,* has become a printing press operator at the Granger Printing Company.

REVISE   Their credit union has a lower interest rate on loans. Our credit union provides a fuller range of services.

TO   *Although their credit union has a lower interest rate on loans,* our credit union provides a fuller range of services.

Phrases.   The second type of subordination is the phrase. A *phrase* is a group of related words that does not have either a subject or a predicate and that acts as a modifier. In the following groups of two-sentence passages, one sentence is turned into a subordinate phrase that modifies an element in the other sentence.

REVISE   The Beta Corporation now employs 500 people. It was founded ten years ago.

TO   The Beta Corporation, *founded ten years ago,* now employs 500 people.

REVISE   Roger Smith is a forest ranger for the State of Michigan. He spoke at the local Kiwanis Club last week.

TO   Roger Smith, *a forest ranger for the State of Michigan,* spoke at the local Kiwanis Club last week.

Single Modifiers.   The third type of subordination is the single modifier, which may be either a one-word modifier or a compound modifier.

REVISE   The file is obsolete. It is taking up valuable storage space.

TO   The *obsolete* file is taking up valuable storage space.

REVISE   The police radio was out of date. It was auctioned to the highest bidder.

TO   The *out-of-date* police radio was auctioned to the highest bidder.

Depending on the context of your writing—your subject, your purpose, and your reader—you may find that, in a sentence, one way of subordinating is more effective than another. In general, a subordinate single modifier achieves some emphasis, a subordinate phrase achieves more emphasis, and a subordinate clause achieves the most emphasis of all. In the following example, one idea has been subordinated in three ways.

REVISE   The display designer's report was carefully illustrated. It covered five pages.

TO   The display designer's *five-page* report was carefully illustrated. (single modifier)

OR   The display designer's report, *covering five pages,* was carefully illustrated. (phrase)

OR   The display designer's report, *which covered five pages,* was carefully illustrated. (clause)

Subordinating to Achieve Emphasis

Just as you can determine the kind of subordinate element that you think is most appropriate in a given sentence, so you can decide, according to the context in which you are writing, which ideas you should emphasize and which ones you should subordinate. In the following sets of examples, two sentences have been combined into one, in two different ways. Notice how the emphasis varies in each set.

REVISE   Blast furnaces are used mainly in the smelting of iron. They are used all over the world.

TO   Blast furnaces, *in use all over the world,* are employed mainly in the smelting of iron. (Subordinates the extent of their use and emphasizes the purpose for which they are used.)

OR   Blast furnaces, *used mainly in the smelting of iron,* are employed all over the world. (Subordinates the purpose and emphasizes the extent.)

REVISE   The document explains how to install the gear. It is written for the mechanic.

TO   The document, *written for the mechanic,* explains how to install the gear. (Subordinates the intended reader and emphasizes the purpose.)

OR   The document, *which explains how to install the gear,* is written for the mechanic. (Subordinates the purpose and emphasizes the intended reader.)

REVISE   Henry Ford was a pioneering industrialist. He understood the importance of self-esteem.

TO   Henry Ford, *who understood the importance of self-esteem,* was a pioneering industrialist. (Subordinates the subject's understanding and emphasizes his pioneering work.)

OR   Henry Ford, *a pioneering industrialist,* understood the importance of self-esteem. (Subordinates the subject's pioneering work and emphasizes his self-esteem.)

If you wish to emphasize something, put it either at the beginning or at the end of the sentence; if you wish to subordinate something, put it in the middle of the sentence.

Avoiding Overloaded Sentences

Subordination is a helpful technique that can enable you to write clear, readable sentences. But, like many useful devices, it can be overdone. Be especially careful not to pile one subordinating clause on top of another. A sentence that is overloaded with subordination will force your reader to work harder than necessary to understand what you are saying. The following sentence is difficult to read because the bottleneck of subordinate clauses prevents the reader from moving easily from one idea to the next.

REVISE   When the two technicians, who had been trained at the company's repair center in Des Moines, explained to Margarita that the new word-processing machine, which Margarita had told them was not working properly, needed a new part, Margarita decided that until the part arrived the department would have its sales letters reproduced by an independent printing supplier.

TO   Margarita told the two technicians that the new word processing machine was not working properly. The technicians, who had been trained at the company's repair center in Des Moines, examined the machine and explained to Margarita that it needed a new part. Margarita decided that until the part arrived, the department would have its sales letters reproduced by an independent printing supplier.

Subordinating everything is as bad as subordinating nothing. For example, study the next three sample paragraphs of a letter from a garage owner to a parts supplier. The first paragraph has too little subordination, the second has too much subordination, and the third illustrates effective subordination.

Example 1: Too Little Subordination

I am returning the parts you sent me, and I am enclosing the invoice that came with them. You must have confused my order with someone else's. I ordered spark plugs, condensers, and points, and I received bearings, piston rings, head gaskets, and valve-grinding compound. I don't need these parts, but I need the parts I ordered. Please send them as soon as possible.

Example 2: Too Much Subordination

You must have confused my order with someone else's, because although I ordered spark plugs, condensers, and points, I received bearings, piston rings, head gaskets, and valve-grinding compound; therefore, I am returning the parts you sent me, along with the invoice that came with them, in the hope that you will send me the parts that I need as quickly as possible because this delay has already put me behind schedule.

Example 3: Effective Subordination

I am returning the parts you sent me, along with the invoice that came with them, because you must have confused my order with someone else's. Although I ordered spark plugs, condensers, and points, I received bearings, piston rings, head gaskets, and valve-grinding compound. Since I need the parts that I ordered and this mix-up is causing an unexpected delay, please send me the parts that I ordered as quickly as possible.

INTRODUCTORY WORDS AND PHRASES

Another way to achieve emphasis is to begin a sentence with an introductory element—a modifying word or phrase that contains the idea you wish to stress. Such a modifier would normally occur later in the sentence.

EXAMPLES   Sales have been good recently.
Recently, sales have been good.

You must work hard to advance.
To advance, you must work hard.

She found several errors while reading the report.
While reading the report, she found several errors.

When you use introductory words and phrases, though, you should watch for two dangers. First, beginning a sentence with a modifying word or phrase may lead you to write a dangling modifier. The first sentence below contains a dangling modifier because the phrase *to advance* cannot logically modify *hard work.* The second sentence corrects the error by making it clear that *to advance* modifies the pronoun *you.*

REVISE   To advance, hard work is required.

TO   *To advance,* you must work hard.

A second danger is that if you begin a sentence with a modifying word or phrase, the meaning of the sentence may accidently be changed. The first of the following sentences instructs the reader to measure the oil that drains over a time period of 15 seconds. The second sentence instructs the reader to wait 15 seconds before measuring the amount of oil that drains into the container—a completely different thought.

EXAMPLES   Measure the amount of oil that drains into the container in 15 seconds.

In 15 seconds, measure the amount of oil that drains into the container.

Once again, make sure that your sentences say exactly what you intend them to say.

PARALLEL STRUCTURE

Parallel structure requires that sentence elements—words, phrases, and clauses—that are alike in function be alike in structure as well. In the following example, the three locations in which a cable is laid are all expressed as prepositional phrases.

EXAMPLE   The cable was laid *behind the embankment, under the street,* and *around the building.*

Parallel structure can produce an economy of language, clarify meaning, indicate the equality of related ideas, and, frequently, achieve emphasis. Parallel structure allows your reader to anticipate a series of units within a sentence. The reader realizes, for instance, that the relationship between the second unit (*under the street,* in the example) and the subject (*cable*) is the same as that between the first unit (*behind the embankment*) and the subject. A reader who has sensed the pattern of a sentence can go from one idea to another more quickly and confidently.

Parallel structure can be achieved with words, with phrases, and with clauses. Whether you use words, phrases, or clauses in parallel structure depends, as it does with subordination, upon the degree of emphasis you wish to create. In general, words in parallel structure produce some emphasis, phrases produce more emphasis, and clauses produce the most emphasis of all.

EXAMPLES If you want to earn a satisfactory grade in the training program, you must be *punctual, courteous,* and *conscientious.* (parallel words)

If you want to earn a satisfactory grade in the training program, you must recognize the importance of *punctuality, of courtesy,* and *of conscientiousness.* (parallel phrases)

If you want to earn a satisfactory grade in the training program, *you must arrive punctually, you must behave courteously,* and *you must study conscientiously.* (parallel clauses)

To make the relationship among parallel units clear, repeat the word (or words) that introduces the first unit.

REVISE The advantage is not in the pay but the greater opportunity.

TO The advantage is not *in* the pay but *in* the greater opportunity.

REVISE The study of electronics is a necessity and challenge to the technician.

TO The study of electronics is *a* necessity and *a* challenge to the technician.

Parallel structure can contribute greatly to the clarity of your writing. But it is more than just a helpful device—sentences that contain faulty parallel structure are often awkward and difficult to read.

REVISE Adina Wilson was happy about her assignment and getting a pay raise.

TO Adina Wilson was happy *about her assignment* and *about her pay raise.*

REVISE   Jason advises his employees to work hard and against relying on luck.

TO   Jason advises his employees *to work hard* and not *to rely* on luck.

REVISE   Check the following items. The dip stick for proper oil level, the gas tank for fuel, the spark plug wire attachment, and that no foreign objects are under or near the mower.

TO   Check the following items: The dip stick *for proper oil level,* the gas tank *for fuel,* the spark plug wire *for proper attachment,* and the lawn *for foreign objects.*

LISTS

You can also consider using lists to achieve emphasis. Lists break up complex statements and allow key ideas to stand out. Be aware, however, that lists are most effective when they are grammatically parallel in structure. When you use a list of phrases or short sentences, each should begin with the same part of speech:

REVISE   Because expenses for the past month have far exceeded budget, the business manager has recommended the following reforms:
1. Employees will not use company telephones for personal calls.
2. For any written copy that is not to go out of house, use low-grade yellow paper rather than bond.
3. Make carbon copies rather than photocopies of all correspondence.

TO   Because expenses for the past month have far exceeded budget, the business manager has recommended the following reforms:
1. Do not use company phones for personal calls.
2. Use low-grade yellow paper rather than bond for any written copy that is not to go out of house.
3. Make carbon copies rather than photocopies of all correspondence.

Notice how much more smoothly the revised version reads when all items begin with imperative verbs.

Lists help focus the reader's attention because they stand out from the text around them. Be mindful, however, not to overuse lists in an attempt to avoid writing paragraphs. When a memo, report, or letter consists almost entirely of lists, the reader is unable to distinguish important from unimportant ideas. Further, the information lacks coherence because the reader is forced to connect strings of separate items without the help of transitional ideas. To make sure that the reader understands how a list fits with the surrounding sentences, always provide adequate transition before and after the list.

If you do not wish to indicate the rank or sequence that numbered lists suggest, you can use bullets, as shown in the list of tips that follows. To type a bullet, use a small "o" and fill it with ink. Following are some tips for using lists:

- List only comparable items.
- Use parallel structure throughout.
- Use only words, phrases, or short sentences.
- Provide adequate transitions before and after lists.
- Use bullets when rank or sequence is not important.
- Do not overuse lists.

OTHER WAYS TO ACHIEVE EMPHASIS

You can create a feeling of anticipation in your reader by arranging a series of facts or ideas in *climactic order*. Begin such a series with the least important idea and end it with the most important one.

REVISE   The hurricane destroyed thousands of homes, ruined some crops, and interrupted traffic.

TO   The hurricane interrupted traffic, ruined some crops, and destroyed thousands of homes.

Emphasis is added at each step as the reader is led from the minor inconvenience of traffic tie-ups, to the more serious problem of partial crop failure, and finally to the hurricane's most devastating impact: the destruction of thousands of homes.

An abrupt change in sentence length can also achieve effective emphasis.

EXAMPLE   We have already reviewed the problems that the accounting department has experienced during the past year. We could continue to examine the causes of our problems and point an accusing finger at all the culprits beyond our control, but in the end it all leads to one simple conclusion. *We must cut costs.*

Sometimes, simply labeling ideas as important creates emphasis.

EXAMPLE   We can do a number of things that will help us to achieve
our goal. We can conduct sales contests in the field; in the
past, such contests have been quite successful. We can increase our advertising budget and hope for a proportionate
increase in sales. We can be prepared to step up production
when the increase in sales makes it necessary. But *most
important,* we can do everything in our power to make sure
that we are producing the best dictating equipment on the
market.

If you don't overuse them, direct statements like *most important* should
make your reader take particular notice of what follows.

Another kind of direct statement is the warning to your reader that
something dangerous is about to follow. Warnings most often appear in
instructions, where they may be brought to the reader's attention by a
special format—the material may be boxed off, for instance—or by atten-
tion-attracting devices like all-capital letters or a distinctive typeface.
Most offices are equipped with typewriters or word processing printers
that can print the alphabet in **boldface** and *italic*. These features can
be used to emphasize important words and phrases in warnings.

WARNING

DO NOT proceed to the next instruction until you have checked
to be sure that the equipment has been unplugged. The electrical power generated by this unit CAN KILL!

Other mechanical devices can be used to achieve a certain amount
of emphasis. A dash within a sentence, for example, can alert the reader
to what follows it. (On the typewriter and word processing equipment
the dash is made by striking the hyphen twice, with no space between
the two.)

EXAMPLES   The job will be done--after we are under contract.
The manager pointed out that our conduct could have only
one result--dismissal.

Italics (indicated on the typewriter by underlining) can be used occasionally to emphasize a word or phrase.

EXAMPLE   `Sales have `<u>`not`</u>` improved since we started the new procedure.`

The problem with devices like italics and the dash is that they are so easy to use that we tend to rely on them too readily, as in the following sentence.

EXAMPLE   `Sales have `<u>`not improved`</u>` since we started the new procedure and are `<u>`not likely`</u>` to improve unless we initiate a more `<u>`aggressive`</u>` advertising campaign.`

Overuse of mechanical devices may cancel their effectiveness. The reader quickly learns that the writer is using the signals to point out unimportant as well as truly important material.

CHAPTER SUMMARY

Effective writing is emphatic writing—it places stress on those facts and ideas that the writer wishes to highlight. Writers can use a number of techniques to make their sentences emphatic.

Ordinarily, the *active voice,* in which the subject of a sentence performs the action, provides greater emphasis than the *passive voice,* in which the subject receives the action. Unless you have a particular reason for using the passive voice, use the active.

In *subordination,* one element in a sentence is given greater stress than another. The less-important element may be expressed as a clause (introduced by words like *who, which, that,* and *although, when,* or *where*), as a phrase, or as a single modifier. Subordination can turn a series of short, subject-verb sentences into one emphatic sentence that pinpoints the relationship of the sentence elements.

Introductory words and phrases allow key ideas in a sentence to be emphasized. (*By keeping a record of the traffic flow through the office,* staff members can better determine the department's space needs.)

Parallel structure achieves economy of language, clarifies meaning, indicates the equality of related ideas, and often creates emphasis. Like subordination, parallel structure may be expressed in words, phrases, and clauses. Note, too, that parallel structure is not just a stylistic device; it is often a necessity in avoiding an awkward or unclear sentence.

Other devices for lending emphasis include using lists (in which the items should be grammatically parallel), arranging ideas in climactic order, changing sentence length, labeling important ideas, and using dashes, boldface, and italics.

EXERCISES

1. Rewrite each of the following sentences so that the verb is in the *active voice*. Whenever a potential subject is not given in a sentence, supply one as you write.

   a. The entire building was spray-painted by Charles and his brother.
   b. It was assumed by the superintendent that the trip was postponed until next Tuesday.
   c. The completed form should be submitted in triplicate to Tim Hagen by the 15th of every month.
   d. The fluid should be applied sparingly and should be allowed to dry for eight to ten seconds.
   e. The metropolitan area was defined as groups of counties related by commuting patterns by the researchers.
   f. The machine tool industry was dominated by two companies— Welland Industries and Machine Tools Unlimited.
   g. Their way to raise capital was to set up a limited partnership.
   h. A test of the equipment should be conducted at the vendor's location.
   i. The brochures and notes from the trade show should be gathered and read carefully.
   j. Images are converted into electronic impulses that can be quickly stored, analyzed, and transmitted by computers in electronic photography.
   k. Reducing absenteeism was a way of enhancing productivity, the company president was told.
   l. Two basic types of business loans are offered by the Small Business Administration: guaranty loans made by private lenders and direct SBA loans.
   m. "Will the new tax laws make leasing rather than purchasing equipment more attractive?" was what the distributor recently asked me.

2. In each of the following, combine the series of short sentences into one unified sentence. Use *subordination* (1) to indicate how the ideas expressed in the sentence relate to each other, and (2) to emphasize the most important idea or ideas.

   a. I recorded my speech on a cassette tape. The cassette tape can be recorded over. It does not need to be erased.
   b. It rained this morning. The construction crew stayed indoors. Members played a game of hearts. Valdez won.
   c. It had snowed for a week. I like to ski. I was delighted.

   d. He studied drafting at a technical school. He joined his brother's firm as a draftsman in 1982.

   e. Thomas Edison was one of America's greatest inventors. Teddy Roosevelt was the twenth-sixth president of the United States. Edison and Roosevelt were friends.

   f. Sales of sewing machines were declining. The management of Presto-Seam became worried. The management decided to initiate a TV ad campaign.

   g. The word-processing group had a backlog of work. No one could type my report. My report is due in two days.

   h. The cost of cotton has increased. All the suppliers have increased their prices. The suppliers are wholesalers.

3. Rewrite the following sentences to eliminate *excessive* subordination.

   a. The duty officer who was on duty at 3:30 A.M. was the one who took the call that there was a malfunction in the Number 3 generator that had been repaired at approximately 9 A.M. the previous morning.

   b. I have referred your letter that you wrote to us on June 20 to our staff attorney who reviewed it in the light of corporate policy that is pertinent to the issue that you raise.

   c. Will your presentation that is scheduled for the 12th of next May and that will answer questions submitted in advance be circulated before the 12th to those who will be attending the workshop?

4. Rewrite the following sentences to make elements within them parallel in construction.

   a. The system is large and convenient, and it does not cost very much.

   b. The processor sends either a ready function code or transmits a standby function code.

   c. The log is a record of the problems that have occurred and of the services performed.

   d. The committee feels that the present system has three disadvantages: it causes delay in the distribution of incoming mail, duplicates work, and unnecessary delays are created in the work of several other departments.

   e. In our first list we inadvertently omitted the seven lathes in room B-101, the four milling machines in room B-117, and from the next room, B-118, we also forgot to include 16 shapers.

   f. This product offers ease of operation, economy, and it is easily available.

g. The manual gives instructions for operating the machine and to adjust it.

h. Three of the applicants were given promotions, and transfers were arranged for the other four applicants.

i. To analyze the data, carry out the following steps: examine all the details carefully, eliminate all the unnecessary details, and a chart showing the flow of work should then be prepared.

j. We have found that the new system has four disadvantages: too costly to operate, it causes delays, fails to use any of the existing equipment, and it permits only one in-process examination.

k. The design is simple, inexpensive, and can be used effectively.

l. Management was slow to recognize the problem and even slower understanding it.

5. Rewrite the following lists to make them parallel in structure.

a. Carry this emergency equipment in your car during long winter trips:

- Chains for tires and towing
- Snow shovel
- Scraper
- Sand or salt
- For minor repairs, a car tool kit
- Flashlight—be sure to check for fresh batteries
- Flares, reflectors
- First aid kit
- Blankets
- Jumper cables are also a good idea

b. Keep these safety tips in mind as you work on your car:

- Wear safety goggles when working under the hood, especially when dealing with the battery.
- The engine should be operated only in a well-ventilated area.
- Fans and belts are dangerous when moving—you or your clothing could get caught in them.
- Avoid contact with hot metal parts, such as the radiator and the exhaust manifold.

5

Revising

One of the enduring legends of American history is that Abraham Lincoln wrote the Gettysburg Address as he made the train trip from Washington, D.C., to Gettysburg. The address is a remarkable accomplishment, even for a writer as gifted as Lincoln. It is the eloquent testimony of a leader with a powerful intellect and a compassionate heart.

But the facts of how the Gettysburg Address was composed do not support the legend. Lincoln actually worked on the address for weeks and revised the draft many times.[1] What Lincoln was doing on the train to Gettysburg was nothing more than what any of us must do before our writing is finally acceptable: he was revising. What is remarkable about the address is that Lincoln made so many revisions of a speech of well under 300 words. Obviously he wanted it to fit the occasion for which it was intended, and he knew that something written "off the cuff" would not satisfy his purpose and audience.

This principle is as true for anyone who writes on the job (which, of course, is what the president was doing) as it was for Lincoln. Unlike the Gettysburg Address, however, most on-the-job writing should not strive for oratorical elegance; the more natural a piece of writing sounds to the reader, the more effort the writer has probably put into revising it.

---

[1] Tom Burnam, *The Dictionary of Misinformation* (New York: Ballantine Books, 1977), pp. 104–106.

REVISING TACTICS

Have you ever found, after writing a first draft that you knew wasn't the best you could do, that you did not know how to improve it? If your answer is yes, you are not alone. All writers—even professional writers— have the same problem at some time or another.

The problem has a simple explanation. Immediately after you write a rough draft, the ideas are so fresh in your mind that you cannot read the words, sentences, and paragraphs objectively. That is, you cannot sufficiently detach yourself from them to be able to look at the writing critically. And to revise effectively, you *must* be critical. You cannot allow yourself to think, "Because my ideas are good, the way I've expressed them must also be good." The first step toward effective revision, then, is to develop a critical frame of mind—to become objective.

As professional writers have learned, there are a number of ways to put distance between yourself and your writing and become objective. Here are two methods that you should always employ:

1. *Allow for a "cooling" period.* Allow a period of time to go by between writing a rough draft and revising it. The ideas will not be as fresh in your mind then, and you can look at the writing itself more objectively. A "cooling" period of a day or two is best, but if you are pressed for time, even a few hours will help.
2. *Pretend that a stranger has written your draft.* Since it is always easier to see faults in others than in yourself, pretend that you are revising someone else's draft. If you can look at your writing and ask, "How could *he* or *she* have written that?" you are in the right frame of mind to revise.

Of course, you may discover your own methods of becoming objective. One student, for example, finds that she can be more critical if she writes her first draft on yellow paper. Another student types his first draft because he cannot be critical when looking at his own handwriting. Some students like to revise with felt-tip pen; others prefer using red or green pencils. Experiment and find out what helps you. The particular methods that work for you are not important. What *is* important is that you develop some technique for becoming objective about your writing—and then use it.

Once you have put the necessary distance between yourself and your writing, you are ready to revise. Again, there is no single method for revision. The following two techniques, however, invariably prove effective:

1. *Revise in passes.* Make several passes through your draft as you revise. The first time you read the draft, look at only one aspect of your writing, such as accuracy or completeness. Then make additional passes, each time looking at a different aspect, such as grammar or spelling. Often, you can spot problems more quickly if you look for only one type than if you look for several types at the same time.

2. *Be alert for your most frequent errors.* Closely related to revising in passes is looking first for the errors that you typically make. One of the most important benefits of taking a writing course is to learn what your weak points are. Make a list of the problems that your instructor has pointed out in your writing, and use that list to guide you as you revise. Also, you might wish to use this chapter as a checklist and run through the headings as you review your draft. A more general "final checklist" appears at the end of this chapter.

If you use a word processor on the job, you can put it to good use as you revise. Its most obvious advantage is that it makes revising in passes so easy. Once you have keyed your draft into the word processor, you can easily make numerous revisions on the video screen, deleting errors and inserting material without having to rekey the entire draft over and over. You can perform the following revision tasks on screen and print the results only when you are satisfied with your text:

- Inserting, deleting, or replacing text anywhere
- Deleting, copying, or moving blocks of text, such as phrases, sentences, paragraphs, or whole pages
- Searching for and replacing individual letters, words, or phrases

As you revise, the system automatically makes "carriage" returns at the end of each line and readjusts margins.

Revising on a word processor has other advantages. Storing text promotes a willingness to explore alternative ways of expressing thoughts, since what is unsatisfactory can be deleted and replaced quickly on screen. Further, some word-processing systems have software that will identify and correct typographical errors and misspellings. Do not, however, rely completely on computerized spell checkers, since they cannot identify errors such as the use of *there* for *their*.

Used thoughtfully in conjunction with the guidelines provided throughout this chapter, the word processor can make revising fast and efficient, thus giving you the chance to revise more and produce clearer, more effective writing. Section C of the Writer's Guide will introduce you to the use of word processors and the writing process.

REVISING FOR ACCURACY AND COMPLETENESS

Above all else, your information must be accurate. Although accuracy is important in all types of writing, it takes on special significance when you write on the job. One misplaced decimal point, for example, can create a staggering budgetary error. Incorrect or imprecise instructions can cause injury to a worker. At the very least, if your writing is not accurate you will quickly lose the confidence of your reader. He or she will be annoyed, for example, if a figure or fact in your writing differs from one in a chart or graph. These kinds of inaccuracies are easily overlooked as you write a first draft, so it is essential that you correct them during revision.

Revision is the time to insert any missing facts or ideas. When you finish your draft, check it against your outline. If any of the main ideas or supporting details you listed are missing from your draft, rewrite your sentences and paragraphs as necessary to incorporate the missing information.

In revising your draft for completeness, you may also think of new information that you failed to include when you were preparing and writing your draft. Always carefully consider such new information in light of your reader and purpose. If the information will help satisfy your reader's need and accomplish the purpose of your writing, by all means add it now. But if the information—no matter how interesting—does not serve these ends, it has no place in your writing.

REVISING FOR BASICS

Grammatical errors, like inaccurate facts or incomplete information, can confuse or irritate your reader and cause him or her to lose confidence in you. Even worse, many of the errors discussed in this chapter are so severe that they can actually alter the meaning of a sentence. Therefore, it is essential that in revising your draft, you check for grammatical correctness.

Following is a survey of common grammatical errors. Each type of error is described briefly here and is then explained in detail in the Handbook section of the Writer's Guide. If you find it helpful, use the survey below as a checklist for grammatical revisions that may be needed.

Agreement

Agreement means that the parts of a sentence, like the pieces of a jigsaw puzzle, fit together properly. The following discussion points out the types of sentences in which problems of agreement occur often.

Subject-Verb Agreement.   A *verb* must agree with its *subject* in number. A singular subject requires a singular verb; a plural subject requires a plural verb. Do not let intervening phrases and clauses mislead you. (See Section 3.4.5 of the Handbook.)

REVISE   The *use* of insecticides, fertilizers, and weed killers, although they offer unquestionable benefits, often *result* in unfortunate side effects.

TO   The *use* of insecticides, fertilizers, and weed killers, although they offer unquestionable benefits, often *results* in unfortunate side effects. (The singular verb *results* must agree with the singular subject of the sentence, *use,* not with the plural subject of the preceding clause, *they.*)

Be careful not to make the verb agree with the noun immediately preceding it if that noun is not its subject. This problem is especially likely to occur when a modifying phrase containing a plural noun falls between a singular subject and its verb.

EXAMPLES   Only *one* of the emergency lights *was* functioning when the accident occurred. (The subject is *one,* not *lights.*)

The *advice* of two engineers, one lawyer, and three executives *was* obtained prior to making a commitment. (The subject is *advice,* not *engineers, lawyer,* and *executives.*)

Words like *type, part, series,* and *portion* take singular verbs even when such words precede a phrase containing a plural noun.

EXAMPLE   A *series* of meetings *was* held to decide the best way to market the new product.

Subjects expressing measurement, weight, mass, or total often take singular verbs even though the subject word is plural in form. Such subjects are treated as a unit.

EXAMPLE   *Four years is* the normal duration of the apprenticeship program.

However, when such subjects refer to the individuals that make up the unit, a plural verb is required.

EXAMPLE   If you're looking for oil, *three quarts are* on the shelf in the garage.

Similarly, collective subjects take singular verbs when the group is thought of as a unit and plural verbs when the individuals are thought of separately.

EXAMPLES   The *committee is* holding its meeting on Thursday. (*Committee* is thought of as a unit.)

The *majority are* opposed to delivering their reports at the meeting. (*Majority* is thought of as separate individuals.)

A relative pronoun (*who, which, that*) may take either singular or plural verbs depending on whether its antecedent (the noun to which it refers) is singular or plural.

EXAMPLES   He is an *employee* who *takes* work home at night.

He is one of those *employees* who *take* work home at night.

A *compound subject* is one that is composed of two or more elements joined by a conjunction such as *and, or, nor, either . . . or,* or *neither . . . nor.* Usually, when the elements are connected by *and,* the subject is plural and requires a plural verb.

EXAMPLE   *Chemistry and accounting are* prerequisites for this position.

A compound subject with a singular and a plural element joined by *or* or *nor* requires that the verb agree with the element nearest to it.

EXAMPLES   Neither the office manager nor the *secretaries were* there.

Neither the secretaries nor the office *manager was* there.

Either they or *I am* going to write the report.

Either I or *they are* going to write the report.

Pronoun-Antecedent Number Agreement. A *pronoun* must agree with its *antecedent,* the noun to which it refers. Like subjects and their verbs, a pronoun must agree with its antecedent in number (singular or plural). (See Section 3.2.3a of the Writer's Guide.)

REVISE   Although the typical *engine* runs well in moderate temperatures, *they* often stall in extreme cold.

TO   Although the typical *engine* runs well in moderate temperatures, *it* often stalls in extreme cold.

Pronoun-Antecedent Gender Agreement.   A pronoun must also agree with its antecedent in gender—masculine, feminine, or neuter. (See Section 3.2.2b of the Writer's Guide.)

EXAMPLE   Mr. Swivet in the accounting department acknowledges *his* responsibility for the misunderstanding, but *Ms.* Barkley in the research division should acknowledge *her* responsibility for *it* also.

Consistency of Tense and Person

Much like agreement errors, illogical shifts in *person* or *tense* can confuse the reader. You would be confused, for example, if someone wrote to you: "If *you* show the guard *your* pass, *one* will be allowed to enter the gate" (shift in person) or "When the contract *was* signed, the company *submits* the drawings" (shift in tense). Your confusion would disappear, however, if the sentences were revised as follows:

EXAMPLES   If *you* show the guard *your* pass, *you* will be allowed to enter the gate. (consistent use of person)

When the contract *was* signed, the company *submitted* the drawings. (consistent use of tense)

Person.   *Person* refers to the forms of a personal pronoun that indicate whether the pronoun represents the speaker, the person spoken to, or the person (or thing) spoken about. If the pronoun represents the *speaker,* the pronoun is in the *first person.* (See Section 3.2.2a of the Writer's Guide.)

EXAMPLE   *I* could not find the answer in the manual.

If the pronoun represents the person or persons spoken *to,* the pronoun is in the *second person.*

EXAMPLE   *You* are going to be a good supervisor.

If the pronoun represents the person or persons spoken *about,* the pronoun is in the *third person.*

EXAMPLE   *They* received the news quietly.

Identifying pronouns by person helps you avoid illogical shifts from one person to another. A very common error is to shift from the third person to the second person.

REVISE   *People* should spend the morning hours on work requiring mental effort, for *your* mind is freshest in the morning.

TO   *People* should spend the morning hours on work requiring mental effort, for *their* minds are freshest in the morning.

OR   *You* should spend the morning hours on work requiring mental effort, for *your* mind is freshest in the morning.

Tense.   *Tense* refers to the forms of a verb that indicate time distinctions. A verb may express past, present, or future time. Be consistent in your use of tense; an unnecessary and illogical change of tense within a sentence confuses the reader. (See Section 3.4.3d of the Writer's Guide.)

EXAMPLE   Before he *installed* the circuit board, he *cleans* the contacts.

This sentence, for no apparent reason, changes from the past tense (*installed*) to the present tense (*cleans*). To be both correct and logical, the sentence must be written with both verbs in the same tense.

REVISE   Before he *installed* the circuit board, he *cleans* the contacts.

TO   Before he *installed* the circuit board, he *cleaned* the contacts.

OR   Before he *installs* the circuit board, he *cleans* the contacts.

The only acceptable change of tense within a sentence records a real change of time.

EXAMPLE   After you *have assembled* Part A [past tense, because the action occurred in the past], *assemble* Part B [present tense because the action occurs in the present].

Dangling Modifiers

Modifiers are words that describe, explain, or qualify an element in a sentence. They can be adjectives, adverbs, phrases, or clauses. A dangling modifier is a phrase that does not clearly refer to another word or phrase in the sentence. You have seen that misplaced modifiers can result in ambiguity; dangling modifiers, by contrast, result in illogical sentences. (See Section 4.3.4d of the Writer's Guide.)

EXAMPLE   While eating lunch in the cafeteria, the computer malfunctioned.

Although the idea of a computer eating lunch in a cafeteria is ridiculous, that is what the sentence actually states. With the dangling modifier corrected, the sentence could read as follows:

EXAMPLE   While *I* was eating lunch in the cafeteria, the computer malfunctioned.

Dangling modifiers often can be humorous, as in the first example. But they can also cause such confusion that your reader misinterprets the meaning of your sentence completely.

One way to correct a dangling modifier is to add a noun or pronoun for the phrase to modify.

REVISE
After finishing the research, the job was easy. (The phrase *after finishing the research* has nothing to modify. Who finished?)

TO
After finishing the research, *we* found the job easy. (The pronoun *we* tells the reader who finished.)

REVISE
Having evaluated the feasibility of the project, the centralized plan was unanimously approved. (Who evaluated the feasibility of the project?)

TO
Having evaluated the feasibility of the project, the *committee* unanimously approved the centralized plan.

REVISE
Keeping busy, the afternoon passed swiftly. (Who was keeping busy?)

TO
Keeping busy, *I* felt that the afternoon passed swiftly.

A dangling modifier can also be corrected by making the phrase a clause.

REVISE
After finishing the research [phrase], the job was easy.

TO
After we finished the research [clause], the job was easy.

REVISE
Having evaluated the feasibility of the project [phrase], the centralized plan was unanimously approved.

TO
Once the committee had evaluated the feasibility of the project [clause], the centralized plan was unanimously approved.

REVISE
Keeping busy [phrase], the afternoon passed swiftly.

TO
Because I kept busy [clause], the afternoon passed swiftly.

Misplaced Modifiers

Another source of ambiguity occurs in the placement of modifiers. The simple modifiers that are most likely to create ambiguity are *only, almost, just, hardly, even,* and *barely.* When you use one of these terms in a sentence, be sure that it modifies the word or element that you had intended it to. In most cases, place the modifier directly in front of the word it is supposed to qualify. (See Section 4.3.4.d of the Writer's Guide at the end of the book for a more extensive discussion of modifiers.)

EXAMPLES   Katrina was the *only* engineer at Flagstead Industries. (The sentence says that Flagstead had one engineer, and she was Katrina.)

Katrina was *only* the engineer at Flagstead Industries. (The sentence says that Katrina had a position at Flagstead no higher than that of engineer.)

Anna Jimenez *almost* wrote $1 million in insurance policies last month. (The sentence says that although Anna Jimenez came close to writing $1 million in insurance policies, she actually didn't write *any*.)

Anna Jimenez wrote *almost* $1 million in insurance policies last month. (The sentence says that Anna Jimenez wrote *nearly* $1 million in insurance policies last month—a very different matter.)

Misplaced phrases can also cause problems. As with simple modifiers, place phrases near the words they modify. Note the two meanings possible when the phrase is shifted in the following sentences:

EXAMPLES   The equipment *without the accessories* sold the best. (Different types of equipment were available, some with and some without accessories.)

The equipment sold the best *without the accessories*. (One type of equipment was available, and the accessories were optional.)

Either of these sentences could be correct, of course, depending on the meaning the writer intends.

A third type of misplaced modifier is a *misplaced clause*. To avoid confusion, clauses should also be placed as close as possible to the words they modify.

REVISE   We sent the brochure to four local firms *that had three-color illustrations*.

TO   We sent the brochure *that had three-color illustrations* to four local firms.

A different kind of ambiguous modifier is the "squinting modifier"—a modifier that could be interpreted as qualifying either the sentence element before it or the sentence element following it.

EXAMPLE   We agreed *on the next day* to make the adjustments.

The reader doesn't know which of the following possible interpretations the writer intended.

MEANING 1   *On the next day* we agreed to make the adjustments.

MEANING 2   We agreed to make the adjustments *on the next day*.

Sentence Problems

A number of errors can make a sentence ungrammatical. The most common such errors are sentence fragments, run-on sentences, and sentences with comma errors.

Fragments.   A sentence that is missing an essential part (*subject* or *predicate*) is called a *sentence fragment*. (See Section 4.3.4c in the Writer's Guide.)

EXAMPLES   He quit his job. (Sentence: *He* is the subject; *quit his job* is the predicate.)

And left for Australia. (Fragment: subject is missing.)

But having a subject and a predicate does not automatically make a group of words a sentence. The word group must also make an independent statement. "If I work" is a fragment because the subordinating conjunction *if* turns the statement into a dependent clause.

Sentence fragments are often introduced by relative pronouns (*who, whom, whose, which, that*) or subordinating conjunctions (such as *although, because, if, when,* and *while*). The presence of any one of these words should alert you to the fact that what follows is a dependent clause, not a sentence, and must be combined with a main clause.

REVISE   The new manager instituted several new procedures. *Many of which are impractical.* (*Many of which* must be linked to *procedures.*)

TO   The new manager instituted several new procedures, many of which are impractical.

A sentence must contain a main, or finite, verb. *Verbals,* which are forms derived from verbs but different in function, will not do the job. (See Section 3.4.2b of the Writer's Guide.) The following examples are sentence fragments because they do not contain main verbs. *Providing, to work,* and *waiting* are verbals and cannot perform the function of a main verb.

REVISE   *Providing* all employees with hospitalization insurance.

TO   The company *provides* all employees with hospitalization insurance.

REVISE   *To work* a 40-hour week.

TO   The new contract *requires* all employees to work a 40-hour week.

REVISE   The customer *waiting* to see you.

TO   The customer waiting to see you *is* from the Labatronics Corporation.

Fragments usually reflect incomplete and sometimes confused thinking. The most common type of fragment is the careless addition of an afterthought.

REVISE   These are my coworkers. A fine group of people.

TO   My coworkers are a fine group of people.

Run-on Sentences. A *run-on sentence,* sometimes called a *fused sentence,* is made up of two or more independent clauses (sentence elements that contain a subject and a predicate and could stand alone as complete sentences) without punctuation to separate them. (See Section 4.3.4b in the Writer's Guide.)

INCORRECT   The new manager instituted several new procedures some were impractical.

Run-on sentences can be corrected in the following ways:

1. Create two separate sentences.

CORRECT   The new manager instituted several new procedures. Some were impractical.

2. Join the two clauses with a semicolon if they are closely related.

CORRECT   The new manager instituted several new procedures; some were impractical.

3. Join the clauses with a comma and a coordinating conjunction.

CORRECT   The new manager instituted several new procedures, but some were impractical.

4. Subordinate one clause to the other.

CORRECT   The new manager instituted several new procedures, some of which were impractical.

5. Join the two clauses with a conjunctive adverb preceded by a semicolon and followed by a comma.

CORRECT   The new manager instituted several new procedures; however, some were impractical.

Revising for Preciseness

The following sign once hung on the wall of a restaurant.

CUSTOMERS WHO THINK OUR WAITERS ARE RUDE
SHOULD SEE THE MANAGER

Several days later the sign was removed after customers continued to chuckle at the sign's unintended suggestion: that the manager was even ruder than the waiters.

In the case of the sign, of course, the customers understood the point that the restaurant owner had wanted to make. But in many types of job-related communication—a report or a letter, for instance—the reader may have difficulty deciding which of several possible meanings the writer had intended to convey. When a sentence (or a passage) can be interpreted in two or more ways and the writer has given the reader no clear basis for choosing from among the alternatives, the writing is ambiguous. Such lack of preciseness is a common source of vagueness in on-the-job writing.

Writing that is precise is so clear that your reader should have no difficulty understanding exactly what you want to say. In checking for precision, look for three likely trouble spots, enemies of precision that may give rise to misinterpretation on your reader's part: faulty comparisons, unclear pronoun reference, and imprecise word choice.

Faulty Comparisons

When you make a comparison, be sure that your reader understands what is being compared.

REVISE   Ms. Jones values rigid quality-control standards more than Mr. Johnson. (Does Ms. Jones value the standards more than she values Mr. Johnson, or does she value the standards more than Mr. Johnson values them?)

TO   Ms. Jones values rigid quality-control standards more than Mr. Johnson does.

When you compare two persons, things, or ideas, be sure that they are elements that can logically be compared with each other.

REVISE   The *accounting textbook* is more difficult to read than *office management*. (A textbook is not the same as a field of study.)

TO   The *accounting textbook* is more difficult to read than the *office management textbook*.

Unclear Pronoun Reference

A *pronoun* is a word that is used as a substitute for a noun. The noun for which the pronoun substitutes is called its *antecedent.* Using a pronoun to replace a noun eliminates the monotonous repetition of the noun. When you use a pronoun, though, be sure that your reader knows which noun the pronoun refers to. If you do not clearly indicate what word, or group of words, a pronoun stands for, your reader may be uncertain of your meaning. When you revise your sentences to correct unclear pronoun references, look especially for three types of errors: ambiguous reference, general (or broad) reference, and hidden reference. (For a further discussion of pronoun reference, see Section 3.2.3b of the Writer's Guide at the end of the book.)

In *ambiguous reference,* there is uncertainty as to which of two or more nouns a pronoun is referring to.

REVISE   Studs and thick treads make snow tires effective. *They* are installed with an air gun. (*What* are installed with an air gun—studs, treads, or snow tires? The reader can only guess.)

TO   Studs, which are installed with an air gun, and thick treads make snow tires effective. (Now it is clear that only studs are installed with an air gun.)

REVISE   We made the sale and delivered the product. *It* was a big one. (Does *It* refer to the sale or to the product?)

TO   We made the sale, which was a big one, and delivered the product. (Now it is clear that the sale, not the product, was a big one.)

REVISE   Jim worked with Tom on the report, but *he* wrote most of it. (*Who* wrote most of the report, Tom or Jim?)

TO   Jim worked with Tom on the report, but Tom wrote most of it.

In a *general* (or *broad*) *reference,* the pronoun—which is frequently a term like *this, that, which,* or *it*—does not replace an easily identifiable antecedent. Instead, it refers in a general way to the preceding sentence or clause.

REVISE   He deals with social problems in his work. *This* helps him in his personal life. (The pronoun *this* refers to the entire preceding sentence.)

TO   Dealing with social problems in his work helps him in his personal life.

REVISE   Mr. Bacon recently retired, *which* left an opening in the accounting department. (The pronoun *which* refers to the entire preceding clause.)

TO   Mr. Bacon's recent retirement left an opening in the accounting department. (Revising the sentence to eliminate the pronoun makes the meaning clear.)

The third cause of unclear pronoun reference is the *hidden reference*. In sentences that contain a hidden reference, the antecedent of the pronoun is implied but never actually stated.

REVISE   Despite the fact that our tractor division had researched the market thoroughly, we didn't sell *many*. (Many what? The pronoun *many* has no stated antecedent in the sentence. The writer assumes that the reader understands that *many* refers to tractors.)

TO   Despite the fact that we had thoroughly researched the market for tractors, we didn't sell *many*. (Now the pronoun *many* has an antecedent, *tractors*.)

OR   Despite the fact that our tractor division had researched the market thoroughly, we didn't sell many *tractors*. (Revising the sentence so that *many* becomes an adjective modifying *tractors* makes the meaning clear too.)

Imprecise Word Choice

As Mark Twain once said, "The difference between the right word and almost the right word is the difference between 'lightning' and 'lightning bug.'" Precision requires that you choose the right word. (See "Choosing the Right Word" in Section A, Part 2 of the Writer's Guide.)

When you write, be alert to the effect that a word may have on your reader—and try to avoid words that might, by the implications they carry, confuse or distract your reader. For example, in describing a piece of machinery that your company recently bought, you might refer to the item as *cheap*—meaning inexpensive. But because *cheap* often suggests "of poor quality" or "shabbily made," your reader may picture the new piece of equipment as already needing repairs.

In selecting the appropriate word, you will want to keep in mind the context—the setting in which the word appears. Suppose you call the new machine "inexpensive" or "moderately priced." Your reader may have confidence that the equipment will work, but may ask, "What does the writer *mean* by inexpensive?" An electric typewriter at $300 might be inexpensive; a small printing press at $30,000 would also be a good buy. The exact meaning of *inexpensive* would depend on the context. For readers who are unfamiliar with the cost of heavy machinery, it might be surprising to learn that a $30,000 press was reasonably priced. It would be up to you, the writer, to provide your readers with a context—to let them know, in this case, what the relative costs of printing equipment are.

The context will also determine whether a word you choose is *specific* enough. When you use the word *machine,* for instance, you might be thinking of an automobile, a lathe, a cash register, a sewing machine—the variety of mechanical equipment we use is almost endless. *Machine,* in other words, is an imprecise term that must be qualified, or explained, unless you want to refer in a general way to every item included in the category *machine.* If you have a particular kind of machine in mind, then you must use more precise language.

REVISE   The maintenance contract covers all the *machines* in Building D.

TO   The maintenance contract covers all the *electric typewriters* in Building D.

Depending on the context, you might need to choose a term even more specific than *electric typewriters.* Figure 5–1 illustrates just how specific a particular context might require you to be. The terminology goes from most general, on the left, to most specific, on the right. Seven levels of specificity are shown; which one would be appropriate depends on your purpose in writing and on the context in which you are using the word.

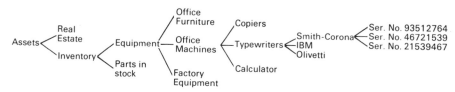

FIGURE 5–1.

For example, a person writing a company's annual report might logically use the most general term, *assets,* to refer to all the property and goods owned by the firm: shareholders would probably not expect a further breakdown. Interoffice memos between the company's accounting and legal departments would appropriately call the firm's holdings *real estate* and *inventory.* To the company's inventory-control department, however, the word *inventory* is much too broad to be useful; a report on inventory might contain the more specific categories *equipment* and *parts in stock*. But to the assistant inventory-control manager in charge of equipment, that term is still too general; he or she would speak of several particular kinds of equipment—*office furniture, office machines,* and *factory equipment.* The breakdown of the types of *office machines* for which the inventory-control assistant is responsible might include *copiers, typewriters,* and *calculators.*

However, even this classification wouldn't be specific enough to enable the company's purchasing department to obtain service contracts for the normal maintenance of its typewriters. Because the department must deal with different typewriter manufacturers, *typewriters* would have to be listed by brand name: *Olivetti, IBM,* and *Smith-Corona.* And the Smith-Corona technician who performs the maintenance must go one step further and identify each Smith-Corona typewriter by serial number. As Figure 5–1 shows, then, a term may be sufficiently specific at one of the seven levels—but at the next level it becomes too broad. Your purpose in writing and your intended reader will determine how specific you should be.

Purpose and audience may sometimes require a general rather than a specific term. To include typewriter serial numbers in a company's annual report, a detailed parts list in a sales brochure, or highly technical language in a letter to the accounting department would, of course, be inappropriate. In all the writing you do, you must decide what your purpose is and who your reader will be, and then select the term that is neither too general nor too specific for the context.

Remember that you must sometimes define terms for your reader. Say you are making a proposal to your boss, who must pass your proposal along to his or her boss for final approval. You may be using terms that your boss's superior will not recognize, because you work with details that will be unfamiliar to someone interested in only the big picture. If you want your proposal to be approved, you would be wise to do everything you can to be sure that your ideas are readily understandable. In some cases you may define specific terms; in others, you may prefer to omit them and write at a more general level.

How you go about defining the terms that need explanation depends on the context. It may often be sufficient to give a brief explanation, in everyday language, of a technical or specialized term.

EXAMPLE   The program then spools the first file (stores the file on magnetic tape until the program is ready to print it) and opens the second file.

Or you may find it easiest to provide a dictionary-type definition.

EXAMPLE   The property includes approximately 1,700 feet of waterside
(land bordering any body of water).

Sometimes it may be necessary to provide a formal definition of a word.
(See Chapter 6 for a complete discussion of formal definition.) To write
such a definition, place the term in a category and show how the term
differs from other members of that category.

EXAMPLE   A lease [*term*] is a contract [*category*] that conveys real estate
for a specified period of time at a specified rent [*how* a lease
differs from other contracts].

REVISING FOR STYLE

Revising for style means examining the ways you have expressed
your ideas. Key stylistic elements include your use of language and your
point of view.

Conciseness

Conciseness is freedom from unnecessary words, and the more concise
your writing, the more effective it will be. Wordiness, as well as stilted
or unpretentious language, can act as a barrier between writer and reader
by making relatively straightforward ideas difficult to understand. You
can achieve conciseness by eliminating any words, phrases, or clauses
that do not contribute to your meaning and any expressions that are
too fancy or obscure. But do not confuse a short sentence with a concise
one; long or short, a wordy sentence is always less readable because of
the extra load it carries. As you revise your writing, be particularly alert
for three types of wordiness: *redundancy,* or the use of a word or words
that do no more than repeat the meaning of something already stated
(*round circle* is an example of redundancy); *padded phrases,* which express
in several words an idea that could easily be said in one (*due to the
fact that* for *because* is an example of a padded phrase); and *affectation,*
the senseless inflation of language to make a message sound more important than it really is (*pore over a tome* for *read a book* is an example of
affectation).

Redundancy.   When a modifying word, phrase, or clause adds no
new information to what a sentence alreadys says, the modifier is redundant.

REVISE   To complete the circuit, join the wires *together* with solder. (The word *together* repeats the thought contained in the word *join*.)

TO   To complete the circuit, join the wires with solder.

REVISE   *Modern* students *today* consider work experience to be as valuable as classroom attendance. (The word *today* repeats the thought expressed by the word *modern*.)

TO   *Modern* students consider work experience to be as valuable as classroom attendance.

REVISE   Our imported products, *which come from abroad,* all have limited warranties. (Since *imported products* can be assumed to be manufactured *abroad,* the clause is not needed.)

TO   Our imported products all have limited warranties.

REVISE   We moved the storage cases into the empty warehouse, *which had nothing in it*. (An *empty warehouse* is understood to have *nothing in it*.)

TO   We moved the storage cases into the empty warehouse.

When they are selected carefully, modifiers—whether adjectives, adverbs, prepositional phrases, or subordinate clauses—can make the words they describe vivid and specific. Modifiers to avoid are those that simply repeat the idea contained in the word they modify. Studying the following list of redundant expressions may sharpen your ability to spot this kind of wordiness.

blue *in color*	to resume *again*
square *in shape*	brief *in duration*
to plan *ahead*	*tall* high-rise
basic essentials	small *in size*
descended *down*	to attach *together*
visible *to the eye*	to cooperate *together*

Padded Phrases.   When an idea that could be stated in one word is buried in an expression that takes several words—and is no clearer than the single word—a padded phrase results.

REVISE   The committee will meet *at an early date*.

TO   The committee will meet *soon*.

REVISE   The contractor will issue regular progress reports *during the time that* the contract is in effect.

TO The contractor will issue regular progress reports *while* the contract is in effect.

REVISE I recently met with the city attorney *with reference to* your case.

TO I recently met with the city attorney *about* your case.

REVISE We missed our deadline *due to the fact that* a strike occurred.

TO We missed our deadline *because* a strike occurred.

REVISE We cannot accept new clients *at the present time.*

TO We cannot accept new clients *now.*

REVISE We have received four complaints *in connection with* the project.

TO We have received four complaints *about* the project.

REVISE *In order* to meet the deadline, we must work overtime.

TO *To* meet the deadline, we must work overtime.

REVISE She was thinking *in terms of* subcontracting much of the work.

TO She was thinking *of* subcontracting much of the work.

There are times, however, when the longer wording is desirable.

EXAMPLE *In terms of* gross sales, the year has been successful; *in terms of* net income, however, it has been discouraging.

Expressions like these must be evaluated individually. If the expression does not contribute to the meaning of the sentence, use its simpler substitute.

  A half-dozen terms are the particular villains of wordiness. When they occur, you should examine your work critically for padded phrases. The words are *case, fact, field, factor, manner,* and *nature.*

REVISE *In many cases,* students profit from writing a term paper.

TO Students *often* profit from writing a term paper. (Sometimes it is necessary, when revising a sentence, to shift the location of the modifier.)

REVISE I was not certain *of the fact that* your cousin is a steelworker.

TO I was not certain *that* your cousin is a steelworker.

REVISE I have been interested *in the fields of* drafting and electronics for several years.

TO	I have been interested *in* drafting and electronics for several years.
REVISE	Speed is also *an important factor.*
TO	Speed is also *important.*
REVISE	The skids were stacked *in an unsafe manner.*
TO	The skids were stacked *unsafely.*
REVISE	The committee seldom considered grievances *of a controversial nature.*
TO	The committee seldom considered *controversial* grievances.

Affectation.   Affectation is the inflation of language to make it more technical or showy than is necessary to communicate information to the reader.

Affectation can be a serious problem in on-the-job writing because it creates a smokescreen that the reader must penetrate to discover the writer's meaning. The following example illustrates the problem.

REVISE	It is the policy of the company to provide the proper telephonic apparatus to enable each employee to conduct the interoffice and intra-business communication necessary to discharge his or her responsibilities; however, it is contrary to company practice to permit telephones to be utilized for personal employee communications.
TO	Your telephone is provided for company business; do not use it for personal calls.

Most people would have to read the first version of the sentence several times before deciphering its message. The meaning of the revised version, which uses direct, simple, and precise language, is evident at a glance.

In your own writing, avoid obscure and legal-sounding words (*discharge responsibilities, aforesaid, hereto,* and so on). Avoid trendy, vogue words such as *parameters* and *up to speed.* Do not use big, imprecise words as a substitute for simple, well-thought-out language. You won't fool anyone. Take a critical look at what you've written to see whether any of the wording should be deflated—replaced with clearer, shorter, down-to-earth words and phrases. Consider the following example.

REVISE	The Model 3211 is a device that provides the capability of performing the printing function to produce reports.
TO	The Model 3211 can print reports.

The first sentence reads like an important pronouncement. Stripped of its pretentious phrases, however, it is actually a simple statement.

In recent years, consumer interest groups and lawmakers have become concerned about the problem of affectation and legal-sounding language in insurance policies, contracts, and other documents. As a result, many states have created "plain English laws," which require that documents be written in clear, understandable language. The following sentences show the effect of revising "legalese" into plain language.

REVISE   I hereby authorize the above repair work to be done along with the necessary material, and hereby grant you and/or your employees permission to operate the car or truck herein described on streets, highways, or elsewhere for the purpose of testing and/or inspection.

TO   You have my permission to make repairs listed on this work order and to use the necessary materials. You or your employees may drive my car or truck to test its performance.

In the revised version, notice the absence of the "high-sounding" phrases *I hereby authorize, hereby grant, herein described, the above repair work,* and *and/or.* Notice that when it is translated into straightforward English, the statement gains in clarity what it loses in pomposity.

If you know the possible reasons for affectation, you will be taking the first step toward avoiding it. The following list addresses the most common reasons for affectation.

- *Impression.* As suggested earlier, one reason writers use pretentious language is that they wish to impress the reader. Creating an impression begins in school, when students try to impress their teachers with fancy words instead of evidence and logic. Later, an employee may want to impress superiors or clients with how well he or she performs on the job.
- *Insecurity.* Writers who are insecure about their facts, conclusions, or arguments may try to protect themselves with a smokescreen of pretentious words.
- *Imitation.* Perhaps unconsciously, some writers imitate poor writing they see around them. In one company, for example, everyone referred to himself or herself in memos as *the writer* instead of *I.* Each new person who joined the company unthinkingly followed the style until the president of the company noticed the practice and told the employees that they could refer to themselves with the normal *I.*
- *Intimidation.* A few writers, consciously or unconsciously, try to intimidate or overwhelm their reader with words—often to protect

themselves from criticism. Such writers seem to feel that the best defense is a good offense.

- *Initiation.* Those who have just completed their training for an occupation often feel that one way to prove their membership is to use technical terminology and jargon as much as possible. Usually, after a few years pass and the novice feels respected by coworkers, the impulse for affectation passes. Supervisors, however, wish the process did not take so long.

- *Imprecision.* Because a writer is having trouble being precise, he or she may find that an easy solution is to use a vague but trendy, pretentious word. It is easier to say "the policy will have a positive impact upon the department" than to explain precisely how the policy will affect the department.

Technical Terminology

Technical terms are standard, universally recognized words that are used in a particular field to refer to specific principles, processes, or devices. Technical terms are useful and sometimes essential in communicating clearly and concisely. For example, the term *divestiture* has a specific, generally understood meaning among readers who have studied management strategies. Similarly, the term *logic gate* would be understood by readers who have studied computer science. If you are certain that *all* your readers (and potential readers) would understand a technical term, use it as an efficient means of communication. If you are at all uncertain, however, you should define the term in everyday language when you first use it.

If your readers are unlikely to understand the concept that a technical term represents, you should explain the concept, perhaps including easy-to-understand examples. Although digressing into an explanation is not as efficient as simply using a technical term, your goal of making your writing easily understandable should be paramount.

Jargon

Jargon is highly specialized technical slang that is unique to an occupational group. If *all* your readers are members of a particular occupational group, jargon (like technical terminology) may provide a time-saving and efficient means of communicating with them. For example, if you were writing to printers or publishers, you might use the term *repro* and be understood. (*Repro* is short for *reproduction,* which in the printing business means the camera-ready copy from which the printing plate is made.)

Jargon enters the language for a variety of reasons, only some of which are defensible. Often, technical terms are cumbersome and abbreviation is desirable. For example, automobiles have a device called a pollution-control valve, which people who work in the automobile industry have shortened to PCV. If you doubt that your reader would understand such technical shorthand, spell the words out.

Also common are words that already have established meanings in everyday speech but have only recently been applied to new concepts and devices. For example, *access*—a noun meaning the ability to enter, approach, communicate with, or pass to or from—has always been part of our language. However, as a transitive verb meaning to get at something, such as a computer file, *access* is very new and should only be used in a specific discussion of computers. Although you can access a computer file, you cannot access a novel. Understandably, the developers of new concepts and devices, in their need to name their creations, rarely have time for elegance. Just remember that this technical shorthand is not a satisfactory substitute for everyday language outside the field in which it is standard.

Yet another type of jargon is used to define occupations euphemistically, and this jargon also must be kept in its place. Good manners dictate that if you are writing to an undertaker and must refer to him by trade, you should use the term *mortician*. Similarly, a garbage collector is a sanitation worker when politeness requires it.

A type of jargon that is indefensible is the useless elongation of standard words. Frequently one hears *analyzation, summarization,* and *notation;* the correct words are *analysis, summary,* and *note.* The additions to such words do not make them mean anything more precise; they simply make them incorrect.

When jargon becomes so specialized that it applies only to one company or subgroup of an occupation, it is referred to as "shop talk." For example, an automobile manufacturer might produce a "pollution-control valve—Model LV-20." In the department where the device is built, it may be referred to as an "LV-20." Obviously, shop talk is appropriate only for those familiar with its special vocabulary and should be reserved for speech and informal memorandums.

Sexist Language

Using masculine pronouns for terms like *everyone, employee, student,* and *technician* could be offensive because many people are sensitive to implied sexual bias in such language.

EXAMPLE   *Everyone* may stay or go as *he* chooses.

When graceful alternatives are available, use them. One solution is to rewrite the sentence in the plural.

REVISE   Every *employee* will have *his* supervisor sign *his* attendance slip.

TO   All *employees* will have *their* supervisors sign *their* attendance slips.

Be careful not to change the pronoun to the plural but leave its antecedent in the singular. The pronoun and its antecedent must always agree.

REVISE   A *technician* can expect to advance on *their* merit.

TO   *Technicians* can expect to advance on *their* merit.

Other possible solutions are to use *his or her* instead of *his* alone or to omit the pronoun completely if it isn't essential to the meaning of the sentence.

REVISE   *Everyone* must submit *his* expense report by Monday.

TO   *Everyone* must submit *his or her* expense report by Monday.

OR   Everyone must submit *an* expense report by Monday.

However, *he or she* can become monotonous when constantly repeated, and a pronoun cannot always be omitted without changing the meaning of a sentence. The best solution, then, is the first one—to use the plural whenever possible.

Point of View

Some writers feel that, especially in job-related writing, it is immodest or inappropriate to use the first-person point of view—that is, to speak of themselves as *I* or *me*. They believe that their material will sound more "objective" or "businesslike" if they refer to themselves in the third person (employing such terms as *the writer, the technician,* or *the reporter*) or if they use the passive voice. Writing of this sort tends to sound stuffy and unnatural, however. In most cases your message will be clearer and easier to follow if you speak of yourself as *I.*

REVISE   *The technician* will complete the wiring and test the system at the end of June.

TO *I will* complete the wiring and test the system at the end of June.

REVISE The tests described in the attached report *were all performed by the writer*.

TO *I* performed all the tests described in the attached report.

Also, in on-the-job writing, avoid the use of *one* as a pronoun, because it is inexact, indirect, and pretentious. The use of *one* does not make your writing more objective; it merely makes a statement sound impersonal, almost as if some nameless, formless being, rather than you yourself, were expressing an idea or making a suggestion.

REVISE *One* can only conclude that the new valves are not effective on the old fire trucks.

TO *I* can only conclude that the new valves are not effective on the old fire trucks.

The use of an impersonal *it is* expression to avoid the pronoun *I* has the same kind of stuffy effect as *the writer* and *one*.

REVISE *It is regrettable that* the material shipped on the 12th is unacceptable.

TO *I regret that* we cannot accept your shipment of the 12th.

The second version is more direct and suggests that the writer is not trying to avoid taking responsibility for what he or she has stated.

Some writers, looking for ways to make their work sound more authoritative or more serious, introduce expressions like *It should be noted that* or *I am inclined to think that* in their writing. Expressions like these only add wordiness.

REVISE *It should be noted that* the gaskets tend to turn brittle after six months in the warehouse.

TO The gaskets tend to turn brittle after six months in the warehouse.

REVISE *I am inclined to think that* each manager should attend the meeting to hear the committee's recommendations.

TO I think that each manager should attend the meeting to hear the committee's recommendations.

The more natural your writing sounds, the more effectively it will communicate.

REVISING FOR MECHANICS

Comma Errors

The most common punctuation problem is the misuse of the comma. This is understandable because the comma has such a wide variety of uses: it links, it encloses, it separates, and it indicates omissions. (For a complete discussion of the comma, see Section 5.1 of the Writer's Guide. Other marks of punctuation are covered there as well.) The following guidelines will help you to use the comma correctly and effectively.

When two independent clauses are joined with only a comma, the error is known as a *comma splice*. (See Section 5.1.6a of the Writer's Guide.) Like a run-on sentence, which also contains improperly connected clauses, a comma splice can be corrected in several ways: (1) joining the two clauses with a comma and a coordinating conjunction, (2) subordinating one clause to the other, (3) joining the two clauses with a semicolon if they are closely related, (4) joining the two clauses with a conjunctive adverb preceded by a semicolon and followed by a comma, or (5) creating two separate sentences.

REVISE   It was 500 miles to the facility, we made arrangements to fly. (comma splice)

TO   It was 500 miles to the facility, so we made arrangements to fly. (comma plus coordinating conjunction)

OR   Because it was 500 miles to the facility, we made arrangements to fly. (one clause subordinated to the other)

OR   It was 500 miles to the facility; we made arrangements to fly. (semicolon)

OR   It was 500 miles to the facility; therefore, we made arrangements to fly. (semicolon, conjunctive adverb, comma)

OR   It was 500 miles to the facility. We made arrangements to fly. (two sentences)

When correcting a comma splice, be sure that the solution you choose correctly conveys the intended meaning of the original sentence.

Do not place a comma everywhere you pause. Although it is true that commas usually signal pauses, *it is not true that pauses necessarily call for commas*. A number of common errors involve placing commas where they do not belong. (See Section 5.1.6b of the Writer's Guide.)

Do not place a comma between a subject and its verb or between a verb and its object.

REVISE   The cold conditions, made accurate readings difficult. (The comma incorrectly separates the subject, *conditions,* from its verb, *made.*)

TO   The cold conditions made accurate readings difficult.

REVISE   He has often said, that one company's failure is another's opportunity. (The comma incorrectly separates the verb, *said,* from its object, *that one company's failure is another's opportunity.*)

TO   He has often said that one company's failure is another's opportunity.

Do not place a comma between the two parts of a compound subject or a compound predicate.

REVISE   The director of the engineering department, and the supervisor of the quality-control section were both opposed to the new schedules. (The comma incorrectly separates the parts of the compound subject, *director* and *supervisor.*)

TO   The director of the engineering department and the supervisor of the quality-control section were both opposed to the new schedules.

REVISE   The director of the engineering department listed five major objections, and asked that the new schedules be reconsidered. (The comma incorrectly separates the parts of the compound predicate, *listed five major objections* and *asked that the new schedules be reconsidered.*)

TO   The director of the engineering department listed five major objections and asked that the new schedules be reconsidered.

In most cases, do not place a comma after a coordinating conjunction such as *and* or *but.*

REVISE   The chairman formally adjourned the meeting, but, the members of the committee continued to argue. (The word *but* is part of the second clause and should not be separated from it by a comma.)

TO   The chairman formally adjourned the meeting, but the members of the committee continued to argue.

REVISE   I argued against the proposal. And, I gave good reasons for my position. (The word *and* is part of the sentence and should not be separated from it by a comma.)

TO	I argued against the proposal. And I gave good reasons for my position.

Do not place a comma before the first item in a series or after the last item in a series.

REVISE	We are considering a number of new products, such as, calculators, typewriters, and cameras.
TO	We are considering a number of new products, such as calculators, typewriters, and cameras.
REVISE	It was a fast, simple, inexpensive, process.
TO	It was a fast, simple, inexpensive process.

Spelling Errors

Following is a list of words that are frequently misspelled in on-the-job writing. This list can serve as a handy reference if you are in doubt about a particular word. If you have trouble with spelling, study the spelling section of the Writer's Guide at the end of the book.

Commonly Misspelled Words

aberration	a lot (*two words*)	architectural
absorption	alcohol	arguing
accelerate	all right (*two words*)	around
accessible	altar (*noun*)	arouse
accommodate	alter (*verb*)	arrangement
achieve	altogether	ascend
acknowledgment	amateur	assert
acquaint	ambivalent	assistant
acquire	analysis	athlete
across	analyze	attach
actual	annual	author
address	anonymous	auxiliary
advice (*noun*)	answer	belief (*noun*)
advise (*verb*)	antiseptic	believe (*verb*)
adviser	apparatus	benefit
aerate	appear	benefited
aggravate	appetite	breathe (*verb*)
airborne	appreciable	brilliant
aisle (*of theater*)	appropriate	buried

business
cafeteria
calendar
captain
carburetor
careful
carrying
category
ceiling
cemetery
certain
changeable
characteristic
chief
choose (*present*)
chose (*past*)
climbed
clothes
column
coming
commit
committed
committee
common
comparatively
conceivable
conceive
concentration
confidant, confidante
  (*noun*)
confident (*adjective*)
conquer
conscience
conscientious
conscious
consistent
continual
continuous
controlled
convenience
copies
corroborate
course
courteous

criteria
criticism
criticize
crowd
crystal
cylinder
dealt
dependent
desirable
despair
desperate
develop
development
diesel
dietitian
difference
different
dilemma
disappear
disappoint
disapprove
disastrous
discipline
discriminate
discussed
disease
dissatisfied
dissection
distinction
doctor
dormitories
drunkenness
ecstasy
efficiency
eighth
electricity
electronics
eligible
eliminate
embarrass
embarrassment
emphasize
enemy
engines

environment
equipment
equipped
especially
essential
exaggerate
exceed
excellent
except
exercise
exhilaration
existence
expense
experience
experiment
explanation
extremely
fascinate
fascinating
February
financial
flourish
forcibly
foreign
foresee
formally (*in a formal
  way*)
formerly (*earlier*)
forth (*forward*)
forty
fundamental
further
gardener
gauge
government
grammar
grateful
grievous
guarantee
guard
guidance
height
identify
imitation

immediately
incidentally
increase
incredible
indelible
independence
indispensable
inevitable
influential
initiate
inoculate
insistent
intellectual
intelligence
interfere
interrupt
invitation
irrelevant
irresistible
irritable
jealous
judgment
knowledge
lead (*verb* and
   noun)
laboratory
led (*verb*)
leisure
length
library
license
lightning
likable
likelihood
likely
loneliness
loose (*adjective*)
lose (*verb*)
lying
maintenance
manageable
management
maneuver
mathematics

meant
miniature
mischievous
misdemeanor
misspelled
morale
mortgage
mysterious
naturally
necessarily
ninety
ninth
noticeable
obstacle
occurred
occurrence
omission
omitted
operate
opportunity
optimistic
origin
oscillate
parallel
particularly
partner
peculiar
perceive
perform
permanent
perseverance
persistent
persuade
pertain
piece
possess
possession
potato
potatoes
practicable
precede
preceding
preference
preferred

prejudice
presence
prevalent
privilege
procedure
proceed
prominent
pronunciation
propeller
protein
prove
psychology
publicly
pursue
realize
really
receipt
receive
recognize
recommend
referred
relevant
relieve
religious
repetition
resemblance
resistance
restaurant
rhythm
ridiculous
safety
salary
scene
schedule
seize
separate
sergeant
shepherd
shoulder
signal
similar
site
sophomore
specimen

speech	technique	undoubtedly
statement	temperament	unnecessary
stopped	temperature	until
straight	tendency	usually
strategy	therefore	vacuum
strength	thorough	vegetable
studying	thought	vertical
subpoena	through	vitamin
succeed	together	Wednesday
suddenness	toward	weird
superintendent	transferred	wholly
supersede	tries	woman
suppress	truly	women
surprise	Tuesday	writing
syllable	twelfth	written
symmetrical		

Also, as you check spelling be sure that you have not substituted a homophone—a word that sounds like another word—for the word that you ought to use. In other words, be sure that you have not used *too* when you meant *two*. (Section 1 of the Writer's Guide provides a list of many of these words.) The ear can play tricks on you, and these mistakes are often hard to catch, since the wrong word is perfectly legitimate when it is used correctly. Further, if you type, be aware of your most frequent typographical errors.

PHYSICAL APPEARANCE

The most thoughtfully prepared, carefully written, and conscientiously revised writing will quickly lose its effect if it has a poor physical appearance. In the classroom or on the job, a sloppy document will invariably lead your reader to assume that the work that went into preparing it was also sloppy. In the classroom, that carelessness will reflect on you; on the job, it can reflect on your employer as well.

Consider Christine Thomas's memo to Harriet Sullivan in Chapter 1. Christine wanted to persuade Harriet. A memo written in sloppy or illegible handwriting on coffee-stained paper would not have helped Christine accomplish her purpose. Similarly, your writing will not accomplish its purpose if it has a poor physical appearance. Neatness counts!

Unless your instructor provides other specific instructions, use the following guidelines to give your writing a neat and pleasing appearance:

1. Use good-quality paper—ruled if you write by hand or nonerasable white bond if you type or use a word processor.
2. Type if at all possible. Otherwise, make sure that your handwriting is neat and readable.
3. If you type or use a word processor, make sure that the ribbon is fresh and the keys are clean so the letters will not fade or smudge. Use the double strike or "overstrike" feature if you use a dot matrix printer.
4. Use at least one-inch margins on the sides of the paper and one-and-a-half-inch margins on the top and bottom.
5. Handle the paper carefully with clean hands so it does not get crumpled or marked with fingerprints.
6. Make sure that the writing is not crowded and that ample white space separates sections.

Good physical arrangement of specific types of writing, such as letters or formal reports, is discussed elsewhere in the book. Refer to the table of contents or the index for page numbers.

REVISION CHECKLIST

The following revision checklist may help you remember the various aspects of revision that this chapter has covered. Refer to it both before and after you write the final draft of any document; you must fix any problems before your reader sees them.

_____Have I allowed a "cooling" period?
_____Is my content complete and accurate?
_____Do all subjects and verbs agree in number?
_____Do all pronouns and their antecedents agree in number and in gender?
_____Are verb tenses accurate and consistent?
_____Are there any dangling or misplaced modifiers?
_____Are all sentences complete and properly punctuated?
_____Is the language precise, unambiguous, and free of unnecessary jargon and sexism?
_____Have I removed all redundancy, padding, and affectation?
_____Is the point of view appropriate and consistent?
_____Are there any comma errors?
_____Are all the words spelled correctly?
_____Is the physical appearance of the document satisfactory?

CHAPTER SUMMARY

Like all good writers, you must revise your writing carefully. The first step toward careful revision is to become objective about your writing—allow for a "cooling" period and then view your draft as if it were written by a stranger. Revise your draft in passes, examining one aspect of your writing at a time, and look for your most common errors first. A word processor permits revision in passes with relative ease.

As you revise, be sure to check your writing for accuracy and completeness. In addition, examine your writing for agreement of subjects and verbs and of pronouns and antecedents, and also for consistency of tense and of person. Eliminate dangling and misplaced modifiers and correct sentence fragments and run-on sentences.

As you check for preciseness, review comparisons for logic and consistency. Clarify the ambiguity of unclear pronoun references by supplying an antecedent to the pronoun that is recognizable immediately. And, according to the context, select words that have no inappropriate associations and are neither too general nor too specific for your purpose and readers.

As you revise for conciseness, strike from your work any redundant modifiers (modifiers that contribute no additional meaning to the words they qualify), any padded phrases (expressions that take several words to convey an idea that one or two words would express just as effectively), and any affectation (inflated language that obscures your message). If you use specialized or technical terms that your reader may be unfamiliar with, provide definitions or easy-to-grasp examples that clarify the terms. Do not use inappropriate jargon as a substitute for direct, well-thought-out language. Avoid implied sexual bias in your choice of pronouns when the antecedent can refer to both men and women. Finally, make your point of view—the way you address the reader—appropriate to the message; in many cases, the first-person point of view will be appropriate.

Remember that even with the most careful revision you will lose your reader's confidence unless your writing has a neat and pleasing physical appearance.

EXERCISES

1. Each of the following sentences contains a faulty comparison. Rewrite each sentence to eliminate the error.

   a. The word-processing machine in the direct mail department operates more efficiently than the customer relations department.

b. The production manager expressed greater appreciation for the temporary help than the sales manager.
c. Julia Valenti, the personnel manager, felt that the applicant was better qualified than Charles Crane, the director of office services.

2. Each of the following sentences contains a "squinting modifier"— that is, a modifier that may qualify either of two elements within the sentence. Locate the squinting modifier and rewrite the sentence in two ways.

a. The transformer that was sparking violently shocked the line operator.
b. The man who was making calculations hastily rose from the desk and left the room.
c. After the committee decided that the work must be completed by Monday, in spite of other commitments, it adjourned immediately.
d. He planned after the convention to take a short vacation.

3. Each of the following sentences contains an unclear pronoun reference. Rewrite the sentences as necessary to eliminate the errors.

a. Many members complained that their representatives made decisions secretly without considering them.
b. Technology has so simplified computer operation that it is now being used in homes.
c. The crane operator did not file a safety grievance and does not plan it.
d. Our company decided to relocate in Grandview Hills, after rejecting Westville and Dale City, which was a difficult decision to make.
e. Anita has held stenographic positions in two insurance companies and in an auto-rental firm, and it should help her in finding a new job.
f. Mrs. Jardina wanted to dictate a letter to her assistant, Mrs. Sanfredini, but she was unable to begin work until after lunch.
g. If you feel that you would like to become a dental hygienist, by all means take a course in it.

4. Each of the following sentences contains a redundant word, phrase, or clause. Rewrite the sentences to eliminate the redundant elements.

a. Our experienced salespeople, who have many years of work behind them, will plan an aggressive advertising campaign to sell the new product.

b. Any two raceway assemblies can be connected together with the plate as shown.

c. The radio announcer kept repeatedly saying, "Buy PDQ brand pretzels!"

d. Dissatisfied employees should give their complaints to the manager who is in charge as supervisor.

e. If you are interested in economics, do not neglect to read the above-mentioned book, which was discussed previously.

5. Each of the following sentences contains at least one padded phrase. Rewrite the sentences to eliminate such phrases.

a. We began the project in the month of April.

b. He opened the conversation with a reference to the subject of inflation.

c. The field of engineering is a profession that offers great opportunities.

d. The process was delayed because of the fact that the chemicals were impure.

e. The personnel manager spoke to the printing-plant supervisor with regard to the scheduling of employee vacations.

f. Due to the fact that Monday was a holiday, we will not be able to complete the job until Wednesday.

6. Each of the following passages contains unnecessary jargon, padded phrases, and affectation. Revise the passages.

a. With reference to the matter that management has declared to be in the best interest of the furtherance of company–employee relations, the president has been authorized and empowered to grant each and every employee, upon the attainment of 30 years of continued and uninterrupted service to the company, an additional period of vacation that shall be of one week's duration.

b. I hereby designate Mr. Samson, who has been holding the position and serving in the capacity of assistant technical supervisor, to be named and appointed to the position and function of deputy director of customer relations. In his newly elevated position Mr. Samson will report, in the first instance, directly to the department director—that is, to me.

c. Purchasers of the enclosed substance should carefully and thoroughly follow the instructions provided herein for the use of the substance, and should in no case whatsoever consume, or otherwise partake of, said substance without proceeding in the manner set forth on the accompanying circular of instructions.

7. In each of the following sentences, select the correct word or words from the two items in parentheses. In some sentences, the choice involves the correct pronoun; in other sentences, it involves the correct verb. After adjusting for agreement, you may need to revise several sentences further to avoid sexism.

   a. The supervisor asked each employee to decide whether (he/they) wanted to work overtime to finish the project.
   b. Her job during the negotiations (was/were) to observe and then report her observations to the manager.
   c. Our line of products (is/are) sold in the West and in the Midwest.
   d. Neither John nor Peter remembered to submit (his/their) work on time.
   e. The Association of Corporate Employees failed because (they/it) never received full support from the member companies.
   f. Any employee who has not completed (his/their) time sheet must do so now.
   g. A number of beneficial products (has/have) resulted from the experiment.
   h. That these figures are contradictory anyone in (their/his) right mind can see.
   i. A staff member is held responsible for any errors that (he or she/ they) may introduce.

8. Revise the following sentences to correct any errors in agreement. The errors may be in subject–verb agreement or in pronoun–antecedent agreement.

   a. A survey of residents in the selected communities show a large potential market for our product.
   b. After each of the printed characters are translated, the report is given to the word processing department.
   c. The committee is planning to submit their recommendations before the end of the week.
   d. The course instructs students in the basics of the subject and provides him with hands-on time.
   e. A project engineer must be able to justify the changes they make in a technician's drawing.

9. Each of the following sentences contains either a dangling modifier or a misplaced modifier. Locate the errors and correct them. Add any necessary words.

   a. An experienced technician, the company was anxious to hire her.
   b. Before taking the training course, it is recommended that the operator read the *Operator's Manual*.

   c. After evaluating the 38 answers, the test was found by the production manager to reveal a serious deficiency.

   d. Hoping to be promoted for her contribution to the project, the vice president's report represents three months of work.

   e. We purchased the store's merchandise that was going out of business.

   f. We are going to install a desk chair for our assistant with a swivel seat.

10. Correct any sentence fragments or run-on sentences in this exercise. Add words and punctuation as necessary.

   a. Judge Ernest Owen rejected the appeal. Eight days after it was made.

   b. You may attend the conference. After you submit your request in writing.

   c. Nice to have talked to you.

   d. Have a profitable meeting.

   e. You can take the Walk-a-Phone with you. Anywhere you need a phone!

   f. They bought the computer for the staff they did not even know how to operate a computer.

   g. The cost of insuring a small business fleet skyrocketed last year combatting that increase has taken on increased importance.

11. Correct the comma faults in the following sentences by adding, changing, or deleting words and punctuation as needed.

   a. The electric voltage in the line was too high, he dared not risk touching it.

   b. An emergency occurs, another committee is born.

   c. Members may pay their dues immediately, they may choose to have a statement mailed to their homes or offices.

   d. The computer's printer has a red, and tan cabinet.

   e. One should never be ashamed to be somewhat sentimental, for, a certain amount of sentimentality makes a person human.

   f. The new law did not put all accountants behind bars, it did make some accountants fearful, though.

   g. The engine overheated, the operator turned it off.

12. The following memorandums were drafted by students requesting tuition reimbursement from their employers for a business writing course. They both contain many examples of the kinds of writing problems discussed in this chapter. Revise each, applying the revision guidelines in this chapter.

a.

```
    DATE:  September 11, 19—-
      TO:  Harold Wells
    FROM:  Norman Hill
 SUBJECT:  Tuition Reimbursement for Business Writing corse
           at Prentice College
```
Dear Mr. Wells.

    I seek tuition reimbursement for the corse Business Writing at Prentice College. In the time I have been employed at the Springfield Steel Co. as an assistant manager, I believe that my managerial skills could be broaden by participation in this corse. This corse would increase my communication skills along with the capacity to deal with others more effectively and efficiently. As far as I observe it, it would be in the best interest of the Company if I enrolled in this corse.

    My enrollment in this corse would be advantageous for a number of reasons;

    First the corse is an adaptation of a work situation. The teacher poses himself not as an teacher, but your manager, the one you write too. He gives the student different situations and teaches the student the right format, wheather its a memorandum or letter. His grading margin is dependant on wheather the manager would be satisfied or not. Included with that he tries to teach the student how to solve each situation with many different methods and technics.

    Another reason why the corse would valuable is because it would make me more verstile in the position I occupy now. This corse would give me a broader range in response letters, reports or article I might be responsible for. Also it will give me the much needed skill to communicate more effectively with the other personnel I don't see.

    Next this corse could be an asset to the company by the new skill I would posess. It would make me more competent to deal with others in a new formal way not known before, such as formal request and memorandums.

    Also the Business Writing corse I would attend could be valuable to employees and future students. Once I learn the proper formats and different styles I will be able to help to broaden others awareness of different formats and styles. Plus I will have the experience of the corse and will be able to recommend the corse.

    My responsibility at Springfield Steel mainly consist of dealing with people on a one to one basis, and refering

problems I see in the warehouse to the manager. The efficiency of one's job could be increased by taking this corse.
It may also install one of the skills one will need to operate
at my most efficient point. This corse would be good for me
as well as the company to create a better manager.

b.

> Date: September 10, 19---
> To: Patrick Allen
> From: Henry Jacobs
> Subject: Tuition Reimbursement to attend a writing class

As of September 1, 19---, I started my new position as
Office Manager. This one requires much more work in the area
of writing, such as letters, memos, and reports compared
to my old job. Because I feel that I am not doing satisfactory
work in these areas of writing, I would like to enroll in a
night class at Prentice College to correct my personal judge-
ment on my writing skills. However, I feel that the company
should reimburse me the tuition of $203.50 for a number of
reasons.

First of all, this writing class will teach me the best
and correct way to write memos, outlines, reports, letters,
proposals, etc. It will also sharpen my other writing skills.
Since not only do many people within the company see my writing but also a large number outside. And I feel this class
is necessary to make sure a good job is done. Good writing
skills can be impressive to our customers, this writing class
will benefit my area of the company.

Second, I feel the tuition should be reimbursed because
I am taking my own free time to improve my work as well as
my job. There is a lot of homework that includes research
for a big formal report. I am doing this for the company and
again, I say, this class will benefit my productivity in
the company as well as being beneficiary.

Finally, the importance of this writing class is great,
but the $203.50 is quite expensive. I feel that since I am
doing this for the company, it can be considered as a training
or workshop expence. And in turn I will provide you and the
company with my best job to benefit it.

As you can see, I have stressed the importance of this
writing class as a benefit to our company as well as making
my job easier and more productive. I feel this class is a
must and tuition should be reimbursed. I will be happy to
elaborate more on this at your request.

part two

THE PROCESS AT WORK

Part One discussed the principles of effective writing that apply to all on-the-job writing tasks. Part Two focuses on the practical applications of these principles. These applications include a grounding in the practical writing strategies basic to all on-the-job writing and explicit guidance on writing the most common types of work-related communications: memorandums, business letters, proposals, forms, and a variety of formal and informal reports. Such aids to communication as tables and illustrations, and the preparation and delivery of oral presentations, are also covered. This section gives extensive treatment to researching your subject, including using the library, interviewing, using questionnaires, and making first-hand observations. As you have seen, researching a subject takes place before the first draft is written. However, the chapter on research appears in Part Two immediately before the chapter on formal reports rather than in Part One because the comprehensive scope of this chapter is more appropriate to the preparation of formal reports than to many other kinds of job-related writing.

Finally, this section ends with a chapter that puts the guidance learned in the rest of the text to its first practical test: finding a job appropriate to your education and abilities.

6

Writing for Specific Purposes

In Part One, you learned that you must establish a *purpose* in writing before you begin to write. Depending on what kind of material you wish to present, on who your reader will be, and on how familiar he or she is with your subject, you can determine your purpose and then choose the most effective way to present your material.

In this chapter, we'll consider a variety of on-the-job writing objectives. You may want to tell your reader how to perform a certain task, or you may need to explain how something works. You may want to describe something or to compare it with something else. To make your subject easier to grasp, you may divide it into logical parts, define key terms, or examine the cause of some event. You may wish to persuade your reader to accept a particular viewpoint. Finally, you may need to summarize your information for readers who have only enough time for an overview.

The techniques discussed in this chapter should help you, first, to establish your purpose, and then to present the information relevant to your purpose in a way that will be clear and convincing to your reader.

INSTRUCTIONS

When you tell someone how to do something—how to perform a specific task—you are giving *instructions*. If your instructions are based on clear thinking and careful planning, they should enable your reader to carry out the task successfully.

To write accurate and easily understood instructions, you must thoroughly understand the task you are describing. Otherwise, your instructions could prove embarrassing or even dangerous. For example, the container of a brand-name drain cleaner carried the following warning:

Use Only as Directed

The instructions then directed the user to

Fill sink with one to two inches of cold water, then close off drain opening.

Users would certainly find it difficult to raise the water level in the sink *before* they closed the drain! Because most users simply ignored the instructions and performed the task according to common sense, no real harm resulted. But suppose such confusing information were to appear in the instructions for administering intravenous fluid or assembling a piece of high-voltage electrical equipment. The results of such inaccurate wording could be both costly and dangerous.

The writer of the drain-cleaning instructions was probably just being careless. Sometimes, though, a writer may not understand an operation well enough to write clear, accurate directions. If you are unfamiliar with a task for which you are writing instructions, watch someone who is familiar with it go through each step. As you watch, ask questions about any step that is not clear to you. Direct observation should help you to write instructions that are exact, complete, and easy to follow.

In writing instructions, as in all job-related writing, you should be aware of your reader's level of knowledge and experience. Is the reader skilled in the kind of task for which you are writing instructions? If you know that your reader has a good deal of technical background, you might feel free to use fairly specialized, technical vocabulary. If, on the other hand, your reader has little or no technical knowledge of the subject, it would be more appropriate to use simple, everyday language— to avoid specialized or technical terms as much as possible.

To test the accuracy and clarity of your instructions, it's a good idea to ask someone who is not familiar with the operation to follow the directions you've written. A first-time user can spot missing steps or point out passages that should be worded more clearly. You may find it helpful, as you observe your tester, to note any steps that seem especially puzzling or confusing.

To make your instructions easy to follow, divide them into short, simple steps. Be sure to arrange the steps in the proper sequence. (Review the information on step-by-step organization, page 25). Steps can be organized in one of two ways. (1) You can label each step with a sequential number.

1. Connect each black cable wire to a brass terminal. . . .
2. Attach one 4-inch green jumper wire to the back. . . .
3. Connect both jumper wires to the bare cable wires. . . .

(2) Or you can use words that indicate time or sequence.

> *First,* determine what the problem is that the customer is reporting to you. *Next,* observe and test the system in operation. *At that time,* question the operator until you believe that the problem has been explained completely.

Keeping the steps in the proper order is not always easy. Sometimes two operations must be performed at the same time. You should either state this fact in an introduction to the instructions or include both operations in the appropriate step.

WRONG 4. Hold the CONTROL key down.
  5. Press the BELL key before releasing the CONTROL key.

RIGHT 4. While holding the CONTROL key down, press the BELL key.

You may find that the clearest, simplest instructions are those whose steps are phrased as "commands." Your instructions will be less wordy, and easier to follow, if you address each sentence directly to your reader.

INDIRECT The operator should raise the access lid.

DIRECT Raise the access lid.

Make instructions concise, but do not phrase them as if they were telegrams. You can write shorter sentences by leaving out articles (*a, an, the*) and some pronouns (*you, this, these*) and verbs, but sentences that have been shortened in this way often have to be read more than once to be understood. The following instruction for cleaning a computer punch card assembly, for example, is not easily understood at first reading.

> Pass card through punch area for debris.

The meaning of the phrase *for debris* needs to be made clearer. Revised, the instruction is understandable at once.

> Pass *a* card through *the* punch area *to clear away* any debris.

Since many people fail to read a set of instructions completely through before beginning a project, you should plan ahead for your reader. If a process in Step 9 is affected by instructions in Step 2, say so in Step 2. Otherwise, your reader may reach Step 9 before discovering that an important piece of information that should have been given in advance was not.

If any special tools or materials are needed for the project, tell your reader at the beginning of the instructions. List any essential equipment at the beginning in a section labeled "Tools Required" or "Materials Required." The reader should not get three-fourths of the way through a project only to discover that a special wrench is necessary for the final steps. The following list of materials appeared at the beginning of a set of instructions for developing film at home.

Materials Required

Exposed film	Towel (paper or cloth)
Developing tank and reel	Scissors
Photographic thermometer	Glassine negative sleeves
Timer (clock or watch)	D-76 developer solution
Funnel (glass or plastic)	Fixing solution (hypo)
Measuring cup (glass or plastic)	Water
Viscose sponge	Storage containers for D-76 and
String	fixing solution (plastic, glass, or
Clothespins	stainless steel)

The instructions, which were written for beginners, continued with a discussion of those terms likely to confuse inexperienced film developers: *developing tank and reel, developer solution,* and *fixing solution.*

In any operation, certain steps must be performed with more exactness than others. Anyone who has boiled a three-minute egg for four minutes understands this principle. Alert your reader to steps that require precise timing or measurement.

You also must warn readers of potentially hazardous steps or materials before the steps are taken or the materials are handled. The conditions that require such warnings are numerous: electrical, chemical, mechanical, biological, and radioactive work, for example, all require some caution. Those handling hazardous materials need to be cautioned about requirements for special clothing, tools, equipment, or other measures they must take to safely complete their task.

When you write instructions, highlight warnings, cautions, and precautions by using special devices that make them stand out from the surrounding text. Warning notices can be presented in a box, for instance. In Figure 6–1, instructions written for maintenance and repair crews of heavy industrial equipment, note the underlined instructions, sepa-

Follow these steps for a typical lockup before all maintenance and repair work:

Step 1. Alert the operator and floor supervisor that you are ready.

Step 2. Identify all sources of residual energy on the machinery.

WARNING

Before beginning work, perform these procedures in the following order:

STEP 3. Place padlocks on the switch, lever, or valve to lock the equipment in the OFF position.

Put tags at this location to indicate that maintenance is in progress.

STEP 4. "Bleed" all hydraulic or pneumatic pressure and all electrical current (capacitance) so that machine components will not accidentally move.

Step 5. Test operator controls.

Step 6. After work is finished, replace all machine safeguards that were removed. Secure and check them to make sure they fit properly.

Step 7. Finally, remove padlocks and clear the machine for operation.

FIGURE 6–1. Set of instructions with precautions made clear.

INSTRUCTIONS

Distribute the inoculum over the surface of
the agar in the following manner:

Step 1. Beginning at one edge of the saucer, thin the inoculum by streaking
back and forth over the same area
several times, sweeping across the
agar surface until approximately
one-quarter of the surface has been
covered.
Sterilize the loop in an open
flame.

Step 2. Streak at right angles to the originally inoculated area, carrying
the inoculum out from the streaked
areas onto the sterile surface with
only the first stroke of the wire.
Cover half of the remaining sterile
agar surface.
Sterilize the loop.

Step 3. Repeat as described in Step 2, covering the remaining sterile agar
surface.

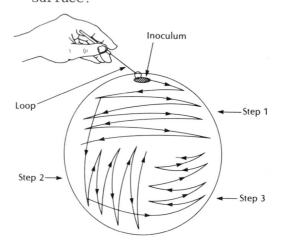

FIGURE 6–2. "Streaking" instructions.

rated by rules from the other steps, directing crews to shut off power sources and "bleed" any residual energy from the equipment before they begin work. Other attention-getting devices include all-capital letters, distinctive typefaces, and the use of colored type. Professional printers and graphic designers can recommend such devices. If you do not have professional printing and design help available, use typefaces available on a standard office typewriter or word processor. Many have changeable type that contains the letters of the alphabet in **boldface** and *italic,* as well as standard typefaces.

Drawings can be a valuable aid when you are giving instructions. Clear, well-thought-out illustrations can make instructions for even the most complex operations quickly understandable by reducing the number of words necessary to explain something. Appropriate pictures and diagrams will enable your reader to identify parts and the relationships between parts more easily than will long explanations. They'll also free you, the writer, to focus on the steps making up the instructions rather than on descriptions of parts. Not all instructions require illustrations, of course. Whether illustrations will be useful depends on your reader's needs and on the nature of the project. Instructions for inexperienced readers should be more heavily illustrated than those for experienced readers. For a full discussion of how to create effective illustrations, see Chapter 13.

Figure 6–2 shows instructions that guide a medical laboratory technician through the steps of "streaking" a saucer-sized disk of material (called *agar*) used to grow bacteria colonies for laboratory examination. The objective is to thin out the original specimen (the inoculum) so that the bacteria will grow in small, isolated colonies. The streaking process makes certain that part of the saucer is inoculated heavily, while its remaining portions are inoculated progressively more lightly. The streaking is done by hand with a thin wire, looped at one end for holding a small sample of the inoculum.

EXPLAINING A PROCESS

When you prepare instructions, your goal is to enable your reader to complete a specific task by following the step-by-step procedure you have outlined. You know that your reader will use your directions to become a *doer.* If, however, you are asked to write an explanation of a *process,* you will have a different purpose in mind: you will be telling your reader how something works or how something is done—but probably not something that your reader will actually be working on or doing himself or herself. The process you explain might be an event that occurs in nature (the tidal pull of the moon), a function that requires human effort (rice harvesting), or an activity in which men and women operate machinery to produce goods or services (automobile assembly-line production).

Just as it is essential for you to be familiar with a task before you can write clear instructions for carrying it out, so you must thoroughly understand a process yourself before you can explain it to your reader. And as in all work-related writing, you must aim your writing at a level appropriate to your reader's background. Beginners, you will probably find, require more basic information, and less technical vocabulary, than do experienced workers.

The explanation of a process has something else in common with written instructions: both kinds of writing are composed of steps. The steps in a process explanation should be as clear, accurate, and complete as those in a set of instructions.

In your opening paragraph, tell your reader why it is important to become familiar with the process you are explaining. Before you explain the steps necessary to form a corporation, for example, you could cite the tax savings that incorporation would permit. To give your reader a framework for the details that will follow, you might present a brief overview of the process. Finally, you might describe how the process works in relation to a larger whole of which it is a part. In explaining the air brake system of a large dump truck, for example, you might note that the braking system is one part of the vehicle's air system, which also controls the throttle and transmission-shifting mechanisms.

A process explanation can be long or short, depending on how much detail is necessary. The following elementary description of the way in which a camera controls light to expose a photographic film, intended for beginning photographers, fits into one paragraph. Note the writer's choice of words and definitions that are designed to communicate the ideas to an audience unfamiliar with the subject. Simple language is used, and specialized terms are defined.

> The camera is the basic tool for recording light images. It is simply a **box** from which all light is excluded except that which passes through a small opening at the front. Cameras are equipped with various devices for controlling the light rays as they enter this opening. At the press of a button, a mechanical blade or curtain, called a **shutter,** opens and closes automatically. During the fraction of a second that the shutter is open, the light reflected from the subject toward which the camera is aimed passes into the camera through a piece of optical glass called the **lens.** The lens focuses, or projects, the light rays onto the wall at the back of the camera. These light reflections are captured on a sheet of film attached to the back wall.

Many process explanations require more details and will, of course, be longer than a paragraph. The following example, which makes up part of a report intended for environmental decision-makers, discusses several methods of surface mining for coal. The writer begins with an overview of the elements common to all the processes, defines the terms important to the explanation, and then describes each separately. Transitional words and phrases serve to achieve unity within paragraphs, and headings mark the transition from one process to the next.

SURFACE MINING OF COAL

The process of removing the earth, rock, and other strata (called <u>overburden</u>) to uncover an underlying mineral deposit is generally referred to as surface mining. Strip mining is a specific kind of surface mining in which all the overburden is removed in strips, one cut at a time. Three types of strip mining methods are used to mine coal: <u>area</u>, contour, and <u>mountaintop removal</u>. Which method is used depends on the topography of the area to be mined.

Area Strip Mining

Area strip mining is used in regions of flat to gently rolling terrain, like those found in the Midwest and West. Depending on applicable reclamation laws, the topsoil may be removed from the area to be mined, stored, and later reapplied as surface material during reclamation of the mined land. Following removal of the topsoil, a trench is cut through the overburden to expose the upper surface of the coal to be mined. The length of the cut generally corresponds to the length of the property or of the deposit. The overburden from the first cut is placed on unmined land adjacent to the cut. After the first cut is completed, the coal is removed and a second cut is made parallel to the first. The overburden (now referred to as spoil) from each of the succeeding cuts is deposited in the adjacent pit from which the coal was just removed. The final cut leaves an open trench equal in depth to the thickness of the overburden plus the coal bed, bounded on one side by the last spoil pile and on the other side by the undisturbed soil. The final cut may be as far as a mile from the first cut. The overburden from all the cuts, unless graded and leveled, resembles the ridges of a giant washboard.

Contour Strip Mining

In areas of rolling or very steep terrain, such as in the eastern United States, contour strip mining is used. In this method, the overburden is removed from the mineral seam in a pattern that follows the contour line around the hillside. The overburden is then deposited on the downslope side of the cut until the depth of the overburden becomes too great for economical recovery of the coal. This method leaves a bench, or shelf, on the side of the hill, bordered on the inside by a highwall (30 to 100 feet high) and on the outer side by a high ridge of spoil.

A method of mining that is often used in conjuction with contour mining is <u>auger mining</u>. This method is employed when the overburden becomes too thick, rendering contour mining uneconomical, and when extraction by underground mining would be too costly or unsafe. In auger mining, an instrument bores holes horizontally into the coal seam. The coal can then be removed like the shavings produced by a drill bit. The exposed coal seam in the highwall is left with a continuous series of bore holes from which the coal was removed.

Mountaintop Removal

In areas of rolling or steep terrain, an adaptation of area mining to conventional contour mining is used; it is called the mountaintop removal method. With this method, entire mountaintops are removed down to the coal seam by a series of parallel cuts. This method is economical when the coal lies near the tops of mountains, ridges, or knobs. If there is excess overburden that cannot be stored on the mined land, it may be transported elsewhere.

DESCRIPTION

When you give your reader information about an object's size, shape, color, method of construction, or other feature of its appearance, you are describing it. The kinds of *description* you will write on the job depends, of course, on where you work and on what you do. Office administrators describe office space and layouts. Equipment maintenance workers write parts and equipment descriptions. And police descriptions of accident scenes are routinely used in court cases. The key to effective descriptions is the accurate presentation of details. To select appropriate details, determine what use your reader will make of the description. Will your reader use it to identify something? Will your reader have to assemble or repair the object you are describing? Which details you include, then, will depend on the task the reader will perform.

Your description may be of something concrete, like a machine, or of something abstract, like computer software. Following is an example of something the reader will never actually see: how and where the different sectors of software are located on a computer disk, that is, its format.

> When the disk initializer prepares a disk for use, it sets the disk to a predefined format, which includes reserving those software areas required by the operating system. Of the available 8,192 sectors, approximately 1,154 sectors are reserved for disk information, system software, and system use. The remaining sectors are available to the user. Initialization of the disk reserves the areas as shown in Figure 6–3.

When describing a physical object (a piece of equipment or a system made up of connected objects), first briefly explain its function and then give an overview of the object or system before describing its parts in detail. The level of detail you must provide will depend on the readers' familiarity with what is being described. You must, of course, become thoroughly familiar with the object before attempting to describe it.

Descriptions can be brief and simple, or they can be highly complex.

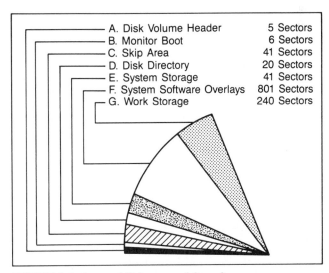

A. Disk Volume Header	5 Sectors
B. Monitor Boot	6 Sectors
C. Skip Area	41 Sectors
D. Disk Directory	20 Sectors
E. System Storage	41 Sectors
F. System Software Overlays	801 Sectors
G. Work Storage	240 Sectors

FIGURE 6–3. Areas of disk reserved for software.

```
┌─────────────────────────────────────────────────────────────┐
│  ─────────────────────────────────────────────────────────  │
│                                                               │
│                   PURCHASE  ORDER                             │
│  ─────────────────────────────────────────────────────────  │
│   Part  No.            Description            Quantity        │
│  ─────────────────────────────────────────────────────────  │
│                                                               │
│   GL/020       Trash compactor bags, 31"×50"  5 cartons       │
│                tubular, non-transparent, 5-   @ 100 per       │
│                mil thickness, including 100   carton          │
│                tie wraps per carton                           │
│  ─────────────────────────────────────────────────────────  │
└─────────────────────────────────────────────────────────────┘
```

FIGURE 6–4. Purchase order.

Simple descriptions usually require only a simple listing of key features. A purchase order, shown in Figure 6–4, is a typical example of simple descriptive writing. Purchase-order descriptions should be clear and specific. An inaccurate or omitted detail may result in the delivery of the wrong item. Even an order for something as ordinary as trash compactor bags needed, in addition to the part number, four specific descriptive details.

Complex descriptions, of course, require more detail than simple ones. The details you select should accurately and vividly convey what you are describing. If it is useful for your reader to visualize an object, for instance, include details—like color and shape—that appeal to the sense of sight. The example that follows is a description of the leaf abnormalities that occur when trees are planted in soil lacking the necessary minerals. The writer, a forester writing for other foresters, offers precise details of the changes in color that were observed.

> Foliage of the black cherry trees showed striking and unusual discolorations in mid-August. Bright red margins extended one half the distance to the midrib and almost to the tip of the leaf. Nearly all leaves were similarly discolored and showed a well-defined line of demarcation between the pigmentation and the normal coloration. By late September, the pigmentation margins had widened and extended to the tips of the leaves. The red deepened in intensity and, in addition, blue and violet hues were apparent for the first time.

The description of leaf abnormalities concentrates on appearance—it tells the reader what the discolored leaves looked like. Sometimes, however, you may want to describe the physical characteristics of an object and at the same time itemize the parts that go into its makeup. If you intended to write a description of a piece of machinery, for example, you would probably find this approach, called the *whole-to-parts method,* the most useful for your purpose. You would first present a general description of the device, since an overall description would provide your reader with a frame of reference for the more specific details that follow—the physical description of the various parts and the location and function of each in relation to the whole. The description would conclude with an explanation of the way the parts work together to get their particular job done.

The paragraph shown in Figure 6–5 describes the assembly of an

The Die Block Assembly (Figure 1) consists of two machined block sections, eight Code Punch Pins, and a Feed Punch Pin. The larger section, called the Die Block, is fashioned of a hard, non-corrosive beryllium-copper alloy. It houses the eight Code Punch Pins and the smaller Feed Punch Pin in nine finely machined guide holes. The guide holes at the upper part of the Die Block are made smaller to conform to the thinner tips of the Punch Pins. Extending over the top of the Die Block and secured to it at one end is a smaller, arm-like block called the Stripper Block. The Stripper Block is made from hardened tool steel, and it also has been drilled through with nine finely machined guide holes. It is carefully fitted to the Die Block at the factory so that its holes will be precisely above those in the Die Block and so that the space left between the blocks will measure .015″ (plus or minus .003″). This space should be barely wide enough to allow the passage of a tape or edge-card. It is here, as the Punch Pins are driven up through the media and into the Stripper Block, that the actual cutting, or punching, of the code and feed holes takes place. The residue (chad) from the hole punching operation is pushed out through the top of the Stripper Block and guided out of

FIGURE 6–5. Illustration to aid description.

the assembly by means of a plastic Chad Collector and Chad Collector Extender.

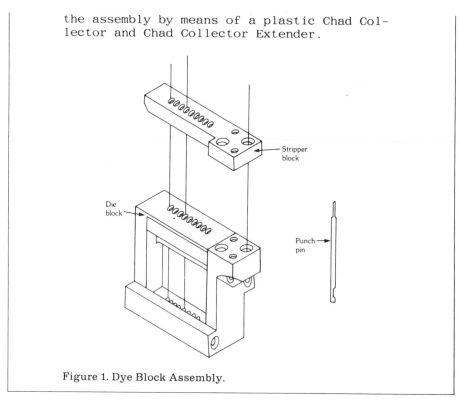

Figure 1. Dye Block Assembly.

FIGURE 6–5, *continued*

electronic typewriter that feeds coded tape or punch cards into the machine. Intended for the typewriter mechanic, this description includes
an illustration of the assembly mechanism.

Illustrations can be powerful aids in descriptive writing, especially
when they show details too intricate to explain in words, as in the following
example showing the operation of a disk unit that uses multiple platters.
Note that each illustration appears immediately after the text that discusses it. To the extent possible, all illustrations should be positioned
this way.

Do not hesitate to use an illustration with a complex description if
the illustration creates a clearer image. Detailed instructions on the
use of illustrations appear in Chapter 13.

The disk pack contains six recording surfaces, each plated with cobalt-nickle to provide long disk life and a high-density magnetic recording surface. Each of the six surfaces is serviced by 12 read/write heads; therefore, each pack is serviced by 72 read/write heads. Of these 72 heads, 64 are available to the user and 8 are reserved for use by the hardware.

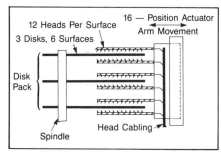

Tracks

A track is the area covered by one read/write head during one complete rotation of the disk. Since 64 read/write heads are available to the user, there are 64 tracks for reading or recording data in each of the 16 positions. Therefore, over the entire recording surface, there are 1,024 tracks available for data.

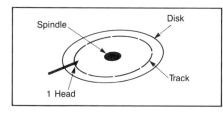

- The area of the disk covered by one read/write head during a revolution is called a track.
- A total of 64 tracks are available in any one of the 16-actuator positions.
- A total of 1,024 tracks are available over the entire 16 positions

Sectors

Each track of the disk is divided into eight addressable units called sectors. Since there are 64 available tracks in an actuator position, 512 sectors are available in each of the 16 positions of the actuator. Therefore, over the entire 16 positions, 8,192 sectors are available for storage. Each sector may contain up to 512 characters.

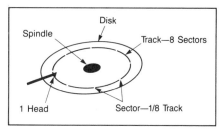

- Each track is divided into eight sectors.
- Each of 16 positions has 512 sectors.
- Each pack has 8,192 sectors.
- Each sector may contain 512 characters.
- Each pack may contain 4,194,304 characters.

COMPARISON

To explain something on the job, you may have to tell how it is like or unlike something else. When you do, you are making a *comparison;* you are saying A is like B.

EXAMPLE   A direct-read water meter gives at-a-glance totals of cubic feet used, just as the odometer of a car provides cumulative readings of miles driven.

Comparisons that point out how things differ are also useful.

EXAMPLE   Air-powered filters attract dust, pollen, and pollutants electrostatically; *they differ from electronic filters in using moving air instead of electricity to generate a charge.*

Comparisons come naturally to us. Think of how often you use comparisons yourself. You regularly compare the merits of television shows, athletic teams, candidates for political office, and the like. In deciding which of two or more items is most suitable for a specific purpose, you automatically weigh the advantages and disadvantages of each one. On the job, you may be called upon to select the best product, the least expensive messenger service, or even the applicant most qualified for a position.

To be sure that your choice will be the best one, you must first determine the basis for making your comparison. For instance, if you were responsible for the purchase of chain saws for a logging company, you would have a number of factors to take into account when establishing your bases for comparison. Because loggers use the equipment daily, you would have to select durable saws, with the right-size engine for the type of wood most frequently cut. Large hardwood trees require high-horsepower saws with thick chains and long bars. Saws used on softwood trees, or used primarily for cutting limbs rather than trunks, can be smaller and lighter. Since chain saws produce noise and vibration, you would want to compare the quality and cost of the various silencers on the market. In considering the various features of chain saws, you would *not* include in your comparison such irrelevant factors as color or place of manufacture. Taking all of these elements into account, you would establish a number of bases for choosing from among the available chain saws—engine size, chain thickness, bar length, antivibration mountings, and noise mufflers.

Once you have decided on what basis (or bases) you will make the comparison, you can determine the most effective method of organization to use for your writing. As long as they strike a proper balance between evenness and difference, comparisons can be organized in several ways. Two methods are used most frequently. In the *whole-by-whole method,* all the relevant characteristics of one item are discussed before those of the next item are considered. In the *part-by-part method,* the relevant features of each item are compared one by one. The following discussion of typical woodworking glues, organized according to the whole-by-whole method, describes each type of glue and its characteristics before going on to the next type.

COMMON WOODWORKING ADHESIVES

WHITE GLUE is the most useful all-purpose adhesive for light construction, but it should not be used on projects that will be exposed to moisture, high temperature or great stress. Wood that is being joined with white glue must remain in a clamp until the glue dries, which will take about 30 minutes.

ALIPHATIC RESIN GLUE has a stronger and more moisture-resistant bond than white glue. It must be used at temperatures above 50°F. The wood should be clamped for about 30 minutes. . . .

PLASTIC RESIN GLUE is the strongest of the common wood adhesives. It is highly moisture resistant—though not completely waterproof. Sold in powdered form, this glue must be mixed with water and used at temperatures above 70°F. It is slow setting and the joint should be clamped for four to six hours. . . .

CONTACT CEMENT is a very strong adhesive that bonds so quickly it must be used with great care. It is ideal for mounting sheets of plastic laminate on wood. It is also useful for attaching strips of veneer to the edges of plywood. Since this adhesive bonds immediately when two pieces are pressed together, clamping is not necessary, but the parts to be joined must be very carefully aligned before being placed together. Check the label before you work with this adhesive. Most brands are quite flammable and the fumes can be harmful if inhaled. For safety's sake, work in a well-ventilated area, away from flames or heat.[1]

As is often the case when the whole-by-whole method is used, the purpose of this comparison is to weigh advantages and disadvantages of each glue for certain kinds of woodworking. The comparison could be expanded, of course, by the addition of other types of glue. In this kind of comparison, organize the paragraphs so that the sequence in which the information is presented is as consistent as the subject matter permits. The comparison of woodworking adhesives first focused on the relative strength of the glue, then noted constraints on its use (such as moisture and temperature conditions), and finally discussed clamping.

If, on the other hand, your purpose were to consider, one at a time, the various characteristics of all the glues, the information might be arranged according to the part-by-part method:

CHARACTERISTICS OF WOODWORKING ADHESIVES

Woodworking adhesives are rated primarily according to their bonding strength, moisture resistance, and setting times.

Bonding strengths are categorized as very strong, moderately strong, or adequate for use with little stress. Contact cement and plastic resin glue bond very strongly, while aliphatic resin glue bonds moderately strongly. White glue provides a bond least resistant to stress.

Moisture resistance of woodworking glues is rated as high, moderate, and low. Plastic resin glues are highly moisture-resistant. Aliphatic resin glues are moderately moisture-resistant; white glue is least moisture-resistant.

[1] *Space and Storage* (Alexandria, Va.: Time-Life Books, 1977), p. 61.

<u>Setting times</u> for these glues vary from an immediate
bond to a four-to-six-hour bond. Contact cement bonds immediately and requires no clamping. Because the bond is immediate, surfaces being joined must be carefully aligned before
being placed together. White glue and aliphatic resin glue
set in thirty minutes; both require clamping to secure the
bond. Plastic resin, the strongest wood glue, sets in four
to six hours and also requires clamping.

With the part-by-part method, comparisons might also be made according
to temperature ranges, special warnings, common uses, and so on. This
approach—making comparisons among a number of possible solutions
to a problem based on a set of criteria by which each possible solution
is evaluated—is sometimes referred to as the problem-solution method.

DIVISION AND CLASSIFICATION

An effective way to approach a complex subject is to divide it into
manageable parts and then go on to explain each part separately. Because
this method is especially well suited to subjects that can be readily broken
down into units, it is used frequently for job-related writing. You might
use this approach, called *division,* to describe a physical object, like a
machine; to examine an idea, like the terms of a new labor-management
contract; or to explain a process, like the stages of an illness.

To explain the different types of printing processes currently in use,
for example, you could divide the field into its major components and,
where a fuller explanation is required, subdivide those components (see
Figure 6–6). The emphasis in division is on breaking down a complex

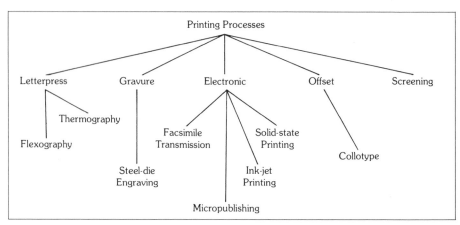

FIGURE 6–6. Division model.

whole into a number of like units—because it is easier to consider smaller units and to examine the relationship of each to the other.

The process by which a subject is divided is similar to the process by which a subject is classified. While division involves the separation of a whole into its component parts, *classification* is the grouping of a number of units (people, objects, ideas, and so on) into related categories. Consider the following list:

Triangular file	Steel tape ruler
Needle-nose pliers	Vise
Pipe wrench	Keyhole saw
Mallet	Tin snips
C clamps	Rasp
Hacksaw	Plane
Glass cutter	Ball-peen hammer
Steel square	Spring clamp
Claw hammer	Utility knife
Crescent wrench	Folding extension ruler
Slip-joint pliers	Crosscut saw
Tack hammer	Utility scissors

How would you group the items in the list? You would begin by asking what they have in common. The most obvious characteristic they share is that they all belong in a carpenter's tool chest. With that observation as a starting point, you can begin to group the tools into related categories. Pipe wrenches belong with slip-joint pliers because both tools grip objects. The rasp and the plane belong with the triangular file because all three tools smooth rough surfaces. By applying this kind of thinking to all the items in the list, you can group each tool according to function (see Figure 6–7).

When dividing or classifying a subject, you must observe some basic rules of logic. First, divide the subject into its largest number of equal units. The basis for division depends, of course, on your subject and your purpose. If you are describing the *structure* of the Wankel rotating combustion engine, for example, you might begin by dividing the subject into its three major parts—the triangular-shaped rotor, the crankshaft, and the housing that contains them. If a more detailed explanation were needed, each of these parts, in turn, might be subdivided into its components. A discussion of the *function* of the same engine, on the other hand, would require a different logical basis for the division; such a breakdown would focus on the way in which combustion engines function: (1) intake, (2) compression, (3) combustion and expansion, and (4) exhaust.

Once you have established the basis for the division, you must apply it consistently. Put each item in only one category, so that items do not overlap categories. An examination of the structure of the rotary combustion engine that listed the battery as a major part would be illogical.

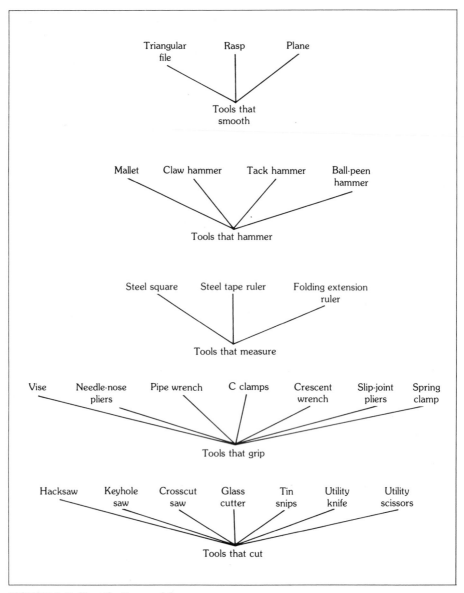

FIGURE 6–7. Classification model.

Although it is part of the car's ignition system (which starts the engine), the battery is not a part of the engine itself. And a discussion of the parts of the ignition system in which the battery is not mentioned would be just as illogical.

In the following example, two Canadian park rangers classify typical park users according to four categories; the rangers then go on to discuss how to deal with potential rulebreaking by members of each group. The rangers could have classified the visitors in a variety of other ways, of course: as city and country residents, backpackers and drivers of recreational vehicles, United States and Canadian citizens, and so on. But for law-enforcement agents in public parklands, the size of a group and the relationships among its members were the most significant factors.

DEALING WITH GROUPS

First, recognize the various types of campers. They can be broken down as follows:

A. Family for weekend stay
B. Small groups ("a few of the boys")
C. Large groups or conventions
D. Hostile gangs

Persons in groups A and B can probably be dealt with on a one-to-one basis. For example, suppose a member of the group is picking wild flowers, which is an offense in most park areas. Two courses of action are open. You could either issue a warning or charge the person with the offense. In this situation, a warning is preferable to a charge. First, advise the person that this action is an offense but, more importantly, explain why. Point out that the flowers are for all to enjoy and that most wild flowers are delicate and die quickly when picked.

For large groups, other approaches may be necessary. Every group has a leader. The leader may be official or, in informal or hostile groups, unofficial. If the group is organized, seek the official leader and hold this person responsible for the group's behavior. For informal groups, seek the person who assumes command and try to deal with this person.[2]

DEFINITION

Accurate definitions are crucial to many kinds of writing, especially for readers unfamiliar with your subject. Depending on your reader's needs, your definition can be formal, informal, or extended.

Formal Definitions

A *formal definition* is a form of classification. In it, you place a term in a class of related objects or ideas and show how it differs from other members of the same class.

[2] A. W. Moore and J. Mitchell, "Vandalism and Law Enforcement in Wildland Areas," in *Proceedings of the Wildland Recreation Conference,* February 28–March 3, 1977, Banff Centre, Alberta, Canada.

DEFINITIONS

Term	Class	Difference
spoon	eating utensil	that consists of a small, shallow bowl on the end of a handle
auction	public sale	in which property passes to the highest bidder through successively increased offers
annual	plant	that completes its life cycle, from seed to natural death, in one growing season

Informal Definitions

In an *informal definition,* a familiar word or phrase is used as a synonym for an unfamiliar word or phrase.

EXAMPLES   An invoice is a *bill.*
Many states have set aside wildlife habitats (or *living space*).
Plants live in a symbiotic, or *mutually benefiting,* relationship with certain kinds of bacteria.
The system is controlled by a photoelectric (*optical*) sensing device.
Equipment functioning with transverse motion (*motion in a straight, continuous line*) can be hazardous.

The advantage of informal definitions is that they permit you to explain the meaning of a term with a minimum of interruption in the flow of your writing. Informal definitions should not be used, however, if the completeness of a formal definition is needed to make the term easier to understand.

Extended Definitions

An *extended definition,* used when more than a phrase or a sentence or two is needed to explain an idea, explores a number of qualities of what is being defined. Some extended definitions may take only a few sentences, while others may run for several paragraphs. How long an extended definition ought to be depends on your reader's needs and on the complexity of the subject. A reader familiar with a topic or an area might be able to handle a long, fairly technical definition, whereas a newcomer to a topic would require simpler language and more basic information.

Compare the language and detail provided in the following two definitions, which explain the chemical concept *pH.* The first definition is intended for people in the graphic arts who need a general understanding of the concept but not a detailed explanation of the principles underlying the concept.

> **pH.** A number used for expressing the acidity or alkalinity of solutions. A value of 7 is neutral in a scale ranging from 0 to 14. Solutions of a lower value are considered acid, while those higher are alkaline.[3]

The second definition of pH, from an article about hydrogen ion activity in human blood, is intended for chemistry students and clinical laboratory technicians. The author assumes that his readers are familiar with chemical symbols (H^+), abbreviations (*mol/liter*), and terms (*ions*).

> About 70 years ago, the pH scale was devised to express hydrogen ion concentration in convenient numbers. The pH value, the exponent of the H^+ concentration in mol/liter with the sign changed from minus to plus, increases as hydrogen ion concentration increases. The normal pH of blood lies between 7.38 and 7.42 and a small change in pH can mean a big change in the H^+ concentration. For example, when pH changes from 7.4 to 7.0, the H^+ concentration increases 2½ fold, from 4×10^{-8} to 10×10^{-8} mol/liter.[4]

Clarifying Definitions

Perhaps the easiest way to define a term is to give specific examples of it. A landscape architect, for example, performed a land-use analysis of a regional park for officials of the Parks Department. Crucial to the analysis were a number of abstract concepts like *form, line,* and *color,* used in precise ways not necessarily corresponding to their everyday use. Without an understanding of these concepts, the officials would be unable to understand the analysis. Specific examples and easy-to-picture details bridge the gap between writer and reader, as in this definition of *form.*

> Form, which is the shape of landscape features, can best be represented by both small-scale features, such as *trees and shrubs,* and by large-scale elements, such as *mountains* and *mountain ranges.*

Another way to define a difficult concept, especially when you are writing for nonspecialists, is to link the unfamiliar to the familiar by means of an analogy (resemblance in some aspects between things that

---

[3] International Paper Company, *Pocket Pal—A Graphic Arts Production Handbook,* 13th ed. (New York: International Paper Company, 1986), p. 201.

[4] John A. Lott, "Hydrogen Ions in Blood," *Chemistry* 51, May 1978, p. 6.

are otherwise not alike). Defining radio waves in terms of their length (long) and frequency (low), a writer develops an analogy to show why a low frequency is advantageous.

> The low frequency makes it relatively easy to produce a wave having virtually all its power concentrated at one frequency. Think, for example, of a group of people lost in a forest. If they hear sounds of a search party in the distance, they all will begin to shout for help in different directions. Not a very efficient process, is it? But suppose that all the energy which went into the production of this noise could be concentrated into a single shout or whistle. Clearly the chances that the group will be found would be much greater.

Some terms are best defined by an explanation of their causes. Writing in a professional journal, a nurse describes an apparatus used to monitor blood pressure in severely ill patients. Called an indwelling catheter, the device displays blood-pressure readings on an oscilliscope and on a numbered scale. Users of the device, the writer explains, must understand what a *dampened wave form* is.

> The *dampened wave form,* the smoothing out or flattening of the pressure wave form on the oscilliscope, is *usually caused by an obstruction* that prevents blood pressure from being freely transmitted to the monitor. The obstruction might be *a small clot or bit of fibrin* at the catheter tip. More likely, *the catheter tip has become positioned against the artery wall* and is preventing the blood from flowing freely.

The most significant point about the occurrence of a dampened wave form is that it is usually the result of a potentially dangerous obstruction. The definition therefore emphasizes cause and indicates what factors may, in turn, produce the obstruction in blood-pressure transmission.

Some writers make a formal definition easier to understand by breaking a concept into manageable parts.

Formal definition   Fire is the visible heat energy released from the rapid oxidation of a fuel. A substance is "on fire" when the release of heat energy from the oxidation process reaches visible light levels.

Division into component elements   The classic fire triangle illustrates the elements necessary to create fire: *oxygen, heat,* and *burnable material* or *fuel.* Air provides sufficient oxygen for combustion; the intensity of the heat needed to start a fire depends on the characteristics of the burnable material or fuel. A burnable substance is one that will sustain combustion after an initial application of heat to start it.

The techniques for dividing the elements of a concept follow the guidelines discussed earlier in this chapter.

Under certain circumstances, the meaning of a term can be clarified and made easier to remember by an exploration of its origin. Because they sometimes have unfamiliar Greek and Latin roots, scientific and medical terms benefit especially from an explanation of this type. Tracing the derivation of a word can also be useful when you want to explain why a word has favorable or unfavorable associations—particularly if your goal is to influence your reader's attitude toward an idea or an activity.

> Efforts to influence legislation generally fall under the head of *lobbying,* a term that once referred to people who prowl the lobbies of houses of government, buttonholing lawmakers and trying to get them to take certain positions. Lobbying today is all of this, and much more, too. It is a respected—and necessary—activity. It tells the legislator which way the winds of public opinion are blowing, and it helps inform him of the implications of certain bills, debates, and resolutions he must contend with.[5]

Sometimes it is useful to point out what something is *not* to clarify what it *is.* A what-it-is-not definition is effective only when the reader is familiar with the item with which the defined item is contrasted. If you say *x* is not *y,* your readers must understand the meaning of *y* for the explanation to make sense. In a crane operators' manual, for instance, a "negative definition" is used to show that, for safety reasons, a hydraulic crane cannot be operated in the same manner as a lattice boom crane.

> A hydraulic crane is *not* like a lattice boom crane in one very important way. In most cases, the safe lifting capacity of a lattice boom crane is based on the *weight needed to tip the machine.* Therefore, operators of friction machines sometimes depend on signs that the machine might tip to warn them of impending danger.
> This is a very dangerous practice with a hydraulic crane. . . .[6]

Problems in Definition

When you use a definition as a means of presenting your material, you should keep in mind a few "don'ts"—pitfalls that may result in confusing, inaccurate, or incomplete definitions.

Avoid *circular definitions,* which merely restate the term to be defined and therefore fail to clarify it.

---

[5] Bill Vogt, *How to Build a Better Outdoors* (New York: McKay, 1978), p. 93.
[6] *Operator's Manual* (Model W-180), Harnischfeger Corporation.

CIRCULAR   *Spontaneous combustion* is fire that begins spontaneously.

REVISED   *Spontaneous combustion* is the self-ignition of a flammable material through a chemical reaction like oxidation and temperature buildup.

Avoid "is when" and "is where" definitions; such definitions overlook what is essential to formal definition—they do not *classify* the term being defined.

"IS WHEN"   A *contract* is when two or more people agree to something.

DEFINITION   A *contract* is a binding agreement between two or more
REVISED   people. (*Binding agreement* is the class of which *contract* is a member.)

"IS WHERE"   A *day-care center* is where working parents can leave their preschool children during the day.

DEFINITION   A *day-care center* is a facility at which working parents
REVISED   can leave their preschool children during the day. (*Facility* is the class of which *day-care center* is a member.)

Do not use definitions made up of terms your readers won't understand. Even informally written material will occasionally require the use of a term in a special sense unfamiliar to your readers; such terms should be defined too.

> In these specifications, the term *safety can* refers to an approved container of not more than five-gallon capacity having a spring-closing spout cover designed to relieve internal pressure when exposed to fire.

CAUSE AND EFFECT

When your purpose is to explain why something happened, or why you think something will happen, cause-and-effect analysis is a useful writing strategy. For instance, if you were asked to report on why the accident rate for the company truck fleet rose by 30 percent this year over last year, you would use cause-and-effect analysis. In this case, you would be working from an effect (higher accident rate) to its cause (bad driving weather, inexperienced drivers, poor truck maintenance, and so on). If, on the other hand, your purpose were to report on the possible effects that the switch to a four-day workweek (ten hours per day) would have on the office staff, you would also use cause-and-effect analysis—but this time you would start with cause (the new work schedule) and look for possible effects (changes in morale, in productivity, in absenteeism, and the like).

The goal of cause-and-effect analysis is to make the relationship between a situation and either its cause or its effect as plausible as possible. The conclusions you draw about the relationship will be based on the evidence you have gathered. *Evidence* is any pertinent fact or argument that helps explain the circumstances of an event. Because not all evidence will be of equal value to you as you draw conclusions, it's a good idea to keep some guidelines in mind for evaluating evidence.

Evidence Should Be Pertinent

The facts and arguments that you gather should be pertinent, or relevant, to your topic. That is, even if the evidence you collect is accurate, you should be careful not to draw from it a conclusion that it does not lead to or support. You may have researched some statistics, for example, which show that an increasing number of Americans are licensed to fly small airplanes. But you cannot use this information as evidence that there is a slowdown in interstate highway construction in the United States—the evidence does not lead to that conclusion. Other, more relevant evidence is available to explain the decline in interstate construction—greatly increased construction costs, opposition from environmental groups, new legislation that transfers highway construction funds to mass transportation, and so on. Statistics on the increase in small-plane licensing may be relevant to other conclusions, however. You could argue that the upswing has occurred because small planes save travel time, provide easy access to remote areas, and, once they are purchased, are economical to operate.

Evidence Should Be Sufficient

Incomplete evidence can lead to false conclusions.

Driver training classes in the schools do not help prevent auto accidents. Two people I know who completed driver training classes were involved in accidents.

Although the evidence cited to support the conclusion may be accurate, there is not enough of it here even to justify making a statement about the driver training program at one school. A thorough investigation of the usefulness of driver training classes in keeping the accident rate down would require many more than two examples. And it would require a comparison of the driving records of those who had completed driver training with the records of those who had not.

Evidence Should Be Representative

If you conduct a survey to obtain your evidence, be sure that you do not solicit responses only from individuals or groups whose views are identical to yours—that is, be sure you obtain a representative sampling. A survey of backpackers in a national park on whether the park ought to be open to off-the-road vehicles would more than likely show them overwhelmingly against the idea. Such a survey should include opinions from more than one interested group.

Evidence Should Be Plausible

Two events that occur close to each other in time or place may or may not be causally related. Thunder and black clouds do not always signal rain, but they do so often enough that if we are outdoors when the sky darkens and we hear thunder, we seek shelter unless we're prepared to get wet. However, if you walk under a ladder and shortly afterward sprain your ankle on a curb, you cannot conclude that walking under a ladder brings bad luck—unless you are superstitious. Although the two events occurred close to each other in time, the first did not cause the second. Merely to say that X caused Y (or will cause Y) is inadequate. You must demonstrate the causal relationship with pertinent facts and arguments.

For example, a driver lost control of his car one summer day and crashed into a tavern. He told the police that the accident had occurred because his car had been in the sun so long and absorbed so much solar energy that he could no longer control it. The cause the driver gave for the accident cannot be taken as either plausible or objective. A careful examination of the event would probably reveal that the driver had been a patron of the tavern shortly before the crash took place. But even this explanation would have to be demonstrated with convincing facts. The police would have to interview other tavern patrons and test the driver to determine breath and blood alcohol levels. If the patrons identified the driver as a recent customer in the tavern, and if the breath and blood tests showed intoxicating levels of alcohol in his system, the evidence would be sufficient to explain why the car had hit the tavern.

Linking Causes to Effects

To show a true relationship between a cause and an effect, you must demonstrate that the existence of the one *requires* the existence of the other. It is often difficult to establish beyond any doubt that one event was *the* cause of another event. More often, a result will have more than one cause. As you research your subject, your task is to determine which cause or causes are most plausible.

When several probable causes are equally valid, report your findings accordingly, as in the following article on the use of an energy-saving device called a furnace-vent damper. The damper is a metal plate fitted inside the flue or vent pipe of natural-gas or fuel-oil furnaces. When the furnace is on, the damper opens to allow the gases to escape up the flue. When the furnace shuts off, the damper closes, thus preventing warm air from escaping up the flue stack. The dampers are potentially dangerous, however. If the dampers fail to open at the proper time, they could allow poisonous furnace gases to back into the house and asphyxiate anyone in a matter of minutes. Tests run on several dampers showed a number of probable causes for their malfunctioning.

> One damper was sold without proper installation instructions, and another was wired incorrectly. Two of the units had slow-opening dampers (15 seconds) that prevented the [furnace] burner from firing. And one damper jammed when exposed to a simulated fuel temperature of more than 700 degrees.[7]

The investigator located more than one cause of damper malfunctions and reported on them. Without such a thorough account, recommendations to prevent similar malfunctions would be based on incomplete evidence.

PERSUADING YOUR READER

Suppose you and a friend are arguing over whether the capital of Maine is Portland or Augusta. The issue is a simple question of fact that can be easily checked in an almanac or an atlas. (It's Augusta.) But suppose you are trying to convince your company that it ought to adopt flexible working hours for its employees. A quick look in a reference book will not settle the issue. Like Christine Thomas in Chapter 1, you

[7] Don DeBat, "Save Energy But Save Your Life, Too," *Family Safety,* Fall 1978, p. 27.

will have to *persuade* management that your idea is a good one. And to achieve your goal—to convince your company to accept your suggestions and act on them—you will probably have to put your recommendations in writing.

In all on-the-job writing, it is important to keep your reader's needs, as well as your own, clearly in mind. This is especially true in persuasive writing, where your purpose may often be to ask your reader to change his or her working procedures or habits. You may think, as Christine Thomas did, that most people would automatically accept a recommendation for an improvement in the workplace. But improvement means change, and people tend to resist change. What you see as an improvement others may see as change for the sake of change. ("We've always done it this way. Why change?") The idea you are proposing may be a threat to a staff member's pet project, or it may make the knowledge and experience that a veteran employee has accumulated seem out of date—so both will probably resist your suggestion. To overcome their resistance, you'll have to convince them that your suggestion has merit. You can do this most effectively by establishing the need for your recommendation and by supporting it with convincing, objective evidence.

Keep in mind, as you seek to persuade your reader, that the way you present your ideas is as important as the ideas themselves. Be thoughtful of your reader's needs and feelings by applying some basic manners in your writing. Avoid sarcasm or any other hostile tone that will offend your reader. If anger shows through in your writing, you will quickly turn the reader against your point of view. Also avoid being overly enthusiastic. Your reader may interpret such an attitude as insincere or presumptuous. Of course, you should not conceal genuine enthusiasm; just be careful not to overdo it.

The following memorandum was written by a supervisor to overcome resistance on the part of employees who had done an excellent job but who were now being asked to change their work habits.

Notice that not everything in this memorandum is painted a rosy hue. Change brings disruption, and the writer points out that fact.

Do not overlook opposing points of view. Most issues have more than one side, and you should acknowledge them. For example, if you were listing reasons why flexible working hours are a good idea, it would be a mistake to overlook the added paperwork that might be required to keep track of separate schedules for all employees. It would be most effective to admit that the paperwork will increase—and then go on to show that the added burden would be more than compensated for by improved employee morale and perhaps by greater productivity. By including differing points of view, you gain several advantages. First, you show your reader that you are honest enough to recognize opposite views when they exist. Second, you can demonstrate the advantage of your

MEMORANDUM

TO: Parts Distribution Section Employees
FROM: Bernadine Kovak, Supervisor *BK*
DATE: April 8, 19—
SUBJECT: Plans for Automated Inventory Control

As you all know, our workload has jumped by 30 percent in the past month. It has increased because we have begun to centralize parts distribution here at Edgewood Division. We no longer have to get parts from the home plant in Lexington.

For us, centralized parts distribution has meant more work. In the next few months the workload will increase another 30 percent. Even a staff as experienced as you are cannot handle such a workload without help—nor will you be asked to.

In the next few weeks we will be installing electronic equipment for the automation of inventory control. Instead of the present manual system of keeping track of parts storage, a small computer will do the memorizing and searching for us.

The new system, unfortunately, will cause some disruption at first. We will have to move most of our parts stock to the new warehouse. We will also have to reorganize the area once the stock is moved. And all of us will have to learn to operate some new equipment.

I would like to put your knowledge and experience to work by having you help the new system get into operation. Let's meet in my office to discuss these improvements on Friday, April 12, at 1 p.m. I'll have details of the plan to discuss with you. I'm also eager to get your comments, suggestions—and most of all—your cooperation.

viewpoint over others. And by bringing up opposing views *before* your coworkers do, you may be able to blunt some of their objections.

SUMMARIZING INFORMATION

A summary is a brief statement containing only the most significant information found in a given document. A good summary condenses the original without distorting its message. By capturing the essence of a three-day convention in a single page, by summing up a week-long business trip in a one-page memo, or by allowing readers to determine quickly and easily whether they need to read the original, a summary can save hours of time.

To make your summary both concise and useful, include:

1. The purpose of the document you are summarizing
2. Its most significant information
3. Its conclusions or results
4. Its recommendations or implications

Do *not* include:

1. Your own opinion or judgment, unless you are making recommendations
2. Information not included in the original
3. Irrelevant information
4. Background information
5. Remarks indicating that you are writing a summary ("This is a summary of . . ." or "The author of this report states . . .")
6. Examples
7. References to anything in the original document ("See the graph on page 3.")
8. Headings
9. Illustrations or tables

Your summary should be able to stand alone, without reference to the original, and should be written at the lowest level, with technical terms and complex data translated into plain English.

To write your summary, first scan the document you are summarizing to get an overall impression. Then read it carefully, highlighting or underlining the most significant information. Look for such obvious signals as headings and highlighted text, and pay special attention to the first and last sentences of each paragraph, since the first is often the topic sentence and the last often summarizes the paragraph. Be careful to focus on principles and not the examples illustrating them. After reviewing the document to make sure that you have not missed anything significant, copy the highlighted and/or underlined information separately. Review this information to see what can be condensed, combined, or eliminated. Then use it to write the draft of your summary, providing the needed transitions and making sure that all the sentences fit together well. When you have tightened and polished your summary to the best of your ability, check it once more against the original document to make certain that you have, in fact, included all the significant information.

CHAPTER SUMMARY

Writing on the job is writing with a purpose. The purpose will always be specific and practical.

When you give someone instructions on how to perform a task, be sure that you understand the task thoroughly. Then present the information at a level appropriate to your reader's background in the subject. Write concisely, addressing yourself directly to the reader. Divide the task into steps, and present each step in its correct sequence. Mention any necessary preparations at the beginning, and provide appropriate warnings where necessary. Use illustrations when they will add clarity.

Most of the guidelines for writing instructions apply to the writing of process explanations as well. Introduce the process by giving the reader pertinent information about its purpose or significance. Then divide the process into steps and present each step in its proper sequence.

Descriptive writing requires the careful selection of pertinent details. Simple descriptions, like parts lists, should be specific and detailed. Complex descriptions, like those of equipment made up of many interacting components, require greater selectivity of details. The whole-to-parts method may be the most effective one for providing your reader with a framework when you are explaining a large or complex subject. Illustrations can be used to clarify descriptive material.

Comparisons show how two or more things are like or unlike one another. For the comparison to be effective, its basis must be valid and consistently applied. Comparisons can be organized on a whole-by-whole or on a part-by-part basis, depending on your reader's needs. The type of organization chosen should be used consistently to avoid confusing the reader.

A complex subject can be made more understandable if it is divided into its largest number of equal parts. Continue the breakdown until it is sufficiently detailed to explain the subject clearly. Classification can be used to group people, ideas, or objects on the basis of their common characteristics. For subjects that can be divided or classified in more than one way, select the basis for the division or grouping that best represents your writing objective. Dealing with all pertinent parts, apply the basis for the division or classification consistently.

Define terms that may be unfamiliar to your readers. Terms can be defined formally, informally, or by extended definition, depending, again, on your reader's needs. To define a term formally, state which grouping, or class, the term belongs to and show how it differs from all other members of the class. To define a term informally, substitute familiar words and phrases for the unfamiliar term. Difficult or important terms can be explained by a variety of methods that extend the original definition. Terms used in a sense different from their accustomed meaning should also be defined. Avoid circular definitions and "is when" and "is where" definitions.

In cause-and-effect explanations, your goal is to establish a plausible relationship between an event and its cause, or between an event and its likely effect. Such explanations require a careful evaluation of the evidence. Is it pertinent? Is it representative? Is it sufficient? Is it merely coincidental? When your evidence is accurate and applicable, state your conclusions carefully. Overstated conclusions will misrepresent your evidence regardless of how pertinent it is.

In persuasive writing, the way in which ideas are presented is as important as the ideas themselves. Take your reader's feelings into account. Avoid a hostile tone, and appeal instead to the reader's good sense. When writing about controversial issues, acknowledge other points of view. The reader will appreciate your honesty, and you can then demonstrate the advantage of your views over the other views.

Summarizing a detailed piece of writing can save your readers time and help them quickly grasp your information. When summarizing, include only what's essential—purpose, significant details, findings, conclusions, and recommendations. Do not include background or irrelevant information or refer to figures and tables in the original. The summary should stand on its own; readers wanting more details can read the original.

EXERCISES

1. Choose one of the following topics to write about. First, decide whether you will develop the topic as a *set of instructions* or as *an explanation of a process*. Then, using the approach you have selected, write a paper, of assigned length, on the topic. Assume that your reader has no knowledge of the topic. Use illustrations where they would be helpful to the reader.

   a. Operation of a photocopy machine
   b. Measurement of blood pressure

c. Cleaning of automobile-battery terminals
d. Purchase of 10 shares of common stock
e. Directions from your home to the nearest commercial airport

2. Write a *description* of one of the following items or of an item of your choice. Specify who your reader will be, and write the description in sufficient detail to permit your reader either to visualize or to locate the item without further assistance. Do not illustrate this assignment.

a. The prominent features (of face, body, clothing, and so on) of a close friend or relative for a "missing persons" bulletin
b. A small mechanical device with no more than five moving parts (pencil sharpener, can opener, etc.)
c. A nonmechanical household or recreational device (rolling pin, tennis racquet, etc.)
d. A piece of land. First give an overview, then establish its location relative to city street or natural boundaries; complete the description with significant details of the land.

3. Write a paper, of assigned length, on one of the following topics by *comparing* the two items cited. Before you begin to write, specify who your reader will be. Make the comparison detailed enough to suit the needs of the reader.

a. Two career choices
b. Two job offers
c. Two products or services with which you are familiar
d. Two persons who are being considered for promotion to the same position
e. A comparison of your choice, organized by either the whole-by-whole method or the part-by-part method (for example, a comparison of two products or appliances designed to do the same job)

4. Choose one of the following topics to write about. First, decide whether you will develop the topic through *division* (separation of a complex whole into several smaller units) or *classification* (grouping of a number of small units into larger, related categories). Then, using the approach you have selected, write a paper, of assigned length, on the topic. Before you begin to write, be sure that you have determined who your reader will be and what your scope will be.

a. Road signs in your area
b. Home-heating methods
c. Hand-held calculators
d. A community service organization in your locality

    e. 35-mm cameras

    f. Recreational or athletic programs in your community

    g. A college library

    h. Safety regulations where you work

    i. Fire extinguishers

    j. The set-up of an office, hospital, or other organization with which you are familiar

5. Write an *extended definition* of a key concept or term related to an occupation or a school subject. Use some or all of the techniques discussed in the chapter for creating extended definitions. Assume that your reader is unfamiliar with the term.

6. Choose one of the following statements to write about. First, decide whether you will develop the topic through *cause and effect* or *persuasion*. Then, using the approach you have selected, write a paper, of assigned length, on the topic. Before you begin to write, be sure that you have determined who your reader will be and what your scope will be.

    a. A dangerous practice or condition in your office or school is likely to cause an accident.

    b. You ought to be promoted to a job with greater responsibility.

    c. Businesses should be encouraged to locate in your community.

    d. Setting up job-training programs in connection with a college will lead to higher employment in your community.

    e. Some aspects of your present job (such as working conditions, equipment, availability of help, organization of your work area) should be changed.

    f. Some aspect of your school (such as the grading system, the library facilities, work programs) should be changed.

    g. Smoking should (or should not) be permitted in public places.

7. Write a summary (approximately 200 words) of the following information.

THE WRITING PROCESS: TECHNICAL WRITING

Writing a technical document is much like writing any document, though in some ways it is more demanding. The writing process can be divided into five major parts: (1) preparing for the writing job, (2) researching, (3) outlining, (4) writing the first draft, and (5) rewriting and polishing the draft.

Preparation. As you prepare to write, you must determine three things: (1) the objective of the writing task, (2) the audience, and (3) the extent to which the subject should be covered. Until you have made these determinations, you cannot proceed effectively.

What do you want your readers to know, or to be able to do, when they have finished reading your document? When you have answered this question, you have established your objective. To be useful, however, an objective must be specific. "Produce a document on the Model 'A' Ford" is too general to be of any help to the writer. "Explain how to operate a Model 'A' Ford" is a specific objective that will serve to keep the writer on the right track throughout the writing process. Without a specific objective, you will inevitably find yourself wandering from the subject.

A speaker explaining the theory of relativity would approach an audience of nuclear physicists quite differently from a high school class. As a writer, you must also adjust your approach to fit your audience. For instance, if your readers were novice programmers, the technical level of your document would be much lower than if they were experienced system analysts.

If you know your objective and the composition of your audience, you should have no difficulty determining the extent to which your subject should be covered. Determining the scope of your coverage should enable you to avoid the common mistake of including too much or too little information. It should also help you avoid being led down side paths that are not directly related to your subject—a time-consuming and wasteful mistake made frequently by beginning writers.

Research. The best and surest way to learn a complex technical subject well enough to write about it is to compile a complete set of notes during research and then to create a working outline from the notes. (In addition to gathering together the necessary information in one place, compiling notes achieves one other major objective—it gets you started on the project. Surely no one ever feels more helpless than the writer who doesn't know where to begin.) Three sources of research material are available: (1) printed material, (2) the personal interview, and (3) your own background and knowledge.

Your starting point in the research process is the available printed material. First read through the material rapidly to get a feel for both the material and the subject; then study the material slowly and deliberately, taking notes and jotting down questions as they arise. (The answers to many of the questions will appear later in the material; however, it is better to jot down questions now and mark them out later than not to jot them down and forget them later.) Take notes on all information that you *may* need; it is easier to delete information that is not needed than it is to go back and try to find information that is needed.

Before going to an interview with a technical expert, formulate a series of exact and to-the-point questions. (Never go to an interview without prepared questions, or with only general questions.) As the interview progresses, the answers to some questions will provoke additional questions. Ask these questions as they arise. If you do not, you will probably find yourself requesting an additional interview later.

The final source of information is your own knowledge and experience. If you are an experienced writer, you have a large reservoir of knowledge about related subjects that you draw on in researching every job. You must use discretion in drawing upon your own knowledge, however, making certain that it is directly applicable to the subject at hand.

Outlining.   The creation of a good final outline is a three-step procedure: (1) organizing your random notes, (2) converting your organized notes into a rough outline, and (3) converting your rough outline into a detailed sentence outline.

After compiling a complete set of notes from the published material, from the personal interview, and from your own knowledge, evaluate your notes carefully and eliminate those that you now feel certain you will not need. If you are still in doubt about any note, include it—you can always eliminate it later if it isn't needed. You now have a body of material with which you are thoroughly familiar. You know the major subjects that you must cover, and you should be able to see how they move logically one to another. First write down the major subjects on a note pad; they should become the major heads you use to tell your readers what they will learn in each section. Then skim through your notes again, jotting down beneath each major head any minor heads you consider necessary. Use the major heads and subheads not only to break your document into logical parts but to guide the readers through the publication as well.

Now you are ready to start creating the rough outline. By designating each major head with a Roman numeral (I, II, etc.) and each minor head, or subhead, with a capital letter (A, B, etc.), you can mark each individual note with its appropriate major head and subhead (II-C, V-A, I-D, etc.). When all the notes are so designated, type the title of your publication. Beneath the title, type the first major head; then, beneath that, type the first minor head. Then type all the notes marked "I-A." Do not attempt to put them in any order at this time (the notes are much too scattered for you to do this effectively at this stage). Then type the second minor head, followed by all the notes marked "I-B," and so on until you have included all the notes under their appropriate major and minor heads. When you have completed this first pass, go over the outline again, concentrating exclusively on achieving the best sequence of your notes. For a long document, this may require several passes.

The major tasks involved in converting the rough outline into a final outline are to write a lead sentence to follow each major head, to provide transition between topics wherever necessary, and to determine where illustrations should be used.

Writing the First Draft.   Your primary objectives in converting your final outline to a first draft are (1) to bring the readers into your writing, (2) to convert notes to sentences and paragraphs, and (3) to simplify and clarify your subject. Do not underrate the professional writing skills required for technical writing. This type of writing makes greater demands upon the basic writing skills than any other. To explain a complex technical subject simply and directly, so that the reader can grasp it quickly and easily, puts the basic writing skills of the best writers to the test.

Rewriting.   If the writing process has been properly executed up to this point, rewriting should not be necessary—only polishing should be required. The process of polishing the draft is a matter of continuing, through successive passes, to smooth out awkward sentences, eliminate needless words and phrases, and ensure transition.

7

Principles of Business Correspondence

Business letters are an essential means of communication among organizations, businesses, and their customers; memorandums (or memos) are an essential means of communication within organizations. Because of their importance, letters and memos should be well written; those that are not may waste considerable time and money. For example, the following poorly written letter was actually sent to a law firm. The staff at the law firm could not understand it, even though a number of attorneys, paralegal assistants, and secretaries were familiar with the case.

Mr. Stewart R. Cassidy
Smith and Jones, Attorneys at Law
1212 Broadway
Hartford, CT 06119

Dear Mr. Cassidy:

In regard to claim on Account #5–861 see enclosed copy of letter received and copy of delivery receipt regarding same. There had been a claim which was disallowed and debtor with-held payment on the bill, and the one we referred to your office for collection, as no pro was mentioned but the one the claim was on was referred to the bill is still open and they still owe Universal, please review and advise.

Sincerely,

Ralph Madison

Ralph Madison

Staff members wrote to Ralph Madison and others at his company without success, and finally the law firm had to send someone to the company to find out what the letter was about.

A letter like this wasted the time of a highly paid staff—and may well have caused a delay in legal services to Ralph Madison's company. Further, carelessly written letters, because they project such a poor image of the writer, can result in loss of another kind. A reader's negative reaction to an unclear or messy letter can cost a firm an important contract or an employee his or her job.

If so much hinges on the preparation of an acceptable letter, why do business people write letters at all? Why don't they rely on the telephone, usually a quicker and easier means of communication? (A letter may be even more expensive than a call: a single business letter can cost well over $5 in labor, stationery, and postage.) A good deal of the time, of course, a telephone call is more appropriate than a letter—when, for instance, an immediate response is needed, or when a person-to-person exchange might smooth over a touchy situation. But there are times when a telephone call cannot replace a letter.

1. Letters provide a permanent, written record of a business transaction.
2. Letters represent a commitment on the part of the writer, as the expression "Put it in writing" indicates. A written promise, conveyed above the signature of an employee who has the authority to act, carries weight that a recollection of a telephone call cannot.
3. Letters provide traveling salespeople, busy executives, and others with a convenient way to receive information and respond (they may be out of the office, or not at their desks, when the phone rings). They can usually set aside time to answer their mail.
4. Letters that are carefully planned can create goodwill—and sometimes stimulate business—even in situations where customers or clients are dissatisfied with a product or service.
5. Letters provide a clear statement of a writer's position, reducing the possibility of a misunderstanding. Similarly, in many cases a recipient of a message needs time to study it. A phone call cannot accommodate careful reflection: if a complicated question is raised on the phone, the answer is often "I'll get back to you on that one."

WRITING LETTERS

The process of writing letters involves basically the same steps that go into most other on-the-job writing. *First,* establish your purpose, your reader's needs, and your scope (see Chapter 1). *Second,* prepare an outline.

(For a letter, an outline may involve little more than jotting down, on a note pad, the points you wish to make and the order in which you wish to make them.) *Third,* write a rough draft from the outline. *Fourth,* set the draft aside for a "cooling" period (see Chapter 5). The cooling period is especially important when a letter has been written in response to a problem. Business letters are not the place to vent emotions. A cooling period, even if it is only a lunch hour, gives the writer a chance to remove any hasty and inappropriate statements made in the heat of the situation. One chief executive of a large company always allows the rough draft of a crucial letter to "cool" overnight before revising and mailing it—regardless of the pressure to send it out right away. This executive believes that a slightly delayed—but appropriate—response is preferable to an immediate reply that may cause misunderstanding later.

For the *fifth* step, revising the rough draft, go over your work carefully, checking for sense as well as for grammar, spelling, and punctuation. Since *format* (the arrangement of the parts of a letter on the page) is a basic element in letter writing, it's a good idea, if you can, to type out a preliminary copy of the letter on paper that is the same size as the stationery you will be using. Set the typewriter at the margins you will use and, as you type, insert the correct spacing between parts of the letter (see pages 176–180). If a secretary or an assistant does your typing, be sure to check his or her work; you will sign the letter, and therefore you are responsible for its appearance and accuracy.

Tone: Goodwill and the Reader's Point of View

A business letter differs in one important way from other kinds of job-related writing: it usually represents a direct communication between one person and another. As a letter writer addressing yourself directly to your reader, you have an opportunity that the writer of, say, a report doesn't have: you are in a very good position to take your reader's needs into account. If you ask yourself, "How might I feel if I were the recipient of such a letter?" you can gain some insight into the likely needs and feelings of your reader—and then tailor your message to fit those needs and feelings. Furthermore, you have a chance to build goodwill for your business or organization. Many companies spend millions of dollars to create a favorable public image. A letter to a customer that sounds impersonal and unfriendly can quickly tarnish that image, but a thoughtful letter that communicates sincerity can greatly enhance it.

Suppose, for example, you are a department-store manager who receives a request for a refund from a customer who forgot to enclose the receipt with the request. In a letter to the customer, you might write, "The sales receipt must be enclosed with the merchandise before we can process the refund." However, if you consider how you might keep the goodwill of the customer, you might word the request this way: "Please enclose the sales receipt with the merchandise, so that we can send your refund promptly." Notice that the second version uses the word *please* and the active voice ("Please enclose the sales receipt"), while the first version uses only the passive voice ("The sales receipt must be enclosed"). In general, the active voice creates a friendlier, more courteous tone than the passive, which tends to sound impersonal and unfriendly. (For a discussion of the active and passive voices, see Chapter 4.) And polite wording, such as the use of *please,* also helps to create goodwill.

However, as a business-letter writer, you can go one step further. You can put the reader's needs and interests first by writing from the reader's point of view. Often, but not always, doing so means using the words *you* and *your* rather than the words *we, our, I,* and *mine.* That is why the technique has been referred to as using the "you" attitude or "you" viewpoint. For example, consider the point of view of the original sentence in the example just given:

```
The sales receipt must be enclosed with the merchandise be-
fore we can process the refund.
```

The underlined words suggest that the writer is centering on his or her need to process the refund. Even the second version, although its tone is more polite and friendly, emphasizes the writer's need to get the receipt "so we can send your refund promptly." (The writer, of course, may want to get rid of the problem quickly.)

But what is the reader's interest? The reader is not interested in helping the business to process its paperwork. He or she simply wants the refund—and by emphasizing that need, the writer encourages the reader to act quickly. Consider the following revision, which is written from the "you" viewpoint:

```
So you can receive your refund promptly, please enclose the
sales receipt with the merchandise.
```

This sentence stresses that it is to the reader's benefit that he or she should act. Consider another example:

```
So that we can complete our file records, please send your
Form 1040-A by March 10.
```

Even though the recipient has little incentive to send the form, the "you" viewpoint can suggest that the recipient's interests are at stake:

> So that your file is complete, please send your Form 1040-A
> by March 10.

Be aware, however, that *both goodwill and the "you" viewpoint can be
overdone.* Used thoughtlessly, both techniques can produce a fawning,
insincere tone—what might be called "plastic goodwill." Consider the
following:

> Thank you so very much for ordering the Trend-Setter Person-
> alized Labels. Obviously, you're a person of extraordinary
> judgment and good taste. You are to be congratulated on your
> fine selection of the one- by three-inch size. You are the
> kind of wonderful person who makes working a joy. Please
> work with us again.

Obviously, the language is full of false praise and sickeningly sweet
phrases. Any attempt at goodwill that is transparently insincere will
be counterproductive.

Direct and Indirect Patterns

In a speech to the Japan Business English Association, Professor
Francis W. Weeks identified one of the most difficult problems in business
correspondence and illustrated it with an anecdote:

> The number one problem, in my opinion, will always be the man-
> ner and style of our approach to people through the medium of written
> communication. One aspect of this problem can be expressed this
> way: "How direct or indirect should our communications be?"
> To be completely direct and forthright, striking to the heart of
> the matter immediately, is also to be blunt and perhaps offensive.
> To be indirect is to be polite and considerate to the reader. "Oh, no"
> say some writers. "To be direct is to be efficient, to save time, effort,
> words, and money. To be indirect is to waste time and be wordy."
> Nearly ten years ago when I had a sabbatical leave of absence
> from the University of Illinois, I was at the Douglas Aircraft Company
> in California studying the communications of their Marketing Depart-
> ment. I remember one day reading a letter from Japan—two pages
> long—written in very good English, but I could not determine what
> the writer was talking about. He seemed to go round and round his
> subject matter without ever coming to the point. I put the letter
> aside intending to go back to it later; then several hours afterwards,
> "the light dawned." He was saying "No." And he was saying it as
> politely and tactfully and indirectly as he knew how.

I know an American executive who would have handled the situation far differently. He would have written "No" in big letters across the face of the letter he was answering and sent it back to the writer.

Even direct, efficient American writers would characterize that as brutal treatment of a correspondent.[1]

Part of the problem, of course, is that notions of courtesy in Japanese business dealings are quite different from those prevailing in the United States. Yet research has shown that, even in America, it is more effective to present good news directly and bad news indirectly.

This principle is true because people form their impressions and attitudes very early when reading letters. As an example, a college student who had applied for a scholarship received a letter explaining that he had not won it. The letter began: "I'm sorry, but you were not awarded the Smith Scholarship." In disappointment, the student threw the letter on his desk and left his apartment. Three days later he picked up the letter and read further. It went on to say that the committee thought his record was so strong that he should call immediately if he were interested in another, but lesser-known, scholarship. The student called but was told that the other scholarship had been awarded to someone else. Since the student had not called immediately, everyone had assumed he was not interested.

Many readers do finish a letter when bad news is presented at the outset, but they generally continue to read with a predetermined opinion concerning what follows. They may be very skeptical about an explanation, or they may reject a reasonable alternative presented by the writer. Furthermore, even when you refuse a request or say "no" one time, you may wish to work with the reader in the future. An abruptly phrased rejection early in the letter may prevent you from reestablishing an amicable relationship.

Consider the thoughtlessness of the rejection letter shown in Figure 7–1. Although the letter is direct and uses the pronouns *you* and *your,* the writer has apparently not considered how the recipient will feel as she reads the letter. There is no expression of regret that Mrs. Mauer is being rejected for the position, nor any appreciation of her efforts in applying for the job: "Sincerely" at the close almost seems hostile. The letter is, in short, rude. The pattern for this letter is Bad news/Explanation/Close. A better general pattern for "bad news" letters is as follows:

1. Buffer
2. Bad news
3. Goodwill

---

[1] Francis W. Weeks, "Current Issues in the Practice of Business Communication in the USA," *Journal of Business Communication* 13, No. 3, Spring 1976, pp. 62–63.

Southtown Dental Center

3221 Ryan Road   San Diego, CA 92217
(714) 321-1579

November 11, 19--

Mrs. Barbara L. Mauer
157 Beach Drive
San Diego, CA 92113

Dear Mrs. Mauer:

Your application for the position of dental receptionist at Southtown Dental Center has been rejected. We have found someone more qualified than you.

Sincerely,

Mary Hernandez

Mary Hernandez
Office Manager

MH/bt

FIGURE 7–1. A poor "bad news" letter.

The "buffer" may be either neutral information or an explanation that makes the bad news *understandable*. Bad news is never pleasant; however, information that either puts the bad news in perspective or makes the bad news seem reasonable maintains goodwill between the writer and the reader.

Consider the revision of the rejection letter, shown in Figure 7–2. This letter carries the same disappointing news as the first, but the writer is careful to thank the reader for her time and effort, to explain why she was not accepted for the job, and to offer her encouragement in finding a position in another office.

Presenting good news is, of course, easier. It is important to remember that good news should be presented early—at the outset, if at all possible. The pattern for "good news" letters should be as follows:

1. Good news
2. Explanation or facts
3. Goodwill

By presenting the good news first, you increase the likelihood that the reader will pay careful attention to details, and you achieve goodwill from the start. Figure 7–3 shows an example of a "good news" letter.

The following additional tips will help you to achieve a tone that builds goodwill with the reader:

1. *Be respectful, not demanding.*

CHANGE   Submit your answer in one week.

TO   I would appreciate receiving your answer within one week.

2. *Be modest, not arrogant.*

CHANGE   My report is thorough, and I'm sure that you won't be able to continue efficiently without it.

TO   I have tried to be as thorough as possible in my report, and I hope you find it useful.

3. *Be polite, not sarcastic.*

CHANGE   I just received the shipment we ordered *six months ago*. I'm sending it back—we can't use it now. Thanks!

TO   I am returning the shipment we ordered on March 12, 1984. Unfortunately, it arrived too late for us to be able to use it.

Southtown Dental Center

3221 Ryan Road   San Diego, CA 92217

(714) 321-1579

November 11, 19--

Mrs. Barbara L. Mauer
157 Beach Drive
San Diego, CA 92113

Dear Mrs. Mauer:

Buffer   Thank you for your time and effort in applying for the position of dental receptionist
at Southtown Dental Center.

Bad news   Since we needed someone who can assume the
duties here with a minimum of training, we
have selected an applicant with over ten
years of experience.

Goodwill   I am sure that with your excellent college
record you will find a position in another
office.

Sincerely,

Mary Hernandez

Mary Hernandez
Office Manager

MH/bt

FIGURE 7–2. A courteous "bad news" letter.

Southtown Dental Center

3221 Ryan Road   San Diego, CA 92217
(714) 321-1579

November 11, 19--

Mrs. Barbara L. Mauer
157 Beach Drive
San Diego, CA 92113

Dear Mrs. Mauer:

Good News   Please accept our offer of the position of dental receptionist at Southtown Dental Center.

Explanation   If the terms we discussed in the interview are acceptable to you, please come in at 9:30 a.m. on November 15. At that time we will ask you to complete our personnel form, in addition to. . . .

Goodwill   I, as well as the others in the office, look forward to working with you. Everyone was very favorably impressed with you during your interviews.

Sincerely,

Mary Hernandez

Mary Hernandez
Office Manager
MH/bt

FIGURE 7–3. A "good news" letter.

4. *Be positive and tactful, not negative and condescending.*

CHANGE   Your complaint about our prices is way off target. Our prices are definitely not any higher than those of our competitors.

TO   Thank you for your suggestion concerning our prices. We believe, however, that our prices are competitive with, and in some cases below, those of our competitors.

Writing Style in Business Letters

Letter-writing style may legitimately vary from informal, in a letter to a close business associate, to formal, or restrained, in a letter to someone you do not know. (Even if you are writing a business letter to a close associate, of course, you should always follow the rules of standard grammar, spelling, and punctuation.)

INFORMAL   It worked! The new process is better than we had dreamed.

RESTRAINED   You will be pleased to know that the new process is more effective than we had expected.

You will probably find yourself relying on the restrained style more frequently than on the informal, since an obvious attempt to sound casual, like overdone goodwill, may strike the reader as insincere. Do not adopt such a formal style, however, that your letters read like legal contracts. Using legalistic-sounding words in an effort to impress your reader will make your writing seem stuffy and pompous—and may well irritate your reader.

Consider the letter shown in Figure 7–4. The excessively formal writing style is full of largely out-of-date business jargon; expressions like *query* (for *request* or *question*), *I wish to state, be advised that,* and *herewith* are both old-fashioned and pretentious. Good business letters today have a more personal, down-to-earth style, as the revision of the letter in Figure 7–5 illustrates.

The revised version not only is less stuffy but more concise. Being concise in writing is important, but don't be so concise that you become blunt. If you respond to a written request that you cannot understand with "Your request was unclear" or "I don't understand your question," you will probably offend your reader. Instead of attacking the writer's ability to phrase a request, consider that what you are really doing is asking for more information. Say so. "I will need more information before I can answer your request. Specifically, can you give me the title and

Amex Laboratories

327 Wilson Avenue   Birmingham, AL 35211
(205) 743-6218

September 7, 19--

Mr. Roland E. Forbes
772 South Wilton Street
Birmingham, AL 35207

Dear Mr. Forbes:

In response to your query, I wish to state
that we no longer have an original copy of
the brochure requested. Be advised that a
photographic reproduction is enclosed herewith.

Address further correspondence to this office
for assistance as required.

Sincerely yours,

E. T. Hillman

E. T. Hillman

ETH:knt
Enclosure

FIGURE 7–4. Poor letter-writing style.

Amex Laboratories

327 Wilson Avenue   Birmingham, AL 35211
(205) 743-6218

September 7, 19--

Mr. Roland E. Forbes
772 South Wilton Street
Birmingham, AL 35207

Dear Mr. Forbes:

Because we are currently out of original copies of our brochure, I am sending you a photocopy of it.

If I can be of further help, please let me
know.

Sincerely,

E.T. Hillman

E. T. Hillman

ETH:knt
Enclosure

FIGURE 7–5. Better letter-writing style.

the date of the report you are looking for?" The second version is a little longer than the first, but it is both more polite and more helpful.

Accuracy in Business Letters

Since a letter is a written record, it must be accurate. Facts, figures, dates, and explanations that are incorrect or misleading may cost time, money, and goodwill. Remember that when you sign a letter, you are responsible for what it says. Always allow yourself time to review a letter before mailing it. Whenever possible, ask someone who is familiar with the situation to review an important letter. Listen with an open mind to any criticisms of what you have said. Make whatever changes you believe are necessary. Again—remember that if you sign the letter, you are responsible for its contents.

A second kind of accuracy to check for is the mechanics of writing— punctuation, grammar, and spelling. In business as elsewhere, accuracy and attention to detail are equated with carefulness and reliability. The kindest conclusion a reader can come to about a letter containing mechanical errors is that the writer was careless. Do not give your reader cause to form such a conclusion.

Appearance in Business Letters

Just as the clothes you wear to job interviews play a part in the first impression potential employers have of you, so the appearance of a business letter may be crucial in influencing a recipient who has never seen you. The rules for preparing a neat, attractive letter are not difficult to master, and they are important—particularly if you type your own letters. First, be sure that the typewriter keys are clean and that the ribbon is fresh. Type as neatly as possible and handle the paper carefully to avoid smudges. If you are using a word processor, print with the "letter quality" setting. (For advice on using a word processor, see the appropriate section in the Writer's Guide.) Type on unruled, white bond paper of standard size and use envelopes of the same quality. Center the letter on the page so that the space between the top of the page and the first line of typing is about equal to the space between the last line of typing and the lower edge. The white space surrounding the typing serves as a frame, a function referred to as the "picture frame" effect. When you use company letterhead, consider the bottom of the letterhead as the top edge of the frame.

A neat appearance alone will not improve a poorly written letter, but a sloppy appearance will detract from a well-written one.

Parts of the Letter

Almost all business letters have at least five major parts. According to variations in the alignment of the parts on the page, letters may be one of several formats. If your employer recommends or requires a particular format and typing style, use it. Otherwise, follow the guidelines provided here.

Heading. The *heading* is the writer's full address (street, city and state, zip code) and the date. The writer's name is not included in the heading because it appears at the end of the letter. In giving your address, do not use abbreviations for words like *Street, Avenue, First,* or *West* (as part of a street or city name). You may either spell out the name of the state in full or use the standard Postal Service abbreviations. The date usually goes directly beneath the last line of the address. Do not abbreviate the name of the month.

EXAMPLE   1638 Parkhill Drive East
Great Falls, MT 59407
April 8, 19--

If you are writing on company letterhead, omit the heading. Type in only the date, placing it two double spaces above the inside address.

Inside Address. The *inside address* is the recipient's full name and address. You can begin the inside address a double space below the date if the letter is long, or on the fifth line below the date if the letter is quite short. The inside address should be flush with (or aligned with) the left margin—and the left margin should be at least one inch wide. Include the reader's full name and title (if you know them) and his or her full address, including zip code.

EXAMPLE   Ms. Gail Silver
Production Manager
Quicksilver Printing Company
14 President Street
Sarasota, FL 33546

Salutation. Place the *salutation* (or "greeting") two spaces below the inside address, also flush with the left margin. In most business letters, the salutation contains the recipient's title (*Mr., Ms., Dr.,* etc.) and last name, followed by a colon. If you are on a first-name basis with the recipient, you would include his or her title and full name in the inside address but use only the first name in the salutation.

EXAMPLES   Dear Ms. Silver:

                Dear Mr. Smith:

                Dear Dr. Smith:

                Dear Captain Smith:

                Dear Professor Smith:

(Note that titles like *Captain* and *Professor* are not abbreviated.)

                Dear George:

(if you are on a first-name basis)

For women who do not have a professional title, use *Ms.* (for either a married or an unmarried woman). If the woman has expressed a preference for *Miss* or *Mrs.,* honor her preference. In cases where you do not know whether the recipient is a man or a woman, you may use a title appropriate to the context of the letter. The following are examples of the kinds of titles you may find suitable:

EXAMPLES   Dear Customer:

(letter from a department store)

                Dear Homeowner:

(letter from an insurance agent soliciting business)

                Dear Parts Manager:

(letter to an auto-parts dealer)

When a person's name could be either feminine or masculine, one solution is to use both first and last names in the salutation.

EXAMPLE   Dear Pat Smith:

In the past, writers to large companies or organizations customarily addressed their letter to "Gentlemen." Today, however, this is inappropriate. Writers who do not know the name or the title of the recipient often address the letter to an appropriate department in the attention line or identify the subject in a subject line in place of a salutation.

EXAMPLES   National Business Systems

                501 West National Avenue

                Minneapolis, MN 55107

                Attention: Customer Relations Department

                I am returning three calculators we purchased that failed to operate when . . . .

```
National Business Systems
501 West National Avenue
Minneapolis, MN 55107


Subject: Defective Parts for XL-100


I am returning three calculators we purchased that
failed to operate when . . . .
```

The Body. The *body* of the letter is, of course, what the letter is about. Begin the body two spaces below the salutation (or below the heading if no salutation appears). Single-space within paragraphs and double-space between paragraphs. If a letter is very short and you want to suggest a fuller appearance, you may double-space throughout and indicate paragraphs by indenting the first line of each paragraph five spaces from the left. The right margin should be approximately as wide as the left margin. (In very short letters you may increase both margins to about an inch and a half.)

Complimentary Close. Start the *complimentary close* or conventional "goodbye" a double space below the body. Use a standard expression like *Yours truly, Sincerely,* or *Sincerely yours.* (If the recipient is a friend as well as a business associate, you can use a less formal close: *Best wishes, Best regards.)* Only the first word of the complimentary close is capitalized, and the expression is followed by a comma. Two double spaces below the complimentary close, and aligned at the left with the close, type your full name. On the next line you may type in your business title, if it is appropriate to do so. Then sign your name in the space between the complimentary close and your typed name. If you are writing to someone with whom you are on a first-name basis, it is acceptable to sign only your given name; otherwise, sign your full name.

EXAMPLE   Yours truly,

Gail Silver

```
Gail Silver
Production Manager
```

Second Page. If a letter requires a second page, carry at least two lines of the body over to page 2. Do not use a continuation page to type only the complimentary close of the letter. The second page should have a heading too, containing the recipient's name, the page number, and the date (never use letterhead for a second page). The heading may go in the upper-left-hand corner or across the page, as shown in the following examples.

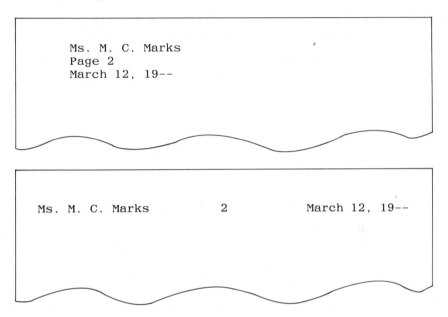

```
        Ms. M. C. Marks
        Page 2
        March 12, 19--
```

```
    Ms. M. C. Marks              2            March 12, 19--
```

Additional Information. Business letters sometimes require additional information—the typist's initials, an enclosure notation, or a notation that a copy of the letter is being sent to one or more named people. Place any such information flush left with the margin, a double space below the last line of the complimentary close in a long letter, two double spaces below in a short letter.

Typist's initials follow two basic patterns. No matter which style you choose, however, the letter writer's initials should appear in capital letters and the typist's initials should appear in lowercase letters. (When the writer is also the typist, no initials are needed.)

EXAMPLES   JTR/pst

(Typist's initials are separated from the writer's initials by a slash.)

JTR:pst

(Typist's initials are separated from the writer's initials by a colon.)

Enclosure notations, which indicate that the letter writer is sending material along with the letter (an invoice, an article, and so on), may take several forms. Choose the form that seems most helpful to your readers. Remember, though, that no matter which form of enclosure notation you select, you should still make a reference in the body of the letter to the fact that material is enclosed.

EXAMPLES   Enclosures: Preliminary report invoice
                          Draft contract

(Enclosures are described briefly if the letter is long and formal, or if the nature of the enclosed items is not obvious.)

Enclosures (2)

or

Encs.

(two or more items)
or

Enc.

(a single item)

(Enclosures are not described if the letter is short and the nature of the enclosures is obvious to the reader.)

A *copy notation* tells the reader that a copy (either carbon or photocopy) of the letter is being sent to one or more named individuals.

EXAMPLE   cc: Ms. Marlene Brier
                    Mr. David Williams

(Brier and Williams receive only the letter.)

cc/enc: Mr. Tom Lee

(Lee receives both the letter and enclosure.)

A business letter may, of course, contain all three items of additional information.

EXAMPLE   Sincerely yours,

Jane T. Rogers

Jane T. Rogers

JTR/pst
Enclosures: Preliminary report invoice
                        Draft contract

cc: Ms. Marlene Brier

Sample Letter Styles

An important factor in the appearance of a letter is its overall format—the arrangement on the page of the five major parts of the letter. The two most common styles of business letters are the full block and the modified block. The *full block style,* which is easier to type because every line begins at the left margin, is suitable only with letterhead stationery (see Figure 7–6). In the *modified block style* the return address, date, and complimentary close are aligned at the right of the center of the page (see Figure 7–7). The remaining elements are aligned at the left margin. All other letter styles are variations of these two basic styles. Again, if your employer recommends or requires a particular style, follow it carefully. Otherwise, choose the style you are most comfortable with and follow it consistently.

Preparing the Envelope

The most widely used form for typing envelopes is the *block* form. Figure 7–8 shows the block form used on business envelopes.

THE MEMORANDUM

The most frequently used form of communication among members of the same organization is the memorandum. Called memos for short, they are routinely used for internal communications of all kinds—from short notes to small reports and internal proposals. Among many other uses, memos

Announce policies	Request information
Confirm conversations	Transmit documents
Exchange information	Instruct employees
Delegate responsibilities	Report results

As this partial list illustrates, memos provide a record of the decisions made and virtually all the actions taken in an organization. For this reason, clear and effective memos are essential to the success of any organization. The widely used slogan, "Put It in Writing," reflects the importance of memos and the care with which they should be written. A carelessly prepared memo sends a garbled message that could baffle readers, cause a loss of time, produce costly errors, or even offend.

Memos play a key role in the management of many organizations because managers use memos (1) to keep employees informed about company goals, (2) to motivate employees to achieve these goals, and (3) to

Letterhead

EVANS & ASSOCIATES
520 Niagara St.
Lexington, KY 40502

(512) 787-1175
TELEX 5-72118

Date   May 15, 19--

Inside
address

Mr. George W. Nagel
Director of Operations
Boston Transit Authority
57 West City Avenue
Boston, MA 02210

Salutation   Dear Mr. Nagel:

Enclosed is our final report evaluating the
safety measures for the Boston Intercity
Transit System.

Body

We believe that the report covers the issues
you raised and that it is self-explanatory.
However, if you have any further questions,
we would be happy to meet with you at your
convenience.

We would also like to express our appreciation to Mr. L. K. Sullivan of your committee
for his generous help during our trips to
Boston.

Complimentary
close
Signature

Sincerely,

Carolyn Brown

Typed name
Title

Carolyn Brown, Ph.D.
Director of Research

Additional
information

CB/ls
Enclosure: Final Safety Report
cc: ITS Safety Committee Members

FIGURE 7–6. Full block letter style (with letterhead).

center

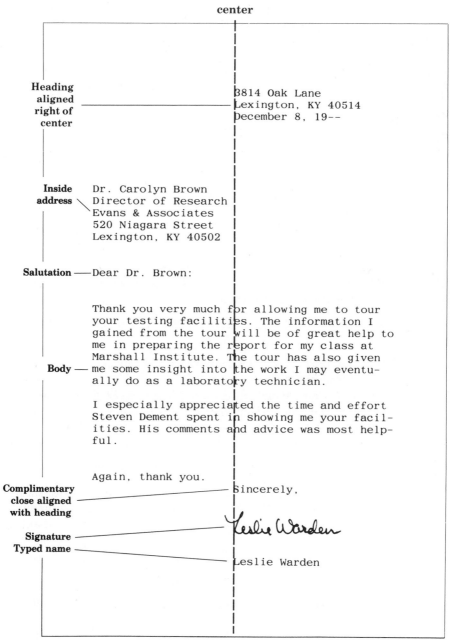

Heading aligned right of center

3814 Oak Lane
Lexington, KY 40514
December 8, 19--

Inside address

Dr. Carolyn Brown
Director of Research
Evans & Associates
520 Niagara Street
Lexington, KY 40502

Salutation —— Dear Dr. Brown:

Thank you very much for allowing me to tour your testing facilities. The information I gained from the tour will be of great help to me in preparing the report for my class at Marshall Institute. The tour has also given **Body** — me some insight into the work I may eventually do as a laboratory technician.

I especially appreciated the time and effort Steven Dement spent in showing me your facilities. His comments and advice was most helpful.

Again, thank you.

Complimentary close aligned with heading

Sincerely,

Signature

Typed name

Leslie Warden

Leslie Warden

FIGURE 7–7. Modified block letter style (without letterhead).

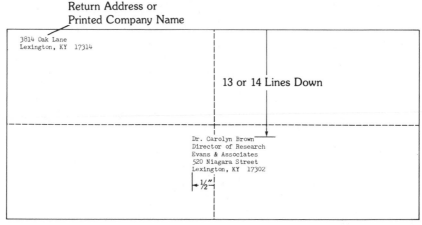

FIGURE 7–8. A #10 envelope, addressed.

build employee morale. Managers who write clear and accurate memos gain respect and credibility. Consider the unintended secondary messages the following notice conveys:

POOR: It has been decided that the office will be open the day after Thanksgiving.

The first part of the sentence ("It has been decided") not only sounds impersonal but also communicates an authoritarian, management-vs.-employee tone: somebody "decides," you work. The passive voice also suggests that the decision-maker does not want to say "I have decided" and thus be identified (in any case, the office staff would undoubtedly know). One solution, of course, is to remove the first part of the sentence.

BETTER: The office will be open the day after Thanksgiving.

Even this statement sounds impersonal, however. A better solution would be to suggest both that the decision is good for the company and that employees should be privy to (if not a part of) the decision-making process.

BEST: Because we must meet the December 15 deadline to be eligible for the government contract, the office will be open the day after Thanksgiving.

This version is forthright and informative, and it helps employees understand the decision.

Memo Protocol

In many organizations, memo writing is governed by protocol, whether written or unwritten. A form of etiquette, protocol acknowledges rank by dictating who receives a memo, and in what order. The following description by a public utility employee illustrates how a memo can confuse rank and lines of authority in both obvious and subtle ways:

> If I put my immediate supervisor's name AND the vice-president's name on the top [following the memo's heading "to"], it says I really report to both equally. If the supervisor's name is on the top and I send a copy to the vice-president, it means that, though structurally I report to the supervisor, I have direct access to the VP.[2]

Although such practices vary, it is important to be alert to the etiquette of routing memos in your organization.

Writing Memos

To produce a memo that is both effective and efficiently written, outline your memo, even if you simply jot down points to be covered and then order them logically. (To review this process, see Chapter 2.) With careful preparation, your memos will be both concise and adequately developed. Adequate development is crucial to the memo's clarity, as the following example indicates.

CHANGE   Be more careful on the loading dock.

TO   To prevent accidents on the loading dock, follow these procedures:
(1) Check . . .
(2) Load only . . .
(3) Replace . . .

Although the original version is concise, it is not as clear and specific as the revision. Don't assume your reader will know what you mean. Readers aren't always careful, and some provide their own interpretations if you are not as specific as possible, so state what you mean explicitly.

Each memo should deal with only one subject. If you need to cover two subjects, write two memos. Multi-subject memos are not only difficult to file (thus easily lost) but also may confuse a hurried reader.

Memo Openings

Although methods of development vary, a memo normally begins with a statement of its main idea. Even if your opening gives the back-

[2] Carla Butenhoff, "Bad Writing Can Be Good Business," *The ABCA Bulletin* 40, No. 2 (June 1977): 12–13.

ground of a problem, the main point should appear early in the first paragraph.

EXAMPLE   As we discussed earlier, because of our inability to serve our present and future clients efficiently, I recommend we hire an additional claims representative and a part—time receptionist.

(Main Idea)

Last year we did not hire new staff because of the freeze on hiring. . . .

(Background Opening)

When your reader is not familiar with the subject or with the background of a problem, provide an introductory background paragraph. Doing so is especially important in memos that serve as records that can provide crucial information months (or even years) later. Generally, longer memos or those dealing with complex subjects benefit most from fully developed introductions. However, even when writing a short memo about a subject familiar to your readers, remind them of the context. Readers have so much crossing their desks that they need a quick orientation. (Words that provide such orientation are shown underlined below.)

EXAMPLE   As we discussed after yesterday's meeting, we need to set new guidelines for . . .

EXAMPLE   As Jane recommended, I reviewed the office reorganization plan. I like most of the features; however, the location of the receptionist and word processor . . .

However, you should *not* state the main point first when (1) the reader is likely to be highly skeptical or (2) you are disagreeing with persons in positions of higher authority. In such cases, a more persuasive tactic is to state the problem first, then present the specific points supporting your final recommendation.

Lists and Headings

Whether or not readers agree with your main idea, using lists is an effective strategy that often gives your points impact in a memo. When points are listed—from most to least persuasive—they stand out rather than becoming lost in a lengthy paragraph. *Be careful,* however, *not to overuse lists.* A memo that consists almost entirely of lists is difficult for readers to understand because they are forced to connect the separate items for themselves. Lists also lose their impact when they are overused.

Using headings is another attention-getting device, particularly in long memos. Headings have a number of advantages:

1. they divide material into manageable segments,
2. they call attention to main topics, and
3. they signal a shift in topic.

Headings also function like the parts of a formal report. Readers can scan the headings and read only the section or sections appropriate to their needs.

Writing Style and Tone

Whether your memo is formal or informal depends entirely on your reader and your objective. Is your reader a coworker, superior, or subordinate? A memo to a coworker who is also a friend is likely to be informal, while a memo written as an internal proposal to several readers or to someone two or three levels higher in your organization is likely to use the more formal style of a report. Consider the following versions of a statement:

To an Equal: `I can't go along with the plan because I think it poses serious logistical problems. First, . . .`

(Informal, casual, and forceful response written to an equal)

To a Superior: `The logistics of moving the department may pose serious problems. First, . . .`

(Formal, impersonal, and cautious response written to the superior about her plan to move the department)

A memo giving instructions to a subordinate should also be relatively formal and impersonal, but more direct—unless you are trying to reassure or praise. Using an overly chatty, casual style in memos to your subordinates may make you seem either insincere or ineffectual. However, if you become too formal, sprinkling your writing with fancy words, you may seem stuffy and pompous, and managers who *sound* stuffy are assumed to *be* stuffy. They may also be regarded as rigid and hence incapable of moving an organization ahead. When writing to subordinates, then, remember that *managing* does not mean *dictating*. An imperious tone—like false informality—will not make a memo an effective management tool. A positive yet reasonable tone is your goal, as in the following example.

EXAMPLE   Because we must meet the December 15 deadline to be eligible for the government contract, the office will be
open the day after Thanksgiving. I am also temporarily
reassigning several members of the office staff as shown
below.

Format and Parts

Memo format and customs vary greatly from organization to organization. The following forms are typical:

- Preprinted half sheets (8½″ × 5½″)
- Message-and-reply forms ("speed messages")
- Regular 8½″ × 11″ letter stationery
- Special 8½″ × 11″ forms with company name or logo

Although there is no single, standard form, Figure 7–9 shows a typical
8½″ × 11″ format with a printed company name.

Some firms also print short purpose statements on the side or bottom
of memos, with space for the writer to check the appropriate box.

EXAMPLE   ☐ For Your Information
          ☐ For Your Action
          ☐ For Your Reply

You can also use this quick-response system for memos sent to numerous
readers whose responses you need to tabulate.

EXAMPLE   I can meet at   1 p.m. ____
                          2 p.m. ____
                          3 p.m. ____

Regardless of the parts included, the element requiring perhaps the
most careful preparation is the subject line title (such as "Schedule for
ACM Electronics Brochure" in Figure 7–9). Subject line titles function
much like the titles of reports: they announce the topic. They are also
an aid to filing and later retrieval. Therefore, they must be accurate.
The memo should deal only with the single subject announced in the
subject line, and the title should be complete.

CHANGE   Subject: Tuition Reimbursement
                        or

         Subject: Time Management Seminar

TO   Subject: Tuition Reimbursement for Time Management
                   Seminar

PROFESSIONAL PUBLISHING SERVICES
MEMORANDUM

TO: Barbara Smith, Publications Manager
FROM: Herbert Kaufman, Vice President *HK*
DATE: April 14, 19—
SUBJECT: Schedule for ACM Electronics Brochure

ACM Electronics has asked us to prepare a comprehensive brochure for their Milwaukee office by August 9, 19—. We have
worked with electronic firms in the past, so this job should
be relatively easy to prepare. My guess is that the job will
take nearly two months. Ted Harris has requested time and
cost estimates for the project. Fred Moore in accounting
will prepare the cost estimates, and I would like you to prepare a schedule for the estimated time.

Additional Personnel

In preparing the schedule, check the following:

    (1) Production schedule for all staff writers
    (2) Available free-lance writers
    (3) Dependable graphic designers

Ordinarily, we would not need to depend on outside personnel;
however, since our bid for the Wall Street Journal special
project is still under consideration, we could be pressed
in June and July. We have to keep in mind staff vacations
that have already been approved.

Time Estimates

Please give me time estimates by April 19. A successful job
done on time will give us a good chance to obtain the contract
to do ACM Electronics' annual report for their stockholders'
meeting this fall.

I know your staff can do the job.

cc: Ted Harris, President
     Fred Moore, Accounting

FIGURE 7–9. Typical memo format.

Remember, too, that the title in the subject line should not substitute for an opening that provides a context for the message.

Capitalize all major words in a title. Do not capitalize articles, prepositions, or conjunctions of less than four letters unless they are the first or last words of the title.

The final step is signing or initialing a memo, a practice that lets the reader know that you approve of its contents. Where you sign or initial the memo depends upon the practice of your organization: Some writers sign at the end of a memo, others sign their initials next to their typed name. Follow the practice of your employer. Figure 7–9 shows a typical memo format.

CHAPTER SUMMARY

To write effective business letters, follow the steps of the writing process discussed in Chapters 1–3: make an outline (which may simply be a list of the points you wish to include in the letter); prepare a first draft and then set it aside for a "cooling" period; revise your work, paying attention to both content and mechanics; and type your final copy according to standard business-letter form.

To establish a tone that is effective and builds goodwill, write from the reader's point of view (the "you" viewpoint). Be careful, however, that you do not overuse these techniques and produce "plastic goodwill." For "good news" letters, be direct; for "bad news" letters, use an indirect pattern.

Writing style in business letters can be informal (in a letter to a close business associate) or formal (in a letter to someone you have never met). The level of formality depends on your purpose and your reader. In general, though, it is best to avoid a style that seems overly chatty.

Because a business letter is a formal written record, it must be accurate. Make sure that your facts, figures, and dates are correct. Every business letter should follow one of the standard letter formats. The two most common ones are the *full block style,* in which all parts of the letter begin at the left margin, and the *modified block style,* in which the return address, the date, and the complimentary close appear just to the right of the center of the page.

A *memorandum* is the chief means of written communication between members of the same organization. In form, a memo may be a brief note; a longer, letterlike document; or an informal report. Memos can play a key role in the effective management of an organization if writers (1) follow memo protocol, (2) organize their memos carefully, (3) prepare useful openings, (4) use lists and headings strategically, (5) adjust the style and tone to the reader, and (6) create a format and subject line title that is appropriate and useful.

EXERCISES

1. Bring to class one business letter that you believe is well written and one that is poorly written. Be prepared to explain your reasons for thinking that one is better than the other. If you are working full- or part-time, you may be able to find letters in your office. Alternatively, obtain letters from friends or relatives, or find examples among the correspondence you receive in the mail.

2. Rewrite the following statement to make it more positive and less blunt.

    I will not pay you because you have not sent the double-jointed widget. If you do not send the right one right away, I will not pay you at all.

3. Rewrite the following passage to make it less unfriendly.

    I wrote for the record you advertised on television, and not only did it take six weeks to get here, but it was the wrong record. Can't you get anything right? I'm canceling payment on my check and sending this record back!

4. Revise the following passage to make it clearer and less pretentious.

    With reference to and in connection with your recent automobile accident, I have been unable to contact you due to the fact that I have been in Chicago on work-related business. I should be back in the office in the neighborhood of the 15th or so. In the unforeseen and unlikely event that I should be delayed, you can utilize Mr. Strawman, of my office, who will also endeavor in your behalf.

5. Find a letter containing bad news that you believe is unnecessarily blunt. Rewrite the letter to protect the goodwill of the organization that sent it. Attach your revision to the original, and submit both to your instructor.

6. Summarize an article on the "you" viewpoint or goodwill from either the *Journal of Business Communication* or the Association for Business Communication *Bulletin*. Limit the summary to 150–250 words. Submit it to your instructor, and (if your instructor so directs) prepare an oral summary for class discussion.

7. Find an example of overdone goodwill. (Mass-produced sales letters, for example, may be useful.) Rewrite the letter or message, retaining goodwill while eliminating poor style.

8. Revise the following statements so they reflect the "you" viewpoint.

   a. I want you to buy this "Handy-Fone" so I can win the sales award for this month.
   b. We must receive a copy of your W-4 Form to complete our files.
   c. Our business is built on our commitment to quality that we pass on to our customers.
   d. I can't finish your income tax calculations until I receive your December receipts. Then I'll be able to file for the expected refund.

9. Improve the business-letter style or memo-writing strategy of the following statements.

   a. As per your request, please find enclosed a copy of the report that was requested by your office.
   b. Persuant to V. B. Lanham's instructions, I have prepared a thorough analysis that your department should have prepared last year.
   c. Records of all long-distance telephonic communications should be submitted prior to the penultimate day of the subsequent month.
   d. You are hereby notified that your vacation schedule must be submitted to my office two months prior to the dates so that I may avoid disruptive interferences. It is hoped this practice will find the acceptance of all staff members. If you have any questions, please feel free to call me. Thanks.

10. You are Manager of Accounting for a company that sells computer software packages throughout the country. You have just received word from the comptroller that there has been a change in the expense allowances for employees using their own automobiles on business. Research done by your company's business office has revealed the need to set different allowance rates for two categories of drivers— "regular" and "nonregular." (Previously, one rate was applied to all employees.)

    "Regular" drivers are those who use their own cars frequently on the job. Typically, these would be employees who regularly drive to their sales territories. "Nonregular" drivers are those employees who only occasionally use their cars on business; most home office personnel would be included in this category.

    The revised allowance is effective immediately. It will be reimbursed according to formulas for each category. "Regular" drivers will receive 20¢ per mile for the first 650 miles driven per month, and 10¢ for each additional mile. "Nonregular" drivers will receive 20¢ per mile for the first 150 miles per month, and 10¢ for each additional mile.

To ensure that these categories are used properly, you want to set up a control procedure. The Accounts Payable supervisor has suggested that the manager of each department notify Accounts Payable, by letter, which employees in his or her department should be classified as a "regular" driver. You agree and decide that Accounts Payable will reimburse those employees not identified by the letter according to the "nonregular" driver formula.

You need to communicate this information to all employees. Prepare a memo to do this.

8

Types of Business Letters

Almost as many types of letters exist as there are reasons for writing. That is why it is important to study the principles discussed in the preceding chapter and apply them to both the situation and your reader's needs. It is helpful to know, however, that many types of letters are so common that standard approaches have been developed to meet specific situations. This chapter is devoted to such letters: primarily the order letter, the inquiry letter, the response to an inquiry letter, the transmittal (or cover) letter, the acknowledgment letter, the complaint letter, the adjustment letter, the refusal letter, the collection letter series, and the sales letter.

Because of its importance to career advancement, the job-application letter is discussed separately in Chapter 15, along with other strategies for finding a job.

THE ORDER LETTER

One of the most common reasons for writing a letter, especially if you work for a small organization or are self-employed, is the need to order supplies or equipment. The equipment may be anything from company letterhead stationery to x-ray film. Obviously, an order letter must be specific and complete if you are to receive the exact item you want. But be careful not to clutter the letter with unnecessary details, such as why you need the items or who will use them. Above all, be accurate.

Since a misspelled word or misplaced decimal point could cause a staggering error, proofread carefully and double-check all price calculations.

Make sure that the order letter contains the following information, as it applies to the item or items you are purchasing.

1. The exact name and part number (if appropriate) of the item.
2. Any useful description of the item: size, style, color, and so on.
3. A description of where you obtained information about the item, such as a catalog page number; you could enclose a photocopy of a page with the item circled.
4. The quantity needed of each item.
5. The price of the item, both unit price and total price, if appropriate.
6. The shipping method: mail, air, express, or, perhaps, simply the "best route."
7. The date of the order and the date by which you need the item (indicate "rush" or other instructions).
8. The place to which the material is to be shipped (make sure you provide the exact and full shipping address).
9. The method of payment: for example, indicate that you have enclosed a check or money order, that you will pay c.o.d. (usually more expensive), or that you have enclosed a purchase order number and the seller is to bill your company.

If you order several items, list them. A list will make your order easier to read.

The example shown in Figure 8–1 is a typical order letter.

If you receive no response to an order letter you may need to send a follow-up letter. If you do send such a letter, be courteous and avoid showing irritation. Identify the order by referring to the date of the original letter, and preferably include a copy of that letter. The example shown in Figure 8–2 is a typical follow-up letter.

THE INQUIRY LETTER

Another common business letter is the inquiry letter, in which the writer requests information from the recipient. Such a letter may be as simple as a note asking the Far 'N' Wide Travel Bureau for a copy of the free brochure "Inexpensive Fly and Drive Vacations" that was offered in a recent issue of your local newspaper; it may be as complex as a letter asking a financial consultant to define the specific requirements for floating a multimillion-dollar bond issue.

There are two broad categories of inquiry letters. The first kind is of obvious benefit to the recipient—you may be asking, for instance, for

WRITE EDITORIAL SERVICES
3209 Mountain View Road
Ft. Collins, Colorado   80523
303-555-1212

September 23, 19--

MEDIA PRODUCTS LTD
1200 Idustrial Park Drive
Boulder, CO   80309

Attention: Sales Department

Please send the following items listed in your August
catalog (CR-801) by November 5, 19--.

8   NEC Ribbons 2000/3000 MS,
        number U-NEC101-12 @ $14.00 each $112.00

3   Boxes of "Clean-Tear" Continuous
        Form paper, 25% rag content,
        number S-LG115-S @ $21.00 each $63.00

1   Posture-Aid Chair, Brown,
        number C-GE1010 @ 105.00 each $105.00

                                TOTAL $280.00

The enclosed check for $310.80 covers the price, sales
tax, and UPS charges. If any of these items are not
available, please return my check and cancel the order.

Sincerely,

James Webber

James Webber
Office Manager

JW:ls
Enclosure: Check

FIGURE 8–1. Order letter.

WRITE EDITORIAL SERVICES
3209 Mountain View Road
Ft. Collins, Colorado   80523
303-555-1212

November 12, 19--

MEDIA PRODUCTS LTD
1200 Idustrial Park Drive
Boulder, CO   80309

Attention: Sales Department

On September 23, I sent you a letter in which I placed
an order for a number of items listed in your August
catalog. I also sent you a check for $310.80.

I have enclosed a copy of that letter, and I request
that you please rush this material to me. If for some
reason you cannot send the material, please cancel my
order and return the check. Thank you.

Sincerely,

James Webber

James Webber
Office Manager

JW:ls
Enclosure: Copy of 9/23 order letter

FIGURE 8–2. Order follow-up letter.

information about a product that a company has recently advertised. The second kind of inquiry letter primarily benefits the writer; an example would be a request to a nonprofit religious organization to send information on the number of worshipers in a geographic area. If the letter of inquiry you are writing is of the second kind, it is particularly important to be considerate of your reader's needs. Your objective in writing the letter will probably be to obtain, within a reasonable period of time, answers to specific questions. You will be more likely to receive a prompt, helpful reply if you follow two guidelines: keep the number of questions to a minimum, so that you do not intrude unduly on the reader's time; and phrase your questions in such a way that the reader will know immediately what type of information you are seeking, why you are seeking it, and what use you will make of it. Be sure, as you write your questions, that you are asking the ones that you had intended to ask. It will be a waste of the reader's time, and a source of frustration to you later on, if you word your questions in such a way that your reader misinterprets them. And your reader will probably find it easiest to answer your questions one by one if you present them in a numbered list.

Your reader may also appreciate it if you offer to send a copy of the document (a proposal for a project, for example) that you plan to prepare based, in part, on the information that you are requesting. As a courtesy, too, you should promise to keep confidential any personal information you may receive. And at the end of your letter, express your thanks to the reader for taking the time and trouble to respond. Do not forget, also, to include the address to which the material is to be sent. (This is most important, of course, if the information will be sent to an address other than the one in your heading.) It is sometimes a good idea to enclose a stamped, self-addressed return envelope, especially if you are writing to someone who is self-employed. A typical inquiry letter appears in Figure 8–3.

RESPONSE TO AN INQUIRY LETTER

Sometimes, of course, you may be the recipient of a letter of inquiry. When you do receive such a letter, first read it quickly to determine whether you are the right person in your organization to answer it— whether, that is, you are the one who possesses both the information and the authority to respond. If you are in a position to answer, do so as promptly as you can, and be sure to answer every question the writer has included. How long your responses should be, and how much technical language you should use, depend, of course, on the nature of the question

P.O. Box 113
University of Dayton
Dayton, OH 45409
March 11, 19--

Ms. Jane Metcalf
Engineering Services
Miami Valley Power Company
P.O. Box 1444
Miamitown, OH 45733

Dear Ms. Metcalf:

Could you please send me some information on heating systems for an all-electric, energy-efficient, middle-priced house that our systems design class at the University of Dayton is designing. The house, which contains 2,000 square feet of living space (17,600 cubic feet), meets all the requirements stipulated in your brochure "Insulating for Efficiency." We need the following information:

1. The proper size heat pump to use in this climate for such a home;

2. The wattage of the supplemental electrical furnace that would be required for this climate; and

3. The estimated power consumption, and current rates, of these units for one year.

We will be happy to send you a copy of our preliminary design report. Thank you very much.

Sincerely yours,

Kathryn J. Parsons

Kathryn J. Parsons

FIGURE 8–3. Inquiry letter.

and on what information the writer has provided about himself or herself. Even if the writer has asked a question that sounds obvious or unimportant to you, be polite. You may point out that the reader has omitted or misunderstood a particular piece of information or has in some other way introduced an error, but be tactful in your correction, so that the reader won't feel foolish or ignorant. If, on the other hand, you see an opportunity to give your reader praise or encouragement, do so. And at the end of the letter, offer to answer any further questions the writer may have.

Sometimes a letter of inquiry sent to a large company arrives at the desk of a staff member who realizes that he or she is not the employee best able to answer the letter. If you have received a letter that you feel you can't answer (because you lack the information or the authority or both), you should do two things. First, find out (if you don't know offhand) who in the company *is* best equipped to answer the letter. Second, forward the letter to that person. Your coworker's letter answering the inquiry should state in the first paragraph that although the letter was addressed to you, it is being answered by someone else in the firm, because he or she is better qualified to respond to the inquiry. Figure 8–4 shows a letter indicating to an inquirer that her letter has been forwarded; Figure 8–5 shows a typical response to the inquiry.

THE TRANSMITTAL LETTER

When you send a formal report, proposal, brochure, or other type of material, you should include with it a short letter called a transmittal (or cover) letter, which identifies what you are sending and why you are sending it. A transmittal letter that accompanies a report may contain the title of the report, a brief description of the report, an acknowledgment of any help received during its preparation, and the authorization or reason for the report. The transmittal letter provides the writer with a record of when and to whom the material was sent.

Written in the form of a standard business letter, the transmittal letter most often opens with a brief paragraph (one or two sentences) explaining what is being sent and why. The next paragraph contains a brief summary of the material or stresses some feature that would be important to the reader. A letter accompanying a proposal, for example, might briefly present convincing evidence that your firm is the best one to do the job. The letter may go on to point out specific sections in the proposal that would be of particular interest to the reader. You might also want to mention any special conditions under which the material

MIAMI VALLEY POWER COMPANY
P.O. BOX 1444
MIAMITOWN, OH 45733

(513) 264-4800

March 15, 19--

Ms. Kathryn J. Parsons
P.O. Box 113
University of Dayton
Dayton, OH 45409

Dear Ms. Parsons:

Thank you for inquiring about the heating
system we would recommend for use in homes
designed according to the specifications outlined in our brochure "Insulating for Efficiency."

Since I cannot answer your specific questions, I have forwarded your letter to Mr.
Michael Stott, Engineering Assistant in our
development group. He should be able to answer the questions you have raised.

Sincerely,

Jane E. Metcalf

Jane E. Metcalf
Director of Public Information

JEM/mk
cc: Michael Stott

FIGURE 8–4. Letter indicating that an inquiry has been forwarded.

MIAMI VALLEY POWER COMPANY
P.O. BOX 1444
MIAMITOWN, OH 45733

(513) 264-4800

March 24, 19--

Ms. Kathryn Parsons
P.O. Box 113
University of Dayton
Dayton, OH 45409

Dear Ms. Parsons:

Jane Metcalf has forwarded your letter of
March 11 about the house that your systems
design class is designing. I can estimate the
insulation requirements of a typical home of
17,600 cubic feet, as follows:

1. We would generally recommend, for such a
   home, a heat pump capable of delivering
   40,000 BTUs. Our model AL-42 (17 kilowatts)
   meets this requirement.

2. With the efficiency of the AL-42, you would
   not need a supplemental electrical furnace.

3. Depending on usage, the AL-42 unit averages
   between 1,000 and 1,500 kilowatt hours from
   December through March. To determine the
   current rate for such usage, check with the
   Dayton Power and Light Company.

I can give you an answer that would apply
specifically to your house only with information about its particular design (such as
number of stories, windows, and entrances).
If you would send me more details, I would be
happy to provide more precise figures--your
project sounds interesting.

Sincerely,

Michael Stott

Michael Stott
Engineering Assistant

FIGURE 8–5. Response to an inquiry letter.

was prepared (limitations in time or money, for instance). The closing paragraph should acknowledge any help received in the preparation of the material, offer additional assistance, or express the hope that the material will fulfill its purpose.

These elements are basic to many transmittal letters. Keep additional remarks brief. The report, pamphlet, or whatever should speak for itself. A transmittal letter should not run beyond a few short paragraphs; it should never exceed one page. Figure 8–6 is a typical letter of transmittal.

Some letters of transmittal are not as detailed as this one—they say essentially "here it is." Figure 8–7 is typical of short transmittal letters.

THE ACKNOWLEDGMENT LETTER

One of the ways to build goodwill in any business is to let customers or clients know that something they sent arrived. A letter that serves such a function is called an acknowledgment letter. It is usually a short, polite note. The examples shown in Figures 8–8 and 8–9 are typical.

THE COMPLAINT LETTER

The best complaint letters do not sound complaining. That statement may sound contradictory, but it's not.

By the time it becomes necessary for you to write a complaint letter (sometimes called a *claim letter*), you may be irritated and angry. If you write a letter that reflects *only* your annoyance and anger, however, you may not be taken seriously—you may simply appear petty and irrational. Remember, too, that the person who receives your letter may not be the one who was directly responsible for the situation about which you are complaining. Venting your anger at someone who was not at fault is neither fair nor useful.

An effective complaint letter—a letter that accomplishes its purpose—should be both firm and well thought out. It should assume, first, that the recipient will be conscientious in correcting the problem. Second, it should indicate that the writer is capable of handling the situation calmly. Finally, the letter should convey that you expect the situation to be corrected.

Although the circumstances and the severity of the problem may

WATERFORD PAPER PRODUCTS
P.O. BOX 413
WATERFORD, WI 53474

(414) 738-2191

January 16, 19--

Mr. Roger Hammersmith
Ecology Systems, Inc.
1015 Clarke Street
Chicago, IL 60615

Dear Mr. Hammersmith:

Enclosed is the report estimating our power consumption for the year as requested by John Brenan, Vice President, on September 4.

The report is a result of several meetings with the Manager of Plant Operations and her staff and an extensive survey of all our employees. The survey was delayed by the temporary layoff of key personnel in Building "A" from October 1 to December 5. We believe, however, that the report will provide the information you need to furnish us with a cost estimate for the installation of your Mark II Energy Saving System.

We would like to thank Diana Biel of ESI for her assistance in preparing the survey. If you need any more information, please let me know.

Sincerely,

James G. Evans

James G. Evans
New Projects Office

JGE/fst
Enclosure

FIGURE 8–6. Long transmittal letter.

ECOLOGY SYSTEMS AND SERVICES
39 Beacon Street
Boston, Massachusetts   02106
617-555-1212

May 23, 19--

Mario Espinoza, Chief Engineer
Louisiana Chemical Products
3452 River View Road
Baton Rouge, LA   70893

Dear Mr. Espinoza:

Enclosed is the final report on our installation of
pollution control equipment at Eastern Chemical Company.
Since your problem is much like Eastern's, I believe a
similar solution would work for Louisiana Chemical.

If your management is interested, I would be happy to
come to Baton Rouge to discuss your needs and make a
preliminary assessment of your facilities. Please call
me collect (ext. 1206) if I can answer any questions.

Sincerely,

Susan Wong, Ph.D.
Technical Services Manager

SW:ls
Enclosure: Report

FIGURE 8–7. Short transmittal letter.

Ecology Systems, Inc.
1015 Clarke Street
Chicago, IL 60615

(312) 719-6620

January 21, 19--

Mr. James G. Evans
New Projects Office
Waterford Paper Products
P.O. Box 413
Waterford, WI 53474

Dear Mr. Evans:

I received your report today; it appears to
be complete and well done.

When I finish studying it thoroughly, I will
send you our cost estimate for the installation of the Mark II Energy Saving System.

Again, thanks for your effort.

Sincerely,

Roger Hammersmith

Roger Hammersmith
Sales Manager

RLH/rlt

FIGURE 8–8. Acknowledgment letter.

ECADS, INCORPORATED

501 BEACH STREET
MIAMI, FL 33167

(305) 834-7200

January 18, 19--

Mr. Joel Baker
3078 Terrace Boulevard
Miami, FL 33117

Dear Mr. Baker:

I received in today's mail the defective part
that we talked about last week on the phone.

As soon as one of our engineers can examine
it, I will phone you.

Sincerely,

Marylin Sanches

Marylin Sanches

MS/bk

FIGURE 8–9. Acknowledgment letter.

vary, effective complaint letters should generally follow the same pattern. They should

1. Identify the faulty item, including invoice numbers, part names, dates, and so forth. (Often it is a good idea to include a photocopy of the bill or contract.)
2. Explain logically, clearly, and specifically what went wrong. (Avoid expressing an opinion of why you *think* some problem occurred if you have no way of knowing.)
3. State what you expect the reader to do to solve the problem to your satisfaction.

Large organizations often have special departments, with such names as "Customer Relations," "Consumer Affairs," or "Adjustments," to handle complaints. If you address your letter to one of these departments, it should reach someone in the company who can be of help to you. In smaller organizations, you might write to a vice president in charge of sales or of service. For very small businesses, write directly to the owner. As a last resort, you may find that a complaint letter photocopied and sent to more than one person in a company will get fast results. Each employee receiving the letter knows (because of the carbon-copy notation) that others, possibly higher in the organization, have received the letter and will notice whether the problem has been solved.

Figure 8–10 shows a sample complaint letter.

THE ADJUSTMENT LETTER

If you, as the manager of the Customer Relations Department of the television company, receive the letter of complaint from Paul Denlinger shown in Figure 8–10, you should take it—and any letter like it—seriously. What is at stake is more than nine tuners. Regardless of how trivial the incident may seem to you, your employer's reputation is on the line. And if the writer, Mr. Denlinger, is satisfied with the way you handle his complaint, he may decide that when the hospital next orders television sets, he'll place the order with your company. What is at stake, then, are both the good name of your company and potential orders of several dozen television sets worth thousands of dollars.

An appropriate response to Mr. Denlinger's letter would be an adjustment letter—a letter that explains to the reader how a complaint he or she has made will be settled. To prepare an adjustment letter, you must first investigate what happened and what you can do to satisfy the cus-

BAKER MEMORIAL HOSPITAL
Television Services
501 Main Street
Springfield, OH 45321

(513) 683-8100

September 23, 19--

Manager, Customer Relations
General Television, Inc.
5521 West 23rd Street
New York, NY 10062

On July 9th I ordered nine TV tuners for your
model MX-15 color receiver. The tuner part
number is TR-5771-3.

On August 2nd I received from your Newark,
New Jersey, parts warehouse seven tuners, labeled TR-413-7. I immediately returned these
tuners with a note indicating the mistake
that had been made. However, not only have I
failed to receive the tuners I ordered, but I
have also been billed repeatedly.

Would you please either send me the tuners I
ordered or cancel my order. I have enclosed a
copy of my original order letter and the most
recent bill.

Sincerely,

Paul Denlinger
Manager

PD:sj
Enclosures

FIGURE 8–10. Complaint letter.

tomer. After you have obtained the facts, you should organize your letter into three basic parts.

1. Refer to the letter of complaint and identify the item or service in question. If your company is responsible for the error, offer an apology early in the letter. Doing so will help you to regain the customer's goodwill.
2. Explain clearly why the error occurred or outline the company policy related to the problem, or do both. This is especially important if you are not able to do everything the customer asks.
3. State specifically what you intend to do or have done to solve the problem. If you are not able to do exactly what the customer asks, give a partial adjustment if possible.

Figures 8–11 and 8–12 show two cirumstances: in the letter shown in Figure 8–11, the company was at fault; in the letter shown in Figure 8–12, the customer was at fault.

THE REFUSAL LETTER

When you receive a complaint letter or an inquiry letter to which you must give a negative reply, you may need to write a refusal letter. Such a letter is difficult to write because it contains bad news. However, you can convey the news tactfully and courteously.

In your letter you should lead up to the refusal. To state the bad news in your opening would certainly affect your reader negatively, as discussed in Chapter 7. The ideal refusal letter says no in such a way that you not only avoid antagonizing your reader but keep his goodwill. To achieve such an objective, you must convince your reader that your refusal is justified *before refusing*. The following pattern is an effective way to deal with this problem:

1. A buffer that establishes a positive tone
2. A review of the facts leading to the bad news or refusal
3. The bad news or refusal itself
4. A goodwill closing

The primary purpose of beginning with a buffer is to establish a pleasant and positive tone. You want to convince your reader that you are a reasonable person. One way is to indicate some form of agreement with, or approval of, the reader or the project. If your refusal is in response to a complaint letter, do not begin by bringing up the reader's disappointment ("We regret your dissatisfaction . . ."). Keep your buffer paragraph positive and pleasant. You can express appreciation for your reader's time

General Television, Inc.
5521 West 23rd Street
New York, NY 10062

Customer Relations
(212) 574-3894

September 28, 19--

Mr. Paul Denlinger, Manager
Baker Memorial Hospital
Television Services
501 Main Street
Springfield, OH 45321

Dear Mr. Denlinger:

Thank you for your letter regarding your order for nine TR-5771-3 tuners. We have shipped the correct tuners by United Parcel; you should receive them shortly after you receive this letter. I have also canceled your original order so that you will not be sent overdue notices and so that we can charge you at our preferred-customer rate.

Please accept our apologies. Evidently a dock worker failed to see your letter in the package, and it was sent to our Rebuilt Parts Department. That is why your note did not come to the attention of our Parts Manager.

To prevent further inconvenience, please send any future packages directly to Mr. Gene Smith, Parts Manager at our Newark facility.

If I can be of any further help, please let me know.

Sincerely,

Susan Siegel

Susan Siegel
Assistant Director

SS/mr

FIGURE 8–11. Adjustment letter—company at fault.

General Television, Inc.
5521 West 23rd Street
New York, NY 10062

Customer Relations
(212) 574-3894

September 28, 19--

Mr. Fred J. Swesky
7811 Ranchero Drive
Tucson, AZ 85761

Dear Mr. Swesky:

Thank you for your letter regarding the replacement of your KL-71 television set.

You said in your letter that you used the set on an uncovered patio. As our local service representative pointed out, this model is not designed to operate in extreme heat conditions. As the instruction manual accompanying your new set states and our engineers confirm, such exposure can produce irreparable damage to this model. Since your set was used in such extreme heat conditions, therefore, we cannot honor the two-year replacement warranty.

However, we are enclosing a certificate entitling you to a trade-in allowance equal to your local GTI dealer's markup for the set. This means you can purchase a new set from the dealer at wholesale, provided you return your original set to the local dealer.

Sincerely yours,

Susan Siegel

Susan Siegel
Assistant Director

SS/mr
Enclosure

FIGURE 8-12. Adjustment letter—customer at fault.

and effort, if appropriate. Stating such appreciation will soften the disappointment and pave the way for future good relations.

Next you should analyze the circumstances of the situation sympathetically. Place yourself in your reader's position and try to see things from his or her point of view. Establish very clearly the reasons you cannot do what the reader wants—even though you have not yet said you cannot do it. A good explanation of the reasons should so thoroughly justify your refusal that the reader will accept your refusal as a logical conclusion. Then state your refusal quickly, clearly, and as positively as possible.

Close your letter with a friendly remark, whether to express your high opinion of the reader's product or merely to wish him or her success in the future.

Figure 8–13 shows a refusal letter sent to a supplier whose product was not selected. Figure 8–14 illustrates a letter refusing an invitation to speak; Figure 8–15, a letter refusing credit; and Figure 8–16, a letter refusing a job offer.

THE COLLECTION LETTER SERIES

With the expansion of credit in recent decades, all companies now need to send collection letters. These letters serve a twofold purpose of (1) helping to collect the overdue bill, and (2) preserving the customer's goodwill.

Most companies send a series of collection letters that become increasingly demanding and urgent, though the number and frequency of letters sent vary from one company to another. Although many firms rely on form letters, a short, personal note will usually motivate a customer to pay a bill faster than will a form letter. Collection letters should be polite; you can demonstrate insistence with the letters' frequency as well as with their tone. The intervals between letters should be long enough for the customer to respond, however. Generally, you should be more patient with a steady, long-time customer than with a new or unknown customer.

The collection process may vary from one business to another. A furrier, for example, might give customers a longer time to pay than would a discount hardware store. Competition is also a factor: if your major competitors gave customers eight months before starting legal action, you should not take action after only two months.

A series of collection letters usually proceeds in three stages, each of which may include several letters. All letters, even form messages, must be courteous and should show genuine concern for whatever problems are preventing prompt payment.

MARTINI REALTY COMPANY
251 West 57th Street
New York, New York 10019

11 February 19--

Mr. Henry Bliss
Abbott Office Products, Inc.
P.O. Box 544
Detroit, MI 48206

Dear Mr. Bliss;

Buffer

Thank you for your cooperation and your patience with us as we struggled to reach a decision. We believe our long involvement with
your company indicates our confidence in your
products.

**Review
of facts
and
Bad news**

However, the Winton Check Sorter has all the
features that your sorter offers and, in
fact, has two additional features that your
sorter does not. The more important one is a
back-up feature that retains totals in its
memory, even if the power fails, so that
sorting doesn't have to start again from
scratch following a power failure. The second
additional feature is stacked pockets, which
are less space-consuming than the linear
pockets on your sorter. After much delibera-
tion, therefore, we have decided to purchase
the Winton Check Sorter.

**Goodwill
close**

Although we did not select your sorter, we
were very favorably impressed with your system and your people. Perhaps we will be able
to use other Abbott products in the future.

Sincerely,

Muriel Johansen

Muriel Johansen
Business Manager

MJ:ct

FIGURE 8–13. Refusal letter.

WATASHAW ENGINEERING COMPANY
301 Decatur Street
Decatur, Illinois 62525

March 26, 19--

George M. Johnson, President
TNCO Engineering Consultants
9001 Cummings Drive
St. Louis, Missouri   63129

Dear Mr. Johnson:

Buffer

I am honored to have been invited to address your regional meeting in St. Louis on May 17. To be considered one who might make a useful contribution to such a gathering of experts is indeed flattering.

Review of facts and Refusal

On checking with those who control the purse strings here a Watashaw Engineering, however, I learned that it would be contrary to company policy for Watashaw to pay my expenses for such a trip. Therefore, as much as I would enjoy attending your meeting, I must decline.

Goodwill close

I have been very favorably impressed over the years with your organization's contributions to the engineering profession, and I am proud to have received your invitation.

Sincerely,

Ralph P. Morgan

Ralph P. Morgan
Purchasing Department

RPM/lcs

FIGURE 8–14. Letter refusing a speaking invitation.

TITUS PACKAGING, INC.
2063 Eldorado Dr.
Billings, Montana 59102

April 14, 19--

Ms. Edna Kohls, President
Graphic Arts Services, Inc.
936 Grand Avenue
Billings, Montana   59103

Dear Ms. Kohls:

Buffer
We appreciate your interest in establishing an open account at Titus Packaging, Inc. In the two years since you began operations, your firm has earned an excellent reputation in the business community.

Review of facts and Bad News
As you know, interest rates have been rising sharply this past year, while sales in general have declined With the current negative economic climate, and considering the relatively recent establishment of your company, we believe that an open account would not be appropriate at this time.

Goodwill Close
We will be happy to review your request around the first of next year, when the economic climate is expected to improve and when your company will be even more firmly established. In the menantime, we will be happy to continue our present cash relationship, with a 6 percent discount for payment made within ten days.

Sincerely,

Marjorie Atkins

Marjorie Atkins, Manager
Credit Department

MA/lcs

FIGURE 8–15. Letter refusing credit.

127 Idlewild Rd.
Boston, MA 02173
October 17, 19--

Ms. Juanita Perez, Director
Personnel Department
Manchester Iron Works, Inc.
Boston, MA   02181

Dear Ms. Perez:

Buffer

I am pleased to receive your **offer** of employment as
an Administrative Assistant in the Executive office.
I was favorably impressed with your company and with
the position as you described it.

Review
of facts
and
Refusal

Since interviewing with you, however, I have been
offered another position that is even more in line
with my long-range goals and have accepted that
position.

Goodwill
close

Thank you for your time and consideration. I enjoyed
meeting with you and your staff.

Sincerely,

Jason L. Wytosh

Jason L. Wytosh

FIGURE 8–16. Letter refusing a job offer.

The first stage of collection letters consists of reminders stamped on the invoice, form letters, or brief personal notes. These early reminders should be written in a friendly tone that emphasizes the customer's good credit record until now. You should remind him of the debt and indicate that you are sure that payment has merely been overlooked. You may even solicit additional business by including promotion for new sales items, as is done in Figure 8–17.

At the second stage, the collection letters are more than just reminders. You now assume that some circumstances are preventing payment. Ask directly for payment, and inquire about possible problems, perhaps inviting the customer to discuss the matter with you. If you have a standard optional payment plan, you might suggest it. Mention the importance of good credit, appealing to the customer's pride and self-esteem as well as sense of fair play. Remind the customer that he or she has always received good value from you. Make it easy to respond by enclosing a return envelope or offering a toll-free telephone number. At this stage, your tone should be firmer and more direct than in the earlier stage, but you should never sound rude, sarcastic, or threatening. Notice how the letter in Figure 8–18 is more direct than the first letter, but no less polite.

The third stage of collection letters reflects a sense of urgency, for the customer has not responded to your previous letters. Although your tone should remain courteous, make your demand for payment explicit. Point out how reasonable you have been, and urge the customer to pay at once to avoid legal action. Again, make it easy to respond by providing a return envelope and a toll-free telephone number, as is done in Figure 8–19.

The effectiveness of a series of collection letters is based on the psychological pressure exerted by frequent requests for payment that become increasingly demanding in tone. Throughout the correspondence, however, you should emphasize your company's willingness to work with the customer to arrange payment. Whenever possible, you want to avoid turning the account over to an attorney or collection agency.

THE SALES LETTER

A sales letter, or letter that promotes a product, service, or store, is a difficult letter to write because it requires both a thorough knowledge of the product or service and a keen awareness of the potential customer's needs. For this reason, many businesses (such as department stores) employ specialists to compose their sales letters. However, if you are employed in a small business or are self-employed, you will probably have to write your sales letters yourself.

ABBOTT OFFICE PRODUCTS, INC.
P.O. Box 544
Detroit, Michigan 48206

30 August 19--

Mr. Thomas Holland
Walk Softly Shoes
1661 East Madison Boulevard
Garfield, AL 36613

Dear Mr. Holland:

With the new school year about to begin, your
shoe store must be busier than ever as students purchase their back-to-school footwear.
Perhaps in the rush of business you've overlooked paying your account of $742, which is
now 60 days overdue.

Enclosed is our fall sales list. When you
send in your check for your outstanding account, why not send in your next order and
take advantage of these special prices.

Sincerely,

Henry Bliss

Henry Bliss
Sales Manager

HB:ew

FIGURE 8–17. Collection letter—first stage.

ABBOTT OFFICE PRODUCTS, INC.
P.O. Box 544
Detroit, Michigan 48206

1 December 19--

Mr. Thomas Holland
Walk Softly Shoes
1661 East Madison Boulevard
Garfield, AL 36613

Dear Mr. Holland:

We are concerned that we have not heard from
you about your overdue account of $742, even
though we have written 3 times in the past 90
days. Since you have always been one of our
best customers, we have to wonder if some
special circumstances have caused the delay.
If so, please feel free to discuss the matter
with us.

By sending us a check today, you can preserve
your excellent credit record. Because you
have always paid your account promptly in the
past, we are sure that you will want to settle this balance now. If your balance is more
than you can pay at present, we will be happy
to work out satisfactory payment arrangements.

Please use the enclosed envelope to send in
your check, or call (800) 526-1945, toll-
free, to discuss your account.

Sincerely,

Henry Bliss

Henry Bliss
Sales Manager

HB:ew

FIGURE 8–18. Collection letter—second stage.

ABBOTT OFFICE PRODUCTS, INC.
P.O. Box 544
Detroit, Michigan 48206

1 March 19--

Mr. Thomas Holland
Walk Softly Shoes
1661 East Madison Boulevard
Garfield, AL 36613

Dear Mr. Holland:

Your account in the amount of $742 is now 180 days overdue. You have already received a generous extension of time, and in fairness to our other customers, we cannot permit a longer delay in payment.

Because you have not responded to any of our letters, we will be forced to turn your account over to our attorney for collection if we do not receive payment immediately. Such action, of course, will damage your previously fine credit rating.

Why not avoid this unpleasant situation by sending your check in the enclosed return envelope within 10 days or by calling (800) 526-1945 to discuss payment.

Sincerely,

Henry Bliss

Henry Bliss
Sales Manager

HB:ew

FIGURE 8–19. Collection letter—third stage.

Whether you write sales letters for a small company or a large one, your first task is to determine whom they should be sent to. One good source of names is a list of past and recent customers; those who have, at some time, purchased a product or service from you may become users again. Other sources are lists of people who may be interested in certain products or services. Such lists, which are often compiled by companies that specialize in marketing techniques, are drawn from the membership rolls of clubs, fraternal and religious organizations, professional societies, and the like. Because these lists tend to be expensive, they should be selected with care.

After you decide whom your mailing list will include, you should prepare your letter carefully. As you do, keep the following points in mind.

1. The opening should attract the reader's attention and arouse his or her interest. Start out, for example, by describing a feature of the product or service that you believe would appeal strongly to your reader's needs. A representative of a company that installs home insulation might use the following opening, addressed to "Dear Homeowner":

   > If you've thought that home insulation is a good idea but too expensive, think again. We can fully insulate your home at <u>no cost to you</u>. Impossible? With the new Federal Energy Tax Credit and the money that we guarantee you'll save . . .

   Be careful, of course, that any claim you make in a sales letter is valid. Mail fraud carries heavy legal penalties.
2. Continue to emphasize the benefits of the product to the reader. Don't exaggerate; you will lose the reader's confidence if your claims sound unreasonable. And don't downgrade a competitor— it smacks of unfair tactics.
3. Make it easy and worthwhile for the customer to respond. You might include a local street map showing how to get to your store, a discount coupon, or instructions for convenient phone-in orders and free delivery.
4. Suggest ways that the reader can make immediate use of the product or service. A sales letter from a fabric store might give instructions for making pillows, bags, and other home-sewn items.

The sales letter in Figure 8–20 is typical. Notice that it is written in a light, friendly tone—sales letters from small, local businesses frequently are, since their purpose is to make the reader feel comfortable about coming to the shop or office. Note that such sales letters are some-

Janice's Cycle Shop
775 First Avenue
Ottumwa, Iowa 52501
(515) 273-5111

April 3, 19--

Mr. Raymond Sommers
350 College Place
Sharpsville, Iowa 52156

Dear Mr. Sommers:

Are you ready to go bike riding this spring--but your
bike isn't?

Janice's Cycle Shop is ready to get your bike in shape
for the beautiful days ahead. We will lubricate all
moving parts; check the tires, brakes, chain, lights,
horn, and all other accessories; and make any minor
repairs all for only $10 and the coupon enclosed with
this letter.

Just stop in any day, Monday through Saturday, between
8:00 a.m. and 9 p.m. We are conveniently located at
the corner of First and Walker. You can pay with cash,
check, or bank credit card.

If you bring your bike in before 10 a.m., you can be
enjoying a spring bike ride that evening.

Happy riding!

Janice's Cycle Shop

FIGURE 8–20. Sales letter.

times "signed" not by an individual but by the shop itself, as is the case in Figure 8–20.

CHAPTER SUMMARY

There are a number of different kinds of business letters that follow established forms. Following are some of the most frequently written kinds.

- An *order letter* is written by a person or organization wishing to make a purchase. The letter should be specific, accurate, and complete, but not cluttered with unrelated details.
- An *inquiry letter* is a request for information. It should state clearly and concisely what information is wanted, who wants it, and what use will be made of it.
- A *response to an inquiry letter* should answer all questions that have been raised and should be phrased politely and tactfully.
- A *transmittal* or *cover letter* accompanies material that is being sent to the recipient. The main purpose of the letter is to identify what is being sent and why it is being sent. The length of the letter varies with the circumstances.
- An *acknowledgment letter,* which reports that something has been received, is sometimes sent as a courtesy.
- A *complaint letter* should be businesslike and logical; it should not sound "complaining." The letter should reflect the fact that the writer is registering the complaint calmly—but it should also indicate that he or she expects the situation to be corrected.
- An *adjustment letter,* often a response to a complaint letter, should explain what caused the problem, specify what is being done to correct it, and, if the company for which the writer works was at fault, apologize for the incident.
- A *refusal letter* should maintain goodwill even though the refusal is clear. When writing this type of letter, you should use an indirect pattern in which the bad news is preceded by a buffer and followed by a goodwill closing.
- A *collection letter series* includes three stages of letters that become increasingly demanding in tone. Throughout the correspondence, however, it should be emphasized that the company is willing to arrange a payment plan, and efforts should be made to retain the customer's goodwill.
- A *sales letter* should catch the reader's attention, arouse the reader's interest, emphasize the benefits of the product or service, and invite the reader to respond.

EXERCISES

1. Prepare a letter of transmittal for either a report or a term paper that you are preparing for a course. Address the letter to the appropriate instructor.

2. The following exercises present situations in which you are asked to respond with different types of correspondence. On the basis of the events described in Exercises *a–e,* write the letters or memos assigned by your instructor. In all exercises, follow the proper format for business letters. Your instructor may ask you to type your letters and envelopes.

   a. Assume that you are writing a letter requesting a free booklet that explains how to clean window-unit air conditioners to achieve better energy efficiency. You must write to an organization called the Energy Conservation Society, located in New York City at 1012 Third Avenue (zip code 10021). You are writing to Nancy Reibold, who is the executive director. You learned about this booklet in an article in *Time* magazine (May 25, 19--). You don't remember the precise title of the booklet.

   b. Assume that you are Nancy Reibold in Exercise *a.* You have received the inquiry letter asking for the booklet. You are out of copies at the moment, however, because you have received more requests for the booklet than you had anticipated. You expect to receive more copies of the booklet within two weeks. Write a response to the inquiry letter explaining the circumstances and telling the reader that you will send the booklet, entitled "Reducing the Cost of Operating Your Window Air Conditioner," as soon as you can.

   c. You are Nancy Reibold's assistant at the Energy Conservation Society (see Exercises *a* and *b*). You have just received 1,000 copies of the booklet from the Jones Printing Company, 105 East Summit Street, New Brunswick, New Jersey (zip code 08910). Both you and Nancy Reibold are very angry. When you opened the box containing the booklets, you discovered that several pages of each booklet had been left unprinted. This is the second printing mistake made by Jones Printing, and the shipment is late as well. Robert Mason, the sales representative for Jones Printing, promised that you would have no problems this time. Nancy Reibold asks you to write a complaint letter to Robert Mason to "get this problem corrected immediately." Write the letter for Ms. Reibold to sign.

   d. Assume that you are Robert Mason (see Exercise *c*). You have received the complaint letter about the printing mistake. After checking, you discover that the booklets sent to the Energy Conservation Society had been subcontracted to another printing firm (ILM Printing Company) because of the backlog of printing jobs at Jones. You know that Jones Printing will not be billed for the booklets if you return them to ILM Printing within five working days. You decide that you must write an adjustment letter to Ms. Reibold quickly. You will need to ask her to return the incorrectly printed booklets.

e. Assume that you are Robert Mason (see Exercise *d*). Send a memo to J. R. Jones, your boss and president of Jones Printing, recommending that ILM Printing Company not be used for future subcontracting work. Use the details from the previous exercises to make the memo convincing.

3. As a class, and with the help of your instructor, create a made-up situation similar to the one in Exercise 2*a–e*. From the events and details you have developed, assign various types of letters to be completed as your instructor requires.

4. Find a catalog for parts or equipment with which you are familiar— for example, stereo components, office supplies, or automobile accessories. Photocopy the pages that give you enough information to order items you need (or would like to have). Write an order letter, address an envelope, and submit the letter, envelope, and photocopies of the pertinent pages to your instructor.

5. Assume that eight weeks have passed since you sent the order letter in Exercise 4. Write an order follow-up letter.

6. You have been designated to write a memorandum to Mark Heller, the head of your engineering department, asking for an extension of the deadline originally set for the completion of your engineering group's current project. Your reasons for asking for the extension are that a vendor delivered needed material seven days late and that one of the key draftsmen in your group missed two weeks of work because of illness.

7. You are the manager of Sunny River Resort. Charles James, director of the State Self-Help Society, has written you requesting the use of your lodge for a two-day meeting of his staff. His letter is as follows:

Dear ――――――:

The Self-Help Society will hold its annual staff meeting on June 15 of this year. We would like to use your lodge for

this two–day meeting, which will include about 50 staff members.

We would need to use your meeting hall from 9 a.m. to 4 p.m.
each day. We would also need an overhead projector, a 16mm
projector, a flip chart, and a podium for the various speakers who will address our group.

Since some of the staff members will stay at the lodge for
two days or more and we will be paying for meals in your dining
room, we would like to use your meeting room free of charge.
I'm sure the exposure your lodge will receive during the
two days will more than pay for the facilities in your meeting
hall.

Please let me know by December 10 if we can use your lodge.

Sincerely,

You will need to write to Mr. James, and you'd like his highly respected
charitable organization to use your meeting room. But you have a
problem: you charge $250 per day to *any* group that uses the meeting
room. The room has a number of fixed and variable costs—you can't
afford to give it away. (Hint: Does it cost money to clean the room,
pay for lighting and air conditioning, supply and repair equipment?
What might happen if others knew you had given the room free?)
Write a letter to Mr. James selling him on the idea of using your
lodge while holding to the position that the $250 fee would apply.
Use tact, a positive tone, and persuasive details to write the letter.

8. You are the manager of a store called Hamon's Fine Clothing. Dr.
   Raymond Warden has purchased two suits (total $575) from you—
   and is six months overdue in paying for them. You've already sent
   several standard-form notices about the late payment. You'll now
   need to start a series of collection letters, but you want to make
   the pace slow. You understood, when you gave Dr. Warden a credit
   line, that he was a well-respected physician in the community. Write
   a series of collection letters, spacing them appropriately (date the
   first letter January 2).

9. You are the manager of BT Discount Auto Parts. Jeff Price, a 23-
   year-old friend of your nephew, owes $325 for parts. You allowed
   him to charge his purchase because your nephew said Jeff was reliable
   and promised to cover Jeff's bill if he didn't pay. It's been two months,
   Jeff has moved across town, and your nephrew says he hasn't seen

Jeff for a month. Your nephew has given you a check, but you'd like to return it by collecting the money from Jeff. Write a collection letter series to Jeff Price, starting with July 1. (You understand that Jeff will be enlisting in the army within five months.)

10. You are Mr. Henry Bliss of Abbott Office Products, Inc., who received the refusal letter that is Figure 8–13. After thinking over the situation, write a memo to R. P. McMurphy, vice president of Engineering (with a copy to Pat Smith, director of Marketing), recommending improvements in the check sorter (or another office system of your choice with your instructor's permission). Collect facts by visiting a local office systems store or examining its catalog.

11. You have recently purchased an electronics repair shop and wish to build your business. You have a mailing list of the previous owner's customers. You understand that many of these customers were unhappy with the previous owner's work. You would like to get them back. You specialize in video equipment (VCRs, televisions, cameras), but you can also work on stereos, digital controls on appliances, and other high-tech equipment (except home computers, which you plan to add if business becomes healthy). When you purchased the shop, you also became an authorized repair service for TEKO products (a line of electronic games and toys).

    The community you serve is relatively affluent, but you understand that one of the complaints against the former owner is that he overcharged customers. Your store is located on East Capitol Drive in a section with a wide variety of appliance stores, restaurants, and even a chain electronics retail store. You are willing to make house calls for large items, such as "giant screen" televisions. You are ambitious and you believe that satisfied customers will improve your business.

    Write a sales letter, addressed to the previous owner's customers, effectively promoting your services.

9

Informal Reports

Reports make up a large part of on-the-job communication. The successful operation of many firms depends on reports that either circulate within the company or are submitted to customers, clients, and others with whom a company does business. It would be difficult, in fact, to find a job in business or industry that did not require, at least on occasion, the writing of reports.

What is a report? Although the term is used to refer to hundreds of different types of written communication, it can be defined as an organized presentation of information, serving an immediate and practical purpose by furnishing requested or needed data.

All reports fall into two broad categories: *formal reports* and *informal reports*. Formal reports, which are explained in detail in Chapter 11, are generally the outgrowth of projects that require many months of work, large sums of money, and the collaboration of many people. Formal reports, which may take several hundred pages, are usually accompanied by a letter of transmittal to the recipient; frequently, such reports have a table of contents and other aids to the reader. Informal reports, on the other hand, normally run from a few paragraphs to a few pages and include only the essential elements of a report (introduction, body, conclusions, recommendations). And informal reports, because of their brevity, are customarily written as a letter—if the report is to be sent outside the company—or as a memorandum—if it is to be distributed within the firm. (See Chapters 7 and 8 for advice on how to write and format letters and memos.)

WRITING THE REPORT

If you will be writing a report on an activity in which you are participating (a special project, for example), it's a good idea to collect information and keep notes as the activity progresses. You may have trouble obtaining all the information later on, when you prepare to write the report.

In determining what notes to take, include all the information that will meet the objective of your report (for example, whatever information will persuade your boss to adopt the plan of action you are proposing) and the needs of your reader (exactly the information that will enable your boss to understand your proposal and to see its logic and benefits).

The purpose of taking notes is to record, in an abbreviated form, the information that will go into your report. The advantage of taking notes is that you don't have to rely on your memory to recollect every detail at exactly the moment when you need to include it in your report. Be careful, however, not to make a note so brief that you forget what you intended when you wrote it. The critical test of a note is whether, a week later, you will still be able to recall all the information and significance that you had in mind when you made the note. (Note-taking is discussed in more detail in Chapter 10.)

Once you have prepared all your notes, organize your outline as explained in Chapter 2. Then work your notes into the appropriate places in your outline.

An informal report is almost always intended for one specific reader or for a small group of readers. Because you will know, in most cases, who your reader will be and how much technical background he or she has, you should be able to determine just how much specialized or technical language to use. You should also have a good idea of how much background information you will need to provide for your reader.

THE PARTS OF THE REPORT

Most reports that you will be called on to write have at least three, and sometimes four, main parts: the introduction, the body, conclusions, and recommendations. The *introduction* serves several key functions: it announces the subject of the report, gives the purpose, and, when appropriate, gives essential background information. The introduction should also concisely summarize any conclusions, findings, and/or recommendations made in the report. Managers, supervisors, and clients find a concise summary useful because it gives them the essential information at a glance and helps focus their thinking as they read the rest of the report. The *body* of the report should present a clearly organized account of the report's subject—the results of a test carried out, the status of a construction project, and so on. The amount of detail you include in the body depends on the complexity of the subject and on your reader's familiarity with the subject. In the *conclusion* of the report, you should summarize your findings and tell the reader what you think their significance may be. In some reports there is a final section giving *recommendations*. (Sometimes the conclusions and recommendations may be combined.) In this section, you would make suggestions based on the data you have presented—suggestions, say, for instituting new work procedures, for setting up new departmental responsibilities, or for hiring new employees.

TYPES OF REPORTS

Because there are so many different types of informal reports, and because the categories sometimes overlap (a trip report, for example, might also be a progress report), it would be unrealistic to attempt to study every type. But it is possible to become familiar with report writing in general and to examine some of the most frequently written kinds of reports. In this chapter we will examine the trouble report, the investigative report, the progress (and periodic) report, the trip report, and the test report. If you master the techniques of writing these kinds of informal reports, you should be able to prepare other kinds as well.

Trouble Report

In many kinds of work you may do, accidents, equipment failures, and work stoppages will occur. Every such incident must be reported, so that its cause can be determined and any necessary steps taken to prevent a recurrence. The record of an accident or a breakdown, a *trouble report*—also called an *accident report* or an *incident report,* depending on the situation—may even be used by the police or by a court of law in establishing guilt or liability. Because it can be vital in preventing further injury or disruption in service, and because it may become legal evidence, a trouble report should be prepared as accurately, objectively, and promptly as possible.

The trouble report should normally be in the form of a memorandum written by the person in charge of the site where the incident occurred and addressed to his or her superior. (Some companies have printed forms for specific types of trouble reports, but even form reports include a section in which the writer must explain in detail what happened.)

On the subject line title of the memorandum, briefly state the nature of the incident you are reporting.

SUBJECT: Personal-Injury Accident in Section A-40

Then, after a brief introductory summary, state exactly when and where the accident or breakdown took place. Describe any physical injury or any property damage—no matter how slight—that occurred. Itemize any expenses that resulted from the incident (for example, an injured employee may have missed a number of workdays, or an equipment failure may have caused a disruption in service to the company's customers). Since insurance claims, worker's compensation awards, and, in some instances, lawsuits may hinge on the information in a trouble report, be sure to include precise data on times, dates, locations, treatment of injuries, the names of any witnesses, and any other crucial information. Include in the report a detailed analysis of what you believe caused the trouble. Avoid any tone of condemnation or blame. Be thorough, exact, and objective, and support any opinion you offer with facts. Mention what has been or will be done to correct the conditions that may have led to the incident. Finally, present your recommendations for the prevention of a recurrence of the trouble (such as increased safety precautions, improved equipment, or the establishment of training programs). If you are speculating on the cause of the accident, make sure that this is clear to the reader; your guess is no doubt an educated one, but it still should be labeled as a guess.

Figure 9–1 shows a trouble report written by the foreman of a loading dock and addressed to the company safety officer. The foreman obtained information from the victim and from the only other witness, whose name and employer he recorded for future reference.

Investigative Report

Although an *investigative report* may be written for a variety of reasons, it is most often produced in response to a request for information. You might be asked, for instance, to check the range of prices that companies charge for a particular item, to conduct an opinion survey among customers, to study a number of different procedures for performing a specific operation, to review a recently published work, and so on. You would then present your findings in a special-purpose report.

An investigative report is usually prepared as a memorandum. Open with a brief introductory summary that includes a statement of the information you were seeking. Then define the extent of your investigation. Finally, state your findings and any recommendations you may have.

MEMORANDUM

      TO: Gerald L. Yeager, Safety Officer
    FROM: Terry I. Washington, Loading Dock Foreman TIW
    DATE: April 20, 19—
 SUBJECT: Personal-Injury Accident in the Loading
            Dock Area

On April 17, 19—, David R. Halbestrum, a dock worker
in my department, accidentally dropped a personal
computer on his left foot, breaking several bones
in that foot.

Accident Description

At approximately 2:15 p.m. on Friday, David was unloading personal computers from a delivery truck.
Normally, the truck would have backed up to the loading dock, an operation that places the bed of the truck
and the loading dock at the same level. However, the
loading dock was full when the truck arrived, so David
decided to take a wheeled dolly out to the truck and
unload it in the waiting area. This meant that he had
to lift the personal computer boxes from the truck
bed, which was about chest-high to him, and lift them
down onto the dolly at ground level. David apparently
underestimated the weight of the first box, and it
slipped from his hands, landing on his left foot.

It was apparent that David's foot was seriously injured, so I immediately summoned a municipal ambu-
lance, which arrived at about 2:25 p.m. and took David
to the emergency room at St. Elizabeth's Hospital.
David's foot was X-rayed and found to have several
broken bones. His foot was placed in a cast and he
was sent home. He expects to return to work on April
22 and I will assign him to clerical duties in the
office until he can resume his duties on the dock.
He will have to wear the cast for six weeks.

The only witness to the accident was the driver of
the truck being unloaded. His name is Willard Jessup,
and he is a driver for Interstate Trucking, Inc.

FIGURE 9–1. Trouble report.

Conclusions About the Cause of the Accident

The accident apparently occurred because of David's
decision to unload the truck in the driveway instead
of waiting for the driver to find a place at the dock.
Since he had never been instructed not to do so, David
cannot be faulted for a decision that seemed logical
to him at the time.

To prevent a recurrence of the accident, I have conducted a safety session with all dock workers, at
which I described David's experience and cautioned
them against unloading trucks at any location except
the loading docks. I have also posted warnings at
three different locations on the loading dock, cau-
tioning against unloading trucks at any other location.

FIGURE 9–1, *continued.*

In the example shown in Figure 9–2, an administrative assistant
reports to a vice president on the relative advantages of leasing vs. purchasing cars for the company fleet and the relative advantages and disadvantages of five different automobiles.

Progress and Periodic Reports

Progress Reports.   The purpose of a progress report is to keep
an individual or a group—usually management—informed of the status
of a project. In answering various questions (Is the project on schedule?
Is it staying within its budget? Is the staff running into any unexpected
snags?), the report lets the reader know precisely what work has been
completed and what work remains to be done. Often the report will
include recommendations for changes in procedure or will propose new
courses of action. Progress reports are generally prepared when a particular stage of a project is reached.

Projects that are most likely to generate progress reports are those
that last for a considerable period of time and are fairly complex. The
construction of a building, the development of a new product, and the
opening of a branch office in another part of town are examples of such
projects. Sometimes, too, a progress report is a specified requirement in
the contract for a project.

DATE: November 23, 19—
TO: Hector Geoffery, Vice President, Opera-
             tions   *WH*
FROM: Willard Hecht, Administrative Assistant
SUBJECT: Purchasing or Leasing Company Automobiles

    As instructed, I have investigated the automo-
tive leasing plans available and compared the relative costs of leasing and of purchasing five different brands of economy cars for our company fleet: the
Pontiac 1000, the Pontiac Sunbird, the Ford Escort,
the Ford Tempo, and the Chevrolet Chevette. All five
cars investigated have four-cylinder engines, automatic transmission, air conditioning, and (except
for the Chevette) front-wheel drive.

The Options

I investigated four alternative options for obtaining the cars.
    1. Cash purchase
    2. Purchase financed through the dealer with
        a $2,000 down payment
    3. Four-year lease
    4. Four-year lease with a purchase option at
        the end of the lease period
    The monthly payment for a lease is determined
by subtracting the predicted value of the car at the
end of the lease period from the price of the car and
dividing by the number of months in the lease period.
(The monthly payment is higher for short lease periods because of the high depreciation rate of new
cars.)
    Before leasing a car, the lessor must pay in ad-
vance the first month's rent, the license and title
fees, and a security deposit. (The security deposit,
determined by rounding up the monthly payment to the
nearest $25, is refunded at the end of the lease if
the car is in good condition.) All automotive leases
limit the number of miles per year the car may be driven
without penalty. The average is 16,000 miles per

FIGURE 9–2. Investigative report.

year. If this mileage is exceeded, the lessor is charged for each extra mile, usually at 6 or 8 cents per mile.

With closed-end leases, the only kind offered by local dealers, the dealer assumes all risks related to the final value of the car except the amount of the security deposit. If there is no extraordinary damage to the car, the dealer returns the security deposit to the lessor; if the car has more than normal wear, the dealer keeps the security deposit for repair costs.

If the lessor leases the car with an option to purchase it at the end of the lease period, the dealer estimates the value he or she believes the car will have at the end of the lease period and writes this value into the lease contract as the price at which the lessor may purchase the car at the end of the lease. The lessor then decides at the end of the lease whether he or she wishes to purchase the car for that price.

Every dealer offers a maintenance contract for an extra $10 to $20 per month. For this extra fee, the dealer agrees to perform all normal maintenance on the car (oil change, tune-up, tire rotations, etc).

The Cars

The Pontiac 1000 is a subcompact car. The interior is quite small and would be uncomfortable for anyone six feet or taller. The controls are easy to reach, but are small and somewhat difficult to use. The seats are cloth covered and quite comfortable. It has a bumpy ride, but it handles well. The body styling is plain.

The Pontiac Sunbird is a compact car. It has a roomier interior than the Pontiac 1000. The seats are cloth covered. The front bucket seats are comfortable, but the rear seat is a bit cramped. All controls are easy to reach and use. The Sunbird has a smooth ride and handles well. The body styling is on the sporty side.

The Ford Escort is a subcompact car. The seats are cloth covered. The front seats are comfortable, but the rear seat is small. The ride is smooth and

FIGURE 9–2, *continued.*

the car handles well. All controls are easy to reach and use. The Escort's body styling is plain.

The Ford Tempo is a compact car. It is larger than the Escort. The interior is cloth, the seats are quite comfortable, and all controls are easy to read, reach, and use. The body styling is aerodynamic and contoured nicely, and the ride is smooth.

The Chevrolet Chevette is a subcompact car. It has a cloth interior, but the front seats are uncomfortable and cramped. Although the controls are easy to reach, the dials and gauges are small and can be difficult to read. The body styling of the Chevette is plain. The ride is choppy and the handling is very stiff.

The Cost

I have summarized the comparative prices to purchase and to lease each of the five cars in Table 1. I have also performed an overall cost analysis on all five cars, comparing the relative cost on each of the following bases:

1. Cash purchase
2. A financed purchase with a $2,000 down payment
3. A four-year lease
4. A four-year lease with a purchase option

I have listed the total cash outlay for each car under each of the four categories in Table 2.

I have also performed a present-worth analysis on the total cash outlay required for each of the five cars under each of the various options. I assumed a rate of return of 9 percent on the funds used. The result of this analysis is shown in Table 3.

The Conclusions and Recommendation

It is evident from the data that the best alternative is to purchase the selected car and finance it with a $2,000 down payment. The advantage of this alternative is that our firm will own the cars, use them for at least four years, and resell each for at least $1,500, regardless of the car selected.

FIGURE 9–2, *continued.*

Table 1. Prices and Monthly Rates

	1000	Sunbird	Escort	Tempo	Chevette
Purchase price	$7,700	$8,600	$6,600	$8,200	$7,500
Finance rate	6.9%	6.9%	8.9%	8.9%	7.9%
Monthly rate of purchase w/$2,000 down	$136	$158	$114	$155	$135
Monthly lease rate	$155	$175	$146	$187	$160
Security deposit	$175	$175	$150	$200	$175
Total for four-year lease	$7,470	$8,430	$7,038	$8,706	$7,710
Miles/year allowed	15,000	15,000	18,000	18,000	16,000
Penalty for exceeding miles/year	6¢/mile	6¢/mile	8¢/mile	8¢/mile	8¢/mile
Engine size (liters)	1.6	1.8	1.9	2.0	1.6
Mileage city/hwy	25/30	24/31	25/30	26/31	25/30

FIGURE 9–2, *continued.*

Table 2. Overall Cost

	1000	Sunbird	Escort	Tempo	Chevette
Purchase price	$8,085	$9,030	$6,930	$8,310	$7,875
Purchase with financing	$8,913	$10,014	$7,502	$9,420	$8,807
Four-year lease	$7,470	$8,430	$6,738	$8,706	$7,710
Four-year lease and purchase	$9,970	$9,345	$9,038	$11,806	$10,010

Table 3. Present-Worth Data

	1000	Sunbird	Escort	Tempo	Chevette
Purchase price	$8,085	$9,030	$6,930	$8,310	$7,875
Purchase with financing	$7,850	$8,779	$6,611	$8,299	$7,760
Four-year lease	$6,589	$7,412	$5,893	$7,632	$6,795
Four-year lease and purchase	$8,335	$9,648	$7,500	$9,706	$8,401

FIGURE 9–2, *continued.*

Of the five cars considered, the Ford Escort appears to be the best value.

I recommend that we purchase Ford Escorts for
our company fleet and that we finance them, with a
$2,000 down payment per car.

FIGURE 9–2, *continued.*

The chief value of a progress report is that it allows management not only to check on the status of a project but to make any necessary adjustments in assignments, schedules, and budget allocations while the project is under way. Progress reports can make it easier for management to schedule the arrival of equipment and supplies so that they will be available when they are needed. And such reports can, on occasion, avert crises. If a hospital had planned to open a new wing in February, for instance, but a shortage of wallboard caused a two-month lag in construction, a progress report would alert hospital managers to the delay—in time for them to prepare alternate plans.

Many projects, of course, require more than one progress report. In general, the more complicated the project, the more frequently management will want to review it. All reports issued during the life of a project should be of the same format. Progress reports to be sent outside the company are normally prepared as letters (see Figure 9–3); otherwise, they can be written as memorandums. The first in a series of reports should identify the project in detail and specify what materials will be used and what procedures will be followed throughout the project. Later reports will contain only a transitional introduction that briefly reviews the work discussed in the previous reports. The body of the reports should describe in detail the current status of the project. And every report should end with any conclusions or recommendations—for instance, alterations in schedule, materials, or procedures.

In the example shown in Figure 9–3, a contractor reports to the city manager on his progress in renovating the county courthouse. Notice that the emphasis is on meeting specified costs and schedules.

Periodic Reports.   Periodic reports perform most of the functions performed by progress reports; the difference between the two is that periodic reports are issued at regular intervals—daily, weekly, monthly, quarterly, annually—rather than at particular stages in a project.

Quarterly and annual reports, because of their length, are usually presented as formal reports (see Chapter 11). Most other kinds of periodic reports seldom run longer than a page or two. Like progress reports, these shorter reports are most often written as memorandums within

HOBARD CONSTRUCTION COMPANY
9032 Salem Avenue
Lubbock, Texas 79409

(806) 769-0823

August 17, 19—

Walter M. Wazuski
County Administrator
109 Grand Avenue
Manchester, NH 03103

Dear Mr. Wazuski:

The renovation of the County Courthouse is progressing on schedule and within budget. Although the cost
of certain materials is higher than our original bid
indicated, we expect to complete the project without
exceeding the estimated costs, because the speed with
which the project is being completed will reduce
overall labor expenses.

Costs

Materials used to date have cost $78,600, and labor
costs have been $193,000 (including some subcon-
tracted plumbing). Our estimate for the remainder
of the materials is $59,000; remaining labor costs
should not be in excess of $64,000.

Work Completed

As of August 15, we had finished the installation of
the circuit breaker panels and meters, of level-one
service outlets, and of all subfloor wiring. The upgrading of the courtroom, the upgrading of the
records-storage room, and the replacement of the air
conditioning units are in the preliminary stages.

Work Schedule

We have scheduled the upgrading of the courtroom to
take place from August 25 to October 5, the upgrading
of the record-storage room from October 6 to November
12, and the replacement of the air conditioning units
from November 15 to December 17. We see no difficulty

FIGURE 9–3. Progress report.

in having the job finished by the scheduled date of
December 23.

Sincerely yours,

Nigel Baldwin

Nigel Baldwin

NB/jsi

FIGURE 9–3, *continued.*

an organization and as letters when sent to clients and customers outside
an organization.

Many kinds of routine information that must be reported periodically—and that do not require a narrative explanation—can be either
recorded on forms or entered into computers. Examples are personnel,
accounting, and inventory records; production and distribution figures;
and travel and task logs.

Preprinted forms have established formats (see Chapter 12), as do
formal reports (see Chapter 11). One- and two-page periodical reports,
however, can be organized in a variety of ways. The standard format of
introduction, body, and *conclusion/recommendations* may serve your
needs. Otherwise, modify the organizational pattern to suit your reader's
reporting requirements. The sample periodic report shown in Figure
9–4 is organized as follows:

- Introduction
- Work performed during this period
- Problems encountered
- Project plans

It could just as well have been ordered as:

- Introduction
- Accomplishments
- Concerns
- Plans

The sample periodic report shown in Figure 9–4 is one of the several
monthly reports that keep the project manager of a computerized docu-
ment-retrieval system (the Document Control System) up to date on
how the training staff is progressing with its work.

MEMORANDUM

TO: James R. Lundy, Project Officer
FROM: Diana F. Talbot, Training Coordinator
DATE: May 3, 19—

SUBJECT: User Training and Assistance for
           April 19—

Introduction

The training staff held one advanced and two basic
training courses in April. In May, we have scheduled
two advanced courses and one basic course. Until enrollment increases, we will consolidate scheduled
classes. The ''Document Control System User's Manual'' will be ready for distribution by May 15.

Work Performed During This Period

Three training sessions were held in April: an advanced course on April 3 and two basic courses on April
13 and 20. To date, 200 staff members have participated in 31 user training sessions since training
was started in June 19—.

Problems Encountered

Scheduled training sessions are not being attended
in sufficient numbers to fill all classes. Until enrollment increases, we will consolidate the number
of scheduled classes to ensure adequate class size.
We encourage potential system users to participate
in scheduled training sessions. These sessions provide the best systematic approach for users to learn
about the advantages that the system offers them as
a review and research tool.

Project Plans

The following classes are scheduled for May:

           May 15 Advanced Course
                  (Materials Staff)

FIGURE 9–4. Periodic report.

```
       May 22  Advanced Course
                  (Records Control Staff)

       May 29  Basic Course
                  (Open to All)

     Final editorial changes are being made in the ''Docu-
     ment Control System User's Manual.'' The cover,
     spine, section dividers, and final artwork for sev-
     eral drawings are nearing completion. The manual will
     be ready by May 15, at which time copies will be dis-
     tributed for each system terminal.
```

FIGURE 9–4, *continued.*

Trip Report

Many companies require or encourage reports on the business trips their employees take. A *trip report* not only provides a permanent record of a business trip and its accomplishments but also enables many employees to benefit from the information that one employee has gained.

A trip report should be in memorandum format, addressed to your immediate superior. On the subject line title give the destination (or purpose) and dates of the trip. After a brief introductory summary, explain why you made the trip, whom you visited, and what you accomplished. The report should devote a brief section to each major event and may include a heading for each section (you needn't give equal space to each event but, instead, elaborate on the more important events). Follow the body of the report with any appropriate conclusions and recommendations.

A sample trip report appears in Figure 9–5.

Test Report

The *test report,* also called the *laboratory report* when the test is performed in a laboratory, records the results of tests and experiments. Normally, those who write test reports do so as a routine part of their work. Tests that form the bases of reports are not limited to any particular occupation; they commonly occur in many fields, from chemistry to fire science, from physics to home economics, from metallurgy to medical technology, and include studies on cars, blood, mercury thermometers, pudding mixes, smoke detectors—the list is endless. Information collected in testing may be used to upgrade products or to streamline procedures.

Because the accuracy of a test report is essential, be sure to take

MEMORANDUM

TO: Robert K. Ford, Manager
      Customer Services
FROM: James D. Kerson, Maintenance Specialist   J.D.K.
DATE: January 13, 19—

SUBJECT: Trip to Smith Electric Co., Huntington,
         West Virginia
         January 3 and 4, 19—

I visited the Smith Electric Company in Huntington,
West Virginia, to determine the cause of a recurring
failure in a Model 247 Printer and to fix it.

Problem

The printer had stopped printing periodically for
no apparent reason. Repeated efforts to bring the
printer back on line would eventually succeed, but
the problem would occur again at irregular intervals.
Neither customer personnel operating the printer nor
the local contract maintenance specialist could
solve the problem.

Action

I went to the customer site the afternoon of January
3 to evaluate the printer. I met with Ms. Ruth Ber-
nardi, the Office Manager, who explained that the
printer stopped and resumed printing unpredictably.
My initial troubleshooting did not reveal the cause
of the problem.

On January 4, I performed standard troubleshooting
procedures but was unable to isolate the cause of the
problem. That afternoon, I resumed troubleshooting
to test all circuit boards and parts and found them
all in working order. I then tested the logic cable
and found that it contained a broken wire. I replaced
the logic cable and then ran all the normal printer
test patterns to make sure no other problems existed.
All patterns were positive, so I turned the printer
over to the customer.

FIGURE 9–5. Trip report.

Conclusion

There are over 12,000 of these printers in the field, and to my knowledge, this is the first occurrence of a bad cable. Therefore, I do not believe the logic cable problem found at Smith Electric Company warrants further investigation.

FIGURE 9–5, *continued.*

careful notes while you are performing the test. When you prepare the report, state your findings in clear, straightforward language. Since a test report should be as objective as possible, it is one of the few writing formats in which the passive voice is usually more suitable than the active voice (see Chapter 4). A test report may be either a letter or a memorandum.

On the subject line title, identify the test you are reporting. If the purpose of the test is not obvious to your reader, explain it in the body of the report. Then, if it is helpful to your reader, outline the testing procedures. You needn't give a detailed explanation of how the test was performed; rather, provide just enough information for your reader to have a general idea of the testing methods. Next, present the data—the results of the test. If an interpretation of the results would be useful to your reader, furnish such an analysis in your conclusion. Close the report with any recommendations you are making as a result of the test.

Figure 9–6 shows one example of a test report. This report does not explain how the test was conducted, because such an explanation is unnecessary. Compare this report with the one shown in Figure 9–7, which does explain how the tests were performed.

Biospherics, Inc.
4928 Wyaconda Road
Rockville, MD 20852

March 14, 19––

Mr. John Sebastiani, General Manager
Midtown Development Corporation
114 West Jefferson Street
Milwaukee, WI 53201

FIGURE 9–6. Test report.

SUBJECT: Results of Analysis of Soil Samples
           for Arsenic

Dear Mr. Sebastiani:

The results of our analysis of your soil samples for
arsenic showed considerable variation; a high iron
content in some of the samples may account for these
differences.

Following are the results of the analysis of 22 soil
samples. The arsenic values listed are based on a wet-
weight determination. The moisture content of the
soil is also given to allow conversion of the results
to a dry-weight basis if desired.

Hole Number	Depth	Moisture (%)	Arsenic Total (ppm)
1	12″	19.0	312.0
2	Surface	11.2	737.0
3	12″	12.7	9.5
4	12″	10.8	865.0
5	12″	17.1	4.1
6	12″	14.2	6.1
7	12″	24.2	2540.0
8	Surface	13.6	460.0

I noticed that some of the samples contained large
amounts of metallic iron coated with rust. Arsenic
tends to be adsorbed into soils high in iron, aluminum, and calcium oxides. The large amount of iron
present in some of these soil samples is probably responsible for retaining high levels of arsenic. The
soils highest in iron, aluminum, and calcium oxides
should also show the highest levels of arsenic, provided the soils have had approximately equal levels
of arsenic exposure.

If I can be of further assistance, please do not hesitate to contact me.

Yours truly,

Gunther Gottfried

Gunther Gottfried
Chemist

GG/jrm

FIGURE 9–6, *continued.*

≡ **Biospherics, Inc.**
4928 Wyaconda Road
Rockville, MD 20852

September 9, 19—

Mr. Leon Hite, Administrator
The Angle Company, Inc.
1869 Slauson Boulevard
Waynesville, VA 23927

Dear Mr. Hite:

On Tuesday, August 30, Biospherics, Inc., performed
asbestos–in–air monitoring at your Route 66 construction site, near Front Royal, Virginia. Six persons and three construction areas were monitored.
In every case, exposure was well below the standards
set by the Occupational Safety and Health Administration (OSHA).

All monitoring and analyses were performed in accor-
dance with ''Occupational Exposure to Asbestos,''
U.S. Department of Health, Education, and Welfare,
Public Health Service, National Institute for Occupational Safety and Health, 1972. Each worker or area
was fitted with a battery–powered personal sampler
pump operating at a flow rate of approximately two
liters per minute. The airborne asbestos was collected on a 37–mm Millipore type AA filter mounted
in an open–face filter holder. Samples were collected
over an 8–hour period.

A wedge–shaped piece of each filter was mounted on a
microscope slide with a drop of 1:1 solution of di-
methyl phthalate and diethyl oxalate and then covered
with a cover slip. Samples were counted within 24
hours after mounting, using a microscope with phase
contrast option.

In all cases, the workers and areas monitored were
exposed to levels of asbestos fibers well below the
OSHA standard. The highest exposure found was that

FIGURE 9–7. Test report.

```
of a driller who was exposed to 0.21 fibers per cubic
centimeter. The driller's sample was analyzed by
scanning electron microscopy followed by energy dis-
persive X-ray techniques which identify the chemical
nature of each fiber, thereby verifying the fibers
as asbestos or identifying them as other fiber types.
Results from these analyses show that the fibers
present are tremolite asbestos. No nonasbestos fi-
bers were found.
                    Yours truly,

                    Gary Willis
                    Gary Willis
                    Chemist


GW/jrm
Enclosures
```

FIGURE 9–7, *continued.*

CHAPTER SUMMARY

Much on-the-job writing consists of various kinds of reports. Informal reports, normally no longer than a few pages, may take the form of a memorandum that circulates within an organization or be prepared as a letter to be sent to someone outside the organization.

The *introduction* of an informal report should state the report's subject and its purpose. In addition, the introduction may summarize the writer's conclusions and recommendations. The *body* of an informal report should present a detailed account of the work or activity being reported on. Any *conclusions* and *recommendations* the writer wishes to offer should close the report.

A *trouble report,* the record of an accident, breakdown, or work stoppage, is usually written as a memorandum. The writer should identify the precise time and place of the trouble, any injury or property damage involved, and any expenses that resulted from the incident. The report should continue with a detailed analysis of the likely cause of the accident or breakdown and should conclude with a statement of what is being done or what will be done to prevent a recurrence of the incident.

An *investigative report* is, in most cases, the presentation of data that the writer has gathered. The report, ordinarily in memorandum format, opens with a statement of the information the writer has sought and goes on to define the extent of the investigation. The report then presents the writer's findings and an interpretation of them if such an analysis is appropriate. The report ends with conclusions and possibly recommendations.

A *progress report* informs the reader of the status of an ongoing project, frequently one that lasts a fairly long period of time. Progress reports issued at regular intervals are called *periodic reports.* By stating precisely what work has been done and what work remains to be completed, these reports can alert the reader to any necessary adjustments in scheduling, budgeting, and work assignments.

A *trip report,* generally a memorandum submitted to the writer's immediate superior following a business trip, includes the destination and the dates of the trip in the subject line title. The body of the report explains why the trip was made, who was visited, and what was accomplished. Any conclusions and recommendations that the writer wishes to present would come at the end of the report.

A *test report* gives the results of a test or experiment. The test reported on is identified in the subject line title. The body of the report states the purpose of the test and, if appropriate, explains the procedures used to conduct the test. The results of the test, and any interpretations that the writer considers helpful to the reader, appear in the body. The report closes with any recommendations the writer may be making as a result of the test.

EXERCISES

1. Write one of the following *trouble reports* in the form of a memo.

   a. You are the traffic manager of a trucking company that has had four highway accidents within a one-week period. Using the following facts, write a *trouble report* to your company president, Millard Spangler.

      • Your company operates intrastate (your state).
      • The four accidents occurred in different parts of the state and on different dates (specify the date and location of each).
      • Each accident has resulted in damage not only to the truck (specify the dollar amount of the damage) but to the cargo as well (specify the type of cargo and the dollar amount of the damage).
      • Only one of the accidents involved another vehicle (truck swerved into a parked car when a tire blew out). Give the make and year of the damaged car and its owner's name.
      • Only one of the accidents involved injury to a company driver (give the name).

- Your maintenance division traced the accidents to faulty tires, all the same brand (identify the brand), and all purchased at the same time and place (identify the place and date).
- The tires have now been replaced and your insurance company, Acme Underwriters, has brought suit against the tire manufacturer to recover damages, including lost business while the four trucks are being repaired (specify the dollar amount of the lost business).

b. You are the dietitian at a hospital. A fire has occurred in the cafeteria, which is under your supervision. Using the following information, write a *trouble report* to the hospital's administrator, Mildred Garnett.

- The chief cook, Pincus Berkowitz, came to work at 5:30 a.m. (specify the date).
- He turned on the gas jets under the grill. The pilot light had gone out, and the jets did not light.
- The cook went to find a match, neglecting to turn off the gas jets.
- He found matches, returned, and lit a match, thus igniting the accumulated gas under the grill.
- The resulting explosion destroyed the grill (estimate the damage) and injured the cook.
- The fire was put out by the security force, but the fire department was called as a precaution.
- The cook was treated by the emergency room physician, then admitted to the hospital's burn unit as a patient, with second-degree burns on his hands, face, and neck.
- He was hospitalized for three days and will be off work for four weeks.

2. You are a personnel specialist assigned to investigate why your company is not finding enough qualified candidates to fill its need for electronics technicians and to recommend a solution to the problem. You have conducted your investigation and determined the following:

- In the past, you recruited heavily from among military veterans. But the absence of a military draft and the offering of attractive reenlistment bonuses to skilled technicians by the military services have all but eliminated this source. Want ads are not producing adequate numbers of veterans.
- The in-house apprentice program, which recruits graduating high school students, has produced a declining number of candidates in recent years because high school enrollment has been declining.

- Several regional technical schools are producing very well-trained and highly motivated graduates. Competition for them is keen, but you believe that an aggressive recruiting campaign will solve your problem.

Write an investigative report to your boss, Cynthia Mitchum, Director of Personnel, explaining the causes of the problem and offering your recommended solution.

3. You have been asked to provide information on *one* of the following topics. Gather the information pertinent to the topic and present the information in an *investigative report*. Your instructor will specify the length of the assignment.

   a. Your energy-consumption habits at home
   b. Your recommendations on the best hotel or motel in your area for out-of-town guests
   c. Which of two local garages that have serviced your car you would recommend to a friend
   d. Which of two local charities you think more worthy of support (specify from among charities in your area)
   e. Which of two or more products or services you use at home or on the job you would recommend to someone and why

4. As the medical staff secretary at a hospital, you must write a *progress report* to the director of the hospital outlining the current status of the annual reappointment of committees. Using the following facts, write the report.

   - A total of 19 committees must be staffed.
   - The Chief of Staff has telephoned each person selected to chair a committee, and you have sent each of them a follow-up letter of thanks from the Chief of Staff.
   - You have written letters to all physicians who are currently on committees but are not reappointed, informing them of the fact.
   - You have written letters to all physicians being asked to serve on committees.
   - You expect to receive replies from those physicians declining the appointment by the 15th of the following month.
   - Once committee assignments have been completed, you will type up the membership of all committees and distribute the membership lists to the complete medical staff.

5. You are a field service engineer for a company that markets diesel-powered emergency generators. You have just completed a five-day

trip to five different cities to inspect the installation of your company's auxiliary power units in hospitals. You visited the following hospitals and cities:

> May 26—New Orleans General Hospital in New Orleans
> May 27—Our Lady of Mercy Hospital in San Antonio
> May 28—Dallas Presbyterian Hospital in Dallas
> May 29—St. Elizabeth Hospital in Oklahoma City
> May 30—Jefferson Davis Memorial Hospital in Atlanta

You found each installation to have been properly done. With the cooperation of the administrators, you switched each hospital to auxiliary power for a one-hour trial run. All went well. You held a brief training session for the maintenance staff at each hospital, teaching them how to start the engine and how to regulate its speed to produce 220 volts of electricity from the generator at 60 hertz. You want to commend your company's sales staff and field personnel for creating a positive image of your company in the minds of all five customers you visited. Write a trip report to José Cruz, Manager of Customer Services, who is your boss.

6. Submit a laboratory *test report,* written in memo form, from a laboratory class that you are taking or have taken.

10

Researching Your Subject

When Tom Cabines, the production manager of the Nebel Printing Company, received a memo from Alice Enkend, chief of the Purchasing Department, asking him how many copies of its holiday calendar a customer had commissioned the firm to print, Tom probably had the answer at his fingertips or would be able to find it after a quick look in his production-scheduling book. Tom's *research*—or tracking down of good information on the topic—probably would be minimal. Suppose, though, that Tom were asked to review current literature on new developments in printing or marketing techniques and to write a report on the subject. How would he go about obtaining the necessary information? For these tasks he *would* have to do some research. He'd probably go first to the library—either the company library, if the firm had one, or the public library.

This chapter will discuss the research facilities most libraries provide and will then consider several other sources of information for a research report: the personal interview, the questionnaire, first-hand observation, and free or inexpensive materials from private and governmental bodies. It will also discuss techniques for systematically recording your research findings (note-taking) and for properly crediting your sources.

Admittedly, the skills discussed in this chapter are used more in college than on the job. Nonetheless, mastery of research techniques in a general sense is valuable: you can apply the methods, if not the specifics, discussed here to a variety of situations throughout your career.

IN THE LIBRARY

The key tools of library research are *reference works,* such as encyclopedias, specialized dictionaries, and handbooks and manuals; the *card catalog,* which represents a listing of books the library owns; *periodical indexes,* which furnish the names of articles in journals, magazines, and newspapers; and published *bibliographies,* which contain the names of books and other materials available. In addition, *computerized retrieval facilities,* through which a researcher can compile a very specialized bibliography from books, periodicals, and other materials, are increasingly common in academic, professional, and law libraries.

Reference Works

Reference works—encyclopedias, dictionaries devoted to special subjects (such as music, chemistry, or medicine), handbooks, manuals, statistical sources, and atlases—are often good places to begin your research, particularly if you know little about your subject. Reference books can provide you with a brief but reliable overview of your subject, and they can also direct you to more specialized sources. Most libraries have a reference librarian who can recommend suitable reference works and assist you in locating them.

Encyclopedias are comprehensive, multivolume collections of articles, usually arranged alphabetically and often illustrated. Some encyclopedias cover a wide range of general subjects, while others specialize in a particular subject. *General encyclopedias* provide the researcher with an overview of a particular subject that can be helpful to someone new to the topic. As a source of background information, the articles in general encyclopedias usually include the terminology essential to an understanding of the subject. Some articles contain bibliographies that can lead the researcher to additional information. The two best-known general encyclopedias are:

> *Encyclopedia Americana.* 30 vols. New York: Grolier. Revised annually.
>
> *The New Encyclopaedia Britannica.* 29 vols. Chicago: Encyclopaedia Britannica, Inc. Revised annually.

Subject encyclopedias provide detailed information on all aspects of a particular field of knowledge. Their treatment of a subject is sufficiently thorough to make it desirable that the researcher have some background information on the subject in order to use the information to full advantage. There are many more specialized encyclopedias than there are general encyclopedias. The following list indicates the range available.

The Cambridge Encyclopedia of Earth Sciences. New York: Crown Publishers, Inc./Cambridge University Press, 1981.

The Encyclopedia of Careers and Vocational Guidance. 6th ed. 3 vols. Chicago: J. G. Ferguson, 1984.

Encyclopedia of Computer Science and Engineering. 2d ed. New York: Van Nostrand Reinhold, 1983.

Encyclopedia of Economics. New York: McGraw-Hill, 1982.

The Encyclopedia of Management. 3d ed. New York: Van Nostrand Reinhold, 1982.

Encyclopedia of Physics. Reading, Mass.: Addison-Wesley, 1981.

Encyclopedia of Statistical Sciences. To be completed in eight volumes. New York: Wiley, 1982–.

Heyel, Carl, ed. *The Encyclopedia of Management*. 3rd ed. New York: Van Nostrand Reinhold, 1982.

International Encyclopedia of the Social Sciences. 17 vols. New York: Crowell Collier and Macmillan, 1968.

Kirk-Othmer Encyclopedia of Chemical Technology. 3rd ed. 24 vols. plus supplements and index. New York: Interscience Publishers, 1978–1984.

McGraw-Hill Encyclopedia of Science and Technology. 6th ed. 20 vols. New York: McGraw-Hill, 1987.

McGraw-Hill Encyclopedia of Science and Technology is supplemented annually by the *McGraw-Hill Yearbook of Science and Technology, 1982–*.

Miller, Benjamin F. *Encyclopedia and Dictionary of Medicine, Nursing and Allied Health*. 3d ed. Philadelphia: Saunders, 1983.

Munn, Glenn G., ed. *Encyclopedia of Banking and Finance*. 8th ed. Boston: Bankers Publishing Co., 1983.

Dictionaries contain definitions, arranged in alphabetical order, of a selection of the words in a language or subject. They also contain information on how words are spelled and pronounced, how they are divided into syllables, and where they originated. *General English-language dictionaries* will give meanings for terms from numerous fields of knowledge. For the meanings of words too specialized for a general dictionary, a subject dictionary is useful. *Subject dictionaries* define the terms used in a particular field, such as business, geography, architecture, and consumer affairs. Definitions in subject dictionaries are generally more current and complete than those found in general dictionaries.

The vocabulary section of the Writer's Guide lists a selection of desk-size English-language dictionaries. Unabridged dictionaries, which are larger and more comprehensive in their coverage, often contain basic terms from many specialized subjects. Four major up-to-date, unabridged English-language dictionaries are:

Funk & Wagnalls Standard Dictionary. New York: Funk & Wagnalls, 1980.

The Random House Dictionary of the English Language, 2nd ed. New York: Random House, 1987.

The Second Barnhart Dictionary of New English. New York: Barnhart/Harper & Row, 1980.

Webster's Third New International Dictionary of the English Language. 3rd ed. Springfield, Mass.: Merriam, 1971.

Following is a selection of subject dictionaries.

Clark, Audrey N. *Longman Dictionary of Geography, Human and Physical.* Harlow, England: Longman, 1985.

Dictionary of Computing. New York: Oxford University Press, 1983.

Dictionary of Geological Terms. 3d ed. New York: Anchor Press/Doubleday, 1984.

Dictionary of the Environmental Sciences. Palo Alto, Calif.: National Press Books, 1973.

A Dictionary of Paper. 3rd ed. New York: American Pulp and Paper Association, 1965.

Dorland's Illustrated Medical Dictionary. 26th ed. Philadelphia: Saunders, 1980.

Graf, Rudolf F. *Modern Dictionary of Electronics.* 6th ed. Indianapolis: Howard W. Sams, 1984.

Harris, C. M., ed. *Dictionary of Architecture and Construction.* New York: McGraw-Hill, 1975.

McGraw-Hill Dictionary of Chemistry. New York: McGraw-Hill, 1984.

McGraw-Hill Dictionary of Earth Sciences. New York: McGraw-Hill, 1984.

McGraw-Hill Dictionary of Scientific and Technical Terms. 2nd ed. New York: McGraw-Hill, 1978.

Means Illustrated Construction Dictionary. Kingston, Mass.: R. S. Means Co., 1985.

Monkhouse, F. J., ed. *A Dictionary of Geography.* 2nd ed. Chicago: Aldine, 1970.

Rosenberg, Harry M. *Dictionary of Computers, Data Processing and Telecommunications.* New York: Wiley, 1984.

Sipple, Charles J. *Computer Dictionary*. 4th ed. Indianapolis: Howard W. Sams, 1985.

Stedman's Medical Dictionary. 24th ed. Baltimore: Williams and Wilkins, 1982.

University Dictionary of Business and Finance. New York: Thomas Y. Crowell, 1972.

Handbooks and *manuals* are usually one-volume compilations of frequently used information in a particular field of knowledge. The information they offer can include brief definitions of terms or concepts, explanations of how certain organizations function, graphs and tables that display basic numerical data, maps, and the like. Handbooks and manuals are a ready source of fundamental information about a subject, although they are usually intended for the researcher with some basic knowledge, particularly in scientific or technical fields. Every field has its own handbook or manual; the following listing shows some typical examples.

American Electrician's Handbook. 10th ed. New York: McGraw-Hill, 1981.

CRC Handbook of Chemistry and Physics. Cleveland: Chemical Rubber Company. Annual.

The College Blue Book: Occupational Education. New York: Macmillan. Annual.

Environment Regulation Handbook. New York: Special Studies Division of Environment Information Center, 1973.

Fallon, William K., ed. *AMA Management Handbook*. 2d ed. New York: AMACOM, 1983.

Fire Protection Handbook. 15th ed. Quincy, Mass: National Fire Protection Association, 1981.

Handbook of Applied Mathematics: Selected Results and Methods. 2d ed. New York: Van Nostrand Reinhold, 1983.

Hunt, V. Daniel. *Handbook of Energy Technology*. New York: Van Nostrand Reinhold, 1982.

Hutchison, Lois Irene. *Standard Handbook for Secretaries*. rev. 8th ed. New York: McGraw-Hill, 1979.

Ludwig, Raymond H. *Illustrated Handbook of Electronic Tables, Symbols Measurements and Values*. 2d ed. Englewood Cliffs, N.J.: Prentice-Hall, 1984.

Matisoff, Bernard S. *Handbook of Electronics Manufacturing Engineering*. 2d ed. New York: Van Nostrand Reinhold, 1986.

McGraw-Hill's National Electrical Code Handbook. 18th ed. New York: McGraw-Hill, 1984.

Merritt, Frederick S., ed. *Building Design and Construction Handbook*. 4th ed. New York: McGraw-Hill, 1982.

Merritt, Frederick S. *Standard Handbook for Civil Engineers*. 3d ed. New York: McGraw-Hill, 1983.

Nash, Edward L., ed. *The Direct Marketing Handbook*. New York: McGraw-Hill, 1984.

Occupational Outlook Handbook. Washington, D.C.: U.S. Government Printing Office. Annual.

Sabin, William. *The Gregg Reference Manual*. 6th ed. Gregg Division. New York: McGraw-Hill, 1985.

U.S. Government Manual. Washington, D.C.: Government Printing Office. Annual.

Statistical sources are collections of numerical data. They are the best source for such information as the height of the Washington Monument; the population of Boise, Idaho; the cost of living in Aspen, Colorado; and the annual number of motorcycle fatalities in the United States. The answers to many statistical reference questions can be found in almanacs and encyclopedias. However, for answers to more difficult or comprehensive questions, you may need to consult works devoted exclusively to statistical data, a selection of which follows:

American Statistics Index. Washington, D.C.: Congressional Information Service, 1978 to date. Monthly, quarterly, and annual supplements.

The American Statistics Index lists and summarizes all statistical publications issued by agencies of the United States government. The publications cited include periodicals, reports, special surveys, and pamphlets.

U.S. Bureau of the Census. *County and City Data Book*. Washington, D.C.: U.S. Government Printing Office, 1952 to date. Issued approximately every five years.

The *Data Book* includes a variety of data from cities, counties, congressional districts, metropolitan areas, and the like. The information, arranged by geographic and political area, covers such topics as climate, dwellings, population characteristics, school districts, employment, and city finances.

U.S. Bureau of the Census. *Statistical Abstract of the United States*. Washington, D.C.: U.S. Government Printing Office, 1879 to date. Annual.

The *Statistical Abstract* includes statistics on social, political, and economic conditions in the United States. Compiled by the U.S. Bureau of the Census, the data include vital statistics and cover broad topics like population, education, and public land. Some state and regional data are given, as well as selected international statistics.

An *atlas* is a collection of maps. Atlases are classified into two broad categories based on the type of information they present—general maps that represent physical and political boundaries and thematic maps that represent a special subject, such as climate, population, natural resources, or agricultural products. Listed below are several well-known general atlases.

> *Hammond Medallion World Atlas.* Maplewood, N.Y.: Hammond, 1982.
>
> *National Geographic Atlas of the World,* 5th ed. Washington, D.C.: National Geographic Society, 1981.
>
> *Rand McNally Cosmopolitan World Atlas.* New Census ed. Chicago: Rand McNally, 1984.
>
> *The Times Atlas of the World,* 2nd rev. ed. Boston: Houghton Mifflin, 1983.

The following are thematic atlases.

> U.S. Department of Agriculture. *Atlas of United States Trees.* Washington, D.C.: U.S. Government Printing Office, 1971.
>
> Environmental Science Services Administration. *Climatic Atlas of the United States.* Washington, D.C.: U.S. Government Printing Office, 1968.

Card Catalog

A *card catalog* is a listing of the books a library owns. It answers some questions that are vital to you as a researcher: Does the library own a particular book by a particular author? What books, if any, on a specific subject does the library own? Where in the library is a given book located?

For most books, there are three cards on file in the catalog: an *author card* (Figure 10–1), a *title card* (Figure 10–2), and a *subject card* (Figure 10–3). Every card is arranged alphabetically in the catalog. Thus, an author card is alphabetized by the author's last name; a title card, by the first important word in the title (*A, An,* and *The* at the beginning of a title are ignored in alphabetizing); and a subject card, by the first word of the subject heading. All three types of cards contain the book's "vital statistics": author's name; title; place of publication; publisher; date of publication; number of pages; the terms *ill., bibliography,* or *index* to indicate whether the book has illustrations, bibliography, or

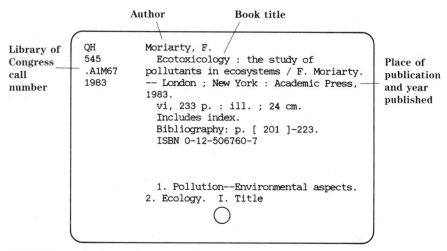

FIGURE 10–1. Author card.

index; the size of the book in centimeters; the major subjects the book covers; and, sometimes, additional information.

Many libraries have transferred their manual card catalog to an on-line computer-retrievable catalog, either for all books in their collections or for books added since they began to computerize their cards. Whether or not the catalog is computerized, author, title, and subject are used to search for books, although the computer may have the additional capacity to retrieve books by any important words in a book title. Search methods for on-line catalogs vary somewhat among libraries. Be-

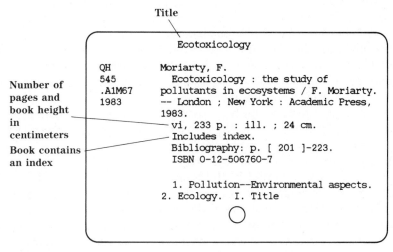

FIGURE 10–2. Title card.

Subject category of this book

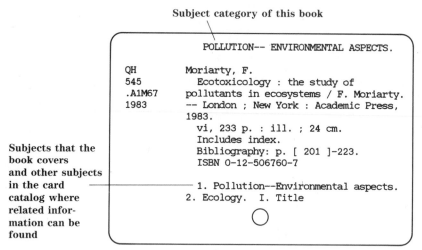

```
                    POLLUTION-- ENVIRONMENTAL ASPECTS.
        QH          Moriarty, F.
        545             Ecotoxicology : the study of
        .A1M67       pollutants in ecosystems / F. Moriarty.
        1983         -- London ; New York : Academic Press,
                     1983.
                        vi, 233 p. : ill. ; 24 cm.
                     Includes index.
                     Bibliography: p. [ 201 ]-223.
                     ISBN 0-12-506760-7

                     1. Pollution--Environmental aspects.
                     2. Ecology.  I. Title
```

Subjects that the book covers and other subjects in the card catalog where related information can be found

FIGURE 10–3. Subject card.

fore beginning an on-line search, read the available instructions or consult a librarian.

If you want to locate a book whose title or author you know, you can look in the card catalog for the book under either its title or its author's name. If, on the other hand, you are trying to find a book on a particular subject and do not have a title or an author in mind, you can look through the card catalog for the subject card or cards that correspond to the topic you are researching. For example, if you were trying to locate information on pollutants in the environment, you would look at cards behind the letter *P* in the card catalog and go alphabetically through the *P*s until you reached the subject cards under the heading *Pollution.* Included under that broad heading would be a number of specific topics, including *Pollution—Environmental Aspects.* The books under each subject heading are arranged alphabetically by authors' last names. The sample card in Figure 10–3 refers to a book that provides an overview of pollutants in the environment.

Some subject cards do not list a particular book but, instead, provide "see also" subject headings that the researcher may want to consult in tracking down additional books (Figure 10–4).

A *call number,* which indicates where on the shelves (or stacks) a book can be found, is located in the upper-left-hand corner of the cards in Figures 10–1 through 10–3. The same call number normally appears on the lower portion of the spine of the book itself. Libraries assign call numbers according to one or both of two systems of classification: the Dewey Decimal System or the Library of Congress System. Check with the librarian about which system or systems your library uses.

OFFICE FURNITURE
see also
FILES AND FILING (DOCUMENTS)

FIGURE 10–4. "See also" Subject card.

You can frequently tell from a book's title what the book is about. Another factor to consider in deciding whether to include a particular book in your research is the author's reputation: Is the writer considered an authority in the field? Has he or she written other, highly regarded books in the field or in a related field? You might check in the card catalog under the author's name to see what other books, if any, the author has written. And you might ask a librarian, an instructor, or someone you know who is familiar with the subject area whether the author has an established reputation in the field. When you obtain a copy of the book you can examine it in the library before deciding whether to use it. Does the book have an index? Indexes are indispensable in tracking down specific topics within a book. Does the book have informative diagrams, charts, tables, and so on? Does it have a comprehensive bibliography that you can use in locating additional material for your research? Is it reasonably up to date? Timeliness is especially important in a fast-changing field like computer technology.

For any book that you decide to include in your research, prepare a three-by-five-inch note card containing the following information: the call number (having the call number handy will enable you to locate the book on the shelves); the author (if the "author" is an organization, indicate that fact); the city of publication; the publisher's name; and the year of publication. When you are ready to prepare a bibliography for your research report, you can do so easily from the information you have recorded on these cards (known as *bibliography cards*). Figure 10–5 illustrates a bibliography card for a book, and Figure 10–6 illustrates a bibliography card for an article in a periodical. Having the author's last name near the upper-left-hand corner of the card will assist you in

QA
76. M367

McCorduck, Pamela

The Universal Machine
New York: McGraw-Hill, 1985

FIGURE 10–5. Bibliography card for a book.

Hackos, Joann

"Using System Analysis Techniques in the Development of Standards and Procedures." *IEEE Transactions on Professional Communication*, Vol. PC-28, No. 3 (Sept. 1985), 25-30.

FIGURE 10–6. Bibliography card for a periodical.

preparing the bibliography, in which the titles of the books and articles you used are arranged alphabetically according to the authors' last names.

Periodical Indexes, Bibliographies, and Abstracting Services

Periodical indexes and bibliographies are lists of journal articles and books. *Periodical indexes* are devoted specifically to journal, magazine, and newspaper articles (the term *periodical* is applied to publications that are issued at regular intervals—daily, weekly, monthly, and so on). *Bibliographies* list books, periodicals, and other research materials published in a particular subject area, such as business, engineering, medicine, the humanities, or the social sciences. *Abstracting services* provide brief summaries of the source cited, giving an idea of its content so that you can judge whether it is relevant to your research. To find a bibliography on your subject, look in the library catalog under the proper term for your topic, then search for the subheading "Bibliography."

Another way to choose the most relevant indexes, abstracts, and bibliographies for your research is to consult the reference librarian or an appropriate guide to the literature, such as the following:

> Sheehy, Eugene P. *Guide to Reference Books.* 9th ed. Chicago: American Library Association, 1976. Supplements are issued irregularly.

> Walford, A. J. *Walford's Guide to Reference Material.* 4th ed. London: The Library Association, 1980–. Vol. 1: Science and Technology, Vol. 2: Social and Historical Sciences, Philosophy, and Religion to be completed in three volumes.

Both of these guides list thousands of reference books, indexes, and other items useful to researchers, annotated and in an arrangement that allows you to find your subject quickly. More specialized guides to the literature include the following:

> Daniells, Lorna M. *Business Information Sources.* rev. ed. Berkeley: University of California Press, 1985.

> Malinowsky, H. Robert, and Jeanne M. Richardson. *Science and Engineering Literature: A Guide to Reference Sources.* Littleton, Colo.: Libraries Unlimited, 1980.

> Robinson, Judith S. *Subject Guide to U.S. Government Sources.* Littleton, Colo: Libraries Unlimited, 1985.

After you have selected the indexes, bibliographies, or abstracts that deal with your subject, consult the instructions in the front of the work or in the first volume of the work if it is a series (see Figure 10–7).

There you will find a key to the abbreviations and symbols used; an explanation of the way information is arranged; a listing of the specific subjects covered; and, for periodical indexes, a listing of the newspapers, magazines, and journals that have been included in the work.

Some of the indexes and abstracts that you are likely to find useful are the following:

Applied Science & Technology Index, 1958–. (Alphabetical subject listing of articles from about 300 periodicals; issued monthly)

Bibliographic Index: A Cumulative Bibliography of Bibliographies, 1937–. (Subject list of bibliographies that appear separately or in books or periodical articles; issued three times a year)

Bibliography and Index of Geology, 1969–. (Bibliography of world literature dealing with the earth sciences; entries are arranged within 29 subject areas; issued monthly)

Bibliography of Agriculture, 1942–. (Listing of literature covering agriculture and allied subjects; issued monthly)

Biological and Agricultural Index, 1964–. (Alphabetical subject listing of biological and agricultural periodicals; issued monthly)

Business Periodicals Index, 1958–. (Subject and title index; issued monthly)

Cumulative Index of the National Industrial Conference Board Publications, 1962–. (Subject index of publications of interest to commerce and industrial managers; issued annually)

Cumulative Index to Nursing and Allied Health Literature, 1965–. (Subject and author index to nursing journals; issued bimonthly)

Current Law Index, 1980–. (Subject, author, cases, and statutes index of about 700 periodicals; issued monthly)

Employment Relations Abstracts, 1958–. (Monthly)

Engineering Index, 1934–. (Alphabetical subject listing; contains brief abstracts; issued monthly)

Essay and General Literature Index, 1900–. (Semiannual index to information on all subjects in collections of articles in books; generally organized by subject, but sometimes by title)

Government Reports Announcements and Index, 1965–. (Semimonthly index of reports arranged by subject, author, and report number)

Index to The Times (London), 1790–. (Monthly)

Monthly Catalog of U.S. Government Publications, 1895–. (Unclassified publications of all federal agencies listed by subject, author, and report number; issued monthly)

New York Times Index, 1851–. (Alphabetically arranged listing of subjects covered in *New York Times* articles; issued bimonthly)

Psychological Abstracts, 1927–. (Abstracts articles dealing with all aspects of psychology and related fields, such as industrial psychology; monthly)

Public Affairs Information Services Bulletin (PAIS), 1914–. (About 1,400 periodicals as well as books, pamphlets, and governmental and international documents are scanned; weekly)

Readers' Guide to Periodical Literature, 1900–. (Monthly index of about 200 general U.S. periodicals, arranged alphabetically by subject)

Safety Sciences Abstracts Journal, 1974–. (Listing of literature on industrial and occupational safety, transportation, environmental and medical safety; issued quarterly)

Social Sciences Index, 1974–. (Alphabetical subject and author listing of about 350 social science periodicals; issued quarterly)

Sociological Abstracts, 1952–. (Monthly abstracting service covering all subjects related to social behavior)

Wall Street Journal Index, 1958–. (Monthly index of business and financial news covered in the *Journal*)

The list above is selective. Many more indexes and abstracting services are published for different fields of research than are described here. Moreover, many of the services listed are available for computerized searching.

Typical of specialized indexes is the *Applied Science & Technology Index.* This index lists, by subject, articles in the fields of aeronautics and space science, chemistry, computer technology and applications, the construction industry, energy resources and research, engineering, fire and fire prevention, food and the food industry, geology, machinery, mathematics, metallurgy, minerology, oceanography, petroleum and gas research, physics, plastics technology, the textile industry, transportation, and other industrial and mechanical arts. In addition, the index covers several branches of engineering—chemical, civil, electrical and telecommunication, environmental, industrial, mechanical, mining, and nuclear. Figure 10–7 shows the explanation that appears at the front of the index (following that page are a key to the abbreviations of journal titles and a listing of all periodicals indexed). Figure 10–8 shows part of a column in the index proper. In the first entry, for example, the index refers to a report on the relationship between academe and industry that appeared in Volume 219 of the periodical *Science* on pages 150 through 151. The issue was published in January 1983; the report is illustrated with diagrams. If this article seemed useful to your research, you would prepare a three-by-five-inch note card recording this information.

After completing your search for periodical articles, locate the neces-

PREFATORY NOTE

The APPLIED SCIENCE & TECHNOLOGY INDEX is a cumulative index to English language periodicals. The main body of the Index consists of subject entries to periodical articles arranged in one alphabet. In addition there is an author listing of citations to book reviews, following the main body of the Index.

Subject fields indexed include aeronautics and space science, chemistry, computer technology and applications, construction industry, energy resources and research, engineering, fire and fire prevention, food and food industry, geology, machinery, mathematics, metallurgy, mineralogy, oceanography, petroleum and gas, physics, plastics, textile industry and fabrics, transportation and other industrial and mechanical arts.

The following engineering disciplines are covered: chemical, civil, electric and telecommunications, environmental, industrial, mining, mechanical, and nuclear.

The Committee on Wilson Indexes of the American Library Association's Reference and Adult Services Division advises the publisher on indexing and editorial policy by means of in-depth contents studies conducted at intervals of several years. The Committee as part of its study prepares a list of periodicals, representative of all subject areas included in the Index, for consideration by the subscribers.

Selection of periodicals for indexing from this list is accomplished by subscriber vote. In voting their preferences subscribers are asked to place primary emphasis on the reference value of the periodicals under consideration. They are also asked to give particular consideration to subject balance in order to insure that no important field be overlooked in proportion to overall index coverage.

While the responsibility for all indexing and editorial decisions rests with The H. W. Wilson Company, every effort is made by the Company to follow the recommendations of the Committee and the subscribers to a given periodical index.

Suggestions for addition or deletion of titles should be brought to the attention of The H. W. Wilson Company, 950 University Avenue, Bronx, N. Y. 10452.

May 1983. Vol. 71. No. 5.

APPLIED SCIENCE & TECHNOLOGY INDEX (ISSN 0003-6986) is published monthly except July, with a bound cumulation each year. Sold only on the service basis; apply to publisher for rates.

FIGURE 10–7. Prefatory note to the *Applied Science & Technology Index.*

ACADEMIC freedom
Academe and industry debate partnership. B. J.
Culliton. Science 219:150-1 Ja 14 '83
Academic freedom and the classified information
system. R. A. Rosenbaum and others. Science
219:257-9 Ja 21 '83
ACCELERATORS (Particles)
CERN reports first vector boson evidence. A. L.
Robinson. Science 219:480 F 4 '83
Laser-driven electron-positron colliders. diags
Phys Today 36:19-21 F '83
Proposing the office of Pan American collabora-
tion [guest editorial] L. M. Lederman. Phys
Today 35:9+ Ag '82; Discussion. 36:107-8 F '83

Numerical control
Surface structure of silicon carbide irradiated
with helium ions with monoenergy and contin-
uous energy distributions. S. Miyagawa and
others. bibl il diag J Appl Phys 53:8697-705 D
'82
ACCIDENTS
See also
Automobile accidents
Burns and scalds
Safety education
ACCIDENTS, Industrial
See also
Burns and scalds
Safety education

FIGURE 10–8. Sample column from the *Applied Science & Technology Index.*

sary periodical volumes in the stacks. Many libraries shelve periodicals alphabetically by title in a separate section of the library. If the periodicals you need are not in your library, you can submit an interlibrary loan request. This service permits you to borrow books and photocopied periodical articles from other libraries that have the materials you need in their collections. Consult your librarian for specific details of the system.

Computerized Information Retrieval

Many libraries—particularly those at large universities—now offer a computer service for the compilation of bibliographies. Computerized information retrieval draws on one or more of the several hundred data bases in searches for pertinent articles on a given subject. Libraries lease access to the data base, a file that can be read by a computer, and communicate with the file through a terminal.

To determine whether a printed index or abstracting service would best serve your needs, or whether you should conduct a computerized search, discuss your research topic with a reference librarian. Some of the reasons you might choose to search by computer rather than manually include: (1) Your topic brings together several different concepts and would require you to search in a printed index under several terms to filter out much irrelevant material. (2) You want the most up-to-date information. (Printed indexes typically are from six weeks to one year

behind the literature they cite; most are three to six months behind.)
(3) You are doing research on a very new concept, perhaps described by
a newly coined word that has not yet appeared as a subject heading in
the printed indexes. (4) Finally, you are searching for a work by a specific
author, but the printed indexes provide only subject access.

The search is conducted by entering key words and phrases on the
terminal to establish the boundaries of the search. Libraries that provide
this service employ a librarian skilled in the strategies that selecting
key words involves: the researcher goes to the librarian and explains
his or her problem, the librarian determines the key words that best
represent the researcher's area of study and enters them on the terminal,
and the screen indicates how many items are available. If the researcher
wishes to expand or limit the number of available items, a different
arrangement of key words is entered. Once a satisfactory number of
items is obtained, the librarian can print out a bibliography.

Suppose, for example, that you were researching the role of super-
tankers in the American merchant fleet. Your librarian might begin the
search with the key words *cargo ships,* and read on the terminal screen
that 874 articles pertain to that broad subject. You do not wish to wade
through this many articles, so the librarian limits the search by entering
the key words *American* and *oil.* The revised number is pared down to
211 articles—still too many for your purposes. You decide that you are
really only interested in articles published during the past year. When
this limitation is entered, the number of pertinent articles is reduced
to a manageable 14. You then request a printout of a bibliography of
the 14 items.

Usually the library will charge a fee based on the data base used,
the results achieved, and the time spent on-line. If you have abstracts
or citations printed out, there may be a delay of a few days, since they
will probably be printed off-line and mailed to save on-line charges. Discuss the policy and anticipated charges with the librarian before proceeding.

Here are some examples of computerized data bases. The frequency
with which they are updated will depend on the vendor through which
your library acquires rights to access the data base.

ABI/INFORM, Dialog, 1971–. Weekly updating.
> (Citations and abstracts of more than 600 business periodicals
> published worldwide, with an emphasis on business concepts
> rather than specific industries or companies)

Aerospace Database, Nexis, 1983–. Biweekly updating.
> (Abstracts of articles dealing with aerospace research and devel-
> opment published in 1,600 periodicals)

Agricola, Dialog, 1970–. Monthly updating.
(Indexes of more than 600 publications worldwide in food and food research)

Biobusiness, Nexis, 1985–. Monthly updating.
(Abstracts from more than 1,000 journals on business applications of biological and biomedical research)

Computer Data Base, Nexis, 1983–. Biweekly updating.
(Abstracts from about 500 periodicals on computers, telecommunications, and electronics)

Management Contents, Dialog, 1974–. Monthly updating.
(Abstracts of about 90 periodicals on management)

National Technical Information Service, Nexis, 1980–. Biweekly updating.
(Abstracts of technical reports and other materials in science and technology)

PTS F&S Indexes, Dialog, 1972–. Weekly updating.
(Indexes of about 2,500 periodicals, with brief summaries, emphasizing a particular company or industry)

Scisearch, Dialog, 1974–. Biweekly updating.
(Indexes of about 4,500 journals in science, technology, and related fields)

This list is meant as illustration only because hundreds of data bases are now available. As always, ask a librarian about the sources—printed or computerized—available for your research needs.

TAKING NOTES

The purpose of taking notes is to condense and record information from the books and articles you have chosen for your research. The notes you take will furnish much of the material for your outline and final written work.

For your notes, you may use either three-by-five-inch or four-by-six-inch cards—but whichever you choose, stick to that size, because when you arrange the cards by topic later on, you may have trouble handling cards of two different sizes. You may well find that the larger-size card is handier: it provides more room for the information and is readily distinguishable from the three-by-five-inch bibliography cards. Make one note per card, on one side of the card only; use ink, since pencil tends to smudge. Near the bottom of each card, identify the source of the information: put in the author's last name (include first name or initials if you have two authors with the same last name) and the page number or numbers on which the material appears in the original source. If you have consulted more than one book or article by an author, include the title as well; for long titles, you may use a shortened form to save space on the card. And be sure to put information from only one source on each card.

As you are taking notes, it's a good idea to make a list of the topics that you will be covering in your research. Then, on the upper-left-hand corner of each note card, enter the appropriate identifying topic (these are sometimes called "slugs"). When you arrange the cards by topic in preparation for working up an outline, you can use the "slugs" as a guide in organizing your material.

Notes can be gathered in one of three ways. The information can be quoted word for word from the original source, as a *direct quotation;* it can be *paraphrased,* or restated in the researcher's own words; or it can be *summarized,* or stated by the researcher in a highly condensed form.

Quoting Directly

A *direct quotation* is an exact, word-for-word copy of an original source. Such quotations, which can be of a word, of a phrase, of a sentence, or, occasionally, of a paragraph, should be used sparingly and chosen carefully. A direct quotation is appropriate when the wording of the original source will support a point you are making, or when you feel that your reader will gain some insight from a particularly well-expressed passage. In both instances, the quoted material should be fairly brief. In addition, such material as policy statements, laws, and mathematical and scientific formulas should ordinarily be quoted exactly. Figure 10–9 shows a note card with a direct quotation on it.

There are two ways of presenting direct quotations. If the quotation you have chosen occupies more than four lines of typed copy, it should be set off from your text. Set-off quotations are usually separated from the text by a double space; every line of the quotation is indented five spaces from the left margin; the quotation is single-spaced; and quotation marks are not needed. It is a good idea to introduce the quotation smoothly—that is, to tell the reader, in your own words, what significance the quotation has for your report.

The county Motor Vehicles Department has strict rules that govern driving during snow emergencies:

Snow emergency is declared when snow or ice creates a road hazard. Under such circumstances driving is pro–

Randomness

"The imposition of order on a very large
number of participants in a system through
the use of randomization or chance has
immediate computational applications."

Mc Corduck, _The Universal Machine_, 250.

FIGURE 10–9. Note card—direct quotation.

hibited on all roads designated ''emergency snow
route'' except when vehicles are equipped with snow
tires or chains. Parking on these designated roadways
is prohibited.[1]

Motorists who get stuck on a snow emergency route without
chains are subject to a $50 fine.

The following note, either at the bottom of the page or at the end
of the paper, would identify the source of the quotation (see the discussion
of documentation):

[1] Citizen's Guide to Public Services in Montgomery
County, Maryland. (Rockville, Md.: Montgomery County,
1971), p. 12.

The second kind of direct quotation, which takes up four lines of
typed copy or less, is run in with the text—it is not set off. It is enclosed
in quotation marks.

When you are planning your remodeling project, don't forget
that residential construction requires a building permit.

```
To obtain a building permit in our area, contact the Depart-
ment of Inspections and Licenses. ''An applicant must submit
an application in duplicate, two sets of blueprints, three
plot plans drawn to scale, and an application for a driveway
apron.''² Once the application has been obtained, it must
be posted at the project site.
```

Again, a note would identify the source.

```
² Citizen's Guide to Public Services, p. 15.
```

There may be times when you want to quote directly from only part
of a passage. Suppose, for example, you saw a sentence like the following
in a company house organ.

```
SpeedMail, Incorporated, just hired two junior-level copy-
writers, who will report to the advertising manager, and a
direct-mail assistant, who will be working closely with the
director of promotion.
```

If you wanted to quote only the portion of the sentence that pertains to
the direct-mail assistant, you would omit the text relating to the copywriters. When you omit material that falls *within a quoted passage,* you
insert *three spaced dots* (called *ellipses*) to indicate where the omission
occurs.

```
SpeedMail, Incorporated, just hired . . . a direct-mail as-
sistant, who will be working closely with the director of
promotion.
```

If, on the other hand, you intended to quote the portion of the sentence
that deals with the copywriters, you would delete the reference to the
direct-mail aide. To indicate the omission of material that comes *at the
end of a quoted passage,* you place *a period followed by three spaced
dots* after the last quoted word.

```
SpeedMail, Incorporated, just hired two junior-level copy-
writers, who will report to the advertising manager. . . .
```

Paraphrasing

A *paraphrase* of a written passage is a restatement of the essential
ideas of the passage in the researcher's own words. Because a paraphrase

does not quote the source word for word, quotation marks are not necessary. When you use paraphrased material in your own work, however, you must credit the source in a footnote.

As you are getting ready to write a paraphrase, you may find it helpful, after you've read the passage, to put it aside for a moment while you decide how to word the paraphrase; this brief period of reflection will give you a chance both to make sure that you understand the writer's message and to prepare your own version of it. When you start to write, pick up the original and refer to it. Check to be certain that you include every important point in the original that is relevant to your topic.

The passage should be paraphrased, of course, according to your topic and the scope of your written work; if the source contains more information than is pertinent to your subject, paraphrase only the material that relates to your purpose in writing. As an example, consider the following passage and two paraphrases of it. The passage discusses the standardization of production in the book industry and how it permitted long-term contracts between book publishers and their printers.[1]

About 15 years ago, the book industry came up with an innovative way to create standards-based long-term contract purchasing where it did not exist naturally. The technique can be applied to many other publishing areas, especially manuals of various kinds in the corporate electronic publishing world.

Books, unlike magazines, are one-time productions, each a little different from the next. Traditionally, each book was put out to several printers for competitive bids. With more than 40,000 new books being published each year, the processing of bids required a small army of purchasing managers in publishing houses, and job planners and estimators in printing firms. In addition, lack of standardization required each book to be produced individually at highest cost.

A number of major publishers and printers analyzed the products they were producing and created standards on which to base long-term contracts. They discovered, for example, that they could reduce more than 100 common page sizes to less than a dozen if they grouped the sizes in clusters and then chose one size for each cluster. This enabled printers to establish standard press settings for faster setup and to purchase paper in standard sizes at minimum cost. They also standardized paper grades and binding styles and materials by types of book.

Unlike magazines, a book publisher could not assign specific books to production slots at the beginning of a contract. However, publishers found that they could predict average monthly production levels by class of book even though they did not know the exact titles to be

[1] Paul D. Doebler, "Standard Practices Play a Role in Cost Management," *EP&P,* December/January 1987, pp. 32–33.

printed each month. So they started writing contracts with printers for blocks of production time to handle specified volumes of work to be produced to predefined standards. Contracts contain unit-pricing structures similar to those in the magazine business. During the contract term, titles are simply assigned production slots. The savings on both sides have been substantial, and costs during the contract life have become predictable.

If your purpose were to gather information to write about how book production was standardized, your paraphrase might read as follows.

Standardized Book Production

More than 40,000 books are published annually in the United States. Until about 15 years ago, each book was produced individually, thus keeping unit printing costs high. At that time, the book industry standardized its products to save on production costs. Publishers and printers agreed to reduce the number of common page sizes from over 100 to fewer than a dozen. This arrangement permitted printers to save time by reducing the number of press settings for faster job startups and to save money by bulk purchasing standard-sized and –graded paper. They made similar savings by reducing binding styles and, as a result, the types of binding materials needed.

If your purpose were to write about how standardization affected the contract arrangements between publishers and printers, your paraphrase might read this way.

Streamlined Book Contracting

About 15 years ago, book publishers and printers standardized book production requirements as a basis for establishing long–term contracts. Prior to standardization, each of the 40,000 books published annually in the United States was bid on competitively by several printers. This process not only made each book expensive to produce, but required publishers to have many purchasing managers and for printers to have numerous job planners and estimators. In a mutual agreement, publishers and printers standardized book sizes from over 100 to fewer than a dozen. Standardization allowed for standard press settings for faster job setups and permitted savings for bulk purchases of standard sized and graded papers and binding materials. Fewer book

sizes also made previously unpredictable contract schedules more predictable because whole classes of books rather
than separate titles could be estimated. Hence, contracts
with printers could be written for blocks of production
time, permitting printers to contain unit costs, assign each
book a production slot, and make costs over the duration of
the contract predictable.

Summarizing

A *summary* is a highly condensed version, in the researcher's own
words, of an original passage. Summary notes present only the essential
ideas or conclusions of the original. As such, they are considerably shorter
than paraphrases of the same passage. As with directly quoted and paraphrased material, the source of summarized information must be credited
in a footnote.

Figure 10–10 shows a note card summary of the following passage.

Now that we have learned something about the nature of elements
and molecules, what are fuels? Fuels are those substances that will
burn when heat is applied to them. Some elements, in themselves,
are fuels. Carbon, hydrogen, sulfur, magnesium, titanium and some
other metals are examples of elements that can burn. Coal, charcoal,
and coke, for example, are almost pure carbon; hydrogen, another
element, is a highly flammable gas. But the most familiar combustible
materials are not pure elements; they are compounds and mixtures.

Wood, paper and grass are principally composed of molecules of
cellulose, a flammable substance. If we examine the chemical makeup
of this compound, we will discover what elements form the basic
fuels in most solid materials. The cellulose molecule contains twenty-
one atoms: six carbons, ten hydrogens and five oxygen atoms: $C_6H_{10}O_5$.
Since oxygen is not flammable (see Oxygen, below), it follows that
the carbon and hydrogen found in most common combustible solids
are the elements that burn. This conclusion becomes even stronger
when we look at common flammable liquids. Gasoline, kerosene, fuel
oils and other petroleum compounds are composed of only carbon
and hydrogen atoms, in varying amounts. These compounds, called
Hydrocarbons (hydrogen + carbon), will all burn.

Other flammable compounds are composed of carbon, hydrogen,
and oxygen atoms in a fixed ratio, making it appear as if there is a
water molecule attached to each carbon atom. A good example is
glucose, a common sugar, which has the formula $C_6H_{12}O_6$. Chemists
call this type of molecule a "hydrated (watered) carbon," or carbohy-
drate. Carbohydrates also burn, but are not to be confused with hydrocarbons.

> Why fuels burn
>
>   The chemical makeup of a substance determines whether it's flammable. Carbon and hydrogen are highly flammable elements, so material made up largely of these elements, called hydrocarbons, are good fuels. Substances made up of carbon, hydrogen, and oxygen, with hydrogen and oxygen in the same proportion as they are in water, are also flammable; they're called carbohydrates. Heat is required before any fuel will burn.
>
>   Meidl, pp. 8-9.

FIGURE 10–10. Note card—summary.

Carbon and hydrogen are only two of the elements which will burn. But, since most common flammable materials contain a combination of carbon and hydrogen fuels, we will limit our discussion of combustion to them at this point.

Fuel, as we have seen, is only one side of the fire triangle. Before it will burn, any fuel requires the addition of heat, another side of the triangle.[2]

Take summary notes to remind yourself of the substance of a research source. Summarized information can also be useful to your reader, because it condenses passages that give more details than the reader needs. (See Chapter 6 for a fuller discussion of summarizing information.)

PLAGIARISM

To use someone else's exact words or original ideas in your writing without giving credit in a reference is known as *plagiarism*. Plagiarism is illegal; in class or on the job it may be grounds for dismissal. Whether the words and ideas come from a published source, or from a fellow student's work, plagiarism is a form of theft for which you can be held accountable.

[2] James H. Meidl, *Flammable Hazardous Materials* (Beverly Hills, Calif.: Glencoe Press, 1970), pp. 8–9.

You may present the words and ideas of another person as long as you give appropriate credit by documenting the passage. Ideas and facts considered "common knowledge" need not be documented. The dates and names of historical events, and many kinds of scientific and statistical information, are common knowledge. Specific examples of common knowledge include the temperature at which water boils, the year the Constitution was ratified, the number of passengers a 747 jetliner can hold, and the area in square miles that Dallas, Texas, occupies.

INTERVIEWING

If you need information that is not readily available in print, you may be able to do some of your research by *interviewing* someone who is an expert on the subject. If, for instance, your subject is nursing-home care in your community, the logical experts to interview would be the directors of several local nursing homes. Sources that can help you decide whom to interview—and how to get in touch with them—include membership lists of professional societies (the membership rolls of large professional organizations are available in many libraries), the yellow pages of the local telephone book, and a firm or organization in your area whose staff includes experts on your subject.

Once you have selected the person or persons you would like to interview, use the following guidelines to help you to obtain the information you need with a minimum of time and trouble for your interviewee and for yourself.

Before the Interview

Always request an interview in advance and make an appointment. You can do so either by telephone or by letter, although a letter may sometimes take too long to permit you to meet a deadline. When you request the interview, explain who you are, what kind of information you are seeking, and why you have chosen to interview this particular expert. Also state that you will schedule the interview at the convenience of the interviewee. Gather some background information about the person and his or her occupation before the interview. You need not exhaust all information sources, of course; let common sense be your guide. How much time will you have before the interview? Is the information difficult to obtain? Be aware, however, that the more preparation you put into an interview, the more you will get out of it.

Your first contact with the interviewee is important because it gives you the opportunity to tell the expert exactly what kind of information you are seeking and allows the interviewee time to prepare for the interview. Some people are made nervous by a tape recorder, so if you would like to use one during the interview, request permission at this point. If the interviewee refuses permission, plan to bring a note pad instead. If you intend to bring a tape recorder, check to see that it's in good working order. However, even a tape recorder that works well can malfunction unexpectedly. Prepare for the worst; bring a writing pad and several pens or pencils to the interview as a backup.

After you have made the appointment, prepare a list of specific questions, based on your writing purpose, that you will ask. Avoid the tendency of the beginning interviewer to ask general rather than specific questions. Analyze your questions to be certain that they are direct and to the point. "Tell me about the kinds of people admitted to Hillcrest Nursing Home" is too broad a request. You will probably get a rambling, general answer in reply. Productive questions would be "What is the average age of persons who come to Hillcrest?" "Are the majority from this vicinity?" "What's the ratio of men to women?" Such queries are much easier to answer than general questions.

Conducting the Interview

Because an interview represents an imposition on someone's time—usually someone who is busy—arrive promptly at the appointed time.

After you arrive and introduce yourself, a few minutes of informal conversation will help both you and the interviewee to relax. But don't drag this period out; an interview is largely straightforward question and response.

During the interview, use the following guidelines:

1. Be pleasant but purposeful. The interviewee knows you are there to get information, so don't be timid about asking your questions. And don't confuse an elementary question on a subject with an ignorant question. If you are too timid, you will go away empty-handed.

2. Refer to the list of questions you prepared in advance, and follow them—don't let yourself become sidetracked. Avoid being rigid, however; if you realize that a prepared question is no longer suitable, go on to the next question.

3. Let the interviewee do most of the talking. Don't try to impress the interviewee with your knowledge of the subject on which he or she is the expert. And don't rebut every point the interviewee makes; after all, you are there to get information, not to debate.

4. Some answers prompt follow-up questions; ask them. "Mr. Bol-chalk, has the automated mail-handling system been as efficient as originally planned?" If the answer is no, you can follow up with "Why?" or "In what specific areas has the system failed?" If the answer is yes, ask details about the differences between the old and the new systems.
5. If the interviewee gets off the subject, be ready with a specific question to direct the conversation back on the track. Your pre-pared list of questions will help.
6. Take only the notes you really need. Obviously, you cannot write down every word of the interview, so concentrate on the important ideas and the key facts and figures. You will be the best judge of how pertinent an idea or a statistic is. If the interviewee is talking too fast, ask him or her to speak more slowly. Anyone who wants to be quoted accurately will be glad to. And if you need a clarification of the facts, politely ask the speaker to explain a point.
7. As the interview is reaching a close, take a few minutes to skim your notes. If you feel there is time, ask for a clarification of anything that is still ambiguous. But be careful not to overstay your welcome.
8. If you use a tape recorder, do not be lulled into a feeling that all your work is being done for you and thereby neglect to ask crucial questions.

After the Interview

As soon as possible after the interview, go over your notes again and fill in any material that is obviously missing. This is the time to summarize the speaker's remarks. Then type or write out the notes in complete sentences. After writing out your notes, select the important information you need and transfer it to your note cards. Observe the same guidelines for creating interview note cards that you used for creat-ing library-research cards. Provide a topic "slug" for each card.

USING A QUESTIONNAIRE

A *questionnaire*—a series of questions on a particular topic, sent out to a number of people—is a sort of interview on paper. It has several advantages over the personal interview, and several disadvantages. A questionnaire allows you to test the thinking of many more people than personal interviews would. It enables you to obtain responses from people in different parts of the country. Even people who live near you may be easier to reach by mail than in person. Those responding to a questionnaire do not face the constant pressure posed by someone jotting down their every word—a fact that could result in more thoughtful answers from questionnaire respondents. And the questionnaire reduces the possibility that the interviewer might influence an answer by tone of voice or facial expression. Finally, the cost of a questionnaire is lower than the cost of numerous personal interviews.

Questionnaires have drawbacks too. People who have strong opinions on a subject are more likely to respond to a questionnaire than those who do not. This factor could slant the results. An interviewer can follow up on an answer with a pertinent question; at best, a questionnaire can be designed to let one question lead logically to another. Furthermore, mailing a batch of questionnaires and waiting for replies take considerably longer than a personal interview does.

The advantages of a questionnaire will work in your favor only if the questionnaire is properly designed. Your goal should be to obtain as much information as possible from your recipients with as little effort on their part as possible. The first rule to follow is to keep the questionnaire brief. The longer the questionnaire is, the less likely the recipient will be to complete and return it. Next, the questions should be easy to understand. A confusing question will yield confusing results, whereas a carefully worded question will be easy to answer. Ideally, questions should be answerable with a "yes" or "no."

```
Would you be willing to work a four-day workweek, ten hours
a day, with every Friday off?

    Yes___

    No___

    No opinion___
```

When it is not possible to phrase questions in such a straightforward style, provide an appropriate range of answers.

```
How many hours of overtime would you be willing to work each
week?

    4 hours___    10 hours___

    6 hours___    More than 10 hours___

    8 hours___    No overtime___
```

And questions should be neutral; they shouldn't be worded in such a way as to lead the respondent to give a particular response.

When preparing your questions, remember that you must eventually tabulate the answers; therefore, try to formulate questions whose answers can be readily computed. The easiest questions to tabulate are those for which the recipient does not have to compose an answer. And questions that require a comment for an answer take time to think about and write. As a result, they lessen your chances of obtaining a response. They are also difficult to interpret. Questionnaires should include a section for additional comments, though, where recipients may clarify their overall attitude toward the subject. If the information will be of value in interpreting the answers, include questions about the recipient's age, education, occupation, and so on. Include your name, your address, the purpose of the questionnaire, and the date by which an answer is needed.

A questionnaire sent by mail must be accompanied by a letter explaining who you are, what purpose the questionnaire will serve, how the questionnaire will be used, and the date by which you would like to receive a reply. If the information provided will be kept confidential, say so in the letter. If the recipient's identity will not be disclosed, state this in the letter too.

Selecting the proper recipients for your questionnaire may be easy or difficult, depending on your needs. If you want to survey the opinions of all the employees in a small shop or a laboratory, you simply send each worker a questionnaire. To survey the members of a club or a profes-

---

October 18, 19--

To: All Company Employees

From: Nelson Barrett, Director *NB*
      Personnel Department

Subject: Review of Flexible Working Hours
         Program

Please complete and return the attached questionnaire regarding Luxwear Corporation's
trial program of flexible working hours. Your
answers will help my staff and me to decide
whether the program is worthwhile enough to
continue permanently.

Return the completed questionnaire to Ken
Rose, Mail Code 12B, by October 28. Your sig-

FIGURE 10–11. Sample questionnaire.

nature on the questionnaire is not necessary. Feel free to raise additional issues pertaining to the program. All responses will be given consideration.

If you want to discuss any item in the questionnaire, call Pam Peters in the Personnel Department at extension 8812.

1. What kind of position do you occupy?

        Supervisory _____

        Nonsupervisory _____

2. Indicate to the nearest quarter of an hour your starting time under flexitime.

7 A.M. _____	8:15 A.M. _____
7:15 A.M. _____	8:30 A.M. _____
7:30 A.M. _____	8:45 A.M. _____
7:45 A.M. _____	9 A.M. _____
8 A.M. _____	Other, specify _____

3. Where do you live?

Talbot County _____	Greene County _____
Montgomery County _____	Other, specify _____

4. How do you usually travel to work?

Drive alone _____	Walk _____
Taxi _____	Bus _____
Train _____	Motorcycle _____
Car pool _____	Other, specify _____
Bicycle _____	

5. Has flexitime affected your commuting time?

FIGURE 10–11, *continued*

Increase: Approx. number of minutes _____ .

Decrease: Approx. number of minutes _____ .

No change _____

6. If you drive alone or in a car pool, has
   flexitime increased or decreased the
   amount of time it takes you to find a
   parking space?

   Increased _____   Decreased _____

   No change _____

7. Has flexitime had an effect on your productivity?

   a. Quality of work

      Increase _____   Decrease _____

      No change _____

   b. Accuracy of work

      Increase _____   Decrease _____

      No change _____

   c. Quiet time for uninterrupted work

      Increase _____   Decrease _____

      No change _____

8. Have you had difficulty getting in touch
   with employees who are on different work
   schedules from yours?

   Yes _____   No _____

9. Have you had trouble scheduling meetings
   within flexible starting and quitting
   times?

   Yes _____   No _____

FIGURE 10–11, *continued*

10. Has flexitime affected the way you feel about your job?

Feel better about   Feel worse about
job   job

Slightly _____   Slightly _____

Considerably _____ Considerably _____

No change _____

11. How important is it for you to have flexibility in your working hours?

Very _____   Not very _____

Somewhat _____   Not at all _____

12. Has flexitime allowed you more time to be with your family?

Yes _____   No _____

13. If you are responsible for the care of a young child or children, has flexitime made it easier or more difficult for you to obtain babysitting or day-care services?

Easier _____   More difficult _____

No change _____

14. Do you recommend that the flexitime program be made permanent?

Yes _____   No _____

15. Do you have suggestions for major changes in the program?

Yes (please specify)   No _____

THANK YOU FOR YOUR ASSISTANCE

FIGURE 10–11, *continued*

sional society, you would mail questionnaires to those who are on a membership list. But to survey the opinions of large groups in the general population—for example, all medical technologists working in private laboratories, or all independent garage owners—is not so easy. Since you cannot include everybody in your survey, you would have to choose a representative cross-section. How would you go about selecting such a cross-section, and how large should such a sample be? Methods of large-scale sampling are beyond the scope of this text. The best sources of information on sampling techniques are research and statistics texts.

The sample questionnaire in Figure 10–11 was sent to employees in a large organization who had participated in a six-month program of flexible working hours. Under the program, employees worked a 40-hour, five-day week, with flexible starting and quitting times. Employees could start the work day between 7 and 9 A.M. and leave between 3:30 and 6:30 P.M., provided that they worked a total of eight hours each day and took a one-half-hour lunch period midway through the day.

OTHER SOURCES OF INFORMATION

Two additional sources of information may prove fruitful in providing you with materials for your research: first-hand observation and experience, and free or inexpensive materials from private and governmental agencies and organizations.

First-Hand Observation and Experience

Why not interview yourself? If your topic deals with something you know well (a hobby or an area of interest, for example), or relates to an occupation you are in or hope to be in, you may already have enough information to get started. Check your home or office for any materials you have acquired on the subject. From your knowledge of the topic, make a rough outline—it will tell you how much you know about the topic, which areas you are strong in, and which areas you are weak in. When your flow of ideas turns to a trickle and then stops, you can expand your knowledge from the other sources discussed in this chapter. For topics that involve a great deal of factual data, you should, in addition, check the accuracy of any facts and figures that you aren't certain about.

Free or Inexpensive Materials from Private and Governmental Agencies and Organizations

In your search for materials on your topic, do not overlook the field of private and governmental agencies and organizations. These include corporations, business and professional associations, nonprofit organizations, and the numerous bureaus and offices of the federal, state, and local governments. Most of these sources distribute free or inexpensive material on virtually any subject. A reference librarian can show you how to go about obtaining material from the agencies and organizations.

When you request information from governmental or private organizations, you must be specific in describing the material or materials you are seeking. If you know the title of a pamphlet or a booklet you want, refer to the title, and to any other information that will serve to identify the pamphlet, in your letter requesting the item. If you are aware that there is a charge for the material, send a check or money order with the request. Doing so will save time for both you and the recipient, because it won't be necessary for the organization to write to you asking for payment before it can send you the materials. One final note: requests for information from private and governmental agencies are usually handled by mail, and postal deliveries can be slow. Therefore, do not rely too heavily on such materials for your research, because the deadline for your written work may arrive before the requested material does.

DOCUMENTATION

By documenting their sources, writers identify where they obtained the facts, ideas, quotations, and paraphrases they have used in preparing a written document. This information can come from books, manuals, correspondence, interviews, software documentation, reference works, and many other kinds of sources. Full, accurate, and consistent documentation allows readers to locate the source of the information given and to find further information on the subject. It also gives proper credit to others so that the writer avoids plagiarism. The sources of all facts and ideas that are not common knowledge to the intended audience should be documented, as should the sources of all direct quotations.

There are three principal methods of documenting sources: (1) *parenthetical documentation*—putting brief citations in parentheses in the text and providing full information in a list of "Works Cited"; (2) *numbered references*—referring to sources with numbers in parentheses or by superscripts in the text and providing full information in a "References" section where the entries are listed numerically in the order of their first citation in the text; and (3) *notes*—using superscript numbers in the text to refer to notes either at the bottom of the page (footnotes) or at the end of the paper, article, or chapter (endnotes). Whatever format you choose, be sure to follow it consistently, in every detail of order, punctuation, and capitalization.

Sometimes a *bibliography* is included at the end of a work. A bibliography is a list of books, articles, or other sources arranged alphabetically at the end of a report or research paper. A bibliography differs from Works Cited, References, or endnotes in that it includes works consulted for background information, in addition to those actually cited in text. For that reason, a bibliography is appropriate only as a supplement to material already listed. The format of entries in a bibliography is identical to that used in the Works Cited or References sections.

Parenthetical Documentation

The following pages describe the parenthetical method recommended by the Modern Language Association of America (MLA) in the *MLA Handbook for Writers of Research Papers, 2nd ed.* This method gives an abbreviated reference to a source parenthetically in text and lists full information about the source in a separate section called "Works Cited."

When documenting sources in text, include only the author and page number in parentheses. If the author's name is mentioned in the text, include only the page number of the source. The parenthetical citation should include no more information than is necessary to enable the reader to relate it to the corresponding entry in the list of "Works Cited." When referring to an entire work rather than to a particular page in a work, mention the author's name in the text, and omit the parenthetical citation.

The following passages contain sample parenthetical citations.

```
Steve Wozniak's first computer was the so-called Cream Soda
Computer, which he and a friend built in 1971, staying up
all night and drinking cream soda (Freiberger and Swaine
205).

According to Freiberger and Swaine, the development of the
BASIC programming language by two Dartmouth professors in
1964 gave ordinary people the means of using the computing
power put in their hands by microprocessor technology and
its commercial exploitation (140).
```

When placing parenthetical citations in text, insert them between the closing quotation mark or the last word of the sentence (or clause) and the period or other punctuation. Use the spacing shown above. If the parenthetical citation follows an extended quotation or paraphrase, however, place it outside the last sentence of the quotation or paraphrase, followed by two spaces between the period and the first parenthesis. Within the citation itself, allow one space (no punctuation) between the name of the author and the page number. Don't use the word *page* or its abbreviation.

If you are citing a page or pages of a multivolume work, give the volume number, followed by a colon, space, and page number (Jones 2: 53). If the entire volume is being cited, identify the author and volume as follows: Smith, vol. 3.

If your list of "Works Cited" includes more than one work by the same author, include the title of the work (or a shortened version if the title is long) in the parenthetical citation, unless you mention it in the text. If, for example, your list of "Works Cited" included more than one work by Alvin von Auw, a proper parenthetical citation for his book *Heritage and Destiny: Reflections on the Bell System in Transition* would appear as in the following sample:

```
In the late seventies, a conflict arose between the Bell
System's engineers and its ''marketeers'' over whether
R & D should determine what the sales force had to market
or marketing research should determine what the technolo-
gists would develop (von Auw, Heritage and Destiny 172-73).
```

Use only one space between the title and the page number.

The works cited in the sample passages given would be listed alphabetically, as follows, in a "Works Cited" section:

```
Freiberger, Paul, and Michael Swaine. Fire in the Valley:
     The Making of the Personal Computer. Berkeley: Osborne/
     McGraw-Hill, 1984.

von Auw, Alvin. Heritage and Destiny: Reflections on the
     Bell System in Transition. New York: Praeger, 1983.
```

The following section explains the content and format of entries in a list of "Works Cited." The format style described is that recommended in the *MLA Handbook for Writers of Research Papers,* 2/e.

Citation Format for Works Cited.   The list of "Works Cited" should begin on the first new page following the end of the text. Each new entry should begin at the left margin, with the second and subsequent lines within an entry indented five spaces. Single-space within entries, and double-space between them.

Author.   Entries appear in alphabetical order by the author's last name (by the last name of the first author if the work has more than one author). Works by the same author should be alphabetized by the first major word of the title (following *a, an,* or *the*). If the author is a corporation, the entry should be alphabetized by the name of the corporation; if the author is a government agency, entries are alphabetized by the government, followed by the agency (for example, "United States. Dept. of Health and Human Services."). Some require more than one agency name (for example, "United States. Dept. of Labor. Bureau of Labor Statistics "). If no author is given, the entry should begin with the title and be alphabetized by the first significant word in the title. (Articles in reference works, like encyclopedias, are sometimes signed with initials; you will find a list of the contributors' initials and full names elsewhere in the work, probably near the introductory material or the index.)

After the first listing for an author, put three hyphens in place of the name for the subsequent entries with the same author. An editor's name is followed by the abbreviation, ed.

McNeill, William H. The Pursuit of Power. Chicago: U of Chicago P, 1982.
———, The Rise of the West. Chicago: U of Chicago P, 1963.

Title. The second element is the title of the work. Capitalize the first word and each significant word thereafter. Underline the title of a book or pamphlet. Place quotation marks around the title of an article in a periodical, an essay in a collection, and a paper in a proceedings. Each title should be followed by a period.

Periodicals. For an article in a periodical (journal, magazine, or newspaper), the volume number (for a magazine or newspaper, simply the date), and the page numbers should immediately follow the title of the periodical. See the sample entries for proper punctuation.

Series or Multivolume Works. For works in a series and multivolume works, the name of the series and the series number of the work in question, or the number of volumes, should follow the title. If the edition used is not the first, the edition should be specified.

Publishing Information. The final elements of the entry for a book, pamphlet, or conference proceedings are the place of publication, publisher, and date of publication. If any of these cannot be found in the work, use the abbreviations n.p. (no publication place), n.p. (no publisher), and n.d. (no date), respectively. For familiar reference works, list only the edition and year of publication.

Following are some sample entries.

Book with One Author

von Auw, Alvin. Heritage and Destiny: Reflections on the Bell System in Transition. New York: Praeger, 1983.

Book with Two or More Authors

Freiberger, Paul, and Michael Swaine. Fire in the Valley: The Making of the Personal Computer. Berkeley: Osborne/ McGraw-Hill, 1984.

Book with a Corporate Author

NEC Home Electronics. PC-8201A User's Guide. Tokyo: NEC, 1983.

Translated Book

Cardos, Fernando Henrique, and Enzo Faletto. Dependency and Development in Latin America. Trans. Marjory Mattingly Urquidi. Berkeley: U of California P, 1979.

Book Edition, If Not the First

Galbraith, John Kenneth. The Affluent Society. 3rd ed. Boston: Houghton Mifflin, 1976.

Multivolume Book

Faber, Mike, and Dudley Seers, eds. The Crisis in Planning. 2 vols. London: Chatto and Windus, 1972.

Book in a Series

Kendrick, John W., and Beatrice N. Vaccar. New Developments in Productivity Measurement and Analysis. Studies in Income and Wealth 44. Chicago: U of Chicago P, 1980.

Work in an Edited Collection

Mundell, Robert A. ''International Monetary Reform: The Optimal Mix in Big Countries.'' Macroeconomics, Prices, and Quantities: Essays in Memory of Arthur M. Okun. Ed. James Tobin, Washington, DC: Brookings Institution, 1983. 285-95.

Report

United States. Dept. of Labor. Bureau of Labor Statistics. Publications of the Bureau of Labor Statistics July–December 1980. Report 641. Washington, DC: US Dept. of Labor, 1981.

Proceedings

De Schutter, J., and G. Bemer, eds. Fundamental Aspects of Appropriate Technology. Proc. of the International Workshop on Appropriate Technology. 4–7 Sept. 1980. Delft, Neth.: Delft UP, 1980.

Paper in a Proceedings

Carr, Marilyn. ''Appropriate Technology: Theory, Policy and Practice.'' Fundamental Aspects of Appropriate Technology. Proc. of the International Workshop on Appropriate Technology. 4–7 Sept. 1980. Ed. J. de Schutter and G. Bemer. Delft, Neth.: Delft UP, 1980. 145–53.

Paper Presented at a Conference

Van Pelt, William. ''Microcomputers and the Business Writing Classroom.'' Midwest Regional Conference, Association for Business Communication. Milwaukee, 18 Apr. 1985.

Journal Article

Stevens, William P., Kathleen C. Stevens, and William Raabe, Jr. ''Communication in Accounting: Readability of F.A.S.B. Statements.'' Review of Business and Economic Research 19 (1983): 110–18.

Magazine Article

Wantuck, Mary–Margaret. ''Bottom Line 101.'' Nation's Business Oct. 1985: 24–32.

Anonymous Article (in Weekly Periodical)

''Western Union Ties PCs and Data Service.'' Infoworld 20 Jan. 1986: 48.

Newspaper Article (On Discontinuous Pages)

> Chira, Susan. ''Minebea: Takeover Quandary.'' New York
>   Times 19 Oct. 1985, national ed.: 21+.

Encyclopedia Entry

> Tannenbaum, Morris. ''Automation.'' Encyclopaedia Britan-
>   nica: Macropaedia. 15th ed. 1982.

Thesis or Dissertation

> Kyj, Myroslaw J. ''The Meaning and Uses of Customer Service
>   in Industrial Products Markets.'' Diss. Temple U. 1985.

Letter from One Official to Another

> Brown, Charles L. Letter to retired members of Bell System
>   Presidents' Conference. 8 January 1982.

Letter Personally Received

> Harris, Robert S. Letter to the author. 3 December 1985.

Personal Interview

> Denlinger, Virgil, Assistant Chief of Police, Alexandria,
>   VA. Personal interview. 15 March 1980.

Computer Software

> Cohen, Michael, and Richard Lanham. Homer: A Computerized
>   Revision Program. Computer Software. Scribner's 1983.
>   Apple II series, 48K for II+ or II, 64K for IIe, disk.

Numbered References

In much scientific and technical writing, the form used to give credit to your information sources differs from the form used in other fields. Information sources are listed in a separate section called "References." The entries in the reference section frequently are arranged according to the order in which they are first referred to in the text. In this system, number 1 in parentheses (1) after a quotation or a reference to a book or an article refers the reader to the information in the first entry in the reference section, number 2 in parentheses (2) refers the reader to the second entry in the reference section, and so on. A second number in parentheses, separated from the first by a colon, indicates the page number in the report or book from which the information was taken— for example, the notation "(3:27)" in the text indicates that the material is found on page 27 of entry 3 in the reference section.

The reference section for relatively short reports appears at the end of the report. For reports with a number of major sections or chapters, the reference section appears at the end of the section or the chapter. (See Chapter 11 for information on the placement of a reference section in a formal report.)

The details of reference systems in the sciences vary widely from field to field. Although the following examples are common in scientific and technical publications, consult publications in your field for precise details.

Book

```
1. Landes, D. S. Revolution in time: clocks and the making
   of the modern world. Cambridge, MA: Belknap/Harvard UP:
   1983.
```

Note that the last name appears first, followed by one or two initials. In the title of the work, only the first word and proper nouns are capitalized, and underlining is not used.

Journal Article

```
2. MacDonald, N. H., Frase, L. T., Gingrich, P. S. and Keenan,
   S. A. The writer's workbench: computer aids for text anal-
   ysis. IEEE Transactions in Communications, 1982, 30:
   105–110.
```

Only the first word and proper nouns in the article title are capitalized, and no quotation marks are used. The journal name is not underlined.

Notes

Notes in publications have two uses: (1) to provide background information or explanations that would interrupt the flow of thought in the text and (2) to provide documentation references.

Explanatory Footnotes. Explanatory or content notes are useful when the basis for an assumption should be made explicit but spelling it out in the text might make readers lose the flow of an argument.

Because explanatory or content notes can be distracting, however, they should be kept to a minimum. If you cannot work the explanatory or background material into your text, it may not belong there. Lengthy explanations should be placed in an appendix.

Documentation Notes. Notes that document sources can appear as either endnotes or footnotes. Endnotes are placed in a separate section at the end of a report, article, chapter, or book; footnotes (including explanatory notes) are placed at the bottom of a text page. Endnotes are easy to type, but readers may find them inconvenient to find and difficult to correlate with the text. Footnotes are tricky to type unless you have a word-processing program that automatically allocates the right amount of space at the bottom of each page. They are, however, convenient for readers.

Use superscript numbers in the text to refer readers to notes, and number them consecutively from the beginning of the report, article, or chapter to the end. Place each superscript number at the end of a sentence, clause, or phrase, at a natural pause point like this,[1] right after the period, comma, or other punctuation mark (except a dash, which the number should precede[2]—as here).

Footnote Format. To type footnotes, leave two line spaces beneath the text on a page, and indent the first line of each footnote five spaces. Begin each note with the appropriate superscript number, and skip one space between the number and the text of the footnote. If the footnote runs longer than one line, the second and subsequent lines should begin at the left margin. Single-space within each footnote, and double-space between footnotes.

```
Assume that this is the last line of text on a page.


    ¹Begin the first footnote at this position. When it runs
longer than one line, begin the second and all following
lines at the left margin.

    ²The second footnote follows the same spacing as the
first. Single-space within footnotes, and double-space be-
tween them.
```

Endnote Format. Endnotes should begin on a separate page entitled "Works Cited" or "References" after the end of the text. The individual notes should be typed as for footnotes. Single-space within notes, and double-space between them, as with footnotes.

CHAPTER SUMMARY

Many information sources are available to you as you research job-related topics. Libraries provide the most complete, systematically arranged body of information. Other sources include the personal interview, the questionnaire, knowledge gained from personal experience, and materials available to you from private and governmental organizations.

The *library* provides the tools for you to find books, articles, reference works, and other materials for your research. Once you have located the materials available in the library, take careful notes and record the sources of your information.

A personal interview with an expert can provide you with up-to-date information not readily available in printed material. Select the person to interview, and obtain some background information on the interviewee. Prepare a list of specific questions to ask; take brief, memory-jogging notes of the answers; and summarize the notes in writing after the interview.

A questionnaire permits you to obtain the views of a group of people without having to go to the time and expense necessary for numerous personal interviews. Take full advantage of the increased number of views a questionnaire provides, and design the questionnaire to produce as much information as you will need without its being a burden to answer. Keep the number of questions brief, and word each one carefully so that the answers marked can be summarized conveniently for your purposes. In a letter accompanying the questionnaire, inform the recipient of who you are, the purpose of the questionnaire, the use to which the answers will be put, and the date by which you would like the questionnaire returned.

Other sources of information include your own knowledge and experience, and the pamphlets, booklets, reports, and other materials provided by companies, professional or trade associations, public-interest groups, and various governmental agencies. To tap your own resources, jot down what you know about a topic and supplement this information with any materials you have available at home or at work. Organize your notes into a rough outline. On the basis of this outline, you can determine particular areas where additional information is needed. You can also pinpoint areas that need to be double-checked for accuracy. A reference librarian can help you to identify the types of information available from private organizations and governmental agencies. Be as specific as possible when you write for this type of material, and enclose any fees that may be required. Allow time for mail handling so that the information will arrive when you need it.

Give complete and accurate credit to all your information sources. Failure to do so will make you guilty of *plagiarism*. Information you quote, paraphrase, or summarize in your text must be documented (1) in brief parenthetical citations in text, with full information in an alphabetical list of "Works Cited"; (2) in numbered references in text that refer to full information in a "References" section where citations are listed numerically in the order of their first citation in text; or (3) in notes that appear either at the bottoms of text pages (footnotes) or in a separate section at the end of a chapter or section (endnotes).

EXERCISES

Note: The exercises in this chapter may be used as the basis for the preparation of a formal report according to the guidelines presented in Chapter 11.

1. Select a topic from your career field or other area of interest. Using the card catalog in your library, locate five books on your topic. Prepare a separate three-by-five-inch bibliography card for each book. (If you prefer, you may use, instead of a note card, a sheet of paper ruled into three-by-five-inch segments.) Follow the instructions on pages 263–265 for preparing a bibliography card for a book.

2. Using the periodical index or indexes in your library, locate five articles, from magazines, newspapers, or journals, on the topic you chose for Exercise 1. Prepare a separate three-by-five-inch bibliography card for each item (or use a ruled sheet of paper as described in Exercise 1). Follow the instructions on pages 263–265 for preparing a bibliography card for an article.

3. If your college library provides computerized information retrieval services, list five data bases the library has access to that are pertinent to your field of study. Note how many periodicals or other sources of information each data base contains, and indicate how frequently each data base is updated. List three periodicals from each data base that publishes articles in your field of study.

4. *Paraphrase* each of the two following paragraphs on a four-by-six-inch note card (or use a sheet of paper ruled into four-by-six-inch segments). Then, on a separate note card, *summarize* the information from each paragraph. Identify each card with a "slug" that states the topic and indicate the source from which the information was obtained.

a. To keep pipes from freezing, wrap the pipes in insulation made especially for water pipes, or in layers of old newspaper, lapping the ends and tying them around the pipes. Cover the newspapers with plastic to keep out moisture. When it is extremely cold and there is real danger of freezing, let the faucets drip a little. Although this wastes water, it may prevent freezing damage. Know where the valve for shutting off the water coming into the house or apartment is located. You may as a last resort have to shut off this main valve and drain all the pipes to keep them from freezing and bursting.[3]

b. The Federal Energy Administration (FEA) estimated in 1976 that annual energy use in the United States was about 75 quadrillion BTUs (or 75 quads), and that use by 1985 would be 98.9 quads. The agency also estimated that even under the most favorable conditions the U.S. cannot expect to gain more than 6 quads from emerging technology by 1990. A more realistic figure, it indicated, might be 2 quads.

The emerging technologies evaluated by FEA included solar, geothermal, and synthetic fuels, but evidently excluded forest biomass. Energy currently obtained from wood is estimated at 1.1 to 1.7 quads. Members of the task force are confident that wood use for energy is increasing greatly, but we have no way of knowing the extent.[4]

5. Using the topic you chose in Exercise 1, complete one or both of the following assignments, depending on your instructor's requirements: (1) create a ten-item sample questionnaire that you could use to gather information on the subject, or (2) interview someone knowledgeable about the subject and submit your rewritten and organized notes of the interview to your instructor. Also submit one of the following with your assignment, as appropriate: a letter to accompany your questionnaire or a letter requesting an interview.

6. Prepare a brief parenthetical citation for each of the following reference items and then create an alphabetically arranged list of "Works Cited" containing full information about each citation.

a. A magazine article beginning on page 80 and ending on page 86 of the April 1987 issue of *Inc.*, by Joshua Hyatt, entitled "Healthy Returns." Your reference is on page 81.

---

[3] Department of Energy, *Winter Survival: A Consumer's Guide to Winter Preparedness* (Washington, D.C.: Government Printing Office, 1978), p. 3.

[4] "Forest Biomass as an Energy Source: Study Report of a Task Force of the Society of American Foresters," *Journal of Forestry* 77, 1979, p. 3.

b. An unsigned "Face-to-Face" interview column in *Inc.* The column runs from pages 23 to 28 and you cite information from page 28.

c. Herman Holtz's book *How to Succeed as an Independent Consultant,* published by John Wiley & Sons in New York in 1983. Your reference is on page 151.

d. An article in *The Washington Post* entitled "Remodeling Is Increasingly Popular," by H. Jane Lehman. The article begins on page 1 and ends on page 10 of Section E of the April 25, 1987, issue. Your citation is on page E-2.

e. A booklet entitled "Exercise and Your Heart," by the Public Health Service of the U.S. Department of Health and Human Services and published in Washington, D.C. by the Government Printing Office in 1983. Your reference is on page 21.

f. Your interview of the City Manager of Plain View, Texas, on March 1, 1987. Her namè is Annette Diggs.

g. An article entitled "Integrating Online Documentation Into the Technical Publishing Process," by Thomas R. Bastrow and Joseph T. Haynes, that appears on pages 37 through 41 of the journal *IEEE Transactions on Professional Communication.* It appears in the December 1986 issue of the journal, volume PC-29, Number 4. You cite information on pages 38 and 39.

h. Computer software distributed by the NCR Corporation in 1984. Issued in disk form, it uses the CP/M 2.2 operating system and is called FirstWord II.

i. The third edition of the reference book *The Penguin Dictionary of Computers* by A. Chandor, J. Grahm, and R. Williamson. The dictionary was published in New York in 1985 by Penguin Books. You cite material from the introduction on page xiii.

j. An article from the 1987 (sixth) edition of the *McGraw-Hill Encyclopedia of Science and Technology,* entitled "Lubricant."

11

Formal Reports

Formal reports are the written accounts of major projects. Projects that are likely to generate a formal report include research into new developments in a field, explorations of the advisability of launching a new product or an expanded service, or an end-of-year review of developments within an organization. The scope and complexity of the project will determine how long and how complex the report will be. Most formal reports—certainly those that are long and complex—require a carefully planned structure that provides the reader with an easy-to-recognize guide to the material in the report. Such aids to the reader as a table of contents, a list of illustrations, and an abstract (brief summary of the report) serve to make the information in the report more accessible. Making a formal topic outline, which lists the major facts and ideas in the report and indicates their relationship to one another, should help you to write a well-organized report.

Most formal reports are divided into three major parts—front matter, body, and back matter—each of which, in turn, contains a number of elements. Just how many elements are needed for a particular report depends on the subject, the length of the report, and the kinds of material covered.

ORDER OF ELEMENTS IN A FORMAL REPORT

The arrangement of the elements in a formal report may vary. Many companies and governmental and other institutions have a preferred style for formal reports and furnish guidelines that staff members must follow. If your employer has prepared a set of style guidelines, follow it; if not, use the format recommended in this chapter. The following list includes most of the elements a formal report might contain.

Transmittal Letter or Memorandum (precedes front matter)

Front Matter
  Title page
  Abstract
  Table of contents
  List of figures
  List of tables
  Preface
  List of abbreviations and symbols

Body
  Summary
  Introduction
  Text (including headings)
  Conclusions
  Recommendations
  Explanatory footnotes
  References

Back Matter
  Bibliography
  Appendixes
  Glossary

TRANSMITTAL LETTER OR MEMORANDUM

When you submit a formal report, you should include with it a brief transmittal (or cover) letter or memorandum that identifies what you are sending and why you are sending it. The letter or memorandum should contain the title of the report, and it may briefly describe it, explain why it was written, and acknowledge significant help received during its preparation.

Written in the form of a standard business letter or memorandum, this transmittal material most often opens with a brief paragraph (one or two sentences) explaining what is being sent and why. The next paragraph contains a brief summary of the report's contents or stresses some feature that would be important to the reader. The correspondence may also mention any special conditions under which the material was prepared (limitations of time or money, for instance). The closing paragraph may acknowledge any help received in preparing the report, or express the hope that the information fulfills its purpose.

These elements are typical of many transmittal letters and memorandums. They should be brief—usually one page. The report that the letter or memorandum accompanies should speak for itself. Examples of long and short transmittal letters are shown in Figures 8–6 and 8–7.

FRONT MATTER

The *front matter,* which includes all the elements that precede the body of the report, serves several purposes: it gives the reader a general idea of the author's purpose in writing the report; it indicates whether the report contains the kind of information that the reader is looking for; and it lists where in the report the reader can find specific chapters, headings, illustrations, and tables. Not all formal reports require every one of these elements. A title page and table of contents are usually mandatory, but whether an abstract, a preface, and lists of figures, tables, abbreviations, and symbols are included will depend on the scope of the report and its intended audience. The front matter pages are numbered with lowercase Roman numerals. Throughout the report, page numbers should be centered near the bottom of each page.

Title Page

The formats of title pages for formal reports vary, but the page should include the following information.

1. *Full title of the report.* The title should indicate the topic and announce the scope and objective of the report. Titles often provide the only basis on which readers can decide whether or not to read a report. Titles too vague or too long not only hinder readers but can prevent efficient filing and information retrieval by librarians and other information specialists. Follow these guidelines when creating the title:

   • Avoid titles that begin "Notes on . . . ," "Studies on . . . ," "A Report on . . . ," or "Observations on. . . ." These notions are evident to the reader. On the other hand, phrases like "Annual Report . . ." or "Feasibility Study . . ." should be used in a

title or subtitle because such information defines purpose and scope.
- Do not use abbreviations in the title. Use acronyms only when the report is intended for an audience familiar enough with the topic that the acronym will not confuse them.
- Do not include the period covered by a report in the title; include that information in a subtitle:

```
EFFECTS OF PROPOSED HIGHWAY
CONSTRUCTION ON PROPERTY VALUES
       Annual Report, 19--
```

2. *Name of the writer, principal investigator, or compiler.* Frequently contributors simply list their names. Sometimes they identify themselves by their job title in the organization (Jane R. Doe, Cost Analyst; Jack T. Doe, Head, Research and Development). Sometimes contributors identify themselves by their tasks in contributing to the report (Jane R. Doe, Compiler; Jack T. Doe, Principal Investigator).
3. *Date or dates of the report.* For one-time reports, you should list the date when the report is to be distributed. For periodic reports, which may be issued monthly or quarterly, list the time period that the present report covers, in a subtitle, as well as the date when the report is to be distributed.
4. *Name of the organization* for *which the writer works.*
5. *Name of the organization or individual* to *which the report is being submitted,* if the work is being done for a customer or client.

These categories are standard on most title pages. Some organizations may require additional information. A sample title page appears in Figure 11–1.

The title page, although unnumbered, is considered page i (small Roman numeral 1). The subsequent pages of the front matter are numbered beginning with page ii.

Abstracts

An abstract is a condensed version of a longer work that summarizes and highlights the major points, enabling the prospective reader to decide whether the work in full is worth reading. Usually 200 to 250 words long, an abstract must make sense independently of the work it summarizes. Depending on the kind of information they contain, abstracts are usually classified as either *descriptive* or *informative.*

The Long–Term Effects of Long–Distance Running
on the Bones and Joints of Male and Female Runners
Aged 50 to 72 Years

Prepared by
Sandra Young, Consultant

Report Distributed: April 15, 19––

Prepared for
Amalgamated Life Insurance Company

FIGURE 11–1. Sample title page.

Descriptive Abstracts.   A descriptive abstract includes information about the purpose, scope, and methods used to arrive at the findings contained in the report. It is thus a slightly expanded table of contents in sentence form. Provided that it adequately summarizes the information, a descriptive abstract need not be longer than several sentences. (See Figure 11–2.)

Informative Abstracts.   An informative abstract is an expanded version of the descriptive abstract. In addition to information about the purpose, scope, and methods of the original report, the informative abstract includes the results, conclusions, and recommendations, if any. The informative abstract thus retains the tone and essential scope of the report while omitting its details.

Which of the two types of abstract should you write? The answer depends on the organization for which you are writing. If it has a policy, comply with it. Otherwise, aim to satisfy the needs of the principal readers of your report. Informative abstracts satisfy the needs of the widest possible readership, but descriptive abstracts are preferable for information surveys, progress reports that combine information from more than one project, and any report that compiles a variety of information. For these types of reports, conclusions and recommendations either do not exist in the original or are too numerous to include in an abstract. Figure 11–3 shows an informative abstract, which is an expanded version of the descriptive abstract shown in Figure 11–2.

Scope.   Include the following kinds of information in an abstract, but bear in mind that at this point your readers know nothing, except what your title announces, about your report:

- The subject of the study
- The scope of the study
- The purpose of the study
- The methods used
- The results obtained (informative abstract only)
- The recommendations made, if any (informative abstract only)

Do not include the following kinds of information:

- A detailed discussion or explanation of the methods used
- Administrative details about how the study was undertaken, who funded it, who worked on it, and the like, unless such details have a bearing on the purpose of the report
- Illustrations, tables, charts, maps, and bibliographic references
- Any information that does not appear in the original

ABSTRACT

      This report investigates the long–term effects
of long–distance running on the bones, joints, and
general health of runners aged 50 to 72. The Amalga-
Purpose   mated Life Insurance Company sponsored this investigation, first to decide whether to underwrite life
insurance for the 19–– U.S. Olympic Marathon Team,
and second to inform its clients about whether long-
distance running is harmful or beneficial to their
health. The investigation is based on recent studies
conducted at Stanford University and the University
Method   of Florida. The Stanford study tested and compared
and   male and female long–distance runners between 50 and
Scope   72 years of age with a control group of runners and
nonrunners. The groups were also matched by sex,
race, education, and occupation. The Florida study
used only male runners who had run at least 20 miles
a week for five years and compared them with a group
of runners and nonrunners. Both studies based findings on medical histories and on physical and x–ray
examinations.

FIGURE 11–2. Descriptive abstract.

ABSTRACT

Purpose

This report investigates the long-term effects
of long-distance running on the bones, joints, and
general health of runners aged 50 to 72. The Amalgamated Life Insurance Company sponsored this investigation, first to decide whether to underwrite life
insurance for the 19—— U.S. Olympic Marathon Team,
and second to inform its clients about whether long-
distance running is harmful or beneficial to their
health. The investigation is based on recent studies

Method
and
Scope

conducted at Stanford University and the University
of Florida. The Stanford study tested and compared
male and female long-distance runners between 50 and
72 years of age with a control group of runners and
nonrunners. The groups were also matched by sex,
race, education, and occupation. The Florida study
used only male runners who had run at least 20 miles
a week for five years and compared them with a group
of runners and nonrunners. Both studies based findings on medical histories and on physical and x-ray
examinations. Both studies conclude that long-distance running is not associated with increased degenerative joint disease. Control groups were more prone

Expanded
Methodology
Discussion

to spur formation, sclerosis, and joint-space narrowing and showed more joint degeneration than runners. Female long-distance runners had somewhat more
sclerosis in knee joints and the lumbar spine area
than matched control subjects. Both studies support
the role of exercise in retarding bone loss with aging
and recommend exercise programs. The investigation
concludes that the life insurance risk factors are
smaller for long-distance runners than for those less
active between the ages of 50 and 72. The investigation recommends that Amalgamated Life Insurance Co.

Conclusions
and Recom-
mendations

underwrite life insurance policies for the 19—— U.S.
Olympic Marathon Team and inform its clients that
an exercise program that includes long-distance running can be beneficial to their health.

FIGURE 11–3. Informative abstract.

Because abstracts may be published independently of the main document, it would make no sense if they referred to any visual material found in the report; therefore, the abstract must make no reference to such material.

Writing Style.   Write the abstract after finishing the report. Otherwise, the abstract may not accurately reflect the original. Begin with a topic sentence that announces at least the subject and scope of the report. Then, using the major and minor heads of your table of contents to distinguish primary from secondary ideas, decide what material is relevant to your abstract. Write clearly and concisely, eliminating unnecessary words and ideas, but do not become so terse that you omit articles (*a, an, the*) and important transitional words (*however, therefore, but, in summary*). Write in complete sentences but avoid stringing a group of short sentences end to end; instead, combine ideas by using subordination and parallel structure. As a rule, spell out most acronyms and all but the most common abbreviations (C°, F°, mph). Finally, as you summarize, keep the tone and emphasis consistent with the original report. For additional information, see "Summarizing Information" in Chapter 6.

An abstract normally follows the title page and is numbered page ii.

Table of Contents

A table of contents lists all the headings or sections of the report in their order of appearance, along with their page numbers. It includes a listing of all front matter and back matter except the title page and the table of contents itself. The table of contents begins on a new page. Note that in Figure 11–4 the table of contents is numbered page iii because it follows the title page (page i) and the abstract (page ii).

Along with the abstract, a table of contents permits the reader to preview the contents of a report and to assess its value. It also aids a reader who may want to look only at certain sections of the report. For this reason, the wording of chapter and section titles in the table of contents should be identical to those in the text.

Sometimes, the table of contents is followed by lists of the figures and tables contained in the report. These lists should always be presented separately, and a page number should be given for each item (see Figure 11–4).

TABLE OF CONTENTS

ABSTRACT   ii
LIST OF TABLES iv

SUMMARY 1
INTRODUCTION 3
THE RESEARCH 4

        The Stanford Study 7
        The Florida Study 9

THE RESULTS 11
CONCLUSIONS AND RECOMMENDATIONS 16

BIBLIOGRAPHY 18

FIGURE 11–4. Sample table of contents.

Preface

The preface is an optional introductory statement that announces the purpose, background, or scope of the report. Sometimes a preface specifies the audience for whom the report is intended, and it may also highlight the relationship of the report to a given project or program. A preface may contain acknowledgments of help received during the course of the project or in the preparation of the report, and, finally, it may cite permission obtained for the use of copyrighted works. If a preface is not included, place this type of information, if it is essential, in the introduction (discussed later in this chapter).

The preface follows the table of contents (and the lists of figures or tables, if these are present). It begins on a separate page titled "Preface."

List of Abbreviations and Symbols

When the abbreviations and symbols used in a report are numerous, and when there is a chance that the reader will not be able to interpret them, the front matter should include a list of all abbreviations and symbols and what they stand for in the report. Such a list, which follows the preface, is particularly appropriate for technical reports whose audience is not restricted to technicians.

Figure 11–5 shows a list of symbols that appear in a report as part of equations that calculate the transfer of heat and water vapor from the surface of cooling ponds. The list is made up of symbols unique to this report. The author assumes that the report readers have a technical education, however, because Btu (British thermal unit), Hg (chemical symbol for mercury), and similar abbreviations are not identified.

BODY

The *body* of a formal report is the text and any accompanying headings, tables, illustrations, and references. In it the author introduces the subject, describes in detail the methods and procedures used, demonstrates how results were obtained, and draws conclusions upon which any recommendations are based. The first page of the body is numbered page 1 (Arabic rather than Roman numerals are used).

Summary

The body of the report begins with a summary that provides a more complete overview of a report than either a descriptive or an informative

SYMBOLS

A	Pond surface area, ft^2 or acres
A_0	One-half the daily insulation, Btu/ft^2
A_n	Surface area of nth segment of the plugflow model, ft^2
C	Cloud cover in tenths of the total sky obscured
C_1	Bowen's ratio, 0.26 mm Hg/°F
C_p	Heat capacity of water, Btu/lb/°F
E_1, E_2	Estimation of equilibrium temperatures using data from offsite and onsite records, respectively, °F
$E(\bar{x})$	Estimation of equilibrium temperature using monthly average meteorologic data, °F
e_a	Saturation pressure of air above pond surface, mm Hg
e_s	Saturation pressure of air at surface temperature, T_S, mm Hg
g	Skew coefficient
H	Heat content, Btu

vi

FIGURE 11–5. List of symbols.

abstract. The summary states the purpose of the investigation and gives major findings, conclusions, and recommendations, if any are to be made. It also provides an account of the procedures used to conduct the study. Although more complete than an abstract, the summary should not contain a detailed description of the work upon which the findings, conclusions, and recommendations were based. The length of the summary is proportional to the length of the report; typically, the summary should be approximately 10 percent of the length of the report.

Some summaries are written to follow the organization of the report. Others highlight the findings, conclusions, and recommendations by summarizing them first, before going on to discuss procedures or methodology.

A summary enables people who may not have time to read a lengthy report to scan its primary points quickly and then decide whether they need to read the report or certain sections of it in full. Because they are often intended for busy managers, summaries are sometimes called "executive summaries."

The executive summary should be written so that it can be read independently of the report. It must not refer by number to figures, tables, or references contained elsewhere in the report. Because executive summaries are frequently read in place of the full report, all uncommon symbols, abbreviations, and acronyms must be spelled out.

Adhere to these additional guidelines when writing an executive summary:

- Write the executive summary last, after completing the report.
- Omit (or define) technical terminology if your readers include people unfamiliar with the topic of your report.
- Make the summary concise, but not brusque. Be especially careful not to omit transitional words and phrases (*however, moreover, therefore, for example, in summary*, etc.)
- Introduce no information not discussed in the report.

Figure 11–6 shows a summary of the report on the effect of running on bones and joints.

Introduction

The purpose of an introduction is to provide your readers with any general information they must have to understand the detailed information in the rest of the report. An introduction sets the stage for the report. In this respect, it resembles the first act of a play in which the audience learns about the characters, their backgrounds, and where the action takes place so it can appreciate what happens from then on. In writing the introduction, you need to state the subject, the purpose, the

SUMMARY

**Background
and
Purpose**

In recent years insurance companies have been
under increasing economic pressure to find better
ways to minimize losses. Thus, Amalgamated Life Insurance Company, like others, has shown increased
interest in the link between exercise and the health
of those it insures. Despite the reported advantages
to overall health of long–distance running, questions have been raised about the long–term physical
impact on bones and joints resulting from long–distance running. Could long–time runners develop
osteoarthritis and degenerative joint diseases?
When Amalgamated considered underwriting life insurance for the 19–– U.S. Olympic Marathon Team, it
sought this information because although the athletes are in excellent physical condition now, the
possibility exists that the strain on bones and
joints from long–distance running could lead to bone
and joint diseases later in life.

Scope

This study, based on research done at Stanford
University and the University of Florida, was undertaken to examine existing information on these effects so that Amalgamated could assess the insurance
risk factors for insuring the U.S. Olympic Marathon
Team. The Stanford study investigated the connection
between long–distance running and bone density and
osteoarthritis (including cysts, bone spurs, joint-
space narrowing, and sclerosis). The Florida study
sought a possible link between running and degenerative joint disease. Based on the findings of these
studies, Amalgamated might also prepare a booklet
for its clients about some of the effects of long-
distance running on health.

Methodology

The researchers at Stanford located 539 runners
and 422 control subjects and evaluated them by questionnaires according to their exercise and dietary
habits and their medical histories. This initial pool
was screened and divided into two study groups of 41
each (18 women and 23 men) matched by age, race, sex,

FIGURE 11–6. Summary.

education, and occupation. The prevalence of sclerosis and bone spur formation in the population at large
made the inclusion of women in this study mandatory.
Then all finalists were combined into an ''all subjects'' study group. All were weighed and given a
physical examination. The impact of their weight on
weight-bearing joints was calculated. The disabil-
ity rate for runners and nonrunners was also established. All participants also had their weight-bear-
ing (ankles, knees, hips) and nonweight-bearing
joints (hands) x-rayed. Finally, all were given bone
density tests. All medical and x-ray examinations
were performed ''blind,'' with the examiners unaware
of the group to which those examined belonged.

    In the Florida study, which focused on degenera-
tive joint disease, all participants were located
and evaluated by questionnaire according to whether
or not they were runners. They also reported their
medical, musculoskeletal, and injury histories.

Methodology
Only men were chosen because there is no difference
in the occurrence of joint disease between men and
women in the population at large. They were divided
into two groups of 23 long-distance runners and 11
nonrunners. Each participant then had an extensive
medical history taken and was given both medical and
x-ray examinations of hips, knees, ankles and feet.
As at Stanford, these were blind tests.

    The test results from both studies showed that
control subjects were more prone to increased spur
formation, sclerosis, and joint-space narrowing
than runners. They also had somewhat more bone degen-

Findings
eration than runners. Runners, on the other hand,
showed increased joint space and bone density. Female
long-distance runners, however, had somewhat more
sclerosis in knee joints and the lumbar spine area
than matched control subjects.

    In general, the researchers concluded that
long-distance running is associated with increased

Conclusions
bone mineral and not with clinical osteoarthritis
or degenerative joint disease, regardless of the

FIGURE 11–6, *continued.*

mileage or number of years spent running. The data
also support the role of exercise in retarding bone
loss with aging and the value of exercise programs.
The Stanford study recommends estrogen and calcium
therapy for women after menopause to retard bone
loss.

Recommen-
dations

Based on the data from these studies, we can conclude that the life insurance risk factors for bone
and joint diseases in long–distance runners between
age 50 and 72 are smaller than for nonrunners in this
age group. Therefore, the Amalgamated Life Insurance
Company should underwrite life insurance for the
19–– U.S. Olympic Marathon Team. Amalgamated should
also inform its clients that an exercise program that
includes long–distance running can be beneficial to
their health.

FIGURE 11–6, *continued.*

scope, and the way you plan to develop the topic. You may also describe how the report will be organized but, as with the informative abstract and the summary, you should exclude the findings, conclusions, and recommendations of the report. Figure 11–7 shows the introduction to the report on long-distance running. The contents of the introduction and the contents of the preface may overlap, but this is not always the case.

Stating the Subject.   In stating the subject, help your reader by including general background information on the history or theory of the subject. You may need to define the topic if it is one that some of your readers will be unfamiliar with.

Stating the Purpose.   The statement of purpose in your introduction should function as a topic sentence does in a paragraph. It should make your readers aware of your goal as they read your supporting statements and examples. It should also tell them why you are writing about the subject and whether your material provides a new perspective or clarifies an existing perspective.

Stating the Scope.   This information tells the reader how much or how little detail to expect. Does your report present a broad survey of the topic, or does it concentrate on one part of the topic? Once you state your scope, stop. Save the details for the main body of the report.

Stating How the Topic Will Be Developed.   In a long report, help your reader by stating how you plan to develop or organize your topic. Is the report an analysis of the component parts of some whole? Is it an analysis of selected parts (or samples) of a whole? Is the material presented in chronological order? Does it move from details to general conclusions, or from a general statement to the details that verify the statement? Does it set out to show whether a hypothesis is correct or incorrect? Providing such information allows your readers to anticipate how the subject will be presented and gives them a basis for evaluating how you arrived at your conclusions or recommendations.

Text

Generally the longest section of the report, the text (or body) presents the details of how the topic was investigated, how the problem was solved, how the best choice from among alternatives was selected, or whatever else the report covers. This information is often clarified and further developed by the use of illustrations and tables and may be supported by references to other studies.

INTRODUCTION

Background

     In recent years, insurance companies have been experiencing increasing economic pressure and have had to find better ways of minimizing losses. Sophisticated computers and more exact data of the latest medical research have helped to calculate risk factors more precisely. Amalgamated Life Insurance Company has also used these data to produce special pamphlets for its clients. The pamphlets describe, for example, the latest findings on the dangers of smoking, a special diet for people with high blood pressure, and the seven warning signs of cancer.

Background

     Such pamphlets have required extensive investigations into the latest research in various fields of medicine. Recently, there has been a growing interest in the relationship between exercise and health. Increased physical activity, especially running, has been found to reduce the risk of cardiovascular disease, to control weight, and to lower blood pressure. However, specific questions have been raised about whether the long–term physical impact on bones and joints associated with long–distance running can be implicated as a factor in the development of osteoarthritis and degenerative joint disease.

     When Amalgamated considered underwriting life insurance for the 19–– U.S. Olympic Marathon Team, its specific objectives in obtaining the latest medical research findings in these areas were twofold:

Purpose

1. To ascertain reliable data for calculating insurance risk factors. (Although the athletes are in excellent physical condition now, would the strain on bones and joints from long–distance running lead to degenerative bone and joint diseases in later life?)

2. To inform the many runners among its clients whether long–distance running is harmful or beneficial to their health.

FIGURE 11–7. Introduction.

**Scope and
Organization**

       Thus, Amalgamated Life Insurance Company spon-
sored this study, which focuses on two recent reports
of research performed at Stanford University and the
University of Florida. The methods by which both research groups selected, screened, and evaluated the
subjects studied and their findings are examined in
detail. This detailed analysis is followed by conclusions and recommendations relevant to Amalgamated's
requirements.

FIGURE 11–7, *continued.*

Most formal reports have no single best organization. How the text is organized will depend on the topic and on how you have investigated it. The text is ordinarily divided into several major sections, comparable to the chapters in a book. These sections are then subdivided to reflect logical divisions in your main sections. The main portion of the text usually ends with a conclusions and recommendations section, depending on the type of information reported. See the sample table of contents (Figure 11–4) for an example of how the text for the report on long-distance running was organized.

Heads.   In formal reports, it is advisable to use *heads* (also called *headings*). These are titles or subtitles within the body of a report that serve as guideposts for the reader. They divide the work into manageable segments, call attention to the main topics, and signal changes of topic.

In long and complicated reports, you may need several levels of heads to indicate major divisions and subdivisions of the topic. There is no one "correct" format for heads, but the following two systems are most widely used.

The unnumbered heading system makes use of the typewriter or word-processing type to differentiate visually among levels of headings. Various systems exist, but the method described in the following guidelines is serviceable and simple.

1. The first-level head is in all-capital letters, is underscored, and is typed flush with the left margin on a line by itself. There is an extra line of space above and below the head.
2. The second-level head is in capital and lowercase letters (that is, the first letter of the first word and of every important word is captalized; prepositions and conjunctions of five letters or more also begin with a capital). Like the first-level head, this head is underscored, is typed flush with the left margin on a line by itself, and has an extra line of space above and below it.
3. The third-level is also in capital and lowercase letters. (Follow the same capitalization guidelines as for second-level heads.) This head is typed flush with the left margin, with an extra line of space above and below, and is not underlined.
4. The fourth-level head is underlined and is indented as a paragraph. The first word of the head is capitalized; the remaining words are not (unless they are proper nouns). The head is typed on the same line as the first sentence of the material it introduces. Therefore, a period generally appears after the head to set it apart from the text that follows. There should be an extra line of space above the head.

The four levels are arranged as follows:

FIRST–LEVEL HEAD

   Begin text here.

Second–Level Head

   Begin text here.

Third–Level Head

   Begin text here.

Fourth–level head. Begin text here.

As you write your report, keep in mind the following guidelines.

1. A new head should signal a shift to a new topic. Lower-level heads should signal shifts to new subtopics within a major topic.
2. Within a topic, all heads at one level should be parallel in their relationship to the topic. Note in the sample table of contents (Figure 11–4) that "THE RESEARCH" (a first-level head) is followed by two parallel second-level heads, both bearing the same relation to the first-level head—they are the specific research studies examined.
3. Too many heads or too many levels can be as bad as too few. They can make the report look cluttered, subdividing the topic too often for your reader to be able to sort out major from subordinate ideas.

The decimal numbering system uses a combination of numbers and decimal points to subordinate levels of heads in a report. The outline below shows the correspondence between different levels of headings and the decimal numbers used.

1. FIRST–LEVEL HEAD

1.1 Second–Level Head

1.2 Second–Level Head

1.2.1 Third–Level Head

1.2.2 Third–Level Head

1.2.2.1 Fourth–Level Head

1.2.2.2 Fourth–Level Head

1.3 Second–Level Head

```
1.3.1 Third-Level Head

1.3.2 Third-Level Head

2. FIRST-LEVEL HEAD
```

Although the second-, third-, and fourth-level heads are indented in an outline or table of contents, as headings they are flush with the left margin in the body of the report. For an example of how the heads help organize a portion of text, see the Writer's Guide at the end of this book.

Note that the first-level heads are typed in all-capital letters; the second-level heads and all subsequent levels of heads are typed in capital and lowercase letters. That is, the first letter of the first word and of every important word is capitalized; prepositions and conjunctions of five letters or more are also capitalized. Every head is typed on a separate line, with an extra line of space above and below the head.

Conclusions

The "Conclusions" section of a report pulls together the results or findings presented in the report and interprets them in light of its purpose and methods. Consequently, this section is the focal point of the work, the goal toward which it is aimed. The conclusions must grow out of the findings discussed in the body of the report; moreover, they must be consistent with what the introduction stated the report would examine (its purpose) and how it would do so (its methodology). For instance, if the introduction stated that the report had as its objective to learn the economic costs of relocating a plant from one city to another, then the conclusions should not discuss the social or aesthetic impact the new plant could have at the new location. Of course, if "costs" are defined in the introduction to include social and aesthetic concerns, then these also must be accounted for in the report and discussed in the "Conclusions" section.

Recommendations

Recommendations, which are sometimes combined with the conclusions, state what course of action should be taken based on the results of the study. Of the three possible locations for a new warehouse, which is the best? Which make of delivery van should the company purchase to replace the existing fleet? Which type of word-processing equipment should the office buy? Should the equipment be leased rather than pur-

CONCLUSIONS AND RECOMMENDATIONS

**Brief State-
ment of
Purpose**

This investigation was undertaken to learn the long-term effects of long-distance running on the bones and joints of male and female runners 50 to 72 years of age. Amalgamated Life Insurance Company sponsored the study and plans to use the results of this investigation in deciding whether to underwrite life insurance for the 19–– U.S. Olympic Marathon Team.

Findings

Clinical and x-ray tests indicate that runners showed positive test results, especially with re-spect to increased joint space and bone density. Fe-male runners, however, had somewhat more sclerosis in knee joints and the lumbar spine area than matched members of the control group.

Conclusions

In general, the research evaluated concluded that long-distance running is associated with in-creased bone mineral, but not with clinical osteoar-thritis or degenerative joint disease. They state that the data support the role of exercise in the re-tardation of bone loss with aging and recommend exer-cise programs. For women, they suggest weight-bear-ing exercises and estrogen and calcium after menopause.

Conclusions

Specifically, for the objectives of this re-port, the life insurance risk factors are smaller for long-distance runners than for the less active population because long-distance runners between the ages of 50 and 72 were in better physical condition than less active members of the control groups.

**Recommen-
dations**

Therefore, the Amalgamated Life Insurance Com-pany should underwrite the life insurance policies for the 19–– U.S. Olympic Marathon Team. Further, Amalgamated should inform its clients that an exer-cise program that includes long-distance running can be beneficial to their health.

FIGURE 11–8. Conclusions and recommendations.

chased? The "Recommendations" section says, in effect, "I think we should purchase this, or do that, or hire them."

The emphasis here is on the verb *should*. Recommendations advise the reader on the best course of action based on the researcher's findings. Generally, someone up the organizational ladder, or a customer or client, makes the final decision about whether or not to accept the recommendations.

Figure 11–8 shows how the conclusions and recommendations from the report on long-distance running were combined.

Explanatory Footnotes

Occasionally, you will need to offer an explanatory comment on an idea mentioned in the main body of the text. This type of footnote is generally placed at the foot of the page on which the comment occurs. Mark the first such footnote on a page with an asterisk (*), the second with a dagger (†), the third with a double dagger (‡), and the fourth with a section mark (§).

A description of the 76 variables identified for inclusion in the regression equations, together with their method of construction, data, source, means, and ranges, is given in Appendix A. The following discussion elaborates on those variables that proved most important in explaining housing price variations.*

---

* The number in parentheses refers to the variable number as used in the regression equation.

References

If, in your report, you refer to material in or quote directly from a published work or other research source, you must provide a list of references in a separate section called "References." If your employer has a preferred reference style, follow it; otherwise, use the MLA documentation guidelines provided in Chapter 10.

For a relatively short report, the references should go at the end of the report. For a report with a number of sections or chapters, the reference section should fall at the end of each major section or chapter. In either case, every reference section should be labeled as such and should start on a new page. If a particular reference appears in more than one section or chapter, it should be repeated in full in each appropriate reference section.

BACK MATTER

The *back matter* of a formal report contains supplemental information, such as the location of additional information about the topic (*bibliography*), clarification of information contained in the report, and more detailed explanation (*appendix*).

Bibliography

The bibliography, which usually appears in the back matter, is the listing, in alphabetical order, of all the sources of information you consulted to prepare the report. Accordingly, the bibliography may be longer than the reference section. Further, because it is arranged alphabetically, it enables a reader interested in seeing whether you consulted a particular source to discover as much at a glance. Figure 11–9 shows the bibliography from the report on long-distance running. Like other elements in the front and back matter, the bibliography starts on a new page and is labeled by name.

Appendixes

An *appendix* contains information that clarifies or supplements the text. Material typically placed in an appendix includes long charts and supplementary graphs or tables; copies of questionnaires and other material used in gathering information; texts of interviews; pertinent correspondence; and explanations too long for explanatory footnotes but helpful to the reader who is seeking further assistance or clarification.

The report may have one or more appendixes; generally, each appendix contains one type of material. For example, a report may have one appendix presenting a questionnaire and a second appendix presenting a detailed computer printout tabulating questionnaire results.

Place the first appendix on a new page directly after the bibliography. Each additional appendix also begins on a new page. Identify each with a title and a heading. Appendixes are ordinarily labeled Appendix A, Appendix B, and so on.

Appendix A

Sample Questionnaire

BIBLIOGRAPHY

Adams, I. D. ''Osteoarthritis and Sport.'' Clinical
Rheumatic Diseases 2 (1976): 523–541.

Bassey, E. J., P. H. Fenton, and I. C. MacDonald, et
al. ''Self–paced Walking as a Method for Exercise
Testing in Elderly and Young Men.'' Clinical
Science of Molecular Medicine 51 (1976): 609–
612.

Jorring, Kurt. ''Osteoarthritis of the Hip.'' Acta
Orthopadica Scandinavica 51 (1980): 523–530.

Jurmain, R. D. ''Stress and the Etiology of Osteoarthritis.'' American Journal of Physics and An-
thropology 46 (1977): 353–366.

Lane, N., D. A. Bloch, and H. H. Jones, et al.
''Long–Distance Running, Bone Density and Os-
teoarthritis.'' Journal of the American Medical
Association 255, No. 9 (1986): 84–97.

McDermott, M., and P. Freyne. ''Osteoarthritis in
Runners with Knee Pain.'' British Journal of
Sports Medicine 17 (1983): 84–97.

Nilsson, B. E., and J. Hernborg. ''The Relationship
Between Osteophytes in the Knee Joints, Osteoarthritis and Aging.'' Acta Orthopadica Scandinavica 44 (1973): 69–74.

Panusch, R. S., C. Schmidt, J. R. Caldwell, et al.
''Is Running Associated with Degenerative Joint
Disease?'' Journal of the American Medical
Association 255, No. 9 (1986): 1152–1154.

Puranen, J., L. Ala–Ketola, P. Peltokalleo, et al.
''Running and Primary Osteoarthritis of the

FIGURE 11–9. Bibliography.

Hip.'' British Medical Journal 1 (1975):
424–425.

U.S. Department of Health, Education and Welfare.
''Healthy People: The Surgeon General's Report
on Health Promotion and Disease Prevention.''
Public Health Service Publication 70–55071
(1979).

FIGURE 11–9, *continued.*

If your report has only one appendix, simply label it "Appendix," followed by the title. To call it Appendix A implies that an Appendix B will follow.

If there is only one appendix, the pages are generally numbered A-1, A-2, A-3, and so forth. If there is more than one appendix, the pages are double numbered according to the letter of each appendix (for example, the first page of Appendix B would be numbered B-1).

Glossary

A *glossary* lists, and then defines, selected terms found in the report. You should include a glossary in your report only if it contains many words and expressions that will be unfamiliar to your intended audience. Arrange the terms alphabetically, with each entry beginning on a new line. Then give the definitions after each term, dictionary style. The glossary, labeled as such, appears directly after the appendix and begins on a new page.

Even though the report may contain a glossary, the terms that appear should be defined when they are first mentioned in the text.

GRAPHIC AND TABULAR MATTER

Formal reports often contain illustrations and tables that clarify and support the text. These materials may be numbered and sequenced in varying ways. The following guidelines show one conventional system for smoothly integrating such materials into the text. For a full discussion of the creation and use of illustrations, see Chapter 13.

Figures

Identify each figure with a title and a number, in Arabic numerals, above or below the figure. For fairly short reports, number figures sequentially throughout the report (Figure 1, Figure 2, and so forth). For long reports, number figures by chapter or by section. According to the latter system, the first figure in Chapter 1 would be Figure 1.1 (or Figure 1–1), and the second figure would be Figure 1.2 (or Figure 1–2). In Chapter 2, the first figure would be Figure 2.1, and so on.

In the text, refer to figures by number rather than by location ("Figure 2.1" rather than "the figure below"). When the report is typed, the figures may not fall exactly where you originally expected.

Tables

Identify each table with a title and a number, centering both of these lines above the table. For fairly short reports, number the tables sequentially throughout the report (Table 2, Table 3, and so on). For long reports, number tables by chapter or by section according to the system described for figure numbering. As with figures, refer to tables in the text by number rather than by location ("Table 4.1" rather than "the above table").

CHAPTER SUMMARY

Formal reports, which are the written accounts of major projects, normally contain three major parts: front matter, body, and back matter. The *front matter* of a formal report may include a title page, an abstract, a table of contents, a list of figures, a list of tables, a preface, and a section for abbreviations and symbols. The *body* of a formal report includes the text of the report, complete with footnotes, headings, tables, illustrations, and references. The text may open with a summary and an introduction and may end with a conclusions and recommendations section. The *back matter* of a formal report may include a bibliography, appendixes, and a glossary. The report should always be identified in a brief transmittal letter or memorandum submitted along with it.

EXERCISES

1. Come to class prepared to discuss the following questions.

   a. Why should a formal report contain a table of contents?
   b. What is the function of a preface in a formal report?
   c. When is a descriptive abstract more appropriate than an informative abstract?
   d. What types of information should *not* appear in an abstract?
   e. What function do heads perform in a formal report?
   f. What is the difference between *conclusions* and *recommendations?*
   g. What is the difference between a *reference section* and a *works cited* section?
   h. What types of material should appear in an *appendix?*
   i. What is the function of a *glossary* in a formal report?

2. Select a feature article from the current issue of *Scientific American* or from a journal chosen by your instructor. Using the article as your starting point, do the following:

   a. Create a formal topic outline, using the guidelines in Chapter 2.

   b. Convert the outline to a descriptive and an informative abstract, and label each accordingly.

   c. Using the outline, create a table of contents for the article as though it were a formal report, using the elements discussed in this chapter that are appropriate.

3. Write a formal report on a topic from your career field or other area of interest. You may want to use the topic you selected and the information you gathered in doing the exercises for Chapter 10. Prepare a topic outline for the report, and submit it for your instructor's review. Include at least the following elements in the report (plus any additional elements your paper may require): title page, descriptive abstract, table of contents, preface, summary, heads, conclusions and/or recommendations, references, and bibliography. Create a transmittal letter for the report addressed to your instructor from you.

12

Proposals and Other Kinds of On-the-Job Communication

Much on-the-job writing—for example, proposals, minutes of meetings, and job descriptions—cannot be classified either as correspondence or as reports. Yet such types of communication can be just as important as the letters, routine memos, and reports that you write. Another kind of communication—the printed form—frequently requires only a minimum of writing and yet can in some circumstances be the most effective and efficient way to communicate. This chapter deals with several of the less-recognized kinds of on-the-job communication: proposals, minutes of meetings, job descriptions, and printed forms.

PROPOSALS

The general purpose of any proposal is to persuade the reader to do something, whether it is (1) to persuade a potential customer to purchase your products and services or (2) to persuade your boss to fund a project you would like to launch. You would write a sales proposal to accomplish the first objective; you would write an internal proposal to accomplish the second. (These types of proposals will be discussed shortly.) Any proposal offers a plan to fill a need, and your reader will evaluate your plan according to how well your written presentation answers his or her questions about *what* you are proposing to do, *how* you plan to do it, *when* you plan to do it, and *how much* it is going to cost.

To answer these questions effectively for your reader, you must be certain that your proposal is written at your reader's level of knowledge. If you have more than one level of audience—a fairly common occurrence, since proposals often require more than one level of management approval—you must take all your readers into account. For example, if your immediate reader is an expert on your subject but the next higher level of management (which must also approve the proposal) is not, you would provide an executive summary written in language that is as nontechnical as possible. You might also include a glossary that explains the technical terms used in the body of the proposal, or appendixes that explain the technical information in nontechnical language. On the other hand, if your immediate reader is not an expert but the person at the next level is, you would write the proposal with the layman in mind and might include appendixes that contain the technical details of your proposal.

Proposals that are short or of medium length basically consist of an introduction, a body, and a conclusion. (Long proposals, as will be discussed, generally contain more elements.) The *introduction* should summarize the problem you are proposing to solve and your solution to it; it may also indicate the benefits that your reader will receive from your solution and the total cost of that solution. The *body* should explain in complete detail exactly (1) how the job will be done, (2) what methods will be used to do it (and, if applicable, the specific materials to be used and any other pertinent information), (3) when work will begin, (4) when the job will be completed, and (5) the detailed cost breakdown for the entire job. The *conclusion* should emphasize the benefits that the reader will realize from your solution to the problem and should urge the reader to action. Your conclusion should have an encouraging, confident, and reasonably assertive tone.

Persuasive Writing

Proposals, by definition, are persuasive writing, since you are attempting to convince someone to do something. Your goal is to prove to your reader that he or she needs what you are proposing to do, that it is practical, and that it is appropriate. For an unsolicited proposal, you may even need to convince your reader that he or she *has* a problem serious enough to require a solution. You would then offer your solution by first building a persuasive case demonstrating the logic of the approach you are proposing. Your facts must lead logically, even inevitably, to your conclusions and your solution.

Give your evidence in descending order of importance; that is, begin with the most important evidence and end with the least important. Anticipate and answer any objections your reader may have to your approach to the problem and your solution to it. Consider any alternative solutions that might be offered and show how yours is superior to them—but be very careful about the tone you use in doing so. For example, the use of sarcasm in describing opposing points of view could very likely backfire.

The tone of your proposal should be positive, confident, and tactful. The following example demonstrates a tone that is arrogant and therefore inappropriate in a proposal.

> The Qualtron Corporation has obviously not considered the potential problem of not having backup equipment available when a commercial power failure occurs. The corporation would also be wise indeed to give a great deal more consideration to the volume of output expected per machine.

The following version of the same passage is timid and therefore equally inappropriate.

> There could perhaps be a possibility of a problem with not having backup equipment available when commercial power fails. Also, it might be advisable to perhaps reconsider the volume of output expected per machine.

The following version of the same passage is positive, confident, and tactful.

> The system should be designed in such a way as to provide backup equipment in the event of a commercial power failure. Also, the system should be based on realistic expectations concerning the output of each machine.

Internal Proposals

An *internal proposal* is normally prepared as a memorandum, by either an employee or a department, and is sent to a higher-ranking person in the same organization for approval. An internal proposal can serve any of three purposes:

1. It can recommend a change in the way something is being done.
2. It can recommend that something be done that is not presently being done.
3. It can recommend a capital appropriation for a large purchase.

As an example of the first kind, a proposal might recommend that the management of multiple manufacturing operations be decentralized.

Typical of the second kind might be a proposal to initiate assigned parking places. The third kind might be a proposal to replace an outdated computer system (Christine Thomas in Chapter 1 wrote just such a proposal).

Writing the Introduction.   The function of the introduction to an internal proposal is to establish that a problem exists for which a solution is urgently needed. The problem, and its negative consequences, must be very clearly presented, even if you think the reader is probably already aware of it—don't make any assumptions. If the person who must approve your proposal is not convinced that a serious problem exists, approval of your solution is unlikely.

After identifying the problem, the introduction should summarize your proposed solution. You might indicate the benefits to be realized from the adoption of your proposal and its total cost. Notice how the following introduction states the problem and then summarizes the writer's proposed solution.

```
TO:       Marge Dundas, Director
          Personnel Resources

FROM:     Leslie Galusha, Manager ⅃𝒢
          Administrative Support Services

DATE:     June 12, 19—

SUBJECT:  Upgrading from Typewriters to Word Processors
```

We are receiving an increasing number of requests to prepare direct mailings that involve sending each recipient an original copy, especially from the Advertising, Public Relations, and Employee Relations Departments. The cost of calling in temporary help to get the typing done is very high, and an abnormal workload results from our efforts to get the extra work done. In addition, the pressure causes much confusion and many frayed nerves.

I propose that we purchase a word processor to enable us to handle the increased workload without the cost and disruption of bringing in temporary help. The following details show the savings and efficiency of the Toshiba EW—100 Word Processor as compared with our present method of dealing with the problem.

Writing the Body.   The body of an internal proposal should provide a detailed description of your solution to the problem. The key word here is *detailed*. Try to put yourself in your reader's position and ask yourself what information *you* would need if you had to make the decision you are asking your reader to make. Then be sure to include all the necessary information. Your presentation of your solution should grow naturally out of your statement of the problem. When applicable, include the following information.

1. A breakdown of costs
2. The methods to be used in achieving the proposed solution to the problem, as well as the equipment, material, and personnel that would be required
3. A detailed schedule for completing the project, possibly broken down into separate tasks

The following sample body is a continuation of the preceding introduction.

Efficiency

The Toshiba EW-100 Word Processor has a merge feature that permits the operator to type the basic letter as one file, substituting a special character for any word or words that will change from one letter to the next (such as name and address), and to type the word or words to be substituted for the special character (such as name and address) as a separate file. Then the operator simply sets up the printer for merge printing and presses the MERGE key. The system automatically types all the letters, substituting the indicated word or words from the second file in each consecutive letter. This operation is many times faster than the best human typist, and it is entirely error-free, once programmed.

Keyboard entry on the Toshiba EW-100 Word processor is much more efficient than it is with a typewriter. Instead of having to ''paint out'' an error or use typewriter correction paper, the operator simply strikes over the error. (The system automatically corrects the error on the diskette.) Because correcting an error is so easy, statistics show that the operator's typing speed increases.

An additional advantage of upgrading from typewriter to word processor is file storage. Rather than using bulky filing cabinets for 8 ½-by-11-inch paper, we can store over 600 pages on a single 8-inch diskette. One single 1 ½-inch diskette container holds ten diskettes, or more than 6,000 pages (double-spaced), thereby reducing our storage requirements dramatically.

Having a Toshiba EW-100 Word Processor and one trained operator would eliminate the need for temporary typists and the
confusion caused by our training these typists while attempting to meet our own deadlines. In short, we could carry
on with our normal office routine. A normal routine not only
would improve our employees' morale but would increase their
efficiency.

Cost Savings

Purchase of the Toshiba EW-100 Word Processor--with a Ricoh
45-characters-per-second daisy-wheel printer--would result in a savings of over $3,500 in the first year, as shown
below.

Purchase price of Toshiba EW-100 with Ricoh printer	$5,000
Cost of temporary typists from Wilson Secretarial Agency last year	$7,400
Typewriter rental from World Office Machines last year	$1,120
Savings the first year ($7,400 + $1,120 − $5,000 = $3,520)	$3,520

Since purchase of the Toshiba EW-100 Word Processor is
a one-time cost, the savings would be substantially greater
after the first year.

Writing the Conclusion. The function of the conclusion of an
internal proposal is to tie everything together, possibly restate your recommendation, and close with a spirit of cooperation (offering to set up a
meeting, supply additional information, or provide any other assistance
that might be needed). Your conclusion should be brief. Notice how the
following continuation of the sample proposal concludes.

On the basis of these facts. I recommend that we purchase a
Toshiba EW-100 Word Processor. Enclosed is a brochure that
describes the Toshiba EW-100 Word Processor in detail. I
will be happy to provide any additional details about the
system, as I understand it, at your request.

Figure 12–1 shows a typical internal proposal. The proposal was written by a plant safety officer to the plant superintendent and recommends changes in the way things are presently being done.

Sales Proposals

The *sales proposal* (or *external proposal*), which is one of the major marketing tools in use in business and industry today, is one company's offer to provide specific goods or services to a potential buyer within a specified period of time and for a specified price. The primary purpose of a sales proposal is to demonstrate that the prospective customer's purchase of the seller's products or services would be a wise investment.

Sales proposals vary greatly in size and relative sophistication. Some may run a page or two and be written by one person; others may be many pages long and be written by several people; still others may take hundreds of pages and be written by a team of professional proposal writers. A short sales proposal might bid for the construction of a single home; a sales proposal of moderate length might bid for the installation of a network of computer systems; and a very long sales proposal might be used to bid for the construction of a multibillion-dollar aircraft carrier.

Your first task in writing a sales proposal is to find out exactly what your potential customer wants. If you can obtain this information from the customer, in writing, you have an advantage. Often, however,

---

```
                           MEMORANDUM

           TO:     Harold Clurman,
                   Plant Superintendent
                                                 FN
           FROM:   Fred Nelson, Safety Officer

           DATE:   August 4, 19--

           SUBJECT:  Safety Practices for Group 333


       Many  accidents  and  near-accidents  have  oc-
       curred  in  Group  333  because  of  the  hazardous
       working  conditions  in  this  area.  This  memo-
       randum  identifies  those  hazardous  conditions
       and  makes  recommendations  for  their  elimina-
       tion.
```

FIGURE 12–1. Internal proposal.

<u>Hazardous Conditions</u>

Employees inside the factory must operate the walk-along crane through aisles that are frequently congested with scrap metal, discarded lumber, and other refuse from the shearing area. Many surfaces in the area are oil-coated.

The containers for holding raw stock and scrap metal are also unsafe. On many of the racks, the hooks are bent inward so far that the crane cannot fit into them properly unless it is banged and jiggled in a dangerous manner. To add to the hazard, employees in the press group do not always balance the load in the racks. As a result, the danger of falling metal is great as the unbalanced racks swing practically out of control overhead. These hazards endanger employees in Group 333 and also employees in the raw-stock and shearing areas, because the crane passes over these areas.

Hazards also exist in the yard and in the chemical building. The present method of dumping strip metal into the scrap bins is the most dangerous practice of all. To dump this metal, the tow-motor operator picks up a rack, with the rack straddling the tow-motor forks, and raises it over the edge of the scrap-metal bin. The operator then rotates the forks to permit the scrap metal to fall from one end of the rack. As the weight shifts, the upright frame at the other end of the rack slams into one of the tow-motor forks (now raised 12 feet above the ground, inside the scrap tub). This method of operation has resulted in two tow-motor tip-overs in the past month. In neither incident was the driver injured, but the odds are great that someone will be seriously harmed if the practice continues.

Group 333 employees must also dump tubs full of scrap metal from the tow motor into the 10-foot-high scrap bins. In order to dump the metal on the tow-motor forks, the operator must raise the tubs high above his head. Because of the unpredictable way in which the

FIGURE 12–1, *continued*.

metal falls from the tubs, many facial cuts and body bruises have resulted. Employees who work in the yard are also subject to danger in winter weather: all employees have been cut and bruised in falls that occurred as they were climbing up on scrap bins covered with snow and ice to dump scrap from pallets that had not been banded.

Finally, nearly all Group 333 employees who must handle the caustic chemicals in the chemical building report damaged clothing and ruined shoes. Poor lighting in the building (the lights are nearly 20 feet above the floor), storage racks positioned less than two feet apart, and container caps incorrectly fastened have made these accidents impossible to prevent.

Recommendations

To eliminate these hazards as quickly as possible, I recommend that the following actions be taken:

1. That Group 333 supervisors rigorously initiate and enforce a policy to free aisles of obstructions.
2. That all dangerous racks be repaired and replaced.
3. That the Engineering Group develop a safe rack dumper.
4. That heavy wire mesh screens be mounted on the front of all tow motors.
5. That Group 333 employees not accept scrap in containers that have not been properly banded.
6. That illumination be increased in the chemical building and that a compulsory training program for the safe handling of caustic chemicals be scheduled.

I would like to meet with you and the supervisor of Group 333 before the end of the month, as your schedule permits. You will have my complete cooperation in working out all of the details of the proposed recommendations.

Copy: Jim Hanchett, Supervisor, Group 333

FIGURE 12–1, *continued.*

you will need to determine what the customer wants on the basis of your experience. You must then determine whether your organization can satisfy the customer's needs. Before preparing a sales proposal, you should also try to find out who your primary competitors are. Then compare your company's strengths with the strengths of the competing firms, determine where you have advantages over your competitors, and emphasize those advantages in your proposal. For example, a small software company bidding for an air force contract at a local base would be familiar with its competitors. If the proposal writer believed that his company had better-qualified personnel than its competitors, he might include the résumés of the key people who would be involved in the project as a way of emphasizing that advantage.

Solicited and Unsolicited Sales Proposals. Sales proposals may be either solicited or unsolicited. The latter are not so unusual as they may sound: companies often operate for years with a problem they have never recognized (unnecessarily high maintenance costs, for example, or poor inventory-control methods). You might prepare an unsolicited proposal for such a company if you were convinced that the potential customer could realize substantial benefits by adopting your solution to the problem. You would, of course, need to persuade the customer of the excellence of your idea and of the need for what you are proposing.

To ensure that you don't waste a lot of time and effort, you might precede an unsolicited proposal with an inquiry to determine whether there is any potential interest. If you receive a positive response, you might then need to conduct a detailed study of the prospective customer's needs and requirements to determine whether, and how, you can be of help to the customer. You would then prepare your proposal on the basis of your study.

An unsolicited proposal must clearly identify the potential customer's problem but at the same time should be careful not to overstate it. Further, the proposal must convince the customer that the problem needs to be solved. One way to do this is to emphasize the benefits that the customer will realize from the solution being proposed.

The other type of sales proposal—the solicited sales proposal—is a response to a request for bids on goods or services. To find the best method of doing a job and the most qualified company to do it, procuring organizations commonly ask competing companies to bid for a job by issuing a *Request for Proposals*. A Request for Proposals may be rigid in its specifications governing how the proposal should be organized and what it should contain, but it is normally quite flexible about the approaches that bidding firms may propose. Normally, the Request for Proposals simply defines the basic work that is to be accomplished.

The procuring organization generally publishes its Request for Proposals in one or more journals, in addition to sending it to certain selected companies that have good reputations for doing the kind of work needed. Some companies and government agencies even hold a conference for the competing firms at which they provide all pertinent information about the job being bid for.

Managers interested in responding to Requests for Proposals scan the appropriate publications regularly. Upon finding a project of interest, an executive in the sales department of such a company obtains all available information from the procuring company or agency. The data are then presented to management for a decision on whether the company is interested in the project. If the decision is positive, the technical staff is assigned the task of developing an approach to the work described in the Request for Proposals. The technical staff normally considers several alternatives, selecting one that combines feasibility and a price that will yield sufficient profit. The staff's concept is presented to higher management for a decision on whether the company wishes to present a proposal to the requesting organization. Assuming that the decision is to proceed, preparation of the proposal is the next step.

When you respond to a Request for Proposals, pay close attention to any specifications in the request governing the preparation of the proposal. Follow the specifications to the letter, even if you don't like them.

Writing a Simple Sales Proposal. Even a short and uncomplicated sales proposal should be carefully planned. The introduction should state the purpose and scope of the proposal. It should indicate the date on which you propose to begin work on the project, the date on which you expect to complete work, any special benefits of your proposed approach, and the total cost of the project. The introduction could also refer to any previous association your company may have had with the potential customer, assuming of course that the association was positive and mutually beneficial.

The body of a sales proposal should itemize the products and services you are proposing to furnish. It should include, if applicable, a discussion of the procedures you would use to perform the work and any specific materials to be used. It should also present a time schedule indicating when each stage of the project would be completed. Finally, the body should include a precise breakdown of the costs of the project.

The conclusion should express your appreciation for the opportunity to submit the proposal, as well as your confidence in your company's ability to do the job to the customer's satisfaction. You might add in the conclusion that you look forward to establishing good working relations with the customer and that you would be glad to provide any additional information that might be needed. Your conclusion could also review any advantages your company may have over its competitors. It should specify the time period during which your proposal can still be considered a valid offer. If any supplemental materials, such as blueprints or price sheets, accompany the proposal, include a list of them at the end of the proposal. Figure 12–2 shows a typical short sales proposal.

PROPOSAL

To Landscape the New Corporate Headquarters
of the
Watford Valve Corporation

Submitted to: Ms. Tricia Olivera,
              Vice President
Submitted by: Jerwalted Nursery, Inc.
Date submitted: February 1, 19--

Jerwalted Nursery, Inc., proposes to land-scape the new corporate headquarters of the Watford Valve Corporation, on 1600 Swason Avenue, at a total cost of $8,000. Landscaping would begin no later than April 30, 19--, and would be completed by May 31.

The lot to be landscaped is approximately 600 feet wide and 700 feet deep. The following trees and plants would be planted in the quantities and sizes given and at the prices specified. They would be positioned as indicated in the enclosed drawing.

4 maple trees (not less than 7 ft.) $40 each	$ 160
41 birch trees (not less than 7 ft.) $65 each	2,665
2 spruce trees (not less than 7 ft.) $105 each	210
20 juniper plants (not less than 18 in.) $15 each	300
60 hedges (not less than 18 in.) $7 each	420
200 potted plants (various kinds) $2 each	400
Total cost of plants	$4,155
Labor	3,845
Total cost	$8,000

FIGURE 12–2. Short sales proposal.

```
All trees and plants would be guaranteed
against defect or disease for a period of 90
days, with the warranty period to begin June
1, 19--.
    The prices quoted in this proposal will be
valid until June 30, 19--.
    Thank you for the opportunity to submit
this proposal. Jerwalted Nursery, Inc., has
been in the landscaping and nursery business
in the Providence area for thirty years, and
our landscaping has won several awards and
commendations, including a citation from the
National Association of Architects. We are
eager to put our skills and knowledge to work
for you, and we are confident that you will
be pleased with our work. If we can provide
any additional information or assistance,
please call.
```

FIGURE 12–2, *continued.*

Writing a Long Sales Proposal. A long sales proposal begins with a *cover letter,* which expresses your appreciation for the opportunity to submit your proposal and for any assistance you may have received in studying the customer's requirements. The letter should acknowledge any previous association with the customer, assuming that it was a positive experience. Then it should summarize the recommendations offered in the proposal and express your confidence that they will satisfy the customer's needs. Figure 12–3 shows the cover letter for the proposal illustrated in Figures 12–4 through 12–11—a proposal that the Waters Corporation of Tampa provide a computer system for the Cookson chain of retail stores.

An *executive summary* follows the cover letter. Addressed to the executive who will ultimately accept or reject the proposal, it should summarize in nontechnical language how you plan to approach the work. Figure 12–4 shows the executive summary of the Waters Corporation proposal. If your proposal offers products as well as services, it should also include a *general description* of the products. Figure 12–5 shows a typical general description.

Following the executive summary and the general description, you explain in detail exactly how you plan to do what you are proposing. This detailed section will be read by specialists who can understand and evaluate your plan, so you can feel free to use technical language and discuss complicated concepts. Figure 12–6 shows one part of the detailed solution appearing in the Waters Corporation proposal, which

The Waters Corporation
17 North Waterloo Blvd.
Tampa, Florida 33607

September 1, 19--

Mr. John Yeung, General Manager
Cookson's Retail Stores, Inc.
101 Longuer Street
Savannah, Georgia 31499

Dear Mr. Yeung:

The Waters Corporation appreciates the opportunity to respond to Cookson's Request for
Proposals dated July 26, 19--. We would like
to thank Mr. Becklight, Director of your Management Information Systems Department, for
his invaluable contributions to the study of
your operations that we conducted before preparing our proposal.

It has been Waters's privilege to provide
Cookson's with retail systems and equipment
since your first store opened many years ago.
Therefore, we have become very familiar with
your requirements as they have evolved during
the expansion you have experienced since that
time. Waters's close working relationship
with Cookson's has resulted in a clear understanding of Cookson's philosophy and needs.

Our proposal describes a Waters Interactive
Terminal/Retail Processor System designed to
meet Cookson's network and processing needs.
It will provide all of your required capabilities, from the point-of-sale operational requirements at the store terminals to the host
processor. The system uses the proven Retail
III modular software, with its point-of-sale
applications, and the superior Interactive
Terminal with its advanced capabilities and
design. This system is easily installed without massive customer reprogramming.

FIGURE 12–3. Cover letter.

Mr. J. Yeung
Page 2
September 1, 19--

The Waters Interactive Terminal/Retail Processor System, which is compatible with much
of Cookson's present equipment, not only will
answer your present requirements but will
provide the flexibility to add new features
and products in the future. The system's
unique hardware modularity, efficient microprocessor design, and flexible programming
capability greatly reduce the risk of obso-
lescence.

Thank you for the opportunity to present this
proposal. You may be sure that we will use
all the resources available to the Waters
Corporation to ensure the successful implementation of the new system.

Sincerely yours,

Janet A. Curtain

Janet A. Curtain
Executive Account Manager
General Merchandise Systems

FIGURE 12–3, *continued.*

EXECUTIVE SUMMARY

The Waters 319 Interactive Terminal/615 Retail Processor System will provide your management with the tools necessary to manage people and equipment more profitably with procedures that will yield more cost-effective business controls for Cookson's.

The equipment and applications proposed for Cookson's were selected through the combined effort of Waters and Cookson's Management Information Systems Director, Mr. Becklight. The architecture of the system will respond to your current requirements and allow for a logical expansion in the future.

The features and hardware in the system were determined from data acquired through the comprehensive survey we conducted at your stores in February of this year. The total of 71 Interactive Terminals proposed to service your four store locations is based on the number of terminals currently in use and on the average number of transactions processed during normal and peak periods. The planned remodeling of all four stores was also considered, and the suggested terminal placement has been incorporated into the working floor plan. The proposed equipment configuration and software applications have been simulated to determine system performance based on the volumes and anticipated growth rates of the Cookson stores.

The information from the survey was also used in the cost justification, which was checked and verified by your controller, Mr. Deitering. The cost-effectiveness of the Waters Interactive Terminal/Retail Processor System is apparent. Expected savings, such as the projected 46% reduction in sales audit expenses, are realistic projections based on Waters's experience with other installations of this type.

FIGURE 12–4. Executive summary.

included several other applications in addition to the payroll application. Notice that this discussion, like that found in an unsolicited sales proposal, begins with a statement of the customer's problem, follows with a statement of the solution, and concludes with a statement of the benefits to the customer.

Essential to any sales proposal are a *cost analysis* and a *delivery schedule.* The cost analysis itemizes the cost of all the products and

---

GENERAL SYSTEM DESCRIPTION

The point-of-sale system that Waters is proposing for Cookson's includes two primary Waters products. These are the 319 Interactive
Terminal and the 615 Retail Processor.

Waters 319 Interactive Terminal

The primary component in the proposed retail
system is the Interactive Terminal. It contains a full microprocessor, which gives it
the flexibility that Cookson's has been looking for.

The 319 Interactive Terminal provides you
with freedom in sequencing a transaction. You
are not limited to a preset list of available
steps or transactions. The terminal program
can be adapted to provide unique transaction
sets, each designed with a logical sequence
of entry and processing to accomplish required tasks. In addition to sales transactions recorded on the selling floor, specialized transactions such as theater tickets
sales and payments can be designed for your
customer service area.

The 319 Interactive Terminal also functions
as a credit authorization device, either by
using its own floor limits or by transmitting
a credit inquiry to the 615 Retail Processor
for authorization.

Data-collection formats have been simplified
so that transaction editing and formatting
are much more easily accomplished. Mr. Sier

FIGURE 12–5. General description of products.

has already been provided with documentation
on these formats and has outlined all data-
processing efforts that will be necessary to
interface the data to your current systems.
These projections have been considered in the
cost justification.

Waters 615 Retail Processor

The Waters 615 Retail Processor is a minicomputer system designed to support the Waters
family of retail terminals. The processor
will reside in the computer room in your data
center in Buffalo. Operators already on your
staff will be trained to initiate and monitor
its activities.

The 615 will collect data transmitted from
the retail terminals, process credit, check
authorization inquiries, maintain files to be
accessed by the retail terminals, accumulate
totals, maintain a message-routing network,
and control the printing of various reports.
The functions and level of control performed
at the processor depend on the peripherals
and software selected.

Software

The Retail III software used with the system
has been thoroughly tested and is operational
in many Waters customer installations.

The software provides the complete processing
of the transaction, from the interaction with
the operator on the sales floor through the
data capture on cassette or disk in stores
and your data center.

Retail III provides a menu of modular applications for your selection. Parameters condition each of them to your hardware environment and operating requirements. The
selection of hardware will be closely related
to the selection of the software applications.

FIGURE 12–5, *continued.*

PAYROLL APPLICATION

Current Procedure

Your current system of reporting time requires each hourly employee to sign a time
sheet; the time sheet is reviewed by the department manager and sent to the Payroll Department on Friday evening. Since the week
ends on Saturday, the employee must show the
scheduled hours for Saturday and not the actual hours; therefore, the department manager
must adjust the reported hours on the time
sheet for employees who do not report on the
scheduled Saturday or who do not work the
number of hours scheduled.

The Payroll Department employs a supervisor
and three full-time clerks. To meet deadlines
caused by an unbalanced work flow, an additional part-time clerk is used for 20 to 30
hours per week. The average wage for this
clerk is $4.25 per hour.

Advantage of Waters's System

The 319 Interactive Terminal can be programmed for entry of payroll data for each
employee on Monday mornings by department
managers, with the data reflecting actual
hours worked. This system would eliminate the
need for manual batching, controlling, and
keypunching. The Payroll Department estimates
conservatively that this work consumes 40
hours per week.

Hours per week	40
Average wage	× 4.25
Weekly payroll cost	$170.00
Annual savings	$8,840.00

Elimination of the manual tasks of tabulating, batching, and controlling can save .25
units. Improved work flow resulting from
timely data in the system without keypunch

FIGURE 12–6. Detailed solution.

```
processing will allow more efficient use of
clerical hours. This would reduce payroll by
the .50 units currently required to meet
weekly check disbursement.

     Eliminate manual tasks                    .25
     Improve work flow                         .75
     40-hour unit reduction                   1.00

     Hours per week                            40
     Average wage                            4.75
     Savings per week                     $190.00

     Annual savings                     $9,880.00

  TOTAL SAVINGS:  $18,720.00
```

FIGURE 12–6, *continued.*

services that you are offering; the delivery schedule commits you to a specific timetable for providing those products and services. Figure 12–7 shows the cost analysis and delivery schedule of the Waters Corporation proposal. Also essential if your recommendations involve modifying the customer's physical plant is a *site preparation description* that details the modifications required. Further, if the products you are proposing to sell require training of the customer's personnel, your proposal should specify the *required training* and its cost. Figure 12–8 shows the site preparation section and Figure 12–9 the training section of the Waters proposal.

To prevent misunderstandings about what your responsibilities will be and what the customer's responsibilities will be, you should draw up a *statement of responsibilities*. The statement of responsibilities, such as the one shown in Figure 12–10, usually appears toward the end of the proposal. Also toward the end of the proposal is a *description of the vendor*. This section should give a factual description of your company, its background, and its present position in the industry. Following this description, many proposals add what is known as an *institutional sales pitch*. Up to this point, the proposal has attempted to sell specific goods and services. The sales pitch strikes a somewhat different chord: it is designed to sell the company and its general capability in the field. Less matter-of-fact than the vendor description, the sales pitch unabashedly sings the company's praises and always concludes the proposal on an upbeat note. Figure 12–11 shows the vendor description and sales pitch sections of the Waters proposal.

COST ANALYSIS

This section of our proposal provides detailed cost information for the Waters 319
Interactive Terminal and the 615 Waters Retail Processor. It then extends these major
elements by the quantities required at each
of your four locations.

319 Interactive Terminal

	Price	Maint. (1 yr)
Terminal	$2,895	$167
Journal Printer	425	38
Receipt Printer	425	38
Forms Printer	525	38
Software	220	--
TOTALS	$4,490	$281

615 Retail Processor

	Price	Maint. (1 Yr)
Processor	$57,115	$5,787
CRT I/O Writer	2,000	324
Matrix Printer	4,245	568
Software	12,480	---
TOTALS	$75,840	$6,679

The following breakdown itemizes the cost per
store.

Store No. 1

Description	Qty	Price	Maint.
Terminals	16	$68,400	$4,496
Digital Cassette	1	1,300	147
Thermal Printer	1	2,490	332
Software	16	3,520	---
TOTALS		$75,710	$4,975

FIGURE 12–7. Cost analysis and delivery schedule.

Store No. 2

Description	Qty	Price	Maint.
Terminals	20	$85,400	$5,620
Digital Cassette	1	1,300	147
Thermal Printer	1	2,490	332
Software	20	4,400	---
TOTALS		$93,590	$6,099

Store No. 3

Description	Qty	Price	Maint.
Terminals	17	$72,590	$4,777
Digital Cassette	1	1,300	147
Thermal Printer	1	2,490	332
Software	17	3,740	---
TOTALS		$80,120	$5,256

Store No. 4

Description	Qty	Price	Maint.
Terminals	18	$76,860	$5,058
Digital Cassette	1	1,300	147
Thermal Printer	1	2,490	332
Software	18	3,960	---
TOTALS		$84,610	$5,537

Data Center at Buffalo

Description	Qty	Price	Maint.
Processor	1	$57,115	$5,787
CRT I/O Writer	1	2,000	324
Matrix Printer	1	4,245	568
Software	1	12,480	---
TOTALS		$75,840	$6,679

The following summarizes all costs.

Location	Hardware	Maint.	Software
Store No. 1	$72,190	$4,975	$3,520
Store No. 2	89,190	6,099	4,400
Store No. 3	76,380	5,256	3,740
Store No. 4	80,650	5,537	3,960
Data Center	63,360	6,679	12,480
Subtotals	$381,770	$28,546	$28,100

TOTAL $438,416

FIGURE 12–7, *continued.*

DELIVERY SCHEDULE

Waters is normally able to deliver 319 Interactive Terminals and 615 Retail Processors
within 120 days from the date of the contract. This can vary depending on the rate
and size of incoming orders.

All the software recommended in this proposal
is available for immediate delivery. We do
not anticipate any difficulty in meeting your
tentative delivery schedule.

FIGURE 12–7, *continued.*

SITE PREPARATION

Waters will work closely with Cookson's to ensure that each site is properly prepared prior to system installation. You will receive a copy of Waters's installation and wiring procedures manual, which lists the physical dimensions, service clearance, and weight of the system components in addition to the power, logic, communication-cable, and environmental requirements. Cookson's is responsible for all building alterations and electrical facility changes, including the purchase and installation of communication cables, connecting blocks, and receptacles.

Wiring

For the purpose of future site considerations, Waters's in-house wiring specifications for the system call for two twisted pair wires and twenty-two shielded gauges. The length of communications wires must not exceed 2,500 feet.

As a guide for the power supply, we suggest that Cookson's consider the following.

1. The branch circuit (limited to 20 amps) should service no equipment other than 319 Interactive Terminals.
2. Each 20-amp branch circuit should support a maximum of three Interactive Terminals.
3. Each branch circuit must have three equal-size conductors--one hot leg, one neutral, and one insulated isolated ground.
4. Hubbell IG 5362 duplex outlets or the equivalent should be used to supply power to each terminal.
5. Computer room wiring will have to be upgraded to support the 615 Retail Processor.

FIGURE 12–8. Site preparation section.

TRAINING

To ensure a successful installation, Waters offers the following training course for your operators.

Interactive Terminal/Retail Processor Operations

Course number: 8256
Length: three days
Tuition: $500.00

This course provides the student with the skills, knowledge, and practice required to operate an Interactive Terminal/Retail Processor System. On-line, clustered, and stand-alone environments are covered.

We recommend that students have department store background and that they have some knowledge of the system configuration with which they will be working.

FIGURE 12–9. Training section.

RESPONSIBILITIES

On the basis of its years of experience in installing information-processing systems, Waters believes that a successful installation requires a clear understanding of certain responsibilities.

Generally, it is Waters's responsibility to provide its users with needed assistance during the installation so that live processing can begin as soon thereafter as is practical.

Waters's Responsibilities

--Provide operations documentation for each application that you acquire from Waters.

--Provide forms and other supplies as ordered.

--Provide specifications and technical guidance for proper site planning and installation.

--Provide advisory assistance in the conversion from your present system to the new system.

Customer's Responsibilities

--Identify an installation coordinator and system operator.

--Provide supervisors and clerical personnel to perform conversion to the system.

--Establish reasonable time schedules for implementation.

--Ensure that the physical site requirements are met.

--Provide competent personnel to be trained as operators and ensure that other employees are trained as necessary.

--Assume the responsibility for implementing and operating the system.

FIGURE 12–10. Statement of responsibilities.

DESCRIPTION OF VENDOR

The Waters Corporation develops, manufactures, markets, installs, and services total business information-processing systems for selected markets. These markets are primarily in the retail, financial, commercial, industrial, health-care, education, and government sectors.

The Waters total system concept encompasses one of the broadest hardware and software product lines in the industry. Waters computers range from small business systems to powerful general-purpose processors. Waters computers are supported by a complete spectrum of terminals, peripherals, data-communication networks, and an extensive library of software products. Supplemental services and products include data centers, field service, systems engineering, and educational centers.

The Waters Corporation was founded in 1934 and presently has approximately 26,500 employees. The Waters headquarters is located at 17 North Waterloo Boulevard, Tampa, Florida, with district offices throughout the United States and Canada.

WHY WATERS?

Corporate Commitment to the Retail Industry

Waters's commitment to the retail industry is stronger than ever. We are continually striving to provide leadership in the design and implementation of new retail systems and applications that will ensure our users of a logical growth pattern.

Research and Development

Over the years, Waters has spent increasingly large sums on research and development ef-

FIGURE 12–11. Description of vendor and institutional sales pitch.

forts to assure the availability of products
and systems for the future. In 19--, our research and development expenditure for advanced systems design and technological inno-
vations reached the $70 million level.

Leading Point-of-Sale Vendor

Waters is a leading point-of-sale vendor,
having installed over 150,000 units. The
knowledge and experience that Waters has
gained over the years from these installations ensure well-coordinated and effective
systems implementations.

FIGURE 12–11, *continued.*

MINUTES OF MEETINGS

Organizations and committees keep official records of their meetings; such records are known as *minutes*. If, in the course of your work, you attend many business-related meetings, you may be asked to serve as *recording secretary* at some of them. The duties of the secretary are to write down and distribute the minutes of a meeting. Usually, at the beginning of each meeting the minutes of the preceding meeting are read aloud if printed copies of the minutes were not distributed to the members beforehand. The group then votes to accept the minutes as prepared or to revise or clarify specific items.

The minutes of meetings should include the following information.

1. Name of the group or committee that is holding the meeting.
2. The place, time, and date of the meeting.
3. The kind of meeting being held (a regular meeting or a special meeting called to discuss a specific subject or problem).
4. The number of members present. If the committee or board is small (ten or fewer), members' names should be given.
5. A statement that the chairperson and the secretary were present, or the name of the substitute if either one was absent.
6. A statement that the minutes of the previous meeting were approved or revised, or a statement that the reading of the minutes was dispensed with.
7. A list of the reports that were read and approved. It is seldom necessary to give a detailed account of the substance of the reports submitted.

8. All the main motions that were made, with statements as to whether they were carried, defeated, or tabled (vote postponed). Do not include motions that were withdrawn. It is also customary to include the names of those who made and seconded the motions.
9. Resolutions that were adopted, written out in full. If a resolution was rejected, make a simple statement to that effect.
10. A record of all ballots, complete with the number of votes cast "for" and "against."
11. The time that the meeting was adjourned (officially ended) and the place, time, and the date of the next meeting.
12. The recording secretary's signature (and typed name) and, if desired, the signature of the chairperson.

Since minutes are often used to settle disputes, they must be accurate, complete, and clear. When approved, minutes of meetings are official and can be used as evidence in legal proceedings.

Keep your minutes brief and to the point. Give complete information on each topic, but do not ramble—conclude the topic and go on to the next one. Following a set format will help you to keep the minutes concise. You might, for example, use the heading TOPIC, followed by the subheadings *Discussion* and *Action Taken,* for each major point that is discussed, as in Figure 12–12.

Keep abstractions and generalities to a minimum and, most important, be specific. If you are referring to a nursing station on the second floor of a hospital, say "the nursing station on the second floor" or "the second-floor nursing station," not "the second floor."

Remember that the minutes you are preparing may be used, at some time in the future, by a lawyer, a judge, or jury members who probably won't be familiar with the situation you are describing—and that you may not be reachable to explain what you wrote. (Even if you are available, you may not remember any of the details of the situation.) After all, the reason for taking minutes is to create a permanent record that will be available if it should be needed—at any time and for any reason.

Be specific, too, when you refer to people. Instead of using titles ("the chief of the Word Processing Unit") use names and titles ("Ms. Florence Johnson, head of the Word Processing Unit"). And be consistent in the way you refer to people. Do not call one person *Mr.* Jarrell and another *Janet* Wilson. It may be unintentional, but a lack of consistency in titles or names may reveal a deference to one person at the expense of another. Avoid adjectives and adverbs that suggest either good or bad qualities, as in "Mr. Sturgess's *capable* assistant read the *extremely comprehensive* report of the subcommittee." Minutes should always be objective and impartial.

If a member of the committee is to follow up on something and

NORTH TAMPA MEDICAL CENTER

Minutes of the Regular Meeting of the
Medical Audit Committee

DATE: July 26, 19—

PRESENT: G. Miller (Chairperson), C. Bloom, J.
Dades, K. Gilley, D. Ingoglia (Secretary),
S. Ramirez, D. Rowan, C. Tsien, C. Voron-
ski.

ABSENT: R. Fautier, R. Wolf

Dr. Gail Miller called the meeting to order at 12:45
p.m. Dr. David Ingoglia made a motion that the June 1,
19—, minutes be approved as distributed. Dr. Carole
Tsien seconded the motion, which was passed.

   The committee discussed and took action on the
following topics.

(1) TOPIC: Meeting Time

   Discussion: A discussion was held on the most
convenient time for the committee to meet.
   Action taken: The committee decided to meet on
the fourth Tuesday of every month, at 12:30 p.m.

FIGURE 12–12. Sample minutes.

report back to the committee at its next meeting, state clearly the member's name and the responsibility he or she has accepted. There should be no uncertainty as to what task the member will be performing for the committee.

When you have been assigned to take the minutes at a meeting, go adequately prepared. Bring more than one pen and plenty of paper. If it is convenient, you may bring a tape recorder as backup to your notes. Have ready the minutes of the previous meeting and any other material that you may need. If you do not know shorthand, take memory-jogging notes during the meeting and then expand them with the appropriate details immediately after the meeting. Remember that minutes are primarily a record of specific actions taken, although you may sometimes need to summarize what was said or state the essential ideas in your own words. Figure 12–13 shows a sample set of minutes that uses a less rigid format than Figure 12–12.

```
                    WARETON MEDICAL CENTER
                    DEPARTMENT OF MEDICINE



             Minutes of the Regular Meeting of the
                    Credentials Committee


     DATE: April 18, 19--


     PRESENT: M. Valden (Chairperson), R. Baron, M.
              Frank, J. Guern, L. Kingson, L. Kins-
              low (Secretary), S. Perry, B. Roman,
              J. Sorder, F. Sugihana

        Dr. Mary Valden called the meeting to order
     at 8:40 p.m. The minutes of the previous
     meeting were unanimously approved, with the
     following correction: the secretary of the
     Department of Medicine is to be changed from
     Dr. Juanita Alvarez to Dr. Barbara Golden.


     Old Business

     None.
```

FIGURE 12–13. Minutes.

New Business

The request by Dr. Henry Russell for staff privileges in the Department of Medicine was discussed. Dr. James Guern made a motion that Dr. Russell be granted staff privileges. Dr. Martin Frank seconded the motion, which was passed unanimously.

Similar requests by Dr. Ernest Hiram and Dr. Helen Redlands were discussed. Dr. Fred Sugihana made a motion that both physicians be granted all staff privileges except respiratory-care privileges, because the two physicians had not had a sufficient number of respiratory cases. Dr. Steven Perry seconded the motion, which was passed unanimously.

Dr. John Sorder and Dr. Barry Roman asked for a clarification of general duties for active staff members with respiratory-care privileges. Dr. Richard Baron stated that he would present a clarification at the next scheduled staff meeting, on May 15.

Dr. Baron asked for a volunteer to fill the existing vacancy for Emergency Room duty. Dr. Guern volunteered. He and Dr. Baron will arrange a duty schedule.

There being no further business, the meeting was adjourned at 9:15 p.m. The next regular meeting is scheduled for May 15, at 8:40 p.m.

Respectfully submitted,

Leslie Kinslow

Mary Valden

Leslie Kinslow
Medical Staff Secretary

Mary Valden, M.D.
Chairperson

FIGURE 12–13, *continued.*

JOB DESCRIPTIONS

To ensure an efficiently functioning organization, most large companies and many small ones find it necessary to specify, in a formal *job description,* the duties of and requirements for many of the jobs in the firm. Job descriptions fulfill several important functions: they provide information on which equitable salary scales can be based; they help management determine whether all responsibilities within a company are adequately covered; they let both prospective and currently working employees know exactly what is expected of them; and, together, a firm's job descriptions present a picture of the organization's structure.

Sometimes plant or office supervisors are given the task of writing the job descriptions of the employees assigned to them. In many organizations, though, an employee may draft his or her own job description, which is then checked over and approved by the immediate superior.

Format for Writing Job Descriptions

Although job description formats vary from organization to organization, the following headings are typical.

- *Accountability*. This section identifies, by title, the person or persons to whom the employee reports.
- *Scope of responsibilities*. This section provides an overview of the primary and secondary functions of the job and states, if it is applicable, who reports to the employee.
- *Specific duties*. This section gives a detailed account of the specific duties of the job, as concisely as possible.
- *Personal requirements*. This section lists the education, training, experience, and licensing required or desired for the job.

Tips for Writing Job Descriptions

If you have been asked to prepare a job description for your position, the following guidelines should be of help to you.

1. Before attempting to write your job description, keep a list of all the different tasks you do in a week or a month. Otherwise, you will almost certainly leave out some of your duties.
2. Focus on content. Remember that you are writing a description of your job, not yourself.
3. List your duties in decreasing order of importance. Knowing how your various duties rank in importance makes it easier to set valid job qualifications.
4. Begin each statement of a duty with a verb, and be specific about what the duty is. Write "Answer and route incoming telephone calls" rather than "Handle telephone calls."
5. Review existing job descriptions that you know have been successful.

JOB TITLE: Welding Supervisor

ACCOUNTABILITY: Reports directly to the Plant Manager

SCOPE OF RESPONSIBILITIES: Is responsible for supervising the work of fifteen welders, for preparing production reports, for maintaining and replacing equipment, and for carrying out such duties as the Plant Manager may specify.

SPECIFIC DUTIES:

Supervises the work of fifteen welders. Evaluates, every six months, the performances of the welders assigned to him or to her. Instructs new employees in safe working habits. Prepares a monthly attendance report. Periodically checks the quality of work by examining tubes and balls for weld splatters and by reviewing the inspector's quality reports. Prepares production reports. Prepares a monthly memorandum itemizing production for the preceding month, including reasons for any failure to meet the production schedule. Maintains and replaces equipment. Maintains accurate logs for each machine. Makes sure that all equipment is in good operating condition and ready for the start of the next shift. Makes sure that all safety devices function properly.
Carries out such duties as the Plant Manager may specify. Meets each week with the Plant Manager and attends special meetings as requested. Attends in-service training programs and keeps up to date on the latest welding techniques.

PERSONAL REQUIREMENTS: Trade or technical college certification or degree in welding. Six years of welding experience. Ability to interact well with employees and management. Desire to stay up to date in the field.

FIGURE 12–14. Job description.

The typical job description shown in Figure 12–14 never mentions the person holding the job described. It focuses, instead, on the job and on the qualifications any person must possess to fill the position.

CREATING BUSINESS FORMS

Because they provide a time-saving, efficient, and uniform way to record data, *business forms* are used for countless purposes in almost all occupations. It is easier and quicker to supply information by filling out a well-designed form than by writing a detailed memorandum, letter, or report. Another advantage the form has over other types of written communication is that on every copy of a form, each particular piece of information appears in the same place—a fact that is especially important when many people are furnishing similar information. If each person providing information sent in an individually written letter, every sheet of paper submitted would be different and would require time-consuming reading and interpretation. In contrast, when the information is supplied on a form, the person filling out the form will have spent less time and effort in furnishing the data, and the person using the information from the form will have a much easier task retrieving and evaluating the data.

Preparing the Form

To be effective, a form should make it easy for one person to supply information and for another person to retrieve and interpret the information. Ideally, a form should be self-explanatory, even to a person who has never seen it before. If you are preparing a form, plan it carefully first. Determine what kind of information you will be seeking and arrange the requests for information in a logical order—logical from the point of view of the person supplying the data and the person receiving it.

Make a draft of the form, putting in all the requests for information you've decided to include and arranging the items in the order you consider the most logical. If any coworkers will be using the form, show the draft to them—you'll be rewarded for the extra time this step takes by the helpful criticism and suggestions you are likely to receive. Once you're satisfied with the draft, you can then prepare a final copy of the form.

Instructions and Captions.   To make certain that entering information on your form will be easy, be sure that you give the proper instructions in the proper place. You've probably had the experience, at some time or another, of starting to fill out a form only to realize too late that you've put your name on the line intended for your street address.

When the instructions are clear and properly placed, the person filling out the form will not be confused about which information goes where.

Instructions, which are used primarily for long, complicated forms, should go at the beginning of the form; they are often preceded by a heading designed to attract the reader's attention.

INSTRUCTIONS FOR COMPLETING THIS FORM

1. Complete the applicable blue–shaded portions on the front of pages 1, 2, and 3.
2. Mail page 1 to the Securi–Med Insurance Company at the address shown above.
3. Give page 2 to your doctor.
4. If services were rendered in a hospital, give page 3 to the hospital.
5. Use the back of page 1 to itemize bills that are to go toward your major medical deduction.

Instructions for distributing the various copies of multiple-copy forms are normally placed at the bottom of the form. These instructions are repeated on every copy of the form.

On the form itself, requests for information are normally worded as captions. Keep captions brief and to the point; avoid unnecessary repetition by combining requests for related pieces of information under an explanatory heading.

CHANGE   What make of car do you drive? _____

What year was it manufactured? _____

What model is it? _____

What is the body style? _____

TO   Vehicle Information

Make _____   Year _____

Model _____   Body style _____

Planning for Responses.   In preparing a form, it is important to provide questions that can be answered simply and briefly. The best responses are check marks, circles, or underlining; next best are numbers, single words, or brief phrases. Sentence responses are the least effective, since they take the most time to write and to read.

Make captions as specific as possible. For example, if a requested date is a date other than that on which the form is being filled out, make the caption read "Effective date," "Date issued," or whatever it may be, rather than simply "Date." As in all job-related writing, put yourself in your reader's place and try to imagine what sorts of requests would be clear to you.

Sequencing of Data.   In designing a form, try to arrange your requests for information in an order that will be most helpful to the person filling out the form. At the top of the form, include *preliminary information,* such as the name of your organization, the title of your form, and any file number or reference number. In the *main portion* of the form, include the entries you need in order to obtain the necessary data. At the *end* of the form, include space for the signature of the person filling out the form and the date.

Within the main portion of your form, the arrangement of the entries will depend on several factors. First, the subject matter of the entries will frequently determine the most logical order. A form requesting reimbursement for travel expenses, for instance, would logically begin with the first day of the week (or month) and end with the last day of the appropriate period. Second, if the response to one item is based on the response to another item, be sure that the items appear in the correct order. Third, whenever possible, group requests for related information together. Fourth, if a form is to move from one individual or one department to another, to be partly filled out by each in turn, put the data to be supplied by the first individual or department at the top of the form, the data to be supplied by the second next, and so on (and each section of the form should, in general, be arranged on the form from left to right and from top to bottom, since that is the way we are accustomed to reading.

In many cases, you'll want to title your form. The title of the form should describe its use and application. A title should be no more than a few words long and should normally be positioned at the top center of your form. If space is critical, the title can be placed at the top left-hand corner of the form.

Designing Forms

When you sit down to prepare the final version of a form, you should pay particular attention to details of design—the arrangement on the page of the entry lines (where the responses will be filled in), and the amount of space provided for the responses.

Entry Lines.   The form can be laid out so that the person completing it supplies information on a writing line, in a writing block, or in square boxes.

The *writing line* is simply a caption.

<table>
<tr><td>_____
(Name)</td><td>_____
(Telephone)</td></tr>
</table>

_____
(Street Address)

<table>
<tr><td>_____
(City)</td><td>_____
(State)</td><td>_____
(Zip Code)</td></tr>
</table>

<table>
<tr><td>_____
(Age)</td><td>_____
(Weight)</td><td>_____
(Height)</td><td>_____
(Sex)</td></tr>
</table>

The *writing block* is essentially the same except that each entry is enclosed in a ruled block, making it impossible for the person filling out the form to associate a caption with the wrong line.

Name		Telephone
Street Address		
City	State	Zip Code
Age	Weight	Height	Sex

When all the possible responses to any question can be anticipated, you can save the person filling out the form time and effort by writing the question on the form, supplying a labeled *square box* for each possible answer, and instructing the person filling out the form to put an X in the box that corresponds to the correct answer. Such a plan will also save you time and effort in retrieving the data. Be sure that your questions are both simple and specific.

EXAMPLE Would you buy another Whapo? ☐ Yes ☐ No

The boxes may either precede or follow the question. Be sure, however, that the boxes and their labels are close enough together that they will be unmistakably associated.

REVISE red ☐ blue ☐ green ☐ yellow ☐

TO red ☐ blue ☐ green ☐ yellow ☐

Spacing. Be sure to provide enough space for the person filling out the form to enter the data. Everyone has filled out a form on which the address, signature, or other item could not possibly fit in the space allowed for it. Insufficient writing space or uneven lines are guaranteed to irritate the person filling out the form and make the information supplied hard to read. In a long form that is poorly designed, errors occur with increasing frequency as the person filling out the form becomes more and more frustrated. And if you have trouble reading responses that are too tightly spaced or that snake around the side of the form, you may introduce additional errors as you retrieve the data.

Forms may be filled out either in longhand or on a typewriter. Always allow sufficient space to accommodate both typewritten and handwritten responses. If you think that at least some people filling it out will use longhand, provide adequate space for a relatively large handwriting. And if you expect that some will reply by typewriter, take their needs into account as well. It is especially important to plan for typewritten responses if you intend to have your form *typeset* (composed on a machine that sets copy for books, newspapers, and other materials). If you do not inform the typesetter that the printed form must be easy to use on a typewriter, those who use a typewriter may have difficulty aligning the form vertically in their machines. The reason is simple: a typewriter types 6 lines to the inch, but the typeset equivalent (the regular text of this book, for example) is 6.0386 lines to the inch. Because of this slight difference in spacing, any typewriter will be off the writing line by the time it nears the bottom of a page-long typeset form. Be sure, then, to remind the typesetter to set *exactly* 6 lines to the inch.

If the form will contain more than one response per line, align the column entries vertically whenever possible, so that the person filling out the form can set tabs on the typewriter (when the tab is pressed, the platen, or roller, automatically moves to a previously set point along the line). As for horizontal spacing, there are two kinds of typewriters: the *elite*, which has twelve characters (both letters and spaces) to the inch, and the *pica,* which has ten characters to the inch. Allow adequate space for responses typed on a pica typewriter.

CHAPTER SUMMARY

Proposals, job descriptions, and minutes of meetings—although not required as frequently as letters, memos, and reports—are nonetheless very important kinds of on-the-job writing. The use of well designed forms is another form of communication that can sometimes, under the right circumstances, be more effective and efficient than writing.

Two kinds of proposals are commonly written in the business world: internal and external. An *internal proposal,* which is written to someone higher in the management structure of an organization, recommends a change or an improvement within an organization. A *sales proposal* (or external proposal) is a document that offers to provide a potential customer with a product or service, or both, at a specific price within a specified period of time. Sales proposals may be unsolicited or solicited; long proposals provide greater detail than short ones and may include such items as an executive summary, a general description of products, a detailed solution, a cost analysis, a delivery schedule, a site preparation section, a training section, a statement of responsibilities, a description of the vendor, and an institutional sales pitch.

Minutes are the official records of business meetings. Written by the designated secretary of the committee or group, they are used to settle disputes and sometimes are even offered as evidence in lawsuits.

Job descriptions specify the duties and requirements for specific jobs. They help management to establish equitable salary scales and determine whether all responsibilities within a company are adequately covered. They also help employees to know exactly what is expected of them in their jobs.

Well-designed *business forms* provide a time-saving, efficient, and uniform way to record and retrieve routine data. Filling in such a form is quicker and easier than writing detailed letters or reports.

EXERCISES

1. Write a proposal in which you recommend a change in a procedure. The procedure should be one with which you are familiar, either at school or at work. The proposal should state the nature of the problem and explain how the new procedure would be put into effect. Give at least three reasons for the change, and support your reasons with

facts that show the advantages of your proposal. Address the proposal to a dean or other school official (if the proposal is school-related) or to your immediate supervisor (if the proposal is work-related).

2. Address an internal proposal to your boss recommending that your company begin a tuition refund plan. Produce at least three major advantages to having a tuition refund plan, and present them in decreasing order of importance.

3. Assume that you are a landscaping contractor and would like to respond to the following Request for Proposals, which appears in your local newspaper:

> Lawn-mowing agreement for the Town of Augusta, Oregon. Weekly mowing of 5 miles of Route 24 median and sidings, 10 acres in Willoughby Park, and 23 acres at Augusta Memorial Golf Course, May 30 through September 30. Proposals are due April 30.

Indicate in your proposal the number of labor-hours that you estimate the contract would require, what you would charge, the ability of your personnel and equipment to do the job, your firm's experience and qualifications, and the weekly schedule that you propose to follow.

4. Write a sales proposal offering to provide 22 new typewriters in replacement for another brand of typewriter presently in use at seven branch offices of a local savings and loan association. The management of the savings and loan association is unhappy with the present typewriters, all of which are leased, and wants them replaced. Your proposal should offer to either sell or lease your brand. It should also offer a maintenance contract, regardless of whether the typewriters are purchased or leased.

5. Attend a meeting of an organization. Go to the meeting prepared to take careful, complete notes of the proceedings (make sure to obtain permission to do so). From the notes you have taken, write up the minutes of the meeting.

6. Attend a business meeting of a local service club (Kiwanis, Toastmasters, Jaycees, etc.). Write the minutes for the meeting. (You must first, of course, obtain permission to attend the meeting and to take its minutes.)

7. Attend a faculty committee meeting, with guidance from and permission of your instructor, and write the minutes of the meeting.

8. Interview someone who holds a job in a field that interests you. On the basis of the information you obtain about the job from the interview, prepare a job description of the position.

9. If you are currently employed, write a description of your job according to the guidelines presented in this chapter. If you are not employed, describe your most recent job (what you did last summer, for example). Try to reconstruct a typical day at that job, recalling as many particulars as possible.

10. Design a weekly time card for factory employees at United Agricultural Products. Employees work Mondays through Fridays, 8 A.M. to noon, 12:30 to 3:30 P.M., and have a half hour for lunch. Include on the time card a column listing the days of the week (vertical column) and columns labeled "Time In," "Time Out" (morning), "Lunch," "Time In," "Time Out" (afternoon), and "Overtime" (horizontal columns). Supervisors are to fill in the times that employees actually arrive at work and leave for the day and the times of their lunch breaks. They are also to fill in the number of hours of overtime (if any) that employees work each day. Include columns for the total hours worked each day and a final box or space for total hours worked for the week. Be sure to leave spaces for the dates that the time card covers and for the signatures of both the employee and the supervisor.

11. Design a form for use by the Medical Staff Secretary of a hospital. The form is for the reappointment of staff physicians for the coming year. It should be designed to obtain the following information: the physician's name, office address, and office telephone number; the physician's status on the hospital's staff (temporary or permanent); the hospital department in which he or she wishes to admit patients (medicine or surgery); the number of the physician's state license; and the physician's birthdate. It should also provide for "yes" and "no" answers about whether the physician in question has attended a satisfactory number of committee meetings, whether the physician has satisfactorily completed all of his or her medical records, and whether the hospital has taken any disciplinary action against the physician during the past year. Finally, the form should provide for the signature of the hospital's Chief of Staff and the date of that signature.

12. Design a form for recording the amount of money you spend each month for the following typical items: housing; food; utilities; transportation (car, bus, subway); insurance (car, life, property, medical);

school; clothing; entertainment; and the like. Include columns that show the amount you budgeted for each item, the amount actually spent, and the difference. Finally, include space for totaling expenses for each column.

13

Creating Tables and Illustrations

The primary purpose of including tables and illustrations in your writing is to increase your reader's understanding of what you are saying. Tables, graphs, photographs, drawings, charts, and maps—often collectively called *visuals* or *visual aids*—can often express ideas or convey information in ways that words alone cannot. Tables allow the easy comparison of large numbers of statistics that would be difficult to understand if they appeared in sentence form. Graphs make trends and mathematical relationships immediately evident. And drawings, photographs, charts, and maps can indicate shapes and relationships in space more concisely and efficiently than text.

By allowing the reader to interpret data at a glance, these visuals encourage faster decision-making. Tables and illustrations should be functional to your writing. If they do not contribute to your reader's understanding, do not use them. When using them is necessary, consider your purpose and your reader carefully. For example, the drawing of a dental x-ray machine for a high school science class would be different from an illustration provided for the technician who repairs such machines.

Many of the qualities of good writing—simplicity, clarity, conciseness, directness—are just as important in the creation and use of visuals. The following general guidelines apply to most visual materials. Detailed guidelines for specific kinds of illustrations are given in the discussion of each type.

1. Keep the information illustrated brief and simple.
2. Present only one or two types of information in each visual.
3. Label or caption each visual clearly.

4. If several visuals are used, number them consecutively. Tables should be numbered separately from other visuals. In a short report or paper, label tables as Table 1, Table 2, and so on; label all illustrations (drawings, photographs, maps, graphs, and so on) as Figure 1, Figure 2, etc.[1]
5. Include a key that identifies any symbols and abbreviations you use in the visual.
6. When appropriate, specify the proportions used, or include a scale of relative distances.
7. To make the visual easier to read, whenever possible use lettering that goes from left to right rather than from top to bottom. (The diagonal lettering in Figure 13–12 is sometimes effective.)
8. Keep terminology consistent. Do not, for instance, refer to something as a "proportion" in the text and as a "percentage" in the visual.
9. Leave enough space around and within the visual for easy viewing.
10. Be certain that the significance of each visual is made clear in the text.
11. Relate the visual to the text around it by referring to it by figure or table number and title.
12. Position the visual as close as possible to the text that refers to it. Unless it is simply impossible, the text reference should precede the figure or table.
13. If more than five visuals appear in a formal report, list them, together with figure/table and page numbers, under a separate heading following the table of contents, labeled "List of Figures" or "List of Tables."

Presented with clarity and consistency, visuals can help your reader focus on key portions of your report. Be aware, though, that even the best visual only supplements, or supports, the text. Your writing must carry the burden of providing context for the visual and pointing out its significance.

A discussion of visuals commonly used in on-the-job writing follows. Your topic will ordinarily determine the best visual material to use.

TABLES

A table is useful for showing large numbers of specific, related data in a brief space. Because a table displays its information in rows and

---

[1] In longer works, such as this book, figures and tables may be double-numbered by chapter or section (for example, the second figure in Chapter 5 would be Figure 5–2).

columns, the reader can easily compare data in one column with data in another. If such data were presented in the text, the reader would read through groups of numbers and possibly not recognize their significance. Tables typically include the following elements (see Figure 13–1):

TABLE 1 RECREATIONAL FRESH-WATER ANGLING BY WATER-BODY TYPE AND GEOGRAPHICAL REGION*

Geographical Regions	Reservoirs	Man-Made Ponds	Natural Lakes & Ponds	Rivers & Streams	Farm Ponds
New England	130	40	570	410	410
Middle Atlantic	710	290	780	1200	630
East North Central	1200	760	3100	1600	1300
West North Central	810	550	1200	970	980
South Atlantic	1100	760	640	1500	1600
East South Central	890	630	190	670	1200
West South Central	1700	610	430	880	1300
Mountain	820	50	280	600	230
Pacific	950	200	820	1400	470
Totals	8300	3900	8000	9200	7800

*In thousands of anglers. Anglers who fished in more than one water body or region are represented in more than one category.

SOURCE: U.S. Department of the Interior

Labels (with pointer lines): Table Number, Caption, Boxhead, Column captions, Stub, Body, Rule, Footnote, Source Line.

FIGURE 13–1. Sample table.

- *Table number.* If you are using several tables, assign each a number; center the number and title above the table. Table numerals are usually Arabic, and they should be assigned sequentially to the tables throughout the text. Tables should be referred to in the text by table number rather than by location ("Table 4" rather than "the above table"). If your report or paper has more than five tables, list table titles, table numbers, and page numbers on a separate page immediately after the table of contents, labeled "List of Tables."
- *Table title.* The title, which is placed just above the table, should describe concisely what the table represents.

- *Column headings.* Headings should be kept brief but descriptive. Units of measurement, where necessary, should either be specified as part of the heading or enclosed in parentheses beneath the heading. Standard abbreviations and symbols are acceptable. Avoid vertical lettering whenever possible.
- *Stub.* The left-hand vertical column of a table is called the stub. It lists the items about which information is given in the body of the table.
- *Body.* The body comprises the data below the column headings and to the right of the stub. Within the body, columns should be arranged so that the terms to be compared appear in adjacent rows and columns. Where no information exists for a specific item, substitute a row of dots or a dash to acknowledge the gap.
- *Rules.* These are the lines that separate the table into its various parts. Horizontal rules are placed below the title, below the body of the table, and between the column headings and the body of the table. They should not be closed at the sides. The columns within the table may be separated by vertical rules if such lines aid clarity.
- *Source line.* The source line, which identifies where the data were obtained, appears below the table (when a source line is appropriate). (Many organizations place the source line below the footnotes.)
- *Footnotes.* Footnotes are used for explanations of individual items in the table. Symbols (*, †) or lowercase letters (sometimes in parentheses) rather than numbers are ordinarily used to key table footnotes because numbers might be mistaken for numerical data within the table.
- *Continuing tables.* When a table must be divided so that it can be continued on another page, repeat the column headings and give the table number at the head of each new page with a "continued" label ("Table 3, continued").

GRAPHS

Graphs, like tables, present numerical data in visual form. Graphs have several advantages over tables. Trends, movements, distributions, and cycles are more readily apparent in graphs than they are in tables. Further, by providing a means for ready comparisons, a graph often shows a significance in the data not otherwise immediately evident. Be aware, however, that although graphs present statistics in a more interesting and comprehensible form than tables do, they are less accurate. For this reason, they are often accompanied by tables that give exact

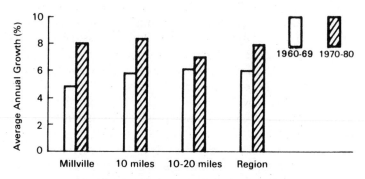

AVERAGE ANNUAL GROWTH RATE
FOR FOUR ZONES AROUND GREATER
MILLVILLE

	Growth (%)[*]	
Area	1960–1969	1970–1980
Millville	4.4	8.0
10 miles	6.0	8.4
10–20 miles	6.1	7.0
Region	6.0	7.8

[*] Data based on assessed market value.

FIGURE 13–2. Figure and table showing the same data.

figures. (Note the difference between the graph and table showing the same data in Figure 13–2.) If the graph remains uncluttered, the exact data can be added to each column, thereby giving the reader both a quick overview of the data and accurate figures. (See Figures 13–11 and 13–12.) There are many different kinds of graphs, most notably line graphs, bar graphs, pie graphs, and picture graphs. All kinds of graphs can now be easily rendered with the aid of computer graphics.

Line Graphs

The line graph, which is the most widely used of all graphs, shows the relationship between two sets of figures. The graph is composed of a vertical axis and a horizontal axis that intersect at right angles. Each axis represents one set of figures. The relationship between the two sets is indicated by points plotted along appropriate intersections of the two axes. Once plotted, the points are connected to one another to form a continuous line, and the relationship between the two sets of data becomes readily apparent.

The line graph's vertical axis usually represents amounts (the vertical axis in Figure 13–3 represents numbers of children), and its horizontal

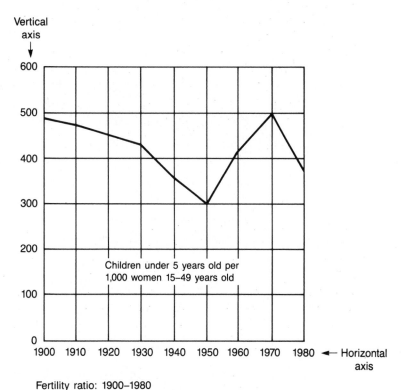

Fertility ratio: 1900–1980

FIGURE 13–3. Single-line graph.

axis usually represents increments of time (the horizontal axis in Figure 13–3 represents ten-year increases).

Line graphs with more than one plotted line are common because they allow for comparisons between two sets of statistics. In creating such graphs, be certain to identify each plotted line with a label or a legend, as shown in Figure 13–4. You can emphasize the difference between the two lines by shading the space that separates them. The following guidelines apply to most line graphs:

1. Give the graph a title that describes the data clearly and concisely.
2. If your report includes several visuals, assign a figure number to each one.
3. Indicate the *zero point* of the graph (the point where the two axes meet). If the range of data shown makes it inconvenient to begin at zero, insert a break in the scale, as in Figure 13–5.
4. Divide the vertical axis into equal portions, from the least amount at the bottom to the greatest amount at the top. Ordinarily, the caption for this scale is placed at the upper left. Lengthy

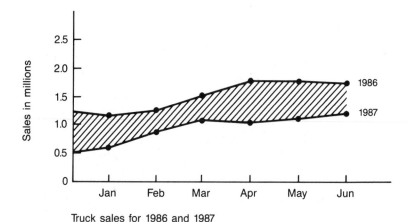

Truck sales for 1986 and 1987

FIGURE 13–4. Double-line graph with difference shaded.

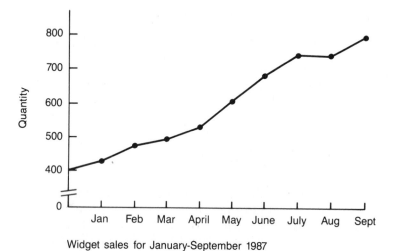

Widget sales for January-September 1987

FIGURE 13–5. Line graph with vertical axis broken.

captions can be placed vertically along the vertical axis, as in Figure 13–4.

5. Divide the horizontal axis into equal units from left to right, and label them to show what values each represents.

6. The angle at which the curved line rises and falls is determined by the scales of the two axes—that is, by the units into which each axis is divided. Therefore, divide the vertical and horizontal scales so that they give an accurate visual impression of the data. The curve can be kept free of distortion if the ratio between the scales is kept constant. See Figure 13–6.

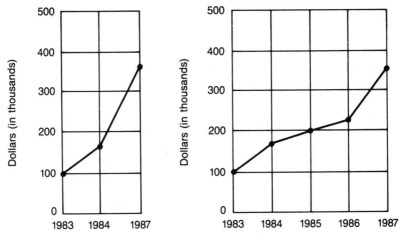

FIGURE 13–6. Distorted curve (left) and distortion-free curve.

7. Hold grid lines to a minimum so that the curved lines stand out. Since precise values are usually shown in a table of data accompanying a graph, detailed grid lines are unnecessary. Note the increasing clarity of the three graphs in Figures 13–7, 13–8, and 13–9.

8. Include a key when necessary, as in Figure 13–8. Sometimes a label will do just as well, as in Figure 13–9.

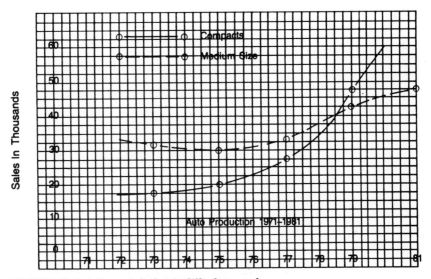

FIGURE 13–7. A line graph that is difficult to read.

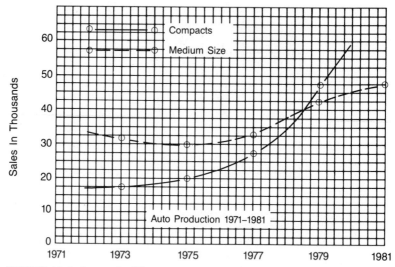

FIGURE 13–8. A more legible version of Figure 13–7.

9. If the information comes from another source, include a source line under the graph at the lower left, as in Figure 13–16.
10. Place explanatory footnotes directly below the figure caption. See Figure 13–13.
11. Make all lettering read horizontally if possible.

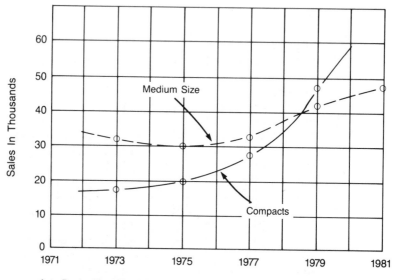

FIGURE 13–9. A clear version of Figure 13–7.

Bar Graphs

Bar graphs consist of horizontal or vertical bars of equal width but scaled in length or height to represent some quantity. They are commonly used to show the following proportional relations:

1. Varying quantities of the same item during a fixed period of time (Figure 13–10)·
2. Quantities of the same item at different points in time (Figure 13–11)
3. Quantities of different items during a fixed period of time (Figure 13–12)
4. Quantities of the different parts that make up a whole (Figure 13–13)

Note that in Figure 13–12, showing refined petroleum prices, the exact price appears at the top of each bar. This eliminates the need to have a table giving the price data accompany the graph. If the bars are not labeled, as they are not in Figures 13–10 and 13–14, the different portions must be clearly indicated by shading, crosshatching, or other devices. Include a key that represents the various subdivisions.

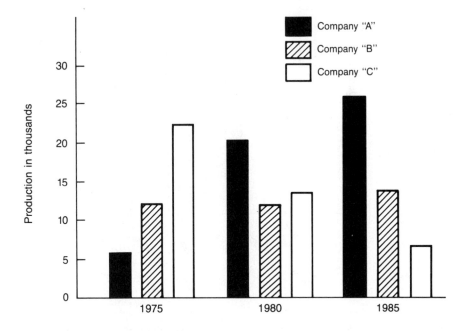

FIGURE 13–10. Bar graph showing quantities of the same item during a fixed period.

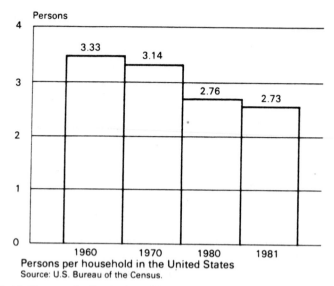

Persons per household in the United States
Source: U.S. Bureau of the Census.

FIGURE 13–11. Bar graph showing quantities of the same item at different points in time.

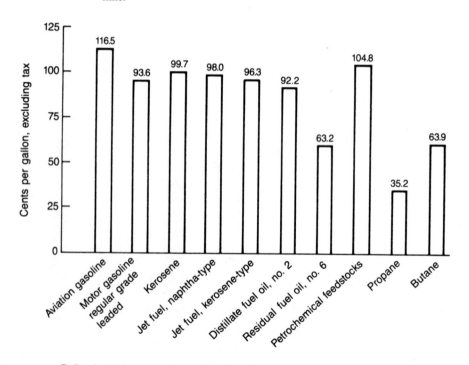

Refined petroleum product wholesale prices, 1982
SOURCE Federal Energy Administration

FIGURE 13–12. Bar graph showing varying quantities of different items during a fixed period (1982).

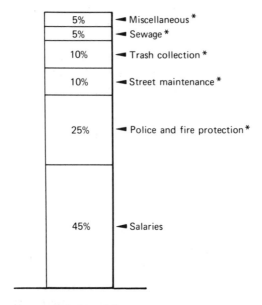

Your municipal tax dollar

* These figures do not include salaries.

FIGURE 13–13. Bar graph showing quantities of different parts making up a whole.

Bar graphs can also indicate what proportion of a whole the various component parts represent. In such a graph the bar, which is theoretically equivalent to 100 percent, is divided according to the proportion of the whole that each item sampled represents. (Compare the displays of the same data in Figures 13–13 and 13–15.) In some bar graphs, the completed bar does not represent 100 percent because all the parts of the whole have not been included in the sample (see Figure 13–14).

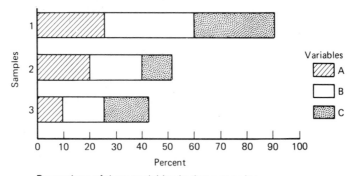

Proportions of three variables in three samples.

FIGURE 13–14. Bar graph in which not all parts of the whole have been included.

Pie Graphs

A pie graph presents data as wedge-shaped sections of a circle. The circle equals 100 percent, or the whole, of some quantity (a tax dollar, a bus fare, the hours of a working day), with the wedges representing the various parts into which the whole can be divided. In Figure 13–15, for example, the circle stands for a city tax dollar and is divided into units equivalent to the percentages of the tax dollar spent on various city services.

The relationships among the various statistics presented in a pie graph are easy to grasp, but the information is often rather general. For this reason, a pie graph is often accompanied by a table that presents the actual figures on which the percentages in the graph are based.

When you construct a pie graph, keep the following points in mind.

1. The complete 360° circle is equivalent to 100 percent; therefore, each percentage point is equivalent to 3.6°.
2. To make the relative percentages as clear as possible, begin at the 12 o'clock position and sequence the wedges clockwise, from largest to smallest.
3. If you shade the wedges, do so clockwise and from light to dark.
4. Keep all labels horizontal and, most important, give the percentage values of each wedge.
5. Finally, check to see that all wedges, as well as the percentage values given for them, add up to 100 percent.

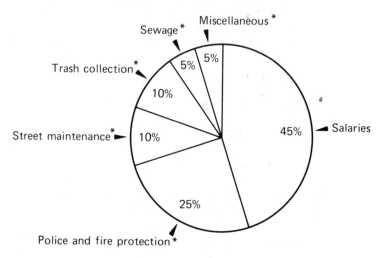

Your municipal tax dollar
* These figures do not include salaries.

FIGURE 13–15. Pie graph.

Although pie graphs have strong visual impact, they also have drawbacks. If more than five or six items of information are presented, the graph looks cluttered. And, unless percentages are labeled on each section, the reader cannot compare the values of the sections as accurately as on a bar graph.

Picture Graphs

Picture graphs are modified bar graphs that use picture symbols to represent the item for which data are presented. Each symbol corresponds to a specified quantity of the item, as in Figure 13–16. Note that precise figures are also included, since the picture symbol can indicate only approximate figures.

Here are some tips on preparing picture graphs:

1. Make the symbol self-explanatory.
2. Have each symbol represent a single item.
3. Show larger quantities by increasing the number of symbols rather than by creating a larger symbol, because if the latter is done it is difficult to judge relative size accurately.

COMPUTER GRAPHICS

Many computer systems, including microcomputers, have sophisticated graphics programs that allow you to create complex six-color graphs, such as multiple bar graphs and pie graphs. By integrating computer graphics and word-processing programs, you can create visuals that can be rapidly inserted anywhere in the text, deleted, or stored for later use. With computer graphics, you can also do the following:

- Use an electronic stylus (a pen with an electronic signal) to draw pictures on a monitor
- Map densities and concentrations in different colors
- Use shading and shadows to create three-dimensional effects
- Create and revise mathematical models, animations, or simulated events
- Use computer-assisted design to direct and automate computer-assisted manufacturing

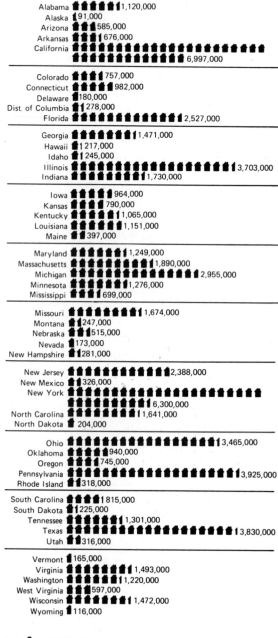

Each ⌂ = 200,000 units

Number of housing units, by states
SOURCE: U.S. Bureau of the Census
FIGURE 13–16. Picture graph.

DRAWINGS

A drawing is useful when you wish to focus on details or relationships that a photograph cannot capture (see Figures 13–17 and 13–18). It can emphasize the significant piece of a mechanism, or its function, and omit what is not significant. However, if the precise details of the actual appearance of an object are necessary to your report or document, a photograph is essential.

To show the proper sequence in which parts fit together, or when it is essential to show the details of each individual part, use an *exploded-view drawing*. (See Figure 13–19.)

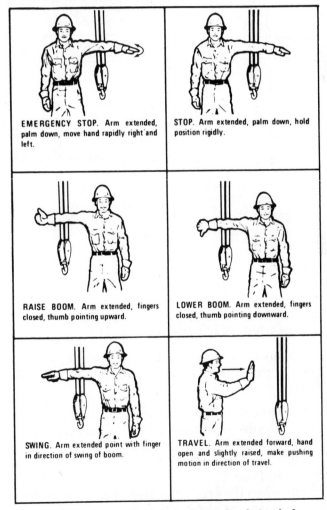

FIGURE 13–17. Drawing showing relationships among hand signals for crane operation. SOURCE: Harnischfeger Corporation.

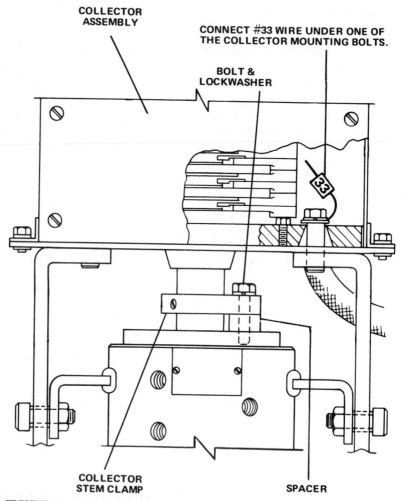

FIGURE 13–18. Cutaway drawing of a collector.
SOURCE: Harnischfeger Corporation.

Many organizations have their own format specifications for draw-ings. In the absence of such specifications, the following tips should be helpful:

1. Give the drawing a clear title and a figure number, both of which should be centered or flush left below the drawing.
2. Place the source line, if there is one, aligned beneath the title.
3. Show the equipment from the point of view of the person who will use it.
4. When illustrating a subsystem, show its relationship to the larger system of which it is a part.

5. Draw the different parts of an object in proportion to one another, unless you indicate that certain parts are enlarged.
6. Where a sequence of drawings is used to illustrate a process, arrange them from left to right and from top to bottom.
7. Label parts in the drawing so that text references to them are clear.
8. Depending on the complexity of what is shown, labels may be placed on the parts themselves, or the parts may be given letter or number symbols, with an accompanying key. (See Figure 13–19.)

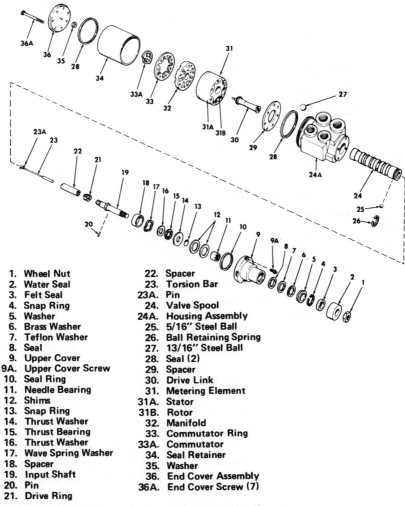

1. Wheel Nut	22. Spacer
2. Water Seal	23. Torsion Bar
3. Felt Seal	23A. Pin
4. Snap Ring	24. Valve Spool
5. Washer	24A. Housing Assembly
6. Brass Washer	25. 5/16″ Steel Ball
7. Teflon Washer	26. Ball Retaining Spring
8. Seal	27. 13/16″ Steel Ball
9. Upper Cover	28. Seal (2)
9A. Upper Cover Screw	29. Spacer
10. Seal Ring	30. Drive Link
11. Needle Bearing	31. Metering Element
12. Shims	31A. Stator
13. Snap Ring	31B. Rotor
14. Thrust Washer	32. Manifold
15. Thrust Bearing	33. Commutator Ring
16. Thrust Washer	33A. Commutator
17. Wave Spring Washer	34. Seal Retainer
18. Spacer	35. Washer
19. Input Shaft	36. End Cover Assembly
20. Pin	36A. End Cover Screw (7)
21. Drive Ring	

FIGURE 13–19. Exploded-view drawing of power steering valve.
SOURCE: Harnischfeger Corporation.

PHOTOGRAPHS

Photographs are vital to many publications. Pictures are the best way to show the surface appearance of an object or to record an event or the development of a phenomenon over a period of time. Not all representations, however, call for photographs. They cannot depict the internal workings of a mechanism or below-the-surface details of objects or structures. Such details are better shown in drawings or diagrams.

Highlighting Photographic Objects

Stand close enough to the object so that it fills your picture frame. To get precise and clear photographs, choose camera angles carefully. A camera will photograph only what it is aimed at; accordingly, select important details and the camera angles that will record these details. To show the relative size of an unfamiliar object, place a familiar object—such as a ruler, a book, or a person—near the object that is to be photographed.

Tips for Using Photographs

Like all illustrative materials, photographs must be handled carefully. When preparing photographs for a report, observe the following guidelines:

1. Mount photographs on white bond paper with rubber cement or another adhesive, and allow ample margins.
2. If the photograph is the same size as the paper, type the caption, the figure number, the page number near which the photograph is to appear, and any other important information on a label and fasten it with rubber cement or another adhesive to the back of the photograph. (Photographs are often given figure numbers in sequence with other illustrations in a publication; see Figure 13–20.)
3. Position the figure number and caption so that the reader can view them and the photograph from the same orientation.
4. Do not draw crop marks (lines showing where the photo should be trimmed for reproduction) directly across a photograph. Draw them at the very edges of the photograph.
5. Do not write on a photograph, front or back. Tape a tissue-paper overlay over the face of the photograph, and then write very lightly on the overlay with a soft-lead pencil. Never write on the overlay with a ball-point pen.
6. Do not use paper clips or staples on photographs.
7. Do not fold or crease photographs.

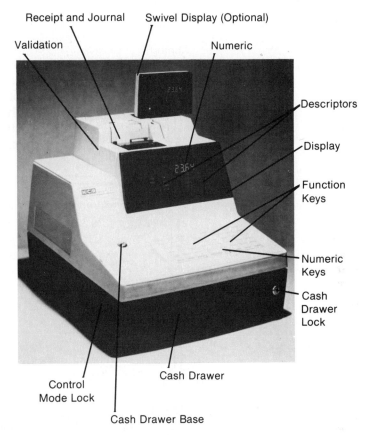

Receipt and Journal Swivel Display (Optional)

Validation Numeric

Descriptors

Display

Function Keys

Numeric Keys

Cash Drawer Lock

Cash Drawer

Control Mode Lock

Cash Drawer Base

FIGURE 13–20. Photograph (cash register).

FLOWCHARTS

A flowchart is a diagram of a process that involves stages, with the sequence of stages shown from beginning to end. The flowchart presents an overview of the process that allows the reader to grasp the essential steps of the process quickly and easily. The process being illustrated could range from the steps involved in assembling a bicycle to the stages by which bauxite ore is refined into aluminum ingots for fabrication.

Flowcharts can take several forms to represent the steps in a process. They can consist of labeled blocks (Figure 13–21), pictorial representations (Figure 13–22), or standardized symbols (Figure 13–23). The items in

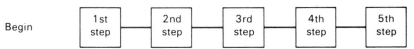

Begin | 1st step | 2nd step | 3rd step | 4th step | 5th step

FIGURE 13–21. Simple block flowchart.

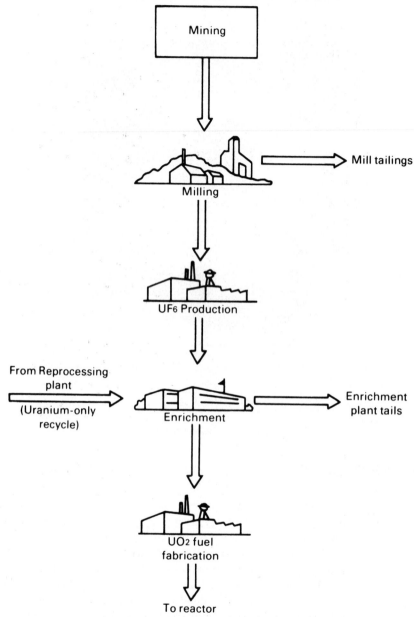

Light-Water Reactor Uranium Fuel Cycle Front-End Operations

FIGURE 13–22. Flowchart using pictorial symbols.

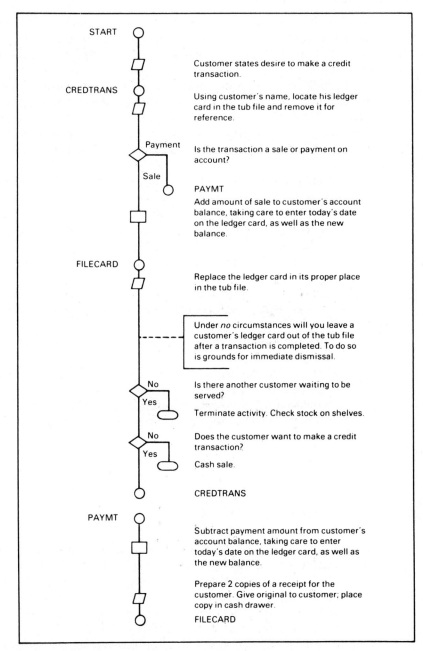

Flowchart of a Credit Transaction

FIGURE 13–23. Flowchart using standardized symbols.

any flowchart are always connected according to the sequence in which the steps occur. The normal direction of flow in a chart is left to right or top to bottom. When the flow is otherwise, be sure to indicate it with arrows.

Flowcharts that document computer programs and other information-processing procedures use standardized symbols. The standards are set forth in *U.S.A. Standard Flowchart Symbols and Their Usage in Information Processing,* published by the American National Standards Institute, publication X3.5. When creating a flowchart, follow these guidelines:

1. Label the flowchart clearly and concisely.
2. Assign the chart a figure number if it is being used in a document that contains five or more illustrations.
3. With labeled blocks and standardized symbols, use arrows to show the direction of flow only if the flow is opposite to the normal direction. With pictorial representations, use arrows to show the direction of all flow.
4. Label each step in the process, or identify it with a conventional symbol. Steps can also be represented pictorially or by captioned blocks.
5. Include a key if the flowchart contains symbols that your reader may not understand.
6. Leave adequate white space on the page. Do not crowd your steps and directional arrows too close together.
7. As with other illustrations, place the flowchart as near as possible to that portion of the text that refers to it.

ORGANIZATIONAL CHARTS

An organizational chart shows how the various components of an organization are related to one another. Such an illustration is useful when you want to give readers an overview of an organization or indicate the lines of authority within the organization. (See Figure 13–24.)

The title of each organizational component (office, section, division) is placed in a separate box. These boxes are then linked to a central authority. If your readers need the information, include the name of the person occupying the position indentified in each box.

As with all illustrations, place the organizational chart as close as possible to the text that refers to it.

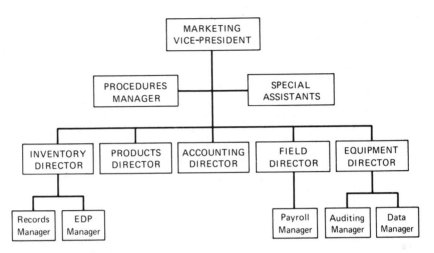

Cramer, Inc., field marketing organization

FIGURE 13–24. Organizational chart.

MAPS

Maps can be used to show the specific geographic features of the area represented (roads, mountains, rivers) or to show information according to geographic distribution (population, housing, manufacturing centers, and so forth).

Bear these points in mind as you create maps for use with your text (see Figure 13–25):

1. Label the map clearly.
2. Assign the map a figure number if you are using enough illustrations (usually five) to justify the use of figure numbers.
3. Make sure all boundaries within the map are clearly identified. Eliminate unnecessary boundaries.
4. Eliminate unnecessary information from your map. For example, if population is the focal point, do not include mountains, roads, rivers, and so on.
5. Include a scale of miles or feet to give your reader an indication of the map's proportions.
6. Indicate which direction is north.
7. Emphasize key features by using shading, dots, crosshatching, or appropriate symbols, and include a key telling what the different colors, shadings, or symbols represent.
8. Place maps as close as possible to the portion of the text that refers to them, but not preceding the first text reference.

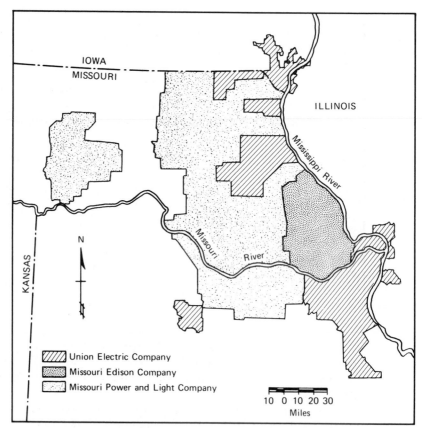

FIGURE 13–25. Map showing service areas of three utilities.
SOURCE: U.S. Nuclear Regulatory Commission.

CHAPTER SUMMARY

Tables and illustrations—graphs, drawings, photographs, charts, and maps—can increase the reader's understanding of what you are saying; they can express ideas or convey information in ways that words alone cannot. To be effective, such visuals must be appropriate to your purpose and suitable to your reader's needs.

A *table* is useful for listing large numbers of specific, related figures in a brief space. A table makes comparisons between figures easy because the figures are arranged in rows and columns.

There are several kinds of graphs. *Line graphs* are used to show the relationship between two or more sets of figures. *Bar graphs* are used to show varying quantities of the same item during a fixed period of time, quantities of the same item at different points in time, quantities of different items during a fixed period of time, or quantities of the different parts that make up a whole. The circle of a *pie graph* equals 100 percent, or the whole, of an element. The wedge-shaped sections into which the circle is divided indicate the percentage of the whole that each division represents. *Picture graphs* are modified bar graphs that use picture symbols to represent the item for which information is given; each symbol corresponds to a specified quantity of the item.

Drawings are invaluable for depicting details of an object or the relationship between objects. Frequently, a drawing is of the outside of an object. When, however, it is necessary to reveal the internal parts of a machine or other object, a *cutaway drawing* is appropriate. An *exploded-view drawing* is used to illustrate the way in which parts fit together or to present the details of each separate part.

Photographs are useful for showing "things as they are" at a moment in time, or for depicting the development of some condition over time.

When you want to present a visual depiction of various stages of a process, choose a *flowchart*. When, on the other hand, your purpose is to show how the various jobs in an organization relate to one another, or to indicate lines of authority within an organization, an *organizational chart* is appropriate. Material on geographical location or distribution can be displayed on a *map*.

EXERCISES

1. Create a table that shows the features of a seasonal maintenance task that you perform over the period of a year. Lawn and automobile care are among the kinds of tasks you may perform on a routine schedule.

2. Create a graph that shows what percentages of the population of the United States owned homes for the periods discussed in the following passage.

> For a growing army of people, realizing the American dream of the good life is closely associated with owning a home. Of 63.4 million occupied housing units counted in the 1970 census, nearly 63 percent (about 40 million) were lived in by their owners. More than 7 million home-owners were added to the U.S. total between 1960 and 1970.
>
> The proportion of owner-occupied homes was 62 percent in 1960 and 55 percent in 1950. In 1940, the first complete housing census found that the owner-occupied proportion was less than 44 percent.[2]

[2] U.S. Bureau of the Census.

3. Prepare a pie graph showing the distribution of 100 companies by type of industry in a survey. Distribution percentages by type of industry is as follows: computer-related, 32%; industrial equipment, 7%; business services, 8%; telecommunications, 10%; media and publications, 10%; consumer goods, 10%; medical and pharmaceutical, 14%; other, 9%.

4. Prepare a bar graph showing how you budget your present income for a typical month.

5. Create a line graph that plots home mortgage interest rates (or population in any U.S. metropolitan area currently over 1 million, or employment in the U.S.. auto industry of both men and women) over the past 20 years. Present the same information in a table.

6. Create a graph that compares sales in thousands of dollars among the various truck parts divisions of the ABC Corporation for 1985, 1986, and 1987. Sales for each division are as follows: axles—1987 ($225), 1986 ($200), 1985 ($75); universal joints—1987 ($125), 1986 ($100), 1985 ($35); frames—1987 ($125), 1986 ($100); 1985 ($50); transmissions—1987 ($75), 1986 ($65), 1985 ($50); clutches—1987 ($35), 1986 ($30), 1985 ($15); and gaskets and seals—1987 ($28), 1986 ($25), 1985 ($20).

7. Modify the following graph so that it can be understood more easily than it can in its present form.

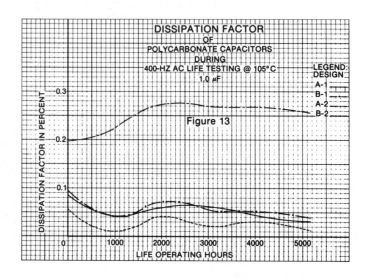

8. Select five drawings from reports, articles, or textbooks. Explain whether or not you think the illustrations make the text more meaningful or easier to follow. Take into consideration how well the illustrations support the ideas presented in the text and whether the illustrations have been correctly placed in relation to the text.

9. Explain whether a photograph or a line drawing would better illustrate features of the following subjects: a dry cell battery (for an article in a general encyclopedia); a flower arrangement (in a florist's brochure); an electrical outlet box (in a wiring instructions booklet); an automobile accident (for an insurance claims adjuster); the procedure for wrapping a sprained ankle (for a first aid handbook); and a tick (in a backpacker's handbook).

10. Beginning at the main entrance and ending at the checkout desk, draw a flowchart that traces the path you follow in locating and obtaining books from your library, as outlined in Chapter 10.

11. Create an organizational chart of a club or group to which you belong.

14

Making an Oral Presentation

Nearly everyone must, at one time or another, make an oral presentation on the job. You may, for example, be asked to report orally on what you learned at a workshop you attended, on the progress of a special project, or on the results of an evaluation program. You may need to present a product or service to potential customers or give cost estimates to a committee. Or a part of your job may be to demonstrate devices to coworkers, give patients instructions for using medical equipment, or show customers how to operate machinery safely. Regardless of the type of job you have, you will very likely need to know how to make an effective oral presentation.

Basically, there are three types of oral presentations: the read speech, the impromptu speech, and the extemporaneous speech.

A *read speech* is delivered by a speaker reading directly from a carefully prepared manuscript. Traditionally, papers were presented as read speeches at meetings held by professional societies. The current trend, however, is for papers to be distributed to the audience beforehand and then summarized by the speaker. The basic weakness of a read speech is that it tends to bore the audience because it does not require the speaker to establish two-way communication with the audience.

An *impromptu speech* is given without advance preparation by the speaker. The impromptu speech is used primarily during a meeting in which the speaker is asked "to say a few words" about something with which she is familiar (often a project with which she is involved). The speaker must then organize her ideas either while she is speaking or in a very short time before she speaks. The only way to prepare for an impromptu speech is to anticipate that you might be asked to report to a group.

By far the most common method of oral presentation is an *extemporaneous speech*. Here, the speaker prepares outlined notes well ahead of the presentation. He then uses his outline only to remind him of what to discuss and in what order to present his material; he does not read from the outline. A goal of extemporaneous speaking is to sound conversational and spontaneous, yet also well organized.

Since it is the most common and appropriate method for most of the speaking you will do, the extemporaneous method is the basis for the following discussion of oral presentations. However, many of the suggestions for delivery apply to the read speech and the impromptu speech as well.

PREPARING AN ORAL PRESENTATION

Preparing an oral presentation is much like preparing to write. You must determine your purpose, analyze your audience, and then organize your ideas and prepare an outline.

Your Purpose

Determine the purpose of your presentation by asking, "What do I want my listeners to know, to be able to do, or to believe after I am finished?" Without a clear purpose, you will not know what to include in your presentation to make it effective, and you will either confuse your listeners or lose their interest.

One way to ensure that you have a specific, clear objective is to write out a statement of your purpose before you develop your presentation. Suppose, for example, that you are the assistant manager of the supply room at Westdale Medical Center. You must present an overview of how the supply room sterilizers, called "autoclaves," work. Your audience will be the new professional employees of the medical center. You might use the following statement of purpose for your presentation: "My purpose in speaking is to explain the function and operation of the autoclave so that new hospital employees will understand it and appreciate its value to the hospital." After preparing such a statement, your next step is to analyze your audience.

Your Listeners

You cannot hope to communicate effectively with your listeners unless you know who they are. Are they coworkers, customers, clients, management, or fellow members of a professional organization? The answer to this question will help you to determine how much knowledge of your subject your listeners already possess. If you are speaking to those in your own occupational field, you know that they understand the terminology of that field—so that you can use it freely. However, if you are speaking to those outside your field, you should carefully define any special terms.

Knowing who your audience is will also help you recognize other factors that might improve your communication with your listeners. An audience composed of management is likely to be interested in the practical aspects of the material you are presenting: costs, scheduling, staff needs, and so on. But if you are speaking to technicians, they are likely to be concerned with the technical details of your presentation.

In preparing an oral presentation, you should pay particular attention to the size of your audience. Facial expressions and gestures that would be effective if you were speaking to half a dozen people sitting around a conference table would be lost on an audience of a hundred workers watching you demonstrate cardiopulmonary resuscitation. With the larger audience, you probably could not rely at all on facial expressions to convey an idea; and instead of pointing with your finger at a chart, you'd have to use a pointer. The size of your audience can also influence the approach you take to your presentation. For a small group of listeners, for instance, you might plan a presentation that is mainly discussion, composed of a short talk and a long question-and-answer period. For a large audience, on the other hand, you would be more likely to prepare a longer, more formally organized presentation with only a brief question-and-answer period.

Your Outline

The development of your subject when speaking differs slightly from the development when writing. Any audience has a limited attention span. A presentation crammed with difficult ideas or numerous statistics is sure either to confuse your listeners or to put them to sleep. Cite facts and figures sparingly, and insert them in such a way that they directly support the major points you wish to make. Put your most important ideas into your opening and closing, where your listeners are more likely to remember them. Unless your presentation is short (under ten minutes), your conclusion should summarize the information presented in the rest of the talk.

There are as many ways to develop a topic in speaking as there are in writing. Several methods are especially good for oral presentations. The particular method of development you choose is less important than the fact that your subject is logically developed.

- *Increasing order of importance* develops your topic from the least important point to the most important point. This leaves the audience with the most important points fresh in their minds.
- *The problem-solution pattern* first describes and analyzes the problem, then presents the criteria for evaluating possible solutions, and finally explains the advantages and disadvantages of each possible solution. Make sure that you are being clear when you define the problem and present the recommended solution.
- *Cause-and-effect,* by stressing the connection between a result and a preceding event, explains why something happened or why you predict that something will happen. This approach can be used effectively in a speech because it holds the interest of the audience much as a detective story does.
- *Specific-to-general* begins with such specific details as statistics, expert opinions, and examples and then goes on to make a general statement that stems logically from the details.
- *General-to-specific* presents a general statement and then follows it with supporting details—statistics, expert opinions, and examples.

When you have determined the best method of development for your subject, create an outline for your presentation. The following example shows how the assistant manager of the supply room at Westdale Medical Center might structure his presentation regarding autoclaves. You will notice that oral presentation outlines are less rigidly logical than outlines for written material (see Chapter 2): the oral presentation outline is not only a map of your method of development but also your cue card or prompter as you speak. Accordingly, you need to tailor it to your own speaking requirements.

<u>OUTLINE</u>

<u>Background Information About the
Autoclave (Sterilizer)</u>

   I. <u>Opening</u>
      A. Ms. Cynthia Lipanski has given you an overview of
         the department—now I would like to give you some
         background about our autoclave sterilizer units.

    B. The points I will cover are explained in greater detail in our department manual, which each of our employees uses.

II. Definitions
    A. Sterilizing kills all living organisms, unlike disinfecting, which merely inhibits the growth of organisms (especially pathogens).
    B. Sterilization kills multiplying organisms (including spores) with steam, under high temperature and pressure, or with gases.
    C. Briefly explain differences between steam autoclaves and ethylene oxide sterilizer (<u>point to units</u>).

III. <u>Materials</u>
    A. Materials that are sterilized include cloth, metal, glass, liquid, rubber, and plastic.
    B. Items that are sensitive to steam must be sterilized with the ethylene oxide unit: rubber goods, electric cords, telescopic lenses, and delicate instruments, for example.
    C. The materials, other than liquids, are wrapped in muslin or placed in <u>peel</u> packages and heat sealed (<u>show instrument and ''peel'' packages</u>).
    D. Liquids, such as saline, are placed in pyrex bottles with closures that allow steam to penetrate.
    E. Each type of material requires precise settings for time, pressure, and temperature (<u>show operators' manual</u>).

IV. <u>Procedure</u>
    A. Operator checks that items are properly wrapped and spaced on the sterilizer cart (<u>point to cart</u>).
    B. Chemical indicators are placed inside the packages, and heat-sensitive tape is used on the outsides.
    C. The operator loads the cart (cooled to prevent condensation) into the sterilizer units.
    D. Although settings are usually pre-set, the operator checks time, temperature, and pressure (<u>show gauges</u>).
    E. The operator closes the door, then pushes the ''lock'' button; the operation proceeds automatically from that point.

      F. Lights on the front of the door will indicate the completion of cycle.

      G. The operator removes the sterilizer cart, using asbestos gloves.

      H. The packages are allowed to cool before they are placed on the storage shelves in the next room.

      I. Westdale's process is more automated than those at smaller hospitals.

  V. <u>Closing</u>

      A. I hope I've given you some idea of how our sterilizer units work.

      B. Are there any questions?

      C. Thank you!

      D. Mrs. Sanches will now demonstrate Unit #2.

The amount of detail you should include in such an outline will depend on both your confidence in front of a group and your familiarity with the subject. Obviously, the more confident and familiar with the subject you are, the less detail you will need. However, you may need to write out and read verbatim those portions that you feel need precise wording, such as important policy statements.

You will also need to decide what physical form of the outline you wish to use as notes for your presentation. Some speakers find that placing the outline in a three-ring binder keeps the pages in order. Other speakers prefer using 4- × 6-inch note cards because they are compact. Use whatever form you find most convenient.

Be careful not to cram the cards with too many notes. You should be able to grasp the information on a card at a glance so that you can maintain eye contact with your listeners. Number the cards so you don't get lost during your presentation.

Using Visual Aids

An important decision to make as you prepare your oral presentation is whether to use visual aids and, if so, what kind. (See Chapter 13.) You can choose graphs, drawings, tables, photographs, or models; you can present them by means of chalkboards, posters, flip charts, or overhead or slide projectors. Well-planned visual aids can add interest and emphasis to your presentation. They can also clarify and simplify your message by reinforcing its key points.

Visual aids can be overdone, of course. Do not attempt to use them to flesh out a skimpy presentation or to focus a disorganized one. In general, use them only if they clarify a point or make your presentation more vivid and concise. It is sometimes helpful, however, to list the major points (usually in key words) on the visual aid so that your listeners can keep them in mind as you discuss each in turn.

Be certain to check the physical arrangement and facilities of the room where you will speak. Does it have a chalkboard? a projector screen? a flip chart? Will a slide or overhead projector be available? Also consider room size. If you plan to use a chalkboard, will the writing be visible to those seated in the back? Everything you use must be tailored to scale. Check to see that nothing obstructs the view of any member of your audience. Keep in mind the following points as you prepare and use your visual aid:

1. Keep the amount of information on each visual aid to a minimum. Try to present only one point on each, and keep numerical data to a minimum.
2. Do not write out sentences; use only words and phrases.
3. Emphasize a visual aid by pointing and referring to it—with physical gestures *and* words.
4. As you discuss the visual aid, be sure that you don't block it with your body.
5. Be careful to talk to your listeners, not to the visual aid.
6. Do not expose the visual aid to the audience until you are ready to discuss it.
7. Give the audience a few seconds to study the visual aid before you begin to talk about it.
8. Remove or cover the visual aid when you are finished with it, lest it distract the audience.

A complete range of visual aids is available. Each has advantages; your choice will depend on the size of the audience and the flexibility that your subject requires.

- A *chalkboard* is easy to use and easy to control; it gives you complete flexibility because you decide what goes on it, what comes off it, and when. Further, it adds animation to your presentation because you must physically put the information on the board. If your information is too extensive conveniently to write out while you speak, put part or all of it on ahead of time. The chalkboard is good with small and medium-sized audiences (up to 40 people). A disadvantage is that it slows you down as you must interrupt your presentation to write on the board as your listeners watch.
- A *poster* is good if it is large enough for your audience to see. Posters can be used for medium-sized and large audiences (40 to 100 people). A common poster size is 2 × 3 feet. Prepare the poster

ahead of time, and make your lettering large enough to be seen comfortably from the back of the room (check this yourself, ahead of time). Felt-tip markers are good writing instruments for posters. Put the poster on the easel only when you are ready to use it; otherwise, it will be distracting to your audience. A disadvantage of posters is that the material on them cannot easily be changed.

• A *flip chart* provides you with good control of what you want the audience to see—you flip it over only when you need to make the next point. You can draw your illustration ahead of time with light pencil lines and fill the lines in with the bold lines of a felt-tip pen during your presentation (sketching it during the presentation helps hold the audience's attention). Flip charts are good for the same size audiences as chalkboards.

• *Slide* and *overhead projectors* can be easy to use if you take the time to learn how to handle them. Do not put a slide or transparency on the screen until you need it. As you prepare your presentation, decide which slides you will use and where each one will go. Have them made up far enough in advance so that you will be able to rehearse with them. You may want to make enough 8 ½- × 11-inch paper copies of each slide or transparency for everyone in the audience and arrange them in the same sequence used during your presentation. If you do, pass them out before your presentation so that the audience can write notes on them. Thus, the audience will have a convenient record of your presentation for future reference.

DELIVERING AN ORAL PRESENTATION

Your oral presentation is most likely to be on a job-related topic. Therefore, you should be able to speak with knowledge and conviction about your subject. This is important because your listeners will have greater confidence in what you say if you speak with conviction.

The key to delivering your presentation well is to practice. Rehearse with your outline and with your visual aids until you know exactly how you want to move from one idea to another. If you practice, you will have no problem with the words you want to use; they will come naturally, and you will have the confidence you need to face your listeners.

Generating Confidence and Enthusiasm

Speaking is like selling. If you believe in your topic, you will be enthusiastic about it, and your audience will find themselves thinking,

"Hey, I didn't know that!" or nodding their heads in agreement as if to say, "I know exactly what you mean!"

You can expect to be nervous. But if you know what you are going to say and how you are going to say it—as you will if you have developed your subject and created a good outline—you can simply relax and talk. Your nervousness won't cause an all-out attack of stage fright. You can strengthen your confidence by being well prepared, by rehearsing, and by speaking in a strong and clear voice. A neat appearance can also add to your self-confidence.

You will have an advantage in delivering your presentation if you can project an image of friendliness; most people react favorably to a friendly approach. Friendliness cannot be faked—it must be honest to be effective. If you are naturally friendly, you can make that quality work to your advantage.

Another aspect of the image you project to your audience is your posture. Stand poised and erect, but not stiff. A slouching posture can harm your credibility with your listeners because they may assume that you lack confidence or don't care how you look or how you come across to others.

Getting and Holding Your Audience

The opening of a presentation can be crucial. It should arouse interest, stimulate curiosity, or impress your listeners with the importance of your subject. You can begin your presentation in a number of ways that will catch the attention of your listeners.

Statement of a Problem.   One way to catch the attention of your listeners is to describe a problem that directly affects them and then suggest a solution to it.

> In the past three months the accident rate in the Press Room has increased by 37%. We've experienced a number of minor accidents and half a dozen serious ones. I've done a thorough investigation of the press area, along with members of Security, and realize that we must set up some new procedures. . . .

Definition.   Although the definition of a word can make a catchy opening, such a beginning should never be contrived—it should be used only if it provides insight into what follows.

> *Diastrophism* comes from the Greek word *diastrophe,* meaning "distortion," and it is applied to the distortion of the earth's crust that created

oceans and mountains. It is not surprising, therefore, that geologists regard . . .

Interesting Fact.   Often an interesting bit of information can be used to stimulate the attention of your listeners.

> A recent survey among retailers in our area revealed that the best way to sell a product is to *give it away*. Does that sound ridiculous? It isn't! And here's why. . . .

You may also be able to use an interesting statistic as an opening.

> Approximately 15,000 requisitions, each containing from one to fourteen separate items, are processed each year by the Purchasing Department. Every item or service that is purchased . . .

Background Information.   The background or history of a subject may be quite interesting and can put the topic in perspective for your listeners.

> The Chinese used bamboo poles to drill for oil; certainly today's giant rigs drilling in a hundred feet of water represent an immense technical advance in the search for oil. But whether four thousand years ago or today, in ancient China or in a modern city, in twenty fathoms of water or on top of a mountain, the object of drilling is and has always been the same—to manufacture a hole in the ground, inch by inch. The hole may be either for a development well . . .

This type of opening can easily be overdone, however. Use it only if the background information is of some value to your listeners. Never use it just to get started.

Quotations.   Occasionally, you can use a quotation to stimulate interest in your subject. To be effective, however, the quotation must be pertinent—not just a loosely related remark taken from a book of quotations simply because the item was listed under the subject heading of your topic. Often an effective quotation is from a respected authority that points to a new trend or development.

> Richard Smith, president of the P. R. Smith Corporation, recently said, "I believe that the Photon projector will revolutionize our industry." His statement represents a growing feeling among corporate . . .

Objective.   In reporting on a project or an activity of some kind, you may wish to open with a statement about the objective of the project.

Such an opening gives your listeners a basis for judging the actual results of the project as you present them.

> Measuring heat transfer has been a costly, time-consuming, and all-too-often inexact procedure. The primary objective of this project was to develop new techniques for measuring heat transfer in a three-phase system. Our first step was to investigate . . .

Forecast.   Sometimes you can use the forecast of a new development or trend to arouse the interest of your listeners.

> In the very near future, we may be able to call our local library and have a videotape of *Hamlet* or of last year's Super Bowl replayed on our wall television. This project and others are now being developed at Wincom Industries. . . .

Delivery Techniques

To deliver an effective oral presentation, observe the following basic "do's and don'ts."

First, when you stand up to speak, *don't rush your opening*. Begin by taking a good look at your listeners, and let them take a good look at you. Then begin your planned opening firmly and authoritatively. Never apologize for inconvenient conditions or tell your listeners how nervous you are (your audience probably won't notice your nervousness—so why call attention to it?).

Try to talk to your listeners about your subject just as you would talk to a friend about it. Be sure to *maintain eye contact* with most of your listeners, not just with one person. Eye contact not only can establish directness of communication with your listeners but can provide you with feedback from them. That is, when you are looking at your listeners, you will probably be able to notice if they begin to look puzzled or confused. Such feedback can serve as a cue that you need to clarify the point you are making.

Be careful not to talk too fast. If you are even a little nervous, speaking too quickly is a real danger. *Do not talk in a monotone;* if you do, you will bore and finally lose your listeners. *Enunciate carefully;* say "going" instead of "gonna," and "don't you think?" instead of "dontchathink?" Try to eliminate fillers like "ah," "like," and "ya-know?" Although such fillers are so common that it may be impossible to eliminate them altogether, make a serious effort to do so. Also, learn to *suppress nervous mannerisms,* such as adjusting your clothing or smoothing your hair.

To emphasize a point, say it—then pause to let its significance register with your listeners—and then repeat the point. You can also achieve emphasis by varying the pitch of your voice, by varying the volume of your voice, and by varying the pace of your presentation. Gestures, too, can create emphasis. A closed fist, for example, can stress an idea dramatically. You can highlight a plea with a palms-up gesture, or indicate the large size of something by making a broad, semicircular motion with one hand. Be sure, though, to use gestures only when they come naturally; in other words, use the same gestures you would in ordinary conversation.

Refer to your notes openly, whether they are on 4- × 6-inch cards or 8½- × 11-inch paper. When you need to look at your notes, do so. Your listeners won't be impatient; they are human too. They won't expect you to be a spellbinding speaker, but they will expect you to be knowledgeable, prepared, and organized.

Rehearse your presentation until you can do it comfortably, in the allotted time, and with no major hesitations. Once you are ready, relax and don't worry about forgetting something. At this point you are not likely to forget a major point, and the sky won't fall if you overlook a minor point.

Concluding

When you are finished, conclude promptly but not abruptly. Don't end as though you were beating a hasty retreat. Plan the ending of your presentation the way you planned your opening. It's your last chance to get your message across, so don't waste it. You may find that it is most effective to conclude with a summary of your main points—so that your listeners will be more likely to remember them. Or, depending on your topic, you might end by making a recommendation, by asking a question, or by using any of the other techniques suggested for written closings in Chapter 3.

Question-and-Answer Period

Depending on the occasion and on your subject, you may want to provide for a question-and-answer session at the end of your presentation. If so, answer questions as completely as time allows or as the question deserves. Be sure that your answers are accurate. Don't be afraid to respond with "I don't know." Be polite and objective in responding to a hostile question, but be prepared to go on to the next question if it becomes evident that the questioner simply wants to argue. Don't play for laughs at a questioner's expense. You'll offend not only the questioner but the rest of your listeners as well.

EFFECTIVE LISTENING

Although you may spend only a small part of your time on the job making oral presentations, you probably spend a great deal of your time listening to other people. You may receive oral instructions, attend workshops sponsored by your employer, or take courses as a part of your continuing education. Whatever the activity may be, it is important to develop effective listening skills.

Tips for Becoming an Effective Listener

You must be motivated to listen—either by an interest in the subject or by a desire to succeed on the job. The following guidelines can help you improve your listening skills.

- Develop a positive attitude toward the speaker. Good listeners assume, for example, that even though the subject may sound dull, the speaker is likely to say something that they can use. Do not allow your own biases or attitudes toward the subject or the speaker to influence your objectivity. Keep an open mind.
- Do not be distracted by a speaker's personality or speaking style; rather, respond thoughtfully to the speaker's words and avoid making judgments too quickly.
- Be prepared. On the job, think and talk about the subject of a meeting or a workshop ahead of time. Preparation should enable you to understand the material better and to remember it more easily.
- Analyze the speaker's words and ideas while you are listening, but don't become so engrossed in your own analysis that you miss important points. Try to spot inconsistencies between the facts and the ideas that you hear. Listen "between the lines." Is the speaker using emotionally charged words? If so, are they appropriate? Can you think of other points that support or reject what the speaker is advocating? Do your own attitudes match those of the speaker? Analyzing a speaker's words and ideas helps you not only to probe the meaning of the subject but to remember key points.
- Take notes. Being a good listener sometimes means being a good note-taker. You may wish to record your own thoughts and questions as you are listening, so that you will remember to verify or ask them after the speaker is finished. The best note-takers record only key words and phrases while they are listening, so that they won't miss anything that is being said.

• When you are not taking notes, look at the speaker. This is not only a courtesy but an aid to concentration and comprehension.

You may not have time or need to follow all these guidelines—if you don't, use the technique or techniques that best help *you* to absorb and remember. You may also find that some of these techniques work better when you are listening to formal oral presentations and others work better when you are listening to one or two people in conversations.

CHAPTER SUMMARY

Oral presentations are in many ways like written presentations.

First, you must determine your objective: is it to inform? to persuade? to arouse your audience to action? Key your objective to the occasion and the audience, and fix it firmly in mind.

Then analyze your audience. Who are they? Are they coworkers? Are they customers? Are they management? Whoever they are, you must gear your presentation specifically to them.

Then gather and organize your information as you would for any communication. Put your outline together using the most suitable method of development: for example, increasing order of importance, problem-solution, specific-to-general, or general-to-specific.

Prepare visual aids if they will help you to achieve your objective. Remember to keep them simple (one idea per visual) and legible. They must be readable by every member of the audience.

Once you have put your material together, rehearse your presentation until you have all the ideas and their order engraved on your mind. Practice with your visuals so that they become a part of your talk, not simply add-ons. Adequate rehearsal gives you the confidence you need to present your material effectively.

The easiest part comes last—the actual presentation. Look at your audience for a moment before you start, then begin talking to them. Watch the people in the audience as you speak—they'll give you the cues you need to adjust your delivery. Speak slowly and distinctly.

Refer to your notes when you need to; the audience expects it. Gesture when it is appropriate. If you have practiced sufficiently, these things will come naturally.

And, finally, conclude your presentation, don't just end it. Summarize your main points or make a firm recommendation.

Much of your time is spent listening to others. Listening is an acquired skill, just as writing and speaking are skills. Ways to increase your effectiveness as a listener are to be motivated to listen (by interest in the subject or by a desire to succeed), to develop a positive attitude toward the presentation, not to be distracted by the speaker's personality or speaking style, to be prepared to receive the information being given you, and to develop an active mind that anticipates and analyzes the information being received.

EXERCISES

1. Come to class prepared to discuss in detail the differences between writing a report and presenting one orally.

2. Deliver a 5-to-10-minute talk on an academic, business, or government policy of which you disapprove. State the reasons for your disapproval, and offer reasons why the policy should be changed or abolished.

3. Deliver a 5-to-10-minute talk explaining the purpose and function of a tool or piece of equipment typically used in your field. If possible, choose a device unfamiliar to someone outside your field. If the item is not too large, bring it to class; otherwise, rely on visual aids to clarify your explanation.

4. Prepare a 5-to-10-minute presentation that argues for or against one of the following topics:

   Flextime at your place of employment
   More campus activities for majors in your field
   Writing proficiency requirement for all graduates
   Writing major to train professional writers
   More writing courses related to your major
   Rental book service at your school bookstore
   24-Hour access to your school library
   Note: Make your topic more specific and get your instructor's approval before you begin.

5. Prepare a 10-to-15-minute talk that argues for or against a controversial issue in your career field. Typical topics would include training or accreditation practices, employment practices, professional or union affiliations, or any legislation (current or pending) that will affect your field.

6. Prepare a 10-to-15-minute talk in which you summarize the findings of a major report. Be prepared to respond to questions.

7. Prepare a 5-to-10-minute talk on why you chose your major field of study.

15

Finding a Job

Before you begin your search for a job, do some serious thinking about your future. Decide first what you would most like to be doing in the immediate future. Then think about the kind of work you'd like to be doing two years from now and five years from now. Once you have established your goals, you can begin your job hunt with greater confidence because you'll have a better idea of what kind of position you are looking for and in what companies or other organizations you are most likely to find that position.

The search for a job can be logically divided into five steps: (1) locating the job you want, (2) preparing an effective résumé, (3) writing an effective letter of application, (4) conducting yourself well during the interview, and (5) sending follow-up letters.

LOCATING THE JOB YOU WANT

A number of sources are available to help you locate the job you want: classified ads, letters of inquiry, trade and professional journals, school placement services, employment agencies, and the advice of friends and acquaintances.

Advertisements in Newspapers

Many employers advertise in the classified sections of newspapers. For the widest selection, look in the Sunday editions of local and big-city newspapers. Although reading dozens of want ads can be tedious, an item-by-item check is necessary if you are to do a thorough job search. The job you are looking for might be listed in the classified ads under any number of titles. A clinical medical technologist seeking a job, for example, might find the specialty listed under "Medical Technologist," "Clinical Medical Technologist," or "Laboratory Technologist." Depending on a hospital's or a pathologist's needs, the listing could be more specific yet, such as "Blood Bank Technologist," "Hematology Technologist," or "Clinical Chemistry Technologist." So play it safe—read *all* the ads. Occasionally, newspapers print special employment supplements that provide valuable information on many facets of the job market. Watch for these.

As you read the ads, take notes on such things as salary ranges, job locations, job duties and responsibilities, and even the terminology used in the ads to describe the work. (A knowledge of the words and expressions that are generally used with regard to a particular type of work can be helpful when you prepare your résumé and letters of application.)

Letters of Inquiry

If you would like to work for a particular firm, write and ask whether it has an opening for someone with your qualifications. Normally, you should send the letter either to the director of personnel or to the specific department head; for a small firm, however, you can write to the head of the firm. Your letter should present a general summary of your employment background or training. It should be brief and to the point, expressing interest in such a job but leaving everything else to your résumé, which you enclose with the letter.

Trade and Professional Journals

In many occupations there are associations that publish periodicals of general interest to members. Such periodicals often contain a listing of current job opportunities. If you were seeking a job in forestry, for example, you could check the job listings in the *Journal of Forestry,* published by the Society of American Foresters. To learn about the trade or professional associations for your occupation, consult the following reference books at a convenient library.

> *Encyclopedia of Associations*
> *Encyclopedia of Business Information Sources*
> *National Directory of Employment Services*

School Placement Services

Check with the career counselors in your school's job-placement office. Government, business, and industry recruiters often visit job-placement offices to interview prospective employees; the recruiters also keep college placement offices aware of their company's current employment needs. While you are in the placement office, ask to see a current issue of the *College Placement Annual*. This publication lists the occupational requirements and addresses of over a thousand industry, business, and government employers.

State Employment Agencies

Most states operate free employment agencies that exist specifically to match applicants and jobs. If your state has one, register with the local employment office. It may have just the job you want; if not, it will keep your résumé on file and call you if such a job comes along.

Private Employment Agencies

Private employment agencies are profit-making organizations that are in business to help people find jobs—for a fee. Choose a private employment agency carefully. Some are well established and quite reputable, but others have questionable reputations. Check with your local Better Business Bureau as well as with friends and acquaintances before signing an agreement with a private employment agency.

Reputable private employment agencies provide you with job leads and help to organize your campaign for the job you want. They may also provide useful information on the companies doing the hiring.

Who pays the fee if you are offered and accept a job through a private agency? Sometimes the employer will pay the agency's fee. Otherwise, you must pay either a set fee or a percentage of your first month's salary on the new job. Before signing a contract, be sure you understand who is paying the fee and, if *you* are, how much you are agreeing to pay. As with any written agreement, read the fine print carefully.

Friends and Acquaintances

Consult with people you know whose judgment you respect. It's especially useful to speak to people who are already working in your chosen field. Family members, friends, neighbors, teachers, members of the clergy—any one of these might provide exactly the job lead you need.

Other Sources

Local, state, and federal government agencies offer many employment opportunities. Local government agencies are listed in the blue pages of your telephone directory under the name of your city, county, or state. For information about jobs with the federal government, contact the U.S. Office of Personnel Management and the Federal Personnel and Management Office, both of which have branches in most major cities. They are listed in the white (or blue) pages of the telephone book under "U.S. Government."

If you are a veteran, local and campus Veterans' Administration offices can provide material on special placement programs for veterans. Such agencies can supply you with the necessary information about the particular requirements or entrance tests for your occupation.

PREPARING AN EFFECTIVE RÉSUMÉ

A *résumé,* the key element in a job hunt, is a summary of your qualifications.[1] It tells a prospective employer about your job objectives, your training and education, your work experience, and your personal data. A résumé itemizes, in one or two pages, the qualifications that you can mention only briefly in a letter of application. On the basis of the information that the résumé supplies, prospective employers can decide whether to ask you to come in for a personal interview. If you do have an interview, the interviewer can base specific questions on the data the résumé contains. For all these reasons, having a résumé is vital.

In preparing to write a résumé, determine what kind of job you are seeking. Then ask yourself what information about you and your background would be most important to a prospective employer in the field you have chosen. On the basis of your answers to this question, decide what sort of details you should include in your résumé and how you can most effectively present your qualifications. Analyze yourself and your background. What jobs have you held? What were your principal duties in each of them? What experience did you gain that would be of value in the kind of job you are seeking? When and how long were you on each job? Consider your education. List the college or colleges you attended, the dates you attended each one, the degree you received, your major field of study, and any academic honors you achieved. The signifi-

---

[1] When a regular typewriter is used, the word *résumé* is spelled without the accent marks.

cant details of your education or training and of any job experience you may have had—along with personal data (your name, address, and so on)—are what make up a résumé.

A number of different formats can be effectively used. The most important thing is to make sure that your résumé is attractive, well organized, easy to read, and free of errors. A common format contains the following:

> Heading
> Personal data (if included)
> Employment objective
> Education
> Employment experience
> References

Underline or capitalize whatever headings you use to make them stand out on the page. Whether you list education or experience first depends on which is the stronger in your background. If you are a recent graduate, list education first; if you have one or more years of related job experience, list experience first. In both cases, list the most recent education or job experience first, the next most recent experience second, and so on.

The Heading

Start with your name, address, and telephone number. These are usually centered on the page. Do not include a date in the heading; if you do, you'll have to keep changing it.

David B. Edwards
6819 Locustview Drive
Topeka, Kansas 66614
(913) 233-1552

Personal Data (Optional)

Federal legislation limits the inquiries an employer can make before hiring an applicant—especially requests for such personal information as age, sex, marital status, race, and religion. Consequently, some job seekers exclude this category because they feel their personal data could have a negative impact on the employer. You may also eliminate this category simply because you need the space for more significant information about your qualifications. However, if you believe the Personal Data category will help you to land a particular job, then include such things as your date of birth and your marital status (it's better to give your date of birth than your age, so your résumé won't become out of date). In any case, you should see yourself through the eyes of your potential employers and provide whatever information would be most useful to them.

Employment Objective

If you have a specific employment objective, include it in your résumé. State not only your immediate employment objective but the direction you hope your career will take.

```
                    EMPLOYMENT OBJECTIVE

A responsible position in an engineering department in
which I may use my training in computer sciences to solve
engineering-related problems.
```

The Employment Objective category enables the employer to identify your purpose quickly. However, avoid using an overly specific employment objective, since an employer might pass you over for similar or related positions in a large company. Ideally, you would write a well-focused, specific résumé for each job. Since this is not feasible, keep your Employment Objective well defined but flexible.

Of course, as yet you may not have a clear objective. You may therefore want to consider excluding the Employment Objective altogether and using one résumé to apply for several different positions.

Education

List the college or colleges you attended, the dates you attended each one, the degree or degrees you received, your major field of study, and any academic honors you earned. If your résumé is relatively short, also give the name of the high school you attended, its location, and the dates you attended.

```
                          EDUCATION

Georgia Institute of Technology, Atlanta; September 19--
      to present.
Expect to receive a Bachelor of Science degree in Engineering
      in June 19--.
```

Major Courses: Calculus I, II, III, IV; Differential Equa-
tions; Methods of Digital Computations; Advanced Com-
puter Techniques; Software Utilization; Special Com-
puter Techniques; Graphic Display.
Activities and honors:
Phi Chi Epsilon—-Honor Society for Women in Business and
Engineering
Society of Women Engineers—-Secretary-Treasurer dur-
ing Junior Year
American Institute of Industrial Engineers—-Secretary
during Senior Year
Engineering Science Club
Doris Harlow Scholarship recipient—-two consecutive
years
Grade average: 3.46/4.00
Dean's List during 6 of 8 semesters
Butler County Community College, Butler, Pennsylvania;
September 19—- to May 19—-

Knoch High School, Saxonburg, Pennsylvania; September
19—- to June 19—-

Employment Experience

List all your full-time jobs, starting with the most recent and working
backward. If you have had little full-time work experience, list part-
time and temporary jobs too. Give the details of your employment, including the job title, dates of employment, and the name and address of the
employer. Provide a concise description of your duties for those jobs with
duties similar to those of the job you are seeking; if a job is not directly
relevant, give only a job title and a very brief description. Specify any
promotions you received. If you have been with one company for a number
of years, highlight your accomplishments during those years. List military
service as a job: give the dates you served, your duty specialty, and
your rank at discharge. Discuss the duties only if they relate to the job
you are applying for.

EMPLOYMENT EXPERIENCE

September 19—- to present

Participated in the Professional Training Program at Computer Systems International, Atlanta, Georgia. Assigned to

```
Design Department, as Production Trainee; to Word-Process-
ing Department, as Clerical Assistant; to Engineering De-
partment, as Programmer Trainee.

April 19-- to September 19--

Lifeguard at Vacationland Amusement Park, Hillstown, Penn-
    sylvania.
Chief lifeguard at end of summer, supervising three other
    lifeguards.
```

Special Skills and Activities

This category usually comes near the end and provides an excellent replacement for the Personal Data category. You may include skills such as knowledge of foreign languages, writing and editing abilities, specialized technical knowledge (such as experience with word processing or a background in electronics), hobbies, student or community activities, professional or club memberships, and published works. Be selective: do not overdo this category, do not duplicate information given in other categories, and include only items that support your employment objective.

A variety of different headings can be used for this category, depending on which skills or activities you wish to emphasize. In Figure 15–2, for example, the heading "Professional Affiliations" is used.

References

You can include references as part of the résumé or provide a statement on the résumé that references will be furnished upon request. Either way, do not give anyone as a reference without first obtaining his or her permission to do so.

```
                        REFERENCES

Furnished upon request.
```

Some résumés, called functional résumés, are arranged not in reverse order of time but according to duties, starting with the job most closely related *in function* to the job you seek. Since this type of résumé relies heavily on experience, it is not one that a recent graduate would normally use.

Do not list your present salary in your résumé. If it is too high, you may automatically price yourself out of a job for which you are applying. If it is too low, any offer you receive might well be less than it might otherwise have been.

As you write your résumé, use action verbs and state ideas concisely. There is no reason to avoid *I* altogether, but it is best not to overuse it.

NOT   I was promoted to shop foreman in June 19--.

BUT   Promoted to shop foreman in June 19--.

Be truthful in your résumé. If you give false data and are found out, the consequences could be serious. At the very least, you will have seriously damaged your credibility with your employer.

Make your résumé flawless before mailing it. If you are not a skilled typist, you may want to have it professionally typed. Printing usually produces more professional-looking copies than does photocopying. This is no time to pinch pennies.

Following are two sample résumés: one by a recent community-college graduate and one by an applicant who has been employed for many years. The writer of the first résumé (Figure 15–1) has had only limited work experience and therefore puts the education section first and gives fairly detailed information about his college work. On the second sample résumé (Figure 15–2), work experience appears first because the applicant has had nine years of full-time employment—a fact that is much more important to a prospective employer than the applicant's educational data.

Organizing Your Résumé by Function Instead of by Job

Some résumés are arranged by type of work experience rather than by job chronology. Instead of listing jobs in sequence, starting with the most recent, this type of résumé lists jobs by the functions performed ("Management," "Project Development," "Training," "Sales," and so on).

The functional arrangement is useful for applicants who wish to stress their skills or who have been employed at one job and wish to demonstrate the diversity of their experience at that job. It is also useful for anyone with gaps in his or her résumé caused by unemployment or illness. Although this type of arrangement can be effective, prospective employers know that it may be used to cover weaknesses, so use it carefully and be prepared to explain any gaps.

The following sample résumés are all for the same person. Figure 15–3 shows a student's first résumé, while Figures 15–4 and 15–5 reflect work experience later in her career (one is organized by job, the other by function). Examine as many résumés as possible and select the format that best suits your goals.

DAVID B. EDWARDS
6819 Locustview Drive
Topeka, Kansas 66614
(913) 233-1552

EMPLOYMENT OBJECTIVE

Position as entry–level programmer or data communications technician, leading to a career in systems analysis and management.

EDUCATION

Associate Degree in Computer Science. Fairview
Community College, Topeka, Kansas.
Graduated June 1983. Dean's Honor List Award re-
ceived for six quarters.

Relevant course work:

Introduction to   Computer Graphics
   Cybernetics   Operating Systems
Programming in COBOL   Design
Programming in FORTRAN   Data Structures
Data Base Management   Technical Writing

Current course work: Programming in PASCAL at Topeka
Technical University Extension.

EMPLOYMENT EXPERIENCE

Computer Consultant--Fairview Community College
Computer Center: advised and trained novice computer users at the College computer center; wrote
and maintained user documentation for the UNIX operating system. November 1983 to present.

Tutor--Fairview Community College: tutored and
advised remedial students in mathematics and computer programming. January 1983 to June 1983.

SPECIAL SKILLS AND ACTIVITIES

Thorough knowledge of the UNIX operating system,
including its word–processing, text–editing, and
file–formatting programs.

FIGURE 15–1. Sample résumé.

Excellent writing and editing skills; practical
experience in documenting computer programs for
beginning programmers and users.

Ability to communicate well with both technical and
nontechnical personnel.

Member of the Fairview Community Microcomputer User's Group, and helped to establish and edit the
Group's monthly newsletter.

FURTHER INFORMATION

References, college transcripts, portfolio of
computer programs, and writing samples available
upon request.

FIGURE 15–1, *continued.*

ROBERT MANDILLO
7761 Shalamar Drive
Dayton, Ohio 45424
Home: (513) 255–4137
Business: (513) 255–3730

EMPLOYMENT OBJECTIVE

Position of greater responsibility and growth potential in the field of technical exhibit design.

EMPLOYMENT EXPERIENCE

Manager, Engineering Drafting Department. Air
Force Orientation Group. Wright–Patterson Air
Force Base, Ohio: official exhibit design, construction, and display agency for the U.S. Air
Force. Manage and control the Engineering Drafting
Department, supervising a staff of 17 Drafting Mechanics. Support engineering design staff; develop, judge, and improve the selection of materials and equipment for design and construction of
exhibits. Write specifications, negotiate with
vendors, initiate and coordinate procurement procedures. June 19–– to present.

Supervisor, Graphic Illustrators. Henderson Advertising Agency, Cincinnati, Ohio. Advanced from
Illustrator to Graphic Technician, and was then
promoted to supervisor of five Illustrators and
four Drafting Mechanics. Monitored and approved
work orders and analyzed work–order requirements.
Selected appropriate media and techniques for orders. Rendered illustrations in pencil or ink.

EDUCATION

Bachelor of Science in Mechanical Engineering
Technology. Edison State College, Wooster, Ohio.
Graduated in June 19––.

Associate Degree in Mechanical Drafting, Wooster
Community College, Wooster, Ohio. Graduated in
June 19––.

FIGURE 15–2. Sample résumé.

PROFESSIONAL AFFILIATIONS

Member of the National Association of Mechanical
Engineers and Draftsmen.

REFERENCES

References, letters of recommendation, and portfolio of original designs and drawings available
upon request.

FIGURE 15–2, *continued.*

CAROL ANN WALKER
273 East Sixth Street
Bloomington, IN 47401
(913) 555-1212

Employment Objective	Position as financial research assistant, leading to a management position in corporate finance.
Education	B.B.A., Indiana University, expected, June 19-- Major: Finance Minor: Computer Science Honors: Dean's List, G.P.A. 3.88/4.00 Senior Honor Society, 19--
Employment Experience	First Bank, Research Department (Bloomington, IN) Intern research assistant: Assisted manager of corporate planning and developed computer model for long-range financial planning. (Summer and Fall semesters, 19--) Martin Financial Research Services Bloomington, IN) Intern editorial assistant: Provided research assistance to staff. Developed a design concept for in-house financial audits. Various part-time jobs to finance education (60%). From 19-- to 19--
Special Skills and Activities	Associate Editor Business School Alumni Newsletter Edited submissions, surveyed business periodicals for potential stories; wrote two stories on financial planning with computer models. President of Women's Transit Program

FIGURE 15-3. Student résumé.

	Coordinated efforts to provide safe nighttime transportation to and from dormitories and campus buildings.
	Amateur Photographer. Won several local awards for nature photos.
References	Available upon request.

FIGURE 15–3. *continued*

CAROL ANN WALKER
1436 W. Schantz Avenue
Dayton, Ohio 45401
(513) 555-1212

Employment   Senior Research Financial Analyst in
Objective   corporate offices of growth and re-
             search-oriented major manufacturing
             company.

Employment Experience
(19-- to present)
  January 19-- to present KERFHEIMER CORPORATION
    (Dayton, Ohio) Senior Financial Analyst (Septem-
    ber 19-- to October 19--) Report to the senior
    vice president for Corporate Financial Planning
    of this $1-billion manufacturer of heavy mining
    and construction equipment, which is also pur-
    chased by various branches of the federal govern-
    ment, including the Department of Defense. Work
    with government procurement officers and engi-
    neers in developing manufacturing cost estimates
    for complex and massive machinery, based on pro-
    totypes developed in our research lab. Develop
    program funding requirements and determine best
    available sources, some of which have been in the
    $100- to $300-million range. Recipient of the
    ''Financial Planner of the Year'' award from the
    Association of Financial Planners.

    Financial Analyst (January 19-- to September
    19--) Reported to the Senior Financial Analyst
    and assisted in the development of funding for
    major Department of Defense contracts for troop
    carriers, digging and earth-moving machines, and
    extension booms. Researched funding options and
    recommended those with the most favorable rates
    and terms. Recommended by the senior financial
    analyst to replace him on his retirement.
  June 19-- to December 19-- FIRST BANK, INC. (Bloom-
    ington, IN) Planning Analyst (September 19-- to

FIGURE 15-4. Advanced résumé: organized by job.

December 19--) Reported to the Manager of Corporate Planning and developed computer models for
short- and long-range planning that saved the
time required to compute costs by 65%.
Education
  Wharton School, University of Pennsylvania (19--
    to present) Graduate Seminars Taken
      Advanced Corporate Planning and Demographics
      Computer Analysis of Corporate Planning
      Theory of Corporate Policies
      Regulation and Corporate Financial Policy
  University of Wisconsin, Milwaukee (June 19--) De-
    gree: M.B.A.
      ''Special Executive Curriculum'': A special
      fast-track program for M.B.A. students who are
      identified as promising and who are sponsored
      by their employer.
  Indiana University (June 19--) Degree: B.B.A.
    (magna cum laude)
      Major: Finance
      Minor: Computer Science
Special Skills and Activities
  Article published in Midwest Finance Journal:
  ''Developing Computer Models for Financial Plan-
  ning.'' (Vol. 34, No. 2, 19--), pp. 122-136.
  Guest Lecturer at Indiana University (June --,
  19--)
  Senior Member, Association for Corporate Finan-
  cial Planning Photographer, Runner, and Member of
  Audubon Society
References and a portfolio of computer financial mod-
els on request.

FIGURE 15–4. *continued*

CAROL ANN WALKER
1436 W. Schantz Avenue
Dayton, Ohio 45401
(513) 555-1212

Employment   Senior Research Financial Analyst in
Objective   corporate offices of growth- and re-
              search-oriented major manufacturing
              company.

Major Accomplishments
  Financial Planning
        • Provided research on funding options that en-
          abled company to achieve a 23% return on invest-
          ment.
        • Developed long-range funding requirements to
          respond to government and military contracts
          that totaled over $1 billion.
        • Developed computer model for long- and short-
          range planning, which saved 65% in preparation
          time.
  Capital Acquisition
        • Developed strategies enabling employers to
          acquire over $1 billion at 3% below market rate.
        • Responsible for securing over $100 million
          through private and government grants for re-
          search.
        • Developed computer models for capital acqui-
          sition that enabled company to increase its
          long-term debt during several major building
          expansions.
  Research and Analysis
        • Developed sophisticated computer models based
          on cutting-edge research applied to practical
          problems of corporate finance.
        • Served primarily as a researcher for 11 years
          at two different types of firms.
        • Recipient of the ''Financial Planner of the
          Year'' award from the Association of Financial
          Planners, a group composed of both academics
          and practitioners.

FIGURE 15-5. Advanced résumé: organized by function.

• Published academic article and am taking doc-
toral-level seminars at the Wharton School,
which are described in the education section
that follows.

Education
Wharton School, University of Pennsylvania (19--
to present) Graduate Seminars Taken
Advanced Corporate Planning and Demographics
Computer Analysis of Corporate Planning
Theory of Corporate Policies
Regulation and Corporate Financial Policy
University of Wisconsin, Milwaukee (June 19--) De-
gree: M.B.A.
''Special Executive Curriculum'': A special
fast-track program for M.B.A. students who are
identified as promising and who are sponsored
by their employer.
Indiana University (June 19--) Degree: B.B.A.
(magna cum laude)
Major: Finance
Minor: Computer Science

Work History
KERFHEIMER CORPORATION (Dayton, Ohio): January
19-- to present
Senior Financial analyst (19-- to 19--)
Financial Analyst (19-- to 19--)
FIRST BANK, INC. (Bloomington, IN) June 19-- to De-
cember 19--
Planning Analyst (19-- to 19--)
Student Intern (19-- to 19--)

Special Skills and Activities
Article published in Midwest Finance Journal:
''Developing Computer Models for Financial Planning.'' (Vol. 34, No. 2, 19--), pp. 122-136.
Guest Lecturer at Indiana University (June 15,
19--) Senior Member, Association for Corporate Financial Planning
Photographer, Runner, and Member of Audubon Society
References and a portfolio of computer financial models on request.

FIGURE 15–5. *continued.*

WRITING AN EFFECTIVE LETTER OF APPLICATION

The letter of application is essentially a sales letter. In it, you are trying to sell your services and, in most cases, will be competing with other applicants. Your immediate objective is to have your letter read by someone in the organization who has authority to screen job applicants; your ultimate goal is to obtain an interview. Therefore, your letter must do three things: catch your reader's attention favorably, convince your reader that you are qualified for the position, and request an interview. Try to accomplish the three objectives in a one-page letter.

Your reader should be able to learn immediately what the purpose of your letter is—you should not waste his or her time with inappropriate formalities or unnecessary details. You should state clearly that you are looking for a job with the organization. It may be a specific job that was advertised or that you learned about from another source, or you may have heard that the company has the kind of position you seek and are writing to inquire whether it has any openings for a candidate with your background. Be sure to tell your reader why you feel you are qualified for the job and that you will be available for an interview. Provide the following information in your letter of application:

1. If you are applying for a specific job, identify the job by title and state how you heard about it. If you are not applying for a specific job, explain that you are seeking a particular kind of position and are writing to inquire whether the organization has any such openings.
2. List your qualifications for the job in summary form. If you are still a student or are a recent graduate and have had little work experience, stress your education; if you have been employed in a related field, emphasize your work background. Then refer the reader to the résumé for other important details.
3. State where you can be reached and when you will be available for an interview.

Send the letter of application to the organization to which you are applying. Include in the letter any information that is pertinent to the particular job or kind of position you are applying for—details that you cannot include in the résumé because it is not written for a specific job.

The start of a letter of application is crucial in catching your reader's attention. One way to begin your letter is to state your employment objective and your interest in fulfilling your goal within the organization to which you are writing.

```
I am looking for a responsible position in an engineering
department in which I may use my training in computer sci-
ences to solve engineering-related problems. I would be in-
terested in exploring the possibility of obtaining such a
position within your firm.
```

Or you could begin the letter of application by naming someone you have met from the organization who has told you about a job (you may have met such a person at a conference or convention, through a friend, and so on). This kind of approach has the advantage of indicating that an employee evidently feels that you may be qualified for the job. Then in the next paragraph of your letter of application, you can give a summary of your qualifications.

```
During the recent NOMAD convention in Washington, a member
of your sales staff, Mr. Dale Jarrett, informed me of a possi-
ble opening for a manager in your Dealer Sales Division. My
extensive background in the office machine industry, I be-
lieve, makes me highly qualified for the position.
```

Once you have opened the letter, your aim is to convince your reader that you are a highly qualified candidate for the position. Expand upon the qualifications you mentioned in the opening and present any additional qualifications that might be particularly appropriate for the specific job. Think carefully about the requirements of the job, and then stress those aspects of your background that would interest a prospective employer most. Highlight any related experience listed in your résumé that is especially pertinent to the job you are applying for. If you are applying for a sales job, for example, indicate that other jobs you have held have taught you how to present a product line effectively. If you are applying for a job as an office manager, indicate any supervisory experience you have had.

Close your letter with a direct request for an interview. If the prospective employer is located near you, you can request that the recipient of your letter either send you a note or call you to set up an appointment. If going on an interview would involve considerable travel expense, let the prospective employer bring up the subject of the interview.

Be sure to type the letter, and make it error-free and attractive.

Following are three sample letters of application. One is by a recent college graduate; the second is by a university student who is about to graduate; and the third is by someone who has had many years of work experience.

The opening paragraph of the first letter (Figure 15–6) states that

                                6819 Locustview Drive
                                Topeka, Kansas 66614
                                June 14, 19--

          Loudons, Inc.
          4619 Drove Lane
          Kansas City, Kansas 63511

          Dear Personnel Manager:

          The Kansas Dispatch recently reported that
          Loudons is building a new data processing
          center just north of Kansas City. I would
          like to apply for a position as an entry-
          level programmer at the center.

          I am a recent graduate of Fairview Community
          College in Topeka, with an Associate Degree
          in Computer Science. In addition to taking a
          broad range of courses, I have served as a
          computer consultant at the college's computer
          center, where I helped train novice computer
          users. Since I understand Loudons produces
          both in-house and customer documentation, my
          technical writing skills (as described in the
          enclosed resume) may be particularly useful.

          I will be happy to meet with you at your con-
          venience and provide any additional informa-
          tion you may need. You can reach me either at
          my home address or at (913) 233-1552.

                                Sincerely,

                                David B. Edwards

                                David B. Edwards

          Enclosure: Resume

FIGURE 15–6. Sample letter of application.

the applicant read in a local newspaper about the company's plan to build a new data processing center. Since the writer is not applying for a specific job opening, he explains what sort of position he is looking for. The second paragraph contains a brief description of the writer's qualifications for the job. In the last paragraph, he indicates where he can be reached to arrange for an interview.

In the second sample letter of application (Figure 15–7), the writer does not specify where she learned of the opening because she does not know whether a position is actually available. Instead, because she is about to graduate, she uses the first paragraph to summarize her educational qualifications. She includes a description, in the second paragraph, of related work experience. In the last paragraph she indicates where she can be reached to set up an interview.

The third sample letter (Figure 15–8) opens with an indication of where the writer learned of the job vacancy. The second paragraph summarizes the candidate's qualifications for the job. The final paragraph asks for an interview and specifies where the writer can be reached.

CONDUCTING YOURSELF WELL DURING THE INTERVIEW

A job interview may last for 30 minutes, or it may take several hours; you may be interviewed by one person or by several, either at one time or in a series of interviews. The job interview is too important to walk into unprepared.

Before the Interview

The interview is not one way. It is also your opportunity to ask questions of your potential employer. In preparation, learn everything you can about the company before the interview. What kind of organization is it? How diversified is it? Is it locally owned? Is it a nonprofit organization? If it is public employment, at what level of government is it? Does it provide a service, and, if so, what kind? How large is the business? How large are its assets? Is the owner self-employed? Is it a subsidiary of a larger operation? Is it expanding? How long has it been in business? Where will you fit in? This kind of information can be obtained from current employees, from such company literature as employee publications, or from the business section of back issues of local newspapers (available in the local library). You may be able to learn the company's

2701 Wyoming Street
Atlanta, Georgia 30307
May 29, 19--

Ms. Laura Goldman
Chief Engineer
Acton, Inc.
80 Roseville Road
St. Louis, Missouri 63130

Dear Ms. Goldman:

I am seeking a responsible position in an engineering department in which I may use my
training in computer sciences to solve engineering problems. I would be interested in
exploring the possibility of obtaining such a
position within your firm.

I expect to receive a Bachelor of Science degree in Engineering from Georgia Institute of
Technology in June, when I will have completed the Computer Systems Engineering Program of the Engineering Department. Since
September 19-- I have been participating,
through the university, in the Professional
Training Program at Computer Systems International, in Atlanta. In the program I was assigned, on a rotating basis, to several staff
sections in apprentice positions. Most recently I have been programmer trainee in the
Engineering Department and have gained a
great deal of experience in computer applications. Details of the academic courses I have
taken are contained in the enclosed resume.

I look forward to hearing from you soon. I
can be contacted at my office (415-866-7000,
ext. 312) or at home (415-256-6320).

Sincerely yours,

Victoria T. Fromme

Victoria T. Fromme

Enclosure: Resume

FIGURE 15-7. Sample letter of application.

522 Beethoven Drive
Roanoke, Virginia 24017
November 15, 19—

Ms. Cecilia Smathers
Vice President, Dealer Sales
Hamilton Office Machines, Inc.
6194 Main Street
Hampton, Virginia 23661

Dear Ms. Smathers:

During the recent NOMAD convention in Washington, a member of your sales staff, Mr. Dale Jarrett, informed me of a possible opening for a Manager in your Dealer Sales Division. My extensive background in the office machine industry, I believe, makes me highly qualified for the position.

I was with the Technology, Inc., Dealer Division from its formation in 1969 to its phaseout last year. During this period, I was involved in all areas of dealer sales, both within Technology, Inc., and through personal contact with a number of independent dealers. Between 1967 and 1969 I served as Assistant to the Dealer Sales Manager as a Special Representative. My education and work experience are contained in the enclosed resume.

I would like to discuss my qualifications in an interview at your convenience. Please write to me or telephone me at 703-449-6743 any weekday.

Sincerely,

Gregory Mindukakis

Gregory Mindukakis

Enclosure: Resume

FIGURE 15–8. Sample letter of application.

size, sales volume, products, credit rating, plant locations, subsidiary companies, new products, building programs, and such information from its annual reports; from publications such as *Moody's Industrials, Dunn and Bradstreet, Standard and Poor's,* and *Thomas' Register;* and from other business reference sources a librarian might suggest. What you cannot find through your research, ask your interviewer. Now is your chance to make certain that you are considering a healthy and growing company.

Try to anticipate the questions your interviewer might ask, and prepare your answers in advance. Following are some of the questions that interviewers typically ask.

- What are your short-term and long-term occupational goals?
- What are your major strengths and weaknesses?
- Do you work better with others or alone?
- Why do you want to work for this employer?
- How do you spend your time?
- What are your most valuable skills?
- What are your top priorities?
- What are your personal goals?

Some of these questions are difficult. Give them careful thought.

During the Interview

Your conduct during the interview is critical.

Promptness. Be sure that you arrive for your interview at the appointed time. In fact, it's usually a good idea to arrive early since you may be asked to fill out an application before you meet your interviewer. Take a copy of your résumé and a pen with you. The résumé will be helpful because it contains much of the same information the application asks for: personal data, work experience, education. Read the form carefully before beginning to fill it out. The application form provides the company with a record for its files—it also gives the company an opportunity to see how closely you follow directions, how thoroughly you complete a task, and how neat you are. Therefore, fill the form out carefully, and proofread it when you are finished. Why risk a careless mistake now?

Appearance. The interview will actually begin before you are seated: what you wear and how you act will be closely observed. The way you dress matters. The rule of thumb is to dress conservatively, avoiding extremes. Be well groomed. For men, a recent haircut and a clean shave are essential; if you wear a beard, have a barber trim it. For women, basic clothes with simple jewelry look most businesslike. Avoid heavy perfume, gaudy lipstick, and gaudy nail polish.

Behavior. Remain standing until you are offered a seat. Then sit up straight (good posture suggests self-assurance), look at the interviewer, and try to appear relaxed and confident. Never chew gum. Don't smoke unless the interviewer invites you to do so. During the interview, you will be a little nervous. This is a natural reaction, and the interviewer expects it. Use this nervous energy to your advantage by channeling it into alertness. Listen carefully and record important information in your memory. Do not attempt to take extensive notes during the interview, although it is acceptable to jot down a few facts and figures.

Responses. When answering questions, don't ramble or stray away from the subject. Say only what you must to answer each question properly and then stop, but avoid giving just "yes" or "no" answers, which usually don't permit the interviewer to learn enough about you. Some interviewers allow a silence to fall just to see how you will react. The burden of conducting the interview is the interviewer's, not yours—and he or she may interpret it as a sign of insecurity if you rush in to fill a void in the conversation. If such a silence would make you uncomfortable, be ready to ask an intelligent question about the company.

Highlight your qualifications for the job you are seeking, but admit obvious limitations as well. Remember also that the job, the company, and the location must be right for *you*. Ask about such factors as opportunity for advancement and fringe benefits (but don't create the impression that your primary interest is security). If the employer seems clearly interested in you, you might also inquire about educational opportunities and, if accepting the job would require you to relocate, recreational and cultural activities in the community.

If the interviewer overlooks important points, bring them up. But, if possible, let the interviewer mention salary first. In the event that you are forced to bring up the subject, put it into a straightforward question. If you have taken the trouble to learn the prevailing salaries in your field, you will be better prepared to discuss salary. If you are a recent graduate, it is usually unwise to attempt to bargain. Many companies have inflexible starting salaries for beginners.

Interviewers look for a degree of self-confidence and for the candidate's apparent understanding of the field in which he or she is applying for a job. Less is expected of a beginner, but even a newcomer must show some command of the subject. One way to impress your interviewer is to ask questions about the company that are related to your line of work. Interviewers also respond favorably to applicants who can communicate, who can present themselves well. Jobs today require interaction of all kinds: person-to-person, department-to-department, division-to-division. Candidates who cannot look the interviewer in the eye or explain why they are applying for the job are not likely to do well in a work situation either.

Conclusion. At the conclusion of the interview, thank your interviewer for his or her time. Indicate that you are interested in the job (if true), and try to get an idea of when you can expect to hear from the company (but don't press too hard).

SENDING FOLLOW-UP LETTERS

After you leave the interview, jot down the pertinent information you obtained (this information will be especially helpful in comparing job offers). A day or two later, if the job is appealing, send the interviewer a brief note of thanks, saying that you find the job attractive and feel you can fill it well (see Figure 15–9).

If you are offered a job you want, write a brief letter of acceptance as soon as possible—certainly within a week. The format for such a letter is simple: begin by accepting the job you have been offered. Identify the job by title and state the exact salary, so that there will be no confusion on these two important points. The second paragraph might go into detail about moving dates and reporting for work. The details will vary, depending on the nature of the job offer. Conclude the letter with a statement that you are looking forward to working for your new employer. Figure 15–10 shows a typical letter of acceptance.

Since, in your job search, you will have applied to more than one organization (it is certainly legitimate to do so) and may receive more than one job offer, you may at some time need to write a letter of refusal. Be especially tactful and courteous because the employer you are refusing has spent time and effort interviewing you and may have counted on your accepting the job. Figure 15–11 shows an example of a job refusal letter. It acknowledges the consideration given the applicant, offers a logical reason for his refusal of the offer, and then concludes on a pleasant note.

2647 Sitwell Road
Charlotte, North Carolina 28210
March 17, 19--

Mr. F. E. Vallone
Personnel Manager
Calcutex Industries, Inc.
3275 Commercial Park Drive
Raleigh, North Carolina 27609

Dear Mr. Vallone:

Thank you for the informative and pleasant interview we had last Wednesday. Please extend my thanks to Mr. Wilson of the Servocontrol Group as well.

I came away from our meeting most favorably impressed with Calcutex Industries. I find the position you are filling to be an attractive one and feel confident that my qualifications would enable me to perform the duties to everyone's advantage.

If I can answer any further questions, please let me know.

Sincerely yours,

Philip Ming

Philip Ming

FIGURE 15–9. Follow-up letter.

2647 Sitwell Road
Charlotte, North Carolina
28210
March 26, 19--

Mr. F. E. Vallone
Personnel Manager
Calcutex Industries, Inc.
3275 Commercial Park Drive
Raleigh, North Carolina 27609

Dear Mr. Vallone:

I am pleased to accept your offer of $865 per month as a junior design draftsman in the Calcutex Group.

After graduation on August 30, I plan to leave Charlotte on Tuesday, September 2. I should be able to find suitable living accommodations within a few days and be ready to report for work on the following Monday, September 8. Please let me know if this date is satisfactory to you.

I look forward to what I am sure will be a rewarding future with Calcutex.

Very truly yours

Philip Ming
Philip Ming

FIGURE 15–10. Acceptance letter.

2647 Peters Road
Charlotte, North Carolina
28210
March 26, 19--

Mr. F. E. Vallone
Personnel Manager
Calcutex Industries, Inc.
3275 Commercial Park Drive
Raleigh, North Carolina 27609

Dear Mr. Vallone:

I enjoyed talking with you about your opening
for a junior design draftsman, and I was
gratified to receive your offer. Although I
have given the offer serious thought, I have
decided to accept a position with a commercial drafting agency. The job I have chosen
will provide me with a greater variety of duties, which I feel will develop my skills
more fully in the long run.

I appreciate your consideration and the time
you spent with me.

Sincerely,

Philip Ming

Philip Ming

FIGURE 15–11. Letter of refusal.

CHAPTER SUMMARY

The search for a job consists of five steps: (1) locating the job you want, (2) preparing an effective résumé, (3) writing an effective letter of application, (4) conducting yourself well during the interview, and (5) sending a follow-up letter.

Sources you can use in locating a job include classified advertisements in newspapers, letters of inquiry, advertisements in trade and professional journals, school placement services, state and private employment agencies, the advice of friends and acquaintances, and local, state, and federal agencies.

Before writing your résumé, determine the exact type of job you are seeking and who the prospective employers are. Then ask yourself what information about you and your background would be most important to those employers. On the basis of your answer to this question, determine what details should be included in your résumé and how you can most effectively present your qualifications. Then prepare your résumé accordingly.

A letter of application must catch your reader's attention, create a desire for your services, and request an interview. Be sure that it includes the specific job for which you are applying (if known), a brief summary of your qualifications for the job, and when and where you can be reached to set up an interview.

Before going to the interview, learn everything you can about your prospective employer. Arrive for the interview promptly. During the interview, highlight strengths you have that could be used in the job you are applying for, demonstrate your knowledge of your field, and project self-confidence. After the interview, make notes of important information you learned during the interview. A day or two later, send the interviewer a brief note of thanks.

If you are offered a job that you plan to accept, send a letter of acceptance to the employer within a few days of receiving the offer. If you have decided to refuse the offer, send a letter as soon as possible, expressing your appreciation for the company's time and effort in considering you for the job.

EXERCISES

1. Find information about the future employment potential of graduates in your major field by using two sources, one of which must be *Occupational Outlook Handbook*. Next, using a large city newspaper, photocopy three job ads for entry-level positions for graduates in your major.

Assume that your instructor has asked you for information about your major so that he or she can advise students seeking information about employment opportunities. Write a memo to your instructor describing the job outlook for such majors, and attach the relevant material you have copied. (Note: Your instructor will indicate the length or the need for any additional information.)

2. Write a letter to a past or present teacher or an employer (or other appropriate person) asking permission to use him or her as a job reference. Be prepared to explain in class why you think this person is especially well qualified to comment on your job qualifications.

3. Write a letter to an actual firm for which you would like to work, asking whether there is a position available for someone with the qualifications you expect to have either at the end of the present semester or when you graduate.

4. Write a letter of application and résumé in response to an advertisement for a job for which you will be qualified upon graduation. Type them neatly on high-quality white bond paper. Make sure they are error- and blemish-free.

5. Assume that you have been interviewed for the job in Exercise 4. Write a follow-up letter expressing thanks for the interview.

6. To prepare for an interview with a prospective employer, list three questions you think the interviewer may ask you, exclusive of the questions given in the text. Then list six questions you would like to ask the interviewer. Arrange both lists from most important to least important. Come to class prepared to discuss both lists.

part three

WRITER'S GUIDE

The Writer's Guide presents important supplemental tools for the writer. Section A contains two parts that focus on language. Part 1 provides sound general advice and a set of rules for improving your spelling. Part 2 contains a systematic treatment of vocabulary building based on the word-part approach. This approach involves learning the meanings of recurring prefixes, roots, and suffixes so that when they appear in an unfamiliar word, you can infer its meaning.

Section B is a comprehensive handbook of grammar, punctuation, and mechanics containing several parts. Part 3 surveys the parts of speech—the functions performed by separate words or groups of words within sentences. Part 4 treats phrases, clauses, sentences, and paragraphs, the larger structures built with words. Part 5 reviews punctuation, the system of symbols that clarifies the structural relationship among words and parts of sentences. And Part 6 covers the mechanics of good writing, such as capitalization and the proper use of symbols.

Section C provides an illustrated introduction to word processing, a technology that business and technical people are using in increasing numbers. This section features a set of guidelines for using word processing to maximum effect for recording ideas quickly and for writing, revising, and creating professionally designed written products.

Section A

Spelling and Vocabulary

1   SPELLING

Personnel managers often reject candidates who make spelling errors on employment applications, résumés, and application letters. Consider, for example, the true story of a college graduate who applied for the position of Assistant Director of Personnel and was rejected for misspelling the word *personnel*.

The reason potential employers react so strongly to spelling errors is simple. Poor spelling reflects negatively on an employee—and, by association, on the employer as well. Everyone makes an occasional error, of course, but a personnel manager may conclude that someone who has overlooked a spelling mistake on something as important as a job application may be careless in his or her work too. Keep in mind that when you apply for a job, an employer must make a judgment based primarily on your résumé, your letter of application, and your interview.

But an even more important reason to learn to be a careful speller is that accuracy in spelling can help you keep the bargain you, as a writer, make with your readers: to assist them in understanding what you are saying. Your job as a writer is to remove roadblocks from the path of communication between you and your readers—and spelling errors, because they can confuse and slow down your readers, create roadblocks.

As you write a first draft, you needn't be concerned about spelling words correctly. Your attention then should focus on what you are saying;

453

to worry about spelling at that point would be a distraction. You can check for and correct spelling errors when you revise; in fact, you should proofread once *just for spelling*. Guard against the natural tendency to concentrate on complex words; pay as much attention to words in common use. It is often the words you use most frequently that trip you up.

If your word processor has a spell checker feature, by all means use it as you make your final revisions. Do not rely completely on the spell checker, however, since no spell checker can identify errors such as the misuse of *there* for *their,* and other similar mix-ups.

Learning to spell requires a systematic effort on your part. The following system will help you learn to spell correctly.

- Keep a dictionary handy, and use it regularly. If you are unsure about the spelling of a word, don't rely on memory or guesswork—consult the dictionary. When you look up a word, focus on both its spelling and its meaning.
- After you have looked in the dictionary for the spelling of the word, write the word from memory several times. Then check the accuracy of your spelling. If you have misspelled the word, repeat this step. If you do not follow through by writing the word from memory, you lose the chance of retaining it for future use. Practice is essential.
- Keep a list of the words you commonly misspell, and work regularly at whittling it down. Do not load the list with exotic words; many of us would stumble over *asphyxiation* or *pterodactyl*. Concentrate instead on words like *calendar, maintenance,* and *unnecessary*. These and other frequently used words should remain on your list until you have learned to spell them.
- Study the following common sets of words that sound alike but differ in spelling and meaning.[1]

affect (verb: to influence)
effect (noun: a result)

all ready (We are *all ready* to go.)
already (Have you finished the work *already?*)

brake (noun: device for stopping)
break (verb: to crack; noun: period of relaxation)

cite (verb: to refer to)
sight (noun: view; something to look at)
site (noun: location)

---

[1] The meanings given here are for identification only—they are not intended to represent every meaning a word may have.

cent (noun: coin)
scent (noun: smell)
sent (verb: past tense of *send*)

coarse (adjective: rough)
course (noun: direction of study; adverb in *of course*)

complement (noun: something that completes something else)
compliment (noun: praise; verb: to give praise)

fair (noun: exhibition; adjective: light-hued, beautiful)
fare (noun: cost of a trip; food served)

foreword (noun: introduction to a book)
forward (adjective and adverb: near or toward the front)

hear (verb: to listen to)
here (adverb: in this place)

its (possessive pronoun: Does the dog have *its* bone?)
it's (contraction[2] of *it is: It's* good to see you.)

lead (noun: a metal—rhymes with *bread*)
lead (verb: to be first—rhymes with *breed*)
led (verb: past tense of verb *to lead*)

may be (verb: It *may be* true, but it's hard to believe.)
maybe (adverb: perhaps—*Maybe* he will visit us.)

pair (noun: set of two)
pare (verb: to trim)
pear (noun: fruit)

peace (noun: absence of war)
piece (noun: small amount)

plain (adjective: ordinary-looking, simple; noun: large field)
plane (noun: aircraft)
plane (verb: to make smooth)

principal (adjective: primary, main; noun: school official)
principle (noun: a controlling idea or belief)

right (adjective: correct, or a direction)
rite (noun: ritual)
write (verb: to create with words)

road (noun: passageway for vehicles)
rode (past tense of verb *to ride*)
rowed (past tense of verb *to row*—to propel a small boat)

---

[2] In a *contraction,* two words are combined and one or more letters are omitted. An apostrophe (') indicates where the letter or letters have been dropped. Contractions are appropriate in some informal writing, but it is best to avoid them in formal contexts.

stationary (adjective: not moving)
stationery (noun: writing paper and envelopes)

their (possessive pronoun—Do you know *their* telephone number?)

there (adverb: at that place)
they're (contraction of *they are*—*They're* going to meet us at the movies.)

to (preposition: toward)
too (conjunction: also; adverb: excessively)
two (number)

weak (adjective: not strong)
week (noun: seven days)

weather (noun: atmospheric conditions)
whether (conjunction: if)

who's (contraction of *who is*—Do you know *who's* coming?)
whose (possessive pronoun: *Whose* coat is this?)

your (possessive pronoun—Is this *your* book?)
you're (contraction of *you are*—*You're* a fine friend!)

The following pages contain a number of rules and some advice to help you improve your spelling. It would be pointless to try to memorize all the rules and reminders. If you have specific problem areas in spelling, however, you would be wise to learn the rules that apply to your particular needs. Note that most of these rules also have exceptions.

1.1   THE SILENT *E* RULE OF THUMB

Words of one syllable that have a long vowel sound usually end in silent *e*. (A *long vowel* is one that is pronounced like the letter's name.) Adding silent *e* to a one-syllable word that has a *short vowel sound* ordinarily gives the vowel a long sound. (Dictionaries vary in the symbols they use to indicate how a word is pronounced. Examine the pronunciation key in the dictionary you use.)

Compare the words in the two lists below.

Short-Vowel Sounds	*Long-Vowel Sounds*
bit	bite
cut	cute
dot	dote
fat	fate
pet	Pete

The silent *e* rule also applies to the accented syllable in some longer words.[3]

com·plete′   con·trive′   re·fuse′

The silent *e* rule does not apply in longer words in which the final syllable is *not* accented.

com·pos′·ite   gran′·ite   hes′·i·tate   op′·pos·ite

If endings are added to the basic word, the silent *e* rule still holds, even if the silent *e* is dropped when the ending is added.

complete, completed   hope, hoping   late, later

1.2 HARD AND SOFT SOUNDS

The letter *c* can sound like a *k* ("hard" *c*) or like an *s* ("soft" *c*). The letter *g* can sound like "guh" ("hard" *g*) or like a *j* ("soft" *g*).

Hard Sound	*Soft Sound*
attic	ace
cog	agent

1.2.1 Hard *C* and Soft *C*

Hard *c* and soft *c* cause problems mostly at the ends of words. The following guidelines will help you to distinguish between hard *c* and soft *c*.

- The sound of *c* is always hard when it is the last letter of a word.

  automatic   economic   electric   spastic   specific

- A long vowel followed by a *k* sound is always spelled with a *k* and a silent *e*.

  eke   fluke   like   take   woke

- A short vowel followed by a *k* sound is spelled *ck* when another syllable follows, except in certain words borrowed from French, such as *racquet*.

  beckon   bracket   picket   pocket   trucker

- An *e* after a *c* almost always indicates a soft *c*.

  ace   ice   piece   place   puce

---

[3] An *accented syllable* receives the emphasis when the word is spoken. The symbol ′ is used here to indicate the accented syllable. Check your dictionary for the symbol it uses.

1.2.2   Hard *G* and Soft *G*

Hard *g* and soft *g* cause problems mostly at the beginnings of words. The following guidelines should help you to distinguish between hard *g* and soft *g*.

- Any *g* followed by a consonant is a hard *g*.

  ghetto   gladly   grain   green

- The *g* in the combinations *gu* and *go* is always hard.

  cargo   goblet   guess   guide

- The *g* in the combination *ga* is always hard except in the word *margarine*.

  gale   gape   garage   gate

- The *g* in the combination *gi* can be either hard or soft.

  fragile   gibber   gift   give

- The *g* in the combination *ge* is usually soft.

  cage   garage   general   germinate   gesture

- The *g* in the combination *gy* is normally soft. Words such as *gynecology* are exceptions.

  gymnasium   gypsum   gyrate   gyroscope

1.3   ADDING TO BASIC WORDS

Words may change spelling according to the way they are used in a sentence. The following rules can serve as a guide in choosing the correct spelling of a plural noun, a verb form, an adverb formed from an adjective, and the comparative and superlative forms of some adjectives (*nicer, nicest*).

1.3.1   Plurals of Nouns

You may have no difficulty spelling a word like *tax, brush,* or *ox*. You may encounter some trouble, though, in spelling the plural forms of these and other words. The general rules for forming the plural of nouns are as follows.

- To form the plural of *most* nouns, add *-s*.

circumstance/circumstances   hat/hats   mule/mules
pen/pens   tie/ties   tool/tools

- To form the plural of nouns that end in *ch, s, sh, ss, x, z,* or *zz,* add *-es.*

branch/branches   brush/brushes   bus/buses
buzz/buzzes   glass/glasses   tax/taxes

- To form the plural of nouns that end in *y* preceded by a vowel, add *-s.*

boy/boys   monkey/monkeys

But if the *y* is preceded by a consonant, change the *y* to *i* and then add *-es.*

filly/fillies   fly/flies

- To form the plural of most nouns that end in *f* and all nouns that end in *ff,* add *-s.*

reef/reefs   roof/roofs   cuff/cuffs

For a few nouns that end in *f,* change the *f* to *v* and add *-es.*

leaf/leaves   loaf/loaves   wolf/wolves

If a noun ends in *fe,* change the *f* to *v* and add *-es.*

knife/knives   life/lives   wife/wives

Note: If there is a *v* in the plural form of a noun, you can usually hear it in the spoken word.

- Some commonly used nouns have a special plural form.

child/children   foot/feet   ox/oxen
tooth/teeth   woman/women   mouse/mice

Consult your dictionary for other plural forms that may be troublesome: nouns ending in *o,* foreign words used in English, a number of scientific and medical terms, and so on.

1.3.2   Adding Verb, Adjective, and Adverb Endings

The general rules for adding endings to verbs, for forming adverbs from adjectives, and for adding the comparative (*-er*) and superlative (*-est*) endings to adjectives are as follows.

- If the word ends in a consonant, simply add the ending.

burn + ing = burning   long + er = longer
small + est = smallest   want + ed = wanted

- If the word ends in silent *e* and the ending begins with a vowel (including *e*), drop the silent *e* of the basic word.

  advise + ory = advisory   base + ic = basic
  desire + able = desirable   fine + est = finest
  landscape + er = landscaper   note + ed = noted

- If the basic word ends in silent *e* and the ending begins with a consonant, simply add the ending.

  care/carefully   like/likely   use/useless

  There are a few exceptions to this rule.

  argue/argument   nine/ninth   true/truly

- If the basic word ends in a consonant and the ending begins with the same consonant, keep both consonants.

  cool/coolly   jewel/jewellike   tail/tailless

- If the basic word ends in *y* preceded by a vowel, simply add the ending.

  betray/betrays/betrayed/betraying
  obey/obeys/obeyed/obeying

  Note: There are three important exceptions to this rule:

  lay/lays/laying   *but*   laid
  pay/pays/paying   *but*   paid
  say/says/saying   *but*   said

- If the basic word ends in *y* preceded by a consonant, change the *y* to *i* before adding the ending, *unless the ending begins with i.*

  copy/copies/copied/copying
  try/tries/tried/trying

- If a verb ends in *ie,* add *-s* or *-d* directly to the word.

  die/dies/died   tie/ties/tied

  But change *ie* to *y* before adding *-ing.*

  die/dying   tie/tying

- When you add *-ly* to most adjectives to form an adverb, simply add the ending. The word *truly* is an exception to this rule.

  careful/carefully   complete/completely   dim/dimly
  nice/nicely   sure/surely   useless/uselessly

When you add the ending *-ly* to most adjectives ending in *cal,* be sure to retain the *a* and both *l*'s.

magical/magically   practical/practically

- When you add *-er, -est,* or *-ly* to an adjective that ends in *y*, change the *y* to *i* before adding the ending.

happy/happier/happiest/happily
noisy/noisier/noisiest/noisily

- When you add *-ly* to adjectives ending in *-ble,* drop the *e* and add only the *-y*.

able/ably   favorable/favorably   incredible/incredibly

1.4   DOUBLING FINAL CONSONANTS

Knowing when and when not to double a final consonant before adding an ending is important. Three things affect the decision: (1) whether the vowel in the basic word is long or short, (2) whether the last syllable of the basic word is accented, and (3) whether the basic word ends in more than one consonant.

1.4.1   The Effect of the Vowel in the Basic Word

For most words of one syllable, double the final consonant only if the preceding vowel is *short*.

flop/flopped	ripe/ripen
let/letting	mate/mated
rip/ripped	tune/tuning

Never double the final consonant of a word if the consonant is immediately preceded by two vowels.

appear/appeared/appearing/appearance
treat/treated/treating/treatment

1.4.2   The Effect of the Word's Accent

In longer words, whether the final consonant is doubled depends on which syllable is accented. When the accent falls on the last syllable of a word, double the final consonant before adding the ending.

> ad·mit'/admitted/admitting   com·pel'/compelled/compelling

When the accent does not fall on the last syllable, do not double the final consonant before adding the ending.

> dif'fer/differed/differing   ex·hib'it/exhibited/exhibiting
> fo'cus/focused/focusing   pro'fit/profited/profiting

1.4.3   The Effect of Final Consonants

When a word ends in more than one consonant, *do not double* the final consonant when adding an ending.

> confirm/confirmed/confirming
> depend/depended/depending/dependence

When a word ends in a double consonant, keep both consonants when adding the ending.

> embarrass/embarrassed/embarrassing/embarrassment
> enroll/enrolled/enrolling/enrollment

1.5   PREFIXES AND SUFFIXES

A *prefix* is a form like *dis-, un-,* or *anti-* that is placed in front of a word to change its meaning. A *suffix* is a form like *-able* or *-ible* that is placed at the end of a word (or word part) to change its meaning. To avoid making spelling errors when you use words that contain prefixes and suffixes, study the following rules.

- When you attach a prefix like *dis-, im-, mis-,* or *un-* to a word that begins with the same letter as the *last* letter of the prefix, be sure to retain the double letters.

  > dis + similar = dissimilar   im + movable = immovable
  > mis + spell = misspell   un + natural = unnatural

- When you attach a suffix that begins with a vowel to a word that ends in silent *e,* you should usually drop the *e.*

  > advise/advisory   continue/continual
  > enclose/enclosure   sane/sanity

- When you attach the suffix *-able* or *-ible* to a word that ends in a soft *c* or a soft *g* sound, retain the *e* of the original word.

change/changeable   manage/manageable
notice/noticeable   service/serviceable

- When you attach suffixes like *-ness* and *-less,* do not change the spelling of the original word.

care + less = careless (retain the *e*—otherwise you are spelling *carless,* "without a car")
drunken + ness = drunkenness (retain both *n*'s)

Note: In a word like *lioness,* the suffix is *-ess* (to indicate female), not *-ness.*

1.6 WORDS WITH *IE* OR *EI*

Among the trickiest words in the English language to spell are *ie* and *ei* words. The following rules of thumb should help you to recognize the correct spelling of these words. The jingle *"i* before *e,* except after *c"* covers rules 1 and 2 below.

1. In most cases, the correct combination following the letter *c* is *ei.*

ceiling   conceive   perceive   receive

2. Many words that are pronounced *ee* are spelled *ie.*

achieve   brief   cashier   field
piece   relieve   tier   yield

3. Many words that are pronounced as a long *a* are spelled *ei.*

eight   freight   rein
veil   vein   weight

4. Words that are pronounced as a long *i* are always spelled *ei.*

height   seismograph   sleight

1.7 CONTRACTIONS

A *contraction* is a form that combines two words, omitting one or more letters, and uses an apostrophe (') to indicate where the letter or letters have been dropped.

cannot/can't   is not/isn't
it is/it's   they are/they're

Remember to place the apostrophe exactly where the letter or letters are deleted.

Be careful not to confuse contractions with words that have the same pronunciation as the contractions.

   its/it's   their/they're   theirs/there's   whose/who's

And do not confuse the presence of the apostrophe to form a contraction with the use of the apostrophe to show possession.

Contraction	*Possession*
can't (can + not)	the woman's voice
don't (do + not)	a student's book

In a contraction, the apostrophe indicates that a letter has been left out. In a possessive form, the apostrophe indicates ownership.

1.8   ABBREVIATED SPELLINGS

In very informal writing, certain words are sometimes spelled in an abbreviated form: *thru* (*through*), *tho* (*although*), and *nite* (*night*). Such abbreviated spellings should be avoided in all job-related writing.

1.9   WORD GROUPS OF FREQUENTLY MISSPELLED WORDS

• Words Ending in *-ery*

| creamery | bravery | effrontery |
| hatchery | imagery | nursery |

• Words Ending in *-ary*

arbitrary	complementary	complimentary	documentary
elementary	fragmentary	imaginary	library
monetary	necessary	primary	tributary

• Words Ending in *-able*

| acceptable | agreeable | avoidable | changeable |
| dependable | manageable | profitable | valuable |

Note: Remember to keep the *e* in *changeable* and *manageable*.

• Words Ending in *-iable*

appreciable   enviable   justifiable
liable   reliable   variable

- Words Ending in *-ible*

audible	combustible	compatible	credible
divisible	eligible	feasible	forcible
illegible	indelible	invincible	negligible
reducible	visible		

- Words Ending in *-ise*

advertise	advise	comprise	compromise
excise	exercise	franchise	revise
supervise			

Note: The noun form of *supervise* is *supervisor;* the noun
    form of advise is *adviser* or *advisor.*

- Words Ending in *-ize*

authorize	energize	familiarize	magnetize
notarize	organize	specialize	stabilize
standardize	subsidize	summarize	synchronize

- Words Ending in *-yze*
    analyze   paralyze

Note: The noun forms are *analysis* and *paralysis.*

- Words Ending in *-eous*

courteous	erroneous	gaseous
heterogeneous	homogeneous	instantaneous
outrageous	spontaneous	

- Words Ending in *-ious*

cautious	contagious	curious	laborious
mysterious	nutritious	previous	repetitious

- Words Ending in *-ous*

anonymous	callous	dangerous	disastrous
grievous	hazardous	intravenous	mischievous
monotonous			

- Words Ending in *-sion*

compulsion	conclusion	conversion	diversion
erosion	expansion	expulsion	extension
occasion	persuasion	propulsion	provision
reversion			

- Words Ending in *-ssion:*

accession	admission	concession
discussion	omission (note one *m*)	recession
remission	succession	transmission

Note: Be sure to distinguish between *intersession* (the period between two *sessions* of the school year) and *intercession* (intervention on behalf of someone).

Words ending in *-cede* and *-ceed* are sometimes troublesome. Study the following lists.

- Words Ending in *-cede*

accede	concede
intercede	precede (to go ahead of someone or something)
recede	secede

The *-ing* forms of these words follow the silent *e* rule: *acceding, conceding, interceding, preceding, receding, seceding.*

- Words Ending in *-ceed*

exceed	proceed (to go forward)	succeed

The *ing* forms are *exceeding, proceeding, succeeding.*

Note: The word *supersede,* "to take the place of something that went before," is often misspelled. It is the only word in common use that has a *-sede* ending.

- Words Ending in *-ence*

magnificence	maleficence	permanence
persistence	pertinence	

- Words Ending in *-ance*

dissonance	malfeasance	perseverance

- Words Ending in *-scence*

effervescence	luminescence	phosphorescence

2 VOCABULARY

Trying to get along with a limited vocabulary is like trying to prepare a five-course meal with only one utensil and a pan. The limited equipment prevents you from dealing successfully with the range of situations you'll find yourself in. A limited vocabulary is a handicap, but it is one you can overcome. The emphasis here is on *you* because there is no magic formula for vocabulary building. It must be done because you want it done. It must also be done systematically and over a period of time. This section provides a system; you must provide the time and desire.

If you stop to think about it, you'll realize that you use at least three different vocabularies, perhaps four. Your largest vocabulary is your *recognition vocabulary,* which includes all the words you recognize and understand in your reading. Your next largest vocabulary is your *writing vocabulary,* which takes in all the words you use in your writing. The third largest is your *speaking vocabulary;* it is smaller than your writing vocabulary because you may consider some words from your writing vocabulary too formal for conversation. And, finally, you may have a limited vocabulary, of from 50 to 1,000 words, that are unique to the particular trade or profession in which you are (or will be) engaged.

You will probably have no trouble in learning your trade, or professional, vocabulary, but you may need to work on improving the other three—especially your writing and recognition vocabularies. One excellent way to do so is by increasing the amount of reading you do and keeping a good dictionary nearby for looking up unfamiliar words. The movement of a word from your recognition vocabulary to your writing vocabulary should be relatively easy. Another effective way to increase your vocabulary is to take a word-part approach, learning the meanings of prefixes and roots of words and, on the basis of those meanings, figuring out the meaning of a new word that contains them. The following pages explore these two methods of improving your vocabulary.

CHOOSING THE RIGHT WORD

Your guideline in choosing the right word should be appropriateness. Is the word or expression you are considering appropriate to both your reader and your purpose? When in doubt about the correct use, exact meaning, or pronunciation of a word, consult a recent edition of a good college or desk dictionary. A compact paperback dictionary may be convenient for checking the spelling of a word, but for a wide range of detailed information about a term, a hardback desk dictionary is essential. The following are considered good desk dictionaries.

- *The American Heritage Dictionary of the English Language.* New York: American Heritage Publishing Company.
- *Funk and Wagnall's Standard College Dictionary.* Rev. ed. New York: Funk and Wagnall's.

- *The Random House College Dictionary.* New York: Random House.
- *Webster's New Collegiate Dictionary.* Rev. ed. Springfield, Mass.: G. & C. Merriam Company.
- *Webster's New World Dictionary of the American Language.* Second college ed. Cleveland: William Collins.

Get into the habit of using a dictionary. As with any reference tool, the more you know about it, the more useful it will be to you. The following is a list of the kinds of information a dictionary entry may provide. Both the order in which the information is given and the form in which it is presented vary; most dictionaries supply a note near the beginning of the volume that explains how the information is arranged and presented in the work. Many dictionaries also include a key to the signs, symbols, and abbreviations that are used. In addition, most dictionaries include, before and after the entry section, a variety of information, such as a pronouncing gazetteer (names of places), a list of common English given names, the names of colleges and universities, and a history of the English language.

1. *Spelling.* Each entry is printed in **bold type.** Occasionally, when there is more than one acceptable spelling, both are given: *catalog, catalogue.*
2. *Syllables.* The word is divided into syllables (if it contains more than one): ox·y·gen. This division provides the correct *hyphenation* of the word—it indicates how the word is divided at the end of the line.
3. *Pronunciation.* The word's pronunciation (how it sounds when spoken) is given, usually in parentheses, by a combination of standard alphabet letters and symbols (the combination is called a *respelling*). Each letter and symbol represents one specific sound; a key to the symbols ordinarily appears at the bottom of every page or every second page of the dictionary. The pronunciation of the word *reserve,* for example, is indicated by the form ri·zûrv'.
4. *Accent.* An accent mark (` or ') indicates which syllable is emphasized when the word is spoken: pri·mar'i·ly. The accent mark ordinarily appears as part of the *respelling* of the word.
5. *Part of speech.* An abbreviation identifies the part or parts of speech the word belongs to: *v.* for *verb; n.* for *noun; pron.* for *pronoun; adj.* for *adjective; adv.* for *adverb; prep.* for *preposition; conj.* for *conjunction; interj.* for *interjection.* If a word functions as more than one part of speech, the different parts of speech are included in the entry.
6. *Definition.* When a word has more than one meaning, each definition is listed, in numbered sequence. The order in which a word's

meanings are listed varies. Some dictionaries present the meanings in historical order, with the oldest meaning first and the most recent meaning last; other dictionaries list the most recent meaning first and the oldest meaning last. (The dictionary's explanatory notes will tell you in what order the meanings are arranged.) If a word has two or more fundamental, and unrelated, meanings, each word is listed as a separate entry; any additional *related* meanings of each word are numbered consecutively within the entry. The word *fan,* for instance, has two separate entries in *The Random House Dictionary:* the first entry includes both the noun that signifies "a device for moving air" and the verb meaning "to move the air"; the second entry applies to the noun *fan* that refers to an "enthusiastic follower."

When a word has one or more specific meanings in one or more special fields (biology, music, literature, architecture, religion, telecommunications, to name just a few), the definitions are introduced by a label that identifies the field. For example, the entry for the word *rest* in *The American Heritage Dictionary* first defines the word according to its most general use—the act of ceasing from work, sleep, death, and so on—and then goes on to define the word according to the way it is used in the specific fields of music, prosody, billiards, and the military.

7. *Example.* To help you understand exactly how a word may be used, some dictionaries provide examples of the word, usually in a phrase or a sentence. The word *serried,* for instance, is defined in *The American Heritage Dictionary* as "pressed together in rows; in close order." The sample sentence that follows is "Troops in *serried* ranks assembled." In examples, some dictionaries italicize the word in question, others abbreviate it, and still others represent the word with a tilde [~].

8. *Picture.* Occasionally, the definition of a word is accompanied by a drawing or a photograph of the object. *The American Heritage Dictionary* in particular has numerous pictures.

9. *Usage.* Usage labels provide information about the standing a word has in relation to current standards of speech. Such a label might indicate that a word is obsolete (no longer in use), primarily British, slang, and so on. Since usage standards change over time, the date of the dictionary is an important factor in determining the accuracy of a given label.

10. *Special uses.* Special uses of a word, or its use in certain expressions, may follow the main body of the definition. The entry for the word *court* in *The American Heritage Dictionary,* for instance, indicates that the word appears in the expressions *out of court* and *pay court to;* each expression is defined.

11. *Synonyms.* For some words, *synonyms* (words that are similar in meaning) are listed and discussed; the discussion, by providing an explanation of the differences in meaning among the synonyms, can help you select the precise word you need.

12. *Antonyms.* For some words, *antonyms* (words that are opposite in meaning) are supplied. The listing may sometimes aid you in selecting the exact word for your context.

13. *Origin.* The origin and history of a word (its *etymology*) appears in some dictionaries following the last definition and in other dictionaries following the part-of-speech indicator.

The following is a typical dictionary entry. It is taken from *The Random House Dictionary* (revised edition, 1975).

op·er·a·tion (op/ə rā/shən), *n.* **1.** the act or an instance, process, or manner of functioning or operating. **2.** the state of something that operates or is in effect (usually prec. by *in* or *into*): *a rule no longer in operation.* **3.** the exertion of force or influence: *the operation of alcohol on the mind.* **4.** a process of a practical or mechanical nature. **5.** *Surg.* a process or act of operating on the body of a patient. **6.** *Math.* a mathematical process, as addition, multiplication, etc., or an instance of its application. **7.** *Mil.* **a.** a campaign, mission, maneuver, or action. **b.** Usually, **operations.** the conduct of a campaign, mission, etc. **c. operations,** a place from which a military campaign or the like is planned and controlled. **8.** a business transaction in securities or commodities, esp. one of a speculative nature or on a large scale. [ME *operacioun* < L *operātiōn-* (s. of *operātiō*)]

Once you've become familiar with the dictionary, make using it a habit. A dictionary can provide great help to you as speaker, reader, and writer. Remember, too, that one of the most effective ways to build a good vocabulary is to read. You will, of course, sometimes run into terms that even a good desk dictionary does not define—especially those terms related to a particular occupation. Many occupations have created special vocabularies to serve their particular requirements, and a number of these vocabularies are large enough and widely enough used to necessitate the publication of specialized dictionaries. If such a dictionary exists in your field, locate one and use it regularly.

THE WORD-PART APPROACH

An effective way to increase your vocabulary is to call on the *word-part* approach when you come across a word you don't know. This technique enables you to work out the meanings of many words when you first see them. A large number of words contain a root, or part, that expresses its primary meaning. In the word *dictate,* for example, *dict,* the root, means "say," "tell," "speak."

The meaning of a word frequently changes when a prefix or suffix is added to the root. A *prefix* is a word part that is placed in front of a root to modify the word's meaning. *Sure* is made *unsure* by the addition of the prefix *un-*. A *suffix* is a word part that is placed after a root. It often tells you what part of speech the word is. Nouns are formed by suffixes like *-ness* (*tightness*), *-ment* (*impediment*), and *-ion* (*coordination*). Many verbs end in *-ate* (*dictate*), *-ize* (*minimize*), and *-ify* (*qualify*). Adverbs are usually recognized by their *-ly* suffixes (*slowly, privately*), while for adjectives the endings *-ous, -ful,* and *-less* are common (*famous, colorful, colorless*).

Sometimes a root can have more than one prefix or suffix. The root *new* and the prefix *re-* form *renew*. The addition of the prefix *non-* and the suffix *-able* makes the word *nonrenewable*. Less common words follow the same pattern. The root *aqua* means "water." This root forms the basis for many words: An *aqualung* is a device used for breathing under water. An *aquacade* is a water sports spectacle in which an *aquaplane* (a board being towed swiftly across water) may be used. An *aquarium* is an enclosure for fish and other *subaqueous* creatures; chemicals dissolved in water form an *aqueous* solution. Once you learn to identify a group of roots and their prefixes and suffixes, you can often work out the meaning of a complex word you have never seen before.

The remainder of this section presents information on roots, prefixes, and suffixes. The word-part under study is listed, defined, and followed by examples of its use in typical sentences.

2.1   ROOTS

2.1.1   act

The root *act* means "do," "move," "put in motion." Typical words are *actuary* (one who calculates insurance premiums) and *activate* (to make active or more active; to put someone on active duty).

EXAMPLES

My insurance agent said that an *actuary* would have to determine the new rates.
To *activate* the mechanism, press the button.

2.1.2   cap, cip

The roots *cap* and *cip* mean "take." Typical words are *capacity* (the ability to take something; the amount that can be contained), *incapacitated* (unable to take on usual work or responsibility), and *recipient* (one who takes or receives).

EXAMPLES

Most babies do not have a *capacity* for large amounts of food.

The injury kept Randall *incapacitated* for weeks.

The *recipients* of the questionnaire were asked to complete it and return it within ten days.

2.1.3   cede, ceed

The roots *-cede* and *-ceed* mean "go" or "move." Typical words are *precede* (to go before), *intercede* (to act on someone's behalf; to attempt to settle a dispute between two people or groups), *proceed* (to go forward), and *exceed* (to move or go beyond).

EXAMPLES

The union stated that negotiations must *precede* any decision.

The attorney attempted to *intercede* on behalf of the juvenile defendant.

After visiting the museum, we will *proceed* to a quaint little café for lunch.

The motorist had *exceeded* the speed limit.

2.1.4   chron

The root *chron* means "time." Typical words are *synchronize* (to arrange two or more things to make them come together in time), *chronic* (continuing over a period of time), and *chronology* (time sequence).

EXAMPLES

The two governments *synchronized* their announcements of the new treaty.

Johnson's *chronic* lateness to work prevented him from receiving a promotion.

The *chronology* of the events was clear from a reading of the pilot's log.

2.1.5   claim, clam

The roots *claim* and *clam* mean "shout." Typical words are *reclaim* (to make available for use; to rescue), *disclaim* (to deny responsibility for or association with something), and *proclamation* (an official public announcement).

EXAMPLES

The urban renewal project will *reclaim* many decaying areas of the city.

Norman *disclaimed* any knowledge of the mistake.

The governor's *proclamation* declared next Monday a state holiday.

2.1.6   clude

The root *clude* means "shut" or "close." Typical words are *include* (to close or contain within), *exclude* (to shut out or refuse admission), and *preclude* (to shut out, or make impossible, beforehand).

EXAMPLES

The warranty *included* both parts and labor.

The new warranty will *exclude* labor.

A busy schedule coming up in October will *preclude* our attending the national convention.

2.1.7   cred

The root *cred* means "believe." Typical words are *credible* (believable), *credence* (believability), *incredible* (not believable), and *credulous* (tending to believe too readily).

EXAMPLES

Vera's version of the event was the most *credible*.

The press gave little *credence* to the official's explanation.

The statistics, *incredible* as they seemed, were nonetheless accurate.

If you are too *credulous*—if you believe everything you hear—you may become the victim of many practical jokes.

2.1.8   cur

The root *cur* means "run." Typical words are *current* (that which runs or flows; at the present time), *cursory* (hasty; not thorough), *recurrent* (occurring or happening again), and *concurrent* (occurring together or at the same time).

EXAMPLES

The rate at which electric *current* flows through the conducting wire is measured in amperes.

The mechanic was not able to determine, from a *cursory* examination, just what had caused the machine to break down.

A *recurrent* dream haunted him all his life.

The *concurrent* scheduling of the meetings meant that we could attend only one of them.

2.1.9 dict

The root *dict* means "speak." Typical words are *dictate* (to speak for recording and transcription; to issue an order or command), *edict* (a proclamation or order), and *jurisdiction* (the area in which one is qualified or has the right to exercise power).

EXAMPLES

The executive *dictated* a letter; her secretary then typed it.

The presidential *edict* commanded citizens not to go out after 10 P.M.

The personnel manager's *jurisdiction* is not restricted to the hiring of employees; he or she administers the medical-insurance programs as well.

2.1.10 frag, fract

The roots *frag* and *fract* mean "break." Typical words are *fragile* (easily breakable) and *infraction* (the breaking of a rule).

EXAMPLES

The instrument is extremely *fragile* and must be handled with great care.

Although the *infraction* of the rule was not serious, the teacher felt that it should not be allowed to go unnoticed.

2.1.11 gress

The root *gress* means "step" or "go." Typical words are *progressive* (favoring change or improvement, especially in political or social affairs; increasing step by step), *digress* (to depart from the subject), and *egress* (the exit or the way out).

EXAMPLES

The *progressive* actions taken by the new administration were praised by the press.

The audience became restless when the speaker *digressed* from the announced topic.

The fire department considered the matter of an emergency *egress* from the building to be a primary concern.

2.1.12 ject

The root *ject* means "to throw." Typical words are *inject* (to force a fluid into a passage; to introduce something new or different into a conversation or other matter), *eject* (to throw out), and *reject* (to refuse to accept, or to throw back).

EXAMPLES

The infection can be controlled by *injecting* medication directly into the bloodstream.

The pilot survived because he was *ejected* from the cockpit and parachuted to earth.

Jerry worked hard on the proposal, but his boss *rejected* it.

2.1.13   mit

The root *mit* means "send." Typical words are *emit* (to send out or send forth), *remit* (to send back, especially money), and *transmit* (to send from one point to another).

EXAMPLES

The electronic cash register *emits* a signal to a central processor.

Please *remit* a total payment of $14.95.

The information is *transmitted* over commercial telephone lines.

2.1.14   sed

The root *sed* means "sit." Typical words are *sedentary* (involving much sitting) and *sediment* (substance that settles to the bottom of a liquid).

EXAMPLES

Desk work is by nature *sedentary*.

Sediment accumulated at the bottom of the pool.

2.1.15   solv

The root *solv* means "free from" or "loosen." Typical words are *absolve* (to free from, especially of guilt), *dissolve* (to loosen or break up), and *solvent* (an agent used to loosen or to dissolve).

EXAMPLES

After the car accident in which his passenger was killed, John never felt completely *absolved* of guilt.

A liquid *solvent* was used to *dissolve* the paint.

2.1.16   spec

The root *spec* means "look at." Typical words are *aspect* (the particular view from which something is considered), *inspect* (to look at closely and critically), *perspective* (a way of looking at things; a point of view that considers the relative proportion of the various elements of a scene), and *specification* (a detailed definition of the requirements of a project or a description of the parts of a whole).

EXAMPLES

The monetary *aspect* of the job was the least of his concerns.

The highway patrol arrived to *inspect* the scene of the accident.

From the *perspective* of the purchaser, the warranty was not a good one.

The *specifications* for the job were published for the benefit of all potential bidders.

2.1.17   tempor

The root *tempor* means "time." Typical words are *contemporary* (existing at the same time, of the same age; modern), *temporary* (for a short time), and *temporize* (to stall for time).

EXAMPLES

Although the two authors were *contemporaries,* their political attitudes were centuries apart.

Ms. Kenka has taken a *temporary* job, from June until September, when she plans to return to school.

The negotiator had instructions to *temporize* until more information could be obtained.

2.1.18   vis

The root *vis* means "to see." Typical words are *vision* (the ability to see) and *supervise* (to oversee the activities of others).

EXAMPLES

The patient was relieved that he still had full *vision* after the eye operation.

College students were hired to *supervise* the playgrounds.

2.2   PREFIXES

2.2.1   a-, an-

The prefixes *a-* and *an-* mean "without." Typical words are *anemia* (without sufficient red blood cells or volume of blood), *apathy* (complete lack of interest or feeling), and *anesthetic* (a drug that dulls the senses, especially the sense of pain).

EXAMPLES

A blood test revealed that the patient suffers from *anemia*.

When only 10 percent of the voting public go to the polls, civic *apathy* is evident.

Before pulling the tooth, the dentist administered an *anesthetic*.

2.2.2 ab-, abs-

The prefixes *ab-* and *abs-* mean "from." Typical words are *abnormal* (removed from the normal) and *abstain* (to keep oneself away from).

EXAMPLES

The man's *abnormal* behavior was caused by excessive drinking.

Drivers are advised to *abstain* from alcohol.

2.2.3 ad- (sometimes spelled ag-, al-, at- when combined with roots that begin with g, l, or t)

This prefix means "to" or "toward." Typical words are *adjoining* (joined to something else), *allocate* (to assign to; to distribute something according to a plan), and *attract* (to draw to or toward).

EXAMPLES

The two families knew each other well because they lived in *adjoining* apartments.

Every city must *allocate* a large sum of money for its transportation system.

Insects are *attracted* to food.

2.2.4 ante-

The prefix *ante-* means "before." Typical words are *anterior* (in or near the front), *anteroom* (a room that comes before another room, as a waiting room), and *antecedent* (an event that occurs before another; the word or phrase to which a pronoun refers).

EXAMPLES

The tumor was located in the *anterior* lobe of the brain.

Because many patients had come to see the doctor, the *anteroom* of the office was crowded.

My *antecedents* were farmers who lived in Wales.

2.2.5   anti-, ant- (before a vowel)

The prefix *anti-* (*ant-*) means "against" or "opposite." Typical words are *antibiotic* (a medicine that acts against bacteria), *antipathy* (a feeling of strong dislike), *antacid* (medicine that acts against acid in the body), and *antonym* (a word that means the opposite of another word).

EXAMPLES

Her fever was lower a few hours after she took the *antibiotic*.

Because I have an *antipathy* to crowds, I avoid the beach on July 4.

He felt better after taking the *antacid* to soothe his upset stomach.

Part of the assignment was to find *antonyms* for a given list of words.

2.2.6   bi-

The prefix *bi-* means "two." Typical words are *biped* (animals with two feet), *bigamy* (marriage to two people at the same time), *biannual* (two times each year), and *biennial* (every two years).

EXAMPLES

Humans and some apes are *bipeds*.

The man was charged with *bigamy* because he had one wife in Akron and another in Indianapolis.

The *biannual* event was held in December and June every year.

The *biennial* event was held in December of years ending in an odd number.

2.2.7   cata-

The prefix *cata-* means "down." Typical words are *catalogue* (a written list; to write down an orderly listing) and *catastrophe* (a sudden and severe downturn in fortune; a disaster).

EXAMPLES

The *catalogue* listed all the products manufactured by the company.

The sudden drop in the stock was a *catastrophe* for many small investors.

2.2.8   circum-

The prefix *circum-* means "around." Typical words are *circumference* (the distance around a circular object), *circumlocution* (a word or expression that says something in a roundabout rather than a straightforward way), *circumspect* (careful to look around at the possible consequences of a deed before acting), and *circumvent* (to go around a problem or an obstacle and thus avoid it).

After measuring the round library table, Jessica announced that its *circumference* was 12 feet.

A person who uses *circumlocution* is probably trying to avoid an issue.

Recognizing the importance of the question, the shop steward tried to be as *circumspect* as possible in answering it.

By apologizing to Ed, Martin hoped to *circumvent* further unpleasantness.

2.2.9 co-, col-, com-, con-

These prefixes all mean "with" or "together." Typical words are *cooperate* (to work together), *coordinate* (to act together), *collaborate* (to work jointly with someone else), *collate* (to put together in order), and *compound* (something formed by the joining of elements or parts).

The problem could be solved if the two sides would *cooperate*.

The nationwide United Fund is a *coordinated* attempt to raise funds for charitable organizations.

The two designers agreed to *collaborate* on the layout drawing.

The office bought a machine that can *collate* a sixteen-page document.

The glossy finish was achieved by the application of a rubbing *compound*.

2.2.10 contra-, contro-, counter-

These prefixes mean "against" or "opposite." Typical words are *contrary* (consistently against), *controversy* (a dispute between those of opposing views), and *countermand* (to cancel or reverse an order).

The views expressed in the book were *contrary* to everything Michael believed.

The school bond issue created a *controversy* in the town; there were strong feelings on both sides of the matter.

The superintendent *countermanded* the foreman's orders.

2.2.11 de-

The prefix *de-* means "down" or "reverse of." Typical words are *decelerate* (to slow down), *demote* (to move down to a lower rank), and *descend* (to go down).

He ran the car off the road because there was no time to *decelerate*.

Unfavorable sales figures forced the company to *demote* several of its junior officers.

The lineman *descended* from the pole after completing the repairs.

2.2.12   dia-

The prefix *dia-* means "across," "thoroughly," or "through." Typical words are *diagonal* (across from corner to corner, through the center), *diagnose* (to identify the nature of an illness; to investigate thoroughly the cause of something), and *diathermy* (a treatment that sends heat through the body).

EXAMPLES

The editor drew a *diagonal* line across the page that was to be omitted from the manuscript.

Lennie was examined by four specialists before one of them was able to *diagnose* his ailment.

A heating pad is one simple device for administering *diathermy*.

2.2.13   dis- (also di-, dif-)

This prefix means "apart" or "not." Typical words are *dilate* (to make larger), *differentiate* (to tell apart), *disjointed* (disconnected, lacking unity), *dissent* (lack of agreement; to disagree), and *disrupt* (to interrupt, especially in a noisy way; to throw into confusion).

EXAMPLES

The medicine that the eye doctor administered caused the pupils of her eyes to *dilate*.

The students were taught to *differentiate* between the two chemicals.

His account of the incident was so *disjointed* that the police were hardly able to follow it.

Martha Sells was the only member of the committee to *dissent* from the majority report.

Sam seemed determined to *disrupt* the meeting because he did not want the resolution to be passed.

2.2.14   e-, ex-

The prefixes *e-* and *ex-* mean "out" or "outside." Typical words are *efficacy* (ability to produce a desired result or outcome), *exhale* (to breathe out), and *exorbitant* (exceeding the customary amount).

EXAMPLES

The chemist was testing a new cancer drug to determine its *efficacy*.

The doctor instructed the patient to take a deep breath and then *exhale*.

The price of the typewriter was *exorbitant;* we had never paid so much for such a machine.

2.2.15   in- (also il-, im-, and ir-)

The prefix *in-*, as well as the alternate forms *il-, im-,* and *ir-,* means "not."[4] Typical words are *insolvent* (not able to pay one's debts; bankrupt), *illegible* (difficult or impossible to read, usually because of unclear or messy copy), *immune* (protected against a disease; not affected by an outcome), and *irrevocable* (irreversible; unable to be reversed or changed).

EXAMPLES

Jim had to move to a less expensive apartment because he had become *insolvent*.

Since the first draft of the paper was *illegible,* I decided to retype my work before I revised it.

Children who have taken flu shots should be *immune* to the disease.

Think carefully before you decide upon a course, since your decision will be *irrevocable*.

2.2.16   inter-

The prefix *inter-* means "between." Typical words are *intervene* (to come between; to interfere), *intermittent* (occurring from time to time; alternately starting and stopping), and *interlinear* (inserted between the lines).

EXAMPLES

Since the two lawyers could not settle the dispute, they asked the judge to *intervene* in the matter.

The patient complained of *intermittent* headaches that would come and go during periods of stress.

I've typed this draft triple-spaced so that you can easily make *interlinear* corrections or changes.

2.2.17   intra-, intro-

These prefixes mean "within." Typical words are *intrastate* (within a state), *intravenous* (within the veins), and *introspection* (examination of one's own thoughts and feelings).

[4] *In-* as a prefix meaning "in, into, within, or toward" is a separate form.

EXAMPLES

The trucking firm was awarded a license to operate on an *intrastate* basis only.

The antibiotic can be taken only by *intravenous* injection.

The *introspection* forced on him by a long period of illness made a striking change in his personality.

2.2.18 micro-

The prefix *micro-* means "small." Typical words are *microfilm* (a small film) and *micrometer* (an instrument for measuring small things).

EXAMPLES

Microfilm requires the use of special equipment to enable the viewer to see the material, the size of which has been reduced considerably.

The tiny specimen could be measured only with a *micrometer*.

2.2.19 para-

The prefix *para-* means "alongside." Typical words are *paraprofessional* (someone who works alongside a professional), *paraphrase* (to rephrase or restate something in one's own words), *parasite* (something that lives off another without giving anything useful in return), and *parallel* (alongside of but at an equal distance at every point, never meeting).

EXAMPLES

The use of *paraprofessionals* is becoming common in schools and hospitals.

When taking notes for a term paper, it is better to *paraphrase* the thinking of others than to quote them directly.

The tree was being slowly destroyed by two different *parasites*.

Railroad tracks are *parallel* to each other.

2.2.20 poly-

Poly- means "many." Typical words are *polygraph* (an instrument that measures changes in heartbeat, blood pressure, and so on and is used as a lie-detector device), *polytechnic* (pertaining to instruction in many arts and sciences), *polyphonic* (combining many different sounds), and *polychromatic* (having many colors).

EXAMPLES

The lie detector test is one of the most common uses of the *polygraph*.

The institute was dedicated to *polytechnic* studies.

The recording technique included a *polyphonic* procedure.
The art department ordered a *polychromatic* scale.

2.2.21   post-

The prefix *post-* means "after." Typical words are *posterity* (that which comes after; future generations), *postmortem* (after death), *postnatal* (after birth), and *postgraduate* (after graduation).

EXAMPLES

We owe it to *posterity* to preserve as much of our natural environment as possible.
The judge ordered a *postmortem* examination to determine the cause of the victim's death.
Postnatal complications can be serious for both the mother and the baby.
The university had acquired a fine reputation for the quality of its *postgraduate* program.

2.2.22   pre-

The prefix *pre-* means "before." Typical words are *preliminary* (going before and leading up to the main part), *preview* (to look at something before it is officially presented), and *preface* (a brief introduction before the text of a book).

EXAMPLES

The court must set a date for a *preliminary* hearing before the trial can be scheduled.
Employees were given a *preview* of the president's presentation to the stockholders.
The *preface* to the speech captured the audience's full attention.

2.2.23   pro-

The prefix *pro-* means "forward," or "forth." Typical words are *propose* (to put forward a suggestion), *proliferate* (to reproduce or increase rapidly), and *profusion* (that which is brought forth in large numbers; an abundance).

EXAMPLES

Frank wanted to *propose* a new method of handling the data, but he could not get the floor.
In the last decade, the use of calculators has *proliferated;* in many offices almost every executive has one.
Grasshoppers appeared that summer in *profusion.*

2.2.24   **proto-** (**prot-** before a root beginning with a vowel)

Proto- means "first" or "fundamental." Typical words are *prototype* (the first form of something, serving as a model for later forms) and *protozoa* (fundamental forms of animal life).

EXAMPLES

The committee voted funds to begin the project but withheld additional financing until the *prototype* proved whether the plan was practical.

Protozoa can be studied only through a microscope.

2.2.25   **super-**

The prefix *super-* means "over" or "beyond." Typical words are *superior* (far above average; higher in rank or authority), *supersede* (to take the place of something), and *superfluous* (more than what is needed).

EXAMPLES

The judges declared XYZ brand car wash to be *superior* to LMO brand.

The directive of June 12 *supersedes* the one dated May 5.

The shipwrecked sailors threw away everything that was *superfluous*.

2.2.26   **sym-, syn-**

The prefixes *sym-* and *syn-* mean "together" or "with." Typical words are *sympathy* (shared feeling; concern for another's distress), *symmetrical* (equal in size, shape, or position of parts on opposite sides of a dividing line), and *synthesis* (the combining of varied elements to form a meaningful whole).

EXAMPLES

The students appeared to be in *sympathy* with the protestors.

Organisms whose right and left sides are mirror images of each other are *symmetrical*.

Dr. Markon's theory of personality is a *synthesis* of psychological ideas taken from Freud, Jung, Horney, and Sullivan.

2.2.27   **trans-**

The prefix *trans-* means "across," "through," or "beyond." Typical words are *transport* (to carry from one place to another), *transfer* (to send from one person or place to another), *transcend* (to go beyond; to surpass), and *transient* (passing quickly, momentary; a visitor, especially to a hotel, who stays only briefly).

It is the company's responsibility to *transport* the goods to the customers. The fee was payment for the *transfer* of the title from the seller to the buyer. Each new generation of computers *transcends* the achievements of the last generation.

Although the thought was a *transient* one, it had made an impression.

2.3   SUFFIXES

Although individual suffixes do convey meaning, their chief function is to indicate a part of speech. For example, the suffixes *-ance, -ion, -ism, -ity,* and *-ment* indicate nouns; the suffixes *-ify* and *-ize* indicate verbs; and the suffixes *-able, -al, -ical, -ive,* and *-ous* indicate adjectives. (See Section 3 of this Guide for a discussion of parts of speech.)

Noun Markers

2.3.1   -ance, -ence

Typical words are *brilliance* (quality of light; great brightness) and *emergence* (act of coming out).

The *brilliance* of the stage lights made the keynote speaker appear unreal.
The river widened at the point of its *emergence* into the sea.

2.3.2   -ion, -ation, -tion

Typical words are *resolution* (the act of solving a problem), *litigation* (the process of taking court action), and *option* (the opportunity to choose; a choice).

The *resolution* of the problem was to be decided at a meeting of top management officials.
Ten persons who were seriously injured when the building collapsed began *litigation,* suing for medical expenses and lost wages.
The student has several career *options* after graduation: she can become a production trainee, enlist in the service, or take a degree in accounting.

2.3.3 -ism

Typical words are *anachronism* (something that is out of its place in time), *socialism* (a political theory that favors society's ownership of the means of production), and *individualism* (the assertion of one's specialness as an individual being).

EXAMPLES

The horse-drawn carriages of New York City are *anachronisms*.
Under *socialism,* all large industry is controlled by the government.
The company encouraged *individualism* in its employees.

2.3.4 -ity

Typical words are *facility* (the ability to do something easily), *authenticity* (the condition of being genuine), and *authority* (the power to command).

EXAMPLES

The *facility* with which Susan handled higher mathematics was remarkable.
Do you have proof of the *authenticity* of this painting—or might it be a fake?
The supervisor did not have the *authority* to dismiss an employee.

2.3.5 -ment

Typical words are *impediment* (an obstacle; something that stands in the way of something else) and *sentiment* (an opinion on a particular matter; a feeling based more on emotion than on thinking).

EXAMPLES

Not knowing how to operate some office machines can be an *impediment* to receiving a promotion.
The *sentiment* among the hospital administrative staff was in favor of working from 8:30 A.M. to 4:30 P.M. rather than from 9 A.M. to 5 P.M..

Verb Markers

2.3.6 -ify

Typical words are *testify* (to make a statement under oath), *justify* (to show that something is reasonable or correct), and *typify* (to be an example of).

Mavine was asked to *testify* during the trial, since she had been a witness to the accident.

You should not try to *justify* your action by claiming that the instructions were so poorly written that you misunderstood them.

I don't believe that the questionable acts of the manager *typify* the company's hiring policies.

2.3.7   -ize

Typical words are *legalize* (to make something lawful), *modernize* (to make something contemporary), and *anesthetize* (to make someone unable to feel pain).

EXAMPLES

The retail industry believed that stores would benefit from *legalized* shopping on Sundays.

The company decided to *modernize* its building, which was old and in poor condition.

The patient was *anesthetized* and felt no pain at all during surgery.

Adjective Markers

2.3.8   -able, -ible

Typical words are *comparable* (able to be compared; similar or equivalent), *indelible* (not able to be removed), *compatible* (able to live together in peace and harmony), and *inevitable* (incapable of being prevented; bound to happen).

EXAMPLES

Do you know in what ways soccer is *comparable* to football?

The tragic experience left an *indelible* mark on her memory.

The two technicians were *compatible* because they had had many similar experiences.

It seemed *inevitable* that the two companies would merge.

2.3.9   -al, -ial

Typical words are *spatial* (relating to space) and *radial* (relating to a radius).

EXAMPLES

An architect must have good *spatial* imagination.

The carpenter cut the bevels with a *radial* saw.

Section B

Handbook of Grammar, Punctuation, and Mechanics

---

3 PARTS OF SPEECH

Part of speech is a term used to describe the class of words to which a particular word belongs, according to its function in a sentence. If a word's function is to name something, it is a noun or pronoun. If a word's function is to indicate action or existence, it is a verb. If its function is to describe or modify something, the word is an adjective or an adverb. If its function is to join or link one element of a sentence to another, it is a conjunction or a preposition. And if its function is to express an exclamation, it is an interjection.

3.1 NOUNS

A noun names a person, place, thing, concept, action, or quality.

3.1.1 Types of Nouns

The two basic types of nouns are proper nouns and common nouns.

(a) Proper nouns. Proper nouns name specific persons, places, things, concepts, actions, or qualities. They are usually capitalized.

EXAMPLES   New York, Abraham Lincoln, U.S. Army, Nobel Prize, Montana, Independence Day, Amazon River, Butler County, Magna Carta, June, Colby College

(b) **Common nouns.** Common nouns name general classes or categories of persons, places, things, concepts, actions, or qualities. The term *common noun* includes all types of nouns except proper nouns. Following are discussions of the basic types of common nouns. Note that many nouns can be placed in more than one of the overlapping categories.

Concrete nouns identify those things that can be detected by the five senses—by seeing, hearing, tasting, touching, or smelling. Concrete nouns can be either count nouns or mass nouns. *Count nouns,* as the term suggests, name things that can be counted or divided; their plurals often end in *s*.

EXAMPLES   human, college, house, knife, bolt, carrot

Mass nouns name things that are not usually counted and do not usually appear in the plural.

EXAMPLES   water, sand, air, copper, velvet

Many words, of course, can serve either as count nouns or as mass nouns, depending on the context in which they are used. If you were to say "I need one brick," *brick* would be a count noun. If you were to say "The building is built of brick," *brick* would be a mass noun.

Abstract nouns refer to things that cannot be detected by the five senses.

EXAMPLES   love, loyalty, pride, valor, peace, devotion, harmony

Collective nouns indicate groups or collections of persons, places, things, concepts, actions, or qualities. They are plural in meaning but singular in form when they refer to groups as units.

EXAMPLES   audience, jury, brigade, staff, committee

3.1.2 Functions of Nouns

Nouns may function as subjects of verbs, as objects of verbs and prepositions, as complements, or as appositives.

EXAMPLES   The *metal* bent as *pressure* was applied to it. (subject of a verb, naming the thing about which the verb makes an assertion)

The bricklayer cemented the *blocks* efficiently. (direct object of a verb, naming the thing acted on by the verb)

The company awarded our *department* a plaque for safety. (indirect object of a verb, naming the recipient of the direct object)

The event occurred within the *year*. (object of a preposition, naming the thing linked by the preposition to the rest of the sentence)

An equestrian is a *horseman*. (subjective complement, renaming the subject of the sentence)

We elected the sales manager *chairman*. (objective complement, renaming the direct object)

George Thomas, the *treasurer,* gave his report last. (appositive, amplifying the noun that precedes it)

3.1.3   Forms of Nouns

With the general exception of mass nouns and abstract nouns, nouns can show number (singular or plural) and possession.

(a)   Singular and plural nouns.   The singular form of a noun refers to one thing, the plural to more than one. Most nouns form the plural by adding *-s*.

EXAMPLE   *Dolphins* are capable of communication with humans.

Nouns ending in *s, z, x, ch,* and *sh* form the plural by adding *-es*.

EXAMPLES   How many size *sixes* did we produce last month?

The letter was sent to all the *churches*.

Our company supplies cafeterias with *dishes* and *glasses*.

Those ending in a consonant plus *y* form the plural by changing the *y* to *ies*.

EXAMPLE   The store advertises prompt delivery but limits the number of *deliveries* scheduled on a single day.

Some nouns ending in *o* add *-es* to form the plural; others add only *-s*.

EXAMPLES   One tomato plant produced 30 *tomatoes*.

We installed two *dynamos* in the plant.

Some nouns ending in *f* or *fe* add *-s* to form the plural; others change the *f* or *fe* to *ves*.

EXAMPLES   cliff/cliffs, fife/fifes, knife/knives, leaf/leaves

Some nouns require an internal change to form the plural.

EXAMPLES   goose/geese, man/men, mouse/mice, woman/women

Some nouns do not change in the plural form.

EXAMPLE   Several *fish* swam lazily in the clear brook while a few wild *deer* mingled with the *sheep* in a nearby meadow.

Most compound nouns joined by hyphens form the plural in the first noun.

EXAMPLE   He provided jobs for his two *sons-in-law*.

If you are in doubt about the plural form of a word, look up the word in a good dictionary. Most dictionaries give the plural form if it is made in any way other than by adding *-s* or *-es*.

(b)   Possessive nouns. The possessive case, indicating ownership, is formed in two ways—either with an *of* clause, as in "the nature *of* the beast," or by adding *-'s*. This discussion will address the *'s* construction, which is generally used with animate nouns.

EXAMPLES   The *chairman's* statement was forceful.

The *Henry's* arm was broken.

The installation of the plumbing is finished except in the *men's* room.

Singular nouns ending in *s* may form the possessive by adding either an apostrophe alone or *'s*. The latter is now preferred.

EXAMPLES   a waitress's uniform *or* a waitress' uniform

an actress's career *or* an actress' career

Plural nouns ending in *s* add only an apostrophe to form the possessive.

EXAMPLE   The architects' design manual contains many illustrations.

With word groups and compound nouns, add the *'s* to the last noun.

EXAMPLES   The *chairman of the board's* report was distributed.

My *son-in-law's* address was on the envelope.

To show individual possession with a pair of nouns, use the possessive with both.

EXAMPLES   Both the *Senate's* and the *House's* galleries were packed for the hearings.

Mary's and *John's* presentations were the most effective.

To show joint possession with a pair of nouns, use the possessive with only the latter.

EXAMPLES   The *Senate and House's* joint committee worked out a compromise.

Mary and John's presentation was the most effective.

Occasionally you will use both an *of* phrase and an *'s* construction.

EXAMPLE   Mary is a colleague *of John's*.

3.2   PRONOUNS

A pronoun is a word that is used as a substitute for a noun. The noun that a pronoun replaces is called its antecedent.

3.2.1   Types of Pronouns

Pronouns fall into several different categories: personal, demonstrative, relative, interrogative, indefinite, reflexive, intensive, and reciprocal.

(a)   Personal pronouns.   The personal pronouns refer to the person or persons speaking (*I, me, my, mine; we, us, our, ours*); the person or persons spoken to (*you, your, yours*); or the person or thing (or persons or things) spoken of (*he, him, his; she, her, hers; it, its; they, them, their, theirs*).

EXAMPLES   I wish *you* had told *me* that *she* was coming with *us*.

If *their* figures are correct, *ours* must be in error.

(b)   Demonstrative pronouns.   The demonstrative pronouns (*this, these, that, those*) indicate or point out the thing being referred to. They also serve as adjectives. In good writing, demonstrative pronouns are avoided because they can lead to ambiguity. (As adjectives, however, demonstratives are not only acceptable but useful.)

EXAMPLES   *This* is my desk.

These are my coworkers.

That will be a difficult job.

Those are incorrect figures.

(c) **Relative pronouns.** The relative pronouns (*who, whom, which, whose,* and *that*) perform two functions simultaneously. They substitute for nouns or preceding ideas, and they connect and establish the relationships between parts of sentences. (Refer to the discussion of independent and dependent clauses in Sections 4.2.1 and 4.2.2.)

EXAMPLES The personnel manager told the applicants *who* would be hired.

The supervisor, *whose* office is next door, keeps those records.

(d) **Interrogative pronouns.** Interrogative pronouns (*who, whom, which, whose, what*) ask questions.

EXAMPLES *Who* went to the meeting in Detroit?

Which copier does two-sided copying?

(e) **Indefinite pronouns.** Indefinite pronouns do not refer to a particular person or thing. They include *all, another, any, anyone, anything, both, each, either, everybody, few, many, most, much, neither, nobody, none, several, some,* and *such.*

EXAMPLE Not *everyone* liked the new procedures; *some* even refused to follow them.

(f) **Reflexive pronouns.** The reflexive pronouns (*myself, yourself, himself, herself, itself, oneself, ourselves, yourselves,* and *themselves*) always end with the suffix *-self* or *-selves.* Reflexive pronouns refer to the subject of the sentence, clause, or phrase in which they appear and turn the action of the verb back upon the subject.

EXAMPLE I asked *myself* the same question.

(g) **Intensive pronouns.** The intensive pronouns are identical in form to the reflexive pronouns, but they perform a different function. They emphasize or intensify their antecedents.

EXAMPLE I *myself* asked the same question.

(h) **Reciprocal pronouns.** The reciprocal pronouns (*one another* and *each other*) indicate relationships among people or things. Use *each other* when referring to two persons or things and *one another* when referring to more than two.

EXAMPLES Sam and Ruth work well with *each other.*

The four crew members work well with *one another.*

3.2.2 Grammatical Properties of Pronouns

(a) **Person.** *Person* refers to the forms of a personal pronoun that indicate whether the pronoun represents the speaker, the person spoken to, or the person (or thing) spoken about. If the pronoun represents the speaker, the pronoun is in the first person.

EXAMPLE   *I* followed the directions in the manual.

If the pronoun represents the person or persons spoken to, the pronoun is in the second person.

EXAMPLE   *You* should report to Ms. Cooper before noon.

If the pronoun represents the person or persons spoken about, the pronoun is in the third person.

EXAMPLE   *They* followed the procedure that *he* had outlined.

Person	Singular	Plural
First	I, me, my	we, ours, us
Second	you, your	you, your
Third	he, him, his	they, them, their
	she, her, hers	
	it, its	

Identifying pronouns by person helps you avoid illogical shifts from one person to another. A very common error is to shift from the third person to the second person.

REVISE   *Employees* must sign the guard's logbook when *you* enter a restricted area.

TO   *Employees* must sign the guard's logbook when *they* enter a restricted area.

OR   *You* must sign the guard's logbook when *you* enter a restricted area.

(b) **Gender.** *Gender* refers to forms of words that designate sex. English recognizes three genders: masculine, feminine, and neuter (to designate objects considered neither masculine nor feminine). The pronouns *he, she,* and *it* indicate gender; only a few nouns (such as *actor* and *actress*) do so.

Gender is important to writers because they must be sure that nouns and pronouns within a grammatical construction agree in gender. A pronoun, for example, must agree with its antecedent noun in gender.

EXAMPLE   Because Wanda Martin supervised *her* sales staff as effectively as Frank Martinez supervised *his,* the company doubled *its* profits.

(See also Section 3.2.3a for a discussion of how sexist language is best avoided.)

(c)   Number.   *Number* signifies how many things a word refers to. A singular pronoun substitutes for a noun that names one thing; a plural pronoun replaces a noun that names two or more things.

EXAMPLE   The manager took *her* break after the employees took *their* breaks.

All singular pronouns (*I, he, she, it*) change form in the plural (*we, they*) except *you.*

EXAMPLE   Since *he* organizes efficiently and *she* supervises effectively, *they* are both valuable employees.

Number is a frequent problem with a few indefinite pronouns (*each, either, neither,* and those ending with *-body* or *-one,* such as *anybody, anyone, everybody, everyone, nobody, no one, somebody, someone*). Since these pronouns are normally singular, they require singular verbs and are referred to by singular pronouns.

EXAMPLE   As *everyone* arrives for the meeting and takes *his* seat, please hand *him* a copy of the confidential report. *No one* should leave without returning *his* copy before *he* goes.

(d)   Case.   Pronouns have forms to show the subjective, objective, and possessive cases. A pronoun is in the *subjective case* when it is used as the subject of a clause or sentence, representing the person or thing acting or existing. The subjective case is also used when the pronoun follows a linking verb, such as *to be.* (A linking verb connects the pronoun with the subject it renames.)

EXAMPLES   *He* is my boss.
My boss is *he.*

A pronoun is in the *objective case* when it indicates the person or thing receiving the action of a verb or when it follows a preposition.

EXAMPLES   Mr. Davis hired Tom and *me.* (not I)
Between *you* and *me,* his facts are questionable.

To test whether a pronoun is in the subjective case or the objective case, try it with a transitive verb (one that requires a direct object—a person or thing to receive the action expressed by the verb). *Hit* is a useful verb for this test. If the form of the pronoun can precede the verb, it is in the subjective case. If it must follow the verb, it is in the objective case.

EXAMPLES   *She* hit the baseball. (subjective case)

The baseball hit *her*. (objective case)

A pronoun in the *possessive case* expresses ownership.

EXAMPLE   He took *his* notes with him on the business trip.

Subjective	Objective	Possessive
I	me	my, mine
we	us	our, ours
you	you	your, yours
he	him	his
she	her	her, hers
it	it	its
they	them	their, theirs
who	whom	whose

If compound pronouns cause problems in determining case, try testing each separately.

EXAMPLES   In his letter, John mentioned *you* and *me*.

In his letter, John mentioned *you*.

In his letter, John mentioned *me*.

To determine the case of a pronoun that follows *as* or *than,* try mentally adding the words that are normally omitted.

EXAMPLES   The director does not have as much formal education as *he* [does]. (You would not write, "Him does.")

His friend was taller than *he* [was tall]. (You would not write, "Him was tall.")

An appositive is a noun or noun phrase that follows and amplifies another noun or noun phrase. A pronoun appositive takes the case of its antecedent.

EXAMPLES   Two systems analysts, Joe and *I,* were selected to represent the company. (*Joe and I* is in apposition to the subject, *systems analysts,* and therefore must be in the subjective case.)

The systems analysts selected two members of our department—Joe and *me*. (*Joe and me* is in apposition to *two members,* which is the object of the verb *selected,* and therefore must be in the objective case.)

The reverse situation can also present problems. To test for the proper case when the pronouns *we* and *us* are followed by an appositive noun that defines them, try the sentence without the noun.

EXAMPLES   (*We/Us*) pilots fly our own planes.

We fly our own planes. (You would not write, "*Us* fly our own planes.")

He addressed his remarks directly to (*we/us*) technicians.

He addressed his remarks directly to *us.* (You would not write, "He addressed his remarks directly to *we.*")

3.2.3   Usage of Pronouns

Pronouns must agree with and clearly refer to their antecedents.

(a)   **Pronoun–antecedent agreement.**   The noun for which a pronoun substitutes is called its antecedent. A personal pronoun in the first or second person does not normally require a stated antecedent.

EXAMPLES   *I* like my job.

You were there at the time.

We all worked hard on the project.

A personal pronoun in the third person usually has a clearly stated antecedent.

EXAMPLE   John presented the report to the directors. *He* (John) first read *it* (the report) to *them* (the directors) and then asked for *their* (the directors') questions.

Agreement, grammatically, means the correspondence in form between different elements of a sentence. A pronoun must agree with its antecedent in person, gender, and number. (See Section 3.2.2 for additional information about these properties of pronouns.)

A pronoun must agree with its antecedent in *person.* If you are describing the necessity of accurate data for laboratory technicians, for example, use either the third person or the second person. Don't mix them. The first sentence following suggests that the technicians are preparing data for someone else (you).

REVISE   If *laboratory technicians* do not update *their* records every day, *you* will not have accurate data.

TO   If *laboratory technicians* do not update *their* records every day, *they* will not have accurate data.

OR   If *you* do not update *your* records every day, *you* will not have accurate data.

A pronoun must agree with its antecedent in *gender*.

EXAMPLE   *Isabel* was already wearing *her* identification badge, but *Tom* had to clip on *his* badge before they could pass the security guard.

Traditionally, a masculine, singular pronoun has been used to agree with antecedents that include both sexes, such as *anyone, everybody, nobody, one, person, someone,* or *student.*

EXAMPLE   *Anyone* who meets this production goal will double *his* bonus.

Many people are now sensitive to an implied sexual bias in such usage. When graceful alternatives are available, use them. One solution is to use *he or she* instead of *he* alone, or *his or her* instead of *his* alone. Another possibility is to omit the pronoun completely if it isn't essential to the meaning of the sentence.

REVISE   *Everybody* completed *his* report on time.

TO   *Everybody* completed *his or her* report on time.

OR   *Everybody* completed a report on time.

Often, the best solution is to rewrite the sentence in the plural. Do not, however, attempt to avoid expressing gender by resorting to a plural pronoun when the antecedent is singular.

REVISE   *Everybody* completed *their* report on time.

TO   The *employees* completed *their* reports on time.

A pronoun must agree with its antecedent in *number*.

REVISE   Because the *copier* has been used so much, *they* have been overheating.

TO   Because the *copier* has been used so much, *it* has been overheating.

Use a singular pronoun with an antecedent like *anyone, each, everybody,* or *everyone* unless to do so would be illogical because the meaning is obviously plural.

EXAMPLES   *Everyone* returned to *his or her* department.

Everyone applauded when I demonstrated our new product for *them.*

Collective nouns may be singular or plural, depending on meaning.

EXAMPLES   The *staff* prepared *its* annual report.

The *staff* returned to *their* offices after the meeting.

A compound antecedent joined by *or* or *nor* is singular if both elements are singular and plural if both are plural.

EXAMPLES   Either the *supervisor* or the *foreman* should present *his* report on the accident.

Neither the *stockholders* nor the *executive officers* wanted *their* company to be taken over by Coast International.

When one of the antecedents connected by *or* or *nor* is singular and the other plural, the pronoun agrees with the nearer antecedent.

EXAMPLES   Either the *receptionist* or the *typists* should go on *their* lunch breaks.

Either the *typists* or the *receptionist* should go on *her* lunch break.

A compound antecedent with its elements joined by *and* requires a plural pronoun.

EXAMPLE   The *architect* and the *designer* prepared *their* plans.

If the two elements refer to the same person, however, use the singular pronoun.

EXAMPLE   The *architect and designer* prepared *his* plan.

(b) **Pronoun reference.** The noun to which a pronoun refers must be unmistakably clear. Pronoun references may be unclear if they are general, hidden, or ambiguous.

A *general* (or *broad*) *reference,* or one that has no real antecedent, may confuse your reader.

REVISE   He sold plumbing supplies in Iowa for eight years; *this* has helped him in his present job as sales manager.

TO   His eight years selling plumbing supplies in Iowa have helped him in his present job as sales manager.

A *hidden reference,* or one that has only an implied antecedent, is another problem.

REVISE   Electronics technicians must continue to study because *it* is a dynamic science.

TO   Electronics technicians must continue to study *electronics* because *it* is a dynamic science.

REVISE   A high-lipid, low-carbohydrate diet is called "ketogenic" because it favors *their* formation.

TO | A high-lipid, low-carbohydrate diet is called "ketogenic" because it favors the formation of ketone bodies.

The third basic problem is an *ambiguous reference,* or one that can be interpreted in more than one way.

REVISE | Susan worked with Jeanette on the presentation, but *she* prepared most of the slides. (Who prepared most of the slides, Susan or Jeanette?)

TO | Susan worked with Jeanette on the presentation, but Jeanette prepared most of the slides.

Ambiguous references frequently occur with the pronouns *it* and *they.*

REVISE | The fire marshal examined the stairway and inspected the basement storage room; *it* had suffered extensive smoke damage.

TO | The fire marshal examined the stairway, which had suffered extensive smoke damage, and inspected the basement storage room.

REVISE | The inspector checked the scales and the time clocks; *they* needed to be leveled again.

TO | The inspector checked the scales and the time clocks; the scales needed to be leveled again.

Do not repeat an antecedent in parentheses following the pronoun. If you feel that you must identify the pronoun's antecedent in this way, you need to rewrite the sentence.

REVISE | The specialist met the patient's mother as soon as she (the specialist) arrived at the hospital emergency room.

TO | As soon as the specialist arrived at the hospital emergency room, she met the patient's mother.

3.3 ADJECTIVES

An adjective modifies or describes a noun or pronoun.

3.3.1 Types of Adjectives

An adjective makes the meaning of a noun or pronoun more exact by pointing out one of its qualities (descriptive adjective) or by imposing boundaries upon it (limiting adjective).

EXAMPLES   a *hot* iron (descriptive)

He is *cold.* (descriptive)

ten automobiles (limiting)

his desk (limiting)

Limiting adjectives include some common and important categories:

Articles (*a, an, the*)
Numeral adjectives (*one, two, first, second*)
Indefinite adjectives (*all, any, each, no, some*)
Demonstrative adjectives (*this, that, these, those*)
Possessive adjectives (*my, his, her, its, your, our, their*)
Interrogative and relative adjectives (*whose, which, what*)

Of these, the forms of the demonstrative, possessive, and interrogative and relative adjectives derive from pronouns and are sometimes called *pronominal adjectives.*

3.3.2 Comparison of Adjectives

Most adjectives add the suffix *-er* to show comparison with one other item and the suffix *-est* to show comparison with two or more other items. The three degrees of comparison are called the positive (the basic form of the adjective), the comparative (showing comparison with one other item), and the superlative (showing comparison with two or more other items).

EXAMPLES   The first ingot is *bright.* (positive degree)

The second ingot is *brighter.* (comparative degree)

The third ingot is *brightest.* (superlative degree)

Many two-syllable adjectives and most three-syllable adjectives, however, are preceded by *more* or *most* to form the comparative or the superlative.

EXAMPLES   The new facility is *more impressive* than the old one.

The new facility is the *most impressive* in the city.

A few adjectives have irregular comparative and superlative degrees (*much, more, most; little, less, least*).

Absolute words (such as *unique, perfect, exact,* and *infinite*) are not logically subject to comparison. After all, something either is or is not unique; it isn't more unique or most unique. Language, however, is not always logical, so these words are sometimes used comparatively.

EXAMPLE   Phase-locked loop circuits make FM tuner performance *more exact* by decreasing tuner distortion.

3.3.3 Placement of Adjectives

When limiting and descriptive adjectives appear together, the limiting adjectives precede the descriptive adjectives, with the article usually in the first position.

EXAMPLE   *the ten gray* cars (article, limiting adjective, descriptive adjective)

Within a sentence, an adjective can precede its noun or follow its noun.

EXAMPLES   The *small* jobs are given priority.

Priority is given when a job is *small*.

In a larger, more complex construction, an adjective may shift from preceding its noun to following it.

EXAMPLES   We negotiated a *bigger* contract than our competitor did.

We negotiated a contract *bigger* than our competitor's.

An adjective is called a predicate adjective when it follows a linking verb, such as *to be*. By completing the meaning of a linking verb, a predicate adjective describes or limits the subject of the verb.

EXAMPLES   The job is *easy*.

The manager was very *demanding*.

An adjective also can follow a transitive verb and modify its direct object (the person or thing that receives the action of the verb).

EXAMPLES   The lack of lubricant rendered the bearing *useless*.
They painted the office *white*.

3.3.4 Use of Adjectives

Nouns can sometimes function as adjectives, especially when precise qualification is necessary.

EXAMPLE   The *test* conclusions led to a redesign of the system.

Frequently, business and technical writing is weakened by too many nouns strung together to serve as modifiers. Therefore, exercise caution when you use nouns as adjectives.

REVISE   The test control group meeting was held last Wednesday.

TO   The meeting of the test control group was held last Wednesday.

OR   The test control group met last Wednesday.

Furthermore, you should avoid general adjectives (*nice, fine, good*) and trite or overused adjectives (a *fond* farewell). In fact, it is good practice to question the need for most adjectives in your writing. Often, your writing not only will read as well without an adjective but may even be better without it. If you need to use an adjective, select one that expresses your meaning as exactly as possible.

3.4 VERBS

A verb is a word, or a group of words, that specifies an action or affirms a condition or a state of existence.

EXAMPLES   The antelope *bolted* at the sight of the hunters.

She *was saddened* by the death of her friend.

He *is* a wealthy man now.

A verb is an essential part of a sentence since the verb makes an assertion about the action or existence of its subject, the someone or something that is its topic. Within a sentence, a verb alone is called a simple predicate; a verb with its modifiers and complements forms a complete predicate. When a subject and a predicate convey a complete thought, they form a sentence (or independent clause). When a subject and a predicate do not convey a complete thought, they form a dependent clause. In contrast to a clause, a phrase is a group of words without the subject-predicate combination.

3.4.1 Types of Verbs

Verbs may be described as either transitive or intransitive; the intransitive verbs include linking verbs.

(a) **Transitive verbs.** A transitive verb requires a *direct object* to complete its meaning. The direct object normally answers the question *whom* or *what* by naming the person or thing that receives the action of the verb.

EXAMPLE   They *laid* the *foundation* on October 24. (*Foundation* is the direct object of the transitive verb *laid*.)

Some transitive verbs (such as *give, wish, cause,* and *tell*) may be followed by an *indirect object* as well as a direct object. The indirect object is usually a person and answers the question "to whom or what?" or "for whom or what?" The indirect object precedes the direct object.

EXAMPLE   Georgiana Anderson *gave* the *treasurer* a *letter*. (*Treasurer* is the indirect object and *letter* is the direct object of the transitive verb *gave*.)

(b)   Intransitive verbs.   An intransitive verb is a verb that does not require an object to complete its meaning. It makes a full assertion about the subject without assistance (although it may have modifiers).

EXAMPLES   The water *boiled*.

The water *boiled* rapidly.

The engine *ran*.

The engine *ran* smoothly and quietly.

(c)   Linking verbs.   Although intransitive verbs do not have objects, certain intransitive verbs may take complements. These verbs are called linking verbs because they link the subject of a sentence to words following the verb. When this subjective complement is a noun (or pronoun), it refers to the same person or thing as the noun (or pronoun) that is the subject.

EXAMPLES   The conference table *is* an antique.

Maria *should be* the director.

When the complement is an adjective, it modifies the subject.

EXAMPLES   The study *was* thorough.

The report *seems* complete.

Such intransitive verbs as *be, become, seem,* and *appear* are almost always linking verbs. Others, such as *look, sound, taste, smell,* and *feel,* may function either as linking verbs or as simple intransitive verbs.

EXAMPLES   Their antennae *feel* delicately. (simple intransitive verb meaning that they have a delicate sense of touch)

Their antennae *feel* delicate. (linking verb meaning that they seem fragile to the touch)

3.4.2   Forms of Verbs

By form, verbs may be described as either finite or nonfinite.

(a)   Finite verbs.   A finite verb is the main verb of a clause or sentence. It makes an assertion about its subject, and it can serve as the only verb in its clause or sentence. Finite verbs may be either transitive or intransitive (including linking) verbs. They change form to reflect person (I *see*, he *sees*), tense (I *go*, I *went*), and number (he *writes*, they *write*).

EXAMPLES   The telephone *rang,* and the secretary *answered* it.

When the telephones *ring,* you *answer* them.

A *helping verb* (sometimes called an *auxilliary verb*) is a verb that is added to a finite or main verb to help indicate mood, voice, and tense. (See the discussions of mood, voice, and tense in Sections 3.4.3b, 3.4.3c, and 3.4.3d, respectively.) Together, the helping verb and the main verb form a verb phrase.

EXAMPLES   The work *had* (helping verb) begun.

I *am* going.

I *was* going.

I *will* go.

I *should have* gone.

I *must* go.

The most commonly used helping verbs are the various forms of *have* (*has, had*), *be* (*am, is, are, was, were*), *do* (*did, does*), *can* (*could*), *may* (*might*), *shall* (*should*), and *will* (*would*). Phrases that function as helping verbs often include *to:* for example, *am going to* and *is about to* (compare *will*), *has to* (compare *must*), and *ought to* (compare *should*).

EXAMPLES   I *am going to* quit.

I *will* quit.

She *has to* get a raise.

She *must* get a raise.

The helping verb always precedes the main verb, although other words may come between them.

EXAMPLE   Machines *will* (helping verb) never completely *replace* (main verb) people.

(b) **Nonfinite verbs or verbals.**   Nonfinite verbs are the verbals (gerunds, infinitives, and participles) which, although they are derived from verbs, actually function as nouns, adjectives, or adverbs.

When the *-ing* form of a verb functions as a noun, it is called a *gerund.*

EXAMPLE   *Seeing* is *believing.*

An *infinitive,* which is the root form of a verb, can function as a noun, an adverb, or an adjective. Because the word *to* usually precedes an infinitive, it is considered the sign of an infinitive.

EXAMPLES   He hates *to complain.* (noun, direct object of the verb *hates*)

The valve closes *to stop* the flow. (adverb, modifies the verb *closes*)

This is the proposal *to select*. (adjective, modifies the noun *proposal*)

A *participle* is a verb form that functions as an adjective. The present participle ends in *-ing*.

EXAMPLE   *Declining* sales forced us to close the branch office.

The past participle may end in *-ed, -t, -en, -n,* or *-d.*

EXAMPLES   What are the *estimated* costs?

Repair the *bent* lever.

Here is the *broken* calculator.

What are the *known* properties of this metal?

The story, *told* many times before, was still interesting.

The perfect participle is formed with the present participle of *have* and the past participle of the main verb.

EXAMPLE   *Having received* (perfect participle) a large raise, the *smiling* (present participle), *contented* (past participle) employee worked harder than ever.

3.4.3   Grammatical Properties of Verbs

Verbs can show person and number, mood, voice, and tense.

(a)   **Person and number.**   Verbs must agree with their subjects in *number* (singular or plural) and *person* (first, second, or third). In the present indicative of regular verbs (see Section 3.4.3b), only the third-person singular differs from the infinitive stem. The verb *to be,* however, is irregular: I *am,* you *are,* he *is,* we *are,* they *are.* (See Section 3.4.4.)

EXAMPLES   I *see* (first-person singular) a yellow tint, but he *sees* (third-person singular) a yellow-green hue.

I *am* (first-person singular) convinced, and they *are* (third-person plural) convinced; unfortunately, he *is* (third-person singular) not convinced.

(b)   **Mood.**   *Mood* refers to the functions of verbs: making statements or asking questions (indicative mood), giving commands (imperative mood), or expressing hypothetical possibilities (subjunctive mood).

The *indicative* mood refers to an action or a state that is conceived as fact.

EXAMPLES   *Is* the setting correct?

The setting *is* correct.

The *imperative* mood expresses a command, suggestion, request, or entreaty.

EXAMPLES   *Install* the wiring today.

Please *let* me know if I can help.

The *subjunctive* mood expresses something that is contrary to fact, conditional, or hypothetical; it can also express a wish, a doubt, or a possibility. The verb *be* is the only one in English that preserves many changes in form to show the subjunctive mood.

EXAMPLES   The senior partner insisted that he (I, you, we, they) *be* in charge of the project.

If the salesman (I, you, we, they) *were* to close the sale today, we would meet our monthly quota.

Most verbs other than *be* do not change form for the subjunctive. Instead, helping verbs show the subjunctive function.

EXAMPLE   *Had I known* that you were here, I would have come earlier.

The advantage of the subjunctive mood is that it enables you to express clearly whether or not you consider a condition contrary to fact. If you wish to express a contrary-to-fact condition or a highly doubtful hypothesis, use the subjunctive; if not, use the indicative.

EXAMPLES   If I *were* president of the firm, I would change several personnel policies. (subjuntive mood)

I *am* president of the firm, but I don't feel that I control every aspect of its policies. (indicative mood)

Be careful not to shift haphazardly from one mood to another within a sentence; to do so makes the sentence unbalanced as well as ungrammatical.

REVISE   Put the clutch in first (imperative); then you should put the truck in gear (indicative).

TO   Put the clutch in first (imperative); then put the truck in gear (imperative).

OR   You should put the clutch in first (indicative); then you should put the truck in gear (indicative).

(c)   **Voice.**   The grammatical term *voice* refers to whether the subject of a sentence or clause acts or receives the action. A sentence is in the active voice if the subject acts, in the passive voice if the subject is acted upon. The passive voice consists of a form of the verb *to be* and a past participle of the main verb.

EXAMPLES   The aerosol bomb *propels* the liquid as a mist. (active)

The liquid *is propelled* as a mist by the aerosol bomb. (passive)

In your writing, the active voice provides force and momentum, whereas the passive voice lacks these qualities. The reason is not difficult to find. In the active voice, the verb identifies what the subject is doing, thus emphasizing the subject and the action. On the other hand, the passive voice emphasizes what is being done to the subject, rather than the subject or the action. As a rule, use the active voice unless you have good reason not to.

EXAMPLES   The report *was written* by Joe Albright in only two hours. (passive voice) (The emphasis is on *report* rather than on Joe and the writing.)

Joe Albright *wrote* the report in only two hours. (active voice) (Here the writer and writing receive the emphasis.)

Things *are seen* by the normal human eye in three dimensions: length, width, and depth. (passive voice) (The emphasis is on *things* rather than on the eye's function.)

The normal human eye *sees* things in three dimensions: length, width, and depth. (active voice) (Here the eye's function—which is what the sentence is about—receives the emphasis.)

Sentences in the passive voice may state the actor, but they place the actor in a secondary position as the object of a preposition ("*by* the normal human eye").

The passive voice has its advantages, however; when the doer of the action is not known or is not important, use the passive voice.

EXAMPLE   The firm *was established* in 1929.

When the doer of the action is less important than the receiver of the action, use the passive voice.

EXAMPLE   Bill Bryant *was cited* for heroism by General Colby.

Be careful about shifting voice within a sentence.

REVISE   We *worked* late last night, and all the tests *were* finally *completed*.

TO We *worked* late last night, and finally we *completed* all the tests.

(d) **Tense.** *Tense* is the grammatical term for verb forms that indicate time distinctions. The six simple tenses in English are past, past perfect, present, present perfect, future, and future perfect. Each of these tenses has a corresponding progressive form that shows action in progress and is created by combining the helping verb *be,* in the appropriate tense, with the present participle (*-ing*) form of the main verb.

Simple	*Progressive*
I begin (present)	I am beginning (present)
I began (past)	I was beginning (past)
I will begin (future)	I will be beginning (future)
I have begun (present perfect)	I have been beginning (present perfect)
I had begun (past perfect)	I had been beginning (past perfect)
I will have begun (future perfect)	I will have been beginning (future perfect)

The *simple present tense* represents action occurring in the present, without any indication of time duration.

EXAMPLE I *use* the calculator.

A general truth is always expressed in the present tense.

EXAMPLE He learned that "time *heals* all wounds."

The present tense can be used to present actions or conditions that have no time restrictions.

EXAMPLE Water *boils* at 212° F.

The present tense can be used to indicate habitual action.

EXAMPLE I *pass* the paint shop on the way to the office every day.

The present tense can be used as the *historical present* to make things that occurred in the past more vivid.

EXAMPLE It is 1865, and the founder of our company is pushing his cart through Philadelphia, delivering fish to his customers. He *works* hard, *expands* his business, and *builds* the firm that still bears his name.

The *simple past tense* indicates that an action took place in its entirety in the past. The past tense is usually formed by adding *-d* or *-ed* to the root form of the verb.

EXAMPLE We *closed* the office early yesterday.

The *simple future tense* indicates a time that will occur after the present. The helping verb *will* (or *shall*) is used along with the main verb.

EXAMPLE   I *will finish* the job tomorrow.

The *present perfect tense* describes something from the recent past that has a bearing on the present—a period of time before the present but after the simple past. The present perfect tense is formed by combining a form of the present tense of the helping verb *have* with the past participle of the main verb.

EXAMPLES   He *has retired,* but he visits the office frequently.

We *have finished* the draft and are ready to begin revising it.

The *simple past perfect tense* indicates that one past event preceded another. It is formed by combining the helping verb *had* with the past participle of the main verb.

EXAMPLE   He *had finished* by the time I arrived.

The *future perfect tense* indicates an action that will have been completed at a future time. It is formed by linking the helping verbs *will have* to the past participle of the main verb.

EXAMPLE   He *will have driven* the test car 40 miles by the time he returns.

3.4.4 Conjugation of Verbs

When a verb is conjugated, all of its forms are arranged schematically so that the differences in tense, number, person, and voice are readily apparent. Following is the conjugation of the verb *drive*. Its principal parts, used to construct its various forms, are *drive* (infinitive and present tense), *drove* (past tense), *driven* (past participle), and *driving* (present participle).

Tense	*Number*	*Person*	*Active Voice*	*Passive Voice*
	Singular	1st	I drive	I am driven
		2nd	You drive	You are driven
		3rd	He drives	He is driven
Present				
	Plural	1st	We drive	We are driven
		2nd	You drive	You are driven
		3rd	They drive	They are driven

Tense	Number	Person	Active Voice	Passive Voice
Progressive present	Singular	1st	I am driving	I am being driven
		2nd	You are driving	You are being driven
		3rd	He is driving	He is being driven
	Plural	1st	We are driving	We are being driven
		2nd	You are driving	You are being driven
		3rd	They are driving	They are being driven
Past	Singular	1st	I drove	I was driven
		2nd	You drove	You were driven
		3rd	He drove	He was driven
	Plural	1st	We drove	We were driven
		2nd	You drove	You were driven
		3rd	They drove	They were driven
Progressive past	Singular	1st	I was driving	I was being driven
		2nd	You were driving	You were being driven
		3rd	He was driving	He was being driven
	Plural	1st	We were driving	We were being driven
		2nd	You were driving	You were being driven
		3rd	They were driving	They were being driven
Future	Singular	1st	I will drive	I will be driven
		2nd	You will drive	You will be driven
		3rd	He will drive	He will be driven
	Plural	1st	We will drive	We will be driven
		2nd	You will drive	You will be driven
		3rd	They will drive	They will be driven
Progressive future	Singular	1st	I will be driving	I will have been driven
		2nd	You will be driving	You will have been driven
		3rd	He will be driving	He will have been driven
	Plural	1st	We will be driving	We will have been driven
		2nd	You will be driving	You will have been driven
		3rd	They will be driving	They will have been driven

Tense	Number	Person	Active Voice	Passive Voice
Present perfect	Singular	1st	I have driven	I have been driven
		2nd	You have driven	You have been driven
		3rd	He has driven	He has been driven
	Plural	1st	We have driven	We have been driven
		2nd	You have driven	You have been driven
		3rd	They have driven	They have been driven
Past perfect	Singular	1st	I had driven	I had been driven
		2nd	You had driven	You had been driven
		3rd	He had driven	He had been driven
	Plural	1st	We had driven	We had been driven
		2nd	You had driven	You had been driven
		3rd	They had driven	They had been driven
Future perfect	Singular	1st	I will have driven	I will have been driven
		2nd	You will have driven	You will have been driven
		3rd	He will have driven	He will have been driven
	Plural	1st	We will have driven	We will have been driven
		2nd	You will have driven	You will have been driven
		3rd	They will have driven	They will have been driven

3.4.5 Subject-Verb Agreement

Agreement, grammatically, means the correspondence in form between different elements of a sentence. Just as a pronoun must agree with its antecedent in person, gender, and number (see Section 3.2.3a), so a verb must agree with its subject in person and number.

EXAMPLES   I *am* going to approve his promotion. (The first-person singular subject, *I,* requires the first-person singular form of the verb, *am.*)

His colleagues *are* envious. (The third-person plural subject, *colleagues,* requires the third-person plural form of the verb, *are.*)

Do not let phrases and clauses that fall between the subject and the verb mislead you.

EXAMPLE   Teaching proper oral hygiene to children, even when they are excited about learning, *requires* patience. (The verb *requires* must agree with the singular subject of the sentence, *teaching,* rather than with the plural subject of the preceding clause, *they.*)

Be careful to avoid making the verb agree with the noun immediately before it if that noun is not its subject. This problem is especially likely to occur when a modifying phrase containing a plural noun falls between a singular subject and its verb.

EXAMPLES   Each of the engineers *is* experienced. (The subject of the verb is *each,* not *engineers.*)

Only Bob, of all the district managers, *has doubled* his sales this year. (The subject of the verb is *Bob,* not *managers.*)

Proper cleaning of the machines and tools *takes* time. (The subject of the verb is *cleaning,* not *machines and tools.*)

Words like *type, part, series,* and *portion* take singular verbs even when such words precede a phrase containing a plural noun.

EXAMPLES   A *series* of directions *was given* to each branch manager.

A large *portion* of most employee handbooks *is devoted* to the responsibilities of the worker.

Subjects expressing measurement, weight, mass, or total often take singular verbs even though the subject word is plural in form. Such subjects are treated as a unit.

EXAMPLES   Ten pounds *is* the shipping weight.

Fifty dollars *is* her commission for each unit she sells.

However, when such subjects refer to the individual units that make up the whole, a plural verb is required.

EXAMPLE   If you need to make change, fifty dollars *are* in the office.

Similarly, collective subjects take singular verbs when the group is thought of as a unit, and take plural verbs when the individuals are thought of separately.

EXAMPLES   The staff *is* reaching its decision. (The staff is thought of as a unit.)

The staff *are* so divided in their opinions that a decision is unlikely to be reached soon. (The staff members are thought of as individuals.)

A book with a plural title requires a singular verb.

EXAMPLE *Monetary Theories is* a useful source.

Some abstract nouns are singular in meaning though plural in form: examples are *mathematics, news, physics,* and *economics.*

EXAMPLES News of the merger *is* on page four of the *Chronicle.*

Textiles *is* an industry in need of import quotas.

Some words are always plural, such as *trousers* and *scissors.*

EXAMPLE His trousers *were* torn by the machine.

The scissors *were* on the table.

BUT A pair of trousers *is* on order.

A pair of scissors *was* on the table.

Modifiers such as *some, none, all, more,* and *most* may be singular if they are used with mass nouns or plural if they are used with count nouns. Mass nouns identify things that comprise a mass and cannot be separated into countable units; count nouns identify things that can be separated into countable units (See Section 3.1.1b).

EXAMPLES Most of the oil *has* been used.

Most of the drivers *know* why they are here.

Some of the water *has* leaked.

Some of the pencils *have* been used.

One and *each* are normally singular.

EXAMPLES One of the brake drums *is* still scored.

Each of the original founders *is* scheduled to speak at the dedication ceremony.

Following a relative pronoun such as *who, which,* or *that,* a verb agrees in number with the noun to which the pronoun refers (its antecedent).

EXAMPLES Steel is one of those industries that *are* hardest hit by high energy costs. (*That* refers to *industries.*)

She is an employee who *is* rarely absent. (*Who* refers to *employee.*)

She is one of those employees who *are* rarely absent. (*Who* refers to *employees.*)

A subjective complement is a noun or adjective in the predicate of a sentence, following a linking verb. The number of a subjective complement does not affect the number of the verb—the verb must always agree with the subject.

EXAMPLE The topic of his report *was* rivers. (The subject of the sentence is *topic,* not *rivers.*)

Sentences with inverted word order can cause problems with agreement between subject and verb.

EXAMPLE From this work *have come* several important improvements. (The subject of the verb is *improvements,* not *work.*)

A compound subject is one that is composed of two or more elements joined by a conjunction such as *and, or, nor, either . . . or,* or *neither . . . nor.* Usually, when the elements are connected by *and,* the subject is plural and requires a plural verb.

EXAMPLE Education and experience *are* valuable assets.

There is one exception to the *and* rule. Sometimes the elements connected by *and* form a unit or refer to the same person. In this case, the subject is regarded as singular and takes a singular verb.

EXAMPLES Ice cream and cake *is* his favorite dessert.

His lawyer and business partner *prepares* the tax forms. (His lawyer is also his business partner.)

A compound subject joined by *or* or *nor* requires a singular verb with two singular elements and a plural verb with two plural elements.

EXAMPLES Neither the *doctor* nor the *nurse is* on duty.
Neither the *doctors* nor the *nurses are* on duty.

A compound subject with a singular element and a plural element joined by *or* or *nor* requires that the verb agree with the element nearest to it.

EXAMPLES Neither the doctor nor the *nurses are* on duty.

Neither the doctors nor the *nurse is* on duty.

3.5 ADVERBS

An adverb modifies the action or condition expressed by a verb.

EXAMPLE The recording head hit the surface of the disk *hard.* (The adverb tells *how* the recording head hit the disk.)

An adverb may also modify an adjective, another adverb, or a clause.

EXAMPLES   The graphics department used *extremely* bright colors. (modifying an adjective)

The redesigned brake pad lasted *much* longer than the original model. (modifying another adverb)

Surprisingly, the machine failed. (modifying a clause)

3.5.1   Functions of Adverbs

An adverb answers one of the following questions.

Where?

EXAMPLE   Move the throttle *forward.*

When?

EXAMPLE   Replace the thermostat *immediately.*

How?

EXAMPLE   Add the solvent *cautiously.*

How much?

EXAMPLES   The *nearly* completed report was lost in the move.

I *rarely* work on the weekend.

I have worked overtime *twice* this week.

Some adverbs (such as *however, therefore, nonetheless, nevertheless, consequently, accordingly,* and *then*) can join two independent clauses, each of which could otherwise stand alone as a sentence.

EXAMPLE   I rarely work on the weekend; *nevertheless,* this weekend will be an exception.

Other adverbs, such as *where, when, why,* and *how,* ask questions.

EXAMPLE   *How* many hours did you work last week?

3.5.2   Comparison of Adverbs

Adverbs, like adjectives, show three degrees of comparison: the positive (the basic form of the adverb), the comparative (showing comparison with one other item), and the superlative (showing comparison with two or more other items). Many adverbs indicate comparison with the suffixes *-er,* or *-est;* alternatively, *more* or *most* may be placed in front of an adverb to indicate comparison. One-syllable adverbs use the comparative ending *-er* and the superlative ending *-est.*

EXAMPLES   This copier works *faster* than the old one.

This copier works *fastest* of the three tested.

Most adverbs with two or more syllables end in *-ly,* and most adverbs ending in *-ly* are compared by inserting the comparative *more* or *less* or the superlative *most* or *least* in front of them.

EXAMPLES   He moved *more quickly* than the other company's salesman.

Of all the salesmen, he moved *most quickly.*

He moved *less quickly* than the other company's salesman.

Of all the salesmen, he moved *least quickly.*

A few irregular adverbs require a change in form to indicate comparison.

EXAMPLES   Our training program functions *well.*

Our training program functions *better* than most others in the industry.

Our training program functions the *best* in the industry.

3.5.3   Adverbs Made from Adjectives

Many adverbs are simply adjectives with *-ly* added, such as *dashingly* and *richly.* Sometimes, the adverb form is identical to the adjective form: examples are *early, hard, right,* and *fast.* Resist the temptation to drop the *-ly* ending from such adverbs as *surely, differently, seriously, consider-ably, badly,* and *really.*

REVISE   The breakdown of the air conditioning equipment damaged the computer system *considerable.*

TO   The breakdown of the air conditioning equipment damaged the computer system *considerably.*

On the other hand, resist the temptation to coin awkward adverbs by adding *-ly* to adjectives (*firstly, muchly*).

REVISE   Firstly, I'd like to thank our sponsor; secondly, I'd like to thank all of you.

TO   First, I'd like to thank our sponsor; second, I'd like to thank all of you.

3.5.4 Placement of Adverbs

An adverb may appear almost anywhere in a sentence, but its position can affect the meaning of the sentence. Avoid placing an adverb between two verb forms where it will be ambiguous because it can be read as modifying either.

REVISE   The man who was making calculations hastily rose from his desk and left the room. (Did the man calculate hastily or did he rise hastily?)

TO   The man who was making calculations rose hastily from his desk and left the room.

An adverb is commonly placed in front of the verb it modifies.

EXAMPLE   The accountant *meticulously* checked the figures.

An adverb may, however, follow the verb (or the verb and its object) that it modifies.

EXAMPLES   The accountant checked the figures *meticulously*.

The gauge dipped *suddenly*.

An adverb may be placed between a helping verb and a main verb.

EXAMPLE   He will *surely* call.

If an adverb modifies only the main verb, and not any accompanying helping verbs, place the adverb immediately before or after the main verb.

EXAMPLES   The alternative proposal has been *effectively* presented.

The alternative proposal has been presented *effectively*.

An adverb phrase, however, should not separate the parts of a verb.

REVISE   This suggestion has *time and time again* been rejected.

TO   This suggestion has been rejected *time and time again*.

To emphasize an adverb that introduces an entire sentence, you can put the adverb before the subject of the sentence.

EXAMPLES   *Clearly,* he was ready for the promotion when it came.

Unfortunately, fuel rationing has been necessary.

In writing, such adverbs as *nearly, only, almost, just,* and *hardly* are placed immediately before the words they limit. A speaker can place these words earlier and avoid ambiguity by stressing the word to be limited; a writer, however, can ensure clarity only through correct placement of the adverb.

REVISE   The punch press *almost* costs $47,000.

TO   The punch press costs *almost* $47,000.

3.6 CONJUNCTIONS

A conjunction connects words, phrases, or clauses. A conjunction can also indicate the relationship between the two elements it connects. (For example, *and* joins together; *or* selects and separates.)

3.6.1 Types of Conjunctions

Conjunctions may be coordinating, correlative, or subordinating. In addition, certain adverbs act as conjunctions.

(a) Coordinating conjunctions. A coordinating conjunction is a word that joins two sentence elements that have identical functions. The coordinating conjunctions are *and, but, for, nor, or, so,* and *yet.*

EXAMPLES   Bill *and* John work at the Los Angeles office. (joining two proper nouns)

To hear *and* to obey are two different things. (joining two phrases)

He would like to include the test results, *but* that would make the report too long. (joining two clauses)

(b) Correlative conjunctions. Correlative conjunctions are used in pairs. The correlative conjunctions are *either . . . or, neither . . . nor, not only . . . but also, both . . . and,* and *whether . . . or.* To ensure not only symmetry but also logic in your writing, follow correlative conjunctions with parallel sentence elements that are alike in function and in construction.

EXAMPLE   Bill will arrive *either* on Wednesday *or* on Thursday.

(c) Subordinating conjunctions. A subordinating conjunction connects sentence elements of different weights, normally independent clauses that can stand alone as sentences and dependent clauses that cannot. The most frequently used subordinating conjunctions are *so, although, after, because, if, where, than, since, as, unless, before, that, though, when,* and *whereas.*

EXAMPLE   He left the office *after* he had finished writing the report.

(d) Conjunctive adverbs. A conjunctive adverb is an adverb that has the force of a conjunction because it is used to join two independent clauses. The most common conjunctive adverbs are *however, moreover, therefore, further, then, consequently, besides, accordingly, also,* and *too.*

> EXAMPLE The engine performed well in the laboratory; *moreover,* it surpassed all expectations during its road test.

3.6.2 Use of Conjunctions

Coordinating conjunctions generally appear within rather than at the beginning of a sentence. There is, however, no rule against beginning a sentence with a coordinating conjunction. In fact, such conjunctions can be strong transitional words and at times can provide emphasis.

> EXAMPLE I realize that the project was more difficult than expected and that you have also encountered personnel problems. *But* we must meet our deadline.

Starting sentences with conjunctions is acceptable in even the most formal English. But, like any other writing device, this one should be used sparingly lest it become ineffective and even annoying.

3.7 PREPOSITIONS

A preposition is a word that links a noun or pronoun (its object) to another sentence element.

3.7.1 Functions of Prepositions

Prepositions express such relationships as direction (*to, into, across, toward*), location (*at, in, on, under, over, beside, among, by, between, through*), time (*before, after, during, until, since*), or figurative location (*for, against, with*). Although only about 70 prepositions exist in the English language, they are used frequently. Together, the preposition, its object, and the object's modifiers form a prepositional phrase, which acts as a modifier.

Many words that function as prepositions also function as adverbs. If a word takes an object and functions as a connective, it is a preposition; if it has no object and functions as a modifier, it is an adverb.

EXAMPLES   The manager sat *behind* the desk in his office. (preposition)

The customer lagged *behind;* then she came in and sat down. (adverb)

3.7.2 Usage of Prepositions

Do not use unnecessary prepositions, such as "off *of*" or "inside *of.*"

REVISE   *Inside of* the cave, the spelunkers turned on their headlamps.

TO   Inside the cave, the spelunkers turned on their headlamps.

Avoid adding the preposition *up* to verbs unnecessarily.

REVISE   Call *up* and see whether he is in his office.

TO   Call and see whether he is in his office.

However, do not omit needed prepositions.

REVISE   He was oblivious and not distracted by the view from his office window.

TO   He was oblivious *to* and not distracted *by* the view from his office window.

If a preposition falls naturally at the end of a sentence, leave it there.

EXAMPLE   I don't remember which file I put it *in.*

Be aware, however, that a preposition at the end of a sentence can indicate that the sentence is awkwardly constructed.

REVISE   Corn was the crop in the field that the wheat was planted *by.*

TO   The wheat was planted next to the corn in the field.

The object of a preposition—the word or phrase following the preposition—is always in the objective case. Despite this rule, a construction such as "between you and *me*" frequently and incorrectly appears as "between you and I."

REVISE   The whole department has suffered because of the quarrel between *he* and Bob.

TO   The whole department has suffered because of the quarrel between *him* and Bob.

Certain verbs (and verb forms), adverbs, and adjectives are used with certain prepositions. For example, we say "interested *in,*" "aware *of,*" "devoted *to,*" "equated *with,*" "abstain *from,*" "adhere *to,*" "conform *to,*" "capable *of,*" "comply *with,*" "object *to,*" "find fault *with,*" "inconsistent *with,*" "independent *of,*" "infer *from,*" and "interfere *with.*"

3.8 INTERJECTIONS

An interjection is a word or phrase of exclamation that is used independently to express emotion or surprise or to summon attention. *Hey! Ouch! Wow!* are strong interjections. *Oh, well,* and *indeed* are mild ones. An interjection functions much as *yes* or *no,* in that it has no grammatical connection with the rest of the sentence in which it appears. When an interjection expresses a sudden or strong emotion, punctuate it with an exclamation mark.

EXAMPLE   His only reaction was a resounding *"Wow!"*

Punctuate a mild interjection with a comma.

EXAMPLES   Well, that's done.

Oh, well, that's done.

Because they get their expressive force from sound, interjections are more common in speech than in writing. They are rarely appropriate to business or technical writing.

---

4 PHRASES, CLAUSES, SENTENCES, AND PARAGRAPHS

Good writing relies upon the writer's ability to put words together that convey a message to a reader in the most effective way. The writer can use a number of tools to help communicate ideas to a reader; among them are phrases, clauses, sentences, and paragraphs.

4.1 PHRASES

Although a phrase is the most basic meaningful group of words, it does not make a full statement. Unlike a clause, it does not contain both a subject (words that name someone or something) and a predicate (words that make an assertion about the subject). Instead, a phrase is based on a noun, a verbal (that is, a gerund, infinitive, or participle), or a verb without a subject.

EXAMPLES   *by August fifth*

operating the machine

has been working

A phrase may function as an adjective, an adverb, a noun, or a verb.

EXAMPLES   The subjects *on the agenda* were all discussed. (adjective)

We discussed the project *with great enthusiasm*. (adverb)

Hard work is her way of life. (noun)

The chief engineer *should have been notified*. (verb)

Even though phrases function as adjectives, adverbs, nouns, or verbs, normally they are named for the kind of word around which they are constructed—preposition, verb, noun, or the three verbals. For definitions of the parts of speech, refer to Section 3 of this Guide.

4.1.1   Prepositional Phrases

A preposition is a word that shows the relationship between the noun or pronoun that is its object and another sentence element. Prepositions express relationships such as direction, location, and time. A preposition, its object, and the object's modifiers form a prepositional phrase, which acts as a modifier.

EXAMPLE   *After the meeting,* the regional managers adjourned *to the executive dining room.*

4.1.2   Verb Phrases

A verb phrase consists of a main verb preceded by one or more helping verbs.

EXAMPLES   Company officials discovered that a computer *was emitting* more data than it *had been asked* for.

He *will file* his tax forms on time this year.

4.1.3   Noun Phrases

A noun phrase consists of a noun and its modifiers.

EXAMPLES   *Many large companies* use computers.

Have *the two new employees* fill out *these forms*.

4.1.4   Participial Phrases

A participial phrase consists of a participle plus its object and any modifiers. A participial phrase functions as an adjective, so it must modify a noun or pronoun and must be placed so that this relationship is clear.

EXAMPLE   *Looking very pleased with himself,* the sales manager reported on the success of the policies he had introduced.

4.1.5   Infinitive Phrases

An infinitive is the root form of a verb (*go, run, talk*), one of the principal parts that is used to construct the various forms of a verb. An infinitive generally follows the word *to,* called the sign of the infinitive. An infinitive phrase consists of the word *to* plus an infinitive and any objects or modifiers.

EXAMPLE   *To succeed in this field,* you must be willing *to assume responsibility.*

4.1.6   Gerund Phrases

When the *-ing* form of a verb functions as a noun, it is called a gerund. A gerund phrase, which also must function as a noun, consists of a gerund plus any objects or modifiers.

EXAMPLES   *Preparing an annual report* is a difficult task.

She liked *running the department.*

4.2   CLAUSES

A clause is a part of a sentence that contains both a subject (the word or group of words that name someone or something as a topic) and a predicate (the main verb and its modifiers and complements that make an assertion about the subject).

Every subject-predicate word group in a sentence is a clause. Unlike a phrase, a clause can make a complete statement because it contains a finite verb (as opposed to a nonfinite verb or verbal) as well as a subject. Every sentence must consist of at least one clause. A clause that conveys a complete thought and thus could stand alone as a sentence is an independent clause.

EXAMPLE   *The scaffolding fell* when the rope broke.

A clause that could not stand alone without the rest of its sentence is a dependent or subordinate clause.

EXAMPLE   I was at the St. Louis branch *when the decision was made.*

A dependent clause may function as a noun, an adjective, or an adverb in a larger sentence; an independent clause may be modified by one or more dependent clauses.

EXAMPLE   While I was in college, I studied differential equations. (*While I was in college* is a dependent clause functioning as an adverb; it modifies the independent clause *I studied differential equations.*)

A clause may be connected with the rest of its sentence by a coordinating conjunction, a subordinating conjunction, a relative pronoun, or a conjunctive adverb. (Refer to Sections 3.2 and 3.6 for discussions of pronouns and conjunctions.)

EXAMPLES   Peregrine falcons are about the size of a large crow, *and* they have a wingspan of three to four feet. (coordinating conjunction)

Mission control will have to be alert *because* the space laboratory will contain a highly flammable fuel at launch. (subordinating conjunction)

It was Robert M. Fano *who* designed and developed the earliest "Multiple Access Computer" system at M.I.T. (relative pronoun)

It was dark when we arrived; *nevertheless,* we began to tour the factory. (conjunctive adverb)

4.2.1 Independent Clauses

Unlike a dependent clause, an independent clause is complete in itself. Although it might be part of a larger sentence, it always can stand alone as a separate sentence.

EXAMPLE   *We abandoned the project* because the cost was excessive.

4.2.2 Dependent Clauses

A dependent (or subordinate) clause is a group of words that has a subject and a predicate but requires a main clause to complete its meaning. A dependent clause can function in a sentence as a noun, as an adjective, or as an adverb.

As nouns, dependent clauses may function in sentences as subjects, objects, or complements.

EXAMPLES   *That human beings can learn to control their glands and internal organs by direct or indirect means* is now an established fact. (subject)

I learned *that drugs ordered by brand name can cost several times as much as drugs ordered by generic name.* (direct object)

The trouble is *that we cannot finish the project by May.* (subjective complement)

As adjectives, dependent clauses can modify nouns or pronouns. Dependent clauses are often introduced by relative pronouns and relative adjectives (*who, whom, whose, which, what, that*).

EXAMPLE   The man *who called earlier* is here. (modifying *man*)

As adverbs, dependent clauses may express relationships of time, cause, result, or degree.

EXAMPLES   You are making an investment *when you buy a house.* (time)

A title search was necessary *because the bank would not otherwise grant a loan.* (cause)

Consult an attorney *so that you will be aware of your rights and obligations.* (result)

Monthly mortgage payments should not be much more *than the buyer earns in one week.* (degree)

Dependent clauses clarify the relationships between thoughts. As a result, dependent clauses can present ideas more precisely than simple sentences (which contain one independent clause) or compound sentences (which combine two or more independent clauses).

REVISE   The sewage plant is located between Millville and Darrtown. Both villages use it. (two thoughts of approximately equal importance)

TO   The sewage plant, *which is located between Millville and Darrtown,* is used by both villages. (one thought, the plant's location, is subordinated to the other, its service area)

REVISE   He arrived at his office early and was able to finish the report without any interruptions. (two thoughts of approximately equal importance)

TO   *Since he arrived at his office early,* he was able to finish the report without interruptions. (one thought, his early arrival, subordinated to the other, his completion of the report)

Subordinate clauses effectively express thoughts that describe or explain another statement. They can state where, when, how, or why an event occurred, thus supplying logical connections that may not be obvious from the context. Too much subordination, however, may be worse than none at all. A string of dependent clauses, like a string of simple sentences, may obscure the important ideas.

REVISE   He had selected classes *that* had a slant *that* was specifically directed toward students *who* intended to go into business. (three dependent clauses of approximately equal importance)

TO   He had selected classes *that* were specifically directed to business students. (one dependent clause emphasizing the most important of the three points)

4.3   SENTENCES

A sentence is a sequence of words that contains a subject and a predicate and conveys a complete thought. A sentence normally has at least two words: a subject (something or someone) and a predicate (an assertion about the action or state of existence of the subject).

EXAMPLE   Sales (subject) declined (assertion about the subject).

To the basic sentence can be added modifiers—words, phrases, and clauses that expand, limit, or make more exact the meanings of other sentence elements.

EXAMPLE   *Computer* sales declined *in August.*

In most sentences, the subject is a noun phrase rather than a single word, and the predicate is a verb or verb phrase with appropriate modifiers, objects, or complements.

EXAMPLE   A good personnel department (subject) screens job applicants carefully (predicate).

Sentences may be classified according to structure (simple, compound, complex) and intention (declarative, interrogative, imperative, exclamatory).

4.3.1   Structure

A simple sentence is often used to make its content stand out in the reader's mind. A compound sentence is used to show that the clauses in the sentence are of equal importance. And a complex sentence is used to show that the clauses in the sentence are of unequal importance.

(a) Simple sentences.   A simple sentence has one clause. In its most basic form, the simple sentence contains only a subject and a predicate.

EXAMPLES   Profits rose.

The strike ended.

Both the subject and the predicate may be compounded to include several items without changing the basic structure of the simple sentence.

EXAMPLES   *Bulldozers and road graders* have blades. (compound subject)

Bulldozers *strip, ditch, and backfill.* (compound predicate)

Likewise, although modifiers may lengthen a simple sentence, they do not change its basic structure.

EXAMPLE   *The recently introduced* procedure works *very well.*

(b) Compound sentences.   A compound sentence combines two or more related independent clauses that are of equal importance.

EXAMPLE   Drilling is the only way to collect samples of the layers of sediment below the ocean floor, but it is by no means the only way to gather information about these strata.[1]

The independent clauses of a compound sentence may be joined by a comma and a coordinating conjunction, by a semicolon, or by a conjunctive adverb preceded by a semicolon and followed by a comma.

EXAMPLES   The plan was sound, *and* the staff was eager to begin. (comma and coordinating conjunction)

The plan was sound; the staff was eager to begin. (semicolon)

The plan was sound; *therefore,* the staff was eager to begin. (conjunctive adverb)

(c) Complex sentences.   A complex sentence contains one independent clause and at least one dependent clause.

EXAMPLE   We lost some of our efficiency (independent clause) when we moved (dependent clause).

A dependent clause may occur before, after, or within the independent clause. The dependent clause can function within a sentence as a subject, an object, or a modifier.

[1] Bruce C. Heezen and Ian D. MacGregor, "The Evolution of the Pacific," *Scientific American* (November 1973), p. 103.

EXAMPLES *What he proposed* is irrelevant. (subject)

We know *where it is supposed to be.* (object)

Fingerprints, *which were used for personal identification in 200 B.C.,* were not used for criminal identification until about 1800. (modifier)

Because complex sentences offer more variety than simple ones, changing a compound sentence into a complex one can produce a more precise statement. When one independent clause becomes subordinate to another, the relationship between the two is more clearly established.

EXAMPLES We moved, *and* we lost some of our efficiency. (compound sentence with coordinating conjunction)

When we moved, we lost some of our efficiency. (complex sentence with subordinating conjunction)

A complex sentence indicates the relative importance of two clauses and expresses the relationship between the ideas contained in them. Normally, the independent clause states the main point, and the dependent clause states a related but subordinate point.

EXAMPLE Although the warehouse was damaged by the fire, all the employees escaped safely from the building.

4.3.2 Intention

By intention, a sentence may be declarative, interrogative, imperative, or exclamatory.

A declarative sentence conveys information or makes a factual statement.

EXAMPLE This motor powers the conveyor belt.

An interrogative sentence asks a direct question.

EXAMPLE Does the conveyor belt run constantly?

An imperative sentence issues a command.

EXAMPLE Start the generator.

An exclamatory sentence is an emphatic expression of feeling, fact, or opinion. It is a declarative sentence that is stated with great force.

EXAMPLE The heater exploded!

4.3.3 Construction

(a) **Parts of sentences.** Within a sentence, every word or word group functions as a sentence element. A *subject* names (and perhaps includes words that describe) the person or thing that is the topic of the sentence.

EXAMPLE   *The new machine* ran.

A verb describes an action or affirms the condition or state of existence of its subject.

EXAMPLE   The new machine *ran.*

A complement is used in the predicate (with the verb) to complete the meaning of a sentence. There are four kinds of complements. The first, the direct object, names the person or thing on which a transitive verb acts. The direct object normally answers the question *what* or *whom.*

EXAMPLES   He wrote *a letter.*

I admire *the boss.*

The second type of complement, the indirect object, names the recipient of the direct object; that is, it names the person or thing that something is done to or for.

EXAMPLE   He wrote *the company* a letter.

The third type of complement, the objective complement, describes or renames a direct object.

EXAMPLE   I like my coffee *hot.*

The last type of complement, the subjective complement, describes or renames the subject of a sentence.

EXAMPLE   The director seems *confident.*

A modifier expands, limits, or makes more exact the meaning of other sentence elements.

EXAMPLE   *Automobile* production decreased *rapidly.*

A connective (a conjunction, a conjunctive adverb, or a preposition) ties together parts of sentences by indicating subordination or coordination.

EXAMPLE   I work hard each week, *but* I relax *when* I play racquetball.

An appositive is a noun or noun phrase that follows and amplifies another noun or noun phrase.

EXAMPLE   Bob, *the personnel director,* just interviewed another engineer.

An absolute is a participial or infinitive phrase that modifies a statement as a whole and is not linked to it by a subordinating conjunction or preposition.

EXAMPLE   *To speak bluntly,* the proposal is unacceptable.

An expletive is a word such as *it* or *there* that serves as a structural filler and reverses standard subject-verb order.

EXAMPLE   *It* is certain that he will go.

Because expletives are meaningless, they are best avoided in business or technical writing.

(b)   Sentence patterns.   Subjects, verbs, and complements are the main elements of a sentence. Everything else is subordinate to them in one way or another. The following are the basic sentence patterns with which a writer works.

EXAMPLES   The cable snapped. (subject–verb)

Generators produce electricity. (subject–verb–direct object)

The test results gave us confidence. (subject–verb–indirect object–direct object)

Repairs made the equipment operational. (subject–verb–direct object–objective complement)

The metal was aluminum. (subject–linking verb–subjective complement)

Most sentences follow the subject–verb–complement pattern. In "The company dismissed Joe," for example, you recognize the subject and the object by their positions before and after the verb. In fact, readers interpret what they read more easily because they expect this sentence order. As a result, departures from it can be effective, if used sparingly for emphasis and variety, but annoying if overdone.

An inverted sentence places the elements in other than normal order.

EXAMPLES   A better job I never had. (direct object–subject–verb)

More optimistic I have never been. (subjective complement–subject–linking verb)

Inverted sentence order can be used in questions and exclamations; it can also be used for emphasis.

EXAMPLES   Have you a pencil? (verb–subject–complement)

How heavy your book feels! (complement–subject–verb)

In sentences introduced by expletives (*there, it*), the subject comes after its verb because the expletive occupies the subject's normal location before the verb. Because expletives are fillers, they are avoided in concise writing.

EXAMPLES There (expletive) are (verb) certain principles (subject) of drafting that must not be ignored. (Compare: "Certain principles of drafting must not be ignored." The meaningful verb of the sentence, *be ignored,* which was buried in a relative clause in the expletive construction, becomes the only verb: the meaningless *are* is unnecessary.) It (expletive) is (verb) difficult (complement) to work (subject) in a noisy office. (Compare: "To work in a noisy office is difficult.")

Unusual sentence order, however, cannot be used often without tiring or puzzling the reader. Instead, a sentence that moves quickly from subject to verb to complement is clear and easy to understand. The writer's problem is to preserve the clarity and directness of this pattern but to write sentences that use more complicated forms to present more information. A skillful writer depends on subordination—the relative weighing of ideas—to make sentences more dense. As the following example shows, a sentence can be rewritten in several ways by subordinating the less important ideas to the more important ones.

REVISE The city manager's report was carefully illustrated, and it covered five typed pages.

TO The city manager's report, *which covered five typed pages,* was carefully illustrated. (adjectival clause)

OR The city manager's report, *covering five typed pages,* was carefully illustrated. (participial phrase)

OR The *carefully illustrated* report of the city manager covered five typed pages. (participial phrase)

OR The *five-page* report of the city manager was carefully illustrated. (modifier)

OR The city manager's report, *five typed pages,* was carefully illustrated. (appositive phrase)

The effective subordination of words, phrases, and clauses produces varied, concise, and emphatic sentences.

4.3.4 Common Sentence Problems

The most common sentence problems are faulty subordination, run-on sentences, sentence fragments, and dangling and misplaced modifiers.

(a) **Faulty subordination.** Faulty subordination occurs (1) when a grammatically subordinate element, such as a dependent clause, actually contains the main idea of the sentence; or (2) when a subordinate element is so long or detailed that it overpowers the main idea. You can avoid the first problem, expressing the main idea in a subordinate element, by deciding which idea is the main idea. Both of the following sentences, for example, appear logical, but each emphasizes a different point.

EXAMPLES   Although the new filing system saves money, many of the staff are unhappy with it.

The new filing system saves money, although many of the staff are unhappy with it.

In this example, if the writer's main point is that *the new filing system saves money,* the second sentence is better. If the main point is that *many of the staff are unhappy,* then the first sentence is better.

The other major problem with subordination occurs when a writer puts so much detail into a subordinate element that it overpowers the main point by its sheer size and weight. In the following example, details are omitted to streamline the sentence.

REVISE   If company personnel do not fully understand what the new contract that was drawn up at the annual meeting of the district managers this past month in New Orleans requires of them, they should call or write the Vice President for Finance.

TO   If company personnel do not fully understand what the new contract requires of them, they should call or write the Vice President for Finance.

(b)   **Run-on sentences.**   A run-on sentence, sometimes called a fused sentence, is made up of two or more sentences without punctuation to separate them. The term sometimes includes pairs of independent clauses separated by only a comma, although these are usually called comma faults or comma splices. Run-on sentences can be corrected by (1) making two sentences, (2) joining the two clauses with a semicolon (if they are closely related and of equal weight), (3) joining the two clauses with a comma and a coordinating conjunction, or (4) subordinating one clause to the other.

REVISE   The training division will offer three new courses interested employees should sign up by Wednesday. (run-on sentence)

OR   The training division will offer three new courses, interested employees should sign up by Wednesday. (comma fault or comma splice)

TO   The training division will offer three new courses. Interested employees should sign up by Wednesday. (period)

OR   The training division will offer three new courses; interested employees should sign up by Wednesday. (semicolon)

OR
The training division will offer three new courses, so interested employees should sign up by Wednesday. (comma plus coordinating conjunction)

OR
Since the training division will offer three new courses, interested employees should sign up by Wednesday. (one clause subordinated to the other)

(c) **Sentence fragments and minor sentences.** A sentence that is missing an essential part (subject or predicate) is called a sentence fragment.

EXAMPLES
She changed jobs. (sentence)

And earned more money. (fragment; it lacks a subject)

But having a subject and a predicate does not automatically turn a clause into a sentence. The clause must also make an independent statement. "I work" is a sentence; "If I work" is a fragment because the subordinating conjunction *if* makes the statement a dependent clause.

Sentence fragments are often introduced by relative pronouns (*who, whom, whose, which, that*) or subordinating conjunctions (such as *after, although, because, if, when,* and *while*). When you use these introductory words, you can anticipate combining the dependent clause that follows with a main clause to form a complete sentence.

REVISE
The accounting department received several new calculators. After its order was processed.

TO
The accounting department received several new calculators after its order was processed.

A sentence must contain a main or finite verb; verbals (gerunds, participles, and infinitives) will not do the job. The following examples are sentence fragments because they lack main verbs. Their verbals (*working, to skip, expecting*) cannot function as finite verbs.

EXAMPLES
Working overtime every night during tax season.

To skip the meeting.

The manager *expecting* to place an order.

Fragments may reflect incomplete or confused thinking. The most common type of fragment is the careless addition of an afterthought.

REVISE
These are the branch tellers. *A dedicated group of employees.*

TO
These are the branch tellers, a dedicated group of employees.

The following examples illustrate common types of sentence fragments.

REVISE   Health insurance rates have gone up. *Because medical expenses have increased.* (adverbial clause)

TO   Health insurance rates have gone up because medical expenses have increased.

REVISE   The engineers tested the model. *Outside the laboratory.* (prepositional phrase)

TO   The engineers tested the model outside the laboratory.

REVISE   *Having finished the job.* We submitted our bill. (participial phrase)

TO   Having finished the job, we submitted our bill.

REVISE   We met with Jim Rodgers. *Former head of the sales division.* (appositive)

TO   We met with Jim Rodgers, former head of the sales division.

REVISE   We have one major goal this month. *To increase the strength of the alloy without reducing its flexibility.* (infinitive phrase in apposition with *goal*)

TO   We have one major goal this month: to increase the stength of the alloy without reducing its flexibility.

Occasionally, a writer intentionally uses an incomplete sentence. This kind of deliberate fragment, called a *minor sentence,* makes sense in its context because the missing element is clearly implied by the preceding sentence or is clearly understood without being stated.

EXAMPLES   In view of these facts, is new equipment really necessary? *Or economical?*

You can use the one-minute long-distance rates any time between eleven at night and eight in the morning. *Any night of the week.*

Minor sentences are elliptical expressions that are equivalent to complete sentences because the missing words are obvious to a reader from the context.

EXAMPLES   Why not?

How much?

Ten dollars.

At last!

This way, please.

So much for that idea.

Although they are common in advertising copy and fictional dialogue, minor sentences are not normally appropriate to business or technical writing.

(d)   **Dangling and misplaced modifiers.**   A *dangling modifier* is a word or phrase that has no clear word or subject to modify. Most dangling modifiers are phrases with verbals (gerunds, participles, or infinitives). Correct this problem by adding the appropriate noun or pronoun for the phrase to modify or by making the phrase into a clause.

REVISE	After finishing the negotiations, dinner was relaxing.
TO	After finishing the negotiations, we relaxed at dinner.
REVISE	Entering the gate, the administration building is visible.
TO	As you enter the gate, the administration building is visible.

A *misplaced modifier* refers, or appears to refer, to the wrong word or phrase. The misplaced element can be a word, a phrase, or a clause.

REVISE	Our copier was used to duplicate materials for other departments that needed to be reduced.
TO	Our copier was used to duplicate materials that needed to be reduced for other departments.

You can avoid this problem by placing modifiers as close as possible to the words they modify. Position each modifier carefully so that it says what you mean.

REVISE	We *just* bought the property for expansion.
TO	We bought *just* the property for expansion.

A *squinting modifier* is ambiguous because it is located between two sentence elements and might refer to either one. To correct the problem, move the modifier or revise the sentence.

REVISE	The union agreed during the next week to return to work.
TO	During the next week, the union agreed to return to work.
OR	The union agreed to return to work during the next week.

Occasionally, a subject and verb are omitted from a dependent clause; the result is known as an *elliptical clause*. If the omitted subject of the elliptical clause is not the same as the subject of the main clause, the construction dangles. Simply adding the subject and verb to the elliptical clause solves the problem. (Or you can rework the whole sentence.)

REVISE	When ten years old, his father started the company. (Could his father have started the company at age ten?)

TO	When *Bill Krebs was* ten years old, his father started the company.
OR	Bill Krebs was ten years old when his father started the company.

(e) **Other sentence faults.**   The assertion made by the predicate of a sentence about its subject must be logical.

REVISE	Mr. Wilson's *job* is a salesman.
TO	*Mr. Wilson* is a salesman.
REVISE	Jim's *height* is six feet tall.
TO	*Jim* is six feet tall.

Do not omit a required verb.

REVISE	The floor is swept and the lights out.
TO	The floor is swept, and the lights *are* out.
REVISE	I never have and probably never will write the annual report.
TO	I never have *written* and probably never will write the annual report.

Do not omit a subject.

REVISE	Although he regarded price-fixing as wrong, he engaged in it until abolished by law.
TO	Although he regarded price-fixing as wrong, he engaged in it until *it was* abolished by law.

Avoid compound sentences containing clauses that have little or no logical relationship to each other.

REVISE	My department is responsible for all company publications, and the staff includes twenty writers, three artists, and four typists.
TO	My department is responsible for all company publications. The staff includes twenty writers, three artists, and four typists.

4.3.5   Effective Sentences

Effective sentences guide the reader and engage his or her attention. They can alert a reader to ideas weighted equally (through parallel structure) or differently (through subordination). In addition, carefully constructed and revised sentences clarify ideas for the reader. Besides highlighting especially significant information, sentences can be varied in length, pattern, and style to avoid boring the reader. Most writers wait until they are revising to concentrate on effective sentences. Then, they can try to eliminate confusion and monotony by building clear, precise, and varied sentences.

(a) Sentence parallelism. Express coordinate ideas in similar form. The very construction of a sentence with parallel elements helps the reader to grasp the similarity of its parts.

> EXAMPLE Similarly, atoms come and go in a molecule, but the molecule remains; molecules come and go in a cell, but the cell remains; cells come and go in a body, but the body remains; persons come and go in an organization, but the organization remains.[2]

(b) Emphatic sentences. Subordinate your minor ideas to emphasize your more important ideas.

> REVISE We had all arrived, and we began the meeting early.
>
> TO Since we had all arrived, we began the meeting early.

The most emphatic positions in a sentence are the beginning and the end. Do not waste these spots by burying the main idea in the middle of the sentence between less important points or by tacking on phrases and clauses almost as afterthoughts. For example, consider the following original and revised versions of a statement written for a company's annual report to its stockholders.

> REVISE Sales declined by 3 percent in 1987, but nevertheless the company had the most profitable year in its history, thanks to cost savings that resulted from design improvements in several of our major products; and we expect 1988 to be even better, since further design improvements are being made. (The sentence begins with the bad news, buries the good news, and trails off at the end.)
>
> TO Cost savings from design improvements in several major products not only offset a 3 percent sales decline but made 1987 the most profitable year in the company's history. Further design improvements now in progress promise to make 1988 even more profitable. (The sentence beginnings emphasize *cost savings* and *design improvements;* the ends stress profits.)

---

[2] Kenneth Boulding, *Beyond Economics* (Ann Arbor: University of Michigan Press, 1968), p. 131.

Reversing the normal word order is also used to achieve emphasis, though this tactic should not be overdone.

REVISE   I will never agree to that.

TO   *That* I will never agree to.

OR   *Never* will I agree to that.

(c) **Clear sentences.** Uncomplicated sentences are most effective for stating complex ideas. If readers must unravel a complicated sentence in addition to a complex idea, they are likely to become confused.

REVISE   Burning fuel and air in the production chamber causes an expansion of the gases formed by combustion, which in turn pushes the piston down in its cylinder so that the crankshaft rotates and turns the flywheel, which then transmits to the clutch the power developed by the engine.

TO   Burning fuel and air in the production chamber causes an expansion of the gases formed by combustion. These gases push the piston down in its cylinder so that the crankshaft rotates. Then the flywheel on the end of the crankshaft transmits to the clutch the power developed by the engine.

Just as simpler sentences can make complex ideas easier to understand, so more complex sentences can make groups of simple ideas easier to read.

REVISE   The industrial park was designed carefully. A team of architects and landscape designers planned it. It has become a local landmark.

TO   The carefully designed industrial park, planned by a team of architects and landscape designers, has become a local landmark.

(d) **Sentence length.** Variations in sentence length make writing more interesting to the reader because many sentences of the same length become monotonous.

Short sentences often can be combined effectively by converting verbs to adjectives.

REVISE   The steeplejack was *exhausted*. He collapsed on the scaffolding.

TO   The *exhausted* steeplejack collapsed on the scaffolding.

Sentences that string together short, independent clauses may be just as tedious as a series of short sentences. Either connect such clauses with subordinating connectives, thereby making some of them dependent, or turn some clauses into separate sentences.

REVISE   This river is 60 miles long, *and* it averages 50 yards in width, *and* its depth averages 8 feet.

TO   This river, *which* is 60 miles long and averages 50 yards in width, has an average depth of 8 feet.

OR   This river is 60 miles long. It averages 50 yards in width and 8 feet in depth.

Although too many short sentences make your writing sound choppy and immature, a short sentence can be effective at the end of a passage of long ones.

EXAMPLE   I believe that man is about to learn that the most practical life is the moral life and that the moral life is the only road to survival. He is beginning to learn that he will either share part of his material wealth or lose all of it; that he will respect and learn to live with other political ideologies if he wants civilization to go on. This is the kind of argument that man's actual experience equips him to understand and accept. This is the low road to morality. *There is no other.*[3]

In general, short sentences are good for emphatic statements. Long sentences are good for detailed explanations and support. Nothing is wrong with a long sentence, or even with a complicated one, as long as its meaning is clear and direct. A sentence that is either noticeably short or noticeably long can be used to good effect because its length will draw the reader's attention. When varied for emphasis or contrast, sentence length becomes an element of style.

(e)   Word order.   When successive sentences all begin in exactly the same way, the result is likely to be monotonous. You can make your sentences more interesting by occasionally starting with a modifying word, phrase, or clause.

EXAMPLES   *Fatigued,* the project director slumped into a chair. (adjective)

Lately, our division has been very productive. (adverb)

Smiling, he extended his hand to the irate customer. (participle)

To learn, you must observe and ask questions. (infinitive)

Work having already begun, there was little we could do. (absolute construction)

In the morning, we will finish the report. (prepositional phrase)

[3] Saul Alinsky, *Rules for Radicals* (New York: Random House, 1971), p. 25.

Following the instructions in the manual, she located and repaired the faulty parts. (participial phrase)

To reach the top job, she introduced constructive alternatives to unsuccessful policies. (infinitive phrase)

Because we now know the results of the survey, we may proceed with certainty. (adverb clause)

Overdoing this technique can also be monotonous; use it with moderation.

Be careful in your sentences to avoid confusing separations of subjects and verbs, prepositions and objects, and the parts of verb phrases. Your reader expects the usual patterns and reads more quickly and easily when they are clear.

REVISE   The manager worked closely with, despite personality differences, the head engineer. (preposition and object separated)

TO   Despite personality differences, the manager worked closely with the head engineer.

This is not to say, however, that subject and verb never should be separated by a modifying phrase or clause.

EXAMPLE   John Stoddard, who founded the firm in 1943, is still an active partner.

Vary the positions of modifiers in your sentences to achieve variety as well as different emphases or meanings. The following examples illustrate four different ways in which the same sentence could be written by varying the position of its modifiers.

REVISE   Gently, with the square end up, slip the blasting cap down over the time fuse.

TO   With the square end up, gently slip the blasting cap down over the time fuse.

OR   With the square end up, slip the blasting cap gently down over the time fuse.

OR   With the square end up, slip the blasting cap down over the time fuse gently.

(f)   Loose and periodic sentences. A loose sentence makes its major point at the beginning and then adds subordinate phrases and clauses that develop the major point. You express yourself most naturally and easily in this pattern. A loose sentence could seem to end at one or more points before it actually ends, as the periods in parentheses illustrate in the following example.

EXAMPLE   It went up (.), a great ball of fire about a mile in diameter(.), an elemental force freed from its bonds(.) after being chained for billions of years.

A compound sentence is generally classed as loose since it could end after its first independent clause.

EXAMPLE   Copernicus is frequently called the first modern astronomer, since he was the first to develop a complete astronomical system based on the motion of the earth.

Complex sentences are loose if their subordinate clauses follow their main clauses.

EXAMPLE   The installation will not be completed on schedule(.) because heavy spring rains delayed construction.

A periodic sentence delays its main idea until the end by presenting subordinate ideas or modifiers first. Skillfully handled, a periodic sentence lends force, or emphasis, to the main point by arousing the reader's anticipation and then presenting the main point as a climax.

EXAMPLE   During the last decade or so, the attitude of the American citizen toward automation has undergone a profound change.

Do not use periodic sentences too frequently, however, for overuse may irritate a reader who tires of waiting for your point. Likewise, avoid the sing-song monotony of a long series of loose sentences, particularly a series containing coordinate clauses joined by conjunctions. Instead, experiment in your writing, especially during revision, with shifts from loose sentences to periodic sentences.

4.4   PARAGRAPHS

A paragraph is a group of sentences that supports and develops a single idea. Like an essay in miniature, it expands upon the central idea stated in its topic sentence (*italicized* below).

> *The arithmetic of searching for oil is stark.* For all his scientific methods of detection, the only way the oilman can actually know for sure that there is oil in the ground is to drill a well. The average cost of drilling an oil well is over $100,000, and drilling a single well may cost over $1,000,000! And once the well is drilled, the odds against its containing any oil at all are 8 to 1![4]

Paragraphs perform three essential functions: (1) they develop the central ideas stated in their topic sentences; (2) they break material

---

[4] *The Baker World*, Baker Oil Tools, Inc.

into logical units; and (3) they create physical breaks on the page, which visually assist the reader.

4.4.1   Topic Sentences

A topic sentence states the central idea of a paragraph; the rest of the paragraph then supports and develops that statement with pertinent details.

The topic sentence is most often the first sentence of the paragraph. It is effective in this position because it lets the reader know immediately what subject the paragraph will develop.

> *The fundamental conception of statistics is that of an infinitely large series of measurements, or population.* Since all observable data is subject to influence by uncontrollable and variable change factors, the values recorded in a series of measurements exhibit corresponding variations. If the mean value is calculated the individual values will be seen to be more or less closely distributed around it. Since the chance factors operate equally in a positive or negative fashion, the distribution is symmetrical. The larger the number of measurements the closer will mean value approach the "true" value of the measured object. Only with an infinite number of measurements, however, will it be identical with the "true" value.[5]

On rare occasions, the topic sentence logically falls in the middle of a paragraph.

> It is perhaps natural that psychologists should awaken only slowly to the possibility that behavioral processes may be directly observed, or that they should only gradually put the older statistical and theoretical techniques in their proper perspective. But it is time to insist that science does not progress by carefully designed steps called "experiments," each of which has a well-defined beginning and end. *Science is a continuous and often a disorderly and accidental process.* We shall not do the young psychologist any favor if we agree to reconstruct our practices to fit the pattern demanded by current scientific methodology. What the statistician means by the design of experiments is design which yields the kind of data to which *his* techniques are applicable. He does not mean the behavior of the scientist in his laboratory devising research for his own immediate and possibly inscrutable purposes.[6]

[5] *Documenta Geigy,* 5th ed. (Ardsley, N.Y.: Geigy Pharmaceuticals, 1956), p. 31.

[6] B. F. Skinner, "A Case History in Scientific Method," *American Psychologist* 2 (May 1956), p. 232.

Although the topic sentence is usually most effective early in the paragraph, a paragraph can lead up to the topic sentence to achieve emphasis. When a topic sentence ends a paragraph, it also can serve as a summary or conclusion, based on the details that were designed to lead up to it.

> Energy does far more than simply make our daily lives more comfortable and convenient. Suppose you wanted to stop—and re-verse—the economic progress of this nation. What would be the surest and quickest way to do it? Find a way to cut off the nation's oil resources! Industrial plants would shut down; public utilities would stand idle; all forms of transportation would halt. The country would be paralyzed, and our economy would plummet into the abyss of national economic ruin. *Our economy, in short, is energy-based.*[7]

Because several paragraphs are sometimes necessary to develop different aspects of an idea, not all paragraphs have topic sentences. In this situation, transitions between paragraphs are especially important so the reader knows that the same idea is being developed through several paragraphs.

> *To conserve valuable memory space, a large portion of the software package remains on disk; only the most frequently used portion resides in internal memory all of the time.* The disk-resident software is organized into small modules that are called into memory as needed to perform specific functions.
>
> **Transition** *The disk-resident portion* of the operating system contains routines that are used less frequently in system operation, such as peripheral-related software routines that are used for correcting errors encountered on the various units, and the log and display routines that record unusual operating conditions in the system log. The disk-resident portion of the operating system also contains Monitor, the software program that supervised the loading of utility routines and the user's programs.
>
> **Transition** *The memory-resident portion* of the operating system maintains strict control of processing. It consists of routines, subroutines, lists, and tables that are used to perform common program functions, such as processing input/output operations, calling other software routines from disk as needed, and processing errors.[8]

In this example, the idea expressed in the topic sentence is developed in three paragraphs, rather than one, so that the reader can more easily assimilate the two separate parts of the main idea.

---

[7] *The Baker World,* Baker Oil Tools, Inc.

[8] *NCR Century Operating Systems Manual,* NCR Corporation.

4.4.2   Paragraph Coherence and Unity

A good paragraph has unity and coherence. Unity means singleness of purpose, based on a topic sentence that states the central idea of the paragraph. When every sentence in the paragraph contributes to the central idea, the paragraph has unity. Coherence means being logically consistent throughout the paragraph so that all parts naturally connect with one another. Coherence is advanced by carefully chosen transitional words that tie together ideas as they are developed. In the following paragraph, the topic sentence and the transitions are italicized.

> *Any company which operates internationally today faces a host of difficulties.* Inflation is worldwide. Most countries are struggling with *other* economic problems *as well. In addition,* there are many monetary uncertainties and growing economic nationalism directed against multinational companies. *Yet* there is ample business available in most developed countries if you have the right products, services, and marketing organization. To maintain the growth NCR has achieved overseas, we recently restructured our international operations into four major trading areas. *This* will improve the services and support which the Corporation can provide to its subsidiaries around the world. *At the same time* it established firm management control, insuring consistent policies around the world. *So* you might say the problems of doing business abroad will be more difficult this year but we are better organized to meet those problems.[9]

A good paragraph often uses details from the preceding paragraph, thereby preserving and advancing the thought being developed. Appropriate conjunctions and the repetition of key words and phrases can help to provide unity and coherence among, as well as within, paragraphs.

> Six high power thyristors connected in a three-phase bridge configuration form the basic armature module. When necessary, the modules are paralleled to meet higher power requirements. The basic armature module is constructed as a convenient *pull-out tray.* All *armature trays* are interchangeable.
>
> For optimum shovel performance it is also desirable to use thyristors in the control of motor fields. These smaller thyristors are also arranged in a *pull-out tray* arrangement called a *field tray.*
>
> Should a fault ever occur in a tray, an *indicator tray* is provided, which by means of pilot lights indicates which tray is the source of the trouble. Through the *pull-out* tray concept, the mine electrician can quickly replace the faulty tray and need not troubleshoot.[10]

[9] *1974 Annual Report,* NCR Corporation.
[10] Harnischfeger Corporation.

5 PUNCTUATION

Punctuation is a system of symbols that help the reader to understand the structural relationships within (and the intention of) a sentence. Marks of punctuation may link, separate, enclose, terminate, classify, and indicate omissions from sentences. Most of the 13 punctuation marks can perform more than one function. The use of punctuation is determined by grammatical conventions and by the writer's intention. Misuse of punctuation can cause your reader to misunderstand your meaning. The following are the 13 marks of punctuation.

apostrophe	'
brackets	[ ]
colon	:
comma	,
dash	—
exclamation mark	!
hyphen	-
parentheses	( )
period	. (including ellipses and leaders)
question mark	?
quotation marks	" " (including ditto marks)
semicolon	;
slash	/

5.1 COMMAS

The comma is used more often than any other mark of punctuation because it has such a wide variety of uses: it can link, enclose, separate, and show omissions. Effective use of the comma depends on your understanding of how ideas fit together. Used with care, the comma can add clarity and emphasis to your writing; used carelessly, it can cause confusion.

5.1.1 To Link

Coordinating conjunctions (*and, but, for, or, so, nor, yet*) require a comma immediately preceding them when they are used to connect independent clauses.

EXAMPLE   Human beings have always prided themselves on their unique capacity to create and manipulate symbols, but today computers are manipulating symbols.

Exceptions to this rule sometimes occur when the two independent clauses are short and each has a single subject and single predicate. However, even in such cases, a comma is preferred.

EXAMPLE   The cable snapped and the power failed.

BETTER   The cable snapped, and the power failed.

5.1.2 To Enclose

(a) **Nonrestrictive and parenthetical elements.** Commas are used to enclose nonrestrictive and parenthetical sentence elements. Nonrestrictive elements provide additional, nonessential information about the things they modify; parenthetical elements also insert extra information into the sentence. Each is set off by commas to show its loose relationship with the rest of the sentence.

EXAMPLES   Our new Detroit factory, *which began operations last month,* should add 25 percent to total output. (nonrestrictive clause)

We can, *of course,* expect their lawyer to call us. (parenthetical element)

Similarly, commas enclose nonrestrictive participial phrases.

EXAMPLE   The lathe operator, *working quickly and efficiently,* finished early.

In contrast, restrictive elements—as their name implies—restrict the meaning of the words to which they apply and cannot be set off with commas.

RESTRICTIVE The boy *in the front row* is six years old.

NON-
RESTRICTIVE The boy, *who is sitting in the front row,* is six years old.

In the first sentence, *in the front row* is essential to the sentence: the phrase identifies the boy. In the second sentence, the nonrestrictive relative clause *who is sitting in the front row* is incidental: the main idea of the sentence can be communicated without it.

Phrases in apposition (which are nonrestrictive and follow and amplify an essential element) are enclosed in commas.

EXAMPLE   Our company, *the Blaylok Precision Company,* is doing well this year.

(b) **Dates.** When complete dates appear with sentences, the year is enclosed in commas.

EXAMPLE   On November 11, 1918, the Armistice went into effect.

However, when only part of a date appears, do not use commas.

EXAMPLE   In November 1918 the Armistice went into effect.

When the day of the week is included in a date, the month and the number of the day are enclosed in commas.

EXAMPLE   On Friday, November 11, 1918, the Armistice went into effect.

(c) **Direct address.** A direct address should be enclosed in commas if it appears anywhere other than at the beginning or end of a sentence.

EXAMPLE   You will note, *Mark,* that the surface of the brake shoe complies with the specifications.

5.1.3 To Separate

Commas are used to separate introductory elements from the rest of the sentence, to separate items from each other, to separate subordinate clauses from main clauses, and to separate certain elements for clarity or emphasis.

(a) **To separate introductory elements.** In general, use a comma after an introductory clause or phrase unless it is very short. This comma helps indicate to a reader where the main part of the sentence begins.

EXAMPLE   *Since many rare fossils never occur free from their matrix,* it is wise to scan every slab with a hand lens.

When long modifying phrases precede the main clause, they should always be followed by a comma.

EXAMPLE   *During the first field-performance tests last year at our Colorado proving ground,* the new motor failed to meet our expectations.

When an introductory phrase is short and closely related to the main clause, the comma may be omitted.

EXAMPLE   *In two seconds* a 20° temperature rise occurs in the test tube.

Certain types of introductory words must be followed by a comma. One such is a name used in direct address at the beginning of a sentence.

EXAMPLE   *Bill,* here is the statement you asked me to audit.

A mild introductory interjection (such as *oh, well, why, indeed, yes,* and *no*) must be followed by a comma.

EXAMPLES   *Yes,* I will make sure your request is approved.

Indeed, I will be glad to send you further information.

An introductory adverb, like *moreover* or *furthermore,* must be followed by a comma.

EXAMPLE   *Moreover,* this policy will improve our balance of payments.

Occasionally, when adverbs are closely connected to the meaning of an entire sentence, they should not be followed by a comma. (Test such sentences by reading them aloud. If you pause after the adverb, use the comma.)

EXAMPLE   *Perhaps* we can still solve the environmental problem. *Certainly* we should try.

(b)   **To separate items from each other.**   Commas should be used to separate words in a series.

EXAMPLE   Basically, plants control the wind by *obstruction, guidance, deflection,* and *filtration.*

Phrases and clauses in coordinate series, like words, are punctuated with commas.

EXAMPLE   It is well known that plants absorb noxious gases, act as receptors of dust and dirt particles, and cleanse the air of other impurities.

Although the comma before the last item in a series is sometimes omitted, it is generally clearer to include it. The following sentence illustrates the confusion that may result from omitting the comma.

EXAMPLE   Random House, Houghton Mifflin, Doubleday and Dell are publishing companies. (Is "Doubleday and Dell" one company or two? "Random House, Houghton Mifflin, Doubleday, and Dell" removes the doubt.)

When adjectives modifying the same noun can be reversed and make sense, or when they can be separated by *and* or *or,* they should be separated by commas.

EXAMPLE   The *dull, cracked* tools needed to be repaired.

When an adjective modifies a noun phrase, no comma is required.

EXAMPLE   He was investigating the *damaged radar beacon system.* (*damaged* modifies the noun phrase *radar beacon system*)

Never separate a final adjective from its noun.

REVISE   He is a conscientious, honest, reliable, worker.

TO   He is a conscientious, honest, reliable worker.

Commas are conventionally used to separate distinct items. Use commas between the elements of an address written on the same line.

EXAMPLE   Walter James, 4119 Mill Road, Dayton, Ohio 45401

Use a comma to separate the numerical elements of a complete date. When the day is omitted, however, the comma is unnecessary. (When a date appears in a sentence, a comma also follows the year. See Section 5.1.2b.)

EXAMPLES   July 2, 1949

                July 1949

Use commas to separate the elements of Arabic numbers.

EXAMPLE   1,528,200

Use a comma after the salutation of a personal letter.

EXAMPLE   Dear John,

Use commas to separate the elements of geographical names.

EXAMPLE   Toronto, Ontario, Canada

Use a comma to separate names that are reversed.

EXAMPLE   Smith, Alvin

(c) **To separate subordinate clauses.** Use a comma between the main clause and a subordinate clause when the subordinate clause comes first.

EXAMPLE   While the test ramp was being checked a final time, the driver reviewed his checklist.

Use a comma following an independent clause that is only loosely related to the dependent clause that follows it.

EXAMPLE   The plan should be finished by July, even though I lost time because of illness.

(d) **To separate elements for clarity or emphasis.** Two contrasting thoughts or ideas can be separated by commas for emphasis.

EXAMPLES   The project was finished on time, but not within the cost limits.

                The specifications call for 100-ohm resistors, not 1,000-ohm resistors.

It was Bill, not Matt, who suggested that the names be changed.

Use a comma to separate a direct quotation from its introduction.

EXAMPLE   Morton and Lucia White said, "Men live in cities but dream of the countryside."

Do not use a comma, however, when giving an indirect quotation.

EXAMPLE   Morton and Lucia White said that men dream of the country-side even though they live in cities.

Sometimes commas are used simply to make something clear that might otherwise be confusing.

REVISE   The year after Xerox and 3M outproduced all the competition.

TO   The year after, Xerox and 3M outproduced all the competition.

If you need a comma to separate two consecutive uses of the same word, rewrite the sentence.

REVISE   The assets we had, had surprised us.

TO   We were surprised at the assets we had.

5.1.4   To Show Omissions

In certain coordinate constructions, a comma can replace a missing, but implied, sentence element.

EXAMPLE   Some were punctual; others, late. (comma replaces *were*)

5.1.5   Conventional Use with Other Punctuation

In American usage, a comma always goes inside quotation marks.

EXAMPLE   Although he called his presentation "adequate," the audience thought it was superb.

Except with abbreviations, a comma should not be used with a period, question mark, exclamation mark, or dash.

REVISE   "I have finished the project.," he said.

TO   "I have finished the project," he said. (omit the period)

REVISE   "Have you finished the project?," I asked.

TO   "Have you finished the project?" I asked. (omit the comma)

5.1.6   Comma Problems

The most frequent comma problems are the comma fault and the use of superfluous commas.

(a)   Comma faults.   Do not attempt to join two independent clauses with only a comma; this is called a "comma fault" or "comma splice." (See also Section 4.3.4b.)

REVISE   The new medical plan was comprehensive, the union ne-gotiator was pleased.

Such a comma fault could be corrected in several ways:

Substitute a semicolon.

TO   The new medical plan was comprehensive; the union ne-gotiator was pleased.

Add a conjunctive adverb preceded by a semicolon and followed by a comma.

TO   The new medical plan was comprehensive; *therefore,* the union negotiator was pleased.

Add a conjunction following the comma.

TO   The new medical plan was comprehensive, *so* the union nego-tiator was pleased.

Create two sentences. (Be aware, however, that putting a period between two closely related and brief statements may result in two weak sen-tences.)

TO   The new medical plan was comprehensive. The union negoti-ator was pleased.

Subordinate one clause to the other.

TO   *Because* the new medical plan was comprehensive, the union negotiator was pleased.

(b)   Superfluous commas.   A number of common writing errors involve placing commas where they do not belong. These errors often occur be-cause writers assume that a pause in a sentence should be indicated by a comma. It is true that commas usually signal pauses, but it is not true that pauses *necessarily* call for commas.

Be careful not to place a comma between a subject and its verb or between a verb and its object.

REVISE   The extremely wet weather throughout the country, makes spring planting difficult.

TO   The extremely wet weather throughout the country makes spring planting difficult.

REVISE   The advertising department employs, four writers, two artists, and one photographer.

TO   The advertising department employs four writers, two artists, and one photographer.

Do not use a comma between the elements of a compound subject or a compound predicate consisting of only two elements.

REVISE   The chairman of the board, and the president prepared the press release.

TO   The chairman of the board and the president prepared the press release.

REVISE   The production manager revised the work schedules, and improved morale.

TO   The production manager revised the work schedules and improved morale.

Placing a comma after a coordinating conjunction (such as *and* or *but*) is an especially common error.

REVISE   We doubled our sales, and, we reduced our costs.

TO   We doubled our sales, and we reduced our costs.

REVISE   We doubled our sales, but, we still did not dominate the market.

TO   We doubled our sales, but we still did not dominate the market.

Do not place a comma before the first item or after the last item of a series.

REVISE   We are purchasing new office furniture, including, desks, chairs, and tables.

TO   We are purchasing new office furniture, including desks, chairs, and tables.

5.2   SEMICOLONS

The semicolon (;) links independent clauses or other sentence elements that are of equal weight and grammatical rank. The semicolon indicates a greater pause between clauses than a comma would, but not so great a pause as a period would.

When the independent clauses of a compound sentence are not joined by a comma and a conjunction, they are linked by a semicolon.

EXAMPLE   No one applied for the position; the job was too difficult.

Make sure, however, that the relationship between the two statements is so clear that a reader will understand why they are linked without further explanation. Often, such clauses balance or contrast with each other.

EXAMPLE   Our last supervisor allowed only one long break each afternoon; our new supervisor allows two short ones.

Use a semicolon between two main clauses connected by a coordinating conjunction (*and, but, for, or, nor, yet*) if the clauses are long and contain other punctuation.

EXAMPLE   In most cases these individuals are corporate executives, bankers, Wall Street lawyers; but they do not, as the economic determinists seem to believe, simply push the button of their economic power to affect fields remote from economics.[11]

A semicolon should be used before conjunctive adverbs (such as *therefore, moreover, consequently, furthermore, indeed, in fact, however*) that connect independent clauses.

EXAMPLE   I won't finish today; moreover, I doubt that I will finish this week.

The semicolon in this example shows that *moreover* belongs to the second clause.

Do not use a semicolon between a dependent clause and its main clause. Remember that elements joined by semicolons must be of equal grammatical rank or weight.

REVISE   No one applied for the position; even though it was heavily advertised.

TO   No one applied for the position, even though it was heavily advertised.

A semicolon may also be used to separate items in a series when they contain commas within them.

EXAMPLE   Among those present were John Howard, president of the Omega Paper Company; Carol Martin, president of Alpha Corporation; and Larry Stanley, president of Stanley Papers.

[11] Robert Lubar, "The Prime Movers," *Fortune* (February 1960), p. 98.

5.3 COLONS

The colon (:) is a mark of anticipation and introduction that alerts the reader to the close connection between the first statement and the one following. A colon may be used to connect a clause, word, or phrase to the list or series that follows it.

EXAMPLE   We carry three brands of watches: Timex, Bulova, and Omega.

A colon may be used to introduce a list.

EXAMPLE   The following corporations manufacture computers:

Control Data Corporation
NCR Corporation
Burroughs

Do not, however, place a colon between a verb and its objects.

REVISE   The three fluids for cleaning pipettes are: water, alcohol, and acetone.

TO   The three fluids for cleaning pipettes are water, alcohol, and acetone.

Do not use a colon between a preposition and its object.

REVISE   I would like to be transferred to: Tucson, Boston, or Miami.

TO   I would like to be transferred to Tucson, Boston, or Miami.

A colon may be used to link one statement to another that develops, explains, amplifies, or illustrates the first. A colon can be used in this way to link two independent clauses.

EXAMPLE   Any large organization must confront two separate, though related, information problems: it must maintain an effective internal communication system, and it must maintain an effective external communication system.

Occasionally, a colon may be used to link an appositive phrase to its related statement if special emphasis is needed.

EXAMPLE   Only one thing will satisfy Mr. Sturgess: our finished report.

Colons are used to link numbers in Biblical references and time designations.

EXAMPLES   Genesis 10:16 (refers to chapter 10, verse 16)

9:30 A.M.

In a ratio, the colon indicates the proportion of one amount to another. (The colon replaces *to*.)

EXAMPLE The cement is mixed with the water and sand at a ratio of 7:5:14.

7:3 = 14:6

A colon follows the salutation in business letters, as opposed to personal letters, where a comma may be used.

EXAMPLES Dear Ms. Jeffers:

Dear Sir:

Dear George:

The first word after a colon may be capitalized if the statement following is a complete sentence, a formal resolution or question, or a direct quotation.

EXAMPLE This year's conference attendance was low: We did not advertise widely enough.

If a subordinate element follows the colon, however, use a lowercase letter following the colon.

EXAMPLE There is only one way to stay within our present budget: to reduce expenditures for research and development.

5.4 PERIODS

A period (.) usually indicates the end of a declarative sentence. Periods also link (when used as leaders) and indicate omissions (when used as ellipses).

5.4.1 Uses of Periods

Although their primary function is to end declarative sentences, periods also end imperative sentences that are not emphatic enough for an exclamation mark.

EXAMPLE Send me any information you may have on the subject.

Periods may occasionally end questions that are really polite requests and questions that assume an affirmative response.

EXAMPLE Will you please send me the specifications.

Periods end minor sentences (deliberate sentence fragments). These sentences are common in advertising but are rarely appropriate to business or technical writing.

EXAMPLE   Bell and Howell's new Double-Feature Cassette Projector will change your mind about home movies. *Because if you can press a button, now you can show movies. Instantly. Easily.*

Do not use a period after a declarative sentence that is quoted within another sentence.

REVISE   "The project has every chance of success." she stated.

TO   "The project has every chance of success," she stated.

A period, in American usage, is placed inside quotation marks.

EXAMPLES   He liked to think of himself as a "tycoon."

He stated clearly, "My vote is yes."

Use periods after initials in names.

EXAMPLES   W. T. Grant, J. P. Morgan

Use periods as decimal points with numbers.

EXAMPLES   109.2, $540.26, 6.9%

Use periods to indicate abbreviations.

EXAMPLES   Ms., Dr., Inc.

Use periods following the numbers in numbered lists.

EXAMPLE   1.
2.
3.

5.4.2   Periods as Ellipses

When you omit words from quoted material, use a series of three spaced periods—called ellipsis marks—to indicate the omission. Such an omission must not change the essential meaning of the passage.

EXAMPLES   "Technical material distributed for promotional use is sometimes charged for, particularly in high-volume distribution to educational institutions, although prices for these publications are not uniformly based on the costs of developing them." (without omission)

"Technical material distributed for promotional use is sometimes charged for . . . although prices for these publications
are not uniformly based on the costs of developing them."
(with omission)

When introducing a quotation that begins in the middle of a sentence
rather than at the beginning, you do not need ellipsis marks; the lowercase
letter with which you begin the quotation already indicates an omission.

EXAMPLES "When the programmer has determined a system of runs,
he must create a systems flowchart to trace the data flow
through the system." (without omission)

The booklet states that the programmer "must create a systems flowchart to trace the data flow through the system."
(with omission)

If there is an omission following the end of a sentence, retain the period
at the end of the sentence and add the three ellipsis marks to show the
omission.

EXAMPLES "During the year, every department participated in the development of a centralized computer system. The basic plan
was to use the computer to reduce costs. At the beginning
of the year, each department received a booklet explaining
the purpose of the system." (without omission)

"During the year, every department participated in the development of a centralized computer system. . . . At the
beginning of the year, each department received a booklet
explaining the purpose of the system." (with omission)

5.4.3 Periods as Leaders

When spaced periods are used in a table to connect one item to
another, they are called leaders. The purpose of leaders is to help the
reader align the data.

EXAMPLE

Weight	Pressure
150 lbs.	1.7 psi
175 lbs.	2.8 psi
200 lbs.	3.9 psi

5.4.4 Period Fault

The incorrect use of a period is sometimes called a period fault.
When a period is inserted prematurely, the result is a sentence fragment.
(See Section 4.3.4c.)

REVISE   After a long day at the office during which we finished the report. We left hurriedly for home.

TO   After a long day at the office during which we finished the report, we left hurriedly for home.

When a period is left out, the result is an incorrect fused (or run-on) sentence.

REVISE   The work plan showed the utility lines they might interfere with construction.

TO   The work plan showed the utility lines. They might interfere with construction.

5.5 QUESTION MARKS

The question mark (?) indicates questions. Use a question mark to end a sentence that is a direct question.

EXAMPLE   Where did you put the specifications?

Use a question mark to end any statement with an interrogative meaning (a statement that is declarative in form but asks a question).

EXAMPLE   The report is finished?

Use a question mark to end an interrogative clause within a declarative sentence.

EXAMPLE   It was not until July (or was it August?) that we submitted the report.

When used with quotations, the question mark may indicate whether the writer who is doing the quoting or the person being quoted is asking the question. When the writer doing the quoting asks the question, the question mark is outside the quotation marks.

EXAMPLE   Did she say, "I don't think the project should continue"?

On the other hand, if the quotation itself is a question, the question mark goes inside the quotation marks.

EXAMPLE   She asked, "When will we go?"

If the writer doing the quoting and the person being quoted both ask questions, use a single question mark inside the quotation marks.

EXAMPLE   Did she ask, "Will you go in my place?"

Question marks may follow each item in a series within an interrogative sentence.

EXAMPLE   Do you remember the date of the contract? its terms? whether you signed it?

A question mark should never be used at the end of an indirect question.

REVISE   He asked me whether sales had increased this year?
TO   He asked me whether sales had increased this year.

When a directive or command is phrased as a question, a question mark usually is not used, but a request (to a customer or a superior, for instance) would almost always require a question mark.

EXAMPLES   Will you please make sure that the machinery is operational by August 15. (directive)

Will you please telephone me collect if your entire shipment does not arrive by June 10? (request)

5.6   EXCLAMATION MARKS

The exclamation mark (!) indicates an expression of strong feeling. It can signal surprise, fear, indignation, or excitement but should not be used for trivial emotions or mild surprise. Exclamation marks cannot make an argument more convincing, lend force to a weak statement, or call attention to an intended irony—no matter how many are stacked like fence posts at the end of a sentence.

The most common use of an exclamation mark is after an interjection, phrase, clause, or sentence to indicate strong emotion.

EXAMPLES   Ouch! Oh! Stop! Hurry!

The subject of this meeting—note it well!—is our budget deficit.

The gas line is leaking! Clear the building!

When used with quotation marks, the exclamation mark goes outside unless what is quoted is an exclamation.

EXAMPLE   The boss yelled, "Get in here!" Then Ben said, "No, sir"! (Ben's statement was not emphatic; the writer is highlighting the unusual nature of his negative reply)

5.7   PARENTHESES

Parentheses ( ) are used to enclose words, phrases, or sentences. Parentheses can suggest intimacy, implying that something is shared between the writer and the reader. Parentheses deemphasize (or play down) an inserted element. The material within parentheses can clarify a statement without changing its meaning. Such information may not be essential to a sentence, but it may be interesting or helpful to some readers.

EXAMPLE   Aluminum is extracted from its ore (called bauxite) in three stages.

Parenthetical material pertains to the word or phrase immediately preceding it.

EXAMPLE   The development of IBM (International Business Machines) is an American success story.

Parentheses may be used to enclose the figures or letters that mark items in a sequence or list. When they appear within a sentence, enclose the figures or letters with two parentheses rather than only one parenthesis.

EXAMPLE   The following sections deal with (1) preparation, (2) research, (3) organization, (4) writing, and (5) revision.

Parenthetical material does not change the punctuation of a sentence. A comma following a parenthetical word, phrase, or clause appears outside the closing parenthesis.

EXAMPLE   These oxygen-rich chemicals, including potassium permanganate ($KMnO_4$) and potassium chromate ($KCrO_4$), were oxidizing agents.

If a parenthesis closes a sentence, the ending punctuation appears after the parenthesis. When a complete sentence within parentheses stands independently, however, the ending punctuation goes inside the final parenthesis.

EXAMPLES   The institute was founded by Harry Denman (1902–1972).

The project director outlined the challenges facing her staff. (This was her third report to the board.)

Use parentheses with care because they are easily overused. Avoid using parentheses where other marks of punctuation are more appropriate.

5.8 HYPHENS

The hyphen (-) functions primarily as a spelling device. The most common use of the hyphen is to join compound words. Check your dictionary if you are uncertain about whether to hyphenate a word.

EXAMPLES   able-bodied, self-contained, carry-all, brother-in-law

A hyphen is used to form compound numbers and fractions when they are written out.

EXAMPLES   twenty-one, one-fifth

Two-word and three-word unit modifiers that express a single thought are frequently hyphenated when they precede a noun (a *clear-cut* decision). If each of the words could modify the noun without the aid of the other modifying word or words, however, do not use a hyphen (a *new digital* computer—no hyphen). If the first word is an adverb ending in *-ly,* do not use a hyphen (*hardly* used, *badly* needed). Finally, do not hyphenate such modifying phrases when they follow the nouns they modify.

EXAMPLES   Our office equipment is *out of date.*

Our *out-of-date* office equipment will be replaced next month.

A hyphen is always used as part of a letter or number modifier.

EXAMPLES   15-cent stamp, 9-inch ruler, H-bomb, T-square

When each item in a series of unit modifiers has the same term following the hyphen, this term need not be repeated throughout the series. For smoothness and brevity, add the term only to the last item in the sequence.

REVISE   The third-floor, fourth-floor, and fifth-floor offices have been painted.

TO   The third-, fourth-, and fifth-floor offices have been painted.

When a prefix precedes a proper noun, use a hyphen to connect the two.

EXAMPLES   pre-Sputnik, anti-Stalinist, post-Newtonian

A hyphen may (but does not have to) be used when the prefix ends and the root word begins with the same vowel. When the repeated vowel is *i,* a hyphen is almost always used.

EXAMPLES   re-elect, re-enter, anti-inflationary

A hyphen is used when ex- means "former."

EXAMPLES   ex-partners, ex-wife

The suffix *-elect* is connected to the word it follows with a hyphen.

EXAMPLES   president-elect, commissioner-elect

Hyphens identify prefixes, suffixes, or syllables written as such.

EXAMPLE   *Re-, -ism,* and *ex-* are word parts that cause spelling problems.

Hyphens should be used between letters showing how a word is spelled (or misspelled).

EXAMPLE   In his letter, he spelled "believed" b-e-l-e-i-v-e-d.

To avoid confusion, some words and modifiers should always be hyphenated. *Re-cover* does not mean the same thing as *recover,* for example; the same is true of *re-sent* and *resent, re-form* and *reform, re-sign* and *resign.*

A hyphen can stand for *to* or *through* between letters, numbers, and locations.

EXAMPLES   pp. 44-46

The Detroit-Toledo Expressway

A-L and M-Z

Finally, hyphens are used to divide words at the ends of typed or printed lines. Words are divided on the basis of their syllable breaks, which can be determined by consulting a dictionary. If you cannot check a word in a dictionary, pronounce the word to test whether each section is pronounceable. Never divide a word so near the end that only one or two letters remain to begin your next typed line. If a word is spelled with a hyphen, divide it only at the hyphen break unless this division would confuse the reader. In general, unless the length of your typed line will appear awkward, avoid dividing words.

5.9   QUOTATION MARKS

Quotation marks (" ") are used to enclose direct repetition of spoken or written words. Under normal circumstances, they should not be used to show emphasis. Enclose in quotation marks anything that is quoted word for word (direct quotation) from speech.

EXAMPLE   She said clearly, "I want the progress report by three o'clock."

Do not enclose indirect quotations—usually introduced by *that*—in quotation marks. Indirect quotations paraphrase a speaker's words or ideas.

EXAMPLE   She said that she wanted the progress report by three o'clock.

Handle quotations from written material the same way: place direct quotations within quotation marks, but not indirect quotations.

EXAMPLES   The report stated, "During the last five years in Florida, our franchise has grown from 28 to 157 locations."

The report indicated that our franchise now has 157 locations in Florida.

Material quoted directly and enclosed in quotation marks cannot be changed from the original unless you so indicate by the use of information in brackets. See Section 5.13 for how to use brackets.

When a quotation is longer than four typed lines, indent each line ten spaces from the left margin. Do not enclose the quotation in quotation marks.

Use single quotation marks (the apostrophe key on a typewriter) to enclose a quotation that appears within another quotation.

EXAMPLE   John said, "Jane told me that she was going to 'hang in there' until the deadline is past."

Slang, colloquial expressions, and attempts at humor, although infrequent in business and technical writing in any case, seldom rate being set off by quotation marks.

REVISE   Our first six months in the new office amounted to little more than a "shakedown cruise" for what lay ahead.

TO   Our first six months in the new office amounted to little more than a shakedown cruise for what lay ahead.

Use quotation marks to point out that particular words or technical terms are used in context for a special purpose.

EXAMPLE   What chain of events caused an "unsinkable" ship like the *Titanic* to sink on its maiden voyage?

Use quotation marks to enclose titles of short stories, articles, essays, radio and television programs, short musical works, paintings, and other art works.

EXAMPLE   Did you see the article "No-Fault Insurance and Your Motor-cycle" in last Sunday's *Journal?*

Titles of books and periodicals are underlined (to be typeset in italics).

EXAMPLE   Articles in the <u>Business Education Forum</u> and <u>Scientific American</u> quoted the same passage.

Some titles, by convention, are neither set off by quotation marks nor underlined, although they are capitalized.

EXAMPLES   the Bible, the Constitution, the Gettysburg Address

Commas and periods always go inside closing quotation marks.

EXAMPLE   "We hope," said Ms. Abrams, "that the merger will be an-nounced this week."

Semicolons and colons always go outside closing quotation marks.

EXAMPLES He said, "I will pay the full amount"; this was a real surprise to us.

The following are his favorite "sports": eating and sleeping.

All other punctuation follows the logic of the context: if the punctuation is part of the material quoted, it goes inside the quotation marks; if the punctuation is not part of the material quoted, it goes outside the quotation marks.

Quotation marks may be used as ditto marks, instead of repeating a line of words or numbers directly beneath an identical set. In formal writing, this use is confined to tables and lists.

EXAMPLE A is at a point equally distant from L and M.
B " " " " " " " S and T.
C " " " " " " " R and Q.

5.10 DASHES

The dash (—) is a versatile, yet limited, mark of punctuation. It is versatile because it can perform all the functions of punctuation (to link, to separate, to enclose, and to show omission). It is limited because it is an especially emphatic mark that is easily overused. Use the dash cautiously, therefore, to indicate more informality, emphasis, or abruptness than the conventional punctuation marks would show. In some situations, a dash is required; in others, a dash is a forceful substitute for other marks.

A dash can indicate a sharp turn in thought.

EXAMPLE That is the end of the project—unless the company provides additional funds.

A dash can indicate an emphatic pause.

EXAMPLE Consider the potential danger of a household item that contains mercury—a very toxic substance.

Sometimes, to emphasize contrast, a dash is also used with *but*.

EXAMPLE We may have produced work more quickly—but our results have never been as impressive as these.

A dash can be used before a final summarizing statement or before repetition that has the effect of an afterthought.

EXAMPLE It was hot near the ovens—steaming hot.

Such a thought may also complete the meaning of the sentence.

EXAMPLE   We try to speak as we write—or so we believe.

A dash can be used to set off an explanatory or appositive series.

EXAMPLE   Three of the applicants—John Evans, Mary Stevens, and Thomas Brown—seem well qualified for the job.

Dashes set off parenthetical elements more sharply and emphatically than do commas. Unlike dashes, parentheses tend to reduce the importance of what they enclose. Contrast the following sentences.

EXAMPLES   Only one person—the president—can authorize such activity.

                  Only one person, the president, can authorize such activity.

                  Only one person (the president) can authorize such activity.

Use dashes for clarity when commas appear within a parenthetical element; this avoids the confusion of too many commas.

EXAMPLE   Retinal images are patterns in the eye—made up of light and dark shapes, in addition to areas of color—but we do not see patterns; we see objects.

A dash can be used to show the omission of words or letters.

EXAMPLE   Mr. A— told me to be careful.

The first word after a dash is never capitalized unless it is a proper noun. When typing, use two consecutive hyphens (--) to indicate a dash, with no spaces before or after the hyphens.

5.11 APOSTROPHES

The apostrophe (') is used to show possession, to mark the omission of letters, and sometimes to indicate the plural of arabic numbers, letters, and acronyms.

5.11.1 Possession

An apostrophe is used with an *s* to form the possessive case of many nouns. (See Section 3.1.3b.)

EXAMPLE   A recent scientific analysis of *New York City's* atmosphere concluded that a New Yorker on the street inhaled toxic materials equivalent to 38 cigarettes a day.

Singular nouns ending in *s* may form the possessive either by an apostrophe alone or by *'s*. The latter is now preferred.

EXAMPLES   a waitress's uniform, an actress's career

a waitress' uniform, an actress' career

Use only an apostrophe with plural nouns ending in *s*.

EXAMPLES   a managers' meeting, the technicians' handbook, a motorists' rest stop

When a noun ends in multiple consecutive *s* sounds, or when the word following the possessive begins with an *s*, the possessive is often formed by adding only an apostrophe. Your ear should tell you when you are stacking up too many sibilants.

EXAMPLES   Jesus' disciples, Moses' sojourn, for goodness' sake, Euripides' plays

With word groups and compound nouns, add the *'s* to the last noun.

EXAMPLES   The chairman of the board's statement was brief.

My daughter-in-law's business has been thriving.

With a series of nouns, the last noun takes the possessive form to show joint possession.

EXAMPLE   Michelson and *Morley's* famous experiment on the velocity of light was made in 1887.

To show individual possession with a series of nouns, each noun should take the possessive form.

EXAMPLE   *Bob's* and *Susan's* promotions will be announced Friday.

The apostrophe is not used with possessive pronouns. (*It's* is a contraction of *it is,* not the possessive form of *it.*)

EXAMPLES   yours, its, his, ours, whose, theirs

In names of places and institutions, the apostrophe is usually omitted.

EXAMPLES   Harpers Ferry, Writers Book Club

5.11.2 Omission

(a)   **Contractions.** An apostrophe is used to mark the omission of letters in a word. Omission of letters in a word and their replacement with an apostrophe produce a *contraction.* Contractions are most often shortened forms of the most common helping verbs. In addition, contractions can reflect negation, combining elements of the word *not* with elements of the helping verb (*don't* for *do not,* for example). Although contractions are in no sense wrong, they are less formal than the longer forms and should therefore be used with caution in writing.

(b)   Abbreviated dates.   An apostrophe can also stand for the first two digits of a year when these digits can be inferred from the context. This device is most common in alumni newsletters and in informal writing; it should be avoided in formal situations.

EXAMPLES   the class of '61

the crash of '29

5.11.3   Plurals

An apostrophe and an *s* may be added to show the plural of a word as a word. (The word itself is underlined or italicized to call attention to its use.)

EXAMPLE   There were five *and's* in his first sentence.

However, if a term consists entirely of capital letters or ends with a capital letter, the apostrophe is not required to form the plural.

EXAMPLES   The university awarded seven *Ph.D.s* in engineering last year.

He had included 43 *ADDs* in his computer program.

Do not use apostrophes to indicate the plural forms of letters and numbers unless confusion would result without one.

EXAMPLES   5s, 30s, two 100s, seven I's

5.12   SLASHES

Although not always considered a mark of punctuation, the slash (/) performs punctuating functions by separating and showing omission. The slash has various names: slant line, virgule, bar, shilling sign.

The slash is often used to separate parts of addresses in continuous writing.

EXAMPLE   The return address on the envelope was Ms. Rose Howard/ 62 W. Pacific Court/Claremont, California 91711.

The slash can indicate alternate items.

EXAMPLE   David's telephone number is (504) 549–2278/2335.

The slash often indicates omitted words and letters.

EXAMPLES   miles/hour (for "miles per hour")
c/o (for "in care of")
w/o (for "without")

The slash separates the numerator from the denominator of a fraction.

EXAMPLES   2/3 (2 of 3 parts); 3/4 (3 of 4 parts); 27/32 (27 of 32 parts)

In informal writing, the slash is also used in dates to separate day from month and month from year.

EXAMPLE   2/28/88

The slash is sometimes used to indicate brackets when a typewriter has no bracket key.

EXAMPLE   The reports stated that "the success of the affirmative action plan at the Westchester/New York/plant should be an inspiration for the industry."

The horizontal lines for the brackets are then penned in neatly.

5.13   BRACKETS

The primary use of brackets ([ ]) is to enclose a word or words inserted by an editor or writer into a quotation from another source.

EXAMPLE   He stated, "Wheat prices will continue to rise [no doubt because of the Russian wheat purchase] until next year."

Brackets are also used to set off a parenthetical item within parentheses.

EXAMPLE   We have all been inspired by the energy and creativity of our president, Roberta Jacobs (a tradition she carries forward from her father, Frederick Jacobs [1910–1966]).

6   MECHANICS

Certain mechanical questions tend to confound the writer on the job. Such questions as whether a number should be written as a word or as a figure, how and where acronyms should be used, whether a date should be stated day-month-year or month-day-year, and many others frequently arise when you are writing a letter or a report. This section of the Writer's Guide is provided to give you the answers to those and other perplexing questions concerning the mechanics of writing on the job.

6.1 NUMBERS

6.1.1 When to Write Out Numbers

The general rule is to write numbers from zero to ten as words and numbers above ten as figures. There are, however, a number of exceptions.

Page numbers of books, as well as figure and table numbers, are expressed as figures.

EXAMPLE   Figure 4 on page 9 and Table 3 on page 7 provide pertinent information.

Units of measurement are expressed in figures.

EXAMPLES   3 miles, 45 cubic feet, 9 meters, 27 cubic centimeters, 4 picas

Numbers that begin a sentence should always be spelled out, even if they would otherwise be written as figures.

EXAMPLE   One hundred and fifty people attended the meeting.

If spelling out such a number seems awkward, rewrite the sentence so that the number does not appear at the beginning.

REVISE   Two hundred seventy-three defective products were returned last month.

TO   Last month, 273 defective products were returned.

When several numbers appear in the same sentence or paragraph, they should be expressed alike regardless of other rules and guidelines.

EXAMPLE   The company owned 150 trucks, employed 271 people, and rented 7 warehouses.

When numbers measuring different qualities appear together in the same phrase, write one as a figure and the other as a word.

REVISE   The order was for *12* 6-inch pipes.

TO   The order was for *twelve* 6-inch pipes.

Approximate numbers are normally spelled out.

EXAMPLE   More than two hundred people attended the conference.

In business or technical writing, percentages are normally given as figures, with the word *percent* written out except when the number appears in a table.

EXAMPLE   Exactly 87 percent of the stockholders approved the merger.

In typed manuscripts, page numbers are written as figures, but chapter or volume numbers may appear either way.

EXAMPLES   page 37

Chapter 2 *or* Chapter Two
Volume 1 *or* Volume One

6.1.2 Dates

The year and day of the month should be written as figures. Dates are usually written in month-day-year sequence, but businesses and industrial corporations sometimes use the European and military day-month-year sequence.

EXAMPLES   August 24, 1988

24 August 1988

The month-day-year sequence may or may not be followed by a comma in a sentence, as in the following examples.

EXAMPLES   The August 24, 1987 issue of *Computer World* has an article . . .

The August 24, 1987, issue of *Computer World* has an article . . .

The day-month-year sequence is *not* followed by a comma.

EXAMPLE   The 24 August 1987 issue of *Computer World* . . .

The slash form of expressing dates (8/24/88) is used in informal writing only.

6.1.3 Time

Hours and minutes are expressed as figures when A.M. or P.M. follows.

EXAMPLES   11:30 A.M., 7:30 P.M.

When not followed by A.M. or P.M., however, times should be spelled out.

EXAMPLES   four o'clock, eleven o'clock

6.1.4   Fractions

Fractions are expressed as figures when written with whole numbers.

EXAMPLES   27 1/2 inches, 4 1/4 miles

Fractions are spelled out when they are expressed without a whole number.

EXAMPLES   one-fourth, seven-eighths

Numbers with decimals are always written as figures.

EXAMPLE   5.21 meters

6.1.5   Addresses

Numbered streets from one to ten should be spelled out except where space is at a premium.

EXAMPLE   East Tenth Street

Building numbers are written as figures. The only exception is the building number *one*.

EXAMPLES   4862 East Monument Street
             One East Tenth Street

Highway numbers are written as figures.

EXAMPLES   U.S. 70, Ohio 271, I94

6.1.6   Writing the Plurals of Numbers

The plural of a written number is formed by adding *-s* or *-es* or by dropping *y* and adding *-ies,* depending on the last letter, just as the plural of any other noun is formed. (See Section 1.3.1.)

EXAMPLES   sixes, elevens, twenties

The plural of a figure should be written with *s* alone.

EXAMPLES   5s, 12s

6.1.7 Redundant Numbering

Do not follow a word representing a number with a figure in parentheses that represents the same number.

REVISE   Send five (5) copies of the report.

TO   Send five copies of the report.

6.2 ACRONYMS AND INITIALISMS

An acronym is an abbreviation that is formed by combining the first letter or letters of two or more words. Acronyms are pronounced as words and are written without periods.

EXAMPLES   radar (*ra*dio *de*tecting *a*nd *r*anging)

COBOL (*C*ommon *B*usiness-*O*riented *L*anguage)

scuba (*s*elf-*c*ontained *u*nderwater *b*reathing *a*pparatus)

An initialism is an abbreviation that is formed by combining the initial letter of each word in a multiword term. Initialisms are pronounced as separate letters. When written lowercase, they generally require periods; when written uppercase, they generally do not.

EXAMPLES   e.o.m. (*e*nd *o*f *m*onth)

COD (*c*ash *o*n *d*elivery)

In business and industry, acronyms and initialisms are often used by people working together on particular projects or having the same specialties—as, for example, engineers or accountants. So long as such people are communicating only with one another, the abbreviations are easily recognized and understood. However, if the same acronyms or initialisms were used in correspondence to someone outside the group, they might be incomprehensible to those readers.

Acronyms and initialisms can be convenient—for the reader and the writer alike—if they are used appropriately. Business writers, however, often overuse them, either as an affectation or in a misguided attempt to make their writing concise.

6.2.1 When to Use Acronyms and Initialisms

Two guidelines apply in deciding whether to use acronyms and initialisms.

1. If you must use a multiword term an average of once each paragraph, introduce the term and then use its acronym or initialism. (See Section 6.2.2.) For example, a phrase such as "primary software overlay area" can become tiresome if repeated again and again in one piece of writing; it would be better, therefore, to use PSOA.
2. If something is better known by its acronym or initialism than by its formal term, you should use the abbreviated form. The initialism A.M., for example, is much more common than the formal *ante meridiem.*

If these conditions do not exist, however, always spell out the full term.

6.2.2   How to Use Acronyms and Initialisms

The first time an acronym or initialism appears in a written work, write out the complete term and then give the abbreviated form in parentheses.

EXAMPLE   The Capital Appropriations Request (CAR) controls the spending of the money.

Thereafter, you may use the acronym or initialism alone. In a long document, however, you will help your reader greatly by repeating the full term in parentheses after the acronym or initialism when the term has not been mentioned for some time. This saves the reader the trouble of searching back to the first time the acronym or initialism was used to find its meaning.

EXAMPLE   As noted earlier, the CAR (Capital Appropriations Request) controls the spending of money.

Write acronyms in capital letters without periods. The only exceptions are those acronyms that have become accepted as common nouns; these terms are written in lowercase letters.

EXAMPLES   laser, scuba, sonar

Initialisms that do not stand for proper nouns may be written either uppercase or lowercase. In general, do not use periods when the letters are uppercase; always use periods when they are lowercase. Two exceptions are geographic names and academic degrees.

EXAMPLES   COD/c.o.d., FOB/f.o.b., CIF/c.i.f., EOM/e.o.m.

CIA, FBI, NASA
U.S.A., U.S.S.R.
B.A., M.B.A.

Form the plural of an acronym or initialism by adding an -*s*. Do not use an apostrophe.

EXAMPLES   MIRVs, CRTs

6.3   ABBREVIATIONS

An abbreviation is a shortened form of a word, formed by omitting some of its letters. Most abbreviations are written with a period; however, in technical and business writing, abbreviations of measurements are generally an exception. In cases where an abbreviation of measurement might be confused with an actual word, the period is used.

EXAMPLES   Mister/Mr.

Avenue/Ave.

September/Sept.

centimeter/cm

inch/in. (the abbreviation *in* could be misread as the word *in*)

Abbreviations, like symbols, can be important space savers in business writing, where it is often necessary to provide the maximum amount of information in limited space. Use abbreviations, however, only if you are certain that your readers will understand them as readily as they would the terms for which they stand. Remember also that a memorandum or report addressed to a specific person may be read by others, and you must consider those readers as well. Take your reader's level of knowledge into account when deciding whether to use abbreviations. Do not use them if they might become an inconvenience to the reader. A good rule of thumb is: When in doubt, spell it out.

In general, use abbreviations only when space is limited. For example, abbreviations are often useful space savers in charts, tables, graphs, and other illustrations. Normally you should not make up your own abbreviations, for they will probably confuse your reader. Except for commonly used abbreviations (U.S.A., P.M.), a term to be abbreviated should be spelled out the first time it is used, with the abbreviation enclosed in parentheses following the term. Thereafter, the abbreviation may be used alone.

EXAMPLE   The annual report of the National Retail Dry Good Association (NRDGA) will be issued next month. In it, the NRDGA will detail shortages of several widely used textiles.

6.3.1 **Measurements**

When you abbreviate terms that refer to measurement, be sure your reader is familiar with the abbreviated form. The following list contains some common abbreviations used with units of measurement. Notice that, except for *in.* (inch), *bar.* (barometer), and other abbreviations that might be mistaken for other words, abbreviations of measurements do not require periods.

amp	ampere	hr	hour
atm	atmosphere	in.	inch
bar.	barometer	kc	kilocycle
bbl	barrel	kg	kilogram
bhp	brake horsepower	km	kilometer
Btu	British thermal unit	lb	pound
bu	bushel	mg	milligram
cal	calorie	min	minute
cm	centimeter	oz	ounce
cos	cosine	ppm	parts per million
ctn	cotangent	pt pint	
doz or dz	dozen	qt	quart
emf or EMF	electromotive force	rad	radian
F	Fahrenheit	rev	revolution
fig.	figure (illustration)	sec	second or secant
ft	foot (or feet)	tan.	tangent
gal	gallon	yd	yard
gm	gram	yr	year
hp	horsepower		

Abbreviations of units of measurement are identical in the singular and plural: one *cm* and three *cm* (not three *cms*).

6.3.2 **Personal Names and Titles**

Personal names should generally not be abbreviated.

REVISE   Chas., Thos., Wm., Geo.

TO   Charles, Thomas, William, George

An academic, civil, religious, or military title should be spelled out when it does not precede a name.

EXAMPLE   The *doctor* asked for the patient's chart.

When it precedes a name, the title may be abbreviated.

EXAMPLES   Dr. Smith, Mr. Mills, Capt. Hughes

Reverend and *Honorable* are abbreviated only if the surname is preceded by a first name.

EXAMPLES   The Reverend Smith, Rev. John Smith (but not Rev. Smith)

The Honorable Commissioner Holt, Hon. Mary J. Holt

An abbreviation of a title may follow the name; however, be certain that it does not duplicate a title before the name.

REVISE   Dr. William Smith, Ph.D.

TO   Dr. William Smith

OR   William Smith, Ph.D.

The following is a list of common abbreviations for personal and professional titles.

Atty.	Attorney
B.A. or A.B.	Bachelor of Arts
B.S.	Bachelor of Science
B.S.E.E.	Bachelor of Science in Electrical Engineering
D.D.	Doctor of Divinity
D.D.S.	Doctor of Dental Science
Dr.	Doctor (used with any doctor's degree)
Ed.D.	Doctor of Education
Hon.	Honorable
Jr.	Junior
LL.B.	Bachelor of Law
LL.D.	Doctor of Law
M.A. or A.M.	Master of Arts
M.B.A.	Master of Business Administration
M.D.	Doctor of Medicine
Messrs.	Plural of Mr.
Mr.	Mister (spelled out only in the most formal contexts)
Mrs.	Married woman
Ms.	Woman of unspecified marital status
M.S.	Master of Science
Ph.D.	Doctor of Philosophy
Rev.	Reverend
Sr.	Senior (used when a son with the same name is living)

6.4   AMPERSANDS

The ampersand (&) is a symbol sometimes used to represent the word *and,* especially in the names of organizations.

EXAMPLES   Chicago & Northwestern Railway

Watkins & Watkins, Inc.

The ampersand may be used in footnotes, bibliographies, lists, and references if it appears in the name of the title being listed. However, when writing the name of an organization in sentences or in an address, spell out the word *and* unless the ampersand appears in the official name of the company.

An ampersand must always be set off by normal word spacing but should never be preceded by a comma.

REVISE   Carlton, Dillon, & Manchester, Inc.

TO   Carlton, Dillon & Manchester, Inc.

Do not use an ampersand in the titles of articles, journals, books, or other publications.

REVISE   Does the bibliography include Knoll's *Radiation Detection & Measurement?*

TO   Does the bibliography include Knoll's *Radiation Detection and Measurement?*

6.5   CAPITAL LETTERS

The use of capital letters (or uppercase letters) is determined by custom and tradition. Capital letters are used to call attention to certain words, such as proper nouns and the first word of a sentence. Care must be exercised in using capital letters because they can affect the meaning of words (march/March, china/China, turkey/Turkey). Thus, capital letters can help eliminate ambiguity.

6.5.1   First Words

The first letter of the first word in a sentence is always capitalized.

EXAMPLE   Of all the plans you mentioned, the first one seems the best.

The first word after a colon may be capitalized if the statement following is a complete sentence or if it introduces a formal resolution or question.

EXAMPLE   Today's meeting will deal with only one issue: What is the firm's role in environmental protection?

If a subordinate element follows the colon, however, use a lowercase letter following the colon.

EXAMPLE   We had to keep working for one reason: pressure from above.

The first word of a complete sentence in quotation marks is capitalized.

EXAMPLE   He said, "When I arrive, we will begin."

Complete sentences contained as numbered items within a sentence may also be capitalized.

EXAMPLE   He recommended two ways to increase sales: (1) Next year we should spend more on television advertising, and (2) Our quality control should be improved immediately.

The first word in the salutation or complimentary close of a letter is capitalized.

EXAMPLES   Dear Mr. Smith:

Sincerely yours,

Best regards,

6.5.2 Specific People and Groups

Capitalize all personal names.

EXAMPLES   Walter Bunch, Mary Fortunato, Bill Krebs

Capitalize names of ethnic groups and nationalities.

EXAMPLES   American Indian, Italian, Jew, Chicano

Thus Italian immigrants contributed much to the industrialization of the United States.

Do not capitalize names of social and economic groups.

EXAMPLES   middle class, working class, ghetto dwellers

6.5.3 Specific Places

Capitalize the names of all political divisions.

EXAMPLES   Chicago, Cook County, Illinois, Ontario, Iran, Ward Six

Capitalize the names of geographical divisions.

EXAMPLES   Europe, Asia, North America, the Middle East, the Orient

Do not capitalize geographic features unless they are part of a proper name.

EXAMPLE   In some areas, mountains such as the Great Smoky Mountains make television transmission difficult.

The words *north, south, east,* and *west* are capitalized when they refer to sections of the country. They are not capitalized when they refer to directions.

EXAMPLES   I may travel south when I relocate to Delaware.

We may build a new plant in the South next year.

State Street runs east and west.

Capitalize the names of stars, constellations, galaxies, and planets.

EXAMPLES   Saturn, Sirius, Leo, Milky Way

Do not capitalize *earth, sun,* and *moon,* however, except when they are used with the names of other planets.

EXAMPLES   Although the sun rises in the east and sets in the west, the moon may appear in any part of the evening sky when darkness settles over the earth.

Mars, Pluto, and Earth were discussed at the symposium.

6.5.4   Specific Institutions, Events, and Concepts

Capitalize the names of institutions, organizations, and associations.

EXAMPLE   The American Management Association and the Department of Housing and Urban Development are cooperating in the project.

An organization usually capitalizes the names of its internal divisions and departments.

EXAMPLES   Faculty, Board of Directors, Accounting Department

Types of organizations are not capitalized unless they are part of an official name.

EXAMPLES   Our group decided to form a writers' association; we called it the American Association of Writers.

I attended Post High School. What high school did you attend?

Capitalize historical events.

EXAMPLE   Dr. Jellison discussed the Boston Tea Party at the last class.

Capitalize words that designate specific periods of time.

EXAMPLES   Labor Day, the Renaissance, the Enlightenment, January, Monday, the Great Depression, Lent

Do not, however, capitalize seasons of the year.

EXAMPLES   spring, autumn, winter, summer

Capitalize scientific names of classes, families, and orders, but do not capitalize species or English derivatives of scientific names.

EXAMPLES   Mammalia, Carnivora/mammal, carnivorous

6.5.5 Titles of Books, Articles, Plays, Films, Reports, and Memorandums

Capitalize the initial letters of the first and last words of a title of a book, article, play, or film, as well as all major words in the title. Do not capitalize articles (*a, an, the*), conjunctions (*and, but, if*), or short prepositions (*at, in, on, of*) unless they begin the title. Capitalize prepositions that contain more than four letters (*between, because, until, after*). These guidelines also apply to the titles of reports and to the subject lines of memorandums.

EXAMPLES   The author worked three years writing the book, *The Many Lives of an Organization.*

The article "Year After Year" describes the life of a turn-of-the-century industrialist.

The report, titled "Alternate Sites for Plant Location," was submitted in February.

6.5.6 Personal, Professional, and Job Titles

Titles preceding proper names are capitalized.

EXAMPLES   Ms. March, Professor Galbraith, Senator Kennedy

Appositives following proper names are not normally capitalized. (The word *President,* however, is usually capitalized when it refers to the chief executive of a national government.)

EXAMPLE   Frank Jones, senator from New Mexico (but Senator Jones)

The only exception is an epithet, which actually renames the person.

EXAMPLES   Alexander the Great, Solomon the Wise

Job titles used with personal names are capitalized and those appearing without personal names are not.

EXAMPLES   John Holmes, Division Manager, will meet with us on Wednesday.

The other division managers will not be present on Wednesday.

Use capital letters to designate family relationships only when they occur before a name or substitute for a name.

EXAMPLES   One of my favorite people is Uncle Fred.

My uncle is one of my favorite people.

Jim and Mother went along.

Jim and my mother went along.

6.5.7 Abbreviations

Capitalize abbreviations if the words they stand for would be capitalized. (See also Section 6.3.)

EXAMPLES   OSU (Ohio State University)

p. (page)

Ph.D. (Doctor of Philosophy)

6.5.8 Letters

Certain single letters are always capitalized. Capitalize the pronoun *I* and the interjection *O* (but do not capitalize *oh* unless it is the first word in a sentence).

EXAMPLES   When I say writing, O believe me, I mean rewriting.

When I say writing, oh believe me, I mean rewriting.

Capitalize letters that serve as names or indicate shapes.

EXAMPLES   vitamin B, T-square, U-turn, I-beam

6.5.9   Miscellaneous Capitalizations

The word *Bible* is capitalized when it refers to the Christian Scriptures; otherwise, it is not capitalized.

EXAMPLE   He quoted a verse from the Bible, then read from Blackstone, the lawyer's bible.

All references to deities (Allah, God, Jehovah, Yahweh) are capitalized.

EXAMPLE   God is the One who sustains us.

A complete sentence enclosed in dashes, brackets, or parentheses is not capitalized when it appears as part of another sentence.

EXAMPLES   We must make an extra effort in sales this year (last year's sales were down 10 percent).

Extra effort in sales should be made next year. (Last year's sales were down 10 percent.)

When certain units, such as chapters of books or rooms in buildings, are specifically identified by number, they are normally capitalized.

EXAMPLES   Chapter 5, Ch. 5, Room 72, Rm. 72

Minor divisions within such units are not capitalized unless they begin a sentence.

EXAMPLES   page 11, verse 14, seat 12

When in doubt about whether or not to capitalize, check a dictionary.

6.6   DATES

In business and industry, dates have traditionally been indicated by the month, day, and year, with a comma separating the figures. (See also Section 5.1.2.)

EXAMPLE   October 26, 1987

The day-month-year system used by the military does not require commas.

EXAMPLE   26 October 1987

A date can be written with or without a comma following the year, depending on how the date is expressed. If the date is in the month-day-year format, set off the year with commas.

EXAMPLE   October 26, 1987, was the date the project began.

If the date is in the day-month-year format, do not set off the date with commas.

EXAMPLE   On 26 October 1987 the project began.

The strictly numerical form for dates (10/26/87) should be used sparingly, and never in business letters or formal documents, since it is less immediately clear. When this form is used, the order in American usage is always month/day/year. For example, 5/7/87 is May 7, 1987.

Confusion often occurs because the spelled-out names of centuries do not correspond to the numbers of the years.

EXAMPLES   The twentieth century is the 1900s (1900–1999).

The nineteenth century is the 1800s (1800–1899).

The fifth century is the 400s (400–499).

6.7   ITALICS (UNDERLINING)

Italics (indicated on the typewriter by underlining) are a style of type used to denote emphasis and to distinguish foreign expressions, book titles, and certain other elements. *This sentence is printed in italics.* You may need to italicize words that require special emphasis in a sentence.

EXAMPLE   Contrary to projections, sales have *not* improved since we started the new procedure.

Do not overuse italics for emphasis, however.

REVISE   This will hurt *you* more than *me*.

TO   This will hurt you more than me!

6.7.1   Titles

Italicize the titles of books, periodicals, newspapers, movies, and paintings.

EXAMPLES   The book *Statistical Methods* was published in 1981.

The *Cincinnati Enquirer* is one of our oldest newspapers.

The *Journal of Marketing* is published monthly for those engaged in marketing.

Italicize abbreviations of such titles if their spelled-out forms would be italicized.

EXAMPLE   The *WSJ* is the business community's journal of record. (reference is to the *Wall Street Journal*)

Put titles of chapters or articles that appear within publications and the titles of reports in quotation marks, not italics.

EXAMPLE   The article "Does Advertising Lower Consumer Prices?" was published in the *Journal of Marketing*.

Do not italicize titles of holy books and legislative documents.

EXAMPLE   The Bible and the Magna Carta changed the history of Western civilization.

Italicize titles of long poems and musical works, but enclose titles of short poems and musical works and songs in quotation marks.

EXAMPLES   Milton's *Paradise Lost* (long poem)

Handel's *Messiah* (long musical work)

T. S. Eliot's "The Love Song of J. Alfred Prufrock" (short poem)

Leonard Cohen's "Suzanne" (song)

6.7.2   Proper Names

Italicize the names of ships, trains, and aircraft, but not the names of companies that own them.

EXAMPLE   They sailed to Africa on the Onassis *Clipper* but flew back on the TWA *New Yorker*.

Exceptions are craft that are known by model or serial designations, which are not italicized.

EXAMPLES   DC-7, Boeing 747

6.7.3   Words, Letters, and Figures

Italicize words, letters, and figures that are discussed as such.

EXAMPLES   The word *inflammable* is often misinterpreted.

I should replace the *s* on my old typewriter.

6.7.4   Foreign Words

Italicize foreign words that have not been assimilated into the English language.

EXAMPLES   *sine qua non, coup de grâce, in res, in camera*

Do not italicize foreign words that have been fully assimilated into the language.

EXAMPLES   cliché, etiquette, vis-à-vis, de facto, siesta

When in doubt about whether or not to italicize a foreign word, consult a current dictionary.

6.7.5   Subheads

Subheads in a report are sometimes italicized; on a typewriter, they are generally underlined.

EXAMPLES   There was no publications department as such, and the writing groups were duplicated at each plant or location. Wellington, for example, had such a large number of publications groups that their publications effort can only be described as disorganized. Their duplication of effort must have been enormous.

Training Writers

We are certainly leading the way in developing first-line managers (or writing supervisors) who not only are technically competent but can train the writers under their direction and be responsible for writing quality as well.

6.8   SYMBOLS

From highway signs to mathematical equations, people communicate in written symbols. When a symbol seems appropriate in your writing, either be certain that your reader understands its meaning or place an explanation in parentheses following the symbol the first time it appears. However, never use a symbol when your reader would more readily understand the full term. Following is a list of symbols and their appropriate uses.

Symbol	Meaning and Use
£	pound (basic unit of currency in the United Kingdom)
$	dollar (basic unit of currency in the United States)
O	oxygen (for a listing of all symbols for chemical elements, see a periodic table of elements in a dictionary or handbook)
+	plus
−	minus
±	plus or minus
∓	minus or plus
×	multiplied by
÷	divided by
=	equal to
≠ or ≠	not equal to
≈ or ≐	approximately (or nearly equal to)
≡	identical with
≢	not identical with
>	greater than
≯	not greater than
<	less than
≮	not less than
:	is to (or ratio)
≐	approaches (but does not reach equality with)
∥	parallel
⊥	perpendicular
√	square root
∛	cube root
∞	infinity
π	*pi*
∴	therefore (in mathematical equations)
∵	because (in mathematical equations)
( )	parentheses
[ ]	brackets
{ }	braces (used to group two or more lines of writing, to group figures in tables, and to enclose figures in mathematical equations)
°F or °C	degree (Fahrenheit or Celsius)
′	minute *or* foot
″	second *or* inch
#	number
*	asterisk (used to indicate a footnote when there are very few)
&	ampersand
♂	male
♀	female
©	copyright
%	percent
c/o	in care of

Symbol	Meaning and Use
a/o	account of
@	at (sometimes used in tables, but never in writing)
´	acute (accent mark in French and other languages)
`	grave (accent mark in French and other languages)
^	circumflex (accent mark in French and other languages)
~	tilde (diacritical mark identifying the palatal nasal in Spanish and Portuguese)
¯	macron (marks a long phonetic sound, as in $c\bar{a}ke$)
˘	breve (marks a short phonetic sound, as in $br\breve{a}cket$)
¨	dieresis or umlaut (mark placed over the second of two consecutive vowels indicating that the second vowel is to be pronounced separately from the first—coöperate)
¸	cedilla (mark placed beneath the letter c in French, Portuguese, and Spanish to indicate the letter is pronounced as s—garçon)
∧	caret (proofreader's mark used to indicate inserted material)
FR	franc (basic unit of currency in France)
Mex $	peso (basic unit of currency in Mexico)
$	peso (Philippine peso)
R	ruble (basic monetary unit of the U.S.S.R.)
¥	yen (basic unit of currency in Japan)

6.9 PROOFREADERS' MARKS

Publishers have established symbols, called proofreaders' marks, which writers and editors use to communicate with printers in the production of publications. A familiarity with these symbols makes it easy for you to communicate your changes to others.

Mark in Margin	Instruction	Mark on Manuscript	Corrected Type
ℓ	Delete	the lawyer's bible	the bible
lawyer's	Insert	The ∧ bible	The lawyer's bible
stet	Let stand	the lawyer's bible	the lawyer's bible
cap	Capitalize	the bible	the Bible
lc	Make lower case	the Law	the law
ital	Italicize	the lawyer's bible	the lawyer's bible
tr	Transpose	the bible lawyer's	the lawyer's bible
⌒	Close space	the Bi ble	the Bible
sp	Spell out	2 bibles	two bibles

Mark in Margin	Instruction	Mark on Manuscript	Corrected Type
#	Insert space	The Bible	The Bible
¶	Start paragraph	¶ The lawyer's...	The lawyer's...
run in	No paragraph	...marks. Below is a....	...marks. Below is a....
sc	Set in small capitals	The bible	The BIBLE
rom	Set in roman type	The (bible)	The bible
bf	Set in boldface	The bible	The **bible**
lf	Set in lightface	The (bible)	The bible
.	Insert period	The lawyers have their own bible	The lawyers have their own bible.
∧	Insert comma	However we cannot....	However, we cannot....
=	Insert hyphens	half and half	half-and-half
O	Insert colon	We need the following	We need the following:
;	Insert semicolon	Use the law don't....	Use the law; don't....
∨	Insert apostrophe	Johns law book	John's law book
∨/∨	Insert quotation marks	The law is law.	The "law" is law.
(/)	Insert parentheses	John's law book	John's (law) book
[/]	Insert brackets	John 1920-1962 went....	John [1920-1962] went....
N	Insert en dash	1920 1962	1920-1962
M	Insert em dash	Our goal victory	Our goal—victory
2	Insert superior type	$3 = 9$	$3^2 = 9$
2	Insert inferior type	HSO_4	H_2SO_4
*	Insert asterisk	The law	The law*
†	Insert dagger	The law	The law†
‡	Insert double dagger	The bible	The bible‡
§	Insert section symbol	Research	§Research

Section C

Word Processing

Word processing enables you to input into a computer such documents as memorandums and reports, edit your text on a video screen, print out a well-formatted paper copy of an edited version of your document, and then store that version electronically for future revision. If the word processor is new to you, try thinking of it as a sophisticated electric typewriter connected to a computer, television screen, and printer. Its main advantage is that once you have input your text, you can easily revise it, deleting errors and inserting corrections, to create a perfect final draft without having to retype the entire document.

Nearly all word-processing systems use the following functions to create and manipulate texts:

- Cursor-controlled editing
- Document formatting and printing
- File storage and retrieval

Cursor-controlled, or "full-screen," editing relies on a cursor, a solid or flashing light that marks your position on the video screen. You move the cursor through your text to perform various editing tasks, such as the following:

- Inserting, deleting, or replacing text anywhere in a document
- Deleting, copying, or moving blocks of text, such as phrases, sentences, paragraphs, or whole pages
- Searching for and replacing individual letters, words, or phrases
- Making automatic carriage returns at the end of each line and automatic readjustments of margins and page "breaks" as you edit

Document formatting commands enable you to create individual or standard formats for your documents that might include the following:

- Fixed margins and automatic indentation
- Automatic page numbering
- Automatic headers and footers
- Automatic notes (footnotes and end notes)
- Multiple copies of your documents using a variety of type sizes and typefaces, including bold and italic

The ability to store a document on a permanent magnetic medium, such as a disk or tape, and then retrieve it allows you to do the following:

- Save all original and revised copies of your documents in an electronic filing system and print a list of your files at any time
- Retrieve the documents at a later date for revision and reprinting
- Merge, copy, and delete documents at will

Writers find the word processor effective for recording ideas quickly when writing first drafts and for extensive rewriting during the revision process. In the business world, the computer is rapidly becoming a primary communication tool for all professionals. Since correspondence, reports, and technical manuals can be quickly generated and revised with this new technology, many companies provide their technical personnel with word processors for everyday use. Businesses are beginning to use computers as effective management tools by linking word-processing technology to other computer applications, such as automatic document preparation, computer graphics, data base retrieval, electronic mail, and "mail-merge" programs that merge large lists of mailing addresses with form letters.

HARDWARE

The term *hardware* refers to the physical parts, or electronic and mechanical components, of a computer. Most word processors use the same basic components. Figure C-1 shows the five basic parts of a typical microcomputer system.

1. The *main system unit* includes three segments: the central processing unit (CPU), internal memory, and disk drive. The CPU is the "brain" that manipulates data and carries out programmed instructions. It uses the computer's internal memory as temporary storage when performing programming tasks and creating temporary working files. The disk drive units, shown as slots A and B in Figure C-1, are standard input/output devices for the transfer

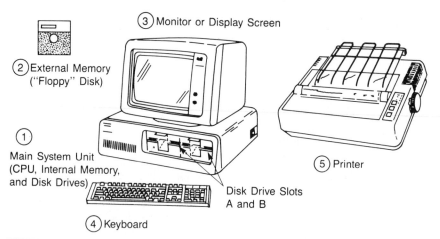

③ Monitor or Display Screen

② External Memory ("Floppy" Disk)

① Main System Unit (CPU, Internal Memory, and Disk Drives)

Disk Drive Slots A and B

⑤ Printer

④ Keyboard

FIGURE C–1. Typical microcomputer system used for word processing.

of information between floppy disks and the computer's internal memory.

2. *External memory* refers to any permanent storage medium, such as flexible or floppy disks on which you can save all your documents. The advantage of floppy disks is that, like cassette tapes, they are portable. You can remove the disks from the computer for safe storage and reinsert them later to retrieve individual documents. A single floppy disk stores approximately 100 to 200 pages of text. Other forms of external memory include hard disks and magnetic tapes capable of storing much larger quantities of data than floppy disks.

3. The *monitor* resembles a common television screen. It displays what you input, the computer's responses, and any documents you retrieve from storage.

4. The computer *keyboard* allows you to input data and commands. It looks like a regular typewriter keyboard but contains several extra keys, including function keys for special operations, such as saving a document, listing files, moving blocks of text, and search and replace commands.

5. The *printer* is similar to a typewriter printing carriage. When you give the appropriate command, the printer prints your text on paper. Microcomputers use three different kinds of printers: dot matrix, letter quality, and laser. Each of these printers produces typefaces of varying quality, as shown in Figure C–2.

Dot matrix printers are fast, reliable printers whose print characters are composed of tiny dots. Although some writers feel that the "computer-generated" look of the dot image is suitable only for draft copies, this

```
This is an example of dot matrix printing.


This is an example of near letter quality
dot matrix printing.


This is an example of letter quality printing.


This is an example of laser printing with
bold, italic and enlarged typefaces.
```

FIGURE C–2. Varying qualities of typeface produced by different printers.

typeface is gaining greater acceptance as more writers use the double strike, or "overstrike," mode (shown in the second example of Figure C–2) to produce near letter quality dot matrix print for memos and informal reports. *Letter quality printers* are slower than dot matrix printers and use a daisy wheel or thimble to print a clear, dark typeface similar to that of an office typewriter. *Laser printers* work on the same principle as photocopy machines by using a jet spraying device to deposit carbon images directly on paper. Laser printers can produce a great variety of high-quality typefaces comparable to professionally printed material.

SOFTWARE AND COMPUTER SYSTEMS

The term *software* refers to precoded instructions or programs, stored on floppy disks, that tell the computer how to execute the commands you input. Such software, which includes word-processing, graphics, and electronic spreadsheet programs, is used by microcomputers. The advantage of the microcomputer is that all software and hardware "stand alone" in an easy-to-use, self-contained system. In a microcomputer or mainframe computer system, individual terminals (keyboard and screen) connect with a large central computer but share the CPU, memory, and word-processing software (usually consisting of "text editor" and "file formatter" programs) with other "users." Although mainframe systems do not provide individual writers with exclusive use of the central computer, they provide huge storage capacity and the ability to communicate with other users through electronic mail messages.

Distributed processing systems link microcomputers together through a central mainframe computer, combining all the advantages of stand-alone microcomputing with large mainframe processing and communications. By linking or "networking" microcomputers through larger computer systems in remote locations, you can transmit documents electronically from one microcomputer to another microcomputer in the same building, across town, or thousands of miles away where the documents can be viewed, printed out, revised, and transmitted back.

WORD PROCESSING AND THE WRITING PROCESS

The word processor is a powerful tool that can help you record your ideas quickly, improve your writing and revising skills, and create professionally designed documents. But remember that good writing is still the result of careful planning, constant practice, and thoughtful revision. In some cases, word-processing technology can initially intrude on the writing process and impose certain limitations that many beginners overlook. The ease of making minor, sentence-level changes and the limitation of a 24-line viewing screen, for example, may focus your attention too narrowly on surface features of the text so that you lose sight of larger problems of scope and organization. Or the fluid and rapid movement of the text on the screen, together with last-minute editing changes, may allow typographical errors and misspellings to creep into the text unexpectedly. Also, as you master the machine and become enamored of its powerful revising capabilities, you may begin to "overwrite" your documents. Inserting phrases and rewriting sentences becomes so easy that you may find yourself generating more text and rewriting more extensively but ultimately saying less. The following tips will help you avoid these initial pitfalls and develop writing strategies that take full advantage of the great benefits offered by word-processing technology.

TIPS ON USING THE WORD PROCESSOR TO IMPROVE WRITING SKILLS

1. Avoid the temptation of writing first drafts on the computer without any planning or outlining. Plan your document carefully by identifying your objective, readers, and scope and by completing your research before you begin writing the draft on the computer.

2. Use the word processor to brainstorm and organize an initial outline for your topic.

3. When you're ready to begin writing, you can overcome "writer's block" by practicing "free writing" on the computer. Free writing means typing your thoughts as quickly as possible without stopping to correct mistakes or complete sentences—concentrate on perfection later.

4. Use the search command to find and delete wordy phrases such as "that is," "there are," "the fact that," "to be," and unnecessary helping verbs such as "will."

5. If the software is available, use spelling checkers and other specialized programs to identify and correct typographical errors, misspellings, and grammar and diction problems. Do not rely completely on computerized spelling checkers, however, since they cannot identify errors such as the misuse of "there" for "their." Maintain a file of your most frequently misspelled or misused words and use the search command to check them in your documents.

6. Avoid excessive editing and rewriting on the screen. Print out a complete paper copy of your drafts periodically for major revisions and reorganization.

7. Always proofread your final copy on paper since the fluidity of the viewing screen makes it difficult to catch all of the errors in your manuscript. Print out an extra copy of your document for your peers to comment on before making final revisions.

8. When writing a single document for multiple readers, use the search command to find technical terms and other data that may need further explanation for secondary readers or inclusion in a glossary.

9. Use the computer for effective document design by emphasizing major headings and subheadings with bold print, by using the copy command to create and duplicate parallel headings throughout your text, and by inserting blank lines (carriage returns) and tab key spaces in your text to create extra white space around examples and illustrations.

10. Keep a standard version of certain documents, such as your résumé and application letters, on file so you can revise them to meet the specific needs of each new job opportunity.

11. Frequently "save" or store your text on disk during long writing sessions and always create an extra or "backup" copy of your documents for safekeeping.

Index

Abbreviated dates, 568
Abbreviated spellings, 464
Abbreviations, 575–577
  capital letters for, 582
  in heading of letters, 176
  list of, in formal reports, 311
Absolute, 531
Abstract, 304–309
Abstract nouns, 489
Abstracting services, 265
Accent mark, 468
Accident reports (trouble reports),
    231–232
Accountability, in job descriptions,
    363
Accuracy
  in business letters, 175
  checking for, 83
  of instructions, 124
  in spelling, 82
Acknowledgment letters, 203
Acquaintances, job leads from, 419
Acronyms, 573–575
  in titles of formal reports, 304
Active voice, 62–66
  for emphasis, 62–66
  in letter writing, 164–166
Address(es)
  in heading of letters, 176
  inside, in letters, 176
  numbers in, 572
Adjective endings, spelling, 501
Adjective markers, 487
Adjectives, 500–503
  adverbs made from, 517
  comparison of, 501
  placement of, 502
  usage of, 502–503
Adjustment letters, 208, 210
Adverb endings, spelling, 517
Adverbs, 515–519
  from adjectives, 517
  comparison of, 516–517
  functions of, 516
  placement of, 518–519

Advertisements, job, 417–418
Affectation, 100–102
Agreement, 84–86
  definition of, 84
  pronoun-antecedent, 85–86
  subject-verb, 84–85, 512–515
Ambiguous pronoun reference, 499–
    500
American Statistics Index, 259
Ampersands, 578
Analogy, definition by, 145–146
Antecedent
  agreement of pronoun with, 497–
    499
  of a pronoun, 499–500
Antonyms, 470
Apostrophes, 566–568
Appearance
  of business letters, 175
  See also Physical appearance
Appendixes, in formal reports, 325–
    328
Appositive, 530
  pronoun, 496
Argumentative writing
  increasing order of importance in,
    33–35
  See also Persuasive writing
Atlases, 260
Attention-getting devices, in instruc-
    tions, 129
Attention line, in place of a salutation,
    177–178
Audience
  of oral presentations, 410–412
  See also Readers
Author card, 260–265
Author/date citation system, 289–294

Back matter of formal reports, 325–
    328
"Bad news" letters, 167–172
  See also Refusal letters
Bar graphs, 383–385

Bibliographies
    at the end of a report or research
        paper, 289
    in formal reports, 325
    in the library, 263–265
Bibliography cards, 263–265
Body of formal reports, 311–325
    conclusions, 322
    explanatory footnotes, 324
    introductions, 313–317
    recommendations, 322–324
    references, 324–325
    summaries, 311–313
    text, 317–322
Body of letters, 178
Body of tables, 377
Boldface type
    for emphasis, 75, 129
Books, *see* Library research
Brackets, 569
Brainstorming, 9–11
Buffer
    in "bad news" letters, 167–172
    in refusal letters, 210, 213
Bullets with lists, 74
Business forms, *see* Forms
Business letters, *see* Letters

Call number, 262
Capital letters, 578–583
    for emphasis, 75
    for heads, 320–322
Captions in forms, 365–366
Card catalog, 260–265
Case of pronouns, 495–497
Cause-and-effect analysis, 148–151
Cause-and-effect development, in oral
        presentations, 405
Central processing unit, 591–592
Chalkboard, for oral presentations,
        408
Charts
    flip, 409
    organizational, 396–397
Checklist, revision, 112
Chronological sequence, 27–29
Circular definitions, 147–148
Claim letters, *see* Complaint letters
Clarifying definitions, 145–147
Classification, as method of develop-
        ment, 140–143
Classification systems of libraries,
        140–143

Classified ads, 417–418
Clauses, 424–427
    elliptical, 536–537
    independent, 525
    misplaced, 89
    subordinate (dependent), 62–67,
        525–527
Climactic order, 74
Closings, 54–57
    See also Conclusion
Coherence of paragraph, 48–52, 545
Collection letters, 213, 218
Collective nouns, 489
College placement offices, 419
Colons, 555–556
Comma errors, 106–108
Comma faults, 552
Commands, instructions as, 125
Commas, 546–553
    to enclose, 547–548
    errors in use of, 106–108, 552–553
    to link, 546–547
    with other punctuation, 551
    problems with, 552–553
    to separate, 548–551
    to show omissions, 551
    superfluous, 552–553
Comma splice, 106
Common knowledge, 279
Common nouns, 489
Comparison(s), 137–140
    of adjectives, 501
    of adverbs, 516–517
    faulty, 92
    part-by-part method for, 138–140
    whole-by-whole method for, 138–
        140
Complaint letters, 203, 208
Complements, 531
Completeness, checking for, 83
Complex sentences, 528–529
Complimentary close, in letters, 178
Compound sentences, 528
Compound subject, 85
Computer software, 593–594
    spell checkers, 594
Computer graphics, 387
Computerized information retrieval,
        269–271
Conciseness
    checking for, 97–102
    of instructions, 125–126
    in letter writing, 172–175

See also redundancy, padded
phrases, and affectation
Conclusion(s)
in formal reports, 322
of informal reports, 231
of oral presentations, 413
of proposals, 336–337
Concrete nouns, 489
Conjugation of verbs, 510–512
Conjunctions, 519–520
coordinating, 519–520
correlative, 519
function of, 519
subordinating, 519
usage of, 520
Connectives, 531
Consistency
of tense and person, 86–87
See also Agreement
Consonants, doubling final, 461–462
Continuation page of letters, 178–179
Contractions, 567–568
spelling, 463–464
Cooling period
in letter writing, 164
before revising, 81
Coordinating conjunctions, 519–520
commas after, 106
Copy notation, 180
Correlative conjunctions, 519
Correspondence, *see* Letters
Cost analysis, in sales proposals, 334–
336
County and City Data Book, 259
Courtesy, in "bad news" letters, 167–
172
Cover letter, for sales proposals, 343
Cursor, 590
Customer Relations Departments,
208

Danger, warnings of, 75
Dangling modifiers, 87–88, 536–537
Dash(es), 565–566
to achieve emphasis, 75–76
within sentence, for emphasis, 75
Data bases, 269–271
Date(s), 571, 683–684
abbreviated, 568
commas in, 547–548
of formal reports,
on letters, 303–304
numbers in, 571

Decimal numbering system, for heads,
321–322
Declarative sentences, 529
Decreasing order of importance, 31–
33
Definitions, 97, 143–148
by analogy, 145–146
circular, 147–148
clarifying, 145–147
dictionary, 468–470
extended, 144–145
formal, 143–144
glossary, 238
informal, 144
"is when" and "is where," 148
in oral presentations, 410–411
problems in, 147–148
with unfamiliar terms, 147–148
Delivering an oral presentation, 409–
413
Delivery schedule, in sales proposals,
347–350
Demonstrative pronouns, 492
Dependent clauses (subordinate
clauses), 62–67, 525–527
Descriptions, 132–137
general, in sales proposals, 343
job, 343
purchase-order, 132–134
vendor, in sales proposals, 350
whole-to-parts technique in, 135
See also Process descriptions
Descriptive abstract, 304–306
Detailed solution, in sales proposals,
343
Dewey Decimal System, 262
Dictionaries, 256–258, 467–470
Direct address, commas in, 548
Direct quotation, 272–274
Directions, *see* Instructions
Disks, 592
Division, 22–24, 140–143
Documentation, 288–296
notes, 295–296
numbered references, 294–295
parenthetical, 289–294
Dot-matrix printer, 592–593
Double spacing, in letters, 178
Doubling final consonants, 461–462
Draft, 43–57
closing of, 54–57
of letters, 163–164

opening of, 52–54
paragraph length in, 48
paragraph unity in, 45–48
revising, *see* Revising
Drawings, 389–391
  instructions with, 129
  See also Illustrations

Editing
  on a word processor, 594–595
Educational background, in resumes,
    422–423
Electronic mail, 591
Ellipses
  in direct quotations, 557–558
  periods as, 557–558
Elliptical clauses, 536–537
Emphasis, 62–76
  active voice for, 62–66
  climactic order for, 74
  introductory words and phrases for,
    70–71
  labeling ideas as important for, 75–
    76
  lists for, 73–74
  parallel structure for, 71–74
  subordination for, 66–70
Emphatic sentences, 538–539
Employment search, *see* Job search
Employment agencies, 419
Employment experience, in resumes,
    423–424
Employment objective, in resumes,
    422
Enclosure notations, 179–180
Encyclopedias, 255–256
  general, 255
  subject, 255–256
Endnotes, 296
  See also Footnotes
English-language dictionaries, 256–
    257
  See also Dictionaries
Entry lines, in forms, 368–369
Enunciation, 412–413
Envelopes, 181, 184
Evidence
  in cause-and-effect analysis, 149–
    150
  in persuasive writing, 152
Exclamation marks, 560
Exclamatory sentences, 529

Executive summaries, *see* Summary
  in sales proposals, 343
Explanation of a process, 129–132
Explanatory footnotes, 295–296
  in formal reports, 324
  for graphs, 382
Expletives, 531–532
Exploded-view drawing, 389
Extemploraneous speech, 403
  See also Oral presentations
Extended definitions, 144–145
External proposals, *see* Sales propos-
  als
Eye contact, in oral presentations,
    412

Facts
  generating ideas and recording, 9–
    12
  interesting, in oral presentations,
    411
  See also Information, Research
Faulty comparisons, 92
Faulty subordination, 532–533
Figures
  in formal reports, 328
  See also Illustrations
Final consonants, doubling, 461–
    462
Finite verbs, 504–505
First draft, *see* Draft
First-hand observation, 287
Flip charts, 409
Flowcharts, 393–396
Follow-up letters
  after job interviews, 444–447
  for order letters, 195, 197
Follow-up questions, in interviews,
    280–281
Footnotes, 296
  author/date system for,
    documentation, 296
  explanatory, *see* Explanatory foot-
    notes
  numbered references, 294–295
  numbers of, 295–296
  second-and-later, 295–296
  for tables, 377
  traditional, 295–296
Forecast, in oral presentations, 412
Foreign words, italics for, 586
Formal definitions, 97

Formal reports, 301–329
  graphic and tabular matter in, 328–329
  order of elements in, 301–302
  See also Back matter of formal reports; Front matter of formal reports
Formality of memos, 187–188
Formal style, in letter writing, 164–166
Format of letters, 176–181
Forms, 365–370
  captions in, 365–366
  designing, 367–370
  instructions in, 365–366
  main portion of, 367
  planning for responses in, 367
  preliminary information in, 367
  sequencing of data in, 367
  spacing in, 369–370
  typeset, 369
Fractions, 572
Fragments, sentence, 90–91, 534–536
Friends, job leads from, 419
"From" line of memo, 188–190
Front matter of formal reports, 303–311
  abstract, 303–311
  list of abbreviations and symbols, 311
  preface, 311
  table of contents, 309–310
  title page, 303–304
Full block style, 181, 182
Fused sentences, *see* Run-on sentences

Gender
  pronoun-antecedent agreement in, 497–499
  of pronouns, 494–495
General description, in sales proposals, 343–347
General encyclopedias, 255–256
General (or broad) pronoun reference, 499–500
General-to-specific sequence, 35–36
  of oral presentations, 405
Generating ideas, 9–11
Gerund phrases, 524
Glossary, in formal reports, 328
"Good news" letters, 169–172

Goodwill
  "good news" letters and, 169–172
  letter writing and, 164–166
Governmental agencies and organizations
  employment opportunities in, 420
  free or inexpensive materials from, 287–288
Grammar, checking, 83
Graphs, 377–387
  bar, 383–385
  line, 378–382
  picture, 387
  pie, 386–387
Greeting, in letters, 176–178
Grid lines, of line graphs, 378–382

Handbooks, 258–259
Hard and soft sounds, 457–458
  spelling, 457–458
Hazardous materials, warnings concerning, 124
Heads (headings)
  in formal reports, 320–322
  of memorandums, 186–187
  of resumes, 421
  of second page, 178–179
  of tables, 375–377
Hidden pronoun reference, 94
Hyphenation, 468
Hyphens, 561–563

Ideas
  generating, 9–11
  organization of, 13–14
Ie or *ei* words, spelling, 463
Illustrations,
  in descriptive writing, 136–137
  in formal reports, 328–329
  instructions with, 129
  See also Drawings
Imitation, affectation and, 100–102
Imperative mood, 507
Imperative sentences, 529
Imprecision, affectation and, 100–102
Impression, wishing to create an, 100–102
Impromptu speech, 402–403
  See also Oral presentations
Inaccuracies
  checking for, 83
  See also Accuracy

Increasing order of importance, 33–35, 405
  organization of information in, 33–35
  in oral presentations, 405
Indefinite pronouns, 493
Independent clauses, 525
Indexes, book, 263
Indexes, periodical, 265–269
Indicative mood, 506–507
Indirectness of letters, 166–172
Indirect object, 525–526
Infinitive phrases, 524
Informal definitions, 144
Informal reports, 229–249
  conclusion of, 231
  introduction of, 230
  investigative, 232–234
  parts of, 230–231
  periodic, 240, 242
  progress, 234, 240
  recommendations in, 231, 242
  test (laboratory), 244, 246
  trip, 244
  trouble (accident), 231–232
Informal style in business letters, 172–175
Information
  checking for accuracy of, 83
  organization of, 20
  See also Facts; Research
Informative abstract, 306–309
Initialisms, 573–575
Initials of writer and typist, on letters, 179
Initiation, affectation and, 100–102
Inquiry letters, 195, 198
  response to, 198, 200
Insecurity, affectation and, 100–102
Inside address of letters, 176
Institutional sales pitch, in sales proposals, 350
Instructions, 123–129
  accuracy of, 124–125
  in active versus passive voice, 64
  conciseness of, 125–126
  in forms, 365–366
  "Materials Required" or "Tools Required" section in, 126
  spatial method of organization in, 30
  step-by-step organization of, 126
  warnings in, 126–129

Intensive pronouns, 493
Interesting facts, in oral presentations, 411
Interjections, 522
Internal proposals, 333–337
Interrogative pronouns, 493
Interrogative sentences, 529
Interviews
  conducting, 280–281
  job, 439–444
  preparation for, 279–280
  self, 9–11
  See also Questionnaires
Intimidation, affectation, and, 100–102
Intransitive verbs, 504
Introduction
  of formal reports, 313–317
  of informal reports, 230
  of internal proposals, 334
  of sales proposals, 341
Introductory words and phrases, 70–71
Investigative report, 232–234
Italics (underlining), 584–586
  for emphasis, 75–76, 129

Jargon, 102–103
Job descriptions, 362–365
Job interviews, 439–444
Job search, 417–448
  follow-up letters, 444–447
  interview, 439–444
  letter of application, 436–439
Job titles, capitalization, 581–582

Keyboard, 592
Kipling, Rudyard, 9

Laser printers, 593
Leaders, periods as, 558
Legalese, 101
Length of paragraph, 48
Letter quality printer, 592–593
Letters,
  accuracy in, 175
  acknowledgment, 203
  additional information in, 179–180
  adjustment, 208, 210
  appearance in, 175
  "bad news," 167–172
  body of, 178
  closings, 55

collection, 213, 218
complaint, 203, 208
complimentary close of, 178
cooling period in writing, 163–164
cover, for sales proposals, 343
direct and indirect patterns for, 166–172
double-spacing in, 178
draft of, 163–164
envelope for, 181, 184
follow-up, after job interviews, 444–447
follow-up, for order letters, 195, 197
format of, 176–181
full block style, 181, 182
"good news," 169–172
heading of, 176
inquiry, 195, 198
inquiry, responses to, 198, 200
inside address of, 176
job application, 436–439
job inquiry, 418
margins of, 178
modified block style, 181, 183
openings, 53
order, 194–195
outlines for, 163–164
parts of, 176–181
refusal, 210, 213, 444
rejection, 167–172
revising, 164
sales, 218, 222, 224
salutation in, 176–178
second page of, 178–179
signature on, 178
steps in writing, 163–164
style of, 172–175
tone, 164–166
transmittal, 200, 203
Letter writers initials, 179
Library of Congress System, 262
Library research, 11, 255–271
card catalog, 260–265
computerized information retrieval, 269–271
periodical indexes and bibliographies, 265–269
reference works, 255–260
Line graphs, 378–382
Linking verbs, 504
Listeners of oral presentations, 404
Listening to oral presentations, 414–415

Lists, for emphasis, 73–74
Loose sentences, 541–542

Manuals, 258–259
Maps, 397–398
Margins of letters, 178
Masculine pronouns, sexist language, 103–104
Mass nouns, 489
"Materials Required" section, in instructions, 126
Measurements, abbreviations for, 576
Mechanics, 569–589
revising for, 106–111
Meetings, minutes of, see Minutes of meetings
Memorandum (memo), 181–190
format, 188–190
openings of, 54, 185–186
closings of, 56–57
protocol, 184–185
special-purpose report, 232
transmittal, 181
Minor sentences, 534–536
Minutes of meetings, 358–362
Misplaced clauses, 89
Misplaced modifiers, 88–90, 536–537
Misplaced phrases, 89
Misspelled words, commonly, 108–111, 464–466
MLA Handbook for Writers of Research Papers, 289–290
Modified block style, 181, 182
Modifiers,
dangling, 87–88, 536–537
misplaced, 88–90, 536–537
redundant, 97–98
single, 67–68
squinting, 89–90, 536
See also Adjectives; Adverbs; Prepositional phrases; Subordinate clauses
Mood of verbs, 506–509
Ms. in salutation of letters, 176–177

Nervous mannerisms, in oral presentations, 412
Newspapers, job advertisements in, 417–418
Nonfinite verbs, 505–506
Nonrestrictive and parenthetical elements, commas used to enclose, 547

Note-taking, 271–279
    direct quotation in, 272–274
    in interviews, 280–281
    paraphrasing in, 274–277
    summary in, 277–278
Notes, 295–296
    for oral presentations, 413
    See also Footnotes
Noun markers, 485–486
Noun phrases, 523
Nouns, 488–492
Number
    pronoun-antecedent agreement in,
        497–499
    of pronouns, 495
    of verbs, 506
Numbered references, 294–295
Numbers (numerals)
    plurals of, 572
    redundant, 573
    when to write out, 570–571

Objective case of pronouns, 495–496
Objective complement, 531
Objective of a project, in oral presenta-
    tions, 403
Observation, first-hand, 287
Omissions
    apostrophes used to mark, 567–568
    commas used to show, 551
Openings, 52–54
Oral presentations, 402–413
    concluding, 413
    delivering, 409–413
    listeners of, 404
    listening to, 414–415
    outlines for, 404–407
    preparing, 403–409
    purpose of, 403
    question-and-answer period after,
        413
    types of, 402–403
    visual aids in, 407–409
Order letters, 194–195
    follow-up letters for, 195, 197
Organization
    of ideas, 4, 5
    of information, 20–37
    See also Outlines
Organizational charts, 396–397
Organization methods (sequence), 25–
    37
    chronological, 27–29

decreasing order of importance, 31–
    33
general-to-specific, 35–36
increasing order of importance, 33–
    35
spatial, 29–31
specific-to-general, 36–37
step-by-step, 25–27
Origin of a word (etymology), 470–487
Outlines, 14, 21–25
    for letters, 163–164
    for memos, 185
    for oral presentations, 404–407
Overhead projectors, 409

Padded phrases, 98–100
Paragraph(s), 45–52, 542–546
    coherence of, 48–52, 545
    definition and functions of, 542–543
    length of, 48
    topic sentences in, 543–544
    transitions between, 544
    unity of, 45–48, 545
Parallel structure, 71–73
Paraphrase, 274–277
Parentheses, 560–561
Parenthetical documentation, 289–
    294
Parenthetical elements, commas used
    to enclose, 547
Part-by-part method for comparisons,
    138–140
Participial phrases, 523–524
Parts of speech, 488–522
    adjectives, 500–503
    adverbs, 515–519
    conjunctions, 519–520
    in dictionary, 468
    interjections, 522
    nouns, 488–492
    prepositions, 520–521
    pronouns, 492–500
    verbs, 503–515
Passes, revising in, 82
Passive voice, 62–66
    in letter writing, 164–166
Period fault, 558
Periodical indexes, 265–269
Periodicals, job opportunities in, 418
Periodic reports, 240, 242
Periodic sentences, 541–542
Periods, 556–559

Person, 86–87
  consistency of, 86–87
  for point of view, 104–105
  of pronouns, 86, 494
  of verbs, 506
Personal data, in resumes, 421–422
Personal names, abbreviations of,
    576–577
Personal pronouns
  See also Pronouns
Personal titles
  abbreviations of, 576–577
  capitalized, 581–582
Persuasive writing, 151–154, 332–333
  See also Proposals
Photographs, 392–393
Phrases, 522–524
  definition of, 522–523
  for emphasis, 67
  introductory, 70–71
  misplaced, 89
  padded, 98–100
  prepositional, 523
  subordination, 67
Physical appearance
  of business letters, 175
  checking, 111–112
  at job interviews, 442–443
Picture graphs, 387
Pie graphs, 386–387
Placement offices, 419
Plagiarism, 278–279
Plain English, 101–102
Plurals
  apostrophe used to show, 568
  of numbers, 572
Plurals of nouns, 490–491
  spelling, 490–491
Point of view, 104–105
  opposing, persuasive writing and,
    152
  reader's, in letter writing, 164–166
Possessive case
  apostrophe used to form, 566–567
  of pronouns, 495–497
Possessive nouns, 491–492
Posters, for oral presentations, 408–
    409
Precision
  revising for, 92
  See also Accuracy
Preface of formal reports, 311
Prefixes, 476–485

Preparation for writing, 4–17
Prepositional phrases, 523
Prepositions, 520–521
Printers, computer, 592–593
Private agencies and organizations,
    free or inexpensive materials
    from, 287–288
Private employment agencies, 419
Problem-solution pattern, for oral pre-
    sentations, 405
Process descriptions, step-by-step se-
    quence in, 129–132
Process explanation, 129–132
Professional journals, job opportuni-
    ties in, 418
Progress reports, 234, 240
Projectors, for oral presentations, 409
Pronoun-antecedent agreement, 497–
    499
Pronoun reference, 499–500
  unclear, 93–94
Pronouns, 93, 492–500
  ambiguous reference, 93
  antecedents of, 85–86, 93, 497–499
  case of, 495–497
  demonstrative, 492
  gender of, 494–495
  indefinite, 493
  intensive, 493
  interrogative, 493
  number of, 495
  person of, 494
  personal, 492
  reciprocal, 493
  reflexive, 493
  relative, 493
  usage of, 497–500
Pronunciation, 468
Proofreaders' marks, 588–589
Proofreading for spelling, 108–111
Proper names, italics for, 585
Proper nouns, 488–489
Proposals, 331–358
  internal, 333–337
  purpose of, 331–332
  sales, *see* Sales proposals
  transmittal letters accompanying,
    343
Punctuation, 546–569
  apostrophes, 566–568
  brackets, 569
  colons, 555–556
  commas, 546–553

dashes, 555–556
exclamation marks, 560
hyphens, 561–563
parentheses, 560–561
periods, 556–559
question marks, 559–560
quotation marks, 563–565
semicolons, 553–554
slashes, 568–569
Purchase order, descriptive writing
in, 132–134
Purpose
determining your, 4, 5
generating ideas and, 4, 5
of oral presentations, 403
statement of, *see* Statement of purpose

Question and answer, as transitional
device, 50–52
Question-and-answer period, 413
Question marks, 559–560
Questionnaires, 12, 281–287
Quotation, direct, 272–274
Quotation marks, 563–565
Quotations, in oral presentations, 411

Reader's background, 6–7
Reader's needs
determining your, 4, 5, 6
generating ideas and, 11
letter writing and, 164–166
Reader's point of view, 7–8
letter writing and, 164–166
Readers, identifying your, 5–8
Readers, multiple, 8
Read speeches, 402
See also Oral presentations
Reciprocal pronouns, 493
Recognition vocabulary, 467
Recommendations
in formal reports, 322–324
in informal reports, 231, 242
Recording secretary, 358
Redundancy, 97–98
Reference section, 324–325
Reference works, 255–260
atlases, 260
dictionaries, 256–258, 467–470
encyclopedias, 255–256
handbooks and manuals, 258–259
statistical sources, 259–260

References
in formal reports, 324–325
in resumes, 424–425
numbered, 294–295
Reflexive pronouns, 493
Refusal letters, 210, 213, 444
Rejection letters, 167–172
Relative pronouns, 493
Repetition of key words and phrases,
as transitional device, 50
Reports
See also Formal reports; Informal
reports
Request for proposals, 340
Research, 254–298
documentation of, *see* Documentation
first-hand observation and experience in, 9–11, 287
free or inexpensive materials from
private and governmental
agencies and organizations,
287–288
interviewing for, 279–281
library, *see* Library research note-
taking for, 271–279
plagiarism and, 278–279
questionnaires, 281–287
Responses
in forms, 367
to inquiry letters, 198, 200
Responsibilities
scope of, in job descriptions, 363
statement of, in sales proposals, 350
Restrained style, in business letters,
172–175
Resumes, 420–435
educational background in, 422–
423
employment experience in, 423–424
employment objective in, 422
personal data in, 421–422
references in, 424–425
sample, 425–435
special skills and activities in, 424
Revising, 80–113
"cooling" period before, 81
affected writing, 100–102
checking for accuracy, 83
checking for completeness, 83
checking for conciseness, 97–102
checking for precision, 92
checking grammar, 83–91

checking physical appearance, 111–112

checking spelling, 82

distancing yourself from your writing, 81

final checklist for, 112

jargon, 102–103

letters, 164

padded phrases, 98–100

in passes, 82

redundant modifiers, 97–98

technical terms, 102–103

unclear pronoun reference, 93–94

word choice, 94–97

your most frequent errors, 82

Revision checklist, 112

Roots of words, 471–476

Rough draft, *see* Draft

Run-on sentences, 91, 533–534

Sales letters, 218, 222, 224

Sales proposals, 337–358

cost analysis and delivery schedule in, 334–336

detailed solution in, 343

executive summary in, 343

general description in, 343

long, 343–358

request for, 340

simple (short), 341–342

site preparation description in, 350

solicited and unsolicited, 340–341

statement of responsibilities in, 350

training section in, 350

vendor descriptions in, 350

Salutation in letters, 176–178

School placement services, 419

Scope

establishing your, 4, 5, 12–13,

stating the, in introduction of formal reports, 313–317

Second page of letters, 178–179

"See also" subject card, 262

Semicolons, 553–554

Sentence fragments, 90–91

Sentence patterns, 531–532

Sentences, 427–442

clear, 539

common problems with, 532–537

complex, 528–529

compound, 528

construction of, 530–532

declarative, 529

effective, 537–542

emphatic, 538–539

exclamatory, 529

faulty subordination in, 532–533

fragments, 90–91, 534–536

imperative, 529

intention of, 529

interrogative, 529

length of, 74, 539–540

loose and periodic, 541–542

minor, 534–536

overloaded with subordination, 69–70

paragraph unity and, 45–48

parallel elements, 538

parts of, 431–432

run-on, 91, 533–534

simple, 528

structure of, 527–529

topic, 46–47, 543–544

transitions between, 49–50

word order in, 540–541

Sequence, *see* Organization methods

Sequencing of data in forms, 367

Sexist language, 103–104

Signature on letters, 178

Silent *e* rule, 456–457

Simple sentences, 528

Single modifiers, 67–68

Singular nouns, 490–491

Site preparation description, in sales proposals, 350

Skills, in resumes, 424

Slashes, 568–569

Slide projectors, 409

Software, *see* Computer software

Source line, in tables, 377

Spatial sequence, 29–31

Speaking vocabulary, 467

Special-purpose report, 232

Specific-to-general sequence, 36–37

in oral presentations, 405

Speeches, *see* Oral presentations

Spelling, 453–467

abbreviated forms of words, 464

checking, 82

commonly misspelled words, 108–111, 464–466

contractions, 463–464

doubling final consonants, 461–462

hard and soft sounds, 457–458

ie or *ei* words, 463

plurals of nouns, 458–459

prefixes and suffixes, 462–463
proofreading for, 108–111
silent *e* rule of thumb, 456–457
verb, adjective, and adverb endings,
   459–461
Spell checker software, 82
Squinting modifiers, 89–90
State employment agencies, 419
Statement of purpose, 5
in introduction of formal report, 317
Statement of responsibilities, in sales
   proposals, 350
*Statistical Abstract of the United
   States,* 259
Statistical sources, 259–260
Step-by-step sequence, 25–27
of process explanations, 130
Stub of tables, 377
Style, in letter writing, 172–175
in abstract writing, 309
revising for, 97–105
Subheads, italics for, 586
Subject, in introduction of formal re-
   ports, 317
Subject card, 260–265
Subject dictionaries, 256–258
Subject encyclopedias, 255–256
Subject line
of memo, 188–190
in place of a salutation, 176–178
Subjective complement, 526
Subjects of sentences, 527–532
Subject-verb agreement, 84–85, 512–
   515
Subjunctive mood, 507
Subordinate clause (dependent
   clauses), 62–67, 525–527
commas used to separate, 550
Subordinating conjunctions, 519
Subordination
for emphasis, 66–70
faulty, 532–533
methods of, 66–69
sentences overloaded with, 69–70
Suffixes, 485–487
Summarizing information, 154–155
Summarizing sentence, as transi-
   tional device, 544
Summary
in formal reports, 311–313
in note-taking, 277–278
Syllables, 468

Symbols, 586–588
list of, in formal reports, 311
Synonyms, 470

Table of contents of formal reports,
   309–310
Tables, 375–377
in formal reports, 329
Taking notes, *see* Note-taking
Technical terms, 102–103
See also Jargon
Tense, 87, 509–510
consistency of, 86–87
Test report (laboratory report), 244,
   246
Text of formal reports, 317–322
Time, numbers to express, 571–572
Title
of books, 581
of films, 581
of formal reports, 303–304
of memorandum, 581
in salutation of letters, 176–178
table, 376
Title card, 260–265
Title pages, for formal reports, 303–
   304
Titles
capital initial letters for, 581
italics for, 584–585
job, 581–582
personal, *see* Personal titles
"Tools Required" section, in instructions, 126
Topic, development of, in introduction
   of formal reports, 317
Topic sentences, 46–47, 543–544
in abstracts, 309
Trade journals, job opportunities in,
   418
Training section, in sales proposals,
   350
Transitional devices, 49–52
in process explanations, 131–132
Transitions
between paragraphs, 50–52, 544
between sentences, 49–50
with lists, 73–74
Transitive verbs, 503–504
Transmittal letters, 200, 203
for formal report, 302–303
Trip report, 244
chronological sequence in, 244

Trouble report (accident report), 231–232
Typefaces
 for emphasis, 75–76
 for warnings or cautions in instructions, 75
Typing
 appearance of letters and, 175
 envelopes, 181, 184
 forms, 367
 quotations, 272–274
Typist's initials, 179

Unabridged dictionaries, 257
Underlining, *see* Italics
Unity of paragraphs, 545
Unnumbered heading system, 320–321
Uppercase letters, *see* Capital letters
Usage labels in dictionaries, 469

Vendor descriptions, in sales proposals, 350
Verbals, 90–91, 505–506
Verb endings, spelling, 459–461
Verb markers, 486–487
Verb phrases, 523
Verbs, 503–515
 conjugation of, 510–512
 finite, 504–505
 forms of, 504–506
 grammatical properties of, 506–510
 intransitive, 504
 linking, 504
 mood of, 506–509
 nonfinite, 505–506
 person and number of, 506
 tense of, 509–510
 transitive, 503–504
 types of, 503–504
 voice of, 507–509
 See also Tense
Veterans, placement programs for, 420

Video screen, 592
Visual aids
 drawings, 389–391
 flowcharts, 393–396
 graphs, *see* Graphs
 maps, 397–398
 in oral presentations, 407–409
 organizational charts, 396–397
 photographs, 392–393
 tables, 375–377
 See also Illustrations
Vocabulary, 466–487
 dictionaries as aid in increasing, 467–470
 word-part approach to increasing, 470–487
Voice of verbs, 507–509

Warnings of danger, 75
 in instructions, 126–129
Whole-by-whole method for comparisons, 138–140
Whole-to-parts technique, 135
Word choice, 94–97
 See also Vocabulary
Word order
 in passive versus active voice, 63–66
Word Processing, 590–595
 for writing drafts, 594
 for revising drafts, 82, 594–595
Word-part approach to increasing your vocabulary, 470–487
Wordiness
 checking for, 97–102
 See also Conciseness
Writer's block, 594–595
Writing block, in forms, 367–369
Writing line, in forms, 365–366
Writing process
 and word processing, 594–595
Writing vocabulary, 467

Zero point of graph, 379

Correction Chart

The following symbols are commonly used in correcting written work. Most of the symbols are keyed to the pages in the text where the problem is discussed.

Symbol	Problem	
ab	abbreviation	464, 573–75, 582
adj	adjective	500–03
adv	adverb	515–19
agr	agreement	84–86, 506, 512–15
amb	ambiguity	92–94, 499–500, 518–19
ap	apostrophe	566–68
awk	awkward	
[ ]	brackets	569
cap	capital letter	578–83
lc	no capital letter (lower case)	578–83
case	grammatical case	495–97
coh	coherence	48–52, 545
:/	colon	555–56
⌃	comma	106–08, 546–53
cf	comma fault	552
dm	dangling modifier	87–88, 536–37
dash	dash	75, 565–66
def	define term	
⸜	delete	
div	word division (syllabication)	563
el	ellipsis (ellipses)	557–58
emph	emphasis	62–76, 538–39
excl	exclamation mark	560
fn	footnote	288–96
frag	sentence fragment	90–91, 534–36
h	hyphen	561–63
ital	italics (underlining)	75, 584–86